St Antony's Series
General Editor: **Jan Zielonka** (2004–), Fellow of St Antony's College, Oxford

Recent titles include:
Celia Kerslake, Kerem Öktem and Philip Robins (*editors*)
TURKEY'S ENGAGEMENT WITH MODERNITY
Conflict and Change in the Twentieth Century

Paradorn Rangsimaporn
RUSSIA AS AN ASPIRING GREAT POWER IN EAST ASIA
Perceptions and Policies from Yeltsin to Putin

Motti Golani
THE END OF THE BRITISH MANDATE FOR PALESTINE, 1948
The Diary of Sir Henry Gurney

Demetra Tzanaki
WOMEN AND NATIONALISM IN THE MAKING OF MODERN GREECE
The Founding of the Kingdom of the Greco-Turkish War

Simone Bunse
SMALL STATES AND EU GOVERNANCE
Leadership through the Council Presidency

Judith Marquand
DEVELOPMENT AID IN RUSSIA
Lessons from Siberia

Li-Chen Sim
THE RISE AND FALL OF PRIVATIZATION IN THE RUSSIAN OIL INDUSTRY

Stefania Bernini
FAMILY LIFE AND INDIVIDUAL WELFARE IN POSTWAR EUROPE
Britain and Italy Compared

Tomila V. Lankina, Anneke Hudalla and Helmut Wollman
LOCAL GOVERNANCE IN CENTRAL AND EASTERN EUROPE
Comparing Performance in the Czech Republic, Hungary, Poland and Russia

Cathy Gormley-Heenan
POLITICAL LEADERSHIP AND THE NORTHERN IRELAND PEACE PROCESS
Role, Capacity and Effect

Lori Plotkin Boghardt
KUWAIT AMID WAR, PEACE AND REVOLUTION

Paul Chaisty
LEGISLATIVE POLITICS AND ECONOMIC POWER IN RUSSIA

Valpy FitzGerald, Frances Stewart and Rajesh Venugopal (*editors*)
GLOBALIZATION, VIOLENT CONFLICT AND SELF-DETERMINATION

Miwao Matsumoto
TECHNOLOGY GATEKEEPERS FOR WAR AND PEACE
The British Ship Revolution and Japanese Industrialization

Håkan Thörn
ANTI-APARTHEID AND THE EMERGENCE OF A GLOBAL CIVIL SOCIETY

Lotte Hughes
MOVING THE MAASAI
A Colonial Misadventure

Fiona Macaulay
GENDER POLITICS IN BRAZIL AND CHILE
The Role of Parties in National and Local Policymaking

Stephen Whitefield (editor)
POLITICAL CULTURE AND POST-COMMUNISM

José Esteban Castro
WATER, POWER AND CITIZENSHIP
Social Struggle in the Basin of Mexico

Valpy FitzGerald and Rosemary Thorp (editors)
ECONOMIC DOCTRINES IN LATIN AMERICA
Origins, Embedding and Evolution

Victoria D. Alexander and Marilyn Rueschemeyer
ART AND THE STATE
The Visual Arts in Comparative Perspective

Ailish Johnson
EUROPEAN WELFARE STATES AND SUPRANATIONAL GOVERNANCE OF SOCIAL
POLICY

Archie Brown (editor)
THE DEMISE OF MARXISM-LENINISM IN RUSSIA

Thomas Boghardt
SPIES OF THE KAISER
German Covert Operations in Great Britain during the First World War Era

Ulf Schmidt
JUSTICE AT NUREMBERG
Leo Alexander and the Nazi Doctors' Trial

Steve Tsang (editor)
PEACE AND SECURITY ACROSS THE TAIWAN STRAIT

James H.S. Milner
REFUGEES, THE STATE AND THE POLITICS OF ASYLUM IN AFRICA

St Antony's Series
Series Standing Order ISBN 978–0–333–71109–5 (hardback)
         978–0–333–80341–7 (paperback)
(outside North America only)

You can receive future titles in this series as they are published by placing a standing order. Please contact your bookseller or, in case of difficulty, write to us at the address below with your name and address, the title of the series and the ISBNs quoted above.

Turkey's Engagement with Modernity

Conflict and Change in the Twentieth Century

Edited by

Celia Kerslake
University Lecturer in Turkish and Fellow of St Antony's College, Oxford University, UK

Kerem Öktem
Research Fellow, St Antony's College, Oxford University, UK

Philip Robins
University Lecturer in Middle East Politics and Faculty Fellow, St Antony's College, Oxford University, UK

In association with St Antony's College, Oxford

First published 2010 by
PALGRAVE MACMILLAN

Palgrave Macmillan in the UK is an imprint of Macmillan Publishers Limited,
registered in England, company number 785998, of Houndmills, Basingstoke,
Hampshire RG21 6XS.

Palgrave Macmillan in the US is a division of St Martin's Press LLC,
175 Fifth Avenue, New York, NY 10010.

Palgrave Macmillan is the global academic imprint of the above companies
and has companies and representatives throughout the world.

Palgrave® and Macmillan® are registered trademarks in the United States,
the United Kingdom, Europe and other countries

ISBN   978–0–230–23314–0   hardback

This book is printed on paper suitable for recycling and made from fully
managed and sustained forest sources. Logging, pulping and manufacturing
processes are expected to conform to the environmental regulations of the
country of origin.

A catalogue record for this book is available from the British Library.

A catalog record for this book is available from the Library of Congress.

10 9 8 7 6 5 4 3 2 1
19 18 17 16 15 14 13 12 11 10

Printed and bound in Great Britain by
CPI Antony Rowe, Chippenham and Eastbourne

Contents

List of Figures

List of Tables

Notes on Orthography and Pronunciation

This volume uses the modern Turkish orthography based on Latin letters. A degree of variation, however, results from the slightly different usage of diacritics by the authors. The names of some Turkish authors, especially those publishing in English language journals, and of some personal and place names are presented without diacritics.

The following letters differ from the English alphabet and are pronounced as shown below:

Ç, ç   'ch' as in 'China'

ğ   When at the end of a word, or before a consonant, lengthens the preceding vowel; when between two vowels, not pronounced.

I, ı   The sound represented by 'a' in 'among'

Ö, ö   Umlauted 'ö' as in German 'Köln'

Ş, ş   'sh' as in 'ship'

Ü, ü   Umlauted 'ü' as in German 'München'

Acknowledgements

The editors would like to express their gratitude to the many individuals who have contributed to this volume and facilitated its publication.

The publication of *Turkey's Engagement with Modernity* is the end result of an initiative launched by the Oxford-based Programme on Contemporary Turkey (PCT), which was funded by an anonymous Turkish benefactor. The project was subsequently supported financially and intellectually by South East European Studies at Oxford (SEESOX with its director Othon Anastasakis), with which the PCT had merged.

Editorial work in such a comprehensive book is crucial, and the able editorial assistance of Elizabeth Angell (New York), and Gökhan Yücel (Oxford), as well as Omar Shweiki's (Oxford) copy-editing was indispensable.

We would also like to thank Carol Davies, Julie Adams, Julia Cook and Anne-Laure Guillerman for their administrative support at different stages of the project.

Our colleagues and students at St Antony's College, the European Studies Centre and the Middle East Centre have contributed to this project with their critical questions, comments and advice. We would especially like to thank Kalypso Nicolaidis and Dimitar Bechev for their active engagement with the subject matter.

Jan Zielonka and Othon Anastasakis, editors of the St Antony's Series, have expedited the publication significantly. Alison Howson, politics publisher at Palgrave Macmillan, and senior editorial assistant Gemma d'Arcy Hughes have managed the production process admirably, with great professionalism and commitment.

Finally, and above all, we are grateful to the authors of this book, who have made possible such an extensive synopsis of Turkey's engagement with modernity in the twentieth century, offering a wide range of topics and differing viewpoints to the reader.

Editors' Preface

Whether it is Samuel Huntington, who situates Turkey right on the fault-line of clashing civilisations, the European Union, which remains undecided whether Turkey is European, or US foreign-policy makers, who at times see the country as an exemplary, 'moderate' Muslim country and at others as a secular democracy, Turkey seems to be at the core of many current intellectual and political debates which preoccupy those who have an interest in international affairs. Questions pertaining to the future of secularism, the relationship between Islam and democracy, the future of the Middle East and Europe all touch upon Turkey, and all these debates can benefit greatly from a substantive examination of the political institutions of the Turkish Republic and the historical evolution of its society and culture in the twentieth century.

Turkey's recent importance for the aforementioned debates corresponds to a growing body of critical and unconventional scholarship on the country's economic, political and social history. In addition to the well-established tradition of a 'high-politics' perspective concentrating on historical figures and institutions, gender-sensitive analysis, social and urban histories and explorations of popular culture have created innovative and challenging ways of approaching the past and present of contemporary Turkey.

In September 2004, St Antony's College hosted a major international conference, convened by Philip Robins, Celia Kerslake and Eugene Rogan, that attempted to gain a grounded insight into Turkey's multiple transformations in this rich but turbulent century, and to recognise the increasingly diversifying field of Turkish studies. The conference was the highpoint of a seven-year series of activities at the University of Oxford organised by the Programme on Contemporary Turkey. *Turkey's Engagement with Modernity* is based on this conference and combines some of its most insightful and innovative contributions.

The resulting volume does not claim to provide a complete overview of all the major issues of importance in the field of Turkish studies. The critical questions of ethno-politics, Kurdish identity, and the destruction of the empire's Armenian communities in the early twentieth century, for instance, are touched upon by authors in one way or another, but not with the depth and breadth that would have been desirable with the benefit of hindsight. The same can be said for the country's rapid, if erratic economic development and the emergence of new industrial bases in central and eastern Anatolia, which has become apparent only in the first decade of the twenty-first century.

Nevertheless *Turkey's Engagement with Modernity* does offer an in-depth insight into a wide range of ideologies, institutions, processes of change, and acts of resistance and critique, which have marked the country's trajectory in the twentieth century and prepared the ground for the twenty-first. We therefore hope that this volume will serve as a reference book for all those students and scholars who wish to understand Turkey's political, societal and cultural complexities through an engagement with its most recent past and with the structural forces that have shaped its evolution.

Synopsis

Tensions of Modernity: Looking Back to a Century of Nationalism

Kerem Öktem

Turkey's Engagement with Modernity explores the structural forces of conflict and change that have marked Turkish history throughout the twentieth century. This volume consists of an introductory essay and 23 individual chapters, grouped into two partly overlapping, yet distinct thematic parts: the first deals with the macro-level of 'State, Politics and International Relations', while the second focuses on the societal and cultural aspects of Turkey's transformation since the late nineteenth century under the heading 'Society and Culture in Flux'.

Andrew Mango introduces the larger debate on the ideologies, forces and personalities that have shaped contemporary Turkey with his essay 'Introduction: Atatürk and Kemalism throughout the Twentieth century'. Today, the Kemalist legacy is being revisited, revised and criticised by a growing number of scholars and public intellectuals, and Kemalist orthodoxy, especially in terms of historiography, is now largely a thing of the past. However, the singular importance of Kemalism persists through its politics and institutions which have contributed so much to the making of modern Turkey. Even in what seems to be unravelling as a new post-Kemalist age, the legacy of the nationalist project, the opportunities it has created and the traumas it has caused remain essential.

The opening section of the book's first part discusses the Kemalist nation building project and the challenges it faced, paying particular attention to both the continuities between Ottoman and Turkish institutions and the ruptures caused by nationalism. The chapters highlight the Ottoman educational legacy, which early republican educators used as a negative 'other' in order to define the new Republic (Benjamin C. Fortna), and the differential predominance of nationalist ideologies in cultural policy, as well as within republican feminist movements. As Yeşim Arat shows, women leaders adopted different strategies in response to state-administered authoritarian feminisim, ranging from an insistence on autonomy for feminist politics to full participation in the dictatorship of the early republic. Murat Belge's discussion of early pan-Turkist literature brings to light the strong anti-humanist and anti-civilisational underpinnings of Turkish nationalism and its distaste for historical realities that do not concur with its own historical imagination. Fully incorporated into the republican state and its institutions, these tropes have continued to shape Turkish politics until today.

The ambivalent and tense relationship between Islam, the military and the state is explored in chapters on the employment of religion by successive Turkish governments since 1880 (Erik-Jan Zürcher), and the societal and political role of Sufi-based communities like the Nurcus and the Gülen movement (Elisabeth Özdalga). Both chapters underline the persistence of Ottoman practices in the republic and the symbiotic relationship between state and religion, despite the initial anticlerical dimension of republican discourse. Feroz Ahmad, with a similar stress on continuity, deciphers the tutelage politics, which the Turkish armed forces have established after the 1960 coup. With vested interests in the economy and the self-defined mission of guarding the secular regime, the armed forces appear responsible for many of the traumatic events that have shaped modern Turkish politics, not least the takeover of the country by General Kenan Evren on 12 September 1980.

The section on institutions and public policy examines the administrative and social legacy of the republic, ranging from the the crises inherent in the political party system and in the Turkish Grand National Assembly (Ersin Kalaycıoğlu), to the changing landscape of higher education. İlterTuran demonstrates, how the military coup of 1980 and the policies of following governments have created a polarised university system. On the one hand, state universities are often strangled by statist ideology and seem increasingly out of touch with universal values. On the other, a new wave of privately funded and managed universities has emerged, some of whom have been developing into instittuions of academic excellence. Zehra F. Kabasakal Arat explores the resilience of gendered policies and discrimination in the labour market, as well as the decreasing rate of labour participation among women in Turkey, a phenomenon partly due to the relative weakness of the welfare state (Sencer Ayata). Halis Akder discusses the history of disease and health campaigns in the republican era, tracing the developmental lines from the 'Ottoman Quarantine' system to republican efforts at combating Malaria.

The last section moves beyond the national framework of politics and policy and looks at 'Turkey as International Actor'. These chapters examine the country's shifting relations with global actors (Henri J. Barkey), the national and international forces shaping Turkey's ever-present, if changing, national security thinking (Ian Lesser), and finally, Turkey's most crucial engagement, namely, its relations with Europe (Nuri Yurdusev). This relationship is shown to exhibit features of confrontation, mutual management and cooperation, all at the same time.

The second part opens with a section on the republican project of cultural rejuvenation, aptly labelled 'Westernisation against the West' (Orhan Koçak), an approach that reveals the paradox between the declared goal of a positively connoted 'Westernisation' and the deep-seated mistrust towards Europe among republican modernisers. Two chapters trace the realisation of this cultural agenda in the fields of literature, where a 'belated modern' tradition eventually connected with the world and created works of high repute (Nüket Esen), and Turkish classical music, which continues to cater to a select circle of sophisticated conoisseurs although failing to attain the popular status some republican nation-builders might have desired (Emre Aracı). Aracı also brings to light the muted history of Western classical music in Turkey before the republic, and the continuty of its institutions.

Building on the republican project of creating a secular high culture, the section on media and popular culture moves into the highly political question of fashion and the production of a republican 'body politic'. Arus Yumul revisits the way the 'Turkish male' was constructed through laws regulating dress, and how his body was imagined through European-style balls and dance events. This section also examines the issue of the changing, if increasingly problematic role of the media, which is facing monopolisation, state intervention and political fragmentation, and has, despite its vibrancy, been as much reflective of the crises in Turkish society as it has been constitutive of some of them (Şahin Alpay, Ayşe Öncü).

The final section on social and urban histories completes the move from a macro perspective to micro histories, discussing the country's modernist architectural heritage and its ideological and sociological underpinnings (Sibel Bozdoğan), and the momentous rural to urban migration that reshaped the cityscapes and social set-up of modern Turkey whilst undermining the traditional power relations of the republic (Jenny B. White). This section, and the book, close with a chapter by Leyla Neyzi on the growing importance of oral history and memory studies in Turkey. Breaking with history as a hegemonic discipline in the service of the state, oral history enables individuals to reconsider Turkey's tortured relationship with its own past, while at the same time empowering them to confront and renegotiate the heavy weight on the collective conscious caused by the hitherto denied memory of assimilation, ethnic cleansing and genocide.

Approaching various aspects of Turkey's societal transformation in the twentieth century from different disciplinary and epistemological angles, the essays in this collection illustrate the deep-seated tensions and conflicts in a fast-changing, heterogenous and vibrant society whose diversity and dynamism have outgrown the unitary-identity model of Kemalist modernism and its racial and anti-Western underpinnings. While Turkey is coming to terms with its many traumas and entering a new, post-Kemalist age, no societal consensus is yet in sight that can entirely replace the legacy of Kemalism. The twenty-first century has begun with an hegemonic struggle between newly forming coalitions of nationalist, isolationist and authoritarian Kemalists and their more globally active, yet no less authoritarian modernist-Islamist contenders. Despite EU-rapprochement, deepening liberalisation and continued commitment to the 'Western world', the outcome of this struggle is far from being resolved.

Notes on Contributors

Editors

Celia Kerslake is Lecturer in Turkish in the Faculty of Oriental Studies at the University of Oxford, and a fellow of St Antony's College. She has published mainly in the field of Turkish linguistics, and is co-author with Aslı Göksel of *Turkish: A Comprehensive Grammar* (Routledge, 2005).

Kerem Öktem is Research Fellow at the European Studies Centre of St Antony's College and an associate of South East European Studies at Oxford. He has worked on new political movements and ethno-politics in Turkey, Turkey's regional neighbourhood, and on the interaction of Muslim immigrant communities and European politics. His latest books are the co-edited *Under the long shadow of Europe. Greeks and Turks in the Era of Post-Nationalism* (Brill, 2009, together with Kalypso Nicolaidis and Othon Anastasakis) and *Mutual Misunderstandings? Muslims and Islam in the European Media* (European Studies Centre, 2009, together with Reem Abou-el-Fadl).

Philip Robins is University Lecturer in politics with special reference to the Middle East, and a fellow of St Antony's College, Oxford. He is currently the Junior Proctor of Oxford University. His most recent book publications are *A History of Jordan* (Cambridge University Press, 2004) and *Suits & Uniforms: Turkish Foreign Policy Since the Cold War* (Hurst/University of Washington Press, 2003). He has published extensively in academic and policy oriented journals on different aspects of the politics and international relations of contemporary Middle East.

Authors

Feroz Ahmad is Professor and Head of the Department of History at Istanbul's Yeditepe University. He has shaped the debate on the role of the Committee of Union and Progress in late Ottoman empire and the early republic with his book *The Young Turks* (Oxford, Clarendon Press, 1969) and has published widely ever since, his latest book being *Turkey: The Quest for Identity* (Oxford, One World, 2003). He is now working on a research project dealing with the Young Turks and the nationalities question.

Halis Akder is Professor in the department of economics at the Middle East Technical University in Ankara. His research has concentrated on agricultural economics and agricultural trade policies, rural poverty, and human development in general. He has published papers, book chapters and reports on these subjects.

Şahin Alpay is Professor of politics at Istanbul's Bahçeşehir University and one of Turkey's leading journalists. He is a regular columnist in the newspaper *Zaman* and it's English version, *Today's Zaman*.

Emre Aracı is a freelance composer, conductor and musicologist based in the UK. His principal research interest covers the European musical tradition in the nineteenth-century Ottoman court. Presently, under the patronage of the Çarmıklı family, he records, performs and broadcasts in this field. He has published biographies of Ahmed Adnan Saygun and Donizetti Pasha and is currently working on the history of Naum Theatre, Istanbul's nineteenth-century Italian Opera House. His CDs include *European Music at the Ottoman Court, War and Peace: Crimea 1853–56, Bosphorus by Moonlight, Istanbul to London*, and the two compilations *Invitation to the Seraglio* and *Euro-Ottomania*.

Yeşim Arat is Professor in the Department of Political Science and International Relations at Boğaziçi University in Istanbul. She has published widely on gender and politics in Turkey, on Turkey's women's movement, and most recently on gender-based violence.

Sencer Ayata is Professor of sociology and Director of the Graduate School of Social Sciences at the Middle East Technical University in Ankara. He has worked on urban societies, poverty and social policy in Turkey.

Henri J. Barkey is the Cohen Professor of International Relations at Lehigh University in Pennsylvania. He is also non-resident Senior Associate at the Carnegie Endowment for International Peace in Washington, DC. His latest publication is *Preventing Conflict Over Kurdistan* (Carnegie Endowment, 2009).

Murat Belge is Professor of comparative literature at Istanbul Bilgi University and one of Turkey's most prolific public intellectuals. As co-founder of İletişim Yayınları and translator of James Joyce, Belge has published a large numbers of books on literature, politics and the social and architectural history of Istanbul. He also has a regular column in the newspaper *Taraf*. His latest publication project deals with fascism and dictatorship.

Sibel Bozdoğan is Lecturer in architecture at Harvard University's Graduate School of Design and member of faculty at Istanbul Bilgi University. She has co-edited the interdisciplinary volume *Rethinking Modernity and National Identity in Turkey* (1997) and is the author of *Modernism and Nation Building: Turkish*

Architectural Culture in the Early Republic (University of Washington Press, 2001).

Nüket Esen is Head of Department and Professor of Turkish language and literature at Boğaziçi University, Istanbul. She specialises in the Turkish novel, literary theory, narratology and Ahmet Mithat, and has published a number of books and articles. Her latest publication is *Orhan Pamuk'un Edebi Dünyası* (Orhan Pamuk's Literary World), co-edited with Engin Kılıç (İletişim Yayınları, 2008).

Benjamin C. Fortna is Head of the Department of History and Senior Lecturer in the modern history of the Near and Middle East at the School of Oriental and African Studies (SOAS) at the University of London. His primary research interest lies in the history of the late Ottoman Empire and the Turkish Republic, with particular attention to education and cultural change. His publications include *Imperial Classroom: Islam, Education and the State in the Late Ottoman Empire* (Oxford: Oxford University Press, 2002) and the co-edited *The Modern Middle East: A Sourcebook for History* (Oxford: Oxford University Press, 2006).

Zehra F. Kabasakal Arat is Juanita and Jospeh Leff Distinguished Professor of Political Science and Women's Studies at Purchase College of the State University of New York (SUNY). Her research focuses on democracy and human rights, with an emphasis on women's rights. Her publications include *Democracy and Human Rights in Developing Countries* (1991), *Deconstructing Images of 'The Turkish Woman'*, (1998), *Non-State Actors in the Human Rights Universe* (2006), *Human Rights Worldwide* (2006), and *Human Rights in Turkey* (2007). She is currently working on a project that examines the changes in human rights discourse and practices in Turkey since the establishment of the Republic of Turkey.

Ersin Kalaycıoğlu is Professor of political science at Istanbul Sabancı University and former rector of Istanbul Işık University. He has directed various survey research projects on political transformation, political values, and electoral behaviour. More recently he has worked on state and civil society in Turkey.

Orhan Koçak is a leading literary critic and editor of the literature journal *Virgül* (The Comma). He has published widely on modern Turkish poets and novelists.

Ian Lesser is Senior Transatlantic Fellow at the German Marshall Fund of the United States and his work focusses on the politics of Turkey, the Middle East and the Balkans. In addition to his co-edited volume *Turkish*

Foreign Policy in an Age of Uncertainty (Rand Corporation, 2003, together with Stephen Larrabee), he is a regular contributor to the Turkey Report series of the German Marshall Funds.

Andrew Mango is a leading expert on Turkey. His *Atatürk: The Biography of the Founder of Modern Turkey* (Overlook, 1999) remains one of the standard works on Mustafa Kemal. His more recent publications are *The Turks Today* (2004) and *Turkey and the War on Terror* (2005).

Leyla Neyzi is an anthropologist, oral historian and associate professor in the Faculty of Arts and Social Sciences at Sabancı University. Her latest publication is the co-edited volume *Memories of Mass Repression: Narrating Life Stories in the Aftermath of Atrocity*, together with Nanci Adler, Selma Leydesdorff and Mary Chamberlain (Transaction Publishers, 2009). She has also published widely in journals such as *History and Memory*, *Comparative Studies in Society and History*, *New Perspectives on Turkey* and *Global Networks*.

Ayşe Öncü is Professor in Sabancı University's Faculty of Arts and Sciences, specialising in cultural politics in Turkey, the media and public spheres, as well as on transcultural spaces of migration. She has published extensively on consumer culture,and the media in Turkey.

Elisabeth Özdalga is Professor of sociology at the Middle East Technical University in Ankara and Director of the Swedish Research Institute in Istanbul. She has published extensively on religious communities and political Islam in Turkey in *Middle Eastern Studies*, *Middle East Critique*, and *Critique*. Her most recent books are the collection *Islamcılığın Türkiye Seyri* (The Trajectory of Islamism in Turkey) (İletişim, 2006) and the edited volume *Late Ottoman Society. The Intellectual Legacy* (Routledge Curzon, 2005).

İlter Turan is Professor of political science at Istanbul Bilgi University, where he has also served as rector between 1998 and 2001. Previously, he worked at Istanbul (1964–93) and Koç Universities (1993–98), in addition to holding visiting appointments at various American universities. His recent writings were published *in South European Society* and *Politics and International Affairs*. He has been a vice president and program chair of the International Political Science Association and is the president of the Turkish Political Science Association.

Jenny B. White is Associate Professor of anthropology at Boston University and former president of the Turkish Studies Association. She is author of *Islamist Mobilization in Turkey* (2002), and *Money Makes Us Relatives: Women's Labor in Urban Turkey* (second edition, Routledge, 2004). She has authored numerous articles on Turkey and lectures internationally on topics ranging from political Islam and civil society to ethnic identity and gender issues. She has also written two historical novels set in nineteenth-century Istanbul, *The Sultan's Seal* (2006), which has been translated into 14 languages, and *The Abyssinian Proof* (2008).

Arus Yumul is Professor and Head of the Department of Sociology at Istanbul Bilgi University. She has worked on issues of ethnic identity, the sociology of everyday life and the body, and published extensively in Turkish journals such as *Düşünen Siyaset, Doğu Batı*, and *Hukuk ve Adalet*.

Nuri Yurdusev is Professor of international relations at the Middle East Technical University, Ankara. He is the author of *International Relations and the Philosophy of History: A Civilizational Approach* (Palgrave Macmillan, 2003) and the editor of *Ottoman Diplomacy: Conventional or Unconventional?* (Palgrave Macmillan, 2004). His articles have been published in various journals, including *Millennium* and *Critique*. His current research interests include the theory and history of international relations, European identity and Ottoman diplomacy.

Erik-Jan Zürcher is the Director of the International Institute of Social History in Amsterdam and chair of the academic committee of the Dutch Higher Education Institute in Ankara. He has published extensively on Turkey's recent history, the role of the Committee of Union and Progress, and the country's EU prospects. His *Turkey: A Modern History*, now in its third revised edition (I. B. Tauris, 2004), is a post-Kemalist revision of Turkish history and has become the standard work in the field.

Introduction: Atatürk and Kemalism throughout the Twentieth Century

Andrew Mango

A discussion about contemporary Turkey cannot help but start with an evaluation of the founding father of the Turkish Republic. Mustafa Kemal Atatürk has shaped modern Turkey, just as Peter the Great has shaped modern Russia. Peter the Great hacked through the ice which surrounded Russia to open a window to the West. Atatürk opened wide windows to the West – windows that were already half open as well as those that had remained shut until his reforms.

The subject of this volume is Turkey's engagement with modernity in the twentieth century. Atatürk was Turkey's greatest, most consistent and most radical moderniser. In Acton's words, all history is contemporary history. So although we are invited to look back to the century that has just ended, our view will depend on our vantage point today in the new millennium. What we think of Atatürk and of his vision, Kemalism, will depend on what we think of Turkey today. Our view of Atatürk will change as Turkey changes, but also as the world changes. The value of collections such as this one lies precisely in the fact that they add an outside perspective to the narrative of facts and events provided by our Turkish colleagues. They are not dependent on foreign scholars and observers to find out what is happening inside their own country, but they may be curious to know what outsiders make of it. I would not be surprised if they found the picture confusing.

Today, Turkey's aspiration to membership of the European Union is foremost in our minds, so let us start by listening to two voices from European institutions. Firstly, to the voice of Walter Hallstein, president of the European Commission, in his speech 40 years ago when Turkey became an associate member of the European Economic Community, the precursor of the Union. 'Turkey', Hallstein said, 'is part of Europe. And here we think first and foremost of the stupendous personality of Atatürk whose work meets us at every turn in this country, and of the radical way in which he recast every aspect of life in Turkey along European lines'.

The second voice is that of Arie Oostlander, *rapporteur* of the European Parliament, in the draft report he presented on 12 March 2003 on Turkey's application for membership of the EU. This is what he said: 'The underlying philosophy of the Turkish state, "Kemalism", implies an exaggerated fear of the undermining of the integrity of the Turkish state and an emphasis on the homogeneity of Turkish culture (nationalism), together with statism, an important role for the army, and a very rigid attitude to religion, which means that the underlying philosophy is itself a barrier to EU membership'. The barrier was lowered somewhat in the final version of the report, which followed three months later (on 19 May 2003). 'The transformation of a state based on Kemalist ideas ... into an EU member state, accepting and sharing the political values we set so much store by in the Union, will be a long drawn-out job', the new text declared. The draft report had claimed that 'the changes demanded are so fundamental that they require the establishment of a new constitution, explicitly based not on Kemalist but on European democratic foundations, with the rights of the individual and the minorities balanced against collective rights in accordance with customary European rights'. The final report omitted the words 'not on Kemalist, but', while repeating the rest of the sentence. But, as we have seen, Oostlander continued to be critical of what he called 'Kemalist ideas'.

So, is this the last word of European institutions on the subject of Kemalism? I do not think so. Oostlander's report was written after 9/11, but before its effect, and the effect of the events that followed – the war in Iraq, the Istanbul, Madrid and London bombings, the massacre of the innocent in Beslan – began to be felt on 'the political values we set so much store by in the [European] Union'. Now, on further reflection, at least some Europeans have begun to argue that the multiculturalism Europe had embraced pushed minorities into ghettos in which extremists found fertile ground, with the result that there were almost certainly more Islamist terrorists in Europe than there had been in Baghdad under Saddam Hussein's tyrannical regime. Many Europeans have rediscovered the value of a unifying national culture along the lines of that advocated by Atatürk, and this rediscovery is leading to changes in education, naturalisation practices and other fields. As more and more Europeans are kidnapped and murdered in unstable states, there is a new appreciation of the virtues of stability which only a strong state can guarantee, and this appreciation casts a new light on the 'statism' which Oostlander found so objectionable in Atatürk's legacy. So too with the critique of Kemalism's 'very rigid attitude to religion' – perhaps Atatürk knew something about religious fanaticism that Oostlander did not.

I would argue that there is another change in the air. The salience of the barbarous behaviour of terrorists has revived the normative use of the word 'civilisation' – not Western civilisation specifically, but civilisation as a universal value. When Atatürk chose universal civilisation as his supreme value, when he summoned his people to join the mainstream of this single civilisation and to contribute to it, he was using current contemporary discourse, before that discourse began to dissolve in the acid of cultural relativism.

Civilisation was, in the words of a contemporary French definition, *'avancement de l'humanité dans l'ordre moral, social, intellectuel, etc'*. Today after two world wars among nations deemed civilised, we may jib at *'moral'*; we may have stronger grounds than ever to distinguish civilisation from morality, but the core definition of civilisation as 'a highly developed state of society', as the OED puts it, has survived in common parlance, carrying to our day the ideals of the European Enlightenment.

Atatürk was not, of course, the first statesman in Turkey to choose civilisation as his ideal. Professor Selim Deringil has provided us with many examples of the normative use of the terms *medeniyet* (civilisation) and *medenî* (civilised) by Ottoman officialdom in the reign of Abdülhamit II. But Atatürk's choice of civilisation as a supreme value was a radical step towards all-round modernisation, without any reservations. Unlike many of his fellow countrymen he was not content to import modern technology alone: he opted for the whole system of modern values current in the most highly developed part of the world, which was centred in the West. In an interview he gave in 1923 to the French writer Maurice Pernot, Atatürk said 'We want to modernise our country. Our whole endeavour is directed at the creation of a modern and, therefore, Western government in Turkey. Is there a single nation which has not turned to the West in its quest for civilisation?' One must note that this statement equating modernisation with westernisation was made to a Westerner. When he addressed his own people, Atatürk spoke of civilisation without any geographical reference.

Atatürk, as is well known, was influenced by the positivist philosophy of Auguste Comte. People who cite this fact usually draw attention to Comte's reliance on what used to be called positive sciences – perhaps empirical sciences is a better term – and his distrust of metaphysical arguments. Atatürk was certainly an empiricist. In his last opening speech in parliament in 1937, he declared boldly 'Our principles should not be confused with the dogmas of books supposed to have come down from heaven. We derive our inspiration not from heaven and the other world, but directly from life'. For a believing Muslim, the book that came down from heaven is of course the Koran. But we must not neglect also the main slogan of positivism – 'order and progress' – a slogan you will find inscribed on the Brazilian flag. Progress, as we have seen, was defined as an advance towards and within universal civilisation. But for this advance to happen, order was essential. In his proclamation to the nation at the time of the Şeyh Sait rebellion in 1924, Atatürk declared, 'The precondition of a happy outcome in every kind of activity, and particularly in economic and commercial development, is tranquillity, law and order secure and strong enough to be beyond the reach of violation.' When Atatürk was to define his policy later as 'peace in the country and peace in the world', he put peace in the country first. In retrospect, this was one of his greatest achievements, which prevented the waste of national resources in civil and external strife, and allowed the use of these resources for the country's development.

Atatürk inherited a state apparatus with a strong administrative tradition. This allowed him to concentrate on creating a Turkish nation out of the Muslim inhabitants of the country. Nation building is a term widely misused today, when, for example, people speak of the American success in nation building in Germany and Japan after World War II. In fact the German and Japanese nations had been built long before the Americans appeared on the scene and helped free these solid nations from the baleful influence of evil rulers. In Turkey, on the other hand, the nation had to be fashioned after the establishment of the Republic. But nation building was not enough, society as a whole had to be rebuilt after the departure of the non-Muslim minorities who had provided most of the skills outside the army and the administration (actually also in parts of the administration) in the multi-ethnic Ottoman state. Turkey's development under and since Atatürk cannot be understood without an appreciation of the extremely narrow skill base on which the republic had to be constructed. As the leader of a poor, illiterate rural society, Atatürk was convinced that his first task was to dispel what he called 'the black cloud of ignorance' which overshadowed his country.

All this was well understood by contemporary Western observers. Writers of books on Turkey old and new may have exaggerated the novelty of Atatürk's approach, but they approved strongly of the direction in which he was taking his country. We find a late echo of this approval in the words I have quoted from European Commission president Walter Hallstein. The Ottoman antecedents of Atatürk's policy were later explained in Bernard Lewis' seminal work, *The Emergence of Modern Turkey*. However when we speak of continuity in the Turkish reform movement, we must bear in mind that it was Atatürk who turned ideas into action. The introduction of the Latin alphabet may have been advocated by Abdullah Cevdet, but the Arabic alphabet continued to be used until Atatürk forced the pace of reform. Women's emancipation may have advanced under the Young Turks, particularly during World War I, when women's labour was needed, but towards the end of that war military police in Istanbul were still arresting women whose skirts were deemed to be too short. The *medrese* religious colleges may have been attached to the ministry of education by the Young Turks, but it was Atatürk who abolished them, sensing that they were, as they are today, even under state supervision, places that produce religious fanatics.

Professor Erik Zürcher, of the generation of scholars that followed Bernard Lewis, stressed Atatürk's use of Muslim solidarity in the Turkish War of Independence and the continuities between Kemalism and the policies of the Young Turks – the Committee of Union and Progress. But here too we must be careful. It is true that Atatürk had been a Unionist and that he worked with former Unionists throughout his life, but he saw the Young Turk leadership – in particular the triumvirate which ruled Turkey during World War I – as setting an example to be avoided. Their foolishness – their adventurism which destroyed the Ottoman state and threatened to destroy the Turkish home-land as well; their constant interference in the administration – taught Atatürk to be wise, to avoid foreign adventures, to delegate power to his ministers and allow his civil servants to do their job. As the Turkish prov-erb put it, the calamity which they caused was worth a thousand words of advice – *bir musibet, bin nasihattan yeğdir.*

In 1964, when Walter Hallstein expressed his admiration for Atatürk and credited him with recasting every aspect of life in Turkey along European lines, the West was engaged in the Cold War with the Soviet Union and was keenly aware of the virtues of order and stability in its part of the world. Atatürk, who had described Bolshevism as 'nonsense' (*safsata*) as early as 1922, was, of course, criticised by Marxists as a petty-bourgeois national-ist. Turkish Marxists and *marxisant* nationalists tried to square the circle by praising him as an anti-imperialist and, of course, as a strong defender of total national independence. But far from being a non-aligned nationalist, Atatürk was strongly in favour of collective security in defence of the sta-tus quo. In 1937 when he quarrelled with his Prime Minister İsmet İnönü, who was afraid that Turkey might be dragged into a war if it helped Britain and France to police the Mediterranean against Italian pirate submarines, Atatürk remarked 'In today's conditions it would even be useful to assign a naval unit to help the British. Can one deny the usefulness of showing that we are in a position to work together with great powers in international affairs and to begin right away to cooperate with them?' Atatürk wanted to join the democratic great powers. The fact that they were imperial powers did not bother him. Anti-imperialism applied only to Turkey's independ-ence and integrity. As for the millions of Muslims ruled by foreigners, it was up to them to develop a national consciousness strong enough to throw off the yoke. A believer in national independence, he nevertheless con-templated – perhaps rather fancifully – relinquishing the presidency of the Turkish Republic to become president of the Balkan Union. It was, it must be admitted, a rare departure from his pragmatism.

Today, *marxisant* intellectuals are in retreat and are to be found mainly sheltering in universities. Now criticism of Atatürk and of Kemalism comes largely from liberals – true liberals, whom we all know and love, and pretend liberals who want to exploit liberal freedoms for their own purposes. The criticism can be explicit as in the case of Mr Oostlander, or implicit, as is usually the case in Turkey where the old practice of blaming not the leader, but his ministers, successors and interpreters is often followed. Or, as is the fashion among liberal academics, the defects they see in Kemalism are blamed not on Atatürk himself, but on the authoritarian tradition he inher-ited from the Ottoman state. When one points out that this line of criti-cism is anachronistic – that the Ottoman state was more tolerant and more successful in administering its subjects than many of its successors have proved to be, and that in Atatürk's time liberal democracy was in retreat in the developed West and that highly developed societies were unable to sustain it, particularly after the great depression of 1929 – critics argue that times have changed, and that Kemalism must change with them. They have a point. Modernisation is, by definition, a continuing process, rather like Trotsky's permanent revolution – but, one hopes, with more constructive results. In any case, change is implicit in Atatürk's otherwise vague principle of *devrimcilik*, which is not made any clearer by being translated as either 'revolutionism' or 'reformism', depending on the translator's inclination. The historian Professor Sina Akşin, one of the most consistent advocates of Kemalism, warns us against what he calls 'frozen Kemalism'. But having said this, one could perhaps venture to point out to liberal critics of Kemalism as a top-down, authoritarian ideology or, at least, cast of mind – that liberalism comes at a price, which not all countries and not all societies can afford to pay at all times. It would of course have been wonderful if the cure for the defects of liberal democracy could have been more liberal democracy, just as the cure for the disadvantages of press freedom were to be more press freedom. Incidentally, Atatürk did enunciate this latter fine principle, but, unsurprisingly, failed to practise it. After 9/11 few of us can ignore the cost of liberal freedoms. After Afghanistan and Iraq, only the wilfully blind can fail to see that the growth of a liberal society is a slow, organic process. Following the first Turkish military coup of 27 May 1960, the youngest member of the National Unity Committee, the ruling junta, said to me: 'Of course we'll be successful, now that virtue has replaced vice'. But the world proved to be a wicked place. Replacing the vice of authoritarianism with the virtue of liberalism is not a guarantee of success, either.

Early Ottoman reformers believed that a constitutional monarchy would solve all the problems of the state. The Young Turks thought that one size fitted all, and sought salvation through the uniform application of their principles irrespective of local conditions. Atatürk pinned his faith on rationalism, saying in his celebrated tenth anniversary address to the nation that he was certain of success because the Turkish nation held aloft the torch of positive science. In 1950 free elections were seen as a panacea. After 1960, the key to progress was believed to lie in measures to prevent the arbitrary use of power by an elected majority in parliament. After 1980, the accent was on subjecting independent institutions to the test of the national interest, while opening up the economy to global competition. Now, it is participatory democracy in politics and fiscal discipline in the economy which are seen as guarantees of success. And of course membership of the European Union is a passport to a radiant future. All these ideas have merit, but all have their downside; all carry a cost.

Let us consider the price Turkey has had to pay for the advent of free elections in 1950. Atatürk had been prudent in fiscal matters and insisted on balanced budgets. True, it was the orthodoxy of the age. He did not rely on foreign aid and credit, even if these were not particularly forthcoming.

In the couple of instances when they were, he did make use of them. But after 1950, fiscal prudence was abandoned – only to be imposed fitfully by the pressure of creditors and the intervention of the military. Self-reliant, perhaps perforce self-reliant, under Atatürk, Turkey developed a dependency culture. The efficiency, self-confidence and traditions of public administration were eroded as it became the plaything of politicians. The downside of free elections is often described by the fashionable term 'populism'. I prefer the old-fashioned term demagogy. Of course, demagogic politicians are not confined to Turkey. Perhaps demagogy and democracy are twin brothers. But a twin brother can be kept in check. Increasing knowledge of the world, coupled with the experience of failed promises, sets a limit to political con men – and the Turkish electorate, like all of us, is learning.

I would also argue that the emergence, and at times the exacerbation, of the conflict between secularists and Islamists, and the problem posed by the spread of Kurdish nationalism, are part of the price Turkey is paying for its adoption of liberal democracy. Foreign critics often cite these conflicts as proof of the failure of Kemalism. I do not agree. When the basilica of Sacré Coeur began construction by public subscription in 1876, with the express purpose of dominating Paris from the hill of Montmartre, secularists saw it as a repudiation of the ideals of the French Revolution. But the ideals have survived and are embraced today by Catholics as well as by secularists in France. In Istanbul a mosque has not been built – yet – to dominate the modern city's hub at Taksim square, and Prime Minister Recep Tayyip Erdoğan, leader of a party with its roots in political Islam, has laid wreaths at the mausoleum of Atatürk and declared his devotion to the principle of secularism. Of course, tension continues between the secularist and the Islamist camps. In France it exploded at the end of the nineteenth century – more than a century after the revolution – when Catholic teaching orders were expelled from the country. Even recently, there was a huge protest demonstration in Paris prompted by the suggestion that the state should contribute to the upkeep of the buildings of Catholic schools. History accelerates, but I for one am not surprised that Turkey has not solved in less than a century a conflict that has lasted two centuries in France and is only now dying down.

Kemalism is also blamed for the failure to accommodate Kurdish nationalism, the one ethnic movement which has stood out against the assimilation of all the Muslim inhabitants of Turkey in the Turkish nation. But could it have been accommodated without endangering law and order and the construction of a modern nation state? Kurdish nationalism first appeared among malcontents within the feudal leadership of the fractious and fragmented Kurdish tribal society. It was inseparable from the threat to law and order which the tribes had always posed. The Kemalists sought to solve it by co-opting part of the feudal leadership in order to isolate the malcontents, and by as much modern development of the area as they could afford.

They built schools and railways, just as the Hanoverians had built roads in the Highlands to subdue the Scottish clans, and the Russians had built the Caucasian Military Highway to subdue the Muslim mountaineers. Critics of Kemalism enumerate successive Kurdish risings as proof of the failure of Kemalist policy. But has there been more mayhem in the Kurdish areas under the Republic than there had been in Ottoman times? I rather doubt it. The suppression of the Dersim rebellion in 1937 when aircraft were used against the rebels (as they had been used by the British against rebellious Kurds earlier in Iraq) figures prominently in Kurdish nationalist historiography as a crime against the Kurdish people. But few remember the punitive expedition against rebels in Dersim launched by the Young Turks in 1909. General Fahrettin Altay, a hero of the Turkish War of Independence, who, as a young officer, had taken part in operations against rebel tribesmen in Dersim, wrote in his memoirs: 'The region of Tunceli [Dersim] had been of old a nest of brigands. After the proclamation of the Constitution, banditry increased considerably among its inhabitants. The time had come to put an end to it'. As I said, that was in 1909.

Kemalists are also accused of exacerbating the Kurdish problem by disestablishing Islam and then by using force to subdue Kurdish disaffection. But the disestablishment of Islam was a precondition of the country's modernisation, irrespective of its effects on Kurdish society. When parts of that society rebelled – and it was always groups within it and not the whole – force had to be used. There is no other way. Here I shall draw a controversial parallel with the defeat of the PKK terrorist campaign. The PKK leader Abdullah Öcalan fled to Syria just as the military were about to take over the government in Ankara in 1980. He lay low while the military were in control, launching his terrorist campaign in 1984 after the civilian government of Turgut Özal had come to power and tried a conciliatory approach to the Kurdish problem. The terrorist campaign would not have lasted for fifteen years, causing more than 35,000 deaths, if the terrorists did not have bases in, and receive help from, foreign states. Finally, the terrorists were defeated when Syria was forced by the threat of Turkish military power to expel Öcalan and close down PKK camps. Within Turkey, most, but not all terrorists were eliminated by the military, which, at the same time, took care to enlist the support of large sections of the local population. It was the defeat of the terrorists which allowed the implementation of liberal policies after force had done its work. Similarly, Atatürk and his ministers used such force as was necessary to manage the Kurdish problem in the hope that the spread of civilisation would gradually solve it. I find an echo of that hope in the words of Prime Minister Erdoğan when he spoke at the opening of an all-weather road in the province of Van. 'Let us open these roads,' he said, 'in order to be able to speak of civilisation and of the European Union'.[1]

Atatürk was a practical statesman who did not allow his vision – today we would call it his mission statement – to divert him from dealing with problems as they arose. When he disowned the Kadro movement with its anti-imperialist rhetoric in the early 1930s, he dismissed one of its proponents as a 'fantasist' (*hayalperest*). His own fantasies, the sun-language theory and the Turkish history thesis which he defended towards the end of his life – did little harm. In the case of language reform, the premises may have been fanciful, but the result – the development of an easily mastered modern Turkish language responsive to the needs of the modern world – has served Turkish society well. Professor Geoffrey Lewis, the doyen of Turkish studies in the UK, has called it 'a catastrophic success'.

From today's vantage point we can see the solidity of the foundations which Atatürk has laid. Tony Blair has done well to include a biography of Atatürk in his holiday reading. I hope he found it both instructive and enjoyable. Of course, there are problems a-plenty in the republic Atatürk founded. These problems derive largely from the population explosion – inevitably in the least-developed parts of the country – from demagogic policies pursued by politicians over the last fifty years, from changes in the outside world. As Atatürk saw it, the task in Turkey is to catch up with the most highly developed part of the world. It may take longer than he expected, but his country has gone a long way along the path he charted. There are still bits of the Middle East in Turkey, but Hallstein's statement that Turkey is part of Europe is a reality rather than an aspiration. I hope that the slippery politicians who rule the member countries of the European Union realise it. If they do not, they should not blame Atatürk and Kemalism to cover up their short-term calculations of profit and loss.

Like all political approaches, Kemalism has its downside. But its core has stood the test of time. I would argue that this core consists of self-reliance, an open attitude to the outside world and an absence of fear in dealings with it, a willingness to follow best practice, a concentration of effort on domestic development and, consequently, prudence in foreign policy. It does not embrace authoritarianism for its own sake, but insists on law and order as the primary duty of the state and its *raison d'être*. And above all, it cherishes rationality in public policy. As I said in my biography of Atatürk, his is an optimistic philosophy. And despite current problems, it is, I think, worth remembering that there is much to be optimistic about in the state of Turkey today.

Bibliography

A. Oostlander (2003) (Rapporteur) Draft Report on Turkey's Application for Membership in the EU (12 March 2003) (Bussels: European Parliament, Committee on Foreign Affairs, Human right, Common Security and Defence Policy).

Part I The State, Its Politics and International Relations

Nation Building and Its Challenges

1
The Ottoman Educational Legacy

Benjamin C. Fortna

Introduction

The topic of the Ottoman educational legacy is both engaging and also rather slippery. The notion of historical legacy is itself not as altogether straightforward as it might first appear. Determining what constitutes the legacy, how it ought to be defined temporally, and for whom it is intended is problematic. Semantically, the term 'legacy' derives from the law of inheritance, and is defined as those properties or assets stipulated to be left as a bequest at the time of death. This implies intention on the part of the legator and acceptance of the legacy on the part of the legatee. It should be immediately apparent that the process by which the Ottoman Empire 'died' and its successor states were born involves no intention on the part of the empire – it made no will and thus could be said, in legal terms to have suffered that problematic fate of dying intestate, a situation renowned for being beneficial only to those in the legal profession.

We are therefore left to contemplate what this legacy might be. Simplest is the tangible inheritance, fixed at time of death. This sort of legacy is the easiest to spot. If we wished, we could easily assemble a sort of educational 'tereke defteri' consisting of an accounting of what the Ottoman Empire had bequeathed to the Turkish Republic, not to mention the other post-Ottoman states. This inheritance would include lists of schools, teachers, curricula, central educational administrative infrastructure, policy memoranda, etc. But immediately we come up against a further problem: what to do with that part of the inheritance that, to put it mildly, did not figure in Republican plans. We think immediately of such parts of the diverse Ottoman educational whole as the *medrese* system, perhaps the pre-eminent feature, historically speaking, of Ottoman education. This system is generally not considered part of the Ottoman educational legacy, because the Republic quickly abandoned it.

Here we encounter the more salient feature of historical legacy: it is not the tangible inheritance that really matters. Or, rather, it is important but not decisive, because it is subject to both historical and historiographical treatment that reflects later conditions and attitudes. The construction of a legacy is subject, in other words, to the manipulation, selective appropriation, creative remembering, and occasionally wilful misrepresentation of both the legatee and the historians and social scientists who invariably reflect, at least to some degree, the legatee's version of events.

It will become clear that one of the most prominent ways in which the Republic treated its Ottoman inheritance in the field of education was by manipulating the Ottoman legacy so as to increase the presumed divide between the Ottoman and Republican periods, even while appropriating much of it in actual practice. Perhaps the first aspect of the Republican attitude to note is the simultaneous wish to separate itself rhetorically from the Empire while taking a pragmatic approach towards adopting tangible aspects of its legacy that would have made Ottoman statesmen proud.

In other words, the Ottoman educational legacy quickly became de-linked from Ottoman realities and intentions, and dependent on post-Ottoman realities and intentions. For the purposes of this chapter, I will consider the Ottoman educational legacy with this shift in mind. But it must be remembered at the outset that this approach involves rather more attention to the Republic's utilisation, appropriation, and construction of this legacy than to the actual Ottoman context that created it in the first place. The Ottoman educational legacy is less about education in the Ottoman Empire than it is about the Republic.

In spite of this inevitably rather skewed perspective, let me come to the defence of the topic at hand. An examination of the Ottoman educational legacy has considerable utility and attractiveness.[1] First, education was emblematic both of the aspirations of the Republic, as it became symbolic (along with the military) of the state's agenda, and of the Republic's varied attitudes towards and responses to the broader Ottoman inheritance. Education was among the most celebrated causes of the early Republican state and the source of many of its most important poses vis-à-vis the public: Mustafa Kemal, later Atatürk, appearing as schoolmaster-in-chief; his highly visible quotations about the importance and purpose of learning in the national cause; and through its campaign of building the institutional and physical infrastructure, via schools, village institutes, the education ministry in Ankara, and so forth. Secondly, education has served as a well-placed barometer to gauge the mix of radical shifts and remarkably smooth continuities that characterise the transition from empire to republic. Thirdly, it offers a perspective for taking the long view, and charting change over a longer time frame than merely that of the early years of the Republic. With time it is remarkable to note that the once-radical Republican changes now seem like a phase of quirky irregularity followed by a longer-term alignment with many aspects of the Ottoman educational trajectory.

The aim of this chapter is to explore the contours of the Ottoman/ Republican juxtaposition with respect to the field of education. I approach this topic by first considering the ways in which it has been treated in the relevant existing literature and then attempting an overall assessment of the Ottoman/Republican relationship as viewed through educational change and continuity.

Treatment in the literature

I begin with an example taken from an early Republican-era reading primer, because it encapsulates an important aspect of the early Republican government's stance towards the Ottoman period. Young Republican readers were being made to disparage the Ottoman past, by characterising it as decadent and reactionary. The author of this particular text, entitled *Cumhuriyet Çocuklarına Türkçe Kıraat* (A Turkish Reader for Republican Children) was Ahmed Cevad [Emre], a transitional late Ottoman and early Republican author of textbooks that reflected the changes affecting state education during the transition from the Ottoman to the Turkish state. The first in this series features a skit entitled 'Yaşasın Cumhuriyet' (Long live the Republic!) (Emre, 1929). Its action centres on Osman, a bossy would-be Padishah, and the heroic Turhan (an old Turkish name meaning chief or nobleman). The names are chosen intentionally to accentuate the difference between the Ottoman imperial past (Osman is the eponym of the Ottoman [Osmanlı] dynasty) and the Turkish nationalist aspect of the Republic. Unsurprisingly, it is Turhan who emerges as the guardian of Republican values against this reactionary Ottoman usurper. Each protagonist is surrounded with a crowd of anonymous partisans, who seem to represent factions in broader society. Here is a taste of the dialogue from the opening lines:

> OSMAN: (rifle on his shoulder, w/ a contingent of children behind him, sternly): Look sharp! Come here all of you and let me see you. (The children stop their playing and look on in astonishment.)
> TURHAN: (bravely): Are we supposed to come on your order?
> OSMAN: Yes, on my order. Leave your games and come here! (He aims his rifle at them, and so do his confederates.)
> TURHAN: What do you want from us?
> OSMAN: You will give me all of your toys and all of your playthings.
> TURHAN: Oh, sir, oh! (Vay beyim vay!) Who do you think you are? You are acting like the evil padishah who robbed the nation. That day has gone, my dear. (O zaman geçti, yavrum.)

Eventually, of course, Turhan and his faction of Republicans win the battle. Turhan's last line is: 'Let's all shout together, "Down with the Sultan; Long live the Republic!"'

While it is faintly possible that this skit represented an actual children's game, this supposition seems rather far-fetched. School textbooks and the children's press of the late Ottoman and early Republican period were invariably didactic, reflecting an authoritarian approach to pedagogy that has proved difficult to dislodge. But the need to draw such a stark line between empire and republic must have been partly due to the well-attested instinct for successor states of the nationalist stripe to denigrate their immediate predecessors and partly due to the fact that, from a child's perspective at least, much less had changed than the rhetoric had suggested.

Before turning from this sort of attempt to use education to propagandise for the Republic and against the Empire, I should mention parenthetically that in recent years Turkey has witnessed an approach that seems calculated to achieve almost the opposite effect. This is the summoning of the Ottoman Empire generally, and on occasion, Ottoman education and learning in particular,[2] to celebrate the empire's history and, only slightly more subtly, to criticise the aggressive secularism and presumed religio-cultural deracination of the Republic. The new curriculum celebrates Ottoman achievements and positions this celebration so as to suit contemporary interests, often for reasons of politics or public relations. What is interesting here, of course, is that the Ottoman past is sufficiently vast to accommodate a wide range of agendas (secular, Islamist, Turkish nationalist, humanist, and so forth.)

Turning to the more scholarly treatment of the Ottoman educational legacy, it should be noted that while there are many examples from the literature to choose from, remarkably few of them touch directly on the question of Ottoman educational legacy. It is interesting to note that until fairly recently, much of the scholarly attention devoted to education in Turkey tended to play down or even ignore completely the question of the Republic's inheritance from the Ottoman Empire.

One of the first scholars to take up the question of the Ottoman antecedents of Republican policy was the late Roderic Davison. His 1981 article entitled 'Atatürk's Reforms: Back to the Roots' was devoted to demonstrating the extent to which key Kemalist concepts and themes were indebted to Ottoman precedents. Davison's tone is deferential, even slightly apologetic. He writes that, 'It is, I think, no derogation from Kemal's achievement that he built on what he found, both concept and institution. The Republic owes much to the Empire; the Empire also owes much to the Republic' (Davison, 1990, p. 243). While it is of course impossible for an inheritance to work in reverse – in other words, for the deceased either to reap tangible benefit from his or her heirs or to pass judgment on how they treat their bequest – what Davison says nevertheless points us towards the reciprocity that is embedded in the historical relationship between an *ancien régime* and its successor. For Davison, making mention of the mutual nature of the Ottoman/Republican debt was perhaps a way of attempting to restore a sense of balance and harmony to a relationship generally regarded otherwise.

By implying that the republic went a long way towards finishing what the empire intended to complete, Davison is actually, in spite of his extremely gentle, guarded tone, saying something that went against the scholarly grain. The prevailing wisdom had, of course, emphasised rupture and discontinuity.

Davison's article shows how the late Ottoman state had laid the ground for much of what would come to pass under Atatürk through twelve separate categories. The last of these thematic points is the most relevant here, namely, the concept of an expanded sphere of governmental activity and responsibility. Davison's prime example of this expansion is state-supported education. He writes, 'The Republic has inherited both the educational goal of the Tanzimat period and the secular school system they created, and has built on them. There is no possibility that the state will again abandon all education to private or religious initiative. The expanded area of state activity begun during the Tanzimat era is irreversible' (Davison, 1990, p. 258).

Davison clearly believed that the general direction of this irreversible shift was essentially positive, as have most who have written on the subject of educational change in the Ottoman and Turkish Republican context. But other voices have argued that the shift involved losses as well as gains. In other words, to return to the legal phrasing of legacy, some aspects of the Ottoman inheritance were dissipated or squandered. For example, Büşra Ersanlı Behar, in a chapter on the 'Ottoman Legacy' in her book *İktidar ve Tarih* (Power and History) makes the point that the richness of the Ottoman historiographical experience did not survive into the early Republic (Ersanlı Behar, 1992, p. 59).

A more typical, and much less critical, view of this transition has been supplied by Joseph Szyliowicz, whose article 'The Ottoman Educational Legacy: Myth or Reality' provides the main scholarly attempt to address the concept of the Ottoman educational legacy head on. In this article Szyliowicz, who has written on Middle Eastern education in the context of modernisation, sensibly begins by evoking the historiographical problems inherent in his subject (Szyliowicz, 1996). Firstly, Mustafa Kemal's reforms were 'explicitly designed to destroy links with the past', and secondly, the fact that different Ottoman territories received their independence at different times, although this is not germane to the Turkish case. He then proceeds, again sensibly, to divide material on Turkey into two categories of the 'material inheritance that the Turkish republic received and then discuss features of the Ottoman educational system that are also characteristic of the contemporary educational scene'. He then divides these characteristics into those with a strong and those with a 'more indirect' link to the Ottoman past. So far so good, for setting out a sort of detective's approach to the Ottoman educational legacy. Problems arise, however, as soon as he sets out the underlying premises and assumptions upon which his understanding of the Ottoman/Republican educational transition is based. What follow are a number of statements that are highly questionable and reveal a number of biases that reflect a more or less unreconstructed Republican position:

'The Turkish republic was not heir to a rich patrimony. Although efforts had been made for over a century to create a modern system of schooling, only limited progress had been achieved by the end of World War I' (Szyliowicz, 1996, p. 285). This is a highly debatable point; the side one takes on this question depends entirely on what baseline one accepts for measuring the 'progress' of the Ottoman educational effort. More recent scholarship tends to see the efforts expended on school construction in the Tanzimat, Hamidian and Young Turk periods as formidable, particularly given the obstacles that had to be overcome in terms of organisation, funding, logistics, and manpower (Somel, 2001; Fortna, 2002).

Szyliowicz's view of the Ottoman efforts is fairly dismissive. 'Another unfortunate legacy the republic inherited from the Ottoman Empire was a conservative orientation'. Seen from the context of nineteenth-century Ottoman realities (and not those of the Republic), it could easily be argued that the Ottoman policy of creating *de novo* an entirely new educational system intended to be independent from the existing *medrese* system, and of drawing inspiration from the latest pedagogical practices in Western Europe, may be labelled a number of things, but 'conservative' would not be one of them. Szyliowicz goes on to praise education of the Ottoman classical period, and then to describe the decline and ossification of the subsequent periods. As for the nineteenth-century reforms, often hailed as exemplary for their Western inspiration and influence, he sets the bar for progressiveness out of reach. The reformers are blamed for not defining 'the problem in terms of overall educational transformation, in terms of introducing Western knowledge in all phases of Ottoman life' (Szyliowicz, 1996, p. 286). It becomes clear that in this view, nothing less than the most radical solution could qualify as 'progress'.

At several points, Szyliowicz's criticism is directed at unwanted phenomena of educational life that appeared in both empire and republic. Perhaps sharing Davison's reluctance to criticise Atatürk's republic, the author finds it convenient to lay these problems at the Ottoman door, leaving unaddressed or at least blurred the question of Republican responsibility for the persistence of such problems as rote memorisation, verbal parroting, overcrowded curricula, the insufficiency of schools and lack of qualified teachers, and the various problems associated with rigid centralisation and authoritarian control.

We thus have a series of statements – there are others – that display a propensity to judge Ottoman education by standards of a later age, as if Szyliowicz were unable, or perhaps unwilling, to attempt to challenge the early Republican attempt to sever the links with the past. While I do not wish to single out Szyliowicz for undue criticism, his article is fairly representative of the prevailing attitude towards the question of Ottoman educational legacy in the early Republic, which has only recently been challenged, either explicitly or implicitly, by such scholars as Aksin Somel, Faith Childress, Barak Salmoni, and others working in the history of Ottoman and/or Turkish education. As a result of their efforts, the frequently unacknowledged (or under-acknowledged) Ottoman precedents for Republican educational successes have recently been restored.

Ruptures and continuities

I would like to turn, in this final section, to an assessment of the extent to which the Ottoman-to-Republican transition in education can be characterised by rupture and by continuity. As mentioned above, an important feature of the early Republic's educational stance was its emphasis on, indeed often its celebration of, a number of striking breaks with the immediate past. As with the political, social, economic, and of course, sartorial changes that it instituted, the Republic intended to portray those in education as new, revolutionary developments.

The most radical, and the most destructive, of these measures was the abolition of almost all religious education. Mostly, of course, this policy meant the closure of Islamic schools, that is, the *medrese* system and the Qur'an schools (although some of these continued in clandestine fashion) (Meeker, 2002, p. 62ff.),[3] but it also meant bringing non-Muslim and foreign schools more closely under state control (although the late Ottoman state had already taken steps in this direction.)

While the Republic continued to expand the educational system along Ottoman lines for the most part, an institutional departure took the form of the Village Institutes (köy enstitüleri) one of the more striking initiatives of the Republic, and one that represented a shift from the cosmopolitan emphasis of Ottoman education to the needs of the Anatolian countryside.

In terms of content, the early Republican period brought education into alignment with the laicism of official state doctrine. In state schools this meant, among other things, an end to prayer and mosques in schools. It also meant that the Islamic and imperial referents were replaced with the cult of the Turkish nation and, gradually, that of Mustafa Kemal, whose sayings and image were with time inserted into the set texts and the iconography of schooling. As Yael Navaro-Yashin has recently argued, this development lay the young Republic open to charges of merely having replaced one cult with another (Navaro-Yashin, 2002).

This replacement was accompanied by a posture of decisive cultural break with the Ottoman past: textbooks skipping over Ottoman history to Turkish history of pre-Islamic times; the break with the Arabic script; and, as we saw with the skit featuring Osman and Turhan, a general denigration of all things Ottoman. The young – and many of the not so young – undoubtedly found this tendency baffling, but then regime change frequently produces curious effects; everything has changed and yet on a daily basis it may appear as if hardly anything has been altered.

In many ways, the boldest elements of Kemalist educational policy have not fared well against the test of time. To name only two examples, the village institutes lasted a mere fourteen years, and the suppression of religion in the educational sphere was later ended by Ataturk's own party as it campaigned for the first openly contested elections of 1950. Indeed, today's Turkey contains in the Gülen schools boarding institutions that bear striking parallels with the secondary schools instituted during the reign of Sultan Abdülhamid II (Turam, 2007). Conversely, it could easily be argued that the biggest successes of Republican education are to be found in those initiatives that followed on from Ottoman policies. For example, Republican successes in the areas of literacy rates, female education, the greater provision of education across the sector and foreign-language instruction, especially at the university level, were all based on initiatives carried over from Ottoman programmes.

I should like now to move onto some of the many areas of continuity and commonality shared between Ottoman and Turkish Republican educational endeavours. The parallels are particularly striking if one allows for a number of symbolic but essentially superficial shifts, such as the replacement of the sultan's insignia – and towards the very end of the Ottoman years, his image – with that of Mustafa Kemal and from 1928, the advent of the Latin script. On a more substantive note, Republican education shared with its Ottoman predecessor numerous aspects of what I referred to earlier as the tangible legacy: school buildings, teachers, central education ministry infrastructure, curricula, and inspectors. And of course, it shared the same students, a subject of considerable academic discussion due to the fact that Young Turk movement arose in late Ottoman schools in the period of Sultan Abdülhamid II (reigned 1876–1909) and many of these individuals went on to play critical roles in the founding and shaping of the Republic. This debate can become a game of praise and blame, especially given the uncomfortable relationship between the Kemalists and the Young Turks after 1923. But we must remember that most students were not activists and probably could not point to very many changes accompanying the shift from empire to republic.

Both the Empire and the Republic shared a range of characteristics and qualities that defined: a) what education is, or is supposed to be; b) what its proper sources and influences were and are; and c) how education ought best to be practiced. Many of these characteristics are also common to almost all other cases of educational expansion, so I will not concentrate on such issues as the struggle for funding, the hope and despair engendered by such ambitious educational plans, or other nearly universal elements. To begin with, in both the late Ottoman and early Republican periods one notices a tension between education as a general, indeed universal concept, and education as a project to be applied to produce a range of specific desiderata. There are echoes in the Republic, for example, of the nineteenth-century Ottoman discussions regarding education as a general good needed to 'catch up' with the West, or as a specific tool required for the proper training of state functionaries, or the means to provide specific vocational skills (Fortna, 2002, Chapter 2; Somel, 2001, p. 173ff.). Those familiar with the current state of higher education in the United Kingdom will note the parallels with the present-day debates over education qua learning versus education qua 'transferable skills', in Hefce-speak. And there are echoes still further back in time to the appearance of the concept of *maarif*, in the terms of Niyazi Berkes, 'the process of becoming acquainted with things unknown', to challenge '`ilm', that is knowledge in the context of the sacred (Berkes, 1963, pp. 99–100).

On both sides of the 1923 divide, a mixture of western and indigenous sources inspired educational initiatives. The buzzwords current in the most up-to-date discussions of educational theory and practice in Western Europe and North America of the day can be found in educational reports and memoranda produced by both the Ottoman and Turkish ministries of education. The systems, curricula and even the buildings that emerged as a result appeared at times to have attained a successful blend of these various elements, a hybrid of East and West that seemed appropriate for either the Ottoman or the Republican context. At other times, as has often been noted, the contradictions became painfully apparent, especially given the extent to which many of its features were imported. France was the common source for a range of educational features, ranging from the general approach to education down to the specifics of course content and architectural plans. The Ottomans found France's centralised plans and eclectic curriculum to their liking, while the Republicans appreciated its laicist approach, as Andrew Mango has recently noted (Mango, 2004, p. 158).

Both Ottoman and Republican educationalists saw education as an arena of contestation, a battleground against unwanted Western influence, especially in the form of missionary schools, but the locally administered minority schools were rarely beyond the suspicion of the relevant ministries. With the Unity of Education (*Tevhid-i tedrisat*) law of 1924, the Republic can be seen to have fulfilled a long-held wish that the Ottoman state lacked only the means to undertake. Both systems approached education as a vehicle for enforcing social discipline, inculcating morality, and fostering patriotism and used the highly centralised, highly hierarchical educational infrastructure borrowed from the French in this attempt. The uniformity and centralised nature of first the imperial and then the national school system was well suited to the practice of curricular vetting and control followed by both states. In this sense, such Republican institutions as first the Council of Educational Policy (Talim ve Terbiye Heyeti) and later the Higher Education Council (Yüksek Öğretim Kurulu, or YÖK) seem very much of a piece with late Ottoman curricular commissions of the sort established by Abdülhamid II.

First Ottoman and then Republican institutions like these have monitored and controlled teachers, textbooks, and the students themselves.

Both systems were highly concerned with uniformity, order, and obedience. Both were equally taken with the 'pedagogical' approach, which, as Mardin has noted, favoured the centralised, uniform curriculum above the more personal relationship between master and apprentice (Mardin, 1997, p. 123). Furthermore, as Akşin Somel has indicated in his impressive study of late Ottoman education, the internalised 'social disciplining' of the late Ottoman period flowed naturally into the early Republican period with, if anything, more attention to social control (Somel, 2001, p. 179ff.). As Somel puts it:

> Though unable to keep the Empire from disintegration, the Hamidian generation of students nevertheless were able to found the Turkish Republic. But their eagerness in order and uniformity continued to display itself in every aspect of the Republican reforms, where even the clothing of individuals became defined and ordered by the administration.
>
> (Somel, 2001, p. 277)

These characteristics shared between empire and republic are hardly unique to the Ottoman/Turkish case. In fact most of them are to be found in other comparable cases of educational history – the Russian/Soviet example comes to mind, but there are also intriguing and suggestive parallels to be found further afield, in China or Vietnam, for example. In my view, these parallels only serve to reinforce the extent to which Ottoman/Turkish educational change was of a piece with worldwide trends, another element of the Ottoman educational legacy.

Conclusion: Education and changing agendas in Empire and Republic

Education is a subject freighted with larger agendas, larger than even the task of raising future generations, and, as we know from listening to countless contemporary politicians, even as they refuse to fund education at a commensurate level, there is nothing more important than that task. In the case of the transition from Ottoman Empire to Turkish Republic, the question of educational legacy is especially fraught, given the extent to which both the late Ottoman Empire and the Turkish Republic invested monetary and political capital in formulating and expanding a centralised educational system. There were different degrees of personal attachment between the leader and the cause of education, of course. It was only very late that images of the sultan were deployed in an educational context, but until then his monogram, and frequently evidence of his personal role as a benefactor of libraries and schools, functioned in the same way. In this Mustafa Kemal was – and of course remains – in a field by himself, but this achievement surely has more to do with the changing context and media of political discourse in the twentieth century than anything else.[4]

Stepping back from 1923, the issue of imperial to republican transition allows us to see the question of the Ottoman educational legacy in broad relief. In the long run, the empire-to-republic shift seems much less abrupt than we have been led to imagine. On the contrary, it appears to fit rather comfortably in a timeline of shifts and adaptations, which reflect the pendular swings and 'corrections' that connect instead of separate the periods involved. As the Tanzimat gave way to the Hamidian period and then to the Young Turk, so also can we see the Young Turk leading on to the single-party period, incorporating the Tevhid-i Tedrisat (unity of education) legislation and the Dil Devrimi (language 'reform'), and then again to the multi-party period with the return of religious education in large numbers, despite the avowed laicism of the state.

The year 1923 probably was much less of an historical watershed than such epochal dates are meant to convey and created far less impermeability than generally supposed. For the Republican elite, of course, the desire to set itself against the Ottoman Empire was understandable and very much in keeping with its contemporaries among the post-Ottoman nation states in the Balkans and the Arab world. The Ottoman legacy proved a temptingly convenient source of blame for problems, whether real or imagined. But for the Republic, like the Ottoman Empire in the Hamidian and Young Turk periods, the way forward in education was largely determined by immediate past precedent. It was by continuing in the direction established as far back as the Tanzimat era that the Republic found its most lasting educational successes. Taking the long view shows us that both Ottoman and early Republican educational efforts were ultimately aiming for the same goal, namely, to provide education that was both Ottoman or Turkish and modern.

Notes

1. For a brief synopsis of education in the late Ottoman and Turkish Republican periods, see Fortna (2002a).
2. In April 1999, for example, an international conference was organised in Istanbul on the subject of Learning and Education in the Ottoman Empire. It was attended by scholars from around the world, with a marked representation from Islamic countries, and by a number of dignitaries from the Organisation of the Islamic Conference, including Sheikh Ahmad Zaki Yamani and a large retinue. The academic level of the papers was extremely variable.
3. See, for example, Meeker's discussion of the underground *medreses* in the district of Of in the province of Trabzon.
4. On the cult of Atatürk as expressed through images of the man, see Navaro-Yashin (2002).

Bibliography

N. Berkes (1963) *The Development of Secularism in Turkey* (Montreal: McGill University Press).

R. Davison (1990) 'Atatürk's Reforms: Back to the Roots', in R. Davison (ed.) *Essays in Ottoman and Turkish History, 1774–1923: The Impact of the West* (Austin: University of Texas Press). Reprint of article originally published in 1981.

A. C. Emre (1929) *Cumhuriyet Çocuklarına Türkçe Kıraat* (Istanbul: Hilmi).

B. Ersanlı Behar (1992) *İktidar ve Tarih: Türkiye'de 'Resmi Tarih' Tezinin Oluşumu (1929–1937)* (Istanbul: Afa).

B. C. Fortna (2002) *Imperial Classroom: Islam, the State, and Education in the Late Ottoman Empire* (Oxford: Oxford University Press).

B. C. Fortna (2002a) 'Turkey – Education System', in *Encyclopedia of Modern Asia*, vol. 5 (New York: Scribners).

A. Mango (2004) *The Turks Today* (London: John Murray).

Ş. Mardin (1997) 'The Ottoman Empire', in K. Barkey and M. von Hagen (ed.) *After Empire: Multiethnic Societies and Nation Building, The Soviet Union and the Russian, Ottoman and Habsburg Empires* (Boulder: Westview).

M. Meeker (2002) *A Nation of Empire: The Ottoman Legacy of Turkish Modernity* (Berkeley: University of California Press).

Y. Navaro-Yashin (2002) *Faces of the State: Secularism and Public Life in Turkey* (Princeton: Princeton University Press).

S. A. Somel (2001) *The Modernisation of Public Education in the Ottoman Empire, 1839–1908: Islamisation, Autocracy and Discipline* (Leiden: E. J. Brill).

J. Szyliowicz (1996) 'The Ottoman Educational Legacy: Myth or Reality', in L. C. Brown (ed.) *Imperial Legacy: The Ottoman Imprint on the Balkans and the Middle East* (New York: Columbia University Press).

B. Turam (2007) *Between Politics and the State: The Politics of Engagement* (Stanford: Stanford University Press).

2
Genç Kalemler and Turkish Nationalism

Murat Belge

This paper examines a single periodical, a literary-cultural journal called *Genç Kalemler* (Young Pens), which was published in Thessaloniki from April 1911 to October 1912. Thirty-three issues were printed throughout this period. The journal has always been well known to students of Turkish nationalism, as it was one of the earliest examples of what one might call a pan-Turkist publication. It was in this journal that Ömer Seyfeddin started his campaign for a purer Turkish language, rid of the Arabic and Persian cumbrances of the composite Ottoman language. Here he collaborated with Ziya Gökalp, who, in addition to being a regular writer, was probably the mentor of the entire project as well as its liaison person with the CUP (Committee of Unity and Progress). Several of the contributors were well-known militants of the nationalist movement. In 1999, the 33 issues of *Genç Kalemler* were transcribed into the new alphabet by Ismail Parlatır and Çetin and published by the Turkish Language Foundation, making the journal much more accessible to scholars (Parlatır and Çetin, 1999).

The compactness of the publication is striking. Here, in this collected volume, amounting to less than 600 pages, one can see several important characteristics of Turkish nationalism, as we have known it in later years, already fully-fledged. By 'certain characteristics', I mean, for instance, the strong xenophobic element and the special bellicosity, the markedly militaristic vocabulary and the insistence on physical strength and victory. However, it is the unique mixture of myth and wish-fulfilment, the manipulation or subordination of facts and truth for the production of a desirable history, which has been such a distinct feature of Turkish nationalist ideology. All this, together with the usual insistence on race, the overtones of social-Darwinism, and the selective attention paid to nationalist experimentation and nation building in the contemporary world, is to be seen in the pages of *Genç Kalemler* – along with a lot of other material, of course, which does not fit these categories.

But this nationalist tone does not quite pervade the journal. The crux of the matter is that during the lifetime of its publication, the Italians decided to occupy the region today known as Libya. This periodical, which started as a cultural journal with a strong patriotic tendency, concentrating on problems of a 'national language', suddenly underwent a transformation and began to acquire the nationalist characteristics listed above. This invasion, later overshadowed by other events, clearly had a major effect on at least some of the Ottoman intelligentsia of the time. For example, Ömer Seyfeddin's well-known story about 'Primo, the Turkish Child' can be put in this context: it was written about a month after the invasion. In retrospect, the invasion and the Turkish response seem to have marked a historical turn of thought which has remained with us ever since. To say the least, it was instrumental in drawing out a lot of accumulated frustration on the part of Turkish intellectuals.

Reticent Turkishness in the empire

I will make a short and hasty excursion through the wide terrain of Turkish nationalism highlighting the landmarks of its development so that I can demonstrate the central position *Genç Kalemler* occupies in this context. The Turks in the Ottoman Empire, at the beginning of the Age of Nationalism, were more or less in the same position as the Germans in the Austro-Hungarian Empire, as told by Musil: feeling that they were running this enterprise called the 'Empire', they were reticent about proclaiming their ethnic origin. However, everyone else in the Empire did so, loudly and with no feeling of shame. Simultaneously, the Turks referred to the 'Ottoman' nation, for a long time, and refrained from emphasising 'Turkishness'. Turkish intellectuals viewed Turkish ethnicity as one among Albanian, Arab, Kurdish, Armenian ethnicities, which all came together to create the Ottoman nation.

These considerations of 'identity' intensified in the Ottoman Empire throughout the 19th century, as they did in many other parts of the world. The Tanzimat reforms, proclaimed in 1839, emphasised the state's will for further 're-organization'. The Tanzimat *firman*, or decree, did not itself start the modernisation movement, but officially endorsed and legalised a process that Mahmud II had started some 15 years earlier. This period ushered in the optimistic ideology of Pan-Ottomanism, the rather naive belief that a state binding itself to the rule of law and placing itself in an equal position *vis-à-vis* all the nationalities (and religious denominations) present in the empire, who thereby became equal 'citizens', would solve the chronic problems of an Empire that was increasingly anachronistic.

For various reasons, the Ottomanist project was not successful. The Tanzimat had followed the Greek War of Independence; on the eve of the last quarter of the century, Serbians and Bulgarians felt ready to repeat the Greek nationalist revolution. The Ottomans, trying to put down the rebellion, found themselves at war with Russia. This war, which lasted from 1877 until

1878, ended in catastrophe for the Ottomans, with the Russian army camping some 25 kilometres from Istanbul. This defeat was the starting point of modern Turkish history, as well as the birth of Turkish nationalist ideology. Its memory has lurked in the national(ist) psyche ever since. This was the first occasion that the Ottoman intelligentsia encountered the fear of total loss of the empire.

It was this fear, more than anything else, that shaped the Turkish national consciousness in the modern era. However, history was determined to treat Turks harshly. The defeat of 1878 was repeated, several times, in the first quarter of the new century, aggravating the fear of imperial dismemberment into a more or less permanent mood of paranoia. The second series of defeats started with the Italian invasion of Libya in 1911, which coincides with the publication of *Genç Kalemler*. But many important transformations of an ideological nature had taken place between these two movements of defeat.

Abdülhamid II, who ascended to the throne in 1876 and soon found himself in a war, correctly assessed that Pan-Ottomanism was not working. It did not persuade the non-Muslim 'subjects' of the Empire to stay within the community. This dilapidated structure had very little to offer to the various people living on its wide lands. The young and energetic ideology of nationalism was strong and getting stronger. Abdülhamid hoped that Islam would be the bond that could hold the empire together. It could be a common ground for Turks, Arabs, Kurds and the converted Caucasians in the East. In the West, the majority of Albanians were Muslims and some Slavs (Pomaks and Torbesh in Macedonia) had also converted. But Abdülhamid II learned, as others also later would, that in an age of nationalism, a common religion was not sufficient to stifle the desire for national independence. Islam was emphasised during his long reign. The spectre of 'Ottomanism' was kept alive, but the 'Ottoman subject' was increasingly defined as a Muslim. During the second Constitutional Monarchy period, Boşo, a Greek member of parliament summed up the Ottoman Christian response to this idea when he said, 'I am as Ottoman as the Ottoman banks'.

Mizancı Mehmed Murad Bey was an important figure among Ottoman intellectuals of the time of Abdülhamid. He was born (1853) and educated in Dagestan, within the Russian Empire, and came to Istanbul in 1873 to be a citizen in the capital of the Caliphate of Islam. He wrote a political novel, the first of its kind in Turkey, in 1891. It is a highly autobiographical novel, where the hero is born in Algeria and educated in France, in Western fashion; he, like his creator, studies medicine and comes to Istanbul with the same motivations as the author.

This hero, Mansur, is presented to us as a 'Muslim hero'. His nationality is not emphasised. However, the two-dimensional pattern of his 'character' can easily be (and was) filled with a national figure. The xenophobia that Murad Bey displayed towards his non-Muslim characters provided the recipe for nationalist literature as it began to form. Mansur is a disappointed hero. In spite of his Western education he (like his creator) hates the West, but this education separates him from his chosen compatriots, who lack rationalism, self-discipline, morality and patriotism. Murad Bey criticises all these 'oriental' traits quite vehemently, but even his Muslim villains cannot reach the level of depravity that is depicted as the natural essence of his non-Muslim characters.

We see in these early attempts at a nationalist literature the 'enemy' already appearing clearly, while the identity of a community defined as 'us' is still quite hazy. This phenomenon is not at all unusual in nationalist literatures. On the contrary, it was the common experience in many cases of nation building. It was also to be inherited by *Genç Kalemler* 20 years later. During the long reign of Abdülhamid, a small minority among the Turkish-Ottoman intelligentsia began to find the Islamist state policy insufficient or perhaps totally undesirable. For them, ethnic origin was much more important than religious affiliation, and consequently a more reliable social tie. The rise of this relatively new ideology proceeded in exact inverse relation with the decline of the belief in Islam as a common bond. Abdülhamid was trying to utilise Islam as an ideological tool in order to keep a multi-ethnic empire from breaking up. Turkism was becoming the nation building ideology of the younger generation of the educated classes.

Turkism and Genç Kalemler

This brings us to *Genç Kalemler*, one of the earliest journals in Turkey to embrace the Turkist ideal. The journal started (taking the place of an earlier literary magazine called *Hüsn ve Şiir*) on 11 April 1911. Many contributed to it, but three people were involved in its publication: Ali Canip, Ömer Seyfeddin and Ziya Gökalp. Gökalp was already an important influence and the 'ideologue' of the CUP. He supplied the main link between the journal and the political group. Ali Canip was 'appointed' editor-in-chief by the Committee, which supplied some money to help its publications. As a result of these influences, we can view it as a semi-official ideological organ of the CUP. But because the CUP itself did not have a systematised ideology at the time, the journal enjoyed more or less complete autonomy.

Italy declared war on the Ottoman Empire on 29 September 1911. Some of the articles of the tenth issue of the second volume were probably already at the printing press by this time. The invasion is mentioned briefly in that issue as the 'Event of the Week'. In this very brief notice, the main empha-sis is on Hakkı Paşa, the Prime Minister (Sadrıazam). He is blamed for the invasion because he had recently been in Italy as the Ottoman ambassador and had failed to predict this movement. In the next issue, published on 27 October, nothing is said about Tripoli. On the twelfth, issued in November, there is a short piece of patriotic prose addressed to the 'glorious flag' by someone called Kemal Nesrin. Çaldıran, the victory in 1515 against Iran, and for some reason, the Battle of Vienna, which was not an Ottoman victory, are mentioned to remind the flag, presumably, about past splendour. The poem mentioned the dead in their graves and calls Italy a 'mad dog'. In the same issue of the journal is a short story by Aka Gündüz, which takes place in Libya, and depicts the Italians murdering Arabs. From this point on, the Italian invasion begins to shape the content of the journal.

This event took place at a point that divides the history of the journal into two almost equal parts. What it was like *before* the invasion is important to understand fully the nature of the change. Understandably, the Turkish language was its primary concern. The first issues contained the beginning of a debate on literature, which continued for a long time, and an investigation of the concept of 'national literature'. However, even this search has more to say about the 'national language' than the possible or desired content of a national literature. An article by Ali Canip, for example, is accompanied by various young writers' answers to a question about the literary worth of four writers of the previous generation, Tevfik Fikret, Cenab Şahabeddin, Halid Ziya and Mehmed Rauf. This is also quite typical, as we see so many times an ideological debate embedded in a generational conflict. The answers printed in the issue are not complimentary to the four writers of established reputation. They have stopped inspiring the new generations, the young writers argue. There is one article in this issue sent from Paris, on Bismarck. This is interesting, since among possible models for nation-state formation, the German and the Japanese cases were usually seen as more consanguine to the Unionist temperament.

With the second volume, an editorial on national language in the beginning becomes a standard feature for the journal. Ömer Seyfeddin is mainly responsible for this topic, but Gökalp and Ali Canip also contribute articles from time to time. Their language is quite heated as they express their opinions, but their proposals are moderate. Their programme for 'purification' resists purging established Arabic or Persian words. They are against the artificial use of obscure words, which they argue are incomprehensible to the majority of the people, and they also oppose the use of foreign (Arabic, mainly) rules of grammar.

The journal carried polemical articles on literature and language, criticising several well-known writers, such as Hüseyin Cahit. Its authors also critiqued people of their own generation, people such as Yakup Kadri or Mehmet Fuat (Köprülü), but one has the feeling that in these cases, their tone is more tolerant, probably because they want to convert such young writers to their own cause.

The journal published a lot of poetry. With very few exceptions, which use militant nationalistic language, these are insipid verses, mostly in the relatively purified Turkish advocated in the editorials on language; mostly versified according to the Turkish system of syllable count rather than in 'aruz', but otherwise conforming to the conventional verse of the previous generations. They are mostly about unrequited love and similar melancholic topics and terribly uninspiring.

Ziya Gökalp's contributions featured a strong nationalism, not only in his poetry but his articles as well. The famous poem 'Turan' appears in the sixth issue in a long article entitled 'The New Language' but more concerned with the subject of literature, Gökalp argues against Bekir Fahri's contention that literature should be international in its appeal. For him, only science can be international; and even language and literature cannot be 'national' – they can only be *ethnic*.

Gökalp contributed a few articles on 'philosophy'. At the end of one of these, he is carried away by his own fervour about the new life and values that Turks are bound to create: 'The Turkish race has not, like other races, degenerated through alcohol and other profanities. The Turkish blood got younger in glorious battles and is like steel ... Turkish intelligence is not on the decline like the intelligences of other nations. Turkish sensitivity has not become effeminate as other sensitivities have. Turkish will-power has not weakened as other will-powers. The hegemony of the future lies in the Turkish endurance. The supermen imagined by the German philosopher Nietzsche are Turks' (Parlatir and Cetin, 1999, p. 239).

Ali Canip's relatively short (five quatrains) poem entitled 'The Soldier' is also interesting, as it features some of the basic themes of Turkish nationalism, in which the 'Soldier' image is all-important. In this poem, we see this image-in-the-making, as the poet tells the soldier what to do. In the future, this relationship will turn around, with the soldier posing as the source of everything right and proper. But at this point, when it is difficult to find military glory, the poet is reminding the soldier of victories of the past and telling him to rejoice in the memory. The wisdom that the 'country will rise on blood' has become a staple of Turkish nationalism ever since. In 'Sen büsbütün uyan ki uyansın bütün vatan' we see both the desire to view the army as the leader of the nation (which will be characteristic of the Turkish model) and the exasperation that this was still far from the truth at the time.

Ömer Seyfeddin was mostly preoccupied with linguistic matters but also produced some short stories. The best-known piece of his from this period is 'Bomba', a story of Bulgarian 'komitacı' forces terrorising other (left-wing) Bulgarian peasants. It is a harsh story, but at least portrays the socialist Bulgarians as human beings, a view that is not the defining feature of his later work. He also published a play in this publication (Parlatır and Çetin, 1999, pp. 152–9). In it, a young Armenian lady lauds Turks and Muslims to the degree of praising polygamy as the most natural form of marriage.

After the Italian invasion of Libya: The anti-civilisationist turn

Ideological change is never abrupt. The Italian invasion did not change the character of *Genç Kalemler* (or the other of the channels of Turkish nationalism at the time) immediately. Some reactions did come early, like Ömer Seyfeddin's story, 'Primo, the Turkish Boy', but others took a longer time to develop. In the third volume of *Genç Kalemler*, issues 17 and 18 are printed together. In this issue we see a name for the first time in the journal's history: Mehmed Ali Tevfik. He occupies more than one half of this rather thick issue. His first contribution is a long article entitled 'India and the Turks', and in a footnote we read that this is the text of a talk he gave at the Union and Progress Club in Thessaloniki about a fortnight before. He talks about the Turkish-Mughal Empire of India with obvious nationalist overtones, but with some effort at impartiality as well. However, at the end of the talk, he assumes a more belligerent anti-Western tone. He condemns the West for the libel of calling Turks 'barbarians' and says 'We shall not listen to the lies and calumnies of Europe any more; we shall listen to history itself', and adds that 'The Turkish nation is on a par with Anglo-Saxon and Latin nations from today and awaits the date of reaching a throne unreachable for other races'.

But Mehmed Ali Tevfik's most interesting contribution to this issue of *Genç Kalemler* is his selection of seven poems, mostly in Petrarchan sonnet form, expressing his reaction to the Italian invasion. The word that is most recurrent in these poems is 'revenge'. It occurs at least once in almost all of them. One addresses the 'Turkish Youth' and tells him to forget immediately 'love, women, flowers' and think only of taking revenge on Italy, leaving its fields in blood, its seas in blood, and its skies in blood (the word 'blood' is also quite recurrent). These poems contain all the elements of nationalist Turkish poetry and discourse. But one interesting point is the identification of Italy with the Roman Empire. Against the Roman image, the author invokes the spirit of Cengiz (Genghis Khan) and Attila of Turkic history. The Cengizes and Atillas of the future are to come and overrun Italy (or Rome) so that places of worship will be razed to the ground, blood will flow in the Tiber, and graves will cover the land.

One earlier poem, by Akil Koyuncu, also deserves special attention, because it anticipates some of the verse written after the Italian invasion. The poem expressed similar sentiments about Crete. One of the rare victories of the Ottoman army at this stage of history was won in the battle over Crete against Greece in 1897. But, nevertheless, after several years of semi-autonomous existence, Crete had voted to join Greece, and this had been another blow to Ottoman pride. In this poem, Koyuncu tells Greeks to stop boasting about being the progeny of Achilles. Greece 'is a black spot on *my* history'! He writes that he wants to, and will one day no doubt, erase it.

In such poems a strange process is occurring: present-day nationalities are identified with antique civilisations (the name of Achilles is obviously a reference to Homer) and then Turks are shown as the destroyers of these civilisations.

Another poem in the same issue, written by Hakkı Süha and dedicated to Ali Canip, echoes quite closely the spirit of Mehmed Ali Tevfik. Here, a second Atilla is expected to put the crescent on the most prominent house of worship, and grab the Italian crown. In the last issue of the journal, Gökalp publishes a poem which is the culmination of this theme, with the refrain, 'Don't forget it, you are Atilla's son'. Two lines are particularly peculiar: 'Don't summon "civilisation", she is deaf/ Leave no stone upon stone, destroy' (Parlatır and Çetin, 1999, p. 571) (If we are to destroy in this fashion, why should we accuse civilisation of being deaf?)

The anti-civilisational element in Turkish nationalism also appears in the long poem by Mehmed Âkif that was picked up to become the National Anthem during the War of Independence. Here, Âkif refers to civilisation as 'a monster with only one tooth remaining'. It is difficult to understand this emotional state. If the West called Turks 'barbarians' and held them responsible for attacking and destroying civilisation, it becomes all the more difficult to understand why these nationalist Turks almost joyfully accepted this accusation. It was probably their frustrated anger that makes them willingly embrace this role of 'destroyer of civilisation'. In their ideology, their thrust for Westernization and modernisation, there is no doubt that the West is 'civilized'. If that is the case, the well-deserved punishment of the West would necessarily involve punishing 'civilisation' at the same time. And the Turk, determined to take his revenge, would not hesitate in fulfilling his duty.

At this point, I would like to make a comparison with the nation-state building process in Greece. Greeks decided to make Athens their capital in 1834 (until then, Nauplion was the capital). At this time, Athens was an unprepossessing small town with a population reduced to less than 5000, most of which was ethnic Albanian. It was not the contemporary state of Athens but its place and prestige in history which influenced this decision. The leaders of the Greek War of Independence were very much 'men of the Enlightenment', admiring pagan Greece more than the Christian Byzantine Empire. This feeling of the native cadres had been reciprocated by European Hellenophiles. In its historical background, Greece had an Athens and a Sparta. The intelligentsia of the early nineteenth century preferred to identify themselves not with Sparta, but with Athens. Such a decision cannot determine everything, but it is very important. Attempts at reviving old traditions are usually very artificial and cannot work. Yet, the kind of tradition that people wish to identify with are important, because this is the outcome of a series of real options.

Turkey did not *really* have a Sparta (nor an Athens); but decided to invent one. The Central Asian steppe, which so many people had tried so hard to abandon, became the 'homeland', described almost as a Garden of Eden. It has since been glorified by generations of nationalistic writers. There is still a certain ambiguity between *Ötüken*, reputedly the capital (composed of tents!) of the warlike Turks, and the Uigur capital where the earliest Turkic writing (and consequently, 'civilisation') was discovered.

The most important reason for this significant difference in the Greek and Turkish mentalities in reconstructing their history at a certain stage of their nation building endeavour is the character of the social strata that acted as the 'founding fathers'. Greece lived without its own state for a half millennium. The Ottomans, replacing the Byzantine Empire, were much closer to it in many ways except for language, in comparison to the Greeks living in the lands of present-day Greece. The Greek forces fought with no regular army and had a state experience only after establishing the nation-state.

The Turks, in contrast, had a long history of a strong state. The Young Turk movement was one of those very rare oppositional movements which had a central ideology of 'saving the state'. The Army was the *force majeure* in the whole enterprise. The underground organisation of the Committee of Union and Progress itself dragged on quite inefficiently until the young army officers in Macedonia began to join after 1905 and suddenly turned it into a powerful movement. The Army kept this role of leadership in the establishment of the Republic as well, and therefore it holds a unique and important place in the entire movement of Turkish modernisation. Ali Canip writes about himself in the 'humour' section, in the second issue, claiming there is an emotional, as well as an intellectual Ali Canip. The former enjoys Cenab's poetry and is inclined to get sentimental. The latter, however, is captivated by Sparta and Nietzsche. Most of his literary friends would agree. Many were officers by profession, such as Ömer Seyfeddin, Kazım Nami, Aka Gündüz, Ferit Tek, Ömer Naci and many others. They believed that Turkey had to take the militarist pathway towards nation-statehood, and this view is reflected in many pages of the *Genç Kalemler*.

Very soon after the Italian invasion, Ömer Seyfeddin published his most blatantly racialist short story, about Primo. Primo is the child of a Westernising Turk and his Italian wife, and is brought up in the Italian way. Kenan Bey, the father, is a pacifist and hates war. Ömer Seyfeddin also adds that he hates Darwin, thus demonstrating the strong influence of social-Darwinism on himself and on his friends in the CUP. Seyfeddin is also an enemy of the Masons (Kenan Bey is one, to be sure) which is a bit surprising as so many of the CUP leaders came from the Masonic lodges of Thessaloniki.

The invasion of Libya disturbed the 'happiness' of this family. Kenan Bey is estranged from his wife, Grazia. But it is their son, Primo, who undergoes the greatest transformation. In some inexplicable way, he decides to become a Turk and stay with his father. He grabs a chair and hits the pictures of Victor Emmanuel and Garibaldi with it. Again for some inexplicable reason, he hates and rejects his mother (which brings great joy to the author): 'Grazia, the effeminate and cowardly symbol of the West, weak, ill and effete, sure to be crushed under the certain triumph of Turan, victorious, young, strong and sharp Turan, was now weeping in great sobs'. This is how the story ends.

Mehmed Ali Tevfik gave a second talk at the club in the city, and this is also reproduced in the journal. This passage is much more interesting in its content and has had long-lasting effects. Tevfik begins his talk by introducing a new concept, that of the 'spiritual homeland'. He says that everybody has a homeland of a physical kind and loves it, but this is not important. What is needed is a 'spiritual homeland', meaning that the present generation is attached spiritually to those who lived before. In this sense, he asserts, 'the main element of spiritual homeland is the graveyard'. He talks of three channels of attachment in this talk, which he begins with a reference to Ernest Renan: 1) to be of the same blood, 2) the feeling of having grown up in a certain way with certain ideas and emotions, and 3) a sense of gratitude. Renan, of course, has nothing to do with the 'blood' argument.

He then gives examples of two nations which have successfully manufactured such spiritual homelands. The first example is the Argentine one, and here Tevfik tells us that the Argentinian schools produced an extremely nationalist education and trained people to admire the greatness of their nation. They learned that Argentina has the greatest soldiers and generals in the world. Tevfik finds this kind of boasting humorous, but hastens to add that 'these are legitimate lies – this is a legitimate tactic to establish the spiritual homeland'. Thus, he implies, Turks should not laugh at Argentinean teachers but must emulate them.

His second example is, unsurprisingly, Japan. In Japan the schools also fed the students with a constant national 'fanaticism'. They were taught to feel only contempt for the Europeans. Tevfik tells us that the Japanese kept the truth about European scientific inventions in science secret, so that Japanese kids had only contempt for the West. In this way, they created the Japanese spiritual homeland. He tells several anecdotes of a militarist tendency. A young soldier misses his wife and secretly comes home to sleep with her one night, but kills her as he returns so as not to repeat the experience. Another Japanese soldier is hit in the face by a bullet, but all the Japanese ladies admire him because his deformity is the outcome of his patriotism. An empress kills her emperor husband with her own hands when he is defeated in battle.

Tevfik then assures us that Turks do not have to create lies to establish the spiritual homeland that makes one discover a divine pleasure in death. He argues that all those high qualities needed for a spiritual homeland are already present in Turkish history. Mehmed Ali Tevfik feels no pressure to camouflage his proposal; quite explicitly, he advocates a conscious distortion of historiography. Reality is not as important as a strong nationalist ideology.

His proposal did not evaporate. Twenty years later, the young Republic of Turkey held its first 'History Congress' under the aegis and the authoritarian eyes of her president, Kemal Atatürk. Yusuf Akçura, a contemporary of Tevfik from Kazan, made a speech toward the end of that meeting in which he stated that a little modification of historical fact would not be considered a great sin, since every other nation was doing the same thing.

The Minister of Education, in his closing speech, said that the message had been understood. The entire 'History Thesis' of the 1930s, together with the accompanying 'Theory of Sun-Language', shows the extent the Republic was prepared to falsify history to obtain a satisfactory historical account, a 'grand narrative' celebrating the feats of the great Turkish nation. The exaggerations of the thirties faded away in time, but the practice of political manipulation of historiography has continued to this day.

Conclusion

It is surprising that this journal, neither very thick nor very long-lived, to which only a handful of the contemporary literati contributed, could play such an effective role in the genesis of Turkish nationalism. Digging up old national myths, or fabricating them when digging was unsuccessful; the close interest in the German and the Japanese models of nationalism; the close interest in Social-Darwinist thought; the complex relationship with the concept of civilisation which quite often leads to a proud proclamation of vandalism; the anti-humanist sub-current in idealising national and racial prowess; and, above all, the tendency to manipulate historical truth to form a desirable nationalist ideology: all of this can be observed in *Genç Kalemler* for the first time and all of this has been with us ever since.

Bibliography

İ. Parlatır and N. Çetin (eds) (1999) *Genç Kalemler Dergisi* (Ankara: Türk Dil Kurumu Yayınları).

3
Nation Building and Feminism in Early Republican Turkey

Yeşim Arat

The nation building project in Turkey has precipitated improvements in women's status and the expansion of women's opportunities. Contemporary feminism, on the other hand, has focused on women's agency in this process. Most post-1980s feminists developed their discourse, if not identity, in opposition to the Kemalist discourse on women's rights. If Kemalists expanded women's rights because, as founding fathers, they knew what women's interests were, feminists claimed they wanted rights because they knew their interests better than men did. Women's agency was at the heart of the controversy. Even today, as Turkey's process of nation building undergoes important structural changes in its desire to become part of Europe, any women's issue that is significant in shaping the contours of the nation state is still about women's agency.

This paper will probe the question of women's agency in the process of nation building in early Republican Turkey. Even though feminists have drawn attention to the instrumental nature of reforms that extended women's rights, women's relationships to those reforms and their engagement in the process still needs to be examined. Feminist scholars have pointed to the significance of women's demands for emancipation prior to the Republic, and analysed how they were ignored and dismissed in the process of nation building and modernisation during the early days of the Republic (Çakir, 1993; Zihnioğlu, 2003). I would like to extend this discussion to the question of women' s engagement and stance towards the modernising reforms and the reformers themselves. Because women benefited dramatically from these reforms, many scholars have assumed and provided research to demonstrate that women of the era endorsed the modernising reforms of the founding fathers eagerly, uncritically and uniformly as subjects of the nation. This paper will argue that feminist women leaders of the day differed from one another in the way they engaged in the process of nation building and modernisation in their country. I will focus on two prominent women, Halide Edip Adıvar, the novelist who actively took part in the War of Independence, and Afet İnan, the adopted daughter of Mustafa Kemal, the founding father of the Republic. Halide Edip was a shrewd critic of the new regime and Afet İnan was its vocal propagandist. Yet both women sought to construct their own subjectivity and articulate their own nationalism and feminism as they engaged in the process of modernisation and nation building defined by the founding fathers.

Women's instrumental roles and agency

With the advent of the new republic, Mustafa Kemal and his friends undertook a well-known series of modernising reforms in Turkey. Arguably, the women of the country were the most important beneficiaries of these reforms. Within a decade or two, women gained a series of rights comparable to those of women in most progressive democracies of the day. Not only were they set free from the restrictions of the Islamic legal code, but they were also enfranchised as citizens equal to men. With the 1926 Civil Code, they gained the rights to divorce and receive equal inheritance to men. Polygamy was abolished and in 1934 women gained suffrage. They were encouraged to seek education and take an active part in public life.

Since the 1980s, Kemalist reforms have been the subject of much controversy. Feminists have demystified the official as well as popular rhetoric that eulogised the Kemalist extension of rights to women. They primarily explored the instrumental nature of the reforms and the functional roles women were expected to play in the modernising nation state. The extension of rights helped the new nation state affirm its secular and national nature as well as its democratic aspirations. The 1926 Civil Code that was so critical in extending women's rights was the most powerful means of secularising the new nation state. The new Civil Code enfeebled the Islamist opposition and undermined any legislative base it might have had to challenge the secularising measures. The new opportunities women attained under the Civil Code undermined Islamic roles for women in society.

On the other hand, extension of rights to women helped consolidate the Turkishness or the national nature of the new republic. The ideologues of Turkish nationalism had claimed that in Central Asia, prior to their acceptance of Islam, the Turks had been proto-feminists. For example, Ziya Gökalp elaborated that men and women ruled together and lived as equals. (Gökalp, 1990, p. 164–7). Therefore, measures giving civil and political rights to women helped the new republic become more truly Turkish. Women's rights thus helped build a Turkish state, one that could be like the more progressive countries in the West without imitating them, by reverting instead to its pre-Islamic roots. Finally, under the authoritarian early Republican regime, the extension of women's rights gave the new state a façade of democracy and liberalism. When fascism in Europe was on the rise, and Turkey had no liberal democratic regime in practice, giving some civil liberties and suffrage to women was a statement of intent.

In the late twentieth century, feminists not only exposed the instrumental nature of these Kemalist reforms, but also emphasised that women's own demands for these rights were ignored. They drew attention to a history of women's writing and organising that had received scant attention till the 1980s (Çakır, 1993, Zihnioğlu, 2003). Women before and during the early Republican period had fought to expand their opportunities, become more educated and engage themselves in public life and professions. They had expressed their needs mostly through writing in women's journals and organising in voluntary associations, but they had explicitly demanded suffrage as well as civil rights (Çakır, 1993; Zihnioğlu, 2003). The Republic, later feminist writers claimed, bypassed these women's demands and aimed to create a tabula rasa where the founding fathers dictated the terms of women's rights reforms independent of women's struggles for these rights. One of the most important contributions of feminist writing after the 1980s was the disclosure of this past. Feminist writing showed how women's struggles for liberation had been duly ignored in the building of the new nation state.

Under the circumstances of the early republic, many women were jubilant as the nation building reforms unfolded. While the reforms might have served to build the national, secular, democratising republic and ignored the struggles of women who fought to extend their rights, they were nevertheless revolutionary. Women's appreciation of the reforms was evident both through their engagement in public celebrations and also through the life stories they narrated in various contexts and occasions (İlyasoglu, 1994). A discourse that contended that 'women owe everything to Atatürk' developed. Yet different women related to Mustafa Kemal and his nation building project differently. Not all women felt that they owed everything to Atatürk, and some women who were intimately involved in the process of nation building wanted to claim their share in the progress towards women's rights in the country. In this paper, I shall look at selected writings of Halide Edip, who has been studied extensively, and of Afet İnan, whose work has been relegated to the realm of Kemalist rhetoric rather than that of social scientific study. By comparing their differing stances towards this project of nation building and modernisation, I will explore the issue of agency that has been so central to feminism.

Halide Edip and Afet İnan

Halide Edip and Afet İnan both worked closely with Mustafa Kemal, Halide Edip during the War of Independence, and Afet İnan thereafter. These two women were seemingly opposites of one another in terms of their relationship to Mustafa Kemal and the regime he installed. Ayşe Durakbaşa, who has studied Halide Edip, claims that Afet İnan was a loyal daughter of the Republic, one who had a mission, whereas Halide Edip was the rebellious daughter (Durakbaşa, 2000, p. 142). Afet İnan's mission was to propagate Kemalist ideology and its reforms, while Halide Edip rebelled against the dictatorship that Mustafa Kemal began building after the War of Independence.

These two women were different from one another in many ways. Halide Edip was born in 1882, 26 years before Afet İnan, who was born in 1908. Edip was the daughter of an Ottoman official at the palace. She was educated at the American College for Girls as one of the first Muslim pupils of the institution, originally founded as a missionary school. At home she took private lessons in French, maths and Eastern literatures. She married her maths teacher in 1901, had two sons, and then divorced him in 1909 because he opted for a polygamous marriage. During the reactionary revolt of 31 March 1909 she escaped to Egypt, and then at the invitation of her British friend Isabel Frye, to England, where she was introduced to literary circles. She began writing novels, engaged in nationalist activism and married Dr Adnan in 1917. In 1919, the couple escaped to Ankara to take part in the nationalist uprising. Halide Edip served in the headquarters of the nationalist forces, translating, reading telegraphic messages, and collecting dispatches, and moved to the front during the later phases of the war. She gained the title of Corporal and later, Sergeant. After the war, however, she and her husband positioned themselves in opposition to Mustafa Kemal, and they had to leave the country in 1926. Halide Edip began publishing her memoirs in 1926 and 1928 in two volumes. In the later volume, which covered the years 1918–23, she told her own story of her experiences in the War of Independence as a testimony in opposition to that of Mustafa Kemal. Edip remained mostly in the US, lecturing and teaching on Turkey and becoming internationally renowned as a Turkish novelist and intellectual.

Afet İnan, on the other hand, had a different background and a different relationship to the regime. She was born in Selanik, attended a French school in İstanbul, and became a teacher at Bursa Teacher's School for Girls. She did not receive the same liberal humanist, Anglo-Saxon upbringing as Edip. Afet İnan met Atatürk in 1925 in İzmir, where she had begun teaching, and became one of Atatürk's adopted children. Atatürk sent her to Lausanne for two years so that she could improve her French. In 1935 she attended the University of Geneva to study social sciences and history, and received her Ph.D. in sociology in 1939. On Atatürk's recommendation, she studied Turkish history to rewrite it in support of nascent Turkish nationalism. Her prolific writing helped legitimise and defend the Kemalist reforms undertaken by the regime. She married after Atatürk's death, had a son and a daughter, and continued writing in celebration of the reforms and propagating Kemalism.

It is interesting to compare Edip and Afet İnan because they were two prominent women leaders during the transition from Ottoman to Turkish Republican times. No other women shared their position among the leading cadres of the new regime. Despite their differences, both worked to establish the new republic, both fought against the colonisation of their country, and both were nationalists and feminists of some kind. Comparing the nature of their nationalism, their views on Mustafa Kemal, feminism, and the foundation of the new republic can shed light on what the women who worked to establish the Republic expected it to become. We can see how their views were reflected, manipulated or dismissed in the process. Despite the differences between the two women, they were both engaged in the project of nation building and modernising Turkey, and both claimed their own agency in the process. Because of the differences between these two women, we can see how resistance to the dictates of the founding fathers could take different, more overt, non-confrontational or subtle forms. Their engagement in the process, especially as they themselves saw it, can improve our understanding of women's agency within the web of power relations they found themselves in during the early Republican era.

Nationalism

Both Halide Edip and Afet İnan were nationalists: they worked to cultivate a Turkish nation. Prior to the War of Independence, Halide Edip worked in the 'Turkish hearths', the branches of a cultural and political society where incipient Turkish nationalism flowered. She developed friendships with prominent Turkish nationalists like Ziya Gökalp, Yusuf Akçura and Hamdullah Suphi. She became famous for her anti-colonialist, nationalist speeches, particularly the one she delivered at a rally at Sultanahmet organised against the Greek occupation of Izmir in 1919. She writes of the occasion when she first heard of the occupation as follows: 'Nothing mattered to me from that moment to the time of the extraordinary march to Smyrna in 1922. I suddenly ceased to exist as an individual: I worked, wrote, and lived as a unit of that magnificent national madness' (Adıvar, 1928, p. 23). Her commitment to nascent Turkish nationalism was not merely one of words. She left her two sons behind to partake in the War of Independence on the side of the nationalists.

Halide Edip's nationalism coexisted with her Western-inspired humanism. She had a deeply rooted liberal humanitarian worldview, cultivated through her Anglo-Saxon education at the American Girls' College. Her appreciation of the individual, her liberal upbringing and her high regard for Western culture always tempered her nationalism. In her memoirs, she narrates in detail how the local Christians maltreated the Turks during the Allied occupation, which protected the Christians. She gives examples of Turkish women harassed in trams and boats by local Greeks or Armenians, who cursed and acted patronisingly towards the Turks. These incidents incited her nationalism. She writes that 'the internal process which was gradually hardening me into an absolute rebel against the enemies of my country, received a check wherever a Westerner appeared who was capable of understanding the desperate position into which the Turks were being pushed ... I felt the fundamental oneness of all those who, regardless of race and creed, dare to believe in truth and reality in a noisy world of politics' (Adıvar, 1928, p. 10). For Edip, there was a 'truth' and 'reality', independent of politics, and it is the truth of humanism. She was ready to give credit to the Greeks as individuals when they exhibited humanism (Adıvar, 1928, p. 300), for example expressing criticism of the war between the two nations or helping fallen soldiers in the field (Adıvar, 1928, p. 306). When Yusuf Akçura narrated that he had seen a Greek soldier and a Turkish soldier lying in each other's arms, she muses 'had they first fought and throttled each other and then realised in the throes of death that they were brothers after all?'

She was also aware that nationalism can be dangerous. Talking to a Greek prisoner of war who reminds her of her younger son after the fight in Sakarya, she concludes: 'Patriotism, which could make people bear the impossible, could transfer itself into this beastliness whenever it took an aggressive form' (Adıvar, 1928, p. 306). When Ismet Paşa asked her to investigate and report on the Greek atrocities in Middle Anatolia, she prefaced her findings, reported in her memoir, with the following apology:

> There is no such thing as a guilty nation. And that one of the obstacles to peace is the hysterical and exaggerated propagating of people's suffering for political purposes. It burdens the younger generations of each nation with the crimes or the martyrdom of their father in which they have had no share. The consequence is either a destructive and pathological feeling of revenge or shame in the generation which is not responsible for the past.
>
> (Adıvar, 1928, p. 307)

The humanist boundaries of Edip's nationalism distinguish it from the official nationalism of the Republican founding fathers. While official Turkish nationalism was sometimes careful to avoid explicit racism in its formal pronouncements, it has been characterised by an ethnic and religious bias against minorities that has shaped policies of the Turkish state.

Afet İnan, on the other hand, was the person whom Mustafa Kemal assigned the task of cultivating ethnic Turkish nationalism. Her studies on the subject defined the parameters of what was officially propagated as Turkish nationalism. Afet İnan explains that Atatürk personally asked her to work on the subject, and she began to do so in a presentation at the 1930 Convention of the Turkish Hearths (Türk Ocakları VI Kurultayı). In this presentation, she posed the question of where the Turks stood in the history of civilisations (İnan, 1981, p. 195). Her conclusion was as follows: 'the highest and first civilised people (kavim) of humanity are the Turks, whose homeland were Altaylar and Central Asia. The Turk is civilisation. The Turk is history' (İnan, 1981, p. 197). She proposed to the Convention that 'radical measures be taken to find out Turkish history and propagate it' (İnan, 1981, p. 196). Her further studies on the subject merely served to bolster this conclusion and present a new image of the Turks, one that provided a nationalist response to the often derogatory images created by Europeans. Interestingly from the perspective of this paper, she credits herself with initiating this study. Although it was Atatürk who instructed her to do so, she emphasises how she influenced him by showing him her French textbooks, in which Turks were described as an invading barbarian race.

Even though Afet İnan attended a French high school and studied in Switzerland to get her Ph.D., she does not exhibit the humanism displayed by Adıvar. Perhaps similarly to Adıvar, she resented the lowly image Turks had in Europe, and felt prompted to change this image. Both women were engaged in the nationalist state-building project, and both attempted to locate themselves as active participants in this process, but they used different blocks to build their state. While both women traced their nationalism to pre-Ottoman Turks, Edip's nationalism was influenced by strains of Ottoman and European thought that are not present in Afet İnan's.

Views on Mustafa Kemal

Both Halide Edip and Afet İnan revered Mustafa Kemal yet the nature and the limits of their reverence differed radically. Halide Edip could be harshly critical of the leader, while Afet İnan worshipped him. Early in *The Turkish Ordeal*, before she narrates the story of her escape to Ankara to join the nationalists, Edip writes of Mustafa Kemal:

> He was the brilliant organiser of the Anafarta victory in Chanak; he was aide-de camp to the sultan; he was a man of extraordinary intelligence and cunning as well as of abnormal ambition. I had met him at a meeting without exchanging words. I had also seen him often walking down the Sublime Port road and thought that he had a remarkably strong face .... I did not trouble myself about the various rumors about his personal ambition, desires for despotism and so on.
>
> (Adıvar, 1928, p. 14)

But after she joined the nationalists and became part of Kemal's inner circle, she became more apprehensive about his disposition towards authoritarianism and self-aggrandisement. She narrates an incident that transformed their relationship, causing her to become suspicious of and distanced from him. In this case, Mustafa Kemal openly and simply insisted that 'every one do as he wishes and commands'. Edip quotes him as saying 'I don't want any consideration, criticism or advice. I will have only my own way. All shall do as I command'. When Edip accosts him and asks 'Me too, my Pasha?' he retorts 'You too'. It is unclear whether Halide Edip would have been as disappointed with Mustafa Kemal had he made a sincere exception to her, but it was after this evening that her relationship with Mustafa Kemal transformed. She decided to write her memoirs and do so in English 'as a faithful record of her experiences during that great ordeal'. She suspected that the story told by Kemal would not accomplish this task, and would serve instead to immortalise him. In her evaluations throughout the memoirs she is very bold and forthcoming in her criticisms of Mustafa Kemal – a stance that many brave men did not undertake for many years, let alone in 1928, when Kemal had the power to demolish any opposition. According to Edip, Mustafa Kemal

was by turns cynical, suspicious, unscrupulous, and satanically shrewd. He bullied, he indulged in cheap street corner heroics. Possessing considerable, though quite undistinguished histrionic ability, one moment he could pass as the perfect demagogue – a second George Washington – and the next moment fall into some Napoleonic attitude. Sometimes he would appear weak and abject coward, sometimes exhibit strength and daring of the highest order. He would argue with all the intricacies of the old-fashioned scholastic till he had become utterly incomprehensible. And then illumine some obscure problem with a flash of inspired clarity....

Of course, one knew all the time that there were men around him who were greatly his superior in intellect and moral backbone, and far above him in culture and education. But though he excelled them in neither refinement nor originality, not one of them could possibly cope with his vitality ... Take any man from the street who is shrewd, selfish and utterly unscrupulous, give him the insistence and histrionics of a hysterical woman who is willing to employ any wile to satisfy her inexhaustible desires, then view him through the largest magnifying glass you can find – and you'll see Mustafa Kemal Pasha.

(Adıvar, 1928, p. 185)

Halide Edip did not merely criticise Mustafa Kemal more sharply than any other member of his close circle, but also compared him unfavourably with other figures in the nationalist movement. According to Edip, Mustafa Kemal was a great leader, but other leaders around him were more intelligent, moral and sophisticated than he was. These men, who deferred to Kemal, were the force behind his various achievements and successes. Throughout her memoirs, Halide Edip carefully credited these powerful figures around Mustafa Kemal and underplayed his role in the independence struggle. Single-handedly, she weaved her own history, revising the official account and providing an alternative story of the War of Independence.

In her memoirs, Halide Edip carefully depicted the War of Independence as a collective effort led by perspicuous generals and Mustafa Kemal.

She respects and is impressed by Fevzi Pasha, the chief of staff, and Ismet Pasha, commander of the Western front for the nationalist army. According to Edip, these men counterbalanced Mustafa Kemal's excesses and his proclivity to radical decisions. She believed that Fevzi Pasha's firm belief in the success of the nationalists was critical in actually winning the war (Adıvar, 1928, pp. 297–8). Mustafa Kemal would sometimes 'attempt the impossible with the greatest zeal and success, but sometimes he would lose heart and easily despair'. Fevzi Pasha, in Edip's words, 'stepped in at these moments and with his strange certitude about our success, kept Mustafa Kemal going (Adıvar, 1928, p. 297). Ismet Pasha, according to Edip, 'had a pleasing and generous disposition and realised the necessity of handling human beings with special care. So he stood like a buffer state between Mustafa Kemal Pasha and those whom he might easily have offended to the disadvantage of the cause' (Adıvar, 1928, p. 297). Of the battle fought in Sakarya, she quotes Fevzi Pasha who claims that the greatest part of the success was due the commissary of the national defence, Refet Pasha's 'timely and swift contribution of fighting material and men' (Adıvar, 1928, p. 293). Refet Pasha, in turn, claims that the Anatolian peasant women carrying ammunition for 'hundreds and hundreds of miles ... on carts or on their backs along roadless wastes, protecting the ammunition with the scanty covers with which they covered their babies who accompanied them tied to their backs' account for the Sakarya success (Adıvar, 1928, p. 293). In her epilogue to TTO, Halide Edip claims that:

> All through the ordeal for independence the Turkish people itself has been the supreme hero – the Turkish people has honored Mustafa Kemal Pasha as its symbol .... Yet in the unending struggle for freedom there can be no real individual symbol, no dictator. There will be only the sum total of a people's sacrifice to bear witness to the guarding of their liberties.
>
> (Adıvar, 1928, p. 407)

Halide Edip disapproved of the political power and stature that Mustafa Kemal had in the new republic. Her writing aimed to portray him in human dimensions. She depicted events and leaders the way she saw them, even if this honest portrayal involved risking her life.

Afet İnan's mission, on the other hand, was different. She idolised Mustafa Kemal and wrote to make others idolise him too. In Afet İnan's writing, in stark contrast to that of Halide Edip, Mustafa Kemal comes to life as a leader who single-handedly won the War of Independence, established a new nation, founded a new state and pioneered a series of radical reforms. There is no recognition of other leaders or of a collective effort behind Mustafa Kemal's victories. Afet İnan writes that 'He has challenged the Sevres Treaty, after a three year period of war, brought Turkey to a victorious stance, with the Lausanne Treaty introduced the New Turkish state to the world' (İnan, 1981, p. 1). She wrote as if Mustafa Kemal had undertaken all these

Herculean tasks on his own. According to Afet İnan, Kemal had opinions and ideas on every topic. He was a commander in battle, a political character in establishing a state, and a revolutionary intellectual in reform movements. Moreover, his opinions 'do not merely relate to the ideas and politics of the day but they exist as guidance for the future' (İnan, 1981, p. 2). His words 'need to be read with care' (İnan, 1981, p. 3). Afet İnan created the aura of a seer or a prophet around Mustafa Kemal.

Like Halide Edip, Afet İnan created her own history of the events that unfolded during Mustafa Kemal's lifetime. She was also intent on being the agent of change and revision, and claimed to provide an objective narration of what she witnessed. She wanted to explain to others how much of a prophet Mustafa Kemal was. Her book *Memoirs and Documents on Atatürk* was written to 'make others hear, in Atatürk's words and with his memoirs, what Atatürk desired for the Turkish nation' (İnan, 1981, p. 3). She claimed that because she heard these stories from Atatürk himself, she was merely transferring his views (İnan, 1981, p. 4). She writes that she tried to narrate the stories she heard from Atatürk literally, just as they were told, and report objectively on what she herself witnessed (İnan, 1981, p. 5). Afet İnan wrote that she assumed it to be a duty for her to explain the stages of his intellectual life to the extent that she knew them (İnan, 1981, p. 5). Afet İnan made it her mission to uphold Mustafa Kemal as Atatürk, and contrary to Halide Edip, she preferred using the name Atatürk rather than Mustafa Kemal when referring to him. Through this mission, she created herself as the Afet İnan she chose to be, and contributed to the writing of an official history that idolised Atatürk at the cost of other important national heroes.

Women and feminism

Halide Edip and Afet İnan's views on Mustafa Kemal were reflected in the way they related to women and women's emancipation in Turkey. Both women were important role models who helped improve women's status in Turkey. Both were very well-educated public figures, lecturers, teachers, and female nationalists working for the establishment of the new republic among a predominantly male group of leaders. Yet their relation to the women of their country, their interpretation of women's emancipation and their feminisms differed.

Both women cared for and appreciated the women of their country, particularly praising rural Anatolian women above urban women. Halide Edip clearly expressed her dislike of the urban socialites who aped Western ways and cultivated friendship with members of Allied Forces (Adıvar, 1928). She always articulated her appreciation of Anatolian women's contribution to the war and recalled the hospitality she was offered both during her flight from Istanbul to Ankara and later throughout her expeditions in Anatolia during the War of Independence. These women were humble and had an 'infectious quality of life' (Adıvar, 1928, p. 373). But while she appreciated women and took her place in the vanguard empowering women, Halide Edip was not a self-declared feminist.

After the 1908 revolution, Edip had founded a women's organisation named Teali-i Nisvan, which aimed to improve women's status. The organization was open only to women who were literate and conceded to attend English lessons (Çakır, 1993, p. 53). Even though Teali-i-Nisvan did not have explicitly political goals, it did help articulate the importance of improving women's social standing in society (Zihnioğlu, 2003, p. 58). Halide Edip's efforts to empower women thus began in Ottoman times. Accordingly, Edip saw women's emancipation in Turkey as a process that had deep roots in both pre-Ottoman Turkish and Ottoman society. In her book *Conflict of East and West in Turkey*, which was based on a series of lectures she delivered in India, she discussed the process of women's emancipation and described women's problems in Turkey.

Edip's view was influenced by Gökalp and she accepted his proposition that women had equal rights in pre-Islamic Turkish society (Adıvar, 1935, p. 196). Even though she was critical of certain Islamic practices, like seclusion and polygamy, her attitude towards Islam was more defensive than dismissive regarding women's position in society. She adopted the common reformist arguments that Islam had extended rights to women in pre-Islamic Arabia and women enjoyed various public activities and professions in the early days of Islam (Adıvar, 1935, pp. 179–82). She acknowledged the roles that women played in Ottoman times regarding public welfare and education, and credited the Constitutional Revolution of 1908 with expanding women's rights. At length, Edip elaborated the secularisation measures that benefited women. She explained how the 1917 Family Law gave greater leverage to women in shaping their marriages through the marriage contract by restricting polygamy and expanding rights of divorce (Adıvar, 1935, p. 196). According to Edip, there was a 'gradual emancipation of Turkish women and their evolution as useful and beneficial social units ... a process that was an integral part of Turkish reform' (Adıvar, 1935, p. 197). She did not view the 1926 Civil Code as the single source of women's emancipation, even though she did acknowledge its supreme importance.

As such, Halide Edip belittled the importance of the 1934 suffrage reform. In *Turkey faces West*, published in 1930, she wrote 'It is perhaps a blessing that [women] have not obtained the vote. Thus they have been protected from the danger of being identified with party politics, and their activities outside the political world could not be stopped for political reasons'(Adıvar, 1930, p. 228). In the *Conflict of the East and West* she expressed a similar opinion more bluntly, writing 'whether they have the legislative vote in the near or far future does not matter so much' (Adıvar, 1935, p. 201). Even though it might be true that the introduction of the 1926 civil code was a more radical step in expanding women's opportunities in society, the right of suffrage was critical in making women more equal to men. It is noteworthy that under the circumstances of the day, even a progressive woman like Halide Edip, who did believe in improving women's status in society, did not consider suffrage that important.

Afet İnan was different; she was an avowed feminist who prided herself on having worked for the feminist cause, particularly for women's suffrage. On the other hand, her feminism was primarily centred on Kemalist prerogatives and dictates. In the preface to her book *Herkesin Bir Dünyası Var*, she listed her articles on women's rights. She explained that in her professional life, the ideal of women's rights had always preoccupied her and had always held an important place in her and her intellectual world (İnan, 1958, p. 1). Afet İnan emphasised that her first public lecture before a large crowd had been on the issue of women's suffrage, and wrote that when her daughter voted in future elections, she wanted her to read her mother's writings on women's suffrage and adopt new ideas on the matter (İnan, 1958, p. 1).

Similarly to Halide Edip, Afet İnan upheld the alleged pre-Islamic roots of Turkish feminism. She proudly agreed with the Ziya Gökalp thesis that ancient Turks had treated women equally to men, and elaborated on the notion that the pre-Ottoman Anatolian states had had feminist practices. According to Afet İnan, Turkish women were heirs to the Amazons (İnan, 1958, p. 100). She did acknowledge that progress on women's rights had been made during the Ottoman reformation, but she primarily saw Ottoman tradition as anti-feminist. Again, much like Halide Edip, she praised the hard-working Anatolian peasant women, particularly their contributions to the War of Independence.

Afet İnan believed the most important achievements for the cause of women's rights had been made by Atatürk after the establishment of the republic. In her writing, she stressed that Atatürk was concerned about women's role in social life and wished to cultivate a class of enlightened women. (İnan 1958, p. 50). She wrote with pride that it was during the Presidency of Atatürk that women's rights were recognised according to democratic principles (İnan, 1958, p. 50). In another context, she asserted with conviction that 'Turkish Women are indebted to the Atatürk era because the Turkish Republic has been assumed to be a progressive country on the issue of recognition of women's rights' (İnan, 1958, p. 62). Contrary to Halide Edip's memoir, in Afet İnan's account the credit for suffrage primarily went to Atatürk. The idea of suffrage was that of Atatürk, the cabinet successfully executed the idea, and the parliament used its good judgement to accept it. Suffrage was the focus of Afet İnan's writing on women's rights.

Despite her veneration of Atatürk and her insistence on his important leadership in women's rights reforms, Afet İnan wrote to affirm the role she played in the process. In different contexts and in different articles, she narrated again and again how she was personally involved in the process of bringing about women's suffrage and how she personally intervened to persuade Atatürk to grant this right. Her story is as follows: when she was teaching civics courses at the Music Teacher Training school, she made students practice voting. A boy objected to her decision to allow the girls to partake in the exercise, because under the prevailing law in the country, women did not have suffrage. Afet İnan wrote that she was, 'as a teacher, very hurt by the objection the student made' (İnan, 1958, p. 20). She dashed to the Marmara residence, where she knew Atatürk and Şükrü Kaya, the minister of interior, would be. She told them of her grief and tried to explain to them that suffrage should be granted to women as well. That very night, Atatürk gathered the members of his cabinet for dinner at his famous 'table' where important issues concerning the country would be debated, and they discussed the topic of women's suffrage. He then urged Afet İnan to study women's suffrage around the world and prepare a paper on the topic. She presented this paper before the political elite at a public conference, and the next day it was published in all the daily newspapers.

Afet İnan related this story frequently in her writings. In her book *Herkesin Bir Ruyası Var*, this story first appears as a note providing background information to the paper she had delivered on the subject (İnan, 1958, p. 20). In her later writings, the story assumes a more central place and is reprinted (İnan, 1958, p. 50). It was important for her to emphasise her role in personally influencing Atatürk's decision to grant suffrage to women. Even a woman like Afet İnan, whose mission in life was to cherish Atatürk, wrote to demonstrate her agency – alleged or actual – in shaping women's rights in Turkey. She vehemently sought to show how she had been able to influence Atatürk, resist his all-encompassing power by modifying his agenda, and induce him to do what she willed.

Conclusion

As different as their stances in the process of nation building were, Halide Edip and Afet İnan both tell stories of resistance and agency. Women might have played instrumental roles in the nation building project, but they were also subjects of this process. Not only did they write their own stories of the process from their own perspectives, but they carefully emphasised their resistance to the founding fathers and their own roles in shaping events. The leaders of the Turkish Republic might have ignored or co-opted women's demands for their rights, but women asserted their agency and offered alternative histories to shape our own histories of this period.

Bibliography

H. Adak (2003) 'National Myths and Self-Na(rra)tions: Mustafa Kemal's Nutuk and Halide Edip's Memoirs and The Turkish Ordeal', *The South Atlantic Quarterly*, vol. 102, no. 2/3, 509–27.

H. E. Adıvar (1928) *The Turkish Ordeal* (New York: The Century Co.).

—— (1930) *Turkey Faces West* (New Haven: Yale University Press).

—— (1935) *Conflict of East and West in Turkey* (Lahore: Ashraf Press).

Y. Arat (1989) *The Patriarchal Paradox: Women Politicians in Turkey* (New Jersey: Fairleigh Dickinson University Press).

Z. Arat (1994) 'Turkish Women and the Republican Reconstruction of Tradition', in F. M. Göçek and S. Balaghi (eds) *Reconstructing Gender in the Middle East* (New York: Columbia University Press).

S. Çakır (1993) *Osmanli Kadın Hareketi* (Istanbul: Metis Yayınları).

A. Daldal (2002) 'Afet İnan, Fuat Köprülü, ve Birinci Türk Tarih Kongresi'nde Tartışmalar', *Toplum ve Bilim*, no. 92, 234–48.

A. Durakbaşa (2000) *Halide Edip: Türk Modernleşmesi ve Feminizm* (İstanbul: İletişim Yayınları).

A. İlyasoglu (1994) 'Religion and Women During the Course of Modernisation in Turkey', *Oral History*, XXIV, 49–53.

A. İnan (1958) *Herkesin Bir Dünyası Var* (Ankara: Türk Tarih Kurumu Basımevi).

—— (1981) *Atatürk Hakkında Hatiralar ve Belgeler* (Ankara: Türkiye İş Bankası Kültür Yayınları).

D. Kandiyoti (1989) 'Women and the Turkish State: Political Actors or Symbolic Pawns?', in N. Y. Davis and F. Anthias (ed.) *Women-Nation-State* (London: The Macmillan Press).

D. Köksal (1994) 'Nationalist Theory in the Writings of Halide Edip', *Turkish Studies Association Bulletin*, vol. 17, 80–90.

Ş. Tekeli (1982) *Kadınlar ve Siyasal-Toplumsal Hayat* (Istanbul: Birikim Yayınları).

Y. Zihnioğlu (2003) *Kadınsız Inkılap* [Revolution without Women] (Istanbul: Metis Yayınları).

Islam, the Military and the State

4
The Importance of Being Secular: Islam in the Service of the National and Pre-National State

Erik-Jan Zürcher

Both in political debates on the current state of affairs in Turkey and in the historiography of the country, the dichotomy of religion and secularism is without doubt the dominant paradigm within which analysis takes place. Observers and commentators (both from within Turkey and from abroad) are so preoccupied with the problem of secularism, or to be more exact: with that of laicism, the separation of religion and state, that one's position on the issue has come to be seen as the yardstick with which any prominent Turkish public figure or intellectual should be judged. Author Orhan Pamuk published his novel *Benim Adim Kirmizi* (*My Name is Red*) to such a degree of worldwide critical acclaim that he is now a Nobel laureate, but the debate on this and subsequent novels by the author in Turkey itself was more about his stance on Islam and westernisation than on the literary merits of his work. The candidature of former Islamist Abdullah Gül for the presidency of the republic, and particularly the fact that, if he were to become president, the first lady would be a woman wearing an Islamic headscarf (türban) in public, caused an uproar. Militant Kemalists in Turkey, led by the army top brass, hinted darkly that Turkey's secular order was in mortal danger. The campaign for the parliamentary elections that were called to clarify the situation caused by the presidential crisis, had as its main issue the threat or otherwise to the secular order and the army's right to interfere in politics to defend that order.

Historical figures are judged on their stance in the secularism debate as much as contemporary ones. Indeed, the contemporary debate on secularism is often structured around historical events and figures from the past: for a long time Prime Minister Adnan Menderes, executed by the military in 1961, was hated by Kemalists as the man who allowed Islam 'back in', but in the 1980s, Izmir International Airport was officially named Adnan Menderes Airport, by people who regarded him as the second great architect of modern Turkey (after Atatürk) and who wanted to make a point about their own political stance. This use of historical figures is thus highly divisive and it is the issue of secularism that divides more than any other. The reappraisal of the once despised 'tyrant' Sultan Abdülhamid II by Islamists (who, in this, tend to follow the lead established by right wing Nakşibendi poet/publicist Necip Fazıl Kısakürek in the 1940s and 50s) is as much an illustration of this phenomenon as is the constant reference to figures like Derviş Vahdeti and Kubılay by hardcore Kemalists. The former was an Islamist firebrand, who as one of the leaders of the 'Muhammedan Union' (*Ittihadi Muhammadi*) and editor of the paper *Volkan* in 1908–9 constantly called for the restoration of religious law. He was accused of instigating the 1909 counterrevolution against the 'secular' Young Turks in Istanbul and convicted and hanged once the Young Turks had regained control of the capital. The latter was the young teacher and reserve officer who confronted a group of radical young mystics that came to the Aegean town of Menemen in 1930 and announced that they were the advance guard of an army of Islam that would bring down the 'infidel' republic. Kubilay paid for his courage with his life when his head was sawn off while the populace of Menemen watched in silence. Both figures, like Menderes and Abdülhamid, thus serve as markers of the boundary between secularism and (political) Islam in contemporary Kemalist discourse.

The other issue, which has dominated the public debate in – and on – Turkey in recent years, is that of Turkey's possible accession to the European Union. In this debate, too, the question whether Turkey is 'truly secular' is constantly raised and the credentials in this field of leading politicians and other public figures are scrutinised. There is nothing on religion or secularism in the official criteria (the so-called Copenhagen criteria) that have to be met by candidate countries and, indeed, the issue of religion was never raised in the negotiations with the ten countries that acceded in 2004. In the Turkish case it is raised in the shape of concern about the depth and irreversibility of Turkey's secular (*laik*) order. Ironically it is Europe, which regards itself as secular (although in fact that secularism is never absolute and in every single European country formal links between state and religion can be demonstrated) that introduces the religious factor into the membership negotiations. This of course feeds into the already existing debate on the issue in Turkey, especially because there are inconsistencies in the European position on the issue that are caused by fundamentally different views on the nature of secularism.

After the 1978–9 revolution in Iran, governments in the West became gravely concerned that Turkey would go the same way. They tended to side with the classic Kemalist interpretation of secularism as a protective shield, guaranteeing (by less than democratic means if need be) the survival of freedom of conscience in the face of the threat of 'Islamic reaction' (*irtica*). This tendency was strengthened when political Islam was identified as the main threat to the West after the end of the Cold War in the early 1990s and, of course, became even more prominent after the terrorist attacks on New York and Washington of 11 September 2001. Fear of a reversal of the Kemalist laicist order is a constant element in the debate on Turkey's accession to the EU. Does Europe risk the entry of a Trojan horse from that vehicle's country of origin?

Side by side with this concern about an Islamic revival, an increasingly fierce critique of the Kemalist interpretation of secularism is also part of the debate. The dominant Christian democrat current in Europe in particular tends to see it as intolerant and unnecessarily restrictive of religious, and religiously inspired, political practice. In taking up this position (which was endorsed by the European Parliament in May 2003), these Europeans seem to side with the interpretation of secularism put forward by Turkish rightwing politicians from Menderes via Demirel and Özal to Erdoğan; an interpretation that sees secularism as an order protecting freedom of conscience *and* religion and makes a distinction between a lay public arena and religiously inspired individuals who should be allowed to function in it and express their religiosity.

There can thus be little doubt that the nature of the relationship between state and religion in Turkey is an important one, but is also an issue on which misconceptions are widespread. Rather than trying to categorise actors along strict and somewhat artificial lines of secular versus Islamist, it is perhaps enlightening to look at the specific policies of successive late Ottoman and Republican Turkish regimes to get a better picture of the position they have taken with regard to the relationship between state and Islam and at the complex relationship between nationalism and religion. In this paper I intend to look in particular at four instances where the state faced acute challenges to its authority and even survival: Sultan Abdülhamid's use of religion to ward of the threats of nationalism and imperialism; the Young Turks' mobilisation of Ottoman Muslims against the perceived threat of the Christian minorities; the use of religion by the Turkish nationalists in their struggle against the occupying forces after World War I and, finally, the attempt of the military rulers of 1980–3 to merge religion and Kemalist nationalism in an effort to break the hold of both socialism and fundamentalism over the Turkish youth. The chapter is based on a critical reading of the recent monographic literature on the topic (Deringil, 1998; Toprak, 1981; Georgeon, 2003; Karpat, 2000; Yavuz, 2003; Poulton, 1997; Seufert, 1997; Bora, 1999; Davison, 1998; Fortna, 2002).

Abdülhamid II and his new moral order

It is now generally recognised that the long reign of Abdülhamid II (1876–1909) in many ways laid the foundations of what became modern Turkey. This is true in the fields of administration (with the expansion of the state bureaucracy and the extension of state control), education and communications (telegraph and railways). It can be argued that it is also true where the management of religion is concerned. Abdülhamid was faced first and foremost with the necessity to rebuild a state and society shattered by the disastrous war against Russia of 1877–8. This war, caused ultimately by separatist Serbian and Bulgarian nationalism, had resulted in huge loss of land and income and a very serious refugee problem as well as a loss of prestige and credibility for the Ottoman ruler. Having lost all confidence in solutions on the basis of a 'unity of the (ethnic) elements' (*ittihadi anasir*) that had been so close to the heart of the Young Ottoman constitutionalists, Abdülhamid started an ideological counteroffensive, which Poulton has likened to Bismarck's *Kulturkampf*. The policy had two fundamental aims. One was to create a new basis for solidarity and national unity. The losses of 1878 had decreased the percentage of Christians in the population from 40 to 20 per cent, so it made sense to try to find this new basis of solidarity in the shared religious heritage of the Muslim majority. This way the embryonic national movements among the non-Turkish Muslim communities (Albanians, Arabs and Kurds) could also be countered. The millions of refugees from the Crimea, the Caucasus and the Balkans, who had after all been forced to flee their homes *because* they were Muslims, could be integrated more easily on the basis of Muslim solidarity. The other aim of Abdülhamid's policies was to increase his authority and effect a degree of bonding with the population by sacralising the institution of the monarchy.

In order to increase solidarity and unity on the basis of Islam, a single, standardized and controlled form of 'national' or Ottoman Islam had to be promoted (although whether we can actually say, as Yavuz does, that the state promoted *Muslim nationalism* is debatable). This led to what Deringil aptly named as the 'Ottomanisation of the Şeriat'. The Hanefi school, which had always been the preferred *mezhep* of the Ottomans, increasingly became the sole recognised authority, even in Arab provinces where the Shafii school had traditionally predominated. The Hanefi interpretation of the religious law was ultimately codified in Ahmed Cevdet Pasha's monumental *Mecelle*, which meant that local judges and muftis to a large degree lost their freedom of interpretation and were expected to refer to a written authoritative text. An officially sanctioned brand of Islam was disseminated through Abdülhamid's fast growing educational network (Fortna's 'Imperial classrooms'), with textbooks on religion and morality being written for the different levels in primary and secondary education and through the distribution of popular and simply written publications such as catechisms (*ilmi hal*). The standardised religious message emphasised loyalty to the state and obedience to the authorities. Its central notion, as Georgeon has pointed out, was that of *ahlak* (morality). The order that the sultan wanted to impose on society was presented as a moral order in which modernisation was encouraged but what was seen as the libertarian excesses of the Tanzimat era were rejected. This moral order clearly appealed to the Sunni Muslim townspeople of Anatolia, but of course Anatolia was far from uniformly Sunni. In its effort to unify the population, the state undertook campaigns to convert the many dissident Muslim communities of Anatolia and Kurdistan to respectable Sunni Islam. Taking his cue from Western missionaries, the sultan sent preachers to the Alevi areas and even had mosques and schools built in Alevi villages. The efforts to increase the authority of the monarchy were based on the sultan's position as caliph. Adülhamid not only used the spurious claim to the caliphate so brilliantly exploited by the Ottoman negotiating team at the Peace of Kücük Kaynarca in 1774 to implicitly threaten the imperialist powers of his day, he also used the caliphate effectively to buttress his regime internally. By emphasising the sacral nature of his office, he could demand not only the loyalty of his subjects, but also the obedience due to the successors of the prophet. Loyalty to the throne thus became a religious duty.

The sultan actively sought the cooperation of religious leaders (primarily Dervish sheikhs) as intermediaries, who could connect with the Muslim community and spread the message. Most famous among these was Abdülhamid's long time favourite Ebulhuda from Aleppo, who was considered to be the 'eminence grise' of the Yildiz palace at the time, but there were many others.

Several authors have pointed out that Abdülhamid was far from unique in his attempts to strengthen his throne by sacralising it. Emperor Francis-Joseph II of Austria and Tsars Alexander III and Nicolas II also tried to effect a bonding with the large majority of their subjects by emphasising their role as defender of the faith and even in Queen Victoria's Britain the monarchy projected a far more Christian and virtuous image than it had under the Georgians.

The Young Turks: 'National' means 'Muslim'

The rule of the Committee of Union and Progress after 1908, and especially after the dethronement of Abdülhamid, is usually contrasted sharply with the preceding era in the historiography of Turkey. There are good reasons for this. The atmosphere of public debate and openness after the revolution contrasted sharply with the suffocating atmosphere of Abdülhamid's final years. Nevertheless the contrast can be overdone. The paradigm of the Young Turks themselves was that of 'Freedom' (*Hürriyet* – the usual description of the 1908 constitutional revolution) and 'Oppression' (*Istibdad* – Abdülhamid's reign) and this is reflected in later history writing. This is especially true for the issues of religion and nationalism.

It is true, of course, that on the ideological level there is a world of difference between Abdülhamid and the Young Turks. The latter were deeply influenced by a popularised version of positivism as well as by Büchnerian materialism. Their political outlook was elitist and authoritarian, but that still contrasted sharply with the autocracy of the former sultan. Nevertheless it can also be argued that there is an underlying ideological relationship.

Abdülhamid consciously tried to shape Ottoman Muslim solidarity into the fulcrum of a reinvigorated Ottoman state and while one can argue about whether this constituted the fostering of an Ottoman-Muslim nationalism or rather a kind of proto-nationalism, there is no doubt that over the years he mobilised Ottoman-Muslim sentiment. In doing so, the sultan was in tune with underlying developments in society, where, as Keyder has argued, a religiously over-determined division of labour between a fast-growing non-Muslim bourgeoisie and an equally fast growing Muslim-dominated state bureaucracy created increasing and ultimately unbearable tensions. The roots of the Committee of Union and Progress (CUP) were to be found in the resentment felt by young Muslim bureaucrats and officers at the change in the balance of power between on the one hand the Christian bourgeoisie and the European powers, who were perceived as being hand in glove with them and the Ottoman state and its servants on the other. The main grievance of the Young Turks against the sultan was that his regime weakened the state and failed to protect the Ottoman nation. Their solution, endlessly repeated in their pamphlets and émigré journals, was to create a modern state (with all the trimmings such as a parliament and a constitution) with a rational, 'scientific' system of administration. They were not, however, anti-Islamic, far from it. As Hanioğlu has shown, it was an unquestioning belief in science and education rather than any democratic sentiment that dominated their thinking. Inspired by positivism, they were vehemently anti-clerical, but with the possible exception of Abdullah Cevdet, the 'atheist philosopher' (*dinsiz mutefekkir*) every one of them saw in a 'true' or 'purified' Islam, a 'rational' religion, which was open to science, a valuable building block of Ottoman reconstruction and a social cement.

In its reconstituted form (from 1906 onwards), the CUP was an organisation of Muslim civil servants and army officers and in its early days was not even open to non-Muslims. It was, in other words, a political movement of Ottoman Muslims for Ottoman Muslims. After the period of compromise, inter-party strife and political turmoil between the constitutional revolution of 1908 and the outbreak of the Balkan War in 1912, the policies of the CUP were a – sometimes awkward – compromise between its professed adherence to the ideal of the 'Unity of the (Ethnic) Elements' (*Ittihadi anasir*), the underlying principle of the Ottoman constitution, and its Ottoman-Muslim nationalism. From 1912 onwards, and certainly after the Unionist coup d'etat of January 1913, Ottoman Muslim nationalism held sway. The Christian communities were now defined as the 'others' and a whole range of 'national' (*millî*) societies, clubs, firms, cooperatives and periodicals were founded in quick succession. Looking at the aims and the membership of these, it is immediately apparent that 'national' now meant 'Ottoman Muslim' only. From 1914 onwards this identification of the CUP with the Muslim majority leads both to the nationalist economic policies of the *Millî iktisat*, through which the committee tried to create a level playing field for Muslim entrepreneurs through state interference in the economy and to the oppressive and ultimately genocidal ethnic policies of the War years. As in Abdülhamid's days, the politics of Muslim solidarity held a special attraction for the large immigrant communities from the Balkans and the Caucasus, who had themselves been victims of religiously inspired persecution. The shared Muslim identity was a perfect path towards integration and it should thus cause no surprise that immigrants, especially Circassians, were so prominent among the CUP militants (especially in the so-called Special Organisation, the *Teskilati Mahsusa*).

Of course, the turn to Muslim nationalism was not due solely to the social make-up of the CUP or to the ideological preferences of its leaders. Just as Abdülhamid's 'Islamic turn' had in part been a rational answer to the changed territorial and demographic realities of the empire, so the appeal to Muslim solidarity of the Young Turks was caused in part by the need to mobilise the population in times of war. Anatolia being the 'soldier's mine' of the empire, appealing to the religious worldview of the peasant population of Anatolia made good sense.

Both elements – religious nationalism (with a strong anti-Greek and anti-Armenian bias) and military necessity – continued to play a role in the post-war era, when, during the 'National Struggle' (*Millî Mücadele*), Ottoman Muslim nationalism reached its apogee. From the Congress of Erzurum in July 1919, through the Congress of Sivas in September of the same year and the final sessions of the Ottoman parliament in early 1920; in the rhetoric of Mustafa Kemal Pasha and others in the National Assembly after April 1920 the struggle was always defined as one of Ottoman Muslims for self determination and against the unjust claims of Armenians and Greeks, and their European supporters. The definition of 'us' and 'them' in religious terms of course persisted until the exchange of populations agreed upon in Lausanne. It was after all Muslims from Greece who were exchanged with Orthodox from Anatolia, without other factors (for instance linguistic ones) playing any role at all (Kitromilidis, 2008; Ladas, 1932).

Sacralisation

Sultan Abdülhamid had made strong efforts to further sacralise his rule by using religious imagery and most of all through the exaltation of the institution of the caliphate. The Young Turks, minor civil servants and officers, were in a totally different position and any sacralisation of their persons was out of the question. They did, however try to sacralise both the committee itself, which was often referred to as a 'Holy Society'(*cemiyeti mukaddes*) and its mission. This came out most clearly with the outbreak of World War I, which was officially declared a Jihad, but it is also visible in the way the person of the sultan-caliph, Mehmet V. Resad, was presented to the public.

Even before the war, during his public visits to Bursa, Edirne and Macedonia in 1910–11, the sultan emphasised the importance of solidarity between the ethnic communities, but he also visited shrines, mosques and Dervish convents and surrounded himself with relics.

During the national struggle after war, sacralisation also took place. In Mustafa Kemal's speeches, the earth of Anatolia is not only sacred in the sense that for any nationalist the national territory is sacred 'because it is drenched in the blood of those who gave their lives for the country'. There is that, to be sure, but he also describes Anatolia as the 'heartland of Islam' (*Islamin harîmi ismeti*). What is at stake, is the rescuing of the *mukaddesat*, the holy traditions. The flavour of the times and the degree to which the struggle was sacralised is perhaps most visible in the text of the Turkish national anthem, the *Istiklal Marsi* (Independence March), written in 1921 by Mehmet Akif. If it were not anachronistic to say so, one would be tempted to say that it describes the struggle entirely in terms of a clash of civilisations, witness verse four:

'Even if a wall of steel surrounds the western horizon
My heart full of belief is a mighty bulwark.
You are full of power, don't be afraid! How can the toothless monster
You call civilisation strangle a religion that is so great?'

Bureaucratising Islam

Another important element of continuity between the Hamidian and Young Turk periods is in the efforts to modernise the state apparatus and extend its hold over the country. As in Abdülhamid's days, integrating Sunni Islam into the state bureaucracy (politicising it in the process) was part of these efforts and a matter of priority for the CUP after the counterrevolution of April 1909 in the capital had shown up the vulnerability of the Young Turk regime. First the Sheikhulislam was given a seat in the cabinet and a Sheikhulislam like Musa Kazim played an important role in legitimising the policies of the Committee. Then, from 1916 onwards, the Sheikhulislam was removed from the cabinet and subordinated to it, with the jurisdiction over Islamic family law, charitable foundations and religious education being transferred to secular ministries. On the face of it these measures contrast sharply with those of the Hamidian era: where Abdülhamid empowered his preferred Islamic authorities and used them as props to his rule, the Young Turks reduced the status and independence of the Islamic authorities. The underlying aim, however, remained much the same: to fully control the Islamic establishment and to use it to strengthen the state. Both regimes, Sultan Abdülhamid as much as the CUP, were extremely suspicious of manifestations of Islam that were outside government control.

This tradition of state control of course reached its apogee during the republic. The image of the Kemalist republic, right from the start was that of a regime that radically broke with the past and introduced a secular, or laicist, order. It is true that the republic took radical measures to limit the influence of Islam on the state within months of its founding. The functions of Caliph and of Sheikhulislam were both abolished by the republic's national assembly in March 1924. At the same time, however, the republic actually *increased* the state's hold over religion. The Presidium for Religious Affairs (*Diyanet Isleri Baskanligi*) that replaced the Sheikhulislamate was given sole responsibility for religious guidance. All imams and muftis were now civil servants. As the central state increased its hold over the country, so did its religious arm: the presidium centrally determined the contents of Friday sermons and instructed muftis on the correct advice to be given to the believers. Over time, the *Diyanet* was turned into a centralised and hierarchical bureaucracy to an extent that had never been achieved by Abdülhamid II. As Davison has pointed out, the state not only restricted religious education – it also fostered it if it could fully control it.

As in the empire, in the republic, too, the state exclusively looked after the religious needs of the Sunni majority, leaving all Muslim dissenters, such as the Alevi, to their own devices. In this respect, the nation state turned out to be as much a Sunni state as the late empire had been.

Morality

If there is one aspect in which there is a clear discontinuity between the late empire on the one hand and the Young Turk and Kemalist eras on the other, it is that of morality. Abdülhamid had sought to base his revived empire on a reinvigorated public morality, the *ahlak* propagated in his school textbooks and in the sermons of the *hatips*. The Young Turks and Kemalists did nothing of the sort. The Unionist policies after 1913 definitely had a secularising character in the social and cultural sphere even when the Unionists were appealing to a sentiment of Muslim nationalism at the same time. The Young Turks and the Kemalists wanted an Islam that was compatible with science and that supported their understanding of the national interest. In the republic this meant that the message was a double one: on the one hand religion was depicted as nothing but the private affair of the believer, on the other the believer was addressed as citizen of the republic with a religious duty to pay taxes and serve in the army (Soymen, 2000, p. 115–17). There were efforts to strengthen the cohesion of society through the strengthening of a morality based on Islam, but they were made by Islamist revivalist movements such as that of Sait Nursi and Süleyman Tunahan. The state only became involved in moral rearmament in the late 1970s.

Kenan Evren: Islam as an antidote

When the Turkish general staff took over power on 12 September 1980, combating the hold of 'foreign' ideologies such as socialism, communism or Islamic fundamentalism over the Turkish youth, Islam was at the top of its agenda. Even in their first proclamation after the coup the generals talked about the need to combat 'perverse' (*sapik*) ideologies. Although the military suppressed the leftist and Islamist movements mercilessly, they also realised that an ideological alternative was needed and that traditional secularist Kemalism had too limited an appeal to be able to do the job. Under the personal guidance of coup leader General Evren (himself the son of an imam), they turned to the ideas of the 'Hearths of the Enlightened' (*Aydınlar Ocakları*). This was an organisation of conservative nationalist academics, politicians and businessmen, founded in 1970 to break the hold of left-wing intellectuals over the political debate. The central element in its ideology, which was developed by its first president, Ibrahim Kafesoglu and called the 'Turkish-Islamic Synthesis', was the idea that Islam and the pre-Islamic culture of the Turks showed up a great number of similarities. Turks were therefore naturally attracted to Islam and destined to be its soldiers. Turkish culture and national identity were shaped by a 2500-year-old Turkic tradition and a 1000-year-old religion, and therefore Islam was not only compatible with Turkish nationalism, but an integral part of it.

The Hearths of the Enlightened had been gaining influence in government circles since Demirel's 'National Front' coalitions in the late seventies, but after the 1980 coup they achieved complete control in the fields of culture and education. The organs of the state were given the task of spreading the message of the Turkish-Islamic Synthesis. Poulton has remarked (without further elaborating the theme) that the ideological policies of Kenan Evren bear a certain resemblance to those of Abdülhamid and indeed, the resemblance is striking, both in the medium and in the message.

Religious education was enshrined in the constitution the military had adopted in 1982. It stated that the state – and the state alone – was charged with religious education and that instruction in religious culture and moral education was to be compulsory in both primary and secondary education. In the textbooks, teaching on Islam was directly linked to values such as nationalism, the unity and indivisibility of the nation, respect for authority and militarism. The Presidium for Religious Affairs was given a constitutional position as well. Its functions were now more than ever completely subservient to the interests of the state and what Yavuz has to say about Hamidian Islam ('in practice religion was subordinate and acted primarily as a shield for the preservation of the state') is true for the Islam of Evren's *Diyanet* as well. The message put out by the presidium in publications such as its *Cep Ilmihali* (Pocket Catechism) is unashamedly nationalist, authoritarian and militarist. National unity was depicted as a religious duty. A special missionary department was set up in 1981 to combat Kurdish separatist agitation in the southeast and Sunni mosques were built in Alevi villages in considerable numbers. The *Diyanet* benefited enormously from the central role it played in the ideological campaign of the military and of their successors. The number of its employees grew from slightly over 50,000 to nearly 85,000 between 1979 and 1989.

So, all the elements that were prominent in Abdülhamid's era were there: the establishment of state control, the use of the mosque and the school, the emphasis on morality (*ahlak*), missionary activity and mosque-building to combat diversity and unify the nation and above all, of course, the attempt to monopolise religious instruction and use it to support the state. The intermediaries were there as well: Fethullah Gülen, who was to become the most prominent religious figure of the 1990s, owed his meteoric rise in part to his support for the coup d'etat of 1980 and his support for the policies of the *Diyanet* afterwards. Throughout the 1980s and early 90s Gülen had privileged access to the seat of political power in Ankara. His movement profited from this privileged position and continued to grow. After the fall of the Soviet Union it developed a network of schools in the Balkans, the Caucasus and Central Asia. It was only when the army top brass made a U-turn and decided to crack down on Islamic organisations from 1997 onwards, that the Fethullahcıs came under pressure and their leader was forced to leave the country and settle in the US.

At the same time, the policies of Kenan Evren also showed up continuities with the Kemalist era in that political activities (or activities that could be interpreted as political in the widest sense) of Islamic movements that were not under state control continued to be regarded as illegal.

Conclusion

What a comparison of these case studies of instances where the Ottoman/Turkish state instrumentalised Islam to achieve political goals seems to show, is an underlying continuity between the late Ottoman Empire and the republic where their 'Islamic' policies are concerned.

Abdülhamid's policies of establishing far-reaching state control over the contents of religious education and instruction; his standardisation of the Şeriat and his attempts to use the religious message to increase loyalty to the throne in a sense presage the Young Turk measures aimed at a further subjugation of Islam to the state. What the Young Turks did during World War I, removing the Sheikhulislam from the cabinet and bringing all forms of education, the administration of Islamic law and the charitable foundations (*evkaf*) under the control of secular ministries, was on the face of it different from what the sultan had done. Where he strengthened the Islamic institutions, the Young Turks weakened them. But both limited the freedom of action of the religious authorities, integrated them further into the state machinery and politicised them. This continued in the Kemalist republic, when all responsibility for religious care and for the charitable foundations was devolved onto a new Presidium for Religious Affairs, directly under the prime minister, which was given extensive powers to centrally determine the message spread in mosques and by muftis.

The early republic clearly broke with the policies of the Hamidian and Young Turk era in the field of education. Both previous regimes had set great store by religious education, centrally determining the curriculum to suit their ideological programme. The Kemalists, by contrast, eliminated religious education altogether. In this area continuity was restored by the neo-Kemalist regime of Kenan Evren after 1980, again determining the content of religious education and using it to buttress loyalty to the state became a priority for the regime.

If there is a strong continuity between the successive regimes in their quest for control over and instrumentalisation of religion, the same is true for the type of argument employed. The debate was never one for or against religion. It was, as Andrews has pointed out, about the *interpretation* of religion. The Hamidian regime, the Young Turks, the Kemalists and the Neo-Kemalists all employed the means at their disposal to argue the case for *true* Islam: loyal to the Caliph in Abdülhamid's case, open to science in that of the Young Turks, private and non-political in that of the Kemalists and nationalist with Evren. This Islam was always opposed by an unacceptable Islam: liberal in the case of Abdülhamid, obscurantist for the Young Turks, political for the Kemalists or fundamentalist in the eyes of Evren's junta.

What the investigation of the four particular case studies has taught us, in addition to further illustrating the above-mentioned continuities, is, I think, the following: in times of crisis, successive Ottoman and Turkish republican regimes have recognised that the Muslim component was so central to the identity of the vast majority of their citizens, that they had no option but to appeal to religion when trying to master the crisis. At the same time we have seen that different types of crisis demand a different kind of appeal to Islam. Abdülhamid II and General Evren were faced by ideological challenges that were felt to be life threatening to their regimes and even to the survival of the state. In the first case, the challenge lay in the centrifugal forces of minority nationalism and in that of political liberalism, in the second case the challenge came from different brands of socialism, from Islamic fundamentalism and – to a lesser extent at the time – from Kurdish separatism. To counter these ideological challenges the rulers had recourse to an appeal to Islamic norms and values, explicitly linked to the political message of dynastic loyalty in the first case and state-centred Turkish nationalism and militarism in the second.

The Young Turks during World War I and the Turkish nationalists of the post-World War I era appealed to religion in a very different manner. Faced with armed conflict, with a life and death battle for the survival of their state, they had to mobilise the largest possible majority on the basis of an appeal to a shared identity. What they were concerned with in the years 1912–22 was to find a new 'national' basis on which to build their state. This they found in the Ottoman Muslim identity. Against the background of the rising tensions between Muslims and non-Muslims in the last decades of the nineteenth century and the Balkan Wars of 1912–13 identities had been shaped primarily on the basis of religious affiliation. The loyalty of the Christian minorities was in serious doubt after the Balkan Wars and there was really no other option but to appeal to the core Muslim population of Anatolia, where most of the Ottoman soldiery was recruited. The same problem presented itself to the resistance movement after World War I. Between 1914 and 1922, sacralisation of the struggle, in the shape of *cihad* or a 'holy ideal' and of the national territory (as earth drenched in the blood of martyrs) certainly took place, but, as the policies of the Young Turks during the war and those of the Kemalists after 1922 showed, Islamisation of state and society was not part of the Young Turk/Kemalist agenda, quite the opposite. The element of 'moral rearmament' was completely lacking and this makes the policies of the Young Turks and early Kemalists during the large-scale armed struggles of their time very different from those either of the preceding Hamidian regime or the junta of 1980–3, who were faced primarily with *ideological* competition. It was the nature of the challenge, which ultimately determined the way in which Islam was instrumentalised, as a basis for a national identity or as a defensive ideology.

Today, the battle lines seem to be drawn more or less as they were in the period between 1950 and 1980. In February 1997, the army, which along with Kemalist civil society organisations and parts of the bureaucracy, had become increasingly alarmed at the growing strength of the Islamist Welfare Party (which had become the biggest party in the land in 1995), presented the government with an ultimatum. Six months later this led to the downfall of Turkey's first Islamist prime minister and in the two years that followed a wide range of measures were taken to strengthen the Kemalist secular order. The army seems to have learnt its lesson and to have distanced itself from the policies of the Evren era with their instrumentalisation of religion. With the perceived ideological danger coming from politicised Islam and the threat to the survival of the unitary nation state coming from Kurdish and Armenian agitation, the army seems to have reverted to a classical Kemalist position based on unyielding laicism and Turkish nationalism. The row about Abdullah Gül's candidature and the 2007 elections, referred to at the start of this article, seem to indicate, however, that hardcore Kemalist laicism still has very limited appeal. The alarmist agitation of the army top brass did not prevent the AKP from gaining a resounding victory. It did so largely without having recourse to the political instrumentalisation of Islam, standing instead on its record of good governance and demanding the right of the elected government to rule without interference. Nationalism on the other hand retains its broad appeal with the Turkish public and ten years after the last 'soft coup' the Kemalist institutions skilfully use the public indignation caused by rather artificial 'Armenian'and 'Kurdish' crises to maintain their autonomy vis-a-vis the democratically elected political leadership.

Bibliography

T. Bora (1999) *Türk Sağının Üç Hali* (Istanbul: Iletisim).

A. Davison (1998) *Secularism and Revivalism: A Hermeneutic Reconsideration* (New Haven: Yale University Press).

S. Deringil (1998) *The Well-Protected Domains: Ideology and the Legitimation of Power in the Ottoman Empire 1876–1909* (London: I. B. Tauris).

B. Fortna (2002) *Imperial Classroom: Islam, the State and Education in the Late Ottoman Empire* (Oxford: Oxford University Press).

F. Georgeon (2003) *Abdulhamid II: Le Sultan Calife* (Paris: Fayard).

Ş. Hanioğlu (1995) *The Young Turks in Opposition* (Oxford: Oxford University Press).

K. H. Karpat (ed.) (2000) *Ottoman Past and Today's Turkey* (Leiden: Brill).

P. Kitromilidis (2008) 'The Greek-Turkish population exchange', in Erik-Jan Zürcher (ed.) *Philologiae et Historiae Turcicae Fundamenta IV: History of Turkey in the Twentieth Century* (Berlin: Klaus Schwarz Verlag).

S. Ladas (1932) *The Exchange of Minorities: Bulgaria, Greece and Turkey* (New York: Macmillan Company).

H. Poulton (1997) *Top Hat, Grey Wolf and Crescent: Turkish Nationalism and the Turkish Republic* (London: Hurst).

G. Seufert (1997) *Politischer Islam in der Türkei. Islamismus als symbolische Repräsentation einer sich moderniesierenden muslimischen Gesellschaft* (Stuttgart: Fraz Steiner).

D. Shankland (1999) *Islam and Society in Turkey* (Huntingdon: Eothen Press).

M. Soymen (2000) *Cep İlmihali* (Ankara: Diyanet Isleri Baskanligi Yayinlari).

B. Toprak (1981) *Islam and Political Development in Turkey* (Leiden: Brill).

H. Yavuz (2003) *Islamic Political Identity in Turkey* (Oxford: Oxford University Press).

5

Transformation of Sufi-Based Communities in Modern Turkey: The Nakşibendis, the Nurcus, and the Gülen Community

Elizabeth Özdalga

As a result of the modern Turkish Republic's constitutional emphasis on secularism, religion has generally been ascribed a marginal, or even a negative or reactionary, role in the country's engagement with modernity. This chapter will focus on some of the Sufi-related communities active in late Ottoman and modern Turkish society. In it, I argue that this marginalisation or denial of the role of religion is strongly coloured by the official ideology, and cannot easily be maintained against more analytical approaches to the history of modern Turkey (Mardin, 1989; Atacan, 1990; Turam, 2007).

The perspective on modernity applied in this article is simple. It derives from Norbert Elias' theory of the civilising process (Elias, 1978 and 1982 [1939]), but builds on a distillation or abstraction of that theory elaborated by Elias himself in *The Society of Individuals* (Elias, 2001 [1989]), a work written half a century after his main opus. As the title of that work suggests, Elias' focus is on the individual and the different ways in which the individual interacts with wider society. The backbone of Elias' theory of modernity is the advanced division of labour – 'increasingly longer chains of interdependencies' – not only in the market proper (trade and production), but on all levels of social life, and encompassing all geographical domains: the local, national and global. In pre-modern society, it is the family and the local community, the village or the tribe, which constitutes the significant 'we' for the individual 'I'. But with the development of a society based on increasingly more complex interrelationships, and a more distinct state organisation to coordinate this complex social configuration, the state also takes on the role of the more significant integration unit – the We – for the individual. In this process, through which the individual is drawn closer to the state and its different formal institutions, the individual becomes relatively more autonomous vis-à-vis the family and other local networks. This transformation means that social belonging or identity is tied to more abstract, less tangible structures, mediated through more elusive sets of imaginations, such as nationhood, religious identities, or beliefs in universal (trans-cultural) values of equality and justice (liberalism), or their opposites: hierarchy and order (authoritarianism).

These processes started to be felt on a larger scale in Turkey during its encounter with modernity throughout the twentieth century. From the point of view of the Sufi-based communities dealt with in this paper, the most striking effect of these transformations is the way that Islam is drawn into a newly emerging political, or public sphere. During this process of growing politicisation, Islam, represented by a great variety of different groups, is not only affected by, but is also involved as an active part in the transformations taking place; much more so than advocates of the official ideology – especially since the establishment of the republic – have been aware of, or willing to admit.

The selection of Sufi-based communities, namely of the Nakşibendis, the Nurcus, and the Gülen community, themselves highlight a transformation from *tarikat* (lodge)-oriented organisations with features of patronage, to looser networks resembling open, voluntary associations. The three communites belong to the same Sufi tradition, with deep roots in history, as well as present society. The Nurcus grew out of the Nakşibendis; and the Gülen community is a branch of the Nurcu movement. This chapter therefore follows the chronological order of the three movements, and will focus on four themes: first, the weakening of *tarikat* organisations; second, new interpretations of Islam in the light of a modernising society (religious 'reformation'); third, the politicisation of Islam, and the diversity of paths chosen by different Islamic communities as actors active in the public sphere; and fourth, Islamic activism operating in a pluralistic context, which should be differentiated from 'political Islam', articulated as an authoritarian ideology including the idea of a utopian 'Islamic state'.

My contention is that the various religious communities and traditions covered by this chapter are highly sensitive to change. This sensitivity is not only one of reactive adjustment to transformations taking place in the larger societal structure, but one in which various religious actors also play an active part. Said Nursi, Sheikh Mehmed Zaid Kotku, Osman Hulusi Ateş and Fethullah Gülen are all examples of religious leaders with pronounced ideas about the predicaments of life in modern society and powerful visions about how to come to terms with them.[1]

The time perspective is that of the 'long century', an expression more often used for the nineteenth than the twentieth century (1789–1914).[2] In this case, however, the long century stretches from the reign of Abdulhamid II (r. 1876–1909) until the first decade of the twenty-first century, with Turkey's now determined efforts to achieve membership of the European Union.

The Nakşibendis

The Nakşibendi order, or *tarikat,* is one of the most widespread and influential Sufi organisations in Turkey. As a Sufi movement it traces its spiritual descent, *silsile*, back to the Prophet, but as a *tarikat* its history dates back to the fourteenth century, when Bahaeddin Nakşibend (1318–89), the epynom of the movement, lived as a leading Sufi sheikh in Buhara in today's Uzbekistan. During the succeeding two centuries, the order spread to areas as distant as Central Asia, Eastern Turkestan, India, China, Afghanistan, and the Ottoman Empire, including the Balkans.

The Nakşibendis trace their *silsile* to Ebubekir, the first caliph, whom they venerate for his exceptional spiritual powers. This bond sets the Nakşibendis apart from most other Sufi orders, who trace their lineages to Ali, the fourth caliph. The Nakşibendis are known for their hostility to Shi'ism, and this factor is nourished by their resentment against the militant Shi'i state established by Shah Ismail in Iran at the beginning of the sixteenth century, in addition to Ebubekir ancestry.

The tendency of generally refraining from ecstatic Sufi rituals and practice 'silent *zikr*', instead of 'loud *zikr*', is a tradition that the Nakşibendis trace back to their Ebubekir ancestry. Sharia, the holy law, is another issue of urgent concern among the Nakşibendis. They are not only well-known for their strong piety, but for their strong sense of social and political responsibility, a tradition that goes back to great leading sheiks such as Hodja Ahrar (1404–90) from Samarkand (Gross, 1999).

Mevlana Khalid

When Abdulhamid II ascended to the throne in 1876 the Nakşibendi order was a social and political power to be reckoned with. It took its strength from a wave of revivalism initated at the beginning of the century by the Kurdish Nakşibendi sheikh and 'renewer' (*mujaddid*) Mevlana Khalid (1776–1826). The factors triggering his success as a leading Sufi *mujaddid* were related to both internal and external effects of the beginning of the modernisation process. Traditionally, the Ottoman rulers had allowed the Kurdish tribes a far-reaching autonomy, which allowed them to organise themselves into relatively large and strong political units, or emirates. Under the spell of modernisation, the Ottoman state also increased its administrative control over more distant areas of the empire,[3] which for the Kurdish regions meant that an authority structure based on larger tribal units and emirates was replaced with a more fragmented tribal structure. With this loss of traditional local or regional political authority, the Sufi sheiks came to be increasingly in demand as arbiters in tribal conflicts and feuds. This demand had an instigating effect on the Sufi orders, especailly the Nakşibendi order, which, in contrast with other orders, like the traditionally influential Kadiri order, was generous in allowing new leaders to establish themselves as Sufi sheikhs. Among the Nakşibendis, sheikh deputies, or *khalifa*s, could establish themselves as independent sheikhs with relative ease, a practice which also facilitated the spread of the order. The Nakşibendis of the Khalidi branch became especially influential in Anatolia, the Balkans (Rumelia), Syria and Iraq (Algar, 1990a; van Bruinessen, 1992).

The Nakşibendis were strong supporters of the Ottoman sultans against both Western, especially British influences, the puritanical (Hanbali) Wahhabi opposition of the Saudi sheiks, and the Ali-oriented Shi'i regime in Iran. However, with the introduction of the Tanzimat, or Westernizing, reforms in 1839, their support for the sultans abated. The order even challanged the modernisers Abdülmecid (1839–61) and Abdülaziz (1861–76) and protested against their grand viziers Ali Pasha and Fuat Pasha, due to the Nakşibendis' burning support for the Islamic law, sharia, and deep suspicion towards the new laws. In Abdülhamid II, however, they found an ally who understood better their patriotism and traditionalism, that is, their reaction against foreign, non-Ottoman and/or non-Sunni influences (Algar, 1990a).

Ahmed Ziyaüddin Gümüşhanevi

A prominent sheikh of the Hamidian period, perhaps the most important Nakşibendi associate of Abdulhamid, was Ahmed Ziyaüddin Gümüşhanevi (1813–93), who was descended from Mevlana Khalid by way of Ahmed Ibn-i Süleyman Halid Hasen al-Şami (1785–1858). He was born in Gümüşhane in the Black Sea region, and under his leadership the order spread from Samsun to Rize. Together with his disciples, or *mürids*, he fought in the Russo–Ottoman War of 1877–8. Still, his major centre of activity was Istanbul, where he put up a *tekke* in Fatih, Iskenderpaşa Cami, which was visited by the sultan. Among his major legacies is a compendium of *hadis*, according to Algar probably the last great work of classical *hadis* scholarship. Studies in Islamic law (*fiqh*) continued to be a characteristic attribute of Gümüşhanevi's branch, including the most prominent sheikh of post-war Turkey, Mehmed Zahid Kotku (1879–1980), who has also been regarded as an erudite authority in this field (Algar, 1990a; 1990b).

Vigorous and insistent commitment to the sharia also meant that the Nakşibendis had strong ties to the *ulema*. Şeyhulislam Musa Kasım (1858–1920) is an example of an influential *alim* who also belonged to the Nakşibendi order (Kara, 1986).

The firm adherence to sharia among the Nakşibendis also led to a distinct sense of responsibility for social issues, and thus involvement in political affairs. A common opinion, therefore, is that the Nakşibendis have a special predilection for politics. Addressing this specific question and discussing it in a broad historical and geographical perspective, Algar draws the conclusion that with the exception of Hodja Ahrar (1404–90) it is difficult to say that any of the historically known Nakşibendi leaders, including Bahaeddin Nakşibend, were particularly involved in political affairs, whether in providing counsel to rulers, or in the direct execution of power (Algar, 1990b). In times of foreign assaults, however, when there was a situation of jihad (war for the defence of Muslim communities against non-Muslim aggression) the Nakşibendis have very often taken an active part. So also in the conflicts between the Ottoman rulers and Shi'i rulers in Iran. Otherwise, it is difficult to claim that the Nakşibendis have been more politically active or militant than some other Sufi orders, like the Kubrawis or the Khalvatis.[4] The alleged rather low political profile of the Nakşibendis changed, however, at the beginning of the nineteenth century and the revivalism initiated by *mujaddid* Mevlana Khalid.

Under the steadily increasing and threatening influence of Western powers, the political situation invited the Nakşibendis to engage themselves in support of the sultan, the ultimate patron of Islam and the sharia. The situation during the nineteenth century could not be ignored by the Nakşibendis, with their spiritually substantiated sense of social responsibility. Algar's analysis here supports other studies concerning the effect of modernisation on Islam's increased involvement in politics (Karpat, 2001; Kara, 2005).

The patriotism of the Nakşibendis led many of them to take part in the Great War and the War of Independence. Many Nakşibendi sheikhs also became members of the first National Assembly, like Servet Efendi (d. 1962) and Hasan Fevzi Efendi (d. 1924) (Algar, 1990b). At the time of the establishment of the modern Turkish republic, however, their close relationship to Abdulhamid II and emphasis on sharia discredited the Nakşibendis in the eyes of the new Kemalist leadership. The history of Turkish secularism is well known. The new government closed all the *tekke*s and forbade tarikat activity by law. The ensuing educational reforms also put an end to Koranic and other forms of religious, namely *medrese*, education. However, except for the revolt led by the Kurdish tribal leader, Sheikh Said, there was no major organised Nakşibendi opposition to the new regime.

The Nakşibendis are known for their obedience or submission (*itaat*) to the existing political power. The history of Osman Hulusi Ateş (1914–96) from Malatya therefore offers an interesting case, showing how a Nakşibendi leader (also of the Khalidi branch) adjusted to secularism and the religious repression of the interwar period. His story is interesting also because it illustrates how a Sufi sheikh in post-war Turkey could become a politically influential person at the local level.

Osman Hulusi Ateş

Osman Hulusi Ateş[5] was born in Darende, a small town west of the provincial capital Malatya, where his father was an *imam*. Hulusi Ateş, who was initiated into the Nakşibendi order at an early age by the sheikh Ehramcızade Ismail Hakkı Toprak (1880–1969), also claimed Nakşibendihood for his own father, but it is not clear whether his father had been a sheikh or just a *mürid*. Hulusi's spiritual father, or *mürşid*, originated from Bukhara, but was born in Sivas, where he also received his *medrese* education. His disciples spread to several different places throughout inner Anatolia, like Malatya, Amasya, Ankara, as well as to Adana and Istanbul.

When the older sheikh died in 1969, two of his alleged 98 *khalifa*s claimed authorisation, or *icazetname*, for sheikhdom; one was Hulusi Ateş, and the other was Hasan Akyol from Sivas, who, having been born in 1895, was almost 20 years older than his rival. Since the deceased sheikh had not left any written *icazetname*, it fell to Hulusi Ateş to secure this authority with his own means. One way in which he could claim spiritual legitimacy was through the alleged prophetic descent of his mother and father. His status as a *seyyid* set him apart from different conflicting groups in the town, and prepared him for the role of mediator and arbitrator, which was expected from a Sufi sheikh. Another way in which he could prove his leadership was by increasing his political power. In the changing sociopolitical conditions of Turkey in the 1970s, he became quite successful as a local power broker, and thereby also consolidated his leadership as a Sufi sheikh.

Ateş achieved this goal through good relations with business people, governmental representatives and the common people in the town on a 'patron-client' basis. Ateş, who was called 'Hulusi Efendi' by his followers, gave his special support and blessing to different projects (especially educational projects), which led prosperous figures, especially business people, to make donations. He established good relations with the district governor (*kaymakam*), so as to secure proper official support in terms of land and building permissions. Representatives from different political parties – he did not favour any one party – became important allies. He also rallied his *mürid*s to supply further support, in the case of school projects through donations of equipment like chairs and tables, and funds necessary to cover scholarships for poor students. In this way Hulusi Ateş helped build and run a secondary school, a religious vocational school, an industrial vocational school and a faculty of theology. Government officials or political representatives involved in this kind of cooperation were not necessarily attached to the brotherhood.

There should be no mistake concerning Hulusi Ateş's role as a moderniser. As a Nakşibendi sheikh he was not only concerned with the spiritual and the moral, but also with worldly matters, and he used his power as a religious leader to coordinate and activate local relationships with the purpose of contributing to a better developed society. Hulusi Ateş was a true moderniser, but he was by no means a militant. He worked in close cooperation with existing institutions, and without raising his voice against the official secularist ideology. Most Nakşibendis followed this pattern, but there were also exceptions, the most renowned being the poet Necip Fazıl Kısakürek, who raised the banner of opposition, and paid for his outspokenness with a large number of court cases and several humiliating imprisonments.

Necip Fazıl Kısakürek

Necip Fazıl (1904–83),[6] the offspring of an Ottoman elite family from Istanbul, was a man of excited emotions, who in the midst of a colourful social life as a banker, poet, playwright, novelist, penman and gambler also struggled with his inner self. According to his own statements, his existential broodings gave him no peace, and one evening on the steamer back from work over the Bosporus to Beylerbeyi, where he was living at that time with his widowed mother, he was confronted by a man who, according to his narrative, followed him with a piercing gaze. Since he was not able to escape the eyes of this man, they started to talk. In this way Necip Fazıl was introduced to the renowned Nakşibendi sheikh Abdülhakim Arvasi. The man in the steamer advised Necip Fazıl to go and see this *mürşid* in the Ağa Camii in Beyoğlu.

Necip Fazıl's relationship with his tutor from the Nakşibendi order lasted for nine years, from 1934 when he first met him, until 1943, when Abdülhakim Arvasi died. He has described his encounter with the sheikh in different books and essays, like *Başbuğ velilerden 33* (*Number 33 of the Leading Sheikhs*, referring to the fact that Abdülhakim Efendi was the thirty-third follower in a *silsile* originating with the prophet Muhammed), *O ve ben* (*He and I*), *Rabıta-i Şerife Abdülhakim Arvasi* (*Abdülhakim Arvasi, The Noble Connection*), and *Tasavvuf Bahçeleri Abdülhakim Arvasi* (*Abdülhakim Arvasi, The Gardens of Mysticism*).

The 'language' available to communicate religious commitment was different from what had existed in pre-republican society. Necip Fazıl strongly rejected the personal dominance characteristic of the traditional Sufi *mürid–mürşid* relationship. It was only in relation to Abdülhakim Arvasi that he showed signs of total devotion. Even this devotion was not absolute, since he would not always obey his sheikh on issues of prayers and other rituals. In terms of inner affection, however, his devotion to Arvasi was total. For Necip Fazıl, his *mürşid* was irreplaceable, and after the death of Abdülhakim Arvasi in 1943, Necip Fazıl never entered into a similar relationship again. The two disciples whom sheikh Abdülhakim had appointed as his possible successors both died before him, and this branch of the Nakşibendi order was broken. The broken chain (*silsile*) became symbolic of the fact that Necip Fazıl had to stand for himself as an autonomous individual. He looked for new ways to communicate his existential experiences. It was not the spoken word of an intimate relationship that mattered, he decided, but the written message directed to an anonymous mass of people.

For many years Necip Fazıl pursued his campaign for Islam (*dava*) through a publication named *Büyük Doğu* (Great East). The magazine carrying this name first appeared in 1943. Just one year later it was closed down for disseminating Islamic propaganda, a blow that was to be repeated over and over again. Financially speaking, it was difficult to publish under such uncertain conditions, and Necip Fazıl often complained about lack of money. Necip Fazıl was also personally affected by state persecution, and was imprisoned several times, though usually for short periods.

The first longer sentence he received lasted from 12 December 1952 to 26 May 1953. He described this shocking experience in *Cinnet müstatili*

(*The Rectangle of Madness*). The book is full of resentful complaints. Necip Fazıl writes that he used to count the seconds, with 24 million seconds to serve. He used to cry very easily and only found consolation in accomplishing his prayers. He did not only conduct his five daily prayers, but would also make up for the ones that he had previously neglected, a practice called *kaza* in Islam. The political liberalisation of the 1950s did not seem to increase his scope of action very much. As a matter of fact, Necip Fazıl's relationship to the Democratic Party and its leader Adnan Menderes was contradictory. *Büyük Doğu* continued to fall foul of the law, while Necip Fazıl is said to have received a salary from the prime minister's special payroll.

From the beginning of the 1960s and until the end of the 1970s Necip Fazıl was engaged in an intensive series of conferences all over the country. When the *Milli Selamet Partisi* (National Salvation Party) was created under the leadership of Necmettin Erbakan in 1972 he gave the party his support, even though with certain reservations. For a couple of years he wrote for the party's daily paper, the *Milli Gazete*, but when the party entered a coalition government with the Republican People's Party (the party of Atatürk) in 1973, his ardour cooled. The compromises of real politics did not suit his disposition. His idealism exceeded the bounds of practical politics, and towards the end of the 1970s he directed his sympathies to an ultra-nationalist party led by Alparslan Türkeş, the *Milliyetçi Hareket Partisi* (the Nationalistic Action Party).

When Necip Fazıl died at the age of 79 in 1983, he was on sick leave from yet another imprisonment. The funeral became a great demonstration for different Islamic groups during an era marked by the suppression of politics after the 1980 military intervention. Necip Fazıl was an intellectual and activist with the ability to unite people from different Islamic groups. He represented an Islamic outlook, but he never appeared as a religious leader. Instead he used his ability to merge an Islamic message with a strongly nationalistic political ideology. Necip Fazıl Kısakürek was one of the first intellectuals in Republican Turkish history to take up Islam as a political ideology. He challenged the official secular nationalism with a nationalism rooted in Islamic beliefs. His revival was built on a combination of religion, national culture and modernity.

The kind of leadership that Necip Fazıl claimed for himself was different from that practiced by the traditional Sufi leaders. It was also alien to the realities of practical politics. Necip Fazıl was too proud, self-seeking and arrogant to engage himself in party politics.[7] His deep desire was to gather everyone who believed in his *dava* under his own single and unquestioned leadership, but since this could neither be a religious, nor a political form of leadership it was channeled into a purely ideological one. In this capacity, he helped articulate Islam as a political force (the politicisation of Islam), an effort that also affected the definition of Turkish national identity. His message was delivered with the help of his strong spirit, his firm belief (*iman*), and his courageous character, which turned him into a kind of intellectual

Hercules, a giant and a hero in the eyes of his followers. This heroism was closely connected to his ability to stand up as an individual against a repressive regime. But Necip Fazıl was not a democrat. He believed in the assertive individual in a Nietzsche-like fashion. He was a true elitist, lacking the slightest scent of populism and opportunism. Such a personality induced fear in both friend and foe, but also with admiration. Necip Fazıl enjoyed great popularity. Tens of thousands of people of different backgrounds – not just a handful of intellectuals – gathered to listen to his many conferences.

Mehmed Zahid Kotku

Returning to mainstream *tarikat*-organised Nakşibendihood, the most well-known Nakşibendi sheikh in modern Turkey is Mehmed Zahid Kotku, a spiritual descendant of Mevlana Khalid and Ahmet Ziyaüddin Gümüşhanevi.[8] Kotku was active in the Iskenderpaşa Camii in Istanbul, which has also rendered the name of this branch of the Nakşibendi order the Iskenderpaşa Dergahı.[9] Coming from the Caucasus (Daghestan), Kotku's family settled in Bursa in 1883. Mehmed Zahid Kotku, who was born in 1897, lost his mother when he was just three-years old. His father, Ibrahim Efendi, who was 16 at the time of migration, was an alleged *seyyid* and completed his education at a *medrese* in Bursa, where he served as an imam in different mosques. He died in 1929.

Mehmed Zahid Kotku received his early education in Bursa, studying not Islamic sciences but commerce. During the First World War he joined the army and served as a combat soldier. After the end of the war he was appointed as a military employee in Istanbul. There he encountered the Gümüşhanevi Tekkesi, which at that time was led by Sheikh Ömer Ziyaeddin Efendi (1849–1921). After the death of the sheikh, he continued his Sufi training under the leadership of Mustafa Feyzi Efendi (1851–1926). At the age of 27, in 1924, Kotku received his Certification of Deputation (permission to guide and teach). By that time he had also learned the Koran by heart.

After the *tekke*s were closed in 1925, Mehmed Zahid Kotku returned to Bursa. When his father passed away in 1929 he took over the position of imam in the village of Izvat, in the province of Bursa. He kept this position for 16 years. In 1945 he was transferred to another mosque in the city of Bursa, where he stayed until 1952, when Sheikh Abdulaziz Bekkine died. Upon his death Kotku went to Istanbul, where he was appointed imam of the Iskenderpasa Camii in 1958, a position he kept until his death in 1980.

Mehmed Zahid Kotku came to Istanbul at the beginning of the Democratic Party period (1950–60), an era in modern Turkish history that was marked by a much more dynamic atmosphere than had existed in the interwar period. A new liberalism and open-mindedness was seen in all spheres of life: political and economic as well as social and religious. New areas of activity opened up, and as a Nakşibendi leader Kotku was as committed to the development and improvement of society as he was to the development of the religious and moral aspects of his fellow citizens. His political inter-ests were also shaped and limited by the main axis of his world view: the individual believer and society. He did not articulate his support for the Democratic Party and later the National Order Party (1969–71) and the National Salvation Party (1972–80) in the name of creating an Islamic state – the polity fell outside of his sphere of interest – but in the hope of favouring and strengthening those whom he thought would promote a bet-ter society. Within the economy he gave high priority to industrialisation, especially to domestic efforts. In this way Kotku resembled Osman Hulusi Ateş: a moderniser, but a moderniser in economic terms and a traditionalist in terms of family values and morals.

People with conservative leanings flocked around Kotku, and with time he became the sheikh of many well-known public figures, like Necmettin Erbakan, Turgut Özal, Korkut Özal, Hilmi Gürel, Nazif Gürdoğan, Lütfü Doğan, and Fehmi Adak, to mention just a few (Yavuz, 1999a).[10]

Establishing a close relationship with a Nakshibendi sheikh meant that the *mürid* had to watch his steps carefully. To practice Islam according to the rules set by the Nakşibendi Sufi order meant accepting a pietistic way of life, in which fasting during Ramadan and praying five times a day were a matter of course, drinking alcohol impossible, and entertainment, if not directly harmful, seen at least as a waste of time. Being a Nakşibendi also meant seriously studying the Koran and Sunna, and other sources of Islamic wisdom. These basic features of Nakşibendi pietism were practices which Erbakan and other people gathering around Kotku had to integrate into their daily lives (Özdalga, 2002).

Discipleship also meant taking the advice of the sheikh on all kinds of issues. Another well-known figure in Turkish politics with close affiliation to the Gümüşhanevi Dergahı, Korkut Özal, has told how he and his friends consulted Mehmed Zahid Kotku on decisive questions. This consultation could be about very personal issues, like marital problems, but also about public questions, like economic and political positions. So, for example, Korkut Özal did not take the final decision to run for the National Salvation Party (NSP) in the 1973 elections until he had got consent from his sheikh (Özal, 1999). The same was true for Necmettin Erbakan, who did not form a party of his own, the National Order Party (NOP), until he had the full support of his *mürşid*, Mehmed Zahid Kotku. This tendency does not mean that the advice of the sheikh was always followed to the letter. Korkut Özal, although considered a staunch follower, admits having failed in this respect (he says he was '95 per cent' loyal), but also points out that Erbakan, more than himself, went his own way.[11]

Esad Coşan

At his death in 1980, the old Sheikh Kotku was succeeded by his son-in-law Esad Coşan, a professor at the Ankara University Faculty of Theology.

Most disciples accepted the new leader, but not all. Necmettin Erbakan, for example, never fully accepted the authority of the younger sheikh, which in time created friction, even hostility, between the Nakşibendi Sufi leader Esad Coşan, and the political leader Necmettin Erbakan.

The period following the 1980 military intervention and the ensuing political repression was marked by disorder and confusion. However, it also led to the establishment of a new political party, ANAP (Anavatan Partisi, Motherland Party), which, under the leadership of another member of the Nakşibendi order, Turgut Özal, initiated new liberalising economic reforms. In the period of economic recovery that followed, new business groups that were connected to different Islamic networks came into being. The economic interest groups around the *Iskenderpaşa Dergahı* developed into one of the most influential alliances, which had ramifications in the media because the groups had their own television channels, newspapers, and magazines, like *Islam, Kadın ve Aile [Women and Family], İlim ve Sanat [Science and Art]*, and *Panzehir*, and their own publishing houses. The Iskenderpaşa Dergahı also founded a health foundation with several hospitals, and a labour confederation, HAKYOL (Hak Yol Işçi Sendikaları Konfederasyonu, Confederation of the Labour Unions of the Right Path). An important reason behind its prominent position, according to Yavuz, was the fact that it had so many powerful personalities among its rank and file (1999a).

Mehmed Zahid Kotku had wholeheartedly supported the National Salvation Party (NSP) during the 1970s. Many of those who joined the party had done so only after having been encouraged by the sheikh, or after having asked his advice.[12] After the closure of all major political parties in Turkey following the 1980 military coup, the political landscape changed dramatically. The new Islamist party formed by Necmettin Erbakan after 1983, the Welfare Party, was much more subjugated to the leader than the former party had been. This change caused resentment in Islamic circles. In Turgut Özal, religious voters had found a faithful Muslim, and Nakşibendi, with more liberal views in ANAP. After this point it was no longer self-evident that the Nakşibendis would support Erbakan's Islamist party. Mehmed Zahid Kotku's successor as the leader of the Iskenderpaşa Dergahı, Professor Esad Coşan, found himself increasingly at cross purposes with Erbakan, and the political support of the sect was thus distributed among different political parties, including ANAP, Demirel's True Path Party, and the ultra-nationalist Nationalist Action Party.

The Nurcus

Leaving the repression of the interwar period behind, the Nakşibendis expanded as a religious movement in the years after 1945. They were especially active in trade and industry, party politics, religious education (*Imam-Hatip* schools) and the media, but they remained faithful to their traditions in matters of religious thought and practices. There were other communities, however, who carried through nothing less than a religious reformation, that is, a new interpretation of the Holy Scriptures, in the midst of the secularising reforms of the 1920s. The leading revivalist of that period was Said Nursi, who originated from a Kurdish tribe with connections to the Halidi branch of the Nakşibendi order. The religious re-interpretation he brought forward inspired a new movement, the Nurcu, which developed partly independently from the other branches of the Nakşibendi order.

Said Nursi

Said Nursi was born in 1873 in the village of Nurs, in the province of Bitlis in southeast Turkey. He was educated at different *medrese*s, some of which were associated with the Nakşibendi order. Said had a good head for studying, but he was also known as an obstinate, even rebellious student, who took pride in challenging his teachers, something which brought him both punishments and expulsions. Around 1890 Said moved to Bitlis, where he continued his studies in *kelam* (theology) and modern sciences. From there he went to Van, where he stayed for about 15 years. There he started to draw up an outline for a local university along the model of al-Ahzar in Cairo. It was planned as a trilingual institution – Arabic, Turkish and Kurdish – offering education in different branches of theology, as well as in the modern sciences. In 1907 he went to Istanbul in order to convince Sultan Abdülhamid to support his project, but the Young Turk revolution of 1908 interrupted his efforts. He persisted in his campaign even after Mustafa Kemal had come to power, but his goal was impossible under the new secularist and nationalist regime. As late as 1951, after the Democratic Party had come to power, Nursi once more brought up the idea of establishing a university in eastern Turkey, but was again blankly refused (van Bruinessen, 1992; Algar, 1980).

Said Nursi supported the Young Turk revolution. He also served as a militia commander both in the Balkan War and in the First World War against Russia. He was taken as a prisoner of war to Russia, but in 1918 he escaped through Germany to Istanbul, where he was active in the Kurdish nationalist organisation *Kürt Teavun ve Terakki Cemiyeti* (Society for Support and Progress of the Kurds) (Zürcher, 1993, p. 177). His patriotism made him antagonistic towards the occupation of Istanbul by the European powers and supportive of Mustafa Kemal's War of Independence. After the war he was invited to Ankara to deliver an address to the National Assembly, but he could not agree with the new leadership about the road to follow after independence, especially concerning the role of religion. Things came to a head after the Sheikh Said rebellion in 1925, after which 46 Kurdish insurgents were sent to the gallows. It does not seem that Nursi had anything to do with this revolt against the new secularist regime, but in the repression that followed a harrowing experience for the nationalist leadership, he was nevertheless exiled to Western Turkey (Algar, 1980; van Bruinessen, 1992).

This event became a turning point in Nursi's life. Afterwards he abandoned political activism and the arenas of conflict and controversy. This
change in his attitude had, however, occurred a couple of years before in
Istanbul, during a visit to the cemetery in Eyüb by the Golden Horn. There,
overlooking the city and seeing such misery after more than ten years of
continuous warfare, he experienced a rare, but tangible, vision of death, as
something that can befall human beings also when corporally alive. From
that moment on he decided to live a different life – leaving the 'old Said'
for the 'new Said' – and withdrew for further meditation to Sarıyer, a village
further along the Bosphorus on the European side. His experience of moral
decline and darkness was strengthened after his encounter with the new
secularist leadership in Ankara in 1923.[13] His exile in 1925 finally confirmed
the rightness of his new orientation (Algar, 1980, p. 319).

Said Nursi turned inwards to his dreams and visions, vital sources for
his Koranic interpretations. He applied the method of 'illuminative wisdom' (*işrak*), once advocated by Shihab al-Din Suhrawardi (d. 1191), who
had carried it on from Avicenna (d. 1037) (Encyclopedia of Islam, 1997,
pp. 119–20). Interpretation is here 'obtained in a flash of light infused
by God into the heart of the Sufi, after a period of contemplation and
asceticism' (Camilla, 1994, p. 16). Nursi's writings, collected in *Risale-i Nur*
(Treatise on the Divine Light), were written in high Ottoman Turkish, and
therefore difficult for the common reader to access. An important issue for
Nursi was bringing about accord between the modern sciences and religion.
According to him, there was no contradiction between these two forms of
knowledge. Rather than challenging and threatening one another, they
complemented and enriched each other. Nursi argued that science should
not be looked upon as an obstacle, but as a resource for believers to widen
their horizons. By obtaining a deeper understanding of nature and the cos-
mos, believers would also raise their consciousness concerning the greatness
of the Creator. There were three ways to acquire Islamic knowledge: through
the Koran, the Prophet and the universe (Yavuz, 2003, p. 159). Nursi's aim
was to deliver a new interpretation of the Koran, which could counter the
scepticism and materialism of his own time. For this purpose he set himself
'face to face with the Koran' (Algar 1980, p. 321).

Said Nursi contemplated the individual believer rather than the community, and the inner, mystical experience rather than personal or communal
behaviour. The traditional Sufi network, the *tarikat* as a form of Sufi organisation, thereby lost its traditional significance in his thought. Under the
spell of Said Nursi's reinterpretations of the Koran, a reformation was imper-
ceptibly taking place, ironically reinforcing the secularising reforms of the
republican regime: ironically, because in spite of Nursi's contemporaneous
reinterpretation, basically in harmony with the spirit of the modernising
secular republic, he was repeatedly accused of being a reactionary, and, as a
result, was exiled from one place to another all over western Turkey.[14]

This antagonism between Nursi and the republican establishment was based on the fact that the latter was eager to remove Islam, not only from the state, but also from society, 'ultimately imprisoning religion in the mosque' (Algar, 1980, p. 328). Since any religious movement outside such a narrow definition was condemned as an offence against secularism, friction was inevitable. Nursi's concerns, on the other hand, were with the secularist and heavily Turkish-oriented nationalist ideology, which curbed contacts with other Muslim peoples (especially Kurds and Arabs); with the way that women were allegedly pushed into the modernising process; and with the prejudice against religious education (Algar, 1980, p. 328). In his criticism Nursi differed from many Nakşibendis, who were not opposed to the heavy pro-Turkish bias of official nationalist ideology (Camilla, 1994). The regime's criticism of Nursi and the *Risale-i Nur* was seasoned with allegations that Nursi was secretly working for the creation of a Kurdish state in Anatolia; or that he had set up a new religious order (*tarikat*), a form of organisation that had been forbidden by law in 1925 (Algar, 1980, p. 329).

With the liberalisation of the post-war period, Nursi's ideas and writings spread to wider circles. He became especially popular among university students, but also found adherents among traditionally pious circles in the smaller towns of Anatolia. His interpretation of Islam touched a sensitive chord among many faithful believers, because, as Mardin argues (Mardin, 1989), it was based on well-known, traditional idioms, like the *umma*, *alim*, sheikh or *pir*, while at the same time transforming their meaning to answer the demands of a society where, to refer to the earlier-mentioned work by Norbert Elias (1991), the old traditional 'we'-relationships – family, tribe, village – were dissolving.[15] The *umma*, for example, takes on the meaning of the nation, or a Muslim 'civil society', in Nursi's thought. A more person-alised view of society, in which the individual takes on more responsibility and autonomy, was spelled out in terms of the well-known Koranic concept *insan* (human being).

The role played by reformers like Said Nursi in Turkey's transition to a modern society is all too often overlooked.[16] The official version of modern Turkish history posits that development was a result of the secularising and modernising reforms initiated by the nationalist republican leadership. The regime saw religious groups, like the Nurcus, as harmless onlookers at best, and at worst as reactionary troublemakers. In fact, it may very well be that they positively contributed to important changes in the underlying mind-set of intellectuals and others who were more closely integrated into the social networks of the common people than were the representatives of the Kemalist elite. During Ottoman times the role of religion was exaggerated by the official state ideology (the legitimacy of the sultan was based on the belief that he protected, but also submitted himself to, Islam), but the rela-tionship has been the reverse during the republic. Since the beginning of the 1920s, the regime's belief in the role of religion as a positive factor in social development and integration has faded, when in fact, religion and changes in religious practices and outlooks have helped in promoting, facilitating, and internalising societal change.

The Nurcu movement was organised as a 'textual community' (Camilla, 1994) a network built up around small circles, from 10 to 70 people each, who gathered for common reading and conversations based around the *Risale-i Nur*. Since the Nurcus were especially active in offering student dormitories, both in larger buildings and in smaller flats, meetings were often held in such '*nur* houses' (*ışık evleri/ houses of light*). These dormitories therefore formed an important venue for the gatherings of the community, where members discussed not only religious matters, but all kinds of issues related to daily life, like work, business, and education. These meetings therefore became important nuclei in the newly emerging public sphere.

The relationship of *Risale-i Nur* to the Koran was, according to Said Nursi, like that of the moon to the sun. His work was but an interpretation of the Koran, and should be read as such. It was supposed to be studied, but not learnt by heart. No single interpretation of Nursi's *Risale-i Nur* could claim absolute authority: interpretations were always done according to the particular reader (Yavuz, 2003, p. 171). The readers were supposed to make a 'hermeneutic leap' from the text to what they experienced as being a meaningful interpretation (Camilla, 1994).

After Nursi's death in 1960, his followers split. The first issue around which controversy occurred was how to manage his legacy: according to one group, the *Yazıcılar* (those who favour [hand]writing), Nursi's writings should be spread by means of handwritten manuscripts. No printing or mass distribution should be allowed, and the texts should be distributed in their original Arabic script. In this way, it was thought, the authenticity and close personal connection to Said Nursi would be preserved. It was not very long, however, until another group established a printing house in 1967 with the purpose of creating a wider dissemination of Nursi's writings. The group published the daily *İttihad*, which was closed by a military court in 1971. The same year, the Izmir daily *Yeni Asya* began to be published.

When Said Nursi was still alive, his followers supported Adnan Menderes and the Democratic Party. When Erbakan set up the National Salvation Party at the beginning of the 1970s, many Nurcus supported him. One group in particular, the members of which became shareholders in the Saudi-based *Faisal Finans*, were elected members of parliament in the 1973 elections. Due to ideological disagreements with Erbakan and dissatisfaction with his increasingly authoritarian leadership, these parliamentarians left NSP before the 1977 elections. This was reflected in the election results: the NSP had got 11.8 per cent of the votes in the 1973 elections, but achieved only 8.6 per cent in 1977.[17] After that, the Nurcus turned to Süleyman Demirel's Justice Party.

The 1980 military intervention also split the Nurcu community. The group around the Izmir daily *Yeni Asya* supported Demirel and opposed the intervention as well as the 1982 constitution, while the group around another prominent Nurcu leader, Fethullah Gülen, known for his nationalist and anti-communist activities, supported the military and the new constitution. While Gülen supported Turgut Özal as prime minister after the 1983 elections, the *Yeni Asya* group rejected him, on the grounds that he was a proxy for the military (Yavuz, 2003).

Thus the Nurcus have split into a large number of networks, among which it is possible to discern three major groups: the *Yazıcılar*, the *Yeni Asyacılar* and the *Gülen cemaati*. This fragmentation is characteristic of most Islamic communities, and contributes to the multiform character of a Muslim public sphere. In spite of this, it is possible to discern an overall consensus concerning the basic principles of the polity: none of the groups discussed in this chapter have been under any decisive influence of the thought of political Islamists, like Sayyid Abu'l al-Ala Mawdudi, Hasan al-Banna or Sayyid Qutb, even if Necmettin Erbakan as leader of the National Salvation Party during the 1970s was flirting with fundamentalist Islamist groups such as the Muslim Brotherhood. Anyway, an Islamic state as an alternative to the existing democratic one has never been on the agenda for the Nakşibendis, nor for the aforementioned Nurcu groups.[18] In spite of this, Turkish secularists within the civil and military administration and other parts of the establishment have watched over these communities extremely carefully. The Nurcus, and among them the Gülen community in particular, have been under strict surveillance by the state, based on an official suspicion that belies their social and educational accomplishments.

Fethullah Gülen

Necip Fazıl once told me ... that Bediüzzaman is a man as great as the architect of Sultanahmet (the Blue Mosque). This great man had great thoughts. But think about the people living on the pontoons under the bridge. What if it fell to my lot to simplify his thoughts into a language understood by them?

(Akman, 2004, p. 73)

Fethullah Gülen, who grew up in Erzurum in north-eastern Anatolia, started his career as religious leader in Edirne – on the opposite side of the country. During the second half of the 1960s he became known as an Islamic activist, serving as a *vaiz* (preacher) in different mosques in and around the western Turkish city of Izmir and organising courses and summer camps intended primarily for university students. As a result of these activities, he was detained for seven months after the military intervention in 1971 (Erdoğan, 1995; Akman, 2004). Gülen's discouraging encounters with the authorities during the 1960s, and especially after the military intervention in 1971, led him to develop a low profile. Eager not to attract too much public attention, he channeled his activities into symbolically less loaded projects, suggesting that building a school is more virtuous than building a mosque, and building a normal (secular) school is more virtuous than building an Imam-Hatip school. Since the mid-1980s, Fethullah Gülen's revivalist movement has developed into one of the most powerful religious communities in Turkey. It has a strong activist orientation, which aims at transforming Said Nursi's visions into practice. For that purpose it especially mobilises young people with high social and educational ambitions. The power of the movement thus comes from its ventures in business (trade, industry and finance), education (around 800 college-type high schools and several universities inside and outside of Turkey),[19] and the media (the daily *Zaman*, magazines, TV channels, publishers), while Nursi's doctrinal legacy is largely left unelabourated. Taken together, the Gülen movement is a diffusely organised group. It combines strong Islamic piety with modern business ethics, is loyal to the state and the nation in spite of the fact that it is rejected by the secular establishment and combines traditional family values, including a conservative view of women, with progressive educational visions and projects, which are seen as important tools in the struggle for the upward mobility of its adherents (Turam, 2004a; 2004b; 2007).

Because the official establishment in Turkey has persistently counteracted the movement, it expanded its activities into Central Asia as soon as the Soviet Union dissolved in 1991. In these areas the movement found fertile ground for its business enterprises as well as its educational missions and nationalistic (Turkish) ambitions. Due to repression, especially after the military's 'soft intervention' in February 1997 and alleged health problems, Fethullah Gülen has been living in Pennsylvania, US, since the end of the 1990s (Yavuz, 2003; Yavuz and Esposito, 2003).

Conclusions

This survey of Sufi-based communities and their significance in Turkey's engagement with modernity has touched on four fields of societal practice: economic, political, ideological, and associational/organisational. In conclusion, I summarise their interactions as follows:

Concerning the economy, the various institutions and organisations of the modern market system (banking and finance, as well as corporations and interest organisations) do not constitute a problem for these groups. On the contrary, actors belonging to the religious communities discussed in this chapter have been willing promoters of capitalism, both on the national and the global levels. There are differences between the communities on some global enterprises and visions, the Gülen community generally being more ambitious in actively promoting global networks than the Nakşibendis. So, for example, those groups within the Nakşibendi order who were affiliated to Necmettin Erbakan and the National Salvation Party of the 1970s and the Welfare Party of the 1980s and 1990s were more narrowly nationalistic in their economic ventures, much like Bülent Ecevit's Democratic Left movement of the same period.

However, there have also been groups within the Nakşibendis who have been more open to global ventures, like those affiliated to the late Prime Minister/President Turgut Özal (d. 1993) and his Motherland Party (ANAP). This tradition has been taken over by the leaders of the Justice and Development Party (established in 2001), who formed governments after the 2002 and following the 2007 parliamentary elections with overwhelming majorities. So on the issue of embracing global perspectives and projects, it seems that there have been important changes over the years within Nakşibendi circles.

Politically, the communities discussed in this chapter are all supporters of the democratic order. The Nakşibendis especially (particularly the people around the Iskender Pasa Cemaati and its leader Mehmet Zahid Kotku, for example Necmettin Erbakan and the brothers Turgut and Korkut Özal) have been active in the political process through their support for establishment of parties like the National Order Party (1969) and the National Salvation Party (1972). These engagements have been decisive in promoting the integration of these Sufi-oriented groups into the political system both on the local and the national level. As a result, the Justice and Development Party, with cadres still sympathetic to Nakşibendi circles (even if not as closely connected as the previous Islamic parties), proved the most decisive political organisation in the struggle for Turkey's integration into the EU. This does not mean that the integration of originally marginal Islamic oppositionist parties has been an easy process, free of conflict and controversy. Such parties have repeatedly encountered repression, especially from the military, and there are still ongoing conflicts related to the role of Islam in Turkish society, for example the issue of the veil. The struggle over 'public space' is still an unsettled issue, which continues to hamper Turkish politics. This was amply illustrated during the spring of 2007, when the election of Abdullah Gül as president was postponed under dramatic circumstances, partly due to the fact that his wife wears a headscarf. Faced with such controversies, the people within the Sufi-based communities are left with an ambivalent attitude of trust and misgivings vis-a-vis the existing state institutions.

In terms of ideology, the role of science and secular education has hardly ever been questioned by the leading Sufi groups discussed in this chapter. In this respect Said Nursi played a pioneering role, both in removing the ideological obstacles to a secular approach to science and in encouraging support for education at different levels. The Gülen community has been especially active concerning public secondary education. The Nakşibendis have been more conservative and restrained in their handling of educational issues. Instead of focusing on the improvement of secular secondary education like the Gülen community, they have given a stronger backing to religious education within the Imam-Hatip schools. This expression of a stronger ideological, Islamist bias on their part also caused considerable friction with the secularist establishment and was one of the decisive issues in the military's move against the coalition government led by Necmettin Erbakan on 28 February 1997.

In terms of the organisational networks of the Sufi communities themselves, important changes have taken place that point in the direction of recognising greater autonomy for the individual. The forerunners in this respect are also found among the Nurcus, especially the Gülen community. Said Nursi taught that the traditional *tarikat* (lodge) organization, built on a close and very personal *mürşid–mürid* (teacher–disciple) relationship belonged to the past. He is believed to have said that 'our time is not a time for *tarikat* organisation'. Instead of organising themselves into *tarikat*s, his followers have gathered in study groups, or 'textual communities'. It is true that the so-called *ışık evleri*, smaller or larger houses or apartment flats organised by Gülen adherents as student dormitories, are 'tight' communities, where the students may be subjected to strong peer pressure from devoted members of the community. But it is also true that at the end of their studies, this kind of life comes to an end and students return to their own families and personal networks. Some of them may, of course, have been recruited for a longer engagement in the movement.

The Gülen organisation is generally loosely structured. It would therefore not be correct to talk about membership in any formal sense. Association with the different networks seems, however, to be open and based on voluntary attachment. Participation is most often based on a young person's individual preference, and does not follow from his/her family relationships. Leaders within the Gülen community have been eager to stress that the character of the association is something different from the traditional *tarikat*. According to this discourse, the approved form of association is the *cemaat* (not as close as the *tarikat*, but still a rather tight community of people, who share basic values and know each other very well). But lately, a new description has appeared, which suggests an even looser form of organisation, namely the *cemiyet* (an association of people from very different walks of life). This new vision was launched in private conversations during the yearly 'Abant meeting' held in Erzurum in early July 2005. In this way the Gülen activists seek to widen their base of recruitment, a sign as clear as any that the movement is trying to stay in tune with the requirements of an urbanising society.

Compared to the Gülen community, the Nakşibendis have been much more eager to hold on to their traditional *tarikat* relationships. This tendency is illustrated in Korkut Özal's narrative of how he became attached to Mehmet Zahid Kotku (Özal, 1999). But his story also tells how, after the death of his *mürşid*, he is deprived of any similar strong relationship.

He respects Kotku's successor, Professor Esad Coşan, but this person does not seem to be a satisfactory substitute for him, and he does not look for another one either. The same was true for Necip Fazıl Kısakürek, who, after the death of his tutor, preferred to stay independent. So, even if more traditional in its organisation, the Nakşibendi *tarikat* organisation also seems to dissolve and be transformed into networks that can serve as effective tools in various political, economic and media-oriented organisations.

The final conclusion to be drawn from the above analysis is that Sufi-based communities are intimately involved in Turkey's engagement with modernity. This chapter has visualised that engagement as a process through which individuals become more autonomous vis-à-vis their family and other primordial relationships, and, by the same token, more involved in various institutions on the national level (Elias, 1991). It is during this difficult and sometimes discouraging course of developments that the Sufi legacy provides a large number of citizens with the conceptual tools for finding a meaningful way to confront the changing realities.

Notes

I want to express my gratitude to the Swedish Research Council (Vetenskapsrådet) in Stockholm for kindly supporting the research underlying this article.

1. The major part of the analysis will be developed through portraits of leading personalities. It may seem as if I have given too much emphasis to individual leaders as agents of change. However, without ignoring the risk of tipping the analysis in a voluntaristic direction, I want to realise the advantage of focusing on personalities, since it facilitates the contextualisation and concretisation of the subject. See Abrams (1982).
2. See Ortayli (1995). In a European context the twentieth century has been remembered as 'the short century'. See Hobsbawm (1995).
3. The way in which the central administration extended its control over the local population with the help of local dignitaries is analysed in detail in the eastern parts of the Black Sea coast in Meeker, 2002.
4. This analysis is not shared by Şerif Mardin, who, in contrast to Algar, contends that '[t]hroughout its history, the Nakşibendi order has always been on the alert for opportunities to use power for what it considered the higher interests of Muslims'. See Mardin (1991, p. 135). My guess would be that the difference of opinion on this question may be caused by the fact that 'power', due to lack of sufficient concrete evidence, remains rather unspecified.
5. For a more detailed and extended analysis of Hulusi Ateş, see Atacan (1999). Atacan's chapter is the main source for this section.
6. For this section, see also Özdalga (1992; 1994).
7. He never let any political party use him for its own purposes. Instead, Necip Fazıl used the existing political parties for his own purposes. This characterisation is from Mehmet Akif İnan, poet and high school teacher of literature and great admirer, or 'disciple', of Necip Fazıl, in an interview in Ankara in 1992.
8. For a more detailed and encompassing portrait of Mehmed Zahid Kotku, see Özal (1999).

9. Other powerful branches in the Istanbul area in the post-war era are: the Erenköy Cemaatı, the İsmail Ağa Cemaatı, and the Menzil Cemaatı. See Yavuz (1999a).
10. Necmettin Erbakan may serve as an example. He affiliated himself during his student years at Istanbul Teknik Üniversitesi with the Nakshibendi order via its Gümüşhanevi Dergahı (branch) in Istanbul. His first inauguration (*intisap*) was to sheikh Hasib Yardımcı. At this sheikh's death in 1949, Erbakan was transferred to Abdülaziz Bekkine, and after his death in 1952, to Mehmed Zahid Kotku.
11. Interview with Korkut Özal in December, 1999.
12. Korkut Özal, Minister of the Interior in one of the coalition governments of the 1970s, discussed his consultation with 'Hocaefendi' before running for membership in parliament (from Erzurum). See Özal (1999, p. 175–6).
13. Algar quotes Nursi saying: 'when I came to Ankara in 1338 (1923), the morale of the people of faith was extremely high as a result of the victory of the army of Islam over the Greeks. But I saw that an abominable current of atheism was treacherously attempting to subvert, poison and destroy their morale' (Algar, 1980, p. 319). Quotation taken from Kısakürek (1969, p. 119).
14. He was accused of establishing secret religious organisations, and/or exploiting religion for political purposes. After leaving Van in 1925 Nursi was moved around to the following places: Burdur (1926), Barla, Eskişehir (trial, prison, 1934), Kastamonu, Denizli (trial, 1943), Emirdağ-Afyon, Afyon (trial, confinement, 1947–9), Istanbul (trial, 1952), Isparta (1953). During a short visit to Urfa in 1960, Said Nursi died (Algar, 1980, pp. 321–4).
15. Mardin uses the expression 'a mobilised rural population' (Mardin, 1989, p. 182).
16. Şerif Mardin is one of very few scholars who have drawn attention to this state of affairs. 'While Said used components of this [traditional] discourse he also transformed it' (Mardin, 1989, p. 163). In spite of the fact that Mardin's biography has become a standard work on Nursi, this observation has not really found its way into the learned public.
17. Based on this, van Bruinessen has estimated that the size of the Nurcu movement during the 1970s was approximately one million, or around 3 per cent of a population of 35 million. The difference between the two elections is 3 per cent in the estimated figure (van Bruinessen, 1992, p. 259).
18. Interview with Korkut Özal in July 2004. The fact that militant Islam has not found a breeding ground in Turkey has led to the apprehension that Turkey's experience with Islam has been qualitatively different from that of other Muslim, especially Arab, countries and/or peoples. For a critical analysis of the notion of Turkish Islam, see Özdalga (2006).
19. Figure given by leading members of the organisation in early 2009. For more detailed figures from the 1990s, see Yavuz (1999b, p. 599).

Bibliography

P. Abrams (1982) *Historical Sociology* (Ithaca: Cornell University Press).
N. Akman (2004) *Gurbette Fethullah Gülen* (Istanbul: Zaman Kitap).
H. Algar (1980) 'Said Nursi and the *Risala-i Nur*: An Aspect of Islam in Contemporary Turkey', in K. Ahmad and Z. I. Ansar (eds) *Islamic Perspectives: Studies in Honour of Mawlana Sayyid Abul A'la Mawdudi* (Jeddah: Saudi Publishing House).
H. Algar (1990a) 'A Brief History of the Naqshbandi Order', in M. Gaborieau, A. Popovic and T. Zarcone (eds) *Naqshbandis: Historical Developments and Present Situation of a Muslim Mystical Order* (Istanbul: ISIS).

H. Algar (1990b) 'Political Aspects of Naqshbandi History', in M. Gaborieau, A. Popovic and T. Zarcone (eds) *Naqshbandis: Historical Developments and Present Situation of a Muslim Mystical Order* (Istanbul: ISIS).

H. Algar (1999) 'From Kashghar to Eyüp: The Lineages and Legacy of Sheikh Abdullah Nidai', in E. Özdalga (ed.) *Naqshbandis in Western and Central Asia: Change and Continuity* (London: Curzon Pres).

F. Atacan (1990) *Sosyal Değişme ve Tarikatlar: Cerrahiler* (Istanbul: Hil Yayınları).

F. Atacan (1999) 'A Portrait of a Naqshbandi Sheikh in Modern Turkey', in E. Özdalga (ed.) *Naqshbandis in Western and Central Asia: Change and Continuity* (London: Curzon Press).

C. E. Bosworth, E. van Donzel, W. P. Heinrichs and G. Lecomte (1997) *Encyclopedia of Islam, vol. ix* (Leiden: Brill).

M. van Bruinessen (1992) *Agha, Shaikh and State: The Social and Political Structures of Kurdistan* (London: Zed Books).

T. N. Camilla (1994) *In the Light of Said Nursi: Turkish Nationalism and the Religious Alternative* [unpublished thesis] (Bergen: Department of History, University of Bergen).

N. Elias (1978) [1939] *The Civilising Process: History of Manners* (Vol. 1) and *State Formation and Civilization* (Vol. 2) (Oxford: Blackwell).

N. Elias (1982) [1939] *The Civilising Process: State Formation and Civilization* (Vol. 2) (Oxford: Blackwell).

N. Elias (1991) *The Society of Individuals* (Oxford, Blackwell).

L. Erdogan (1995) *Fethullah Gülen HocaEfendi: 'Küçük Dünyam'* [Fethullah Gülen HocaEfendi. 'My little world'] (Istanbul: AD Yayinlari).

P. Evans, D. Rueschmeyer, and T. Skocpol (eds) (1985) *Bringing the State Back In* (Cambridge: Cambridge University Press).

J. Gross (1999) 'The *Waqf* of Khoja Ubayd Allah Ahrar in Nineteenth Century Central Asia: A Preliminary Study of the Tsarist Record', in E. Özdalga (ed.) *Naqshbandis in Western and Central Asia: Change and Continuity* (London: Curzon Press).

Ü. Günay (2002) 'Türkiye'de Toplumsal Değişme ve Tarikatlar', *İslamiyat Dergisi*, vol. 5, no. 4, 141–62.

S. Hall and B. Gieben (eds) (1992) *Formations of Modernity* (Cambridge: Polity Press).

R. Hefner (2000) *Civil Islam: Muslims and Democratization in Indonesia* (Princeton: Princeton University Press).

E. Hobsbawm (1995) *The Age of Extremes: The Short Twentieth Century 1914–1991* (London: Abacus).

I. Kara (1986) *Türkiye'de İslamcılık Düşüncesi* [Islamist thought in Turkey] (Vol. 1) (Istanbul: Risale).

I. Kara (2005) 'Turban and Fez. *Ulema* as Opposition', in E. Özdalga (ed.) *Late Ottoman Society: The Intellectual Legacy* (London: Routledge).

K. Karpat (2001) *The Politicisation of Islam: Reconstructing Identity, State, Faith, and Communit in the Late Ottoman State* (Oxford: Oxford University Press).

N. F. Kısakürek (1969) *Son Devrin Din Mazlumları* (Istanbul: Büyük Doğu Yayınları).

N. F. Kısakürek (1989) *Başbuğ Velilerden 33* (Istanbul: Büyük Doğu Yayınları).

Ş. Mardin (1989) *Religion and Social Change in Modern Turkey: The Case of Bediüzzaman Said Nursi* (New York: State University of New York Press).

Ş. Mardin (1991) 'The Naksibendi Order in Turkish History', in R. Tapper (ed.) *Islam in Modern Turkey: Religion, Politics and Literature in a Secular State* (London: Tauris).

M. Meeker (2002) *A Nation of Empire: The Ottoman Legacy of Turkish Modernity* (London: University of California Press).

I. Ortaylı (1995) *İmperatorluğun En Uzun Yüzyılı* [The Longest Century of the Empire] (İstanbul: Hil Yayınları).

K. Özal (1999) 'Twenty Years with Mehmed Zahid Kotku: A Personal Story', in E. Özdalga (ed.) *Naqshbandis in Western and Central Asia: Change and Continuity.* (London: Curzon Press).

E. Özdalga (1992) 'East and West as Symbols of Good and Evil: Turkish Muslim Intellectuals Facing Modernity', in B. Utas and K. Vikör (eds) *The Middle East Viewed from the North* (Bergen: Alma Mater Forlag AS).

E. Özdalga (1994) 'Necip Fazıl Kısakürek: Heroic Nationalist in the Garden of Mysticism', *Meddelanden* (Swedish Research Institute in Istanbul, Stockholm), no. 19, 5–27.

E. Özdalga (2000) 'Worldly Asceticism in Islamic Casting: Fethullah Gülen's Inspired Piety and Activism', *Critique*, no. 17, 83–104.

E. Özdalga (2002) 'Necmettin Erbakan: Democracy for the Sake of Power', in M. Heper and S. Sayari (eds) *Political Leaders and Democracy in Turkey* (Lanham, Maryland: Lexington Books).

E. Özdalga (2003) 'Secularizing Trends in Fethullah Gülen's Movement: Impasse or Opportunity for Further Renewal?', *Critique: Critical Middle Eastern Studies*, vol. 1, no. 12, 61–73.

E. Özdalga (2006) 'The Hidden Arab: A Critical Reading of the Notion of Turkish Islam', *Middle Eastern Studies*, vol. 42, no. 4, 551–70.

A. Özdemir and K. Frank (2000) *Visible Islam in Modern Turkey* (London: Macmillan).

B. Turam (2004 a) 'The Politics of Engagement between Islam and the Secular State: Ambivalences of 'Civil Society', *British Journal of Sociology*, vol. 55, no. 2, 259–81.

B. Turam (2004 b) 'A Bargain between the Secular State and Turkish Islam: Politics of Ethnicity in Central Asia', *Nations and Nationalism*, vol. 10, no. 3, 353–74.

B. Turam (2007) *Between Islam and the State: The Politics of Engagement in Turkey* (Stanford: Stanford University Press).

J. B. White (2002) *Islamist Mobilization in Turkey: A Study in Vernacular Politics* (Seattle: University of Washington Press).

H. Yavuz (1999a) 'The Matrix of Modern Turkish Islamic Movements: The Naqshbandi Sufi Order', in E. Özdalga (ed.) *Naqshbandis in Western and Central Asia: Change and Continuity* (London: Curzon Press).

H. Yavuz (1999b) 'Towards an Islamic Liberalism? The Nurcu Movement and Fethullah Gülen', *Middle East Journal*, vol. 53, no. 4, 584–605.

H. Yavuz (2003) *Islamic Political Identity in Turkey* (Oxford: Oxford University Press).

H. Yavuz and J. Esposito (eds) (2003) *Turkish Islam and the Secular State: The Gülen Movement* (Syracuse: Syracuse University Press).

E. J. Zürcher (1993) *Turkey: A Modern History* (London: I. B.Tauris).

6
Military and Politics in Turkey

Feroz Ahmad

There is a widely accepted myth that the roots of Turkey's army date back to ancient times. Professor Ismail Kayabali and Cemender Arslanoglu claimed on Army Day (26 August 1976) that the Turkish armed forces have served the nation for 2185 years (Kayabali and Arslanoglu). More realistically, we can trace the origins of the modern Turkish army back to the 1820s, when Sultan Mahmud II destroyed the unruly Janissary corps, which had long since lost any military effectiveness, and founded a new Ottoman army on modern lines.

Sultan Abdülhamid II (1876–1909) perceived this modernised army as a potential threat to the tradition-based absolute rule that he sought to establish. One of the measures he took was to divide his army between the so-called *mektepli* or war academy-trained officers and the *alaylı* or officers who had risen from the ranks thanks to royal patronage and were therefore loyal to the Sultan. The mektepli had been educated in the modern military schools and academies and been taught not only modern methods of warfare, often by foreign military advisers, but had acquired such secular values as patriotism and nationalism, and the ideas of liberty, fraternity and the rule of law, ideas which had emerged from the French revolutionary tradition. The alaylı officers were loyal to the status quo and its institutions, more tradition-bound and therefore alienated by the ideas that flourished after the constitutional revolution in July 1908. They, along with members of the rank and file revolted in April 1909 and many were purged from the army after the rebellion failed.

The mektepli officers were the progressive-minded officers who formed the backbone of the Ottoman army and supported the reformist policies of the Committee of Union and Progress (CUP). But with the purge of alaylı officers after 1908, the mektepli died in large numbers in the many wars the empire waged between 1908 and 1922. Had these enlightened officers been a larger part of Mustafa Kemal's supporters after the formation of the republic, his reforms would probably have taken root more firmly (*Cumhuriyet*, 18 March 1990; Turfan, 2000).

The army played a predominant role in winning the national struggle, though the part played by the mainly civilian 'Defence of Rights Associations' throughout Anatolia ought not to be discounted. On 17 February 1920 the Ottoman Parliament adopted the National Pact (*Misak-i Milli*) and for the first time the word 'Turkey' was included in the text and became part of diplomatic vocabulary. In order to create a nation, regimes need what may be described as a 'territorial reference point' and that was now Anatolia for both the Sultan's regime in Istanbul and the Nationalists in Ankara.

The Treaty of Sevres

Europe's idea of the new 'Turkey' was incorporated in the Treaty of Sevres of August 1920. The Sultan was left with a fragmented Anatolia which he accepted under duress; 'a weak existence is preferable to total annihilation' noted the Sultan's Privy Council (Jaschke and Pritsch, 1929, p. 37; Rustow, 1959).[1] Had the Allies succeeded in imposing the Treaty of Sevres, the new Turkey would have been a truncated religious state under the Sultan-Caliph. But such a state was totally unacceptable to the Nationalists, who had launched an armed struggle to liberate the territory awarded by the armistice to the Muslims of Anatolia. Only after they had won the war in 1922 could they forge the new Turkey.

It is fair to assume that the majority of the people, including the army and the officer corps, would have preferred continuity under a constitutional monarchy led by the Sultan-Caliph. Such a regime provided continuity as well as legitimacy that would have given the new state prestige throughout the Muslim world and a say in world affairs. Even after the Kemalists carried out what amounted to a political coup d'état by having the Grand National Assembly in Ankara declare Turkey a republic, such senior officers as Kazim Karabekir, Ali Fuad Cebesoy, and Rauf Orbay (all sons of Ottoman pashas) still hoped that the Caliph could in time become president. In October 1922, General Refet Bele had tried to persuade Sultan Vahdettin to dismiss the 'phantom government' of Istanbul and recognise Ankara, thereby joining the Nationalists. But Vahdettin had refused (Mango, 1999, p. 363). The generals, as well as some former Unionists, believed that though the empire had gone, its institutions along with its religious ideology could be maintained in the new republic. Had they come to power there would have been no question of the new Turkey becoming secular and carrying out the reforms that led to modernity in Turkey rather than mere modernisation (Rustow, 1959).

Even before the rivalry between the generals was resolved in Mustafa Kemal's favour, in December 1923 the Assembly passed a law to end military involvement in politics; commanders had to choose between their military careers and politics, and officers on active service could not be deputies (Mango, 1999, p. 400). After 1926, when the opposition had been defeated, the Republican People's Party (RPP) played the dominant role, becoming the instrument for formulating and implementing policy. The new regime shifted its focus on reform from the military to the social and economic spheres. There was a nation to be created, and the military was expected to serve a purely defensive purpose, especially to ward off any threat from Mussolini's Italy. The protocol between the provincial governor and the military commanders also changed, so that governors received the generals, and the generals received the governors whenever they came on official visits (Madanoglu, 1982, pp. 82–3).

Marshal Fevzi Çakmak, who had been appointed Chief of Staff in 1921, was ideally suited to keep the army out of politics. But he personally exercised considerable influence and was left free of constraints from both the cabinet and the assembly, making him virtually independent of political control. The new army was devoted to the defence of the Republic, and Çakmak was given all the authority to deal with that. He would veto the construction of new railways and roads or the industrialisation of certain regions of Anatolia if he believed that a potential enemy could use them. Cemal Madanoglu, a junior officer in the 1920s and one of the leaders of the 1960 coup d'état, learned to his surprise that Çakmak would not permit the construction of factories in the Diyarbakir-Urfa region for strategic reasons (Madanoglu, 1982, p. 135). Though the state was run largely by civilian institutions – the RPP, the Assembly, and the new bureaucracy, 'the separation of military and civilian spheres ... was never complete or watertight'. Fevzi Çakmak was able to act independently of civil authority 'if he thought the defence of the Republic was threatened' (Rustow, 1959, pp. 549–50).

The Kemalist regime was transitional in nature, and the position of the officers continued to decline between 1920 and 1950, if representation in the assembly is any guide. 'The ratio of retired military officers continued to fall from one sixth in 1920 to one eighth in 1943, and one twentieth in 1950' (Rustow, 1959, pp. 549–50; Frey, 1965). Moreover, Celal Bayar, a civilian, replaced Ismet Inönü, the general, as prime minister in November 1937. Bayar's cabinet lasted until 11 November 1938, the day after Atatürk's death and Inönü's election as the new president. Though Inönü was master of the RPP bureaucracy he was also supported by Fevzi Çakmak and the army; Çakmak is said to have rejected the offer of the presidency.[2]

Marshal Fevzi Çakmak retired on 1 January 1944, having served as Chief of Staff since 1921. The reason given was that he had reached the age of retirement, but few people found that convincing.[3] In fact, the resignation marked an impending change in policy, a change that Cakmak might well have resisted had he remained Chief of Staff. Turkey's benevolent neutrality towards Nazi Germany had angered the Allies, and in February 1944 Anglo-American aid to Turkey was terminated. Ankara responded in March by annulling the notorious 'Wealth Tax' law that had victimised the non-Muslim minorities, and in April ended sales of chrome to Germany after receiving an Anglo-US note. On 18 May, the government put anti-Soviet pan-Turanists, many of whom were in the army, on trial. The next day, President İnönü denounced racism and Turanism as subversive ideologies that contradicted Turkey's foreign policy (Ozdogan, 1990, pp. 109–10).[4] Finally on 23 February 1945 Ankara declared war on the Axis powers so as to join the UN. In June, Moscow's call for the modification of the Turkish-Soviet border and the joint defence of the Straits as a condition for renewing the 1925 Treaty pushed Turkey into seeking US guarantees. That was a defining event for the Turkish military.

Western orientation and NATO-membership

The radical transformation of the armed forces came as a result of the Pentagon's decision to give modern arms to Turkey in order to confront the Soviet Union on its southern border, impeding its advance towards the oil fields of the Middle East (Pach, 1991, pp. 88–129).[5] This decision to arm Turkey and the 'Free World' coincided with the post-war economic downturn and the fear of another depression. Against this background, the National Security Council in Washington proposed 'a vast program of militarization of the economy'. It called for a 'rapid and sustained build-up of the political, economic, and military strength of the free world', which can be achieved only if it is recognised 'by this Government, and the American people, and all free peoples, that the cold war is in fact a real war in which the survival of the free world is at stake' (Chomsky, 1982, pp. 21–2). Consequently the role of the military in Turkey changed dramatically. Since 1923 it had been purely defensive; after 1946 it became offensive, especially after Turkey joined NATO in 1952.

Despite the transition to multi-party politics, the generals saw themselves as allies of the RPP and the single-party regime. They were upset by İnönü's defeat in the 1950 election and offered to carry out a coup to prevent the Democrats from coming to power. İnönü prevented the generals from any hasty act and allowed the DP to form the new government. However, one of the first acts of Prime Minister Adnan Menderes was to purge officers thought to be loyal to İnönü. While İnönü remained active in politics the Democrats suffered from the so-called İnönü complex. They were never sure about the loyalty of the military and always regarded İnönü's political activity with suspicion and fear. Had İnönü resigned in 1950, the history of democratic Turkey might have been more stable (Ahmad, 1977, p. 30ff.; Birand, 1995, pp. 63–4).

As Turkey's military was integrated into NATO's structure, new organisations were created within it so as to fight communism with ideas, money, and equipment from the US. While such organisations were founded throughout NATO, they were directed from the HQ in Brussels. Turkish officers were trained to combat 'internal subversion', and there was a large contingent of Americans at various bases throughout the country providing such training. A number of junior officers, such as the future putschist

Alparslan Türkeş, then a captain, were sent to the US for further training. There they worked with officers from other countries and imbibed the 'free world ideology' and the threat that the Soviet Union posed. When Türkeş returned to Turkey he was appointed to the Guerilla School at Çankırı to teach the lessons that he had learned in the US (Yalcin and Yurdakul, 1999, pp. 37–9; Birand, 1995, pp. 63–4).

By the early 1950s the government had lost control of its military intelligence to the US Central Intelligence Agency (CIA). Ahmet Salih Korur, undersecretary to Prime Minister Menderes, found that the Americans controlled Turkey's National Security Organisation or MET *(Milli Emniyet Teşkilatı)*. He stated that 'they influenced MET by giving money. American intelligence [i.e., the CIA] read all our files. I saw that the [training] school in Istanbul, the Istanbul organisation, the interrogation organisation at Yeşilköy were under American control. The Americans paid the salary of the school director in Istanbul directly to him, as well as the salaries of the Yeşilköy body. In fact, they paid the salaries of the entire MET ... and therefore the entire service was accountable to them and they used our officials as though they were theirs. The officials who monitored communications, especially telephones, were also in their pay'.

When Ahmet Salih Korur related his findings to the Prime Minister, Menderes ordered that all money coming from the CIA be put into the MET budget and all relations between individuals and the Americans be terminated. He explained: 'Let's not offend the Americans, as we will always require the CIA. But let's prevent our officials taking money directly from the Americans. Let them help us with technology, of which they have plenty and which our service needs urgently. We will be happy if they help us in this way. This is not a matter of pride. That is how we saw it and conducted the relationship' (Mumcu, 1990).[6]

Ironically, the Democrats themselves brought the military into politics by declaring martial law following the events of 6–7 September 1955. They had hoped that planned attacks on Greek businesses would demonstrate to the world how Turkish people felt about Greek claims to Cyprus. The attacks degenerated into anarchy and the government was forced to proclaim martial law in order to restore order in Istanbul and Izmir (Dosdogru, 1993; Yalcin and Yurdakul, 1999, pp. 48–51). The Democrats undermined their position further by taking anti-democratic measures against the opposition RPP. In 1957, Samet Kuşçu, a staff officer, informed the security service of an impending coup, leading to the 'Nine Officers' Incident'. But nothing came of the information.

The 27 May 1960 coup and the army's emergence as political actor

The government should have woken up after the Kuşçu incident but failed to do so. When the coup took place in May 1960, the government learned of its approach from its intelligence only after the students of the War School demonstrated. But the government was too weak to act, and as Uğur Mumcu noted: 'Only strong governments can prevent a coup. A government that has lost its legitimacy falls like leaves in autumn'. Later, Süleyman Demirel, leader of the Justice Party, Prime Minister, and finally President, claimed that Menderes had had no warning of the impending coup, even though MET was led by a civilian diplomat. But the May coup was unique, because junior officers outside the High Command carried it out. State intelligence was caught unawares(Mumcu, 1990)[7].

The 1960 coup undermined the process of Turkey creating a civil society, a process that began with the establishment of multi-party politics in 1945. Paradoxically, the junta of 38 officers who seized power also aided this process by transforming the political map of Turkey and giving the country a radically new and liberal constitution and institutions such as the Constitutional Court.[8] Political life was also opened up to the Left, with permission granted for the formation of a socialist party and trade unions to bargain collectively with their employers.

The very size of the junta, called the National Unity Committee (NUC), made consensus virtually impossible. Therefore dissidents were purged from its ranks on 13 November 1960. The so-called Fourteen radicals who were expelled from the NUC, wanted the junta to remain in power for some years so as to carry out structural reforms to transform political life in the direction of corporatism and away from democracy and pluralism. The 'Fourteen' were not arrested, put on trial, or imprisoned; they were given sinecures and exiled. Alparslan Türkeş, the most prominent radical, was sent to the Turkish embassy in New Delhi. The junta did not want to alienate any of the following the radicals might have had in the armed forces. Despite this precaution, there were still active officers who felt aggrieved for being left out of the NUC although they too had been part of the conspiracy. Led by Colonel Talat Aydemir, they made two abortive attempts on 22 February 1962 and 20–21 March 1963 to overthrow the government.

The generals (and the politicians) were dismayed by the continuing instability and decided to restore the hierarchical authority in the armed forces. They therefore formed the Armed Forces Union (AFU – *Silahli Kuvvetler Birliği*), 'an umbrella organisation designed to embrace and control all dissident elements in the armed forces' (Ahmad, 1977, pp. 168–72). The generals were given constitutional authority under Article 111 of the 1961 Constitution, which established the National Security Council (NSC – *Milli Güvenlik Kurulu*). This body was to consist of important ministers from the cabinet (civilians) as well as the Chief of the General Staff and representatives of the armed forces. The President of the republic, a retired general after the coup, or in his absence the prime minister, presided over the NSC. Its function was to assist the cabinet 'in making decisions related to national security and coordination'. As if this role was not broad enough to make the generals very influential in

Turkey's political life, in March 1962 the legislature passed a bill increasing the NSC's powers, enabling it virtually to interfere in the deliberations of the cabinet through regular consultation and participation in preparatory discussions (Ahmad, 1977, p. 181). Turkey had become a 'national security' state.

The creation of the National Security Council established the political authority of the military for the foreseeable future, making the generals 'guardians of the nation'. The law establishing the Army Mutual Assistance Association (OYAK – *Ordu Yardımlaşma Kurulu*), passed on 3 January 1961, began the process of integrating the military into the rapidly expanding economic structure of the country. The creation of OYAK was the third defining event in the changing identity of the military. The first such event had been the founding of a national army – out of what was formerly the imperial Ottoman army – by the Republican regime. The second defining event was Turkey's membership of NATO, when the army was transformed into a 'free-world' or 'NATO' army. Despite the continuing rhetoric in support of Kemalism, statism, one of the six pillars of Kemalism, was abandoned in favour of free-market capitalism and the armed forces became the economic and political partners of Turkey's bourgeoisie.

OYAK's regulations permitted regular officers to invest 10 per cent of their salaries in the fund, to be reimbursed at a later date. This service cushioned the officer class from inflation and allowed them to lead a middle-class life of consumption and comfort, a life that they had been deprived of before the coup. With state support OYAK became one of the most profitable enterprises in Turkey, despite economic downturns (Akca, 2004).[9] OYAK continued to diversify and in 2004 moved into personal pensions (Bireysel Emeklilik), potentially a lucrative market with Turkey's growing middle class. It also enjoyed a captive market in the armed forces, and up to 25 per cent of those working in the armed forces had signed up by 2004 (Milliyet, 23 January 2004). OYAK continued to be profitable. On 15 May 2004, Hürriyet reported that in 2003 the holding had made a profit of TL 661.4 trillion and its total assets had grown by 32 per cent to TL 2.2 quadrillion.

The generals took measures to prevent any other attempts at coups d'etat from outside the High Command. In July 1965, the Assembly passed a law creating a new National Intelligence Agency (*Milli Istibaharat Teşkilatı*, better known by its Turkish acronym MIT) to replace MET. The civilian leadership of the intelligence organisation, which was thought to be in the pay of the CIA, was purged and placed under Brigadier-General Fuat Doğu for the next five years. MIT became the body that collected information for the NSC (Yalcin and Yurdakul, 1999, pp. 122–8; Ozdemir, 1989, pp. 176ff.).

The military had remained in control of Turkey's political life even after the return to elected governments in 1961. In 1965 the neo-Democrat Justice Party won the election and formed a government on its own. But power remained firmly in the hands of the generals, with Cevdet Sunay succeeding Cemal Gürsel as president and the ambitious General Cemal Tural becoming Chief of the General Staff. Apart from MIT, the military had its own intelligence to watch all activities within the armed forces. The military even began to intimidate its critics; an example of this was the beating up of Ilhami Soysal, a journalist who criticised the generals for living extravagantly thanks to the privileges they enjoyed and the special housing allotted to them (The press, 9 September 1966; Yalcin and Yurdakul, 1999, pp. 129–30).[10] Relations between Washington and Ankara cooled after President Johnson sent Prime Minister Inönü the now notorious 'Johnson letter' in June 1964. Inönü was told not to use arms given by NATO to attack Cyprus during the crisis over the island. As a result, the General Staff decided to form a special force, the Army of the Aegean, totally independent of commitments to NATO. As the US Sixth Fleet no longer found Turkish ports very hospitable because of demonstrations by nationalist and leftist militants, the Pentagon began to favour using port facilities in Greece after the 'Colonels' coup' in Athens in April 1967.

The political situation in Turkey deteriorated dramatically during the latter half of the 1960s. Strikes, the activities of the left-of-centre opposition RPP, the criticisms from the Workers' Party of Turkey, demonstrations against the US presence in Turkey, violence by the Maoist Left, and rightwing '*komandos*' organised by the Nationalist Action Party made the task of governing the country virtually impossible. Finally, the government's attempt to pass labour legislation so as to curb the growing influence of DISK – the Confederation of Revolutionary Workers – led to a huge protest by the workers of the industrial region around Istanbul. On 16 June 1970 the city on both sides of the Bosporus was paralysed, and units of the First Army were called in to quell the protest, while tanks guarded factories and government buildings. The Right described the event as 'the dress rehearsal for a revolution'.

For the Right, virtually all the problems of the day stemmed from the 1961 constitution, which was deemed too liberal and therefore a luxury for Turkey at its stage of underdevelopment. The answer was to amend the constitution, but Demirel's government lacked the votes to do so. Brigadier-General Fuat Doğu's explanation for the prevailing disorder was probably the one accepted by the High Command as well. He was in charge of MIT at the time, and he placed the blame squarely on the 1961 constitution, university autonomy, the autonomy of Turkey's Radio and Television (TRT), freedom of the press, an independent judiciary, the unions, the left wing of the RPP, and finally the senate with its 27 Life Senators, former members of the NUC, the men who had carried out the 1960 coup. Doğu Pasha's solution was simple: amend the constitution, declare martial law and arrest all the leftists on the MIT list (Yalcin and Yurdakul, 1999, p. 188).

The coup of March 1971, the CIA and Cyprus

The generals' memorandum of 12 March 1971 forced PM Demirel to resign and introduced a period of military rule that lasted until the election of

1973. At the time it was rumoured that the generals had intervened in order to prevent a coup from below and to maintain the 'chain of command'. On the twenty-fifth anniversary of the intervention, General Dogan Gures, the former chief of the general staff and True Path Party's deputy for Kilis, stated that 'the 12th March memorandum prevented progress towards a military coup' (Zaman, 12 March 1996).[11]

Until the general election of 1973, the generals governed through an 'above-party' coalition that included a number of technocrats who were expected to carry out the reforms that the Demirel government had failed to bring about. Martial law was declared on 26 April, and the repression of the Left began in earnest. The government also increased the military budget for 1971, noting that 'Turkey broke a record in NATO by increasing her defence expenses by 30 percent in 1971. Turkey's armed forces are the largest in NATO after those of the United States. The defence budgets of other NATO countries have increased negligibly over the last five years. In the Netherlands the increase was 36 percent, in Norway 43 percent, in Greece 71 percent, whereas in Turkey it was 76 percent' (*Turkish Digest*, July 1972).[12]

Cevdet Sunay's term as president ended on 28 March 1972, and he became an ex-officio member of the Senate. Who would succeed him became the question of the day. General Faruk Gürler, one of the generals who had forced Demirel's resignation on 12 March, seemed to be the military's choice. He was commander of the land forces, and in August 1972 had been appointed Deputy Chief of Staff, replacing the unpopular Memduh Tağmaç. But in the fifteenth round of the presidential election on 16 April 1973, the Assembly elected Senator Fahri Korutürk as Turkey's sixth president. He was a retired admiral and ambassador who had become an independent 'Contingent Senator' (one of the contingent of 15 Senate members appointed by the president). Gürler's failure to be elected president was seen as the politicians' revenge for the military's 12 March intervention. Nevertheless Admiral Korutürk was a military man, albeit considered a moderate in comparison to Faruk Gürler.

The general election of October 1973 came as a surprise and an embarrassment to the generals. It brought to power Bülent Ecevit's RPP with social democratic aspirations. He had opposed the memorandum regime in contrast to Ismet Inönü, the grand old man of the party, and defeated him for the party's leadership. The other party whose electoral success the generals were unhappy with was the openly Islamist National Salvation Party, led by the quixotic Necmettin Erbakan. These two parties with contrasting views on laicism formed an unstable coalition.

The coalition limped along until the government decided to intervene in Cyprus after the Greek-Cypriot National Guard coup, supported by Athens, ousted Archbishop Makarios on 15 July 1974. Ankara demanded the restoration of Makarios and the legitimate government in Cyprus and then intervened on 20 July as one of the guarantors of the 1960 constitution.

Ecevit told Joseph Sisco, Nixon's envoy, that 'The United States and Turkey have both made mistakes – the United States by preventing Turkish military action, and Turkey by accepting. We should not make the same mistake again ... We have done it your way for ten years and now we are going to do it our way' (Stern, 1977, pp. 119–20).[13]

At the height of his popularity, Ecevit resigned on 18 September 1974. He hoped that an early election would bring his party to power without the need for a coalition partner. He made a grave miscalculation, for the parties of the Right refused to permit an early election. After a period of political uncertainty and a long ministerial crisis, Süleyman Demirel was able to form a coalition of parties of the Right only in December 1975. His cabinet came to be known as the 'First Nationalist Front Government'. Meanwhile in February 1975, the US Congress imposed an arms embargo on Turkey in retaliation for its intervention and occupation of northern Cyprus.

With the parties of the Right in power, especially the Nationalist Action Party, violence in the streets of Turkey's cities became endemic. The military could have intervened at any time in order to stop the bloodshed, but seemed to be waiting for an appropriate moment when it would be seen as the saviour of the nation. The Maraş massacre of Alevis by extreme right militants in December 1978 forced Ecevit, now back in power, to impose martial law in thirteen provinces as the only way to stop the violence and halt the revolt against the state. Martial law was just a step away from direct military rule.

By late 1978, Turkey's importance to the West had begun to increase dramatically because of the rapidly deteriorating situation in Iran. There was even talk in the press of an operation from Turkey to save the Shah (*Hürriyet*, 19 November 1978).[14] Further east in Afghanistan a communist government had come to power that was to lead to Soviet intervention. A stable Turkey became essential for the Western strategy in the region, and aid to modernise the army, weakened by the embargo, increased. Western leaders who met in Guadeloupe agreed on the need for multilateral aid to Turkey. Washington was anxious to restore relations with Turkey, but US policymakers wanted maximum freedom to manoeuvre within its bases, for example, the freedom to supply Israel, a freedom it did not enjoy in 1973. Washington was worried about the existing instability both in Iran and Turkey and the pessimism that this generated in the region. Turkey's military had to be modernised and brought back into the Western fold. There was speculation when Defence Minister Hasan Esat Isik resigned in January 1979. He was considered a hardliner in his relations with the US, and the generals wanted him out of the way; he had been excluded from talks with Warren Christopher when Washington's envoy met Ecevit and the generals earlier in the week. Even Ecevit was considered an obstacle to the negotiations because he personally wanted to play a role in the détente rather than leave negotiations to the generals.

The partial senate and by-elections of 14 October 1979 were a huge defeat for Ecevit. He resigned two days later, making way for Demirel's minority government. The strategic importance of Turkey continued to grow as a result of the crisis in the region. The occupation of the US embassy in Tehran by 'revolutionary guards' (4 November); the occupation of the Grand Mosque in Mecca by pro-Iran Islamists (20 November), and Soviet intervention in Afghanistan on behalf of their client (26 December) triggered a new stage in the struggle against political Islam, as well as the beginning of the 'second cold war'. The military in Ankara was alarmed by such developments (Birand, 1987, pp. 166ff.).

There was another development that required the military's attention, related to its partnership in the economy: the rise of globalisation. In December Demirel's appointment of Turgut Özal as his undersecretary in charge of the economy signalled a radical departure. The government declared its dedication to promoting a 'free market' economy, removing virtually all obstacles that stood in the way. Soon after that, Ozal launched his economic programme known as the 'Decisions of 24th January' [1980], a programme that required severe belt-tightening by workers and consumers. He declared that he needed five years of social peace before the economy would be stabilised: no more collective bargaining and strikes, or demonstrations for an Islamic state in Turkey.

Violence, globalisation and the 12 September 1980 coup

What Özal required was provided by the generals when they intervened on 12 September 1980 and forced Prime Minister Demirel to step down. In March 1971 the junta had calculated that the 'fine tuning' of the constitution and various institutions would be sufficient to put the system on an even keel. This time the new junta decided that a total overhaul was required, with a new constitution and institutions designed to strengthen the state. The military banned all political and social groups – including all parties – from the country's political life, though not TUSIAD and other business circles, which did not have difficulty in partially filling the vacuum so created (Ilkin, 1993).

Turkey was under military rule throughout the 1980s, even though parliamentary rule was restored after the election of November 1983. Supported by Washington, the generals totally disregarded criticism from Europe concerning the lack of democracy and the violation of human rights. For the Pentagon, it was stability that mattered. The 1982 Constitution was put to a referendum on 7 November and approved by 91 per cent of the voters, thus providing an element of legitimacy for the generals.

The junta that was in power for three years, from September 1983 called itself the National Security Council (NSC). It was headed by Chief of Staff Kenan Evren and included the four chiefs of the armed forces (army, navy, air force, and gendarmerie). Martial law commanders ran the country; the armed forces had been 'transformed into an institution of militarism … One sign of the advent of militarism is the assumption by a nation's armed forces of numerous tasks that should be reserved for civilians' (Johnson, 2004). That was certainly the case in the Turkey of the 1980s. With the aim of modernising the air force, in September 1983 Turkey agreed to buy 160 F-16 fighters from General Dynamics Corporation of St Louis, Missouri over the next ten years. These fighters were to be assembled and manufactured in Turkey, an important step in the development of the Turkish arms industry. In March 1989, Turgut Özal inaugurated the Mürted facilities of TÜSAŞ Aerospace Industries, where the F-16 was to be assembled. US Ambassador Robert Strausz-Hupé described the new facilities as 'an important milestone in Turkey's continuing advance towards a more complete technological, economic, and political integration with the West' (Turkey Today, March 1989).

After political life was restored, new parties formed, and an election held on 6 November 1983, the military suffered a setback when its party, the Nationalist Democracy Party (NDP) led by retired General Turgut Sunalp, failed to win. The victory of Turgut Özal's Motherland Party was seen as a slap in the face for the NSC as well, as General Evren came out strongly against Özal days before votes were cast. But Sunalp's defeat and Özal's victory were a triumph for the cosmopolitan, globalising wing of the military, for Özal had been their man ever since he launched his economic programme on 24 January 1980. This was a working partnership until Özal's death in 1993, even after Kenan Evren retired as president in November 1989 and Özal succeeded him as Turkey's second civilian president.

However, under PM Özal some saw a turning point in the civilian–military relationship when the military failed to have their candidate appointed Chief of Staff and Özal intervened. This is how the event unfolded in June 1987. When Necdet Urug was about to retire as Chief of Staff he made it known that his candidate, Gen. Necdet Oztorun, commander of the land forces, would be his successor. This was normal practice and well within the principle of hierarchy. But under the constitution, the President appointed the Chief of Staff on the recommendation of the PM. On 29 June Özal announced that he wanted General Necip Torumtay to succeed Urug, and Necdet Oztorun resigned the following day.

This is described as a coup staged by Özal against the generals; in fact it was President Kenan Evren's coup against his own comrades. Necdet Oztorun and others said as much in interviews after the event, though Ozturun noted that Evren would gain nothing from this. But what was the real meaning of this incident?

The incident was the manifestation of a factional rivalry or even struggle within the High Command between self-styled Kemalists and those who might be described as 'cosmopolitans'. In 1983 the Kemalists won when they prevented Bulent Ulusu from forming the junta's party. Instead, their candidate,

Turgut Sunalp, was to form the NDP. Necdet Urug's retirement in 1987 provided the opportunity for the 'cosmopolitans' to turn the tables on their rivals. Urug, it was rumoured, had planned to consolidate his faction's position into the twenty-first century. Necip Torumtay was a genuine 'cosmopolitan', who spoke English fluently, liked music, and whose wife painted. Moreover, he was close to the Pentagon. Oztorun, on the other hand, represented the tradition of Fevzi Çakmak's army and was not well suited to deal with his NATO counterparts. As for President Evren, he hoped to win civilian support to stay on as president after his term expired in 1989. But that did not happen, and Özal's election seemed to suggest that the civilians had finally broken the hold of the generals over the presidency. Turgut Özal's ambition was to control the armed forces as Menderes had tried to do in the 1950s. But he failed to appoint his man, General Recep Ergun, as commander of the land forces and potentially the future chief of staff. General Kemal Yamak replaced Necdet Oztorun and Recep Ergun became Özal's adviser.

Some observers of the Turkish political scene concluded that Torumtay's appointment was 'an important victory by the government over the corporate interests of the military' (Hale, 1994, p. 8). That is how it seemed at the time, especially when Özal, the civilian, succeeded Evren as president. But the military's position had become so strong with the 1982 Constitution that the army no longer needed a president from within their ranks to dominate the political life of the country.[15]

After the fall of the Berlin wall and the collapse of the Soviet bloc in November 1989, politicians such as Demirel, now the leader of the True Path Party, called for MIT to be placed in the hands of civilians and for civil society to assume responsibility for the regime so as to prevent any further coups. He declared: 'If civil society understands its own interests, assumes responsibility for them, and gives a democratic response, then there will be no need for a coup. If the people do not raise their voices, if they applaud coups, that means they are encouraging a coup. If civil society is anxious about anything, if it awaits a coup and then applauds it, there is nothing one can do to prevent a coup'. While he opposed abolishing the National Security Council or the National Intelligence Organisation, for such institutions were part of every state, he supported reform of these institutions. As matters stood, the leaders of MIT were always military men, recommended to the government by the General Staff. That is why MIT (or MET under CIA control) had not warned the government of the 1960 coup, the 1971 Memorandum, or the 1980 seizure of power. On 16 March 1990, a journalist in *Cumhuriyet* commented: 'Generally speaking, the government knows what is going on in Angola, but knows nothing about what goes on in Ankara. That comes from the influence of the military wing [of the NSC]. Thus in today's climate the thing to do is to civilianise National Intelligence. Thus criticism of the soldiers and the organisation would end. That raises the question of what kind of a new MIT Turkey should have'.[16] Two days later, Uğur Mumcu concluded that the question was not one concerning MIT but one requiring the democratisation of the entire apparatus of state; the question of the undersecretary who headed MIT had to be considered in that light. If that were not done, it would not matter whether the undersecretary was a soldier or a civilian. MIT's undersecretary ought to be a civilian, but before that the state ought to be democratic from top to bottom. That was the only way to prevent another coup.[17]

Saddam Hussein's invasion of Kuwait in August 1990 and the first Gulf crisis brought civil–military relations to the fore in Ankara. President Özal wanted Turkey to play an active role in the coming war and he acted independently of his ministers. That led to the resignation of Foreign Minister Ali Bozer on 11 October, because at a White House meeting between Özal and Bush, Bozer had been excluded while Secretary of State James Baker had not. A week later Defence Minister Safa Giray also resigned because he opposed Özal's assertive policy. However, the most dramatic resignation came on 3 December when Chief of Staff Necip Torumtay resigned. Özal believed that after the war Iraq would be partitioned and a federated Kurdish state would emerge in northern Iraq. It could join Turkey in a future federation. But Torumtay found such an idea dangerous and prevented its implementation by resigning rather than following orders to occupy Mosul and Kirkuk. It was also rumoured that the Pentagon did not want Özal to go any further than support US forces. Turkey's direct intervention might cause problems with Arab allies, just as Israel's active intervention would. Torumtay's resignation ended that possibility. Until that point, Özal had made policy virtually on his own, with almost total disregard for his prime minister, Yildirim Akbulut, and the cabinet, even bypassing the NSC. He was said to have relied on his kitchen cabinet, which included some retired generals.[18]

Unstable politics, continuing tutelage: The 1990s

After the 1989 general election, Turkey had begun to lapse into unstable coalition politics. Parties and politicians became more and more unpopular, because of their opportunism and corruption. Only the military increased in popularity, because soldiers were considered upright and honest, especially as the army had been waging war against the PKK, the Workers' Party of Kurdistan, since 1984 and the death of 'martyrs' (Turkish troops killed in action) was reported daily in the media. A survey conducted by the University of Anatolia asked whether people's confidence in certain groups and institutions had increased or decreased. It found that public confidence had decreased in virtually all groups and institutions save the military. The results were published in *Cumhuriyet* (7 June 1996), see also Table 6.1.

After witnessing the success of US forces in the Gulf War, Turkey's military decided to reform the armed forces so as to meet the challenges of contemporary warfare. The Gulf War proved to be another defining event, and the

Table 6.1   Public Confidence in institutions

	Increasing	Unchanged	Decreasing
1. Politicians	2.2		85.5
2. Local administration	16.5	43.7	39.9
3. Army	59.9	36.2	8.0
4. Unions	13.0	44.5	41.6
5. The private sector	28.5	45.1	26.4
6. Educational institutions	14.8	35.2	50.0
7. Universities	20.7	49.1	30.2
8. IMF, World Bank	6.9	47.5	45.6
9. Television	16.4	41.8	41.8
10. Newspapers	5.6	28.3	66.1

Pentagon once again became the critical ally. When General Ismail Hakki Karadayi, the new chief of staff, visited Washington in August 1994, all aspects of defence cooperation between the two countries were discussed. PM Tansu Ciller, as did most other politicians, agreed with the need to modernise the armed forces, and she said that her government planned to allocate $2 billion yearly for the next decade to accomplish that end.[19] In November 1994 she became the first PM of Turkey to visit Israel, a country that was to play an important role in the modernisation of the armed forces, providing Turkey with new technology necessary to wage modern warfare. A strategic partnership began to take shape.

Internally the military became more concerned about the rise of political Islam in the country. The generals claimed that 'reaction' (*irtica*) was becoming a greater threat to stability than 'separatism', the code word for the Kurdish insurrection. On 14 March 1990 *Cumhuriyet* reported that 146 commissioned and non-commissioned officers had been expelled from the armed forces, and there was alarm that 'religious reactionaries' were trying to penetrate the military at all levels. As the military did not recruit graduates from the Imam-Hatip schools, the Islamists were coaching pupils from middle school so that they could enter the military. As a result it was estimated that 50 'Islamised' students had initially succeeded in joining the military; within four years the number had risen to 200.

The election of December 1995 confirmed the worst fears of both the military and secularists in Turkey. The Islamist Welfare Party (Refah Partisi) had won. Attempts were made to form a government that would exclude Welfare. But when the secular parties of the right failed to establish a stable and coherent government, in June 1996 Welfare's leader, Necmettin Erbakan, was allowed to form a coalition with the True Path Party. The

Islamists were in principle hostile to Israel, and in opposition Erbakan had even led 'Free Jerusalem' demonstrations. But as prime minister, Erbakan could do nothing to stop the developing relationship with Israel. As other agreements were signed between Turkey and Israel, PM Erbakan confessed that any change in his country's foreign policy was unlikely.

28 February 1997: The postmodern coup and gradual EU-engagement

In October 1996 opposition leader Mesut Yilmaz floated rumours of a military coup against Erbakan after he returned from his humiliating visit to Libya. But a coup was unlikely as the generals were already in control of Turkey's political life thanks to their control of the NSC. On 4 February 1997 a convoy of tanks sent through the town of Sincan, on the outskirts of Ankara, was sufficient to intimidate the Islamist local administration and the government that had permitted the staging of 'Jerusalem Night' on 31 January. On 28 February, the NSC ordered a clampdown on Islamists, in a set of decisions that came to be known as the '28th February Process'. General Çevik Bir, the deputy chief of staff, stated that in Sincan 'we restored the democratic balance'. On 18 June 1997 PM Erbakan resigned and the coalition collapsed. In August the Assembly, following up on the most important of the 28 February decisions, passed a law extending compulsory secular education from five to eight years so as to weaken the hold of Islamists on the youth.

By the mid-1990s, Turkey had begun to consider carrying out the reforms necessary to become a candidate for membership of the European Union. One of these reforms required that the military be brought under parliamentary control. A body known as the 'Western Working Group' (Bati Calisma Grubu), attached to the General Staff, aroused controversy. Some supported it because its job was to keep track of the activities of Islamists who were seen as a threat to the secular republic. But PM Mesut Yilmaz disagreed. In an interview (*Hürriyet*, 11 September 1997) he stated that the Group was no longer necessary because his government would meet any threat. But nothing was done to end the Group. In January 2000, the office of the General Staff would even be accused in the press of supporting the Turkish Hizbullah's activities against the PKK, accusations the General Staff strenuously denied. So heated was the controversy regarding the military's role that President Demirel had to warn politicians to be careful not to drag the army into politics.[20]

Turkey's exclusion from the list of candidates for consideration for EU membership at the Luxembourg summit in December 1997 proved traumatic. This decision was thought to strengthen the military and play into the hands of the Islamists, weakening civil society. A humiliated Mesut

Yilmaz declared that he would seek a strategic partnership with the US. But such an option no longer existed and Turkey was forced to pursue the EU option. Europe was beginning to define itself against the US even within NATO, especially with talk of an alternative military force. The factionalism in the military between the Kemalists and the cosmopolitans continued into the twenty-first century. With the capture of the PKK leader Abdullah Öcalan in February 1999, Turkey became more nationalistic. The Kemalist faction's fortunes were now in the ascendant; it refused to declare victory in the war against the PKK and accept a negotiated solution. The General Staff issued a statement on 18 March declaring they would never recognise the PKK as a legal body. And in his Bayram message (28 March), Chief of Staff Hüseyin Kıvrıkoğlu promised that 'The Turkish army would risk lives to uphold the country's territorial integrity, democracy, and secularism'. For the moment the nationalists had the upper hand and the election of 18 April also proved to be their triumph, with the victory of Ecevit's 'Democratic Left', in fact a party of the Right, and the Nationalist Action Party. Both parties had benefited from Öcalan's capture.

At the Helsinki meeting of 10 December 1999 the EU accepted Turkey's candidacy with two preconditions: firstly, relations with Greece must be normalised, and secondly, reforms must be undertaken to meet the so-called Copenhagen criteria on human rights and the rights of minorities. The press hailed the EU decision as historic, marking a turning point in the country's modern history. Only the nationalist press urged caution. But the country, if surveys are to be believed, was committed to EU membership.

Both TÜSIAD and MÜSIAD (the associations of businessmen and industrialists of Istanbul and Anatolia respectively) supported 'constitutional reform' and the 'democratisation of the administration': the General Staff to be attached to the Defence Ministry, the powers of the NSC to be decreased, its duties and responsibilities defined in the constitution, and a civilian appointed as its secretary (Aksam, 4 April 2000). It took some time for politicians and bureaucrats to support these reforms. In August 2001 Mesut Yilmaz agreed and noted that unless the power of the generals was limited and freedom-curbing laws lifted, Turkey would not be able to enter the EU. When Deputy PM Devlet Bahceli, leader of the Nationalist Action Party saw the reforms 'as a plot against Turkey's unity', Mesut Yilmaz, his partner in the cabinet, accused him of 'hiding behind the army'. The military seemed to be supporting Bahceli's arguments. Retired General Suat Ilhan declared that EU membership was against Turkey's history and contradicted the Kemalist revolution. He said Turkey would 'either be a state of the EU or preserve the independent nation state founded by Atatürk'. But after the NSC meeting of 30 May (press, 31 May 2002) Chief of Staff Kivrikoglu announced in unequivocal terms that 'joining the EU was a geopolitical necessity'.

On 8 January 2003 Chief of Staff General Hilmi Özkök, who succeeded Hüseyin Kıvrıkoğlu, was also convinced that Turkey's future was in the European Union. He defined the military's consensus regarding the issue.

The Turkish Armed forces have always been the pioneers of modernisation. Membership of the EU will be the most effective tool to realise that goal. The Turkish army is already in Europe because of NATO. For this reason, it is a very great injustice to claim that the Turkish armed forces are against EU membership. The Turkish armed forces are not against the EU; on the contrary, membership is a means of harmonization within the EU. But what we want to emphasize is that we want to enter the EU not at any cost, but on an equal footing, protecting our national and geographical integrity.

The military felt more secure about the future of Turkey with a secular-minded president in Cankaya. Before President Demirel's term expired in 2000, the Chief of Staff met PM Ecevit and told him what the armed forces expected from the next president, who was after all the Commander-in-Chief of the armed forces. Ahmed Necdet Sezer, who was elected Turkey's tenth president on 5 May 2000, was the kind of civilian president the military wanted. He was a judge who had headed the Constitutional Court, was secular and a liberal willing to see the constitution amended so as to permit free discussion regarding such issues as Kurdish rights.

In October 2001 parliament began amending the constitution so as to bring Turkey closer to the EU, a process that still goes on. Later the NSC even accepted education in Kurdish, even though earlier the nationalists had characterised that as 'separatist activities directed by the PKK, a terrorist organisation, an issue that would threaten the country's security'. In January 2002 the parliament approved a draft law amending the NSC law in line with an earlier constitutional amendment of the previous year. The Deputy PM and the Justice Minister were added to the NSC, giving civilian members the majority. Moreover, NSC decisions were to be considered 'recommendations' to the cabinet.[21]

Waning hegemony: The army in the 2000s

Washington continued to believe that the military still played the commanding role in defence and foreign affairs. Thus when Vice President Dick Cheney arrived in Ankara in March 2003 to obtain the government's support for the coming attack on Iraq, he asked that Chief of Staff Kıvrıkoğlu be present when he met Prime Minister Ecevit, knowing that Ecevit was an opponent of war.[22] Some months earlier, Murat Yetkin had written that, much to its surprise, the General Staff had received a message from the US Defence Cooperation Bureau in Ankara that the US expected 'full and complete cooperation' from Turkey's armed forces. The generals found the request odd, as such decisions were political and required approval from the Grand National Assembly.[23]

The general election of November 2002 brought the Justice and Development Party (known by its Turkish initials as AKP) to power with a large majority. Because of its Islamist antecedents, some feared that the military might object. However, that did not happen, and a journalist close to the generals had predicted as much.[24] Chief of Staff Hilmi Özkök, who arrived in Washington on the day of the election, described the election as democratic and therefore supported by the armed forces. But in Istanbul, a retired general emphasised the military's continued support for laicism and warned that religion could take Turkey back to medieval times (*The Press*, 4 November 2002).

After the visit to Ankara by Paul Wolfowitz, a Republican, neo-conservative hawk close to generals and the media, the Pentagon was convinced that Ankara would support the US attack on Iraq. That is how it seemed before US plans were thrown into confusion on 1 March 2003 when parliament vetoed the measure permitting the US to open a northern front. On 31 January the NSC had endorsed the plan to station foreign troops in Turkey. A month later (27 February), the Defence Minister announced that Ankara had reached an agreement on military cooperation with the US. But the AKP government wanted to cover itself by letting the generals and the NSC make the decision so that it would seem like a 'state', not a 'party' decision. The generals opted to leave the decision to parliament, convinced that the motion would be passed. However, some 100 AKP deputies violated party discipline and voted against the measure. The RPP opposition also voted against the measure, so as to embarrass the government. Both the military and the government had miscalculated (Filkins, 2003).

The Chief of Staff had supported the deployment of US troops in Anatolia and the opening of a northern front because that would give Ankara a voice in the post-war situation in Iraq. Moreover, the war would be shorter and less painful if Ankara backed Washington. He therefore urged parliament to reconsider. He admitted that 100 per cent of Turkey, not 94 percent, was opposed to the war. But he said: 'Turkey is not capable of preventing the war on its own. Our choice isn't between good and bad. Our choice is between bad and worse ... If we don't participate, we will suffer the same harm from war. However, our losses won't ever be compensated and we won't ever have a say in the aftermath'.[25]

Erdogan had already stated that he would introduce a new resolution permitting the deployment of US troops. But that was too late, for the US military had decided to adopt 'Plan B' and attack from the south. However, the Pentagon and the neo-conservatives in Washington held the Turkish generals responsible for the failure of the passage of the resolution and seemed determined to humiliate and punish them.[26] The military's (and

TÜSIAD's) willingness to send Turkish troops to Iraq was rejected by the Kurds of northern Iraq. Despite all the gestures from the generals, on 4 July US forces in northern Iraq seized eleven members of Turkey's 2000-strong Special Forces in Süleymaniye and took them to Kirkuk. They were accused of planning the assassination of the Kurdish leader. This incident triggered a crisis between Washington and Ankara, Turkey closing down its border with Iraq at Habur. The Turkish media reported that the generals in Ankara were considering closing Turkish air space if the soldiers were not released, denying the US the use of Incirlik, and sending more troops into northern Iraq. After phone calls to Washington, the Turkish soldiers were released two days later, but talk of a crisis between Ankara and Washington continued.[27]

This incident strengthened the military's resolve to enter the EU, and more measures were passed to meet Europe's requirements. After a meeting between Erdoğan and Özkök, the press noted on 22 May that the generals had given the government the green light to pass all measures necessary. On 6 August President Sezer signed into law the seventh European Union harmonisation package that parliament had passed earlier. The structure of the NSC – long a bastion of Turkish military power and influence – was changed. From now on the NSC general secretary was to be appointed by the prime minister and approved by the president, the council was to meet bi-monthly instead of monthly and, most importantly, the NSC became an advisory rather than an executive body (Belge, 2004).[28]

Joining the EU had become a priority for the military. They understood that after the failed resolution Washington no longer saw Turkey as a 'strategic partner'. The Pentagon had begun to cultivate Bulgaria in 2001 and build bases at Burgas.[29] The generals believed that the military would have a role to play if Europe created its own defence force and all the problems with its neighbour, Greece, would be resolved 'in a week once Turkey joined the EU'. In January 2004, the NSC gave the 'green light' to Cyprus joining the EU later in the year; this despite the fact that Cyprus had been considered a 'life and death issue' for the military (*The Press*, 24 January 2004).

The military was so committed to joining the EU that most generals rejected the idea of playing the role of 'the key country' that Washington seemed to be assigning to Ankara in its 'Great Middle East Project' to create a new, democratic region with 'moderate Islam'. The Milliyet of 15 April 2004 reported President Sezer's statement at the War Academy that 'moderate Islam' would be a step backward for Turkey. Under the AKP government, maintaining the secular order remained the principal issue on the minds of the generals. This issue of secularism, along with such questions as the headscarf and the status of Imam-Hatip schools, was hotly debated. But the governing party seemed willing to compromise, and the army supported the government's reforms to meet EU criteria (Milliyet, 15 April 2005).

There was tension when the AKP wanted to change the status of the Imam-Hatip schools. The generals opposed the government's bill that would allow Iman-Hatip graduates to compete for university places on equal terms with other candidates. The next day, on 5 May, the press reported that Erdoğan had ordered the party to remain silent and not respond to the Chief of Staff's statements, thus maintaining harmony between the AKP and the army. But the end of President Sezer's term in office in April 2007 raised tension to a new level. The army had relied on Sezer, an ardent secularist, to veto any legislation that threatened the secular order. The AKP leadership could have avoided controversy by nominating a candidate who was conservative but without an Islamist past, thus appeasing the opposition. Instead it nominated Foreign Minister Abdullah Gül, one of the party's founders and with deep roots in Islamist politics. The generals responded by posting a memorandum on their website hinting at intervention if Gül's election went ahead. They also called for a social reaction to Gül's appointment, and there were huge demonstrations in Istanbul on 29 April, and subsequently in other cities.

Prime Minister Erdoğan responded by announcing an early general election for 22 July. Without an effective opposition, the AKP won by 47 per cent of the vote and 341 of the 550 parliamentary seats. It was politically difficult for the army to oppose the programme of a democratically elected government with such a large majority and Abdullah Gül was duly elected Turkey's eleventh president on 28 August.

The day before Gül's election, General Büyükanıt issued another stern warning on the armed forces' website: 'Our nation has been watching the behaviour of centres of evil, who systematically try to corrode the secular nature of the Turkish Republic. Nefarious plans emerge in different forms every day ... The military will keep its determination to guard social, democratic and secular Turkey'. However, President Gül swore to respect secularism 'one of the main principles of our Republic, a precondition for social peace'. But relations with the army were strained. The top brass boycotted Gül's swearing-in ceremony in parliament, the Chief of Staff refused to call Gül 'my president' even though he was Commander-in-Chief, nor were the headscarf-wearing wives of the prime minister and the president invited to 'Victory Day' celebrations on 30 August.

There has been a slow and steady erosion of secular values under AKP rule that has led to a response from the army. Soon after the public prosecutor presented an indictment to the Constitutional Court charging the AKP and its leaders with undermining the secular regime so as to establish an Islamic state, the press of 5 April 2008 published excerpts from an interview that Chief of Staff Yaşar Büyükanıt gave to a defence magazine. He spoke of 'creeping Islamism', noting that 'Certain circles have always exploited religion since the foundation of the Turkish Republic. Reactionary forces continue anti-secular activities at home and abroad via legal institutions like associations and foundations ... Providing internal security and homeland security are the military's duties, as defined by the Constitution'.

Turkey's EU membership prospects are as unclear as ever. In the last few years, the military has lost much of its legitimacy as 'master of the country' and 'guardian of the republic'. To what extent the military will be able to reinvent itself as a professional army acting in the spirit of the armies of democratic countries remains to be seen. If it does succeed in doing so, this will be a sea change in civil-military relations in Turkey and the Middle East.

Notes

Newspaper articles are cited in the Endnotes and the text, but not in the Bibliography.

1. Kemalettin Sami Paşa describes the birth of the national army during the national struggle in Sami, 1962, pp. 7–9.
2. Bozdag, a prominent researcher and journalist, claims that he was informed that Atatürk had written a secret will, kept in the Presidential library at Cankaya. In this will Ataturk is said to have stated that 'Let Marshal Fevzi Çakmak be the president after me'. Bozdag related this to Ihsan Sabri Caglayangil in the 1980s. See *Sabah* (24 March 2002).
3. Sinan Omur, gives text of Inönü's letter. This is a hagiographical account of Çakmak's life and his military and political career but nevertheless useful. See, Omur (1965, pp. 74–6).
4. Ozdagan's thesis remains the most analytical monograph on the subject.
5. Colman McCarthy reviewing John Tirman's (1997) *Spoils of War: The Human Cost of America's Arms Trade* (New York: Free Press) in Guardian Weekly, 15 February 1998, wrote: 'By Tirman's numbers, Ankara might as well be a satellite army of the United States. From 1984 to 1993, Turkey received $6 billion in military aid. During 1991 to 1995, Washington supplied four-fifths of Turkey's military imports'.
6. Andreas Papandreou also found that Greek intelligence was controlled by the CIA when he entered government. See his memoirs, Papandreou (1971).
7. On the 1957 conspiracy see Ahmad (1977).
8. For the changes brought about by the 1960 regime see Hale (1994, pp. 119ff.). This book provides an excellent study of the subject. See also Ahmad (1977, pp. 147ff.).
9. In OYAK'S fortieth anniversary report, the press of 27 November 2001 noted that OYAK had become one of Turkey's biggest corporations, with stakes in 26 companies involved in automobiles, cement, finance, food, chemicals, and the service sector.
10. Both Prime Minister Demirel and leader of the opposition Ismet Inönü sent Soysal messages of sympathy.
11. He said that '12 March Memorandum "askeri darbeyi ilermeyi engelledi"'. On 21 January 1972, the Daily Telegraph (London) published a list of countries where the CIA had been actively involved in politics between 1947 and 1971 and Turkey was one of them. The paper listed the military coup of 27 May 1960 and the intervention of 12 March 1971 when the 'CIA help[ed] in overthrow of Menderes government by General Gürsel' and 'CIA agents [were] active in engineering the resignation of government following military action', respectively. Demirel, (1977) published the original from the Daily Telegraph, 'Where the CIA Has Worked', page following 270ff. In December 1976, Ihsan Sabri Caglayangil,

the Justice Party government's foreign minister in Demirel's coalition, also spoke about the CIA's involvement in the 12 March intervention.

12.   Turkey's increase was considerable if we compare its GDP with that of the other NATO countries. The International Institute for Strategic Studies in London wrote that the defence budget amounted to $995 million, 3.7 per cent of GNP. See IISS (1974) cited in Tamkoc (1976, p. 203).

13.   Turkish forces occupied roughly the part of the island that Turkey had been promised under the Acheson plan of 1964. The Turkish solution was said to have been welcomed in Washington by Kissinger. See also O'Malley and Craig (2001).

14.   Earlier in February 1977, Gen Alexander Haig, Supreme Allied Commander in Europe, that is, the head of NATO, had asked Congress to lift the embargo on Turkey because 'We need flank solidarity in NATO to face the emerging Soviet threat'.

15.   See Hikmet Ozdemir's interview with Fehmi Koru in *Zaman* (8 August 1989); Ozdemir discusses the question of the military in greater detail in his book *Rejim ve Asker*.

16.   See Hakki Erdem's article in *Cumhuriyet* (16 March 1990).

17.   See Ugur Mumcu, 'Sivillesme' in *Cumhuriyet* (18 March 1990).

18.   On 8 November 2001, the daily newspaper *Sabah* reported that Gunes Taner, a member of Özal's cabinet, said that Özal had asked Torumtay how many troops would be killed if Turkey invaded Kirkuk. Torumtay did not answer but Gunes Taner had replied, about 30,000–40,000. Later, Torumtay complimented him on his military knowledge.

19.   'Turkey plans to spend $150 billion over the next 30 years on defence – roughly double its current expenditure on what is already the second largest military force in NATO' in Guardian Weekly (1996, vol. 155, no. 16, p. 4). There was much discussion of the military's plan to modernise. *Cumhuriyet* (20 March 2000) wrote about Turkey's plans to invest in the arms industry: the first stage of the projects, amounting to $20 billion was to be completed within ten years. The total expenditure on arms projects should surpass $150 billion with the goal of making Turkey the most important military power in the region. Turkey would have AWACS and 561 helicopters, giving it the strongest air force in the region. In Washington on 30 March, 2000, Defence Secretary William Cohen said that Turkey would join a $200 billion US programme to develop and build the versatile new joint strike fighter. Asked to comment on his country's arms purchases, Ambassador Baki Ilkin replied: 'We are restructuring the army so that it has more mobility and rapid action units. We are surrounded by a lot of crises, in the Balkans, Kosovo, internal troubles in Georgia, the Caucasus, and we are following developments in Iraq'. Washington Post, 17 March 2000. The military decided to import modern battle tanks and attack helicopters for the new mobile army. But by 2004, there was also talk of building a state-of-the-art tank in Turkey. A group consisting of Nurol Holding, the Koc and Karamehmet Groups were to form a consortium, perhaps marking the beginning of a Turkish 'military-industrial complex'. See Yigit Bulut, *Radikal* (18 May 2004); and Tolga Aliner, 'Savunma cephesinde yeni kararlar', *Radikal* (19 May 2004). See also M. A. Kislali, 'TSK degisiyor', *Radikal* (12th March 2004). Chief of Staff Hilmi Ozkok declared that in future the armed forces would rely on brain instead of brawn.

20.   Over the years there was much discussion in the press about the military's role in illegal activities regarding surveillance and violence against 'enemies of the state'. The general staff finally admitted that it had kept files on freemasons, Satanists,

and other enemies. See *Radikal* (11 March 2004); the headline read: 'Kara Kuvvetleri Yasalari Cignedi', that is 'The army has broken the law'.

21. But the reforms left intelligence in the hands of the military. See, *Radikal* (31 August 2003). Ahmet Insel, a critic of the so-called deep state noted that the 'official deep state is none other the National Security State'. After 12 September 1980, the NUC emerged as a state within the state. It not only concerned itself with military and foreign policy matters, but also internal politics, including economics and culture'. The NSC and its secretary general also directed the secret activities of the state and were able to do things that the government of the day knew nothing about. It even carried out operations against its own citizens who were seen as a threat to the state and described as 'internal enemies'. In time the NSC began to see itself as the real state, the one who defined the mission of the state. This had been unnecessary in the golden age of the Republic (1923–1945) when party and state had been one. See *Radikal* (28 August 2003) 'Derin devlet', and Insel's article, 'Milli guvenlik devletinde yeni perde', *Radikal Iki* (7 September 2003).

22. See Murat Yetkin, *Radikal* (19 March 2003).

23. See Murat Yetkin, *Radikal* (7 September 2002).

24. See Mehmet Ali Kislali's interview with Nese Düzel, *Radikal* (19 August 2002).

25. See Chief of Staff Özkök's interview with Elefterotipia (Athens), reported in the press (19 October 2003).

26. See Mehmet Ali Birand's interview with Nese Düzel, 'Amerika en cok askerlere kizgin', *Radikal* (19 May 2003) and *The Economist* (12 July, 2003), 'A Partnership at Risk?'.

27. The Turkish press (5 July 2003) following gave this incident wide coverage. It was also covered in the West. See 'Turkey Military Raps US Over Iraq Arrests', in *Washington Post* (7 July 2003); *The Economist* (12 July 2003) 'A Partnership at Risk?'.

28. See also, *The Economist* (31 July 2003) 'A Revolution of Sorts – Taming the Generals, and Knocking on Europe's Door'.

29. On 8 June 2003, *Radikal* (supplement) published the translation of a report prepared for the Center for Strategic and International Studies (CSIS), Washington, DC by its Turkey Project Director, Bulent Aliriza, 'Turkiye ve ABD yeni arayista'.

Bibliography

F. Ahmad (1977) *The Turkish Experiment in Democracy 1950–1975* (Boulder, CO: Westview press).

I. Akca (2004) 'OYAK'in 37 sirketi var', in H. Goktas and M. Gülbay (eds) *Kisladan Anayasaya Ordu* (Istanbul: Metis Yayinlari).

S. Andreski (1968) *Military Organisation and Society* (Berkeley and Los Angeles: University of California Press).

M. Belge (2004) 'Avrupa Birligi'ne girersek ordu memleketin sabihi olmaktan cikar', in H. Goktas and M. Gülbay (eds) *Kisladan Anayasaya Ordu* (Istanbul: Metis Yayinlari)

M. A. Birand (1987) *The Generals' Coup in Turkey* (London: Brassey's Defence Publishers).

M. A. Birand (1995) *Demirkirat* (Istanbul: Milliyet Yayinlari).

N. Chomsky (1982) *Towards a New Cold War* (New York: Pantheon).

H. Demirel (1977) *12 Mart'in Icyüzü* (Istanbul: Yeni Asya Yayinlari).

H. Dosdogru (1993) *6–7 Eylul Olaylari* (Istanbul: Baglam Yayinlari).

D. Filkins (2003) 'In Defeat of U.S. Plan, Turks See a Victory for Democracy', *New York Times*, 5 March.

F. Frey (1965) *The Turkish Political Elite* (Cambridge, MA: MIT Press).

W. Hale (1994) *Turkish Politics and the Military* (London: Routledge).

M. E. Han (1967) *Efendi Degil, Dost: siyasi bir otobiyografi* (Istanbul: Istanbul: Matbaasi).

IISS (1974) *The Military Balance 1974–1975* (London: IISS).

S. Ilkin (1993) 'Businessmen: Democratic Stability', in M. Heper, A. Oncu and H. Kramer (eds) *Turkey and the West* (London and New York: I. B. Tauris).

G. Jaschke and E. Pritsch (1929) *Die Türkei seit dem Weltkriege: Geschichskalender, 1918–1928* (Berlin: No publisher mentioned).

C. Johnson (2004) *The Sorrows of Empire* (New York: Metropolitan Books).

I. Kayabali and C. Arslanoglu (n.p. and n.d.) *Doruk Türk Ordusu Tarihi* [The Complete History of the Turkish Army].

M. A. Khan (1967) *Friends Not Masters: A Political Autobiography* (New York, London, Karachi: Oxford University Press).

C. Madanoglu (1982) *Anilar, 1911–1938* (Istanbul: Cagdas Yayinlari).

B. O'Malley and I. Craig (2001) *The Cyprus Conspiracy: America, Espionage and the Turkish Invasion* (London and New York: I. B. Tauris).

A. Mango (1999) *Atatürk the Biography of the Founder of Modern Turkey* (Woodsctok and New York: The Overlook Press).

U. Mumcu (1990) 'CIA-MIT', *Cumhuriyet*, 17 March.

H. Ozdemir (1989) *Rejim ve Asker* (Istanbul: Afa yayinlari).

G. G. Ozdogan (1990) *The Case of Racism-Turanism: Turkish Nationalism during the Single-Party Period, 1931–1944* [unpublished Ph.D. thesis] (Istanbul: Bogazici University).

C. J. Pach (1991) *Arming the Free World: The Origins of the United States Military Assistance program, 1945–1950* (Chapel Hill and London: The University of North Carolina Press).

A. Papandreou (1971) *Democracy at Gunpoint: The Greek Front* (London: Deutsch).

K. S. Pasa (1962) 'Milli Ordu Nasil Dogdu Nasil Kazandi', *Yakin Tahrihimiz*, vol. 3, pp. 7–9.

D. A. Rustow (1959) 'The Army and the Founding of the Turkish Republic', *World Politics*, vol. 11, no. 4, pp. 513–52.

H. Sharabi (1988) *Neopatriarchy* (New York: Oxford University Press).

L. Stern (1977) *The Wrong Horse* (New York: Times Books).

M. Tamkoc (1976) *The Warrior Diplomats* (Salt Lake City: University of Utah Press).

J. Tirman (1997) *Spoils of War: The Human Cost of America's Arms Trade* (New York: Free Press).

N. Turfan (2000) *Rise of the Young Turks – Politics, the Military and Ottoman Collapse* (London: I. B. Tauris).

H. Turgut (1995) *Sahinlerin Dansi – Türkeş'in Anilari* (Istanbul: ABC Yayinlari).

S. Yalcin and D. Yurdakul (1999) *Bay Pipo: Bir MIT Gorevlisinin Siradisi Yasami: Hiram Abas* (Istanbul: Dogan).

Institutions and Public Policy

7
The Turkish Grand National Assembly: New Challenges and Old Problems

Ersin Kalaycıoğlu

Turkish politics has been shaped by a fragmented, polarised, and volatile party system (Ergüder, 1980–1, pp. 48–51; Özbudun, 1981, pp. 237–8; Ergüder and Hofferbert, 1988, pp. 84–94; Özbudun, 2000, pp. 74–80, see also Table 7.1). As a corollary of the party system, the legislative party system suffered from a similar malaise as it moved from a two-party structure, under the influence of a predominant Democrat Party (DP) in the 1950s, to a moderate, pluralist party format in the 1960s and 1970s. The same trend seemed to have re-appeared in the aftermath of the last democratic breakdown from 1980 to 1983. Indeed, Özbudun recently argued that 'all three maladies of the Turkish party system in the 1970s (volatility, fragmentation and polarisation) have reappeared, if anything in worse form' in the 1980s and 1990s (Özbudun, 1997, p. 88 and see Table 7.2). The data in Tables 7.1 and 7.2, as well as the fact that two smaller parties (each winning 4–8 per cent of the national vote at every national election) could not win any parliamentary seats and thus are not included in Table 7.2, gives the impression that Turkey moved from a moderate pluralist party system toward an extreme pluralist one during the 1980s and 1990s (Table 7.2).

The last breakdown of Turkish democracy occurred in 1980 and the military was at the helm of the government between 1980 and 1983. The 1983 elections were neither free nor fair, since the military remained in power and dictated the procedures. The military government of the day sifted through all the political parties and candidates who presented themselves for the electoral competition and eliminated all those it deemed harmful. Prior to the 1983 elections, the government had alre ady altered the election laws and established a very high national threshold of 10 per cent. The apparent objective of such a modification was to disable all smaller extreme right- and left-wing parties from entering the Turkish Grand National Assembly (TGNA). However, the former formula of proportional representation (d'Hondt's largest average), which had been in use since the 1961 general elections, was preserved. Consequently, only three political parties managed to field candidates. Among them the Populist Party (HP), and the Nationalist

Table 7.1   Volatility and fragmentation in the party system

Elections	Volatility	Fragmentation of votes	Fragmentation of seats	Effective number of parties
1961	–	0.71	0.70	3.3
1965	24.5	0.63	0.63	2.6
1969	11.4	0.70	0.59	2.3
1973	28.4	0.77	0.70	3.3
1977	18.3	0.68	0.60	2.5
1983	–	0.66	0.61	2.5
1987	–	0.75	0.51	2.0
1991	16.6	0.79	0.71	3.5
1995	23.0	0.83	0.77	4.3
1999	22.6	0.84	0.79	4.8
2002	43.9	0.81	0.46	1.9

Sources: Ergun Özbudun (2000, p. 77). The Table entries for the 1999 and 2002 elections are calculations by the author, using the same methods described by Özbudun.

Democracy Party (MDP) were encouraged or indirectly established by the military government as the 'loyal' government and opposition parties. The third party was established by the former 'Minister of the State' who was in charge of the economy of the military government between 1980 and 1983, Turgut Özal. He and his Motherland Party (ANAP) could not be barred from entering the electoral process, and they represented the only civilian alternative to the MDP and the HP. Interestingly enough, 45 per cent of the eligible electorate ended up supporting ANAP at the polls, and it emerged as the largest parliamentary group in the TGNA. However, the 1983 elections should be considered a 'transition' election, rather than a democratic one.

If we discount the 1983 elections, Turkey has been experiencing free, competitive national elections since 1987. The same electoral formula has been in use, with some alterations, namely, the 10 per cent national threshold for qualification for a seat in the TGNA and the d'Hondt formula. The height of the threshold kept the party system from veering towards an atomistic multi-partyism, yet it failed to stop any of the extreme right-wing parties from gaining seats in the TGNA. The TGNA enjoyed a moderate, pluralist three-party system during the 1980s, which eventually grew to a four and then a five party format, with two small parties that received 4–8 per cent of the national vote each, hence failing to gain any representation in the TGNA, but nonetheless, influencing the competition and the outcome of the elections. Hence, if we are to follow Sartori's formulation in determining relevant parties in a party system (Sartori, 1976, pp. 119–30) and consider the coalition and blackmail potentials of the Turkish political parties, the Turkish

Table 7.2 Election results and the distribution of seats in the TGNA (1983-2002) (%)

Political parties elections		CHP %	MHP %	ANAP %	HP %	MDP %	SHP %	DYP %	RP/FP+ %	DSP %	AKP %
1983	Vote	–	–	45.1	30.5	23.3					
	Seat			52.8	29.2	17.7					
1987	Vote			36.3	–	–	24.4	19.9	–	–	
	Seat			64.9	–	–	22.0	13.1	–	–	
1991	Vote			24.0	–	–	20.6	27.2	16.7(*)	–	
	Seat			25.7	–	–	19.7	39.7	13.1(*)	–	
1995	Vote	10.7	–	19.6	–	–	–	19.2	21.4	14.6	
	Seat	8.9	–	24.0	–	–	–	24.5	28.7	13.8	
1999	Vote	–	18.0	13.2	–	–	–	12.0	15.4	22.2	
	Seat	–	23.5	15.6	–	–	–	15.5	20.2	24.7	
2002	Vote	19,4	–	–	–	–	–	–	–	–	34,3
	Seat	32,4	–	–	–	–	–	–	–	–	66,0

Notes: Only those parties that could win enough votes to be represented in the National Assembly are included in the Table.

(*) These cells refer to the Welfare Party Alliance, which includes RP, Nationalist Work Party (MÇP), which later was converted into the MHP, and Reformist Democracy Party (IDP), which is now the Nation Party (MP).

CHP = Republican People's Party (left-of-centre, secular); MHP = Nationalist Action Party (ultra-nationalist, anti-Communist); ANAP = Motherland Party (right-of-centre, liberal/conservative); HP = Populist Party (praetorian, left-of-centre); MDP = Nationalist Democracy Party (praetorian, right-of-centre); RP = Welfare Party (Islamist, 'National Outlook'); SHP = Social Democratic Populist Party (left-of-centre, secular); DYP = True Path Party (right-of-centre, nationalist, conservative); DSP = Democratic Left Party (left-of-centre, nationalist), AKP = Justice and Development Party (conservative, liberal, Islamist).

(+) FP = Virtue Party in the 1999 elections, which was more or less the continuation of the RP under a different name, after the former was banned by the Constitutional Court. The FP was also banned, and the AKP and Felicity Party (SP, Islamist) were established in 2001 to replace the FP. Blank cells indicate that the party represented in the corresponding column did not exist at the time of the corresponding national election.

Sources: Kalaycıoğlu (1999a, p. 48). Official Gazette (Resmi Gazete) (2002) November 10, no. 24932.

party system should be characterised as a form of extreme pluralism, with seven political parties throughout the 1990s. Indeed, the number of political parties in the TGNA increased towards the end of the tenure of each assembly to double-digit figures.[1]

The proclivity in the Turkish parliamentary party system towards a form of extreme pluralism seems to have come to an abrupt end during the 3 November 2002 elections. In 2002 there were only two significant political parties, which were overwhelmingly preferred by the voters, and at this time the Turkish party system started to show signs of a potential two-party or predominant party format.

Ostensibly, the TGNA has been performing within the context of a political system characterised by volatile voting behaviour of fragmented blocs of voters. Consequently, the TGNA has operated under the influence of an unstable political system that has experienced recurring economic and political crises, which deeply influenced its institutional characteristics. In this paper, I will examine those institutional characteristics of the TGNA in detail.

The Turkish Grand National Assembly: Structure and change

The Turkish Grand National Assembly is a special institution, distinguished from all other political structures and institutions of the Turkish Republic. Formerly, the Grand National Assembly (GNA), which later assumed the title of the Turkish Grand National Assembly (TGNA), predates the political system to which it gave birth by more than three years. The GNA was established on 23 April 1920 as an institution of popular representation, constituting the font of all political legitimacy. It functioned as the sole source of political authority in a nebulous state mechanism, which was embedded within its structural confines (Soysal, 1969, pp. 12–13; Özbudun, 1992, p. 6). The 'Grand National Assembly Government' (popularly known as the 'Ankara Government') of 1920–3 also confronted, competed, and clashed with the Ottoman government in Istanbul (popularly known as the 'Istanbul Government'), and provided an alternative to the political regime the latter represented. Finally, the GNA emerged as the political structure symbolising national resistance to the international occupation of the Turkish homeland in the immediate aftermath of World War I. Thus, the TGNA constitutes not only a fundamental and indispensable structure of popular representation and representative democracy in Turkey, but it also symbolises liberation from occupation, and the national sovereignty of the Turkish Republic.

The nationalist forces of the Grand National Assembly Government won the War of Liberation and the Turkish Republic was established in 1923. The Grand National Assembly was redesigned as the legislature according to a Westminster model of democracy in 1924 (Soysal, 1969, p. 11). In practice, the majority group of the former GNA was organised as the Republican People's Party (CHP) and continued to dominate the legislative activities of what was to become the TGNA. Led by the charismatic leader and hero of the War of Liberation, Mustafa Kemal Atatürk, who assumed the Presidency of the Republic and leadership of the CHP simultaneously, the TGNA began to operate under the dominance of the CHP majorities. The CHP also controlled the executive branch of the government in a single-party regime from 1923 to 1945. The democratic regime of the early republican era was a short-lived experiment, which failed to survive the first major challenge to the young Republic in 1925. Hence, the TGNA became the ceremonial plenary body of a single-party government from 1925 to 1945.

The overall party structure of the TGNA eventually evolved into a two-party format with a distinct slant towards predominant one-party rule by the CHP between 1946 and 1950, and later by the Democrat Party (DP) until the breakdown of democracy by means of a young officers' coup on 27 May 1960. Until 1960, Turkey had a regime of unchecked and uncontrolled dominance of the TGNA by a party majority, where the role and effectiveness of the opposition were minimal. The style of rule differed little according to which of the two parties, the CHP or the DP, was at the helm of government. The CHP and the DP legislative elites were quite alike in their parliamentary socialisation. The leader of the DP was none other than the last Prime Minister of Atatürk's presidency. Other leading figures of the DP had also spent many years among the ranks of the CHP parliamentary group of the single-party era. Consequently, the attitudes of the CHP and the DP elites toward parliamentary opposition were quite similarly contemptuous. It was unsurprising that the relations between the CHP and DP between 1945 and 1960 eventually degenerated into a 'no-holds-barred-war' (Frey, 1975, p. 65). The TGNA was replete with what Frey called an 'in-group versus out-group orientation', which had been inimical to any kind of open political competition, and undermined all semblance of legitimacy of the opposition (out-group, enemy) in the eyes of the in-group (allies) (Frey, 1975, pp. 65–7).

By 1961, Turkey had a new constitution and a new political regime. The TGNA, had an upper chamber for the first time, the Senate. The political regime of the 1961 Constitution was based on the premise that the unchecked and unbalanced power of the legislative majorities of the previous era constituted the primary cause of the breakdown of the democratic regime of the 1950s. Therefore, the 1961 Constitution erected various constitutional and legal restrictions on the absolute power of legislative majorities. The Senate was one such structural design within the legislative system, intended to check the excesses of the majorities of the GNA, the lower chamber of the TGNA. The establishment of the Constitutional Court, the introduction of measures that guaranteed independence of the judiciary from the executive branch of government, the creation of judicial oversight of decisions of the public bureaucracy, and finally, the extension of autonomous status to the Turkish Radio and Television agency and the universities were all intended to check the power of the party group(s) of the majority of the lower chamber of the TGNA. The deviation from the majoritarian model of democracy became complete with the adoption of proportional representation, as incorporated in d'Hondt's largest average formula, in 1961. In the meantime, the military closed down the DP, imprisoned most of its leading figures and executed the former PM, Minister of Finance and Foreign Affairs. A scramble to fill the vacuum left behind by the political exit of the DP combined with the new electoral system, which enabled small parties to survive and even thrive, contributed to the eventual development of a moderate pluralist (Sartori, 1976, pp. 130ff.) party system in Turkey. Coalition governments also emerged as a novelty, though they seem not to have been welcomed or trusted by the major political forces of the country. The new and more cumbersome rules of the political game failed to render Turkish democracy sustainable. In the midst of a bloodbath the military conducted another coup and suspended the activities of the TGNA for three years in 1980.

The performance of the Senate failed to impress the major pressure groups of the country, such as the leading industrialist and employers associations, TÜSİAD, TİSK and the military. Unlike many other regimes with upper chambers, Turkey possessed neither the vestiges of a landed aristocracy that would participate in the politics of the country, nor a federal system, the regional distinctions of which might need protecting in the process of political decision-making. Hence, the Senate seemed to serve no other purpose than to frustrate the majority of the lower chamber of the TGNA, and slow down the legislative process on partisan and ideological grounds, especially when the opposition had the majority in the Senate. When the same party controlled both the Senate and the National Assembly, the Senate failed to act as an intra-legislative control. In the 1982 Constitution, the Senate was abolished. The new military regime trimmed the powers of the Constitutional Court and the higher courts, and either curtailed or fully abolished the autonomy of the Turkish Radio and Television Agency and the universities. A constitutional order that emphasised stability and security, to the detriment of liberty and mass political participation, was thus established through the political regime of the 1982 Constitution. Concomitantly, the regime drew up new electoral laws to check the representativeness of electoral outcomes with governability. Hence, each province was allotted a single seat in the unicameral TGNA, irrespective of the number of voters registered in the province, and the remaining seats were distributed in proportion to the size of the electorate registered in each province. Consequently, relatively sparsely populated provinces received a disproportionate amount of representation, to the detriment of such metropolitan areas as Ankara, Istanbul, and Izmir. Additionally, the 10 per cent national threshold further eroded the proportionality between the distribution of the votes and seats in the TGNA (Kalaycıoğlu, 2002, p. 58). Hence, a peculiar electoral system emerged, functioning as a majoritarian system when the voters tended to vote for one party, and a representative one when they tended to support many political parties. Consequently, the electoral system failed to improve the stability of political the system, and provided many opportunities for political conflicts that were reflected in the legislative system.

The challenge of legislative institutionalisation

How has the TGNA fared, given so much tinkering with its structure and the political regime (constitutions) of the country? How far was the TGNA able to develop its institutional mettle within the socio-political and economic environment and the constitutional order in which it had to function?

A political structure institutionalises when the political actors serving in and outside of the structure widely accept and value its organisation and procedures as legitimate answers to recurring political problems (Huntington, 1968, p. 12; Feibleman, 1956, p. 52; cf. Lenski and Lenski, 1974, p. 53). A legislative structure interacts with many political actors. Voters, pressure groups, voluntary associations, public bureaucracy, and the judiciary and the executive branches of the government are almost constantly in contact with the legislative branch of the government. The internal actors are primarily the deputies, who are elected for defined periods of tenure, and only serve for long periods when successful in getting re-elected. However, there are also the bureaucratic staff of the legislature, who help and advise the deputies and serve many masters throughout their long careers. The acceptance and respect for values, norms, rules of conduct, and procedures of the legislature by all those actors within and without, interacting with it, are critical to the institutionalisation of a legislature.

Hence, the rules of legislative conduct, norms, and values gain value and stability in the eyes of the political actors who perform within and outside it, as a legislature institutionalises. Consequently, institutionalisation of a legislative body is manifested stable performance of its main tasks and functions. Persistence through adaptation to the changing political environment, which presents various challenges to a legislature, is a sign of institutionalisation. However, the mere survival of a legislative organisation alone does not necessarily indicate that it has been institutionalised (Huntington, 1968, pp. 13–17). Institutionalisation also necessitates that the legislature be valued, respected, and even trusted by the other political actors who engage in political transactions with it. The most important political interface for the deputies of a legislative organisation is the one shared with the voters, who the former purport to represent. A legislative organisation is a structure built around the interactions between the represented (people, voters) and their representatives (deputies, members of the parliament). Hence, for a legislative organisation to persist, it is critical that it become valued and supported by the very voters who elect its main actors. It is only when a legislature gains stability, while simultaneously gaining value and trust in the eyes of the voters, that it begins to institutionalise.

Institutionalisation provides stability and clarity to the internal mechanisms of a structure. The institutional actors know what roles to perform, and which norms, and rules of conduct to follow under what circumstances. As political structures institutionalise, new roles and rules emerge to deal with new circumstances and the changing demands of the political actors who engage with them. Institutionalised political structures tend to develop complex customary and often written rules of conduct, which are internalised by their older members (seniority) and are learned by each cohort of incoming members. Consequently, institutionalisation is correlated with increasing complexity of the internal structures, multiplicity of roles, and rules of conduct. Seniority increases in importance, both as a value and as a practice. In legislative organisation where the *de jure* equality of the members reigns supreme, establishing norms and rules of conduct that are internalised and then passed on to the incoming new members, is difficult to say the least. However, studies have shown that institutionalised legislatures manage to accomplish the hard task of developing procedures of socialisation for their new recruits (Fenno,1966, pp. 58–68; Polsby, 1975, p. 218; Matthews, 1985, pp. 37–8). Such a practice also leads to a final, yet similarly critical characteristic of an institutionalised political organisation.

The increased complexity of the political structures creates the new challenge of enabling the organisation to function in harmony as roles and rules multiply. New roles and rules load the structure, as new actors playing new roles demand to be reckoned with. Consequently, a problem of coherence eventually emerges. If unsolved, the incoherence of increased complexity undermines the performance of the political structure, which falters and risks breaking down. Consequently, a political organisation institutionalises when it can not only gain widespread value, support and confidence, but also when it can successfully and simultaneously marry increased complexity with coherence (Huntington, 1968, pp. 22–4).

In view of the preceding definition of institutionalisation, I will now track the stability, support and trust, the respect paid to rules, norms and parliamentary procedures (standing order, *içtüzük*), and the overall performance of the Turkish Grand National Assembly.

Stability

The overall development of the TGNA since its establishment in 1920 has been characterised by a number of severe shocks and disruptions to its membership and activities. In 1950, a major landslide at the polls resulted in a wave of new deputies, which completely swept away the accumulated experience of the former assemblies. However, previous assemblies had functioned under the predominance of a single party regime of the CHP. Therefore, the 1950 assembly was the first democratic assembly of the TGNA, except for the short-lived experience of multi-party contestation in

1924–5. The disturbances and disruptions continued after 1950. In 1960, the TGNA was closed down briefly by means of a military coup. A similar breakdown of the Turkish legislative system occurred in 1971, when the TGNA was sidelined as a military junta ruled the country behind the scenes and through a 'rubber stamp' assembly until 1973. In 1973, the TGNA returned to democratic rule, yet for only seven more years. Another military coup in 1980 closed down the TGNA for another three years, until 1983. In 1983, Turkey began to move toward multi-party politics, which started to show signs of pluralism only after 1987. Consequently, it is hard to argue that the TGNA of the post-1945 era is a political organisation that has hosted patterns of behaviour, procedures, and acts that were stable or valued.

Similarly, the Grand National Assembly, which in its initial stages functioned as the locus of all political authority and decision-making, at par with the state, eventually evolved into a legislative organ of the state, subservient to the executive branch of the government. In the 1920s and the 1930s, the single party rule of the CHP governments and the charismatic leadership of Mustafa Kemal Atatürk and other elites, such as İsmet İnönü and Celal Bayar, subjected the TGNA to the will of the powerful executives in practice. However, the Constitution and the laws of the country still accorded the TGNA the unique power of being the font of all political legitimacy. Nevertheless three military coups and two constitutions later, the 1982 Constitution relegated the TGNA to the role of subservient assembly of a political regime fully dominated by the executive branch of the government, under the leadership of a politically and legally omnipotent Presidency and an extremely powerful Prime Minister. Under the circumstances, it is hard to assume that the TGNA was legally accorded much value, except as a rubber stamp of political legitimacy, in the 1982 constitutional regime of Turkey.

Parallel to the diminishing role of the TGNA in the political system, membership of the TGNA lost much value and stability. In fact, when compared with those national legislatures that demonstrate high levels of institutionalisation, the TGNA demonstrates remarkably high turnover rates and short tenures for its members (see Table 7.3, and Figures 7.1a and 7.1b). Furthermore, the turnover rates have recently been on an upward trend, which indicates a similar erosion of the TGNA's institutionalisation. Under the circumstances, it is logical to assume that new members dominate the TGNA, so that change and radical uprooting of the institutional norms and rules of conduct occur, to the detriment of seniority and professionalism. As cogently argued by Nelson Polsby (1971) and Thomas Saalfeld (1997), high membership turnover rates occur when legislatures are young and yet uninstitutionalised. Eventually, turnover rates drop, at times even sharply down to a range of 20–30 per cent. Saalfeld argued that in 1949 the Bundestag held 410 new members, which fell to between 91 and 130 in the aftermath of the federal elections of the 1980s. These findings indicate that legislative

Table 7.3   Legislator stability in Turkey: New deputies in the TGNA (1920–2002)

Year	%	Arithmetic mean per regime
1920	77	
1923	63	
1927	37	
1931	39	
1935	34	
1939	32	
1943	33	
1946	41	44.5[a]
1950	81	
1954	51	
1957	53	61.7[b]
1961	84	
1965	50	
1969	53	
1973	57	
1977	47	58.2[c]
1983	85[1]	
	91[2]	
1987	50[1]	
	54[2]	
1991	60[1]	
	63[2]	
1995	55[1]	
	57[2]	
1999	56[2]	
2002	81[2]	67[d]

Notes: This rate includes all those who had not had any previous legislative experience as elected deputies of the Grand National Assembly, or senators, constituent assembly members in 1961 and consultative assembly members in 1981–2, unless indicated otherwise.

1) Includes all those deputies who had not previously served as deputies in any legislative assembly.
2) Includes only those deputies who had not previously served as elected deputies in the Grand National Assembly.
a) Arithmetic mean for the single party era, and the 1946 assembly.
b) Arithmetic mean for the free and fair elections of the two-party era.
c) Arithmetic mean for the 1961–80 multi-party era.
d) Arithmetic mean for the former deputies of the Grand National Assembly only in the post-1983 multi-party era.

Sources: Kalaycıoğlu, 1988, p. 51; Frey, 1965, p. 164; Tachau and Good, 1973, p. 555.

service, merit and seniority gain value through increasing numbers of senior members serving long, and in some cases, lifelong careers. When merit and seniority coincide, they provide a very strong source of authority and power in a legislature (Fenno, 1966, pp. 167–82). Fenno observed that in a legislative setting where party discipline does not exist, such as the US Congress,

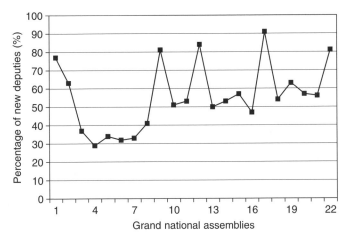

Figure 7.1a New deputies in the TGNA (1920–2002)
Source: Loewenberg and Patterson (1979, pp. 110–12) and the Turkish data are from Figure 7.1a.

the experience and expert knowledge that emerges with seniority contributes to the emergence and sustenance of norms, values and unwritten rules of conduct (Fenno, 1966, pp. 166–263).

Rates for the 1987, 1991, 1995, 1999, and 2002 assemblies are produced from 18th, 19th and 20th Assembly Albums, and 21st and 22nd Assembly figures were calculated from the information provided in the www.tbmm.gov.tr.

The TGNA suffers from a cycle of turnover of its deputies (see Figure 7.1a), which undermines the establishment of norms, rules of conduct, and professionalism, as well as expertise in legislative procedures. The TGNA seems to be in a constant state of fluidity, whereby the huge majority of about 70 per cent or more of its members serve for only one single term, and thus a huge majority of deputies act with no accumulated expertise in how the standing commissions work. The percentage of deputies serving in the commissions with no previous expertise hovers around a stunning 90 per cent (see Table 7.4). The current standing commissions of the TGNA have shown no deviation from that pattern of expertise and seniority in commission membership (see Table 7.4). The newly elected deputies are often associated with change and represent 'anti-establishment' parties and ideologies. They have often been the champions of anti-establishment election campaigns, which cast the previous assemblies as congregations of deputies seething with corruption. Consequently, new deputies dissociate themselves from the values and norms of such previous assemblies. Under the circumstances, entrenchment of norms, values and rules of conduct fail to materialise.

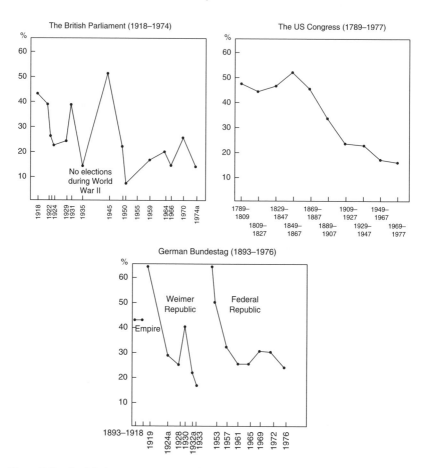

Figure 7.1b   Legislative turnover rates: A comparison
Source: Loewenberg and Patterson (1979, pp. 110–12) and the Turkish data are from Figure 7.1a.

It becomes almost impossible to pass such practices from one cohort to the next, for the attrition rate among senior members is so high that there are too few to emerge as role models.

Finally, with such a high turnover rate, the majority of the deputies are cognisant of the fact that they are unlikely to be in the TGNA for long. Most will not be re-elected, and those re-elected will not survive more than two or three elections. The election laws, when married with uninstitutionalised political parties (the current ruling AKP was only established on 14 August, 2001), provides for arbitrary rule of strong leaders, who then decide who will enter the ballot list and at what rank in every electoral

Table 7.4 The turnover rates in the commissions of the TGNA

Commission on	2002–4*	1983–7	1975–83	1971–5	1967–71	1964–7
Justice	92	83	100	100	86	84
Constitution	88	78	95	96	86	88
Public works, construction, transportation and tourism	83	91	100	100	100	95
Foreign affairs	88	78	95	93	100	95
Interior affairs	92	87	100	100	95	88
State economic enterprises	97	83	–	–	–	–
National education, culture, youth affairs	84	100	100	96	81	84
National defence	96	91	100	96	85	80
Economic planning and budget	77	85	98	91	94	89
Health, family, labour and social services	96	78	100	96	86	80
Industry, technology and commerce	92	91	100	96	100	86
Agriculture, forestry and village affairs	91	87	100	43	86	84
Auditing of the governmental expenditures	–	–	–	–	95	90
Petitions	86	94	–	–	–	–
Accounts of the TGNA	64	91	–	–	–	–
Environment	90	–	–	–	–	–
Human rights	83	–	–	–	–	–
European Union harmonisation	93	–	–	–	–	–
Arithmetic mean per column	**87.8**	**86.9**	**98.9**	**91.5**	**91.2**	**86.9**

Notes: *Percentages of those without any previous legislative experience in the TGNA commissions are reported in this column. All other columns consist of the percentages of those deputies who lost their commission seats.
– Incomplete or missing information.
Sources: Kalaycıoğlu, 1990, p. 208 and the 2002–4 figures are calculated from information provided at www.tbmm.gov.tr

district. Consequently, irrespective of what a deputy does in the TGNA, he or she will only get elected if he or she has the support of the leader of the party and if the voters support the party at the same time. It has been enormously difficult to satisfy both of those conditions in Turkish politics. Hence, the game of legislative politics operates in a setting where careers are astonishingly short, decided by the caprice of the party leaders, and the volatile voting patterns of the electorate. Deputies are increasingly pressured to demonstrate their existence and value to the party leaders and their constituents or interest groups in their constituencies. Such pressures do not necessarily promote rule-abiding behaviour, or prevent corruption.

Legislative rules of conduct and norms at risk

The TGNA has an elaborate set of written rules incorporated in its Standing Orders (İçtüzük), which are as important as the constitution of the country in the conduct of legislative affairs. The Standing Orders incorporate many rules, which regulate almost all critical activities that take place during the legislative process. Obviously, parliamentary procedures do not operate only within the confines of written rules. Norms, customs, traditions, rituals, and other unwritten rules of conduct play a critical role in ordering and civilising the interactions between deputies belonging to different constituencies and parties. They constrain the behaviour of the deputies, so that their manners stay within the confines of courtesy, and civility. Political ideologies and interests clash on the floor, commissions, and elsewhere in the TGNA. The bickering among the political classes can easily degenerate into a 'no-holds-barred-war' (Frey, 1975, p. 65). What matters most in keeping the political interactions from degenerating into conflict is, in part, the value accorded to the Standing Orders, norms and customs.

The Standing Orders of the current TGNA date back to 1973. Indeed, the parliamentary procedure of the TGNA is still regulated by means of a Standing Order of an assembly and political regime that have been rendered defunct by a military coup. Previously, it had taken the TGNA 12 years to draw up a new Standing Order in accordance with the 1961 Constitution. The 1973 Standing Orders of the TGNA were devised by the leading Justice Party (AP) parliamentary group, in a highly partisan manner. Without consulting the opposition parties, or even the main opposition party at the time, the CHP. They constituted the imprint of the AP government's vision of the legislative branch of government. Although the document has out-lived its usefulness, it still serves as the glossary of written regulations, which guide the parliamentary procedures of the TGNA. Since 1983, the TGNA has failed to draw up a new Standing Order in agreement with the spirit of the 1982 Constitution. This fact should be taken as a sign of the lack of cooperation between the political party groups, who could not negotiate the rules of conduct for the parliamentary game of which they are players. It seems as if the TGNA is very slow to adapt to the changing political regimes of the country. In and of itself, such a fact bodes ill for the adaptability and the institutionalisation capacity of the TGNA.

The Standing Orders of the TGNA stipulate various rules of conduct, from how to request the floor in order to address the General Assembly, to the style to be used in addressing the floor, and similarly, stipulate that the deputies be tactful in referring to their colleagues and other political actors, and refrain from being rude, and abrasive. Proper oral and behavioural conduct is

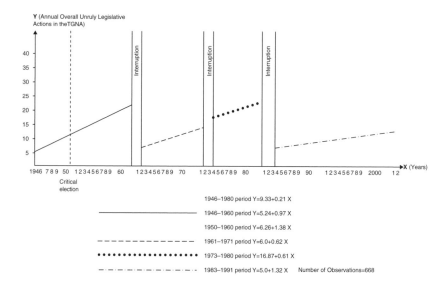

Figure 7.2 Trends of unruly legislative actions in the TGNA (1946–2002)
Source: Kalaycıoğlu (1988, p. 53; 1998, p. 104) and the data for 1992–2002 era were collected by Mustafa Oğuz of Sabancı University.

stipulated in writing in the Standing Orders. The deputies also mention that unwritten rules, norms and customs exist (Kalaycıoğlu, 1997, pp. 202–3). However, the floor debates of the TGNA have periodically been replete with examples of rule violations and misconduct since the 1950s (Kalaycıoğlu, 1988, pp. 52–3; 1999b, pp. 103–4; see Figure 7.2), and since 1997 this has been the case in the commissions as well. Such rule violation undermines the orderly conduct of business and the due process of legislation in the TGNA.

A close examination of Figure 7.2 indicates that regard for the orderly conduct of legislative bus iness tends to break down in periods of extra-parliamentary political instability, that is, right before every military coup. The mounting tension in the political system tends to create repercussions in the TGNA, which precipitate insults, threats, physical assaults, and protestation of various sorts, from banging on the desks by whole party groups of deputies to mass attacks on the deputy addressing the floor, with increasing frequency and variety. Such breakdowns of rule-abiding legislative behaviour diminish in periods immediately after the coups and during the re-institution of democratic politics. However, with the re-introduction of democratic politics, the disregard for the rules of proper legislative conduct tends to rise to prior levels (see Figure 7.2). The trends for unruly legislative behaviour in the 1945–60, 1961–80, and 1983–2002 periods have all been positive, and until 1991 similar in magnitude (Kalaycıoğlu, 1998, p. 104), which clearly indicates that the power of the norms and customs instilling orderly legislative behaviour have been too weak to constrain such dysfunctional or, at times, even anomic behaviour. Only in recent years has the trend shown some indication of decreasing, which shows a drop in the number of unruly acts. However, although the frequency of such acts decreased, their severity increased, and there were even some deaths due to fistfights on the floor of the TGNA, with such fighting sometimes spilling over into the lobby as well. Therefore, it is still not possible to argue that rule-abiding legislative behaviours are gaining ground and thus that legislative rules and roles are valued and respected by the deputies of the TGNA.

What seems more interesting is that rule violating behaviour during the floor debates has recently been extended to the major standing commissions. In the summer of 1997, when the new legislation on the eight years of mandatory elementary school education was taken up by the TGNA, the Welfare Party (RP) deputies used raucous behaviour to disrupt the due process of various standing commissions, which were assigned the task of carrying out the 'technical work' on the government-sponsored education bill. Prior to the 1982 Constitution, no such disruptive behaviour was observed in the meetings of the standing commissions of the TGNA. The Welfare Party (RP) plurality seemed to have reached a critical mass with the ability to disrupt the due process of legislative procedure in the 1995 elections. Thus, as a radical party with an Islamic portfolio, the RP was able to convert the commissions into an arena of ideological conflict and political warfare over something they considered a critical issue, religious education. The same pattern continued in the aftermath of the 1999 elections in the TGNA. However, with the predominance of the Justice and Development Party (AKP) in the TGNA following the 3 November 2002 national elections, the frequency of rule-violating behaviour has ebbed, and the conduct of legislative behaviour has become much more orderly. In the meantime Turkey has not experienced a serious political crisis, and the legislative opposition of the CHP has seemed resigned to accepting their ineffective status, and has not been pressured to act in dramatic ways to keep its competitors, such as the Democratic Left Party (DSP) at bay. The current two-party format in Turkey has not been challenged or perturbed by any outside challenger, or any major political crisis. Therefore, it is too early to tell whether the norms and values of orderly legislative conduct are taking hold, or whether the TGNA is just going through a period of stasis since the elections of 3 November 2002. The current, dramatically high turnover rate, and the large number of newly elected deputies serving for the first time in the TGNA, makes it hard to be optimistic about a sudden drive toward legislative institutionalisation in Turkey.

Confidence in the TGNA

Feelings of confidence and/or trust in the legislative institutions not only provide for the survival of the legislative system, but also indirectly contribute to the very survival of representative democracy. When viewed from a comparative perspective, confidence in national legislatures seems to be rather shallow (see Table 7.5). Indeed, an examination of Table 7.5 indicates that even national legislatures such as those in Iceland or the UK can only muster 52.8 and 48 per cent of popular support, respectively (see Table 7.5). Other legislative institutions in consolidated democracies, such as the

Table 7.5 Confidence in the national legislature (1990)

Countries	Some confidence	High confidence	Total	Coefficient of variation
	%	%	%	
US	34.1	7.6	41.7	0.34
Germany (Federal)	43.4	6.8	50.2	0.29
Austria	34.5	5.8	40.3	0.31
Belgium	37.5	4.0	41.5	0.33
Denmark	35.7	5.6	43.1	0.31
Finland	29.3	3.9	33.2	0.34
France	39.1	4.3	43.4	0.35
Netherlands	49.4	3.2	52.6	0.28
UK	36.6	11.6	48.2	0.35
Ireland	37.1	12.8	49.9	0.33
Spain	31.6	5.2	36.8	0.36
Sweden	37.9	7.5	45.4	0.32
Italy	26.3	4.2	30.5	0.38
Iceland	43.4	9.4	52.8	0.30
Japan	23.8	4.5	28.3	0.33
Canada	31.4	5.6	37.0	0.32
Norway	**50.8**	7.9	58.7	0.27
Portugal	33.0	4.2	37.2	0.36
Brazil	*17.7*	5.6	*23.3*	**0.52**
Chile	36.3	**27.1**	63.4	0.32
India	45.5	19.6	65.1	0.32
Korea (South)	26.5	7.4	33.9	0.40
Czechoslovakia	39.9	4.1	44.0	0.32
Hungary	31.3	7.8	39.1	0.39
Poland	48.7	24.1	**72.8**	0.25
Turkey (1990)	28.8	26.4	55.2	0.40
(1996/7)	34.0	16.5	50.5	0.46

Notes: Those percentages reported in italics are the lowest and the figures in bold are the highest percentages per column.
Coefficient of Variation is calculated as V = standard deviation/arithmetic mean. The coefficient of variation measures the homogeneity of the percentages reported in the same row. The more the value of V approaches '0', the more the homogeneity of the row percentages becomes (Nachmias and Nachmias, 1987, pp. 388–9).
Source: Turkish Values Surveys of 1990 and 1996/7.

French Parliament or the US Congress, do little better, with only 43.4 and 41.7 per cent of popular confidence, respectively. Italians, Japanese, Finns, and Brazilians seem to have less confidence in their national legislatures, with only 20–30 per cent of the population registering any confidence in those institutions. About 55 per cent of the Turkish adult population in 1990 and 50 per cent in 1996–7 registered confidence in the TGNA (Kalaycıoğlu, 1999b, pp. 105–6). However, right after the most severe financial crisis of the country in 2001, confidence in the TGNA declined sharply. A more recent study reported that the TGNA had won the trust of about 37 per cent of the voting age population, a somewhat higher proportion than that of the least-trusted institution of the country, the political parties (23 per cent) (Adaman, Çarkoğlu and Şenatalar, 2002, p. 38). However, even such a dip in confidence in the TGNA does not rate it much lower than the Italian or Spanish national legislatures (see Table 7.5). Consequently, there is either a global crisis of confidence and trust with representative democracy and its most critical institution, the national legislature, or comparatively speaking, the TGNA does not seem to be suffering from lack of political confidence or popular trust.

It is hard to assume that Turkish politics and society are experiencing similar challenges to those faced by post-industrial societies of North America and Europe such as the rising demands of direct democracy. There is scant evidence that voters are demanding to take part more than usual in the local and national politics of Turkey (Falay et al., 1996, pp. 67–8). There is not much evidence indicating increased activism calling for more popular input in the affairs of the country, either. Demands for referenda are occasionally voiced in Turkey; yet other institutional mechanisms of direct democracy, such as initiative and recall votes, are practically unknown. The recent use of such mechanisms in California, and the electoral success of Arnold Schwarzenegger, failed to attract much attention in Turkey. It is virtually impossible to argue that the Turkish voters are rising up to demand more political power and responsibility in local or national politics. On the contrary, the political interface between the people and their representatives still revolves around demands for personal favours (*kayırılma*) such as jobs, healthcare, job promotion or transfer, and postponement of mandatory military service for men, in exchange for their support at the polls. Patron–client relations built around lineage (*akrabalık*), tribalism (*aşiret*), regional solidarity (*hemşehrilik*), and religious brotherhood (*tarikat*), still dominate the relations between the deputies of the TGNA and the voters. Indeed, many deputies who are elected from the metropolitan cities still serve their 'hemşehri' from other and remote parts of the country unrelated to their constituency. Their own family backgrounds and tribal, regional, or religious ties become functional in the constituency services provided by the deputies of the TGNA. In practice, the deputies of the TGNA are intensely involved in personal relations with the voters, in a way that constitutes what is referred to in the US as 'casework' (Kalaycıoğlu, 1995, pp. 46–7, 52–3).

Currently, the most important and visible political activity of the electorate is centred around establishing and maintaining personal links with some deputies of the TGNA in return for favours and personal benefits. Such connections constitute immaculate patronage relations, which often work to promote some special and even personal interests to the detriment of others, as well as the laws and regulations of the land. Consequently, to the extent that the patronage relations work, the voters feel well served by their deputies. Indeed, there is evidence that such a feeling contributes to the relatively high level of support extended to the TGNA in Turkey (Kalaycıoğlu, 1980, pp. 131–7). However, such patronage relations also undermine law enforcement and increase corrupt practices in the political system.

Interestingly enough, patronage relations help sustain a high level of support for the legislative system in Turkey, yet, paradoxically, images of patronage linkages in the media also trigger anger and at times disgust about legislative politics in Turkey. There is still not much evidence that the voters perceive the complexities of patronage relations in representative democracy in Turkey. Patronage linkages constitute the same infrastructure that helps voters acquire various services, while undermining law enforcement and promoting corrupt practices in the country. It seems that the success of the popular demand for favouritism through representative democracy fuels political corruption in Turkey. Unless the popular demand for favouritism subsides, there is little chance of ridding Turkish politics of corruption.

It is also a matter of fact that the TGNA provides the only channel of political influence for some of the disadvantaged in Turkey. The TGNA is the only political structure where even a *'çulsuz'* (*sans-culotte*) can approach a political authority (deputy) and expect a welcoming reception, however lacking in substance it may be. Nevertheless we have evidence that such a welcome gives the impression that the voter in question is treated as if he or she were 'somebody'. In essence, the powerless tend to receive much less than they ask for in their interactions with the deputies of the TGNA. However, they seem to enjoy a sense of being treated as respectful citizens from those interactions. Hence, it is little wonder that the TGNA receives widespread support even from the disadvantaged sectors of Turkish society (Kalaycıoğlu, 1980, pp. 132–5; 1995, p. 57).

Conclusion

The volatility and fragmentation of the party system creates a very high turnover rate of deputies in the TGNA. The military interventions produced new constitutions, election laws, and political parties, which in turn led Turkish politics to operate under conditions of constant flux, making the institutionalisation process of the TGNA suffer dearly. A system that operated with an unsettled regime, laws that constantly change with bewildering speed and complexity, and political actors who also enter and exit the political scene frequently produced a very high turnover rate of deputies. Consequently, the vocation of deputy failed to emerge as a valued professional career, and instead became that of a profiteer, who occupies a parliamentary seat for three to four years and does his or her best to raise enough pecuniary benefits to offset the expenditure and loans accumulated to finance campaign expenditure. The image of a deputy as 'professional politician' is thus damaged. Polls tended to indicate that people have become distrustful of 'professional politicians' and perceive them as conniving and sly profiteers, who will engage in any kind of deal for pecuniary benefits. However, the people seem also to be cognisant of the fact that however untrustworthy the deputies may be, they still provide the best chance to access some services of the state agencies and the public bureaucracy. Barristers are not any more trusted than deputies of the TGNA in Turkey, however, they still get the business of their clients, since their knowledge of the law provides their clients with the best opportunity to seek justice. It is no wonder that a plurality, and in some assemblies, a majority of the deputies in Turkey have been lawyers.

The relations between the represented and their representatives tend to be quite functional. The represented purport to support the deputies at the polls and the deputies pretend to help them with finding jobs, gaining promotions or transfers to new departments, or even getting a bed in a state hospital. The deputies know that their casework does not guarantee re-election, yet they also know that callous attitudes towards the demands of their constituents will definitely undermine their chances of getting re-elected. So, it is highly prudent for deputies to appear to be intensely involved in casework. The constituents also seem to know very well that the deputies of the TGNA will not be much help unless they can establish some kind of personal or proximal relationship through blood ties, regional bonds, or religious brotherhood solidarity with the deputy in question. Even then, they may receive much less than they ask for. However, they also seem to calculate that using the office and services of a deputy will help in dealing with the state agencies. In the meantime, sitting in the office of the deputy, eating one or two lunches at the deputy's expense at the TGNA restaurant facilities, and a photo opportunity with the deputy will not hurt, either. Constituents will at least get the satisfaction of being treated as the rightful citizens of the land, whatever the outcome of their contact may be.

The history of the TGNA has been one of several crises undermining its drive toward institutionalisation. The shift from two-party to single-party rule in the early 1920s, back to a two-party system between 1946 and 1960, away from two-party system to a moderate pluralist one between 1961 through 1980, toward extreme pluralism in the 1990s, and finally back to a two-party format in the 2000s, involved a huge and complicated list of parties and leaders. These changes, irrespective of whether they occurred through military coups or popular support at the polls, had the same effect of high turnover rates and very short tenure for the deputies, which produced an assembly that suffered from lack of legislative merit, seniority and professional ethics. The vocation of deputyship has become so tenuous and disrespected that during interviews, the deputies resented the fact that the author of this article referred to them as 'professional politicians'. The deputies themselves seemed to put very little emphasis on their vocation and the professional ethics accompanying it. Indeed, some did not even know what such a profession consisted of. Consequently, the TGNA has been plagued with crises of suspension, frequently changing political regimes and legal procedures, and has experienced high turnover (deputies). Indeed, the history of the TGNA has become one of de-institutionalisation, rather than institutionalisation. Turkey has tried to consolidate its democracy, while simultaneously undermining the development of a pivotal institution in any democracy. The Grand National Assembly played a major role in the War of Liberation and the establishment of the Republic that followed. However, its role will continue to be much more humble in the consolidation of democracy in Turkey.

Notes

1. Even today, the TGNA hosts three political parties, although only two parties and 12 independent deputies won seats during the 3 November 2002 elections. Two independent deputies decided to join ranks with the True Path Party (DYP) recently. Indeed, one of the independent deputies, Ağar, has become the new the leader of the DYP. For a more thorough discussion of the electoral laws and their consequences in Turkey, see Kalaycıoğlu (2002, pp. 55–71).

Bibliography

F. Adaman, A. Çarkoğlu and B. Şenatalar (2002) *Household View on the Causes of Corruption in Turkey and Suggested Preventive Measures* (Istanbul: Tesev).

Ü. Ergüder (1980–1) 'Changing Patterns of Electoral Behavior in Turkey', Boğaziçi *University Journal (Social Sciences)*, vol. 8–9, pp. 45–69.

Ü. Ergüder, and I. R. Hofferbert (1988) 'The 1983 General Elections in Turkey: Continuity or Change in Voting Patterns' in M. Heper and A. Evin (eds) *State, Democracy and the Military: Turkey in the 1980s* (Berlin, New York: Walter de Gruyter).

Y. Esmer (1995) 'Parties and the Electorate: A Comparative Analysis of Voter Profiles of Turkish Political Parties' in Ç. Balim, E. Kalaycioglu, C. Karatos, G. Winrow and F. Yasamee (eds) *Turkey: Political, Social and Economic Challenges in the 1990s* (Leiden, New York; Köln: E. J. Brill).

Y. Esmer (2002) 'At the Ballot Box: Determinants of Voting Behavior' in S. Sayari and Y. Esmer (eds) *Politics, Parties, and Elections in Turkey* (Boulder, London: Lynne Rienner).

N. Falay, E. Kalaycıog˘lu and U. Özkirimli (1996) *Belediyelerin Mali Yönetimi: I'ktisadi ve Siyasal Bir Çözümleme* (Istanbul: TESEV Yayınları).

J. K. Feibleman (1956) *The Institutions of Society* (London: G. Allen).

Richard F. Fenno Jr (1966) *The Power of the Purse: Appropriations Politics in the Congress* (Boston: Little, Brown, and Co.).

Frederick W. Frey (1965) *The Turkish Political Elite* (Cambridge, MA: MIT Press).

Frederick W. Frey (1975) 'Patterns of Elite Politics in Turkey', in George Lenczowski (ed.) *Political Elites in the Middle East* (Washington DC: American Enterprise Institute for Public Policy Research).

S. P. Huntington (1968) *Political Order in Changing Societies* (New Haven and London: Yale University Press).

E. Kalaycıoğlu (1980) 'Why Legislatures Persist in Developing Countries: The Case of Turkey', *Legislative Studies Quarterly*, vol. 5, no. 1, pp. 123–39.

E. Kalaycıoğlu (1988) 'The 1983 Parliament in Turkey: Changes and Continuities', in M. Heper and A. Evin (eds) *State, Democracy and the Military: Turkey in the 1980s* (Berlin, New York: Walter de Gruyter).

E. Kalaycıoğlu (1994) 'Elections and Party preferences in Turkey: Changes and Continuities in the 1990s', *Comparative Political Studies*, vol. 27, no. 3 (October), pp. 402–24.

E. Kalaycıoğlu (1995) 'The Turkish Grand National Assembly: A Brief Inquiry into the Politics of Representation in Turkey', in Ç. Balim, E. Kalaycioglu, C. Karatos, G. Winrow and F. Yasamee (eds) *Turkey: Political, Social and Economic Challenges in the 1990s* (Leiden, New York, Köln: E. J. Brill).

E. Kalaycıoğlu (1997) 'Constitutional Viability and Political Institutions in Turkish Democracy', in A. Baaklini and H. Desfosses (eds) *Designs for Democratic Stability: Studies in Viable Constitutionalism* (Armonk, New York and London: M. E. Sharpe).

E. Kalaycıoğlu (1999a) 'The Shaping of Party Preferences in Turkey: Coping with the Post-Cold War Era', *New Perspectives on Turkey*, (Spring), vol. 20, pp. 47–76.

E. Kalaycıoğlu (1999b) 'Türkiye'de Siyasal Rejimin Evrimi ve Yasama Sistemi' [Evolution of the Political Regime and the Legislative System in Turkey], in Z. Rona (ed.) *Bilanço 1923–1998: Türkiye Cumhuriyeti'nin 75 Yılına Toplu Bakış Uluslararası Kongresi, I. Cilt: Siyaset - Kültür – Uluslararasi İlişkiler* (Istanbul: Tarih Vakfi Yayinlari).

E. Kalaycıoğlu (2002) 'Elections and Governance', in S. Sayari and Y. Esmer (eds) *Politics, Parties and Elections in Turkey* (Boulder, London: Lynne Rienner).

Ş. Mardin (1975) 'Centre-Periphery Relations: A Key to Turkish Politics?', in Engin D. Akarlı with Gabriel Ben-Dor (eds) *Political Participation in Turkey: Historical Background and Present Problems* (Istanbul: Boğaziçi University Press).

G. Lenski and J. Lenski (1974) *Human Societies: An Introduction to Macrosociology* (New York: McGraw-Hill).

D.R. Matthews (1985) 'Legislative Recruitment and Legislative Careers', in G. Loewenberg, S. C. Patterson and M. E. Jewell (eds) *Handbook of Legislative Research* (Cambridge, Boston: Harvard University Press).

D.Nachmias and C. Nachmias (1987) *Research Methods in the Social Sciences* [Third Edn] (New York: St. Martin's Press).

National Report: Turkey 2002 (2002) (Ankara: The Republic of Turkey, Ministry of Environment and UNDP).

E. Özbudun (1981) 'The Turkish Party System: Institutionalization, Polarization, and Fragmentation', *Middle Eastern Studies*, vol. 17, no. 2 (April), pp. 228–40.

E. Özbudun (1992) *1921 Anayasası* (Ankara: Atatürk Kültür, Dil ve Tarih Yüksek Kurumu, Atatürk Araştırma Merkezi Yayınları).

E. Özbudun (1997) 'Civil Society and Democratic Consolidation in Turkey', in E. Özdalga and S. Persson (eds) *Civil Society, Democracy and the Muslim World* (Istanbul: Swedish Research Institute) [Transactions vol. 7].

E. Özbudun (2000) *Contemporary Turkish Politics: Challenges to Democratic Consolidation* (Boulder, London: Lynne Rienner).

N. Polsby (1971) 'Institutionalisation of the US House of Representatives', in H. Hirsch and M. D. Hancock (eds) *Comparative Legislative Systems: A Reader in Theory and Research* (New York: The Free Press).

T. Saalfeld (1997) 'Professionalization of Parliamentary Roles in Germany: An Aggregate Level Analysis: 1949–1994', in W. C. Müller and T. Saalfeld (eds) *Members of Parliament in Western Europe: Roles and Behavior* (Portland, OR and London: Frank Cass).

G. Sartori (1976) *Parties and Party Systems: A Framework for Analysis*, Vol. I (Cambridge: Cambridge University Press).

M. Soysal (1969) *Dinamik Anayasa Anlayışı: Anayasa Diyalektiği Üzerine bir Deneme* (Ankara: Ankara Üniversitesi Siyasal Bilgiler Fakültesi Yayını).

F. Tachau and M. D. Good (1973) 'The Anatomy of Political and Social Change: Turkish Parties, Parliaments and Elections, Comparative Politics', vol. 5, no. 4, pp. 551–73.

N. Yalman (1973) 'Some Observations on Secularism in Islam: The Cultural Revolution in Turkey', *Daedalus*, vol. 102, pp. 139–62.

8
University Governance in Turkey

İlter Turan

Introduction

Since 1946, when the Turkish political system made a first transition to democracy, the Turkish university system has often been one of the focal points of political debate. The stakeholders include the universities themselves, the Inter-university Council, the Committee of University Rectors, the Council on Higher Education (CHE), the Ministry of National Education (MNE), the Council of Ministers, the President of the Republic, parliamentary parties, professional associations, graduate associations of various universities, representatives of various types of high schools, as well as a host of others. Not only are they often pitted against each other in this complex power game, but many are divided among themselves as well. To the outside observer, the difficulties encountered in operating a university system may appear to be somewhat unusual. To those familiar with the context and the tradition of higher education that has prevailed since the beginning of Ottoman modernisation, they probably seem natural.

This chapter examines the evolution and characteristics of university governance in Turkey. Governance here denotes how Turkish universities, under the constraint of legal and institutional frameworks, work within the context of broader society to perform their multiple roles. The following includes a historical review, focusing on change through time, and a discussion of its contemporary characteristics.[1]

Origins of Turkey's university system

An inscription on the main gate of Istanbul University features the date 1453, the year of the city's Ottoman conquest. The beginning of the modern university system is more commonly traced to the *Darülfünun*, the Ottoman House of Sciences. This institution was first conceived in an 1845 report addressing educational reform. It opened in 1863 but closed in 1865 after being destroyed by a fire (Baskan, 2001, pp. 21–32; Erdem, 2004, p. 196).

It experienced a number of 'false starts', finally opening in 1900 (Lewis, 1961, pp. 181–2).

Although the Darülfünun was a university,[2] it belonged to a system of professional schools established by the government throughout the nineteenth century to train men to meet specific needs especially in the military domain. These included engineering schools, military medicine schools and veterinary medicine schools, military colleges, a staff college, schools of commerce and public administration, all located in Istanbul. Taken together, these were expected to strengthen the defence capabilities of the country. Training young generations in Western knowledge and science, the reformers felt, would lead to a modern transformation and the salvation of the Ottoman state (Alkan, 2004, p. 91).

The development of new educational institutions to avert further decline appears to have produced a set of fundamental understandings of the role of education in society that has continued ever since. First in this set is a view of education as the major instrument available to the state for the transformation of society. The Ottoman state had judged that it had to Westernise to stand up to European powers. Yet, the content of education borrowed from the West transmitted positivist and materialist ways of thinking and sympathy for prevalent European political ideologies, including democracy and constitutional government. Observing this, Abdülhamid II under whose reign modern schools registered major growth, introduced courses on religion and morals to counter the 'corrupt tendencies of Westernisation'. He failed, however, losing his throne to the modernising elite. The outcome of this process was an understanding that institutions of higher learning train model people, equipped with not only the proper knowledge and skills but also the proper ideology to serve the needs and purposes of the state. Alkan notes that the development of 'official ideology' and its transmission to later generations through state schools is a product of this period (Alkan, 2004, p. 81).

The second understanding is a corollary of the first: institutions of higher learning are not just centres of independent thinking, research and professional training; they should also offer ideological training to future leaders of society.[3] This stance has proven to be particularly problematic when the ideology held by the 'institutions of the state' and those of the 'institutions of elected governments' diverged under the conditions of political competition.

The third understanding is that the state is exclusively responsible for higher education. To meet its growing needs for educated people, the Ottoman state developed a state-run system of higher education. The new schools produced individuals whose skills were not in demand except by the state, and whose values were hardly in harmony with the traditions of society. These continued to expand against the traditional institutions that relied mainly on Islamic charity and inadvertently began to produce counter-elites. Bureaucrats and political leaders wanted the state to monopolise higher education so as to continue with modernisation. Traditional institutions of religious learning were abolished in 1924. As the state was now the sole provider of higher education, it became firmly established that it had the exclusive responsibility to provide free education.

The university system under the republic

University development during the republic went through six stages, exemplified in important legal changes. The first begins with the founding of the republic in 1923 and ends in 1933 with the closing of the Darülfünun. The second, marked by the opening of Istanbul University, ends in 1946 with the enactment of a new Universities Law. The third begins in 1946 and ends in 1961when the law was changed to enhance university autonomy. The fourth runs between 1961 and 1973 when another law aiming to establish a centralised system while limiting their administrative autonomy was accepted. The fifth is from 1973 to 1981, a period of social and political turmoil with the universities constituting an ideological battleground between right and left wing student and faculty. An incoming military junta restored order and passed a new Universities Law in 1981, leading to the current stage.

1923–46: The continuation of tradition

While closing down the traditional institutions, the Republican government retained the schools that had been established as part of the modernisation programmes, including the Darülfünun. The Darülfünun, which was to develop into a full university, presented two problems. Firstly, it was academically inadequate with poorly trained staff and it made little effort to improve itself. The Minister of Education, Reşit Galip, complained as early as 1924 that despite enjoying the privileges including autonomy, the Darülfünun had failed to deliver the progress that the Turkish intelligentsia expected of it (Milli Eğitim Bakanlığı, 1998, p. 8). Secondly, the Darülfünun seemed not to be interested in assuming a role in advancing the republican revolution.

To deal with the problem, a study was commissioned from a Swiss professor. Albert Malche's report of 1932, identified many of the problems that would plague the system in later years. These included lack of scholarly interaction among various parts of the university, confinement of faculty activity to teaching, lack of research and publications, lack of interaction between faculty and students, teaching of courses based on a single textbook and an emphasis on theoretical matters without relating them to the actual problems of society (Malche, 1939, pp. 6–12).

The government allowed some discussion of the matter in public until the legislature suddenly passed Law 2252[4] on 31 May 1933, abolishing the Darülfünun and authorising the Ministry of Education to establish Istanbul University by 1 August 1933. The law comprising 14 articles, dealt with those who lost their jobs, the creation of new positions and budgetary matters. On 10 October 1934, the Council of Ministers accepted the Statute of Istanbul University (Milli Eğitim Bakanlığı, 1998, pp. 13–22) which placed it under the authority of the Ministry. The university rector was nominated by the Minister of Education, appointed by the council of ministers and approved by the president. The deans were appointed by the minister upon the rector's recommendation.

It is noteworthy that the bill was read and voted on without debate (T. B. M. M. Zabıt Ceridesi, 1933, pp. 465–7). Indeed, the Darülfünun were not held in high esteem by the political elites. The idea that something had to be done was widely shared. With the closure, nearly two-thirds of the faculty lost their jobs. The ordeal showed that the Darülfünun had lacked the institutional élan to resist abolition. Political authority wanted to ensure that the new university would conform to the spirit of reforms.

1933–46: Beginnings of institutionalisation and professionalisation

The 1933 reform did not establish an elaborate system of university organisation and administration or offer criteria for faculty recruitment and promotions. Reducing its autonomy, the bill tried to bring about a rapid transformation of the Darülfünun. The brief and imprecise nature of the law conformed to the recommendations of the Malche report that the new system be flexible so as to enable adjustments when needed.[5] The law also made it clear that the university was answerable to the Ministry of Education.[6] After the university adjusted its political stance by joining the republican establishment, the government did not interfere in its daily affairs.

A significant development facilitating the closure of the Darülfünun was the arrival of German professors. After Hitler's rise to power, Atatürk invited well-known German professors wanting to leave Germany to assume teaching positions in Turkey. These scholars, hired on a contractual basis with higher pay, lectured in German with interpreters but were expected to learn Turkish in three years. Their presence had important outcomes. They came from a well-established university system and so tried to turn Istanbul University (and later Istanbul Technical and Ankara universities) into quality, professional institutions. They trained new scholars, developed libraries, prepared textbooks and built a European university environment in which to train Turkish scholars. Since they were not part of the domestic political debate, their presence restrained both the university's politicisation and government's interference.

The government eventually created two new universities, Istanbul Technical and Ankara, by bringing together institutions established earlier by different ministries to meet their needs. These included the engineering schools under the direction of the Ministry of Public Works. They were consolidated into Istanbul Technical University[7] in 1944. The law school of the Ministry of Justice, the Faculties of Language, History and Geography of the Ministry of Education and the School of Public Administration merged into Ankara University as part of the university reforms of 1946.[8]

1946–60: Universities during Turkey's first democratic experiment and its failure

The opening of institutions of higher learning during the 1930s and early 1940s were isolated events. No standard organisational and administrative model or method of faculty recruitment and promotions was followed. Since the government planned further expansion, the need for a common framework was evident. Equally important, pressures for democratisation had been mounting,[9] enticing the government to adopt a more accommodating approach. They led to the preparation of a new universities bill. In his introductory remarks, the prime minister spelled out the new line of thinking that universities should become autonomous and employ standard criteria in faculty recruiting, training and promotions. Noting that institutions of knowledge could not be administered by a single centre, he proposed that universities elect their own members. An inter-university council, headed by the Ministry of Education, would address common concerns (Üniversiteler Kanunu Tasarısı, 1946, pp. 3 and 7). Despite a liberal outlook, however, the prime minister also noted that the Ministry would govern the system, overseeing the universities.[10]

An ideological mission was added to the bill in the Committee on Education stating that a major responsibility of universities was to help young people to develop a 'national character', and strong attachment to the principles of the revolution.[11] While the government bill had emphatically referred to contemporary democratic principles, the Committee replaced them with stronger nationalistic language. The particular amendment, surprisingly, elicited no discussion.[12] Similarly, nobody objected to the idea of having the Education Ministry head the universities.

Law no. 4936 was accepted on 13 June 1946. Comprising 81 articles, it offered an organisational framework for Turkish universities, many features of which have remained to this day. Universities are comprised of faculties (colleges), where each faculty, made up of a number of chairs (departments) run by elected chairpersons, is run by an elected dean. An executive and an academic committee, elected from among faculty members work with the dean to administer the faculty. The university is headed by an elected rector. The two-tiered committee system of faculties is replicated in the executive committee and the senate. Rectors and university representatives meet at an Inter-University Council to address common concerns and set standards, including the selection of post Ph.D. habilitation (Doçentlik) examination juries. The law specified the qualifications needed to enter and hold academic jobs and foresaw a competitive recruitment process. Promotions at all levels required either the taking of exams and/or submitting one's academic record to review by academic committees. The law marked a change towards professionalisation.

Law no. 4936 was also a clear step in developing a modern university system (Lewis, 1961, p. 438). It viewed universities as trusted institutions and gave them autonomy. It anticipated, it seems correctly, that autonomy would be exercised within the limits of republican ideology. The faculty, for example, had not invoked autonomy against the expulsion of several faculty members from Ankara University in 1948 under highly questionable accusations of propagating communism.

The elections of 1950 ended the rule of the Republican People's Party, which had governed unchallenged ever since the establishment of the republic. The victorious Democrats (DP) were anxious to curb the arbitrary power of the Republican modernisers in the bureaucracy who saw this as an attempt to undo the republican revolution. As part of the republican establishment, the universities shared the bureaucrats' apprehension regarding the Democrats' ulterior intentions. The DP, on the other hand, mobilised the masses to show that they were now commanding the bureaucratic-intellectual elite. Government-opposition relations grew progressively worse, dragging universities into the political struggle. This derived partly from the universities' self perceived role as defenders of the republican revolution, and partly from the Republican People's Party, which saw the universities as a natural ally.

Under conditions of political competition, the powers accorded to the Ministry of Education eventually became its Achilles' heel. The DP government, responding to the political challenge, attempted to increase government control of universities. A law in 1953 had defined the making of political statements and writings as infractions of discipline leading to possible expulsion. A 1954 law, on the other hand, had empowered the Ministry to place professors under ministerial control or terminate their employment (Erdem, 2004, pp. 202–3; Shaw and Shaw, 1977, p. 411). After 1957, the opposition became increasingly convinced that the DP would not leave power through ordinary elections. It mobilised all its resources to bring the government down. Feeling insecure, the government turned to authoritarian measures. The prime minister publicly insulted the professors. The Ministry of Education removed vocal administrators from their posts and later expelled them for making political statements or engaging in political activity.[13] Such behaviour reinforced the universities' determination to affect political change. In the spring of 1960, anti-government demonstrations by students became widespread. Failing to contain them, the government, called on the army for help. On 27 May 1960, the National Unity Committee ousted the DP government, arrested its deputies, and assumed political power. In the words of Karpat:

> The revolution skyrocketed the intelligentsia's prestige, along with that of the military. ... The military consulted with university professors and (they) were associated with the key decisions such as the drafting of a new constitution and the trial of democratic deputies.
>
> (Karpat, 1973, p. 264)

Despite the political volatility that characterised the universities during the 1950s, the DP government had continued opening new universities to accommodate the growing demand of a rapidly increasing population. Ege University in Izmir and Black Sea Technical University in Trabzon were opened in 1955, to be followed by Atatürk University in Erzurum in 1957 and the Middle East Technical University (METU) in Ankara in 1959. Among these, METU was established by special legislation. Modelled on American universities and run by a Board of Trustees, it was met with uniform hostility by the other universities.

Unrestrained autonomy and political degeneration: 1961–73

The members of the 1960 junta, believing in social engineering through legal change, made amendments to the constitution and university laws. Soldiers and professors alike felt that checks should be introduced to prevent parliamentary majorities from resorting to the authoritarianism of the Ottoman Empire. This was done by extending constitutional protection to the critical institutions of the republican state, including the universities. In Article 120 of the 1961 constitution, universities were given full autonomy. After specifying that only the state may establish universities, the first paragraph defined universities as public institutions possessing academic and administrative autonomy. The next explained that they are administered by organs whose members are elected from among the faculty. The third stipulated that a university organ may not be dissolved or faculty members dismissed by any external authority. Conducting research and publishing findings were to be free from interference. Faculty members could become members of political parties but not assume administrative responsibilities except at the national headquarters.

During parliamentary debate, a motion to allow private universities under state control was introduced, but quickly turned down by a majority suspecting that unless universities were state institutions, they would represent interests counter to those of the state. A rather curious logic appears to have been employed in rejecting the proposal. A politician coming from an academic background argued that placing private institutions under state control would violate university autonomy because the state might force these institutions to teach only those ideas that it liked. The freedom and autonomy of state universities, on the other hand, was guaranteed. Then his genuine concern surfaced: these institutions might well defend 'foreign' interests, political and economic doctrines or even religious ones (Öztürk, 1966, p. 3270).

Pursuant to constitutional change, Law 4936 of 1946 underwent substantial revisions.[14] All references to the Ministry of Education were dropped in Article 13 dealing with the Inter-University Council. The chair would now rotate among university rectors. The Minister could neither call nor attend its meetings. The provision empowering the Minister as the head of the system exercising control over universities was also abolished. This liberation, however, came with a long-term political cost. The role the universities played in the 1960 military revolution, their role in writing a new constitution and a new university law and their willingness to rid the institution of members who deviated from institutional preferences[15] may have served the short-term interests of universities, but led to their identification by the public as partisan institutions.

By 1964, the pre-1960 political balance had begun to return. That year, the DP's successor Justice Party (JP) replaced the RPP-led coalition that was favoured by the leaders of the military coup. Committed to restoring the state-politics balance in favour of the latter, the JP won the 1965 elections overwhelmingly. It was interested in enhancing the government's control over the universities. Student-based violence after 1967 provided the government with a justification for proceeding.

The roots of political turmoil from 1967 until the 1980 military intervention have not been sufficiently analysed. It appears that the liberal atmosphere following the 1961 Constitution opened the way for the diffusion of socialist thinking among the younger faculty and students of major urban universities. Why? The advent of competitive politics and an expanding private sector had undermined the status of intellectuals and bureaucrats as tutelary elites. Their claim of a mission to modernise society and therefore political power was no longer found sufficiently persuasive. Under the circumstances, Marxist–Leninist thinking about the vanguard of the proletariat proved attractive because it accepted tutelary rule by a political class. 'Ignorant masses' were quickly renamed as the 'the working class', while the bureaucratic elite became the 'vanguard of the proletariat'.

To counter the socialist youth and establish a balance in the streets, the government promoted jingoistic nationalism through supporting the development of nationalist, 'anti-communist' youth movements, preparing the conditions of a breakdown of order in universities. In addition, it promoted the growth of new universities with nationalist faculty and students. Starting in 1967, all educational centres, especially those in major urban centres like Istanbul and Ankara, came to be characterised by incessant turmoil. Gangs of students fighting and killing each other on ideological grounds, and the occupation of university buildings leading to the closing of universities became commonplace. Politics was too polarised to produce solutions. The government, judging the 1961 constitution too restrictive of government powers and otherwise too liberal, wanted, but failed to change it. With incessant public disturbances and daily deaths, the Armed Forces issued a powerful ultimatum to the government on 12 March 1971, demanding the formation of a national unity coalition. Five caretaker governments were formed until the 1973 elections. Formed under the Sword of Damocles of a military intervention, the government changed the laws that made it difficult to maintain public order and to exercise firmer control over public institutions. The universities law was severely revised.[16]

The failed attempt to discipline the universities: 1973–81

As universities became trouble spots, the almost total immunity they had enjoyed against the government since 1960 began to erode. The 12 March ultimatum gave successive right-wing coalitions the opportunity to bring about change. Prepared without consulting the universities, changes focused on two areas: redefining universities' ideological orientation, and increasing government control. The 'reform' was considered by the parliament in late May. The debate reflected ideological concerns. Many complained that the youth had abandoned national traditions and were won over by foreign ideologies. A party spokesman reminded colleagues of what a former prime minister had said: 'Our universities have professors, who like incubators, are in the business of producing communists'. He then added, 'Before anything else, we must train people with belief, but truly enlightened people. That is the only way to guarantee the future of this country' (T. B. M. M., 1973, pp. 482–3).

Many changes came. One was redefining the mission of universities to include inculcating students with national traditions. Another was making certain that students who had participated in 'anarchical' events were not hired as graduate assistants.[17] A third was empowering the government to take over universities that failed to maintain teaching or became a centre for challenging fundamental republican values such as indivisibility of the country on linguistic, religious, racial or social class grounds. A fourth was the establishment of a monitoring council comprising the Prime Minister, the Education Ministry, the Minister of Justice, representatives of the State Planning Organisation and the National Security Council, as well as three former rectors of universities selected by lottery. The council would monitor violations of discipline among the faculty and staff and initiate disciplinary procedures if the university or faculty administrations failed.

Ideological concerns constituted the basic motivation for changing the administrative structure of universities, but there were others. An agency that studied and planned the country's long-term higher education was lacking. The new universities encountered faculty shortages, while over-staffed established universities remained disinterested. The expansion of existing universities was unsystematic or unresponsive to societal demands. There was no reliable system of monitoring faculty performance. Budgetary allocations to universities were insufficient while students contributed almost nothing. The central remedy was the creation of a Council of Higher Education, comprised of university representatives and relevant agencies of the government. The Council would, among other resolutions, do the following:

- prepare short and long-term plans to meet the country's human resource needs
- ensure that higher education would be developed according to the economic development plans
- propose expansion of the existing educational programmes
- determine the needs of other institutions of higher learning and the way universities can render assistance to them, develop programmes to achieve that end and to monitor these programmes
- determine tuition fees.

Law 1750 went into effect in July 1973. The traditional urban universities judged that the new law infringed their constitutionally guaranteed auto-nomy. In the aftermath of the autumn 1973 elections, with the normalisa-tion of political life, Istanbul, Istanbul Technical and Ankara universities and the Republican People's Party, went to the Constitutional Court separately to argue that some key articles of the law were unconstitutional. In its December decision, the Court agreed. 'National customs and traditions' were vague and could not define the mission of universities. Imprecise and arbitrary criteria could not be used in hiring graduate assistants; the government could not decide on its own to take over a university, only university administrations could decide to close down the institution; universities could not initiate tuition fees. The Council on Higher Education was also deemed unconstitu-tional. Within two years, the new law looked like the one it had replaced.

The incumbent coalition government, looking like a confederation of ministries each conducting its own policy, was preoccupied with violence and public disorder not unlike those that had produced the 1971 military ultimatum. It proved incapable of producing a coherent legislative response to the decision of the Constitutional Court. The attempt by the military and right-wing coalitions to discipline the universities had ended in failure.

On 12 September 1980, the military intervened directly. In identifying the culprits for the country's dire state of affairs, the commanders placed uni-versities high on the list. The head of the National Security Council (NSC), General Kenan Evren, criticised the universities for having failed 'to pick up the fallen national flag, while complaining about salaries'. The NSC, decided to overhaul the entire constitutional arrangement. On 6 November 1981, Law no. 2547[18] was enacted during the constitution's suspension. The new constitution came into effect in November 1983.

The new national university system: Wearing a straitjacket since 1981

The military intervention came at a time when all civilian institutions had suffered declines in their credibility. The National Security Council viewed universities led by professors and students accused of using their own political ends, as a threat to domestic peace. These allegations, however questionable, were widely accepted. No constituency supported universities when they came under the junta's attack. The generals soon discovered that they could shape the universities as they wished. They produced the longest and the most detailed universities law to date.

Under the influence of their own training, the generals viewed university education as professional training. They also thought that an important mission of the university was indoctrination. They were convinced that if the youth had been better indoctrinated about Atatürk's ideas and achievements, they would not have been attracted to 'alien' ideologies.[19] The purposes university education would serve, some contradictory, were expressed in Article 5 which described the goals of higher education as training students:[20]

- To be deeply attached to Atatürk's nationalism, guided by his principles and reforms
- To feel pride and honour in being Turkish, and to bear the moral, ethical, cultural, humanistic and national values of the Turkish nation
- To be imbued with love of family, country and the nation and to hold the interests of society above those of the individual
- To be aware of their responsibilities toward the Turkish state and to render these into daily behaviour
- To possess powers of free and scientific thinking, a broad view of the world, and respect for human rights
- To develop physically, mentally, ethically and emotionally in a balanced and healthy way
- To acquire a profession; to possess the knowledge, skills, modes of behaviour and the general culture that this profession requires in order contribute both to one's own material well being and happiness, and to the development of their country and to meet its needs.

The description did not stop there but continued with references to the indivisibility of the country, joining contemporary civilisation, conducting research etc. The next article elaborated further on the ideological orientation of universities, where a reference to 'national traditions and customs' rejected by the Constitutional Court in 1975 as being too vague reappears. The Council of Higher Education was re-established as the central organ to which universities are responsible. All institutions of higher learning are integrated into university frameworks under the Council's authority. Decisions of existing universities to establish new faculties, research centres, departments; the opening of new universities; finalising the number of students to be admitted, creating and eliminating faculty positions, appointing deans, nominating candidates for rector are examples of its powers. Even the determination of curricula was initially its prerogative. When viewed in totality, it is clear that the administrative autonomy of universities was largely destroyed. The election of university functionaries is substituted with a system of appointments by some higher authority, although faculty members eventually retrieved some say in the identification of candidates.

In line with the tradition established in the constitution of 1961, the universities are treated as state institutions, protected against incursion by daily politics. The Ministry of Education has no real role in university governance. Most of the Council's members and its chair are appointed by agencies of the state like the presidency and NSC. Rectors are also appointed by the President of the Republic.

At the beginning, the junta was highly influential on how the Council operated. It is at this time that a common organisational scheme was devised for all universities. Accordingly, the name of each subunit, such as faculty or department, were to be made the same across the system. Departments bearing the same name would have standard curricula. The same courses with the same contents would be offered by the same-named departments nationwide. Members of faculty of each rank were expected to teach a minimum number of hours. Those without sufficient teaching hours would be asked by the Council of Higher Education to move to institutions that needed teaching faculty. Associate professors could not be promoted at the same institution and could not be rehired by their former university until after two years.

As the military's power receded after the transition to competitive politics, the Council became more amenable to changes. Standardised course contents were dropped and departments were given some choice in devising their programmes. Changing the organisational scheme became possible; strict adherence to teaching loads was relaxed and promotion within the same institution was allowed. Emphasis on the inculcation of ideology was, however, retained. The law and the constitution have also undergone liberalising revisions over time. Most recently, the representative of the National Security Council[21] was removed from the Council of Higher Education in order to conform to EU expectations of reducing the military's role in politics.

Relations between the Justice and Development Party (AKP) government since 2002 and the Council have been problematic. Viewing itself as representing the interests of the state and protected by the constitution and the laws against the interventions of politicians, the Council has worked hard to defend what it considers to be regime values against the government. One critical value has been secularism. The Council has taken a firm stand against admitting female students who cover their heads, ostensibly for religious reasons, to classes and exams and even to campus, denying them a university education. Similarly, it has devised a system of admissions where the graduates of preacher training schools (Imam Hatip Lisesi) are favoured for admission to faculties of theology but put at a disadvantage in seeking admission to other departments. The current government with broad appeal among religious constituencies, wants both policies changed as part of a reform package. The Council of Higher Education, backed by other state institutions including the NSC, a number of university rectors and, until recently, the President, had not been accommodating. Although, there is currently an AKP elected president and a new Council chair appointed by him, a confrontational mood between the government and the universities continues to prevail.

Despite much criticism, however, the Council of Higher Education has become an indispensable part of the university system which, in itself, seems firmly established and difficult to alter in fundamental ways. Its historical evolution, and the interaction between politics and academics, has produced a stable set of characteristics that will be discussed in the following section.

Fundamental characteristics of the university system

As may have become evident in the preceding discussion, the Turkish university system has acquired a set of characteristics over time. These will be examined briefly in the following pages.

Universities are institutions of political indoctrination: Viewing universities as agents of political indoctrination is a legacy of Turkish modernisation. The idea of training the modernising elites was narrowed down and redefined during the early republic to supporting the republican state and its values, in particular secularism. Rendering universities agents of indoctrination fails its mission and generates problems. Depicting universities as centres of free-thinking, expression and research and then asking them to inculcate ideology is contradictory. Understandably, the universities should not become home to organisations against the integrity of the state and the regime, but they must be open to the discussion of highly diverse ideas.

It is far from clear that universities are realising their mission of indoctrination. The direct indoctrinating instrument is a mandatory course entitled 'History of the Turkish Revolution' in which the virtues of the republican regime and the reforms of Atatürk are extolled. The outcome, however, seems to be different from that intended. Most students view the course as a burden to be passed with minimum effort. This lack of esteem often reduces the course to mere formality. Secondly, efforts to produce a standard content textbook, have not appealed to faculty. The ensuing content variety undermines the course's purpose. Thirdly, the course has provided a platform for faculty to propagate their own ideologies. Using university education for indoctrination is an unnecessary feature of the system, but it is a taboo to suggest its elimination. It would be met with accusations that this would help deconstruct Atatürk's legacy.

Universities identify with 'state' concerns and positions: since the advent of competitive politics, when a distinction between the state and the government became meaningful, Turkish universities have identified themselves as state institutions. Such a distinction, as used in Turkish, assumes that society has some interests that are above the concern of everyday politics and hence elected politicians. These are tended to by institutions of the state such as the military and the bureaucracy. While this stance has given universities some protection against encroachments from politicians, it has also guided them to cooperate with other state institutions and to adopt 'state' positions on public policy questions. Until recently, for example, the Council for Higher Education has displayed a highly cooperative attitude toward the NSC, undermining the role of the universities as centres offering critical thinking on national problems. The Council for Higher Education adopts policy positions and encourages university administrators to follow suit. It has been common for university senates to issue declarations supporting or protesting policies, groups or even countries. This reinforces impressions that Turkish universities are illiberal institutions. This picture is not wholly accurate in that individual members of faculty feel little constraint in expressing divergent opinions and, particularly at established universities, opinion on all matters is diverse and debate among faculty, lively.

There is another dimension of identifying with the state: the restraining of the government. Being a state institution rests on the assumption that this is a way of maintaining the autonomy necessary to ensure freedom of thought and expression. Yet, administrators have often appealed to autonomy to escape accountability rather than to ensure freedom. Even today, if less so, administrators may withhold promotion to faculty on thinly veiled ideological grounds but they reject plans to increase governmental oversight because autonomy would be threatened.

Universities are part of the public services: The laws view state universities, the core of the system, as public services, subject to the rules and regulations of government agencies. This introduces sometimes trivial but often serious constraints on how universities conduct their business. On the trivial side, for example, are the cases of students taking their professors to administrative courts to get their grade changed because grading is an 'administrative' act. On the more serious side is the fact that all professors are paid on a seniority-based civil-service scale. Administrators have little means to reward those who perform better. Similarly, they have no discretionary resources to attract new faculty or keep those offered better terms elsewhere. The 'subjugation' to cumbersome procedures makes it extremely difficult to manage research grants. To pursue research projects from acquiring private funding sources and carrying them out faces endless inflexibilities only circumvented by bending rules. Universities are not governed by a set of rules that match the nature of the public service they offer.

The university system is highly centralised: The university system has become highly centralised since 1981. Until then, it had been comprised of reasonably autonomous units. The 1981 law required compliance to a standard organisational–operational model allowing for no variety among universities, placing them under the control of the Council for Higher Education. The establishment of departments, programmes or research centres; determination of the number of students admitted to each department, level of admission scores employed, rules of transferring to different programmes or institutions, and preparing student disciplinary codes, all became prerogatives of the Council.

A society that is growing more sophisticated and developing highly differentiated needs requires a much more flexible and responsive university system which is cognisant of the individual student's preferences and interacts freely with its environment. This is impossible without dismantling central control. The mindset behind the current system aims at maximising order and discipline, not responding to societal needs. A new framework has to be created.

There is one positive outcome of the centralised system. Pressured by the Council, the Inter-University Council has produced improved instruments for measuring foreign language competence and scholarly achievements of faculty. Its main negative feature is that it has prevented universities from experimenting with innovative ideas and programmes.

The structure of governance excludes important stakeholders: A university has many stakeholders. The current system acknowledges the state and to lesser extents the government and faculty. The faculty is involved in the rector's nomination and in daily administration while the state runs the centrally administered system with a view to maximising security and ideological conformity. Other stakeholders hardly participate in university governance. In many societies, for example, graduates constitute a resource of ideas and finance. They have no formal role in Turkish university governance. Similarly, the business world that employs graduates is excluded. The nomination of candidates to the position of rector is seen as an exclusive faculty concern, overlooking the fact that students, staff, graduates and the community are also stakeholders. Formal structures allowing stakeholders to contribute to democratic governance of universities are lacking. This exclusionary stance, justified by appeals to autonomy and guardianship of the republican regime deprives the universities of resources and other beneficial opportunities.

Students do not contribute to meeting the cost of university education: Education is free at state universities in Turkey, apart from a small enrollment fee that varies between universities and departments. Attempts to introduce tuition fees have always been met with student demonstrations. State responsibility for free higher education became entrenched when the 1960 constitution stated it openly and the Constitutional Court declared private universities unconstitutional.[22]

It is difficult to defend a system of free tuition. As an individual's educational level rises, the benefits that accrue also rise, rendering it reasonable for her/him to contribute to its financing. Furthermore, many who gain admission to Turkish universities pay for their earlier education in two ways. Firstly, many expensive private high schools advertise that more of their graduates gain admission to universities. Secondly, many students enroll in expensive preparatory programmes for taking the admission test. We may also add that a substantial number of students seek to gain admission to state and private universities at the same time, suggesting that they may have the ability to pay. The proposition that students cannot afford tuition calls for empirical scrutiny.

State institutions operate with insufficient budgets: State institutions have rightly complained that current funding does not sufficiently meet their needs. Libraries often fail to maintain journal subscriptions or acquire recent publications; buildings are poorly maintained, other needs neglected and salaries are abysmally low, particularly in urban settings. Turkey must allocate a greater percentage of its national budget to state universities yet, there is no indication that public funding will increase substantially soon. Therefore, any future reform of the university system will have to consider higher tuition at state universities, even if lower than those of the growing private university system.

The universities operate in a seller's market: Turkish universities meet only part of the demand. In June 2004, for example, more than 1,900,000 high-school graduates took the entrance exam. A quarter gained admission to a university, many becoming students in universities and departments they did not want. Although in many instances the value added to an individual by higher education is not high, higher social status, the possibility of serving as an officer during military service for men, perceived improved job prospects and other considerations contribute to a swelling demand. Except at a few outstanding institutions, students are insensitive to quality of education. Being assured of students, the universities are not under pressure to improve performance.

Measures of faculty performance and institutional performance exist but work with limited success because reward and penalty mechanisms are lacking. For faculty, there is no system of rewards for those performing above average. For universities, retaining teaching faculty is paramount. The Council for Higher Education cannot do much either, since it wants universities to take on students, however underperforming they might be. Exceptions to this unpromising picture exist. Some universities have recently taken prominent institutions abroad as a reference to benchmark their activities. In most institutions some faculty, especially younger members with degrees from abroad conduct research and publish internationally. A system-wide instrument measuring publications to qualify for the habilitation exam encourages publishing among junior faculty. All universities have adopted some performance standards for promotion. Despite these, demand for universities exceeds supply, undermining pressures for evaluation and improvement.

Private institutions: A new actor in the system

Mainly through the efforts of the first head of the Council for Higher Education, Dr İhsan Doğramacı, the 1982 Constitution contained a provision for opening private universities subject to state oversight and control (Article 130). A year later, the idea was incorporated into the existing Universities Law.[23] The novelty was met with considerable ideological resistance from state universities. The first private institution opened five years later under the leadership of Dr Doğramacı was Bilkent University. Believing that private universities should develop and sensing that one alone would always be in jeopardy, he encouraged the opening of others. In Istanbul, Koç and in Ankara, Başkent University opened their doors in 1993. The openings accelerated after 1996 so that they are now an indispensable part of the system with more than 25 in operation.

Each private university has a board of trustees that appoints the rector with the Council's approval. On paper, their organisational–administrative model looks much like state universities but, there is variety between them of vision, mission and administration. Private institutions have been established by a variety of actors:

- Family based business conglomerates as a philanthropic undertaking, for example, Koç, Sabancı
- Independently wealthy men with a philanthropic orientation, for example, Has, Bilkent
- Foundations active in other fields moving into higher education – for example, Başkent by the Kidney Foundation, Haliç by Children with Leukemia Foundation
- Foundations that operated primary and secondary schools but wanted to move into higher education, for example, Yeditepe, Işık
- Commercial primary and secondary school owners that wanted to add a university to their line of activities. For example, Kültür, Bahçeşehir, Doğuş
- Quasi public bodies with significant resources e.g. Istanbul Ticaret established by the Istanbul Chamber of Commerce, Izmir Ticaret by similar means in Izmir.

- Building contractors that decided to go into the field of education, for example, Maltepe, Beykent
- Consortia of philanthropic businessmen and cooperating academicians, for example, Fatih and Istanbul Bilgi

Such a wealth of founders produces a variety of governance patterns but private university history is too brief to suggest patterns. In cases such as Koç and Sabancı established by family conglomerates, university administration is left to 'managers' with boards offering guidelines. More typical, however, is where trustees closely monitor what happens and offer their 'wisdom and skills' even if not solicited, on the running of the institution daily. This may change over time as they are replaced through retirement or natural causes, and the faculty develops a stronger *esprit de corps* but currently it is a problem. Interventionist tendencies of the trustees have prompted some rectors to seek the increase of Council intervention to balance trustee power.

There is one dimension of private universities that legitimises trustee intervention. State universities are funded from the national budget. They are assured that faculty and staff salaries will always be paid. Bankruptcy and closing are not contemplated. At private institutions income is not guaranteed but raised from tuition and charitable contributions. Most universities do not yet have income-yielding portfolios, while grants and gifts are limited and sound financial management is needed. Yet, administrators are academics with limited financial skills and trustee intervention may be useful for financial health.

Through time, some private universities will predictably become more institutionalised; relations between administrators and trustees will stabilise. Others may experience difficulties with some terminating their activities.

Private universities and the national university system

The legislation on private universities is imprecise, confusing and sometimes contradictory. For example, the constitution exempts their administrative and financial operations from central control, limiting regulation to academic matters. Yet the Council for Higher Education scrutinises them on everything. The inspectors study budgets, question administrative decisions and even suggest how the university should be run. The Council's policy has been to bring private institutions into the state fold. Private institutions have not presented a united front against this tendency. Some have tried to appease the Council to gain its favour while others have ignored its directives or actively opposed it. Since the directives sometimes lack a solid legal basis, the Council may not push institutions into obedience unless there is a clear violation, it may withhold cooperation on other matters. If an institution is weak internally (e.g. does not have a sufficient qualified faculty, fails to attract a sufficient number of students etc.) and cannot mobilise external support (e.g. not enjoy sufficient public esteem, has poor public relations, little political or external financial support), it is more likely to accommodate the Council.

For several reasons, state universities have wanted private institutions to submit fully to the system to which they are subject. First, there still exist some administrators who believe that university education is a state responsibility. Second, some feel that private universities attract inferior students and accommodate them academically to sustain enrollments. It has become evident through time that this logical claim bears little relationship to empirical reality. Third, some administrators are concerned that private institutions are stealing valuable faculty which could be prevented if they were not allowed. This concern is exaggerated, at the time of their founding, private institutions recruited from public universities, now they are recruiting largely new Ph.D. holders, many trained abroad. Similarly, some administrators have argued that state financial aid to some private institutions is taking money away from them. Again the sums have been small, totalling annually half the budget of a mid-sized state university. Fourth, some have feared that private institutions are a way of undermining the cohesive 'republican' stand of state universities. Finally, the greater freedom of action and flexibility private institutions enjoy may have elicited feelings of jealousy.

The Council for Higher Education is dominated by people with state university backgrounds, many questioning the appropriateness of private universities. Yet they have gained acceptance and legitimacy. The relations between private universities and the Council, how much they can deviate from the structure of the university system, whether they can conduct innovative experiments in administration and education, and the extent to which their views and needs will be accommodated in the future will depend on larger societal changes. As society becomes more democratic, the administrative system less centralised and the scope of politics expands away from the state, private universities will become more autonomous actors. Political change is in that direction.

The impact of private universities on the system of higher education

Private universities have changed the landscape of higher education. Many are simply teaching institutions, repeating what most state universities do. They have increased capacity but they are not a force for change or innovation. Irrespective of its nature, however, there is an important difference between a private and a state university. In the former, relations between the faculty, university, bureaucracy and students tend to be friendlier. This partly derives from disgruntlement of the overworked, underpaid faculty and staff at state universities. But, there is also an attitudinal difference since private institutions appeal to a narrower segment of the demand within which there is competition to attract students. Spaces are not always filled and students may transfer and this encourages service responsiveness.

The private institutions have greater flexibility in administration and finance, more capable of seizing opportunities in the national and international environment than state institutions. For example, they are more successful in working with diplomatic missions in inviting lecturers, organising conferences, running scholarship programmes, organising film festivals etc. because they make decisions and financial commitments quickly and are more punctual in realizing them. Similarly, they have been more open to international contacts, initiating bilateral relationships, developing student exchanges and hiring foreign faculty.

Faculty performance is generally more closely scrutinised and sanctioned at private institutions. Criteria of performance vary although the minimum is fulfilling teaching obligations, and for many, that is sufficient. That may explain why many private universities prefer to offer standard salaries based on rank and years of service rather than performance based differentiated salaries. Those universities that value research and publications like Bilkent and Koç reflect the differences in performance to their salaries. Sabancı and Bilgi, on the other hand, employ a strategy of positive reinforcement by giving monetary rewards to those who have published. These practices show that performance associated rewarding is possible. This has encouraged some state universities to find resources to reward their own faculty's research and publications.

The evaluation of institutional performance has also been a by-product of the opening of private universities. Statistics on annual publications by university faculty were initially developed to compare the performance of the first private university with those of state institutions. Slowly, the evaluation of institutional performance has made its way into the system. Currently, high performance brings only prestige but it has generated a renewed emphasis on research and publication. Turkey has moved up in the global ranking of scientific publications in recent years.

Finally, the efforts of private universities to publicise their facilities, activities, international cooperation, advantages and achievements so as to increase applications, have prompted some state universities to do the same. These have helped meet the needs of high school seniors who welcome any information they can get on where they can go, what they can study, what facilities they may find, whether they can stay in a dorm, or whether they are able to get a scholarship.

Conclusion

In this paper I have traced the development of the Turkish university system and its major characteristics. As is evident, the system has never been able to rid itself of the ambivalence generated by a conflict of interest between being a professional academic organisation and being a defender of republican values. In the meantime, the economic, social and political environment of Turkish universities has been changing. These processes integrating Turkey into the international system, particularly the EU, has intensified pressures for further professionalisation. Economic and political change, on the other hand, has challenged the ideological mission of universities and their tutelary orientation toward society.

Change is always painful. The university system does not appear capable of initiating change itself, nor does it have sufficient built-in flexibilities to allow it to accommodate pressures for change. In the past, major changes have all been brought about during non-democratic interludes under military pressure. There is a need for change again. The universities are not enthused and there is little consensus among them as to what kind of change, if any, i s desirable. Change will likely be introduced again from outside the university system, but this time probably by an elected government.

Notes

I wish to acknowledge my appreciation of my graduate assistants, Burç Beşgül and Oya Memişoğlu who helped find texts of laws, minutes of the parliamentary debates and many other documents.

1. The author started his career at the Faculty of Economics, Chair of Political Science of Istanbul University in 1964 and remained there until 1984 when he moved to the then recently established Faculty of Political Science where he served as the chair of International Relations. In 1993, he joined the faculty at the newly opened private Koç University. Five years later, he moved to Istanbul Bilgi University and served as its Rector during 1998–2001. He continues to teach at Bilgi.
2. The Darülfünun was comprised of a medical school, a law school, a faculty of letters, a faculty of sciences and a school of divinity. Cf. Milli Eğitim Bakanlığı (1998, p. 8).
3. Frederick W. Frey refers to the outcome as 'bifurcation of society based on educational achievement', pointing out that 'On the one side were the "modernists" influenced by a Western oriented, secular education and desiring to remold Turkey into an effective state respected by the West', in Frey (1965, p. 37).
4. Law No. 2253 İstanbul darülfünununun ilgasına ve Maarif Vekaletince yeni bir Üniversite kurulmasına dair kanun, 31 Mayıs 1933 in Düstur (1933) Üçüncü Tertip, Teşrinisani 1932–Teşrinievvel 1933 (Ankara: Başvekalet Matbaası)
5. The Prime Minister, introducing the Universities bill to the National Assembly. See Üniversiteler Kanunu Tasarısı ve Milli Eğitim ve Bütçe Komisyonları Raporları (1946, 1/579 – 27 Nisan, p. 3).
6. Shaw and Shaw note that ministerial control of the new university surpassed that over the Darülfünun. Cf. Shaw and Shaw (1977, p. 387).
7. Law no. 4619 dated 12 July 1944.

8. Law no. 4936 dated 13 June 1946, Article 78.
9. For factors creating pressures for democratic change, see for example, Turan (1969).
10. Ibid., p. 8
11. Ibid, p. 18.
12. For the debate, see T. B. M. M. Tutanak Dergisi (1946) *Cilt* 24, 11–13 June.
13. For example, the Dean of the Faculty of Political Science of Ankara University was taken into 'ministerial' custody for politically inspired criticism of government. This was followed by faculty resignations and student boycotts. See the chronology in Robinson (1963, p. 318). Shaw and Shaw attribute the 'political intransigence' of the faculty members in part to poor pay and lack of sufficient opportunity for promotion under a German inspired system of chairs. Cf. Shaw and Shaw (1977, p. 410).
14. Law no. 115, enacted 27 November 1960 was signed immediately by the president and published in the Official Gazette the next day. It went into effect within 24 hours of its enactment in the parliament. Usually, this procedure takes longer.
15. The junta, the National Unity Committee, decided with the probable cooperation of some university professors to terminate the employment of 147 members of the faculty of various ranks, but mainly professors failing to extend unqualified support to. Laws no. 114 and 115 that brought the important changes to Law 4936.
16. The developments of this period are aptly summarised in Eric J. Zürcher (1993, pp. 261–86 passim). The particular interpretation relating to universities is offered not by Zürcher, however, but by the author.
17. The tradition in most Turkish universities is the hiring of graduate assistants with the intention that they will eventually become permanent faculty members. The ideological sensitivity displayed at their recruitment stage is hardly surprising.
18. In its original form Law 2547 was accepted by the NSC prior to the adoption of a new constitution. The constitution, rather than constituting a framework for the new law, was devised to legitimise the existing situation. This removed any grounds to challenge the law on constitutional grounds.
19. The military subscribing to the ideology of the nation state thought that political competition could take place only within this framework.
20. Law no. 2547.
21. The military committee that assumed political power in 1980 called itself the National Security Council, but it is used here to refer to a military–civilian agency that is concerned with the questions that its name indicates.
22. In 1965, a law had allowed the Ministry of Education to authorise the opening and operation of 'high' schools that gave diplomas equivalent to university diplomas (Law no. 625, 18 June 1965). Schools pursuing open admission policies for tuition paying students were opened. State universities immediately identified these as diploma mills although their faculty came from state universities on a part time basis, and challenged their existence at the Constitutional Court. On 12 January 1971, the Court agreed that Article 120 of the constituiton made the state exclusively responsible for higher education (Decision 1971/3 published in the Official Gazette on 26 March 1971). The private institutions were incorporated into the state system.
23. Law no. 2880 dated 19 August 1983 that added 15 articles to Law no 2547. These changes hardly fit in with the rest of the law which was devised with only state universities in mind.

Bibliography

M. Ö. Alkan (2004) 'İmparatorluk'tan Cumhuriyet'e Modernleşme ve Ulusçuluk Sürecinde Eğitim', in K. H. Karpat (ed.) *Osmanlı Geçmişi ve Bugünün Türkiyesi* (İstanbul: İstanbul Bilgi Üniversitesi).

G. A. Baskan (2001) 'The Development of Higher Education in Turkey', *Gazi Eğitim Fakültesi Dergisi*, vol. 21, no. 1, pp. 21–32.

F. H. Erdem (2004) 'Türkiye'de Devlet-Üniversite İlişkisinin Siyasal Analizi', *Muhafazakar Düşünce*, vol. 1, no. 1, Summer, p. 196.

F. W. Frey (1965) *The Turkish Political Elite* (Cambridge: MIT Press).

İstanbul Darülfünununun İlgasına ve Maarif Vekaletince Yeni Bir Üniversite kurulmasına dair kanun (1933) *Düstur*, Üçüncü Tertip, Teşrinisani 1932-Teşrinievvel 1933 (Ankara: Başvekalet Matbaası).

H. K. Karpat (1973) 'Social Groups and the Political System After 1960', in K. H. Karpat (ed.) *Social Change and Politics in Turkey: A Structural-Historical Analysis* (Leiden: E. J. Brill).

B. Lewis (1961) *The Emergence of Modern Turkey* (London: Oxford University Press).

A. Malche (1939) *İstanbul Üniversitesi Hakkında Rapor* (İstanbul: Maarif Vekaleti).

Milli Eğitim Bakanlığı Yüksek Öğretim Genel Müdürlüğü (1998) *Cumhuriyetin 75. Yılında Yüksek Öğretim* (Ankara: Milli Eğitim Basımevi).

K. Öztürk (1966) *İzahlı, Gerekçeli, Anabelgeli ve Maddelere Göre Tasnifli Bütün Tutanakları ile Türkiye Cumhuriyeti Anayasası, Cilt III* (Ankara: Türkiye İş Bankası Kültür Yayınları).

R. D. Robinson (1963) *The First Turkish Republic: A Case Study in National Development* (Cambridge: Harvard University Press).

S. Shaw and E. K. Shaw (1977) *History of the Ottoman Empire and Modern Turkey, Vol. II* (London: Cambridge University Press).

T. B. M. M. Tutanak Dergisi (1973) 22 May, I. oturum.

T. B. M. M. Tutanak Dergisi (1946) *Cilt 24*, 11–13 June.

T. B. M. M. Zabıt Ceridesi (1933) Altmış dördüncü inikat, 31.V. 1933, Devre 4, İçtima 2.

I. Turan (1969) *Cumhuriyet Tarihimiz* (İstanbul: Çağlayan).

Üniversiteler Kanunu Tasarısı ve Milli Eğitim ve Bütçe Komisyonları raporları (1946) 1/579 – 27 Nisan.

E. Zürcher (1993) *Turkey: A Modern History* (London: I. B. Tauris).

9
Opportunities, Freedoms and Restrictions: Women and Employment in Turkey

Zehra F. Kabasakal Arat

Introduction

Although the terms are usually used interchangeably, 'work' and 'employment' are different concepts, and the distinction is particularly important to the construction of gender roles. While work includes labour that yields products and services that are essential to the sustainability of the family and society, if the value generated as a result of work has only a 'use value' rather than a 'market value', it is not included in employment and income statistics. The term 'employment' is usually used in reference to enumerated labour; people are considered to be employed if they receive wages or salaries for their labour or earn income by running their own businesses through self-employment. (Although, exceptions exist, for example in the case of female labourers in the agricultural sector of Turkey discussed later in this paper.)

Feminist theory and literature point to the social and economic importance of women's work and the recognition of the value of women's 'invisible' labour has been on the agenda of the advocates of women's rights for some time. Nevertheless most feminists also seek to increase women's employment, especially in the formal economy, for at least two reasons. First, they view women's employment outside the home as a way of breaking down gender barriers and undermining 'traditional' gender roles that define women's place as being at home. Second, they expect employment to enhance women's financial independence, which in turn would allow a woman to make her own choices and participate in the decision-making processes in the family, work place, social organisations, and political institutions. Consequently, improvements in women's employment are expected to pave the way towards women's liberation, empowerment, and gender equality.

In this paper, I examine women's employment in Turkey and explore the factors that have contributed to the low rate of female participation in the work force. I highlight two institutions that are particularly important in defining public attitudes and setting the cultural and structural constraints for women's employment: the state and religion. Although the secularisation project of the Kemalist leadership treated the state as a counter-force containing and controlling the influence of religion, I contend that the two institutions have consorted in forging a patriarchal gender ideology. Together they have created a normative/cultural milieu that reinforces women's dependency on men and restricts both women's rate of participation in the workforce and their employment opportunities. I later examine some developments since the 1980s and argue that they have led to an increase in women's demand for employment and legal reforms, but the opportunities have remained limited and as yet have failed to serve an emancipatory or empowering function. Among these interrelated factors that yielded a mixed outcome regarding women's employment in recent years, I discuss the following: the economic hardship caused by the restructuring of the Turkish economy according to neoliberal theory and the IMF-imposed structural adjustment programme; the rise of the women's movement; Turkey's candidacy of the European Union (EU) and the EU membership criteria; the rise of Islamist politics and the Justice and Development Party (AKP); and the legal reforms adopted since the 1990s.

The patterns and conditions of women's employment

Since the Second World War, women around the globe have made steady progress in a few areas. In addition to the improvements in literacy and education and attaining voting rights, women's participation in the labour force increased significantly. While the rate of progress has varied from one country to another, even in places where the change has been most profound, women still lag behind men on all political, social and economic indicators. As for employment, despite the increase in women's employment, women hold jobs and positions that are lower both in status and pay; they face insecurities, discrimination, sexual harassment, unfavourable work conditions, and the burden of household responsibilities alongside their work outside the home.

Women's employment in Turkey, being subject to all of these problems, does not appear to be atypical. However, Turkey deviates from the global pattern by sustaining a *decline* in women's participation in the workforce. Table 9.1 shows an overall decline in the economic activity rate from 83.7 per cent in 1955 to 48 per cent in 2006, which can be partially explained by an increase in educational opportunities (thus, entering the workforce is delayed) and improvements in life expectancy (thus, the retired population expands). However, the decline in the female economic activity rate is significantly higher and cannot be explained solely by improvements in education and health in Turkey.

In 1955, 72 per cent of the female population aged 15 and older was economically active, but with a steady decline, the activity rate fell to

Table 9.1 Economically active population rates, 1955–2006 (percentages for population 15 years of age or over)

Year	Total	Female	Male	Active female per 100 active male
1955	83.7	72.0	95.3	76
1960	79.6	65.3	93.6	69
1965	74.3	56.6	91.8	61
1970*	64.9	50.2	79.5	62
1975*	64.5	47.3	80.9	55
1980*	63.2	45.9	80.2	56
1985*	61.2	43.7	78.5	55
1990	56.6	34.1	79.7	44
1995	54.1	30.9	77.8	41
2000	49.9	26.6	73.7	37
2005	48.3	24.8	72.2	35
2006	48.0	24.9	71.5	35

Notes: For pre-1990 rates, the 'Unknown' is excluded in calculating percentages.
*Includes population 12 years age and over.
Sources: For 1955–85, State Institute of Statististics, Türkiye'de Kadın Bilgi Ağı, Table 5.2 www.die.gov.tr/tkba/istatistikler.htm (visited: 1 June 2004); for 1990–2006, Statistical Institute of Turkey, Statistical Indicators, 1923–2007, Table 91. http://www.tuik.gov.tr/yillik/Ist_gostergeler.pdf (visited 17 May 2009).

24.9 per cent in 2006. The 47.1 points of decline for women (47.1%) far exceeds the 23.8 points of decline noted for males (23.8%) during the last six decades. Moreover, while there were 76 economically active females for every 100 economically active males in 1955, in 2006 there were only 35 females. In fact, as reported in Table 9.2, the female share of the overall labour force declined from 43.1 per cent in 1955 to 36 per cent by 2000. These statistics clearly show that women's presence in the economy has been diminishing, and the gap between men and women has been increasing.

Traditionally, the main area of economic activity for women has been the agricultural sector, where women are typically employed as unpaid workers in family farms. Women's employment is expected to decline with economic development, due to the mechanisation of agriculture and urbanisation, but then as new employment opportunities emerge, women's economic activity rate starts to increase again (Boserup, 1990). In other words, a U-shaped relationship is observed between economic development and women's economic activity rate (Boserup, 1990). Moreover, it is noted that since transnational corporations have largely relied upon cheap female labour in developing countries, the economic activity rate of women increased in many developing countries during the recent phase of globalisation (Tinker, 1991; Wood, 1995).

In Turkey, however, we observe an inverse linear relationship between women's economic activity rates and development. Although the agricultural sector has been shrinking and women's participation in other economic

Table 9.2 Economically active female population by activity area (population 15 years of age or over)

Economic activity	% of economically active female population		% female within total economically active population	
	1955	2000	1955	2000
Total	100.00	100.00	43.1	36.0
Agriculture, hunting, forestry, fishing	95.64	75.16	53.3	56.6
Mining and quarrying	.02	.03	1.9	2.8
Manufacturing	2.28	6.59	16.5	18.8
Utilities	.008	.09	2.6	8.5
Construction	.04	.21	2.6	1.6
Trade, restaurants, hotels	.28	3.73	4.4	13.7
Transportation, communication, storage	.08	.69	2.3	7.4
Finance, insurance, real estate, business services	–	2.87	–	7.4
Community, social and personal services	1.13	10.47	11.9	3.7
Other	.51	.05	21.3	15.0

Sources: State Institute of Statistics (2004) *Statistical Indicators, 1923–2002* (Ankara: State Institute of Statistics) Tables 1.15 and 1.16.

sectors has been increasing, the displaced agricultural female labourers have not been fully absorbed by the non-agricultural sectors. As seen in Table 9.2, while 95.64 per cent of the economically active females worked in agriculture in 1955, by 2000 this figure fell to 75.16 per cent. Nevertheless agriculture remained the main area of employment for women; in 1955, females constituted more than half of the agricultural labour force (53%), and they continued to do so in 2000, even showing a small increase (56.6%). Although other activity areas recorded an increase in female participation, the improvements have been modest. As noted in Table 9.2, the most dramatic change was in the service sector (women's economic activity rate in trade, restaurants and hotels increased from .28% to 3.73%, and in community, social and personal services increased from 1.13% to 10.47%). In manufacturing, the percentage of the economically active female population increased from 2.28 per cent to 6.59 per cent, but the representation of women in this sector remained virtually the same, with only a 2.3 point increase from 16.5 per cent to 18.3 per cent.

In Turkey, women's economic participation rates have always been lower in urban areas. According to the 2007 data, 32.7 per cent of rural and 20.2 per cent of urban women were economically active, 83 per cent of rural female workers were employed in agriculture and 77 per cent of them worked as unpaid family workers (Başbakanlık, 2009, p. 22). Among the wage-labourers in the agricultural sector, the most disadvantaged segment includes women and children, because their wages are not only small but also tend to be paid to the man who is the head of the household (Özbay, 1991, p. 43).

Lack of access to their own earnings is a problem experienced by many women and girls. The most striking example is the carpet-weaving industry in rural areas, in which girls and young women work at home or in workshops all day, in some places from sunrise to sunset, but the carpets are marketed by male members of the family who collect and spend the money, often without any input from the women who earned it (Berik, 1984). Studies also show that women do not have much control over their earnings, even if they are directly paid, and invariably they spend all or most of their income on family needs (Başbakanlık, 1999, p. 172).

Women's earnings tend to be lower in all economic sectors and occupations, regardless of the educational level of the employees and the size of the workplace. According to a 2003 survey, on average men earn 42 per cent more than women (Türkonfed, 2007, p. 33). A comparative sector analysis, conducted in 1994, finds the largest gap in the agricultural sector, in which men earned 4.3 times more than women, and the only occupational area where the earnings of women and men approximated equality involved administrative, executive and managerial positions (State Institute of Statistics, 2004, Table 6.1).

However, women's promotion and representation rates in managerial positions have been low in all sectors. In 1999, among the women holding administrative ranks, more than two-thirds were unit heads (75.9%), 18 per cent branch directors, and 5.8 per cent department heads, and only 1.5 per cent were deputy general directors or vice-presidents (Başbakanlık, 1999, p. 36). In Turkey, educated and skilled female workers tend to concentrate in the public sector, and as revealed by the 1994 data, among public sector employees women held 65.9 per cent of the positions in legal services, 65.7 per cent in health services, 43.4 per cent in educational services, and 34.3 per cent in general administrative services; however, only 17 per cent of the judges and prosecutors were women; there were no female provincial governors (*Vali*), and out of 806 of the appointed governors to towns (*Kaymakam*), only 3 were women (Başbakanlık, 1999a, pp. 35–6). In 1990, while 44 per cent of the teachers employed by the Ministry of Education were women, women constituted only 7 per cent of school principals (Kabasakal, 1998, p. 226), and the situation was worse by 2003, when women's share of teaching positions increased to 67 per cent but their representation among principals declined to 4 per cent (Çelikten, 2005, p. 208). The 1990 Census indicated that within the health sector, women constituted 53 per cent of all personnel, 55 per cent of paramedics and 26 per cent of doctors; yet their representation in health administration remained very low (Başbakanlık, 1999a, pp. 35–6).

An area of employment where women in Turkey fare more favourably than women in many other countries has been academia; according to the 1998 statistics, women constituted 34.2 per cent of the faculty in universities, with a significant representation in natural sciences (35.6%), medicine (36.9%) and engineering (25.8%) (Acar, 1998, p. 313). However, women's representation declines in higher ranks (e.g., as opposed to 41.5 per cent of research assistants, only 22.2 per cent of full professors were women), as well as in administrative positions (15.9%) (Acar, p. 1998, p. 319).

Women's representation in management in the private sector has not been any better. Although there may be a few highly visible women managers who not only reach the top in their corporation but also play leadership roles in their respective industries (e.g., Gülay Sabancı and Arzuhan Doğan Yalçındağ), reviewing the findings of nearly forty years of research, which report that women constitute 3–4 per cent of top management in manufacturing, Hayat Kabasakal concludes that 'there has been no increase in the percentage of senior management positions filled by women in the manufacturing sector from the 1960s to the 1990s' (Kabasakal, 1998, p. 226).

Women who work as wage-labourers are also concentrated in certain areas and seldom move up to supervisory and managerial positions. In her study of industrial employment, Yıldız Ecevit points out that women's work in factories is separated from men's both horizontally and vertically:

> Women participate in certain stages of the production process and occupy the space that particular activity takes place. They usually don't work with men. When the production process requires working together, women and men are separated in terms of the tasks that they perform. Vertical segregation refers to the place of men and women in the factory hierarchy. While women are usually unskilled labourers, men are both skilled and unskilled labourers. Moreover, they [men] hold important supervisory positions ... The best position that a woman can acquire is group leadership, which is likely to happen only if all members of the group are women.
>
> (Ecevit, 1998, p. 277).

She further notes that although the form of the sex-based division of labour varies depending on the production type and industry, similar patterns and concentrations can be observed in most places: women in 'unskilled' and men in 'skilled' jobs; women in labour-intensive and men in capital-intensive activities; women in manual and men in machine work; women in 'light' and men in 'heavy' work; women in assembling pieces and men in producing the whole; women in the preparatory and finalising stages of production and men in the core of the production process (Ecevit, 1998,

p. 278). Moreover, what constitutes 'unskilled' or 'light' work is not defined objectively; for example women are assigned to assemble cans when the work is done manually and requires some muscle strength and skill, but the work is given to men when the process is mechanised and demands no skill or strength (Ecevit, 1998, p. 282).

Ecevit's study of the textile factories in Bursa reports that employers frequently argue that what keeps women from acquiring supervisor and management positions are their high level of absenteeism and their lower levels of education and training. Yet, she finds that contrary to those claims, men are *preferred* for supervisory positions over women even where equally educated and experienced female workers exist; she also notes that whenever the introduction of a new technology requires training, men are recruited and allowed to use the machinery (Ecevit 1991, pp. 64–7). The latter practice results in the concentration of female workers in 'unskilled', labour-intensive and lower-paying jobs. Ecevit explains the gender differences in specialisation, rank and wages by the employers' biases about women's natural skills (e.g., dexterity, fitness for boring and tedious jobs), assumptions about women's physical fitness, and the belief that men are the main providers for families and should thus be better paid – views that she finds to be common among union leaders as well (Ecevit, 1991, p. 73–4).

Işık Urla Zeytinoğlu's review of some research findings explains why women have limited and poor employment opportunities in urban areas in similar words: 'Most employers and managers are men, and they have negative attitudes toward women and prefer to hire men. Women are hired for jobs that do not attract men, or for jobs in which employers believe that women will be more obedient employees than men, willing to work in poor conditions, and less likely to unionise or strike' (Zeytinoğlu, 1998, p. 188).

Consequently, many poor urban women, who have to work, seek their chances in the informal sector (Başbakanlık, 1999b, pp. 29–37). Although statistics on the occupational distribution of the workforce in the informal sector in urban areas are not available, it is well known that a considerable number of women, especially the first and second generation of immigrant women, work in private homes as maids and 'cleaning women'. Wages, work conditions, and 'benefits' obtained through work in this kind of employment vary depending on the means, generosity and temperament of the employers (Kalaycıoğlu and Helga Rittersberger, 1998). Nevertheless a report, issued in May 2009, confirms that female employment in the informal sector has been higher than that of males and the gap is wider in rural areas:

In Turkey, although the employment in the informal sector has been over 45 per cent on the average, in 2000, it was 73.8% in rural areas (91.4% female and 64% male) and 28.8% in urban areas (30% female and 28.5% male); in year 2007, it was 66.6% on average (89.1% female and 55.3% male) and 33.4% in urban areas (36.6% female and 32.5% male).

While this figure [the informal sector share of the active workforce] was approximately 88% in agricultural activities, in 2007, it approached 32% in non-agricultural activities. These [findings] imply that informal sector employment concentrated in the agricultural sector in rural areas, especially among those who worked as unpaid family labourers. In 2007, while 22.7% of those who worked as unpaid family workers were male, women constituted 77.3% of them.

(Başbakanlık, 2009, p. 23)

The concentration of female labour in the informal sector exacerbates the problem of access to health care and social security. 98.7 per cent of women in the agricultural sector and 66.4 per cent of women in non-agricultural sector work are without any social security benefits (Türkonfed, 2007, p. 29). Turkey is in the process of creating a uniform social security system that combines three social security systems, Sosyal Sigortalar Kurumu (SSK), BAĞ-KUR, and Emekli Sandığı, which cover mainly wage workers, self-employed people and housewives, and civil servants, respectively. As of March 2007, among those who are insured, 58 per cent of women are covered by the SSK, 33 per cent by Emekli Sandığı, and 15 per cent by BAĞ-KUR (Başbakanlık, 2009, p. 23). Although the legislation process in 1983 yielded two laws that attempted to establish a social security system in the agricultural sector – the Agricultural Workers Social Security Law (no. 2925) and the Social Security Law for the Self-Employed in Agriculture (no. 2926) – these laws have been ineffective since they make subscription voluntary, not mandatory. A study on the female wage labourers in agriculture finds that 66.8 per cent of them are not covered by any social security system (Yıldırak et al., 2003).

Workers in Turkey acquired the right to unionise, exercise collective bargaining and strike in the 1960s, and a constitutional amendment of 1995 granted the same rights (except the right to strike) to civil servants. Although the overall rate of unionisation has been over 50 per cent, women's representation in both union membership (at around 15%) and administration has been dismal. Consequently, unions have not been responsive to the needs of female workers, such as childcare services and facilities (Özbay, 1991, pp. 52–3 and n.8). Meryem Koray, a long time observant of worklife and labour unions in Turkey, notes that gender discrimination in task assignment, promotion and lay-offs has not even been included in unions' agendas (Acar, Ayata and Varoğlu, 1999, p. 11).

Factors that contribute to women's low and declining participation in the workforce

The gap between the male and female economic participation rates is typically explained by women's lower level of educational attainment, gender bias of and discrimination by employers, women's household responsibilities and reproductive function, and patriarchal cultural norms about women's role and place in the society. These are interrelated factors that exacerbate each other's impact, and in Turkey, too, their interactive and cumulative impact works against women's employment.

Education

An important area where women recorded significant progress in Turkey has been education. While 90.2 per cent of the female population six years of age or older was illiterate in 1935, this rate had fallen to 19.4 per cent by 2000. However, the progress has not been equal for both sexes. In 1935, females constituted 57.7 per cent of the illiterate population; by 2000, this figure soared to 75.5 per cent (State Institute of Statistics, 2004, Table 3.2).

Not surprisingly, similar gaps have been observed in educational attainment levels, since schooling rates for girls decline as the education level increases (Gök and Ilgaz, 2007). The representation of girls in vocational education also tends to be lower, and the bulk of the vocational schools that are designed for or more likely to be attended by girls do not provide training that involves marketable or demanded skills. The Girls' Institutes and their graduates in particular excel in home economics and good housekeeping rather than training for or acquiring skilled jobs.[1] Another set of popular vocational school for girls has been those that offer religious education and train priests. 45.71 per cent of students in *imam hatip* high schools have been girls (Türkonfed, 2007, p. 53). However, since imam and hatip positions in mosques are not open to women, education in these institutions does not lead to employment for their female graduates.

The primary and secondary education system and curricula have also perpetuated cultural norms and gender roles that are based on an understanding that childcare, cooking, cleaning and other household tasks are women's responsibilities (Arat 1994a; Gümüşoğlu, 1998). The fact is, overburdened and restricted by these responsibilities, women cannot seek or compete for jobs in the formal economy and when they do so they face discrimination based on the same cultural norms and understandings of gender roles. These patriarchal norms remain pervasive due to their support by important and powerful institutions.

However, the empowering impact of higher education and its direct link to employment cannot be dismissed. Feride Acar juxtaposes the findings of two studies: A study of women who obtained higher education shows that nearly 70 per cent of these women worked and their work was supported by their family, 94 per cent had chosen their partners in marriage, 89 percent indicated that they participate equally in family decisions, 61 per cent believed that household chores should be equally shared by the partners and 35 per cent found their spouses' contribution to the housework inadequate; on the other hand, a study conducted in the urban slums, where the education level is low, finds that less than 10 per cent of women worked, 20 per cent of them had married a relative, 80 per cent consulted their husbands on all issues, and only half of them stated that their husbands ever consulted them before making a decision (Acar, 2003).

Patriarchal norms: Their institutional foundations and pervasiveness

As in most other countries, two powerful institutions, religion and state, have been most influential in dictating the norms and rules that shaped women's lives in Turkey. As a successor to the multicultural Ottoman Empire, the Republic of Turkey encompasses a diverse population that subscribes to different belief systems. However, Islam, which is followed by over 98 per cent of the citizens, has been paramount in shaping the cultural outlook of the country.

As a world religion that has been spreading for nearly one-and-a half millennia, Islam cannot be defined in singular terms, and like all aspects of its teachings, the gender ideology of the religion is open to interpretation. Nevertheless along with other Abrahamic religions, Islam was introduced to and shaped by patriarchal cultures, and more importantly, the major religious authorities devised and transmitted interpretations that placed women into a subordinate position. As I wrote elsewhere, like all religious texts, the holy Qur'an embodies complex and conflicting messages, some of which can be interpreted in favour of women by liberation theologies (Arat, 2000). The popularised versions of interpretations, however, have been highly gendered and employed toward affirming the subordination of women. While a comprehensive analysis of gender ideology in Islamic sources is beyond the purpose and space allocated to this paper, I will highlight a few Qur'anic references that are frequently invoked and used to reinforce women's dependency on men and restrict women's economic role and freedom.

Although the Qur'an allows women to own property under their own names, even after entering into a marital contract, it establishes an imbalance by assigning men inheritance rights that are twice those of women (Sura 4, verse 11). Instead of contextualising it, this element of inequality has been perpetuated and is often justified by Islamic jurists as a requirement of the responsibility assigned to men for serving as the *providers of their families*, also specified in the Qur'an (Sura 65, verses 6–7). However, assigning that task as a gender role creates and maintains other gender roles that subordinate women. In fact, verse 34 of sura 4 states:

> Men are managers of the affairs of women
> for that God has preferred in bounty
> one of them over another, and for that
> they have expended of their property.
> Righteous women are therefore obedient,

guarding the secret for God's guarding.
And those you fear may be rebellious
admonish; banish them to their couches,
and beat them. If they then obey you,
look not for any way against them;[2]

While the Qur'an does not require the concealing of women and the segregation of sexes, due to some sayings that are attributed to the Prophet and an interpretation of the veiling practised by the Prophet's wives as an ideal to be followed by all Muslim women, Muslims in many countries, including some in Turkey, have embraced veiling and the segregation of the sexes as requirements of the religion. An extension of these veiling and segregation practices has been the seclusion of women, with the definition of a woman's proper place as home, and of her presence in public places (without the company of a male member of the family) and interaction with other men as transgression. The cumulative effect of these interpretations has been the promulgation of the notion of an ideal household that is headed by a man who provides for his family and keeps his wife and female members of the family at home to raise children and fulfil other domestic responsibilities.

The modern Turkish state has also played a role in the perpetuation of patriarchal norms. In the 1920s, the Kemalist leadership launched a modernisation project that involved Westernisation and secularisation of the society, and encouraged women's participation in the public domain – including their participation in the economy. Its policies resulted in an increase in women's educational and employment opportunities. However, although the regime made a deliberate attempt to end the use of religion as the main guide and source of public and private law, the above-mentioned morality and gender roles, attributed to Islam, were followed by the secularist political leadership, as well.

Despite the somewhat feminist stance evident in the 1926 Family Law, which ended some discriminatory practices (e.g., polygamy, unequal inheritance rights, divorce by repudiation by men) or in the expansion of education opportunities for women, the overall approach of the regime fell short of seeking gender equality or empowerment of women. The secular yet still patriarchal approach of the regime maintained women's dependence on men. This approach can be observed in laws and administrative policies pursued since the 1920s (Arat, 1994b). For our purposes, I highlight the legal provisions that reflect the intention of sustaining male dominance and restricting women's employment. (The relatively recent changes in these laws are discussed in the last section, under 'Legal Reforms').

Family law of 1926: The Civil Law failed to establish full legal equality between the sexes and contained several articles and clauses that placed men first among equals. The Law identified the man as the head of the union of marriage (Article 152/I). According to this law, the right and responsibility of deciding the place of residence belonged to the husband (Article 152/II). It was also the husband's responsibility to provide for his wife and children (Article 152/II). Although the father and mother shared the guardianship responsibilities, in case of a disagreement, the right of guardianship would be given to the father (Article 263). The union of marriage was represented by the husband (Article 154). Although the wife had some representative rights, they were limited to legal representation in matters that dealt with providing 'the continuous needs of the house' (Article 155). The wife could take a job or engage in a craft only with the 'explicit or implicit permission' of the husband (Article 159/I). The husband, on the other hand, could require his wife to contribute to the family budget to 'a reasonable extent' (Article 190). Upon marriage, the wife had to assume and use the husband's family name (Article 153/I). The wife was held responsible for taking care of the house (Article 153/II). However, she was never given the primary role, and in fact, Article 153/II specified that 'to the extent that she can, the wife serves as the assistant and consultant of her husband to pursue the happiness of the family'.

Labour laws: The regulation of the labour market and work through legislation was not attempted until the 1950s. Various employment laws and the Civil Servant Law were mainly gender neutral (Zeytinoğlu, 1998, pp. 191–2), but by the same token, they were silent on some women's issues. The Labour Law (no.1475), enacted in 1972, applied to 'workers,' defined as individuals 'employed under a labour contract and earning a wage' (Article 1), including those in the private and public sectors and engaged in both manual and non-manual labour. Assuming a protective posture toward female workers, Article 69 of the Law no. 1475 imposed a ban on 'night work' by women and children. Similarly, Article 68 prevented the employment of women of all ages and male children for work that took place under ground or water. It further restricted employment for women by banning them from jobs that involved physically demanding, dangerous and poisonous activities to prevent an impact on the reproductive function of women. Consequently, women had not been able to participate in better-paying industrial jobs in mining, construction, and heavy metal and manufacturing industries (Kazgan, 1979).

The discriminatory clauses of the Civil and Labour laws, together, tended to preserve the sexual division of labour as well as women's dependence on men, both socially and economically. Society henceforth has not treated 'work' as a right of women, or as a means for fulfilling women's individual needs. Labour laws also failed to assist women and accommodate their needs – such as providing equal pay for comparable work, job security in case of pregnancy and childbirth, protection against sexual discrimination in hiring/firing or sexual harassment, or any assistance for childcare.

An attempt was made to protect maternity and motherhood under Article 70 of the Labour Law, which banned women from work for six weeks prior to and six weeks after the birth. However, by introducing maternal leave as a 'ban' rather than a 'right' of women, lacking provisions that would guarantee a sufficient amount of leave after birth in case of late deliveries, allowing the employer to unilaterally end the contract at the end of the maternity leave (Article 13/a), the law undermined its own protective provisions. Moreover, maternity leave was organised differently in various labour laws that applied to women in different occupations (e.g., the workers, the press employees, civil servants, etc.) (Başbakanlık, 1999, pp. 93–4). Childcare facilities did not become a concern of legislators until the 1980s.

Despite secularist claims, the thinking underlying the legislation that gave man the upper-hand in managing family affairs, designated him the head of the household, and made women's employment conditional upon the husband's approval has overlapped with the patriarchal religious discourse. Both the state and religion have set the norms that defined 'women's proper place as home' and women's employment (or earning money) as relevant only as a supplement. Moreover, both institutions have reinforced the power of men within the family and allowed them to define what is proper for their wives.

Public attitudes toward women's employment

A survey study of values conducted in 1990 found that 86 per cent of the sample population approved of working couples, but 80 per cent believed that being a housewife can be as satisfactory as working outside the home; more importantly, however, more than half of the participants (52%) advocated that priority should be given to male applicants in cases of limited employment opportunities and high unemployment (Acar, Ayata and Varoğlu, 1999, p. 8).

A study of human resource administrators in the public sector revealed that the majority of administrators considered submissiveness to be the most important characteristic of women employees, believed that women's presence in the public sector had negative consequences, and subscribed to the notion that women's biological functions and emotional nature prevented them from being objective and successful in decision making (Acar, Ayata and Varoğlu, 1999, p. 13). According to another study, conducted by the General Directorate on the Status and Problems of Women, the public views the employment of a woman as acceptable and legitimate only after she fulfils her responsibilities as a wife and mother – a finding that the researchers use to explain why urban women's participation in the workforce peaks at the ages of 20–24 and sharply declines at the ages of 25–29, during which women tend to marry and start having children (Başbakanlık, 2000, p. 17). The average length of working life for a woman is noted as eight years, after which she leaves the workforce for family-related reasons such as marriage, pregnancy or caring for a sick family member (İlkkaracan, 1998, pp. 286 and 291). Women, too, may think of employment outside the home as inappropriate and undesirable.

The majority of working women indicate that they work because of financial need; otherwise, they would prefer to stay at home.[3] Women's lack of desire for work is understandable given the fact that most of them work in highly demanding, insecure jobs for low wages, while still carrying the burden of fulfilling the household responsibilities. The role of stress and work conditions in shaping their attitude toward work becomes clearer in the light of the survey results that show that the most common response to the question 'as a woman what would be the priority changes that you would like to make in your life', is 'to go to school and work as a career woman' (İlkkaracan, 1998, p. 298). Studies also indicate that even when their earnings are substantial and constitute nearly half of the family income, women tend not to see their earnings as a major contribution, but treat it as supplementary income useful to meet some daily needs (Başbakanlık, 1999a, b, pp. 170–5; Kalaycıoğlu and Rittersberger, 1998, p. 226; Ecevit, 1991).

Recent developments

The year 1980, which witnessed a military coup d'état that led to three years of military rule, is considered a turning point in the Turkey's history for many reasons. Following this upheaval, some developments that took place after the country returned to civilian rule in 1983, set new trends. Changes in four areas are particularly important for our purposes: the change in economic policies; Turkey's candidacy of the European Union; the rise of the women's movement; and the rise of Islamist politics and the Justice and Development Party (AKP). These largely simultaneous and interrelated developments have affected women's lives but not in a single direction; they created both opportunities and hardships.

Economic policies

The military coup enabled the implementation of the IMF structural adjustment policies (SAP) adopted by the civilian government in January 1980 without any public resistance and opposition. The underlying philosophy of the SAP was later internalised by several political leaders that dominated post-1980 politics, starting with Turgut Özal, whose Motherland Party was brought to power by the first elections after the military coup, in 1983. The Özal government's trademark and legacy was economic liberalisation and shifting Turkey's industrialisation strategy from import-substitution to an export-oriented one. An inevitable impact of the economic liberalisation policies, along with the implementation of other requirements of the IMF, which were later reinforced by the economic criteria of the EU membership and thus have been guiding the Turkish economy for nearly four decades, was the deterioration of the already wide income gaps. Between 1987 and 1994, the income share fell for all quintiles except for the highest one (which marked an increase from 49.9% to 54.9%), and consequently the GINI Coefficient for income inequality rose from .44 to .49 (Human Development Report, Turkey, 1998, p. 43).

Although the shift to export-led industries created some opportunities for women in labour-intensive industrial sectors such as textiles, the new sectors have not been impressive in the quality or number of jobs that they have created. In fact, investments in the industrial sector and its employment capacity declined, especially for women (Ecevit, 1991, pp. 108–10) who sought employment opportunities in the service sector. Despite the noted increase in this sector, the jobs created could not compensate for the losses in the agricultural sector nor the increase in the population.

A large portion of employment in the service sector has been within the public sector, but that sector has been targeted by the SAP that called for both privatisation and reducing the government sector. The privatisation and reform of state-owned economic enterprises led to the dismissal of a number of workers (Tansel, 2005), with reductions taking place especially in the Ministries of Education, Health and Social Security, and Transportation, which have been traditionally major employers of women (Ecevit, 1991, p. 111). Consequently, unemployment rates have increased, and in 2007, the female unemployment rate reached 10 per cent on average and 17.4 per cent in the non-agricultural sector. The unemployment among young urban women who have graduated from high school (17.7%) is nearly twice as high as the unemployment rate among men in the same category (9.2%) (Başbakanlık, 2009, p. 23).

The economic hardship was further intensified by the SAP that also required freezing wages and restricting subsidies, which resulted in the deterioration of income distribution and the decline of real wages (Ecevit, 1998, p. 37) and pushed more family members into the workforce. The end result has been the expansion of the informal sector, which provides insecure and marginal jobs, substandard work conditions, and low pay.

Labour analysts agree that the official employment figures do not match the reality because they exclude or underestimate the informal sector, which has become increasingly important for women (Özbay, 1991, p. 46; Ecevit, 1991, pp. 11314 and 1998, pp. 57–71; Human Development Report, 1998). Women cannot compete well with men in the institutionalised labour market. In addition to the educational disadvantages, they 'are less mobile in the labour force due to domestic obligations and are more vulnerable to the bottlenecks created by traditional values' (Human Development Report, 1998, p. 48). Noting the significant amount of time spent by women on housekeeping and childcare, as well as on production of food and other consumer goods for family consumption, Özbay argues:

> In sum, even if some of their activities can be referred to as 'economic activity' [employed] women are primarily housewives. Thus, they use at

least part of their labour at home. In economics, consumption oriented production at home is excluded in labour-related discussions. However, when the issue is approached sociologically, it is observed that the lower activity and productivity rates of the female workforce compared to male workforce, the difficulty in identifying the 'active' women, the concentration of [women's labour] in low status jobs, all stem from the necessity of engaging female labour in consumption oriented activities at home. This necessity is generated by social values, in fact by laws. In other words, female labour is not completely unfettered even in capitalism.

(Özbay, 1991, p. 53)

In fact, those women who work as unpaid labourers in agricultural and non-agricultural sectors, as well as waged labourers who work irregularly or who perform income-earning activities at home, tend to define themselves as 'housewives' rather than as 'working-women' (İlkkaracan, 1998, p. 289).

The European Union and international law

In addition to the radical policy shifts in economy, the Özal government took bold political steps to better integrate Turkey with the Western economies and international organisations, especially with the European Union. Thus, acting on Turkey's long-time aspirations to join the EU, Özal formally applied in April 1987 and in the same year, perhaps in order to demonstrate Turkey's commitment and strengthen its chances of being accepted to the EU, he moved toward recognising the jurisdiction of the European Human Rights Court (a process that was finalised by the Akbulut government in December 1989).

Successive Turkish governments also intensified the ratification of international human rights treaties, including the United Nations Convention for the Elimination of All Forms of Discrimination Against Women (CEDAW). After ratifying CEDAW in 1985, Turkey also became a party to the Optional Protocol to the Convention in October 2002. In order to fulfil the state's obligations under the Convention, the government made some institutional arrangements. In 1990, the government established the Directorate General on the Status and Problems of Women under the Ministry of Work and Social Security, as the national executive office that would coordinate state efforts; and when it designated a state ministry responsible for women and family, it brought the Directorate under the Office of the Prime Ministry. Offices on women were also created within different ministries and state agencies, including the Ministry of Labour, State Planning Organisation and the State Institute of Statistics. These offices, which focus on women and their rights, and other administrative agencies created to monitor and oversee human rights practices and policies – for example, the parliamentary

Commission on Human Rights, the State Ministry responsible for human rights issues, the Coordinating High Commission of Human Rights (İnsan Hakları Koordinatör Üst Kurulu) – have helped increase the attention given to women's issues, even though they lack the institutional power and funds necessary to accomplish significant change.

The watchful eyes of the EU pressured the government to undertake legislative and administrative reforms that would help improve women's status, and women's organisations in Turkey used Turkey's bid for the EU membership as leverage to press for a reform agenda. Although, the European Parliament, the Council of Europe and various women's organisations in European countries have paid attention to the problems and improvements in areas that concern women, the overall impact of the EU on women's employment opportunities and lives has not always been positive.

While the EU's political criteria for membership – human rights, democracy and rule of law – stimulate reforms that recognise and protect women's civil and political rights, its economic criteria, which calls for privatisation, competitiveness and flexible labour markets, are in sync with the IMF's neo-liberal policies and aggravate the economic problems and hardship faced by women (Arat and Smith, forthcoming 2010). The recent social security reform may serve as a case in point.

Social Security and Public Health Insurance Law (no. 5510), which was legislated first on 31 May 2006 but considered void after the Constitutional Court rejected 22 of its articles, was finally adopted by the parliament with some minor revisions on 17 April 2007. This 'gender neutral' law includes certain provisions that not only effectively remove some of the rights granted to women by the previous legislation but also includes certain provisions that make it harder for women to gain access to social security and health benefits. The law was subject to protest by various women's groups and health professionals, but the EU was completely silent on the protested items and endorsed the law.

Women's movement

A significant change in Turkish politics involved the emergence of a women's movement in the mid-1980s and the proliferation of women's organisations (Sirman, 1989). Although sceptical of the state agencies and concerned about being co-opted by the state (Ecevit, 2007), women's organisations engaged in the legislative reform process. They embraced the CEDAW and used it and other international human rights instruments to pressure the state, at times collaborating with state agencies to implement the convention provisions and improve women's conditions. Women's activism, combined with the government's desire to improve Turkey's prospects of joining the EU, yielded some changes in laws that were favourable to women.

The rise of Islamist politics and the AKP

The rise of Kurdish nationalism and Islamist politics, which both included organised militia groups, arguably caused the most divisive and disruptive events in the post-1980 period, the scars of which will continue to affect the nature of politics in Turkey for some time. Islamists groups have also pursued their power struggle through party politics, protests, and street demonstrations. They have challenged the secularist state by problematising the policy that bans the wearing of headscarves at universities and by public employees in government offices as a human rights issue. Framing the ban as a violation of religious freedom, Islamist groups and parties sought to mobilise women. Islamist women, however, reframed the headscarf ban not only as an issue of religious freedoms and rights but also an issue of sexual discrimination that violates women's rights to education and employment. Thus, while challenging the secularist state and demanding Islamist women's right to enter the public space and seek education and employment, Islamist women also raised questions about the traditional interpretations of the religion that emphasise sexual division of labour, prescribe segregation of sexes and define women's place in the home and attempted to separate these cultural norms from the essence of Islamic principles (İlyasoğlu, 1998). They have also participated in the women's movement and have collaborated with secular women's groups in pressuring the government on a range of issues such as the implementation of CEDAW and amending the constitution in favour of gender equality.

The power struggle of the Islamists resulted in a landslide victory of an Islamist party, the Justice and Development Party (Adalet ve Kalkınma Partisi, AKP), during the November 2002 elections, and the AKP formed a majority government that ruled for five years. After another round of successful campaigning and elections in July 2007, it returned to parliament as the largest party and resumed governance of the country.

The ideological stance of the AKP has been subject to debate. The predecessor of the AKP, the Welfare Party (WP) headed by Necmettin Erbakan in the 1990s, attempted to close the limited number of women's shelters, defined women's primary roles as housewives and mothers, and supported segregation of the sexes and limiting women's economic participation – to only four hours, two days each week. The leaders of the AKP, some of whom were prominent figures in the WP, broke ties with the Erbakan group. Defining themselves as 'Conservative Democrats', they have claimed to be religious yet not Islamist. Although the electoral success of the AKP can be largely explained by its ability to convince a large segment of the electorate, the extent to which the party leadership has changed its gender approach and will be able to resist its conservative members' and constituencies' remain questionable. Parliamentary debates during the legislative reforms (especially on women-related articles of the Constitution and the Penal

Code, which took place in spring and autumn of 2004, respectively) revealed the persistence of traditionalism among the AKP deputies, indicating that women may have more foes than allies within the ranks of the governing party.

Their desire to keep adultery as an offence against public morality in the Penal Code, opposition to the failed constitutional amendment that would protect affirmative action toward gender equality, and insistence on keeping a provision of the new Civil Code that requires a wife to take the husband's last name are but a few instances that raise scepticism about the AKP's commitment to gender equality. Resistance to change in favour of gender equality appears be stronger at the local level. A self-help booklet for newlyweds prepared and distributed by the Altındağ municipal government in Ankara demonstrated the persistence of patriarchal values among AKP members. Promoting traditional gender roles, opposing women's education, and supporting men's control in the family, the booklet became a target of protests by women's groups in late 2005. Consequently, its distribution was stopped by an order of the central government. Some women's groups also raise concerns about the overall 'Islamisation of public life' during the last few decades, particularly since the AKP came to power, and are sceptical about the Islamist feminists' ability to be a powerful interpretive voice that would surpass the traditionalist and patriarchal interpretations of religious norms.

Legal reforms

Starting in the late 1980s, state institutions started to liberalise and amend the discriminatory aspects of some laws. A milestone in the legal reform process was the Constitutional Court's decision of 29 November 1990, which itemised the articles of the Civil Law that violated the principle of equality of sexes, which is protected by the Constitution and included in several international conventions to which Turkey has become a party (Başbakanlık, 1999, p. 64). Consequently, Article 159 of the Civil Law, which made a woman's employment conditional on her husband's approval, was abolished by a Constitutional Court decision that became effective upon its publication in the Official Paper on 2 July 1992. The Constitutional Court annulled some other provisions of the Civil Law and other legislation on the basis of their being in violation of the principle of equality of sexes (e.g., provisions on adultery in the Penal Code, which defined the act of adultery differently for men and women, were annulled in 1996).

The protection of women against domestic violence was incorporated into the Law on the Protection of Family (no. 4320), enacted on 14 January 1998. The Law listed the forms of violence and unacceptable behaviour (Article 1), defined the obligations of the state and the procedures to be followed, and set the penalty for the violators of the 'protection decision' by the court at imprisonment ranging from three to six months (Article 2).

The overhaul of the Civil Code did not take place until November 2001, when a new Civil Law (no. 4721) was issued. The new law, which entered into force on 1 January 2002, marks a drastic shift toward equality by employing the term 'spouse' instead of gender-specific references and avoiding allusions to sexual division of labour and responsibilities within marriage. It defines marriage as a union in which 'spouses are obliged to maintain the happiness of the union together and attend to the care and education of the children jointly' (Article 185). Together, they choose their domicile; manage the union; and contribute to the family expenses with their labour and wealth, according to their ability (Article 186). Both of the spouses represent the union throughout their life together (Article 188). As for employment and work, the Law notes: 'Neither of the spouses would need the permission of the other in choosing an occupation or work. However, the peace and interest of the union of marriage is considered in occupation and work choices and their performance' (Article 1992). Article 202 also specifies that the joint property regime is the default for the wealth acquired by the spouses during the marriage, for those who marry after the law enters into force. However, the law maintains patrilineal norms by requiring the woman to take the family name of the man upon marriage, and allowing her to use her maiden name before the husband's last name only upon the approval of a written petition submitted to the office of population registration (Article 187).

The legal reforms also include laws and regulations that are directly related work. An important effort to assist pregnant women and working mothers was the Regulation on Conditions of Work for Pregnant or Nursing Woman, Nursing Rooms and Day-care Nurseries in 1987. The Regulation entitles women to a paid leave for medical check-ups during the first trimester of pregnancy and one month after the delivery. It also dictates: 'In workplaces that employ 100–150 female workers, regardless of their age and marital status, there has to be a nursing room, for the care of the children age of 0–6 and for the lactating women to nurse their children, provided by the employer within the 250-meter vicinity of the women's work-site'. Despite its good intentions, the regulation has failed to create such facilities; on the other hand, it is argued that the specification of the number of female workers employed in defining the employer's obligation worked against women, because employers have tried to keep the number of female workers under 100 to avoid opening a nursery (Acar, Ayata and Varoğlu, 1999, p. 9; Zeytinoğlu, 1998, pp. 192–3; Başbakanlık, 1999, p. 94).

The new Labour Law (no.4857), enacted on 22 May 2003 and entered into force on 10 June of the same year, has addressed some shortcomings of the previous Labour Law (no. 1475). Article 74, which covers issues of maternity and pregnancy, entitles women to paid leave for periodic medical check-ups during pregnancy; increases the length of maternity leave before and after birth to eight weeks for a total of 16 weeks, and extends it to

18 weeks in case of multiple-births; allows women to use the time unused during late pregnancy after the delivery; permits reduction in the work load during pregnancy and extension of leave as dependent on the medical report by a doctor; and entitles each woman with infant children to have up to one-and-half-hours of nursing breaks, the timing, frequency and length of which are to be determined by the woman herself. The Law also assures that none of these periods of leave count toward the annual vacation of the employee (Article 55), and imposes a fine of TL 500 million on the employer or employer's representative who violates these provisions (Article 104).

However, the new labour law also bans women from work that takes place underground or underwater, and assigns the authority of determining women's employment for 'heavy and dangerous' work or work at night to a regulation issued by the Ministry of Work and Social Security, upon consultation with the Ministry of Health (Articles 72 and 73, respectively).

The legislative reforms of the last decade also included amendments to the Constitution itself. A law enacted on 3 October 2001 amended Article 41 on the protection of family, revising the first paragraph that defined the family as 'the foundation of Turkish society' with the addition of a clause describing it as 'based on equality of the spouses'. The equality and non-discrimination clause (Article 10) was amended in May 2004 to add a paragraph that reads: 'Women and men have equal rights. The state is obliged to realise this equality in life'. The Penal Code, which has been notorious for restricting freedoms yet tolerating violence against women (e.g., rape and honour killings) by allowing reduced sentences or dropping charges if the rapist agrees to marry his victim, was replaced by a new law in October 2004. The new law falls short of meeting all demands of women's groups but removes all gender biases of the previous law, recognises marital rape as a crime, and increases penalties for crimes committed against family members.

Conclusion

Given the conditions and characteristics of women's employment in Turkey, it is not surprising that the main reason women work is economic need. Since women enter the labour force out of necessity, rather than choice and face various hardships and obstacles to advancement, employment has been far from emancipatory or empowering for most women. Moreover, the prevailing culture leads women in Turkey to remain more 'family and marriage oriented'; their life planning is not based on living alone or heading a family but is instead geared toward marriage (Başbakanlık, 1999, p. 176).

Only urban upper-class women (both secular and Islamist), who hold professional jobs and are able to buy the labour of other women (and quite a few of them are able to do so, thanks to the skewed income distribution and availability of cheap labour from immigrant women), are likely to see employment as a means to self-fulfilment and economic independence. Yet, even within those strata, only a few women climb up the ladder and even fewer reach important decision-making positions at work. Nevertheless some survey studies provide evidence that an increase in women's participation in the workforce and improvement in their position and conditions at work may make employment more desirable for women and help them gain more control over their lives, family affairs and household decisions (Başbakanlık, 1999; Erman, 1998, p. 217; İlkkaracan, 1998). Such progress, however, would require overcoming the biases that have been prevalent within all segments of the society and reinforced by essentially patriarchal laws.

The recent changes in the law are promising. They at least remove one category of normative support that was previously granted to discriminatory practices. With some pressure from both national and international organisations, such as women's organisations, human-rights groups, the European Union (EU), and the United Nations, the Turkish government and other state agencies may also take concrete steps toward implementing the new laws. The EU, in particular, has a powerful hand and is likely to achieve some progress in eliminating legal obstacles to women's employment. However, the EU may undo what it achieves in the legal domain with the policies that it pushes in the economic domain. As EU member countries pursue economic and social policies that indicate a shift from a commitment to social welfare and security to increasing productivity and trade competitiveness, the economic criteria for membership and the rising tide of neoliberalism may lead the EU to require Turkey to follow polices that would only aggravate the current trend and push more and more workers, especially women, into the informal sector and undercut their social security.

Also questionable are the intentions of the ruling party. While women's rights find some supporters among AKP members and parliamentarians, the numeric and political strength of these individuals is not clear or reassuring. In addition to the parliamentary debates and municipal initiatives that reveal the persistence of the traditionalist gender approach among the AKP deputies and mayors, Recep Tayyip Erdoğan, the Prime Minister and head of the AKP, has repeatedly rejected women's demand for an electoral quota system that would help in improving women's representation in parliament.

Notes

1. For information on Girls' Institutes, their significance and patriarchal ideological underpinnings, see Tan (1979) and Arat (1994a).
2. *The Koran Interpreted* (1955). The root of the Arabic words that are translated here as 'managers of the affairs' and 'beat' and their 'authentic' intentions and meanings have been a subject of dispute among conservative and modernist exegetes. For various modernist/feminist exegeses, see Barazangi (1997); Engineer (1992); Wadud (1999). For a brief review of the different interpretations of the verse, see Stowasser (1998; 1994).

3. In Ecevit's study of factory workers, this group constitutes 83 per cent of the women (Ecevit, 1991, p. 59). Yıldırak et al. found that 46.4 per cent of agricultural wage-workers would rather be housewives (p. xv). Tekeli (1982) considers the sentiment to be common among relatively better educated, white-collar urban women.

Bibliography

F. Acar (1998) 'Türkiye Üniversitelerinde Kadın Öğretim Üyeleri', in *75 Yılda Kadınlar ve Erkekler* (Istanbul: Türkiye Ekonomik ve Toplumsal Tarih Vakfı).

F. Acar, A. Ayata and D. Varoğlu (1999) *Cinsiyete Dayalı Ayrımcılık: Türkiye'de Eğitim Sektörü Örneği* (Ankara: T.C. Başbakanlık, Kadın Statüsü ve Sorunları Genel Müdürülüğü).

F. Acar (2003) 'Toplumsal Cinsiyet ve Değişim Dinamikleri', in *Türk Alman Diyaloğuna Katkılar: Hak ve Cinsiyet* (Haburg: Körber-Stıftung).

A. Akin, S. Üner, D. Aslan, Ç. Esin and A. Coşkun (2004) *Türkiye'de Toplumsal Cinsiyet ve Sağlık (Gender and Health in Turkey)* (Ankara: T.C. Başbakanlık, Kadın Statüsü ve Sorunları Genel Müdürülüğü).

Z. F. Arat and T. Smith (forthcoming 2010) 'The EU and Human Rights in Turkey: Political Freedom without Social Welfare?', in H. Carey (ed.) *What Difference Does the EU Make for Democratization and Human Rights?* (Lanham: Rowman and Littlefield).

Z. F. Arat (2000) 'Women's Rights in Islam: Revisiting Qur'anic Rights', in P. Schwab and A. Pollis (eds) *Human Rights: New Perspectives, New Realities.* (Boulder, CO: Lynne Rienner Publishers).

Z. F. Arat (1998) 'Educating the Daughters of the Republic' in Z. F. Arat (ed.) *Deconstructing Images of The Turkish Woman* (New York: St. Martin's Press).

Z. F. Arat (1994a) 'Liberation or Indoctrination: Women's Education in Turkey', *Journal of Economics and Administrative Studies*, vol. 8, no. 1–2, pp. 83–105.

Z. F. Arat (1994b) 'Kemalism and Turkish Women', *Women and Politics*, vol. 14, no. 4, pp. 57–80.

N. H. Barazangi (1997) 'Muslim Women's Islamic Higher Learning as a Human Right', in M. Afkhami and E. Friedle (eds) *Muslim Women and the Politics of Participation: Implementing the Beijing Platform* (Syracuse, NY: Syracuse University Press).

T. C. Başbakanlık (2009) Türkiye'de Kadının Durumu (Ankara: T. C. Başbakanlık, Kadının Statüsü Genel Müdürlüğü).

T. C. Başbakanlık (2000) *Türkiye'de Kadınlara Ait Girişimlerin Desteklenmesi* (Ankara: T. C. Başbakanlık, Kadının Statüsü ve Sorunları Genel Müdürülüğü).

T. C. Başbakanlık (2000) *Sağlık Sektöründe Kadın* (Ankara: T. C. Başbakanlık, Kadın Statüsü ve Sorunları Genel Müdürülüğü).

T. C. Başbakanlık (1999a) *Yeni Üretim Süreçleri ve Kadın Emeği* (Ankara: T. C. Başbakanlık, Kadın Statüsü ve Sorunları Genel Müdürülüğü).

T. C Başbakanlık (1999b) *Çalışmaya Hazır İşgücü Olarak Kentli Kadın ve Değişimi* (Ankara: T. C. Başbakanlık, Kadın Statüsü ve Sorunları Genel Müdürülüğü).

G. Berik (1984) *Women Carpet Weavers in Rural Turkey: Patterns of Employment, Earnings and Status* (Geneva: ILO).

E. Boserup (1990) *Economic and Demographic Relations in Development* (Baltimore: Johns Hopkins University Press).

M. Çelikten (2005) 'A Perspective on Women Principles in Turkey', *International Journal of Leadership in Education*, vol. 8, no. 3, pp. 207–21.

Y. Ecevit (2007) 'Women's Rights, Women's Organizations and the State', in Z. F. Kabasakal-Arat (ed.) *Human Rights In Turkey: Policies And Prospects* (PA: University of Pennsylvania Press, 2007).

Y. Ecevit (1998) 'Türkiye'de Ücretli Kadın Emeğinin Toplumsal Cinsiyet Temelinde Analizi', in *75 Yılda Kadınlar ve Erkekler* (Istanbul: Türkiye Ekonomik ve Toplumsal Tarih Vakfı).

Y. Ecevit (1991) 'Shop Floor Control: The Ideological Construction of Turkish Women Factory Workers', in N. Redclift and M. T. Sinclair (eds) *Working Women: International Perspectives on Labour and Gender Ideology* (New York: Routledge).

A. A. Engineer (1992) *The Rights of Women in Islam* (New York: St. Martin's Press).

T. Erman (1998) 'Kadınların Bakış Açısından Köyden Kente Göç ve Kentte Yaşam', in *75 Yılda Kadınlar ve Erkekler* (Istanbul: Türkiye Ekonomik ve Toplumsal Tarih Vakfı).

Y. Ertürk and N. Kardam (1999) 'Expanding Gender Accountability? Women's Organizations and the State in Turkey', *International Journal of Organization Theory and Behavior*, vol. 2, pp. 167–97.

F. Gök and D. Ilgaz (2007) 'The Right to Education: The Turkish Case', in Z. F. Kabasakal-Arat (ed.) *Human Rights In Turkey: Policies And Prospects* (University of Pennsylvania Press, 2007).

F. Gümüşoğlu (1998) 'Cumhuriyet Döneminde Ders Kitaplarında Cinsiyet Rolleri', in *75 Yılda Kadınlar ve Erkekler* (Istanbul: Türkiye Ekonomik ve Toplumsal Tarih Vakfı).

İ. İlkkaracan (1998) 'Kentli Kadınlar ve Çalışma Yaşamı', in *75 Yılda Kadınlar ve Erkekler* (Istanbul: Türkiye Ekonomik ve Toplumsal Tarih Vakfı).

İnsan Hakları Koordinator Üst Kurulu (1999) *İnsan Hakları Açısından Kadının Durumu, Sorunları ve Çözüm Önerileri* (Ankara: İnsan Hakları Koordinatör Üst Kurulu).

H. Kabasakal (1998) 'A Profile of Top Women Managers in Turkey', in Z. F. Arat (ed.) *Deconstructing Images of 'The Turkish Woman'* (New York: St. Martin's Press).

S. Kalaycıoğlu and H. Rittersberger (1998) 'İş İlişkilerine Kadınca Bir Bakış: Ev Hizmetlerinde Çalışan Kadınlar', in *75 Yılda Kadınlar ve Erkekler* (Istanbul: Türkiye Ekonomik ve Toplumsal Tarih Vakfı).

G. Kazgan (1979) 'Türk Ekonomisinde Kadınların İşgücüne Katılması, Mesleki Dağılımı, Eğitim Düzeyi ve Sosyo-Ekonomik Statüsü' (Women's Participation in the Workforce, Occupational Distribution, Educational Level, and Socioeconomic Status within the Turkish Economy), in N. Abadan-Unat (ed.) *Türk Toplumunda Kadın* (Istanbul: Ekin Yayınları).

The Koran Interpreted (1955) [Translation by Arthur J. Arberry] (New York: MacMillan Publishing).

F. Özbay (1991) 'Türkiye'de Kadın ve Çocuk Emeği', *Toplum ve Bilim*, no. 53, pp. 41–54.

N. Sirman (1989) 'Feminism in Turkey: A Short History', *New Perspectives on Turkey*, vol. 3, pp. 1–34.

State Institute of Statistics (2004) Türkiye'de Kadın Bilgi Ağı, available at www.die.gov.tr/tkba/istatistikler.htm

B. Stowasser (1994) *Women in the Qur`an, Traditions, and Interpretations* (New York: Oxford University Press).

B. Stowasser (1998) 'Gender Issues and Contemporary Quran Interpretation', in Y. Y. Haddad and J. Esposito (eds) *Islam, Gender, and Social Change* (Oxford: Oxford University Press)

M. Tan (1979) *Kadın: Ekonomik Yaşamı ve Eğitimi* (Ankara: Türkiye İş Bankası Kültür Yayınları).

A. Tansel (2005) 'Public-Private Choice, Wage Differentials, and Gender in Turkey' *Economic Development and Cultural Change*, vol. 53, no. 3, pp. 453–77.

Ş. Tekeli (ed.) (1982) *Kadınlar ve Siyasal Tomplumsal Hayat* (Ankara: Birikim Yayınları).

I. Tinker (ed.) (1991) *Persistent Inequalities: Women and World Development* (New York: Oxford University Press).

United Nations Development Programme (1998) *Human Development Report: Turkey* (Ankara: UNDP).

A. Wadud (1999) *Qur'an and Woman: Rereading the Sacred Text from a Woman's Perspective* (New York: Oxford University Press, 1999).

Türkonfed (2007) *İş Dünyasında Kadın* (Women in Work Life) (İstanbul: Turkish Enterprise and Business Confederation).

A. Wood (1995) *North-South Trade, Employment, and Inequality: Changing Fortunes in a Skill-Driven World* (New York: Oxford University Press).

N. Yıldırak, B. Gülçubuk, S. Gün, E. Olhan and M. Kılıç (2003) *Türkiye'de Gezici ve Geçici Kadın Tarm İşçilerinin Çalışma ve Yaşam Koşulları ve Sorunları* (Ankara: Tarım-İş).

I. U. Zeytinoğlu (1998) 'Constructing Images as Employment Restrictions: Determinants of Female Labour in Turkey', in Z. F. Arat (ed.) *Deconstructing Images of 'The Turkish Woman'* (New York: St. Martin's Press/Palgrave Macmillan).

10
Poverty, Social Policy and Modernity in Turkey

Sencer Ayata

The major household surveys carried out in Turkey in the last five years indicate that the incidence of absolute poverty varies between three to 5 per cent of the population, while nearly one-third of the families in the survey are identified as economically vulnerable (Buğra and Sınmardemir, 2004). Turkey's standing in the Human Development Index (HDI) lags considerably behind the country's international economic ranking; in other words Turkey is conspicuously poor in terms of social indicators and social development (Akder, 2004). Marked social class, gender and regional inequalities in Turkish society continue to exist, and despite impressive improvements in macro-economic indicators in the last few years, there has been no corresponding move towards creating a more egalitarian social order (World Bank, 2000; Yalman, 2004). Global economic conditions tend to increase job and income instability, making poverty almost a permanent state for increasing numbers of people and weakening traditional mechanisms of mutual help and solidarity (Sönmez, 2002). Finally, the social security regime in Turkey is highly inefficient and inadequate, and political efforts towards creating a more just and egalitarian society remain weak.

The relative weakness of the welfare state and social policy in Turkey can be seen as a matter of limited economic capacity and an outcome of insufficient government funds to build a powerful social security framework. A low level of social spending is undoubtedly associated with the low average per capita income of the country, and equally significant factors such as inadequate taxation and the prevalence of a vast, unregistered informal economy seriously limit the size of the government budget. Some analysts put the blame on the high level of military spending dictated by the urgencies of both Turkey's highly centralised power structure and a highly unstable regional and political environment. From the opposite point of view, others have argued that mobilisation from below is too weak to push political actors towards the further expansion of the welfare state. In recent years, some observers have drawn attention to the role of global economic competition and specifically, the dominance of neo-liberal economic policies that emphasise reduced government spending. Furthermore, Turkey has major divisions and cleavages that generate continuous ethnic and religious conflict and tension, causing a major drain on economic resources, impeding the establishment of a favourable investment climate. Finally, it can be argued that the weakness of commitment to social policy in Turkey is related to the Turkish political culture, in which issues of poverty, social inequality and social policy rarely, if at all, constitute the main substance of political and public debate.

In this study I discuss only the political aspect of this particular problem, what I call the 'weak commitment' to poverty reduction, social policy and the welfare state in Turkish politics. Politics as an explanatory factor is crucial, in that developing, formulating and implementing social policies is above all the responsibility of political actors, political parties and the governments. As Hall (Hall and Midgley, 2004, p. 65) argues, specific anti-poverty interventions are related to overarching development strategies and the wider context of values and ideologies. Following this idea, I examine poverty and social policy, in the generic sense of support for the well-being of citizens provided through social action (Alcock, 2002, p. 3), from the point of view of the ideological standpoints of the major political movements and parties in Turkey. This raises three main questions: How do Turkey's major political actors and traditions perceive poverty? What measures and tools do they prioritise in their approaches to poverty reduction and social policy? And how were these perceptions and approaches shaped by their ideology, specifically their conceptions of development, change and modernity?

Late Ottoman social policy

Despite significant changes involving the increasing centralisation of the state, the commercialisation of agriculture and the geographical mobility of the population, the vast majority of the population in the late Ottoman Empire lived in isolated villages, deprived of adequate infrastructural services and the advanced agrarian economic relations characteristic of modern industrial societies. The frequent wars of the period resulted in serious shortages of both manpower and livestock in the rural countryside (Çavdar, 2003, p. 103–31). In most parts of the country transportation facilities were inadequate, roads sparse and imperfect, motor vehicles few, railway transport absent and modern communication services poor. Health services were thoroughly insufficient, as evidenced by frequent epidemics; for instance, 14 per cent of the rural population suffered from malaria, and 9 per cent from syphilis, while tuberculosis was extremely widespread all over the country. Less than one quarter of villages had primary schools (Timur, 1971, p. 55). The cities, and specifically the coastal provinces in Anatolia, were expanding rapidly as a result of massive immigration of the Muslim populations from the Balkans, Crimea and Caucasia (Georgeon, 1999, p. 172).

The coastal provinces benefited from growing cash crops of cotton, silk, tobacco and raisins, as well as developments in export–import trade, education, and modern transportation facilities such as the railway. Nevertheless industry remained weak and poverty swept the rapidly growing cities such as İstanbul and İzmir.

In Ottoman society, poverty was conceived in traditional terms as referring to the permanent poor, the victims of natural disasters, war veterans and the destitute (elderly, sick, disabled, orphans). Such people needed to be fed, clothed and provided with fuel in winter. The Ottomans saw the task of helping the poor and the needy first and foremost as the responsibility of benevolent individuals and pious foundations. In other words, the traditional welfare system depended on the mobilisation of the meagre resources of individuals, families and local communities, which ultimately depended on arousing individual sentiments such as pity, compassion, mercy and fear of God. In late Ottoman society however, both the pious foundations and guild-centred occupational group solidarity were losing their effectiveness as instruments of social welfare and social policy. The existing welfare services were both inefficient and insufficient, and their organisation on a larger scale necessitated the intervention of the state. The Western-educated elites wanted the government to play a more prominent role in providing education, health and insurance services for the people. In a similar vein, the elites tended to see both social legislation and social insurance as major responsibilities to be undertaken by the state.

An early step in social legislation was the government's attempt to regulate working conditions in the coal mines. In the second half of the nineteenth century, the state introduced retirement funds and social insurance schemes to provide social security for civil servants and their families. A fund for military officers was established as early as 1866, and it was followed in 1981 by a fund for civil servants (Talas, 1992, p. 187). The government established a specialised department of government to undertake welfare services. These steps laid down the beginnings of a corporatist system of social-welfare provision based on employment status differences.

A recent study on the origins of modern social welfare in Turkey draws attention to the key role played by Sultan Abdülhamit, who acknowledged that state welfare spending could provide new opportunities for communication between the ruler and his subjects (Özbek, 2002). Abdülhamit tried to strengthen the palace against the bureaucracy and by way of extension, emphasised a patrimonial style of administration over rational-bureaucratic approaches. The distribution of welfare during his reign (1876–1908) was highly personal and patrimonial. The benefits allocated to the urban poor were presented as alms, or as personal gifts and favours from the Sultan; for instance, meat and various kinds of food were freely distributed in the mosque courts in İstanbul after Friday prayers. Abdülhamit conceived social policy as a person's *hayrat*, that is, a good deed in the traditional Islamic sense; such activity involved a broad category of services including not only social assistance to the poor, but also the construction of inns, bathhouses and bridges as well as the opening of new schools and hospitals. The benefits, however, were often allocated arbitrarily without using standard criteria; for instance, stipends were provided for the needy according to individual petitions and the amount of support varied from one individual case to another. Finally, there was a strong emphasis on public display and ceremony in welfare provision (Özbek, 2002).

Since the government budget was highly restricted, the Sultan's spending on good deeds remained minimal. Furthermore, only 6 per cent of the total welfare spending was diverted to social assistance. In order to reach as many people as possible, the benefits were reduced to small, almost symbolic amounts. On the other hand, charity was regarded as a religious activity, since benefits were distributed through religious institutions such as the mosques, the religious networks and particularly the Sufi brotherhoods. In addition, government funds were overwhelmingly directed to leading religious centres such as İstanbul and Hicaz (Özbek, 2002). This particular strategy complemented Abdülhamit's broader policy of supporting the conservative *ulema* and the Sufi *tarikat* leaders to provide legitimacy for his rule (Zürcher, 1995). By contrast, the Young Turks, who took control of the government in 1908 tried to introduce a modern, secular, bureaucratically organised conception of social welfare (Özbek, 2002). The different approaches of the Sultan, on the one hand, and the Young Turks, on the other, were similar in content and style to the divergences in social policy orientation between secular Western and conservative Islamic political parties in the Republican period.

The new republic

The modernising elites' conception of poverty took shape as an outcome of the historical encounters of the Ottoman Empire with the Western world, and as such it was expressed mainly in cross-cultural or cross-national terms to emphasise the social and economic backwardness of the new nation. During the early years of the Republic, Atatürk stated that wealth and poverty were the factors that fundamentally distinguished the Western world from the East; the West was prosperous and the East was poor. He said, 'we are poor people struggling to maintain our independence; the country is devastated from one end to the other; everywhere you hear the owls singing; the people have no roads, no riches, indeed have nothing; the whole population is in a pitiful state of utter poverty and destitution. The country needs improvement, prosperity, welfare' (Timur, 1971, p. 191). The Republican leaders thought that the only solution was modernisation, conceived of as the wholesale transformation of an agricultural and traditional country of poor and illiterate peasants into a modern, secular and industrial state.

Modernisation involved a move from ignorance to science/rationality, backwardness to civilisation, and poverty to opulence. In this sense, the very notion of modernity implied an end to the poverty of the nation.

One major aspect of modernisation entailed attaining the contemporary state of civilisation; hence, the Republican leadership argued for the wholesale adoption of Western culture and institutions to combat parochialism and ignorance. Cohn, for instance, argues that the educated elites were indeed ashamed of the backwardness of the villages and the ignorance of the peasants whom they wanted to change and modernise. Webster's (1939, p. 144) account of village life clearly states what actually worried the early Republican elites: 'Villages even lacked coffee houses. Mail arrived once a week. There was not a single radio instrument for receiving news and music from the outside world. No traffic passed through. Not a single resident with an educational background'. In order to join the ranks of the civilised, such ignorant rural people had to be educated and schooled in Western culture (Mango, 2005, pp. 55–6). Therefore, the government's priority was to implement a cultural project to change the traditional values and attitudes of the people by providing them with secular education, reducing gender inequalities in society and undermining the power of the reactionary Islamic forces held responsible for the ignorance of the masses.

The second priority was economic in nature. In the eyes of the founders of the Turkish Republic, the late Ottoman Empire had essentially been a de facto colony, subordinate to and exploited by the developed industrial nations. They believed that emancipation from domination would come through industrialisation, which would provide a solid material basis for national sovereignty and independence (Tezel, 1982, pp. 132–3). Hence, the fight against poverty was also a part of a broader strategy of economic and social development.

The secular-modernist tradition has clearly favoured state-provision of social welfare and state-directed social policy above informal and traditional forms of welfare provision. The new elite believed that the latter methods were under the control of reactionary religious forces. The state intervened in the social sphere to undertake various social security measures and implement social policies based on the understanding that the population of the country was a productive force, indispensable for economic development. In this vein, the early Republican governments focused on education; during the period of single-party rule the number of children in primary school increased from 341,941 to 1,591,039; middle school students from 5905 to 65,168; and high school students from 1241 to 21,440 (Tezel, 1982, p. 90). Similarly, the early Republican governments tackled the problem of the health condition of the population. In 1923, life expectancy at birth was only 33 years; in 1928, there were only 1078 doctors in the country and the number of patients per doctor was 12,223. The improvements in this sphere were considerable; the number of doctors increased to 3020 while the number of persons per doctor was reduced to 6890 (Çavdar, 2003, pp. 192, 269, 344; Tezel, 1982, p. 91). The Ministry of Hygiene and Social Assistance was responsible for the prevention of ill health and the government focused its extension of health services on smaller administrative units and primary health care provision (Yazgan, 1974, pp. 81–91). The health reform programme had multiple aims, including the lining and covering of wells used for drinking water, construction of water pipes for domestic purposes and of sanitary outdoor toilets, and efforts to keep sewage and filth out of the water supply, drain mosquito breeding swamps, open public baths and set up medicine chests (Webster, 1939, pp. 189, 264).

The state saw its objective as providing for the well-being of the poor; an economic policy approach that Boratav and Özuğurlu (2004, p. 6) have called 'benevolent paternalism'. According to this particular outlook, the government, as the supreme regulator in the society, assumes a major role in improving the living standards of the poor people. The policies of the single party towards wage labour, urban working class and issues of social policy varied significantly over time in response to changes in the domestic economy and world economic conditions. The government passed legislation to protect employees in industry and workers employed by foreign companies by setting minimum wages as well as maximum work hours and age limits. Insurance funds were established for retirement and health and measures to protect children and pregnant women were taken (Talas, 1992, pp.78, 86, 88). On the other hand, the state restricted trade unions, collective bargaining and the right to strike in order to curb the potential political power of organised labour. The solidaristic of the early Republic aimed to create a unified and cohesive society and effectively eliminate class conflict. Hence, where social legislation was concerned, workers were approached as individuals rather than as a collectivity (Kuruç, 2005). Finally, the regulatory framework developed by the government was exclusive, segmented and highly fragmented. Workers in private and public services in different departments of the state were each covered by a different insurance fund (Talas, 1992, p. 96). In social security, the state gave priority to civil servants and workers in the formal sector. The Labour Law excluded workers in agriculture, small enterprises and the transportation industry, as well as the outworkers.

At the founding of the Republic, a very high proportion of the families in the rural countryside (17%) had no land at all, while 62 per cent were poor small-scale farmers. Furthermore, land was fragmented and seasonal unemployment widespread. The most important rural reform undertaken by the Republican government was the abolition of the tax on agricultural output (*aşar*), from which all farmers, large and small, benefited significantly. As Boratav and Özuğurlu (2004, p. 4) argue, the economic conditions of the peasants changed for the better until the 1940s. Specifically, the 1920s was a golden age for peasants, as they benefited from increased investments in agriculture, favourable terms of trade between agricultural and industrial goods and high rates of economic growth. Tezel (1982), on the other hand, points out that during single-party rule the government remained irresolute between two conflicting objectives: drastic measures to improve the economic condition of the peasants on the one hand, and sensitivity to the interests of the landowners who gave their support for the War of Independence, on the other. Hence, despite two major legislative attempts, the single-party government failed to pass the land reform bill in the national assembly as a result of opposition from the representatives of the landed upper classes.

During the Second World War, hundreds of thousands of men were conscripted, economic growth was negative, real wages declined and peasants retreated to subsistence farming. The government exercised food rationing in the cities in order to protect the urban population from the threat of food scarcity and starvation. In the country as a whole there was a sharp decline in living standards. The single-party government began to emphasise social reform with a new vigour in the aftermath the war. It established a new Ministry of Work responsible for improving the living standards of the working people and enacted a law that paved the way for free trade union activity in 1947.

In summary, although the Republic viewed the fundamental objective of protecting the weak and vulnerable as a primary aim of the state, the new state did not perceive the heart of the poverty problem as one of social inequality. Instead, it considered the elimination of poverty and other social objectives as derivatives of the grand project of cultural transformation and economic development.

The centre-right

The roots of the centre-right tradition in Turkish politics go back to the Democrat Party (DP), which came to power with an overwhelming majority after winning the first genuinely competitive elections in 1950. The party was closely linked to the commercial bourgeoisie and big landowners. It took a liberal position in economic matters and gave rise to a new approach to politics described as 'parliamentary populism' (Boratav and Özuğurlu, 2004, p. 10). After the DP was closed down following the 1960 military coup, the Justice Party (JP) of Süleyman Demirel ruled the country either single-handedly or in coalition governments until it, too, was closed down by another military regime in 1980. The ideology of the centre-right combines elements of traditional religious culture, economic liberalism and a conception of democracy emphasising the power of the majority (Cizre, 2002). In this particular period, the scope of social security expanded significantly, the government took important steps towards the institution of modern industrial relations, and living standards increased as a result of economic policies based upon import-substitution policies. Both the centre-right and the centre-left political parties were trying to respond to the major challenge of massive displacement of labour in agriculture and the problem of re-embedding the uprooted population in the cities. There was a consensus among the main political parties about emphasising the responsibilities of the state towards the poor. The rapid expansion of the welfare state in Europe in these years also influenced the political parties and governments in Turkey in the direction of social reform.

The centre-right parties conceived of the poor in three different ways. Firstly, they saw the peasants and the new migrants in the cities as poor. The cure for this generalised state of poverty was seen as one of rapid economic growth that would increase employment and the living standards of the population. The second conception identified poverty as absence of social security, and the solution for this particular problem was foreseen as the expansion of the welfare state. Finally, the poor were perceived as the victims of personal or family misfortune, sickness, accident or natural disaster. In such cases, the state was obliged to provide the necessary safety net. In addition, the centre-right political parties emphasised the role of customary, fundamentally religious methods of social welfare provision. Their underlying assumption was that mutual help and communal solidarity, both in the form of the rich helping the poor and the mutual assistance between members of the extended family and neighbours, were powerful elements of social welfare in Turkish society.

Many Justice Party MPs were upwardly mobile people coming from the non-privileged sections of Turkish society. Their early life experiences made them well aware of the suffering of the ordinary people – Demirel himself had first-hand experience of village life and poverty. He described poverty as a form of oppression, arguing that his sympathy for the poor and their suffering and his ambition to relieve their pain underlay his political struggle (Demirel, 2004, pp. 324–30). The JP was strongly committed to the belief that members of society's lower income groups deserved a minimum of social welfare. In his address to the JP Congress in 1965, Süleyman Demirel underlined the close relationship between economic development and social welfare; 'Development is a human cause, a cause for human dignity. Economic development is a *cihad* (an Islamic holy war) that needs to be waged in order to eliminate such evils as poverty, hunger, ignorance and ill health' (Şahinoğlu, 1966, p. 32). The JP programme recognised the fundamental role and duty of the state in promoting measures to reduce income inequalities, provide welfare for the poor and reduce regional and economic disparities through education and increased social security. The party's major policy targets included the introduction of unemployment insurance and legal coverage for agricultural workers, a reduction in unemployment, an increase in the scope of social security among the urban and rural populations alike, and the development of Eastern Anatolia.

The main developments in social policy between 1950 and 1980 involved the above-mentioned measures. Additionally, the state established old age pensions for insured workers in 1950, followed in 1957 by insurance for the disabled, the elderly, the victims of work accidents and the family of deceased workers (Talas, 1992, p. 191). Furthermore, in the 1960's and 1970's the increased pace of industrialisation led to the expansion of the organised working class and the increasing weight and influence of these workers in society and in politics. As a response, the government created the Ministry of Work and Social Assistance in 1960 to coordinate social welfare policies. The Social Insurance Law of 1964 was an attempt towards unifying the fragmented legislative and security regime (Talas, 1992, p. 194). In 1972, Demirel's government established a new insurance scheme covering the self-employed and expanded the scope of the Labour Law and minimum wage practice. The regime took measures to enable the families of insured workers to benefit from the health services of the Social Insurance Institution (SSI). Finally, in the 1970s, the government also established an old age pension for uninsured senior citizens.

In addition to legal social policy measures, the centre-right governments adopted populist policies with profound consequences for the rural and urban poor. They saw the basis of the legitimacy of their power mainly in the periphery, and claimed to be culturally closer to the religious countryside, asserting that they were the true representatives of the economic interests of the agrarian population. The JP government invested heavily in rural infrastructure, and extended extensive subsidies to the agricultural sector. The economic policies of the centre-right governments made a clear commitment to increasing agricultural productivity and modernising agriculture, while opposing policy measures that involved the redistribution of landed property. Factors such as a shortage of capital and skills, rapid mechanisation of agriculture, fragmentation of holdings, financial difficulties and heavy dependence on a single crop created massive rural poverty and unemployment.

In the cities, the poor migrants built their houses on expropriated land that belonged to the state in order to avoid paying rent for accommodation. Some migrants were even able to extend their houses and build shops on the ground floor to earn additional income. The government contributed to the consolidation of the houses and neighbourhoods of the poor by developing basic infrastructural services such as electricity, sewage, roads, public transport, water, schools, parks, and medical centres. Furthermore, the houses were authorised through successive amnesties that made the occupiers legal owners of the property with proper title deeds. This system has become a major source of upward social mobility for millions of migrant families in the big cities.

Nevertheless the centre-right and centre-left approaches of this period differed significantly in their understanding of the welfare state. For the centre-left, social justice involved increased social equality and the minimisation of income and status differences between different social groups. For the centre-right, however, the core principle of social justice was one of providing a minimum standard of income and social security for all people. What really mattered to the centre-right political parties were not abstract principles but pragmatic considerations (Demirel, 2004, p. 321). Whereas Ecevit, the leader of the centre-left in the 1970s, dreamed of a Turkey where there would be no oppressors and exploiters, for Demirel, success in politics was to be measured by providing infrastructural services (Mango, 2005, p. 78). As a matter of fact, the centre-right tradition, following the dominant economic policy discourse of the 1960s and 1970s, emphasised a strategy of development based on mobilising funds for industrial investments. Hence, governments were advised to limit social spending so as to promote capital formation, economic growth and employment opportunities. The understanding was that increased welfare spending should not function as income redistribution and that rises in real wages should result from productivity increase. The centre-right view would not tolerate hatred of private property and wealth or allow political interventions to deter investments that created employment (Adalet Partisi, 1972, pp. 5–6, 11–12). The leading Justice Party firmly believed that competition, freedom of enterprise, a full-fledged market economy and dynamic international trade would generate economic growth, increased revenues for the state and greater spending on social security. In the party manifesto the most important measure for increasing social justice was declared to be the increase of jobs and rising incomes, whereas the greatest source of injustice was identified as unemployment (Adalet Partisi, 1977, pp. 178–9). The party also rejected nationalisation as a viable poverty reduction strategy. The JP emphasised that social justice should not be understood as making individuals equal; since the cake was too small, dividing it further would not make anyone happy. Demirel for instance, has argued that there is not a single developing country in the world that has a comprehensive welfare system; for him the core of social justice was economic growth (Demirel, 2004, pp. 324–30).

There was a brief return to conventional populism between 1991 and 1993 under the short-lived Demirel coalition government, but from the early 1980's onwards the neo-liberal agenda began to dominate politics and shape the scope of social policy. The neo-liberal approach underlined the importance of free markets, entrepreneurship and profit-seeking, with a stress on policy measures involving tax reduction, cuts in public spending, privatisation, and depression of wages (Hall and Midgley, 2004, p. 77). The neo-liberals tried to facilitate market mechanisms and promote the interests of the business community with the view that what is good for business is also good for the poor. Import substitution policies were abandoned and the economy was increasingly opened to foreign capital and global competition in order to attract capital and promote access to global markets. On the other hand, the state established safety net programmes and social funds to address the poverty problem. The Social Solidarity and Assistance Fund (SSAF) was created by a law enacted in 1986 as an off-budget fund with the objective of providing social assistance (food aid), medical aid, support for education and micro credit schemes for the poor. A similar measure was the Green Card, which provides free health care for people who are not covered by any social security organisation (Buğra and Keyder, 2003, p. 38). This residual approach to state-directed social policy was initially proposed by the Motherland Party of Turgut Özal in the 1980s, carried on by the younger generation of the centre-right leaders of the 1990s (Çiller, 1994 and 1995; Yılmaz, 1999), and later consolidated by the Justice and Development Party (JDP) that came to power in 2002.

The centre-left

As a result of the rapid expansion of the domestic market and rapid growth in agriculture and industry in the 1960s and 1970s, social and economic issues took greater priority in public debate and discussion (Bila, 1999, pp. 212, 217). In the 1970s the RPP, the party of the Westernising elites that founded the Turkish Republic, was increasing its votes, winning almost all local and general elections against its main opponent the centre-right JP. The labouring poor, including the peasants, artisans, shopkeepers and workers, were the main target of centre-left policy and propaganda. During the rising tide of the centre-left in the 1970s, social inequality became the central idea in conceptualising poverty and reducing wealth and income differences through redistribution was seen as an indispensable policy for the elimination of this poverty. The policy priority of the centre-left RPP was not economic development per se, but the creation of an egalitarian society with a more balanced distribution of wealth and income. In other words, the promotion of social equality and the well-being of working people were seen as policy objectives as significant as accelerated economic growth. The new social democratic point of view proposed that it would be impossible to achieve high rates of economic growth without spreading social welfare among the whole population. Hence policies of increasing social justice should not be postponed for the sake of accelerating investments.

   The RPP was influenced by both the ideas and policies of the social democrats in Europe and the discourses of the Turkish socialist left. In the early 1960s the RPP, before adopting the centre-left position, passed new laws introducing a minimum wage, equal pay for equal work, freedom of trade union activity, collective bargaining rights and the right to strike, in accordance with the liberal spirit of the 1960 Constitution. The party emphasised the ideals of equality, solidarity and supremacy of labour in order to distinguish itself from the liberal right (Coşkun, 1978, pp. 95–104; Koloğlu, 2000, pp. 65–108). The RPP adopted a highly critical attitude towards usurers, big landowners and large-scale monopolistic enterprises which, they thought, were exploitative and oppressive forces opposing the interests of both the people and the state. On the other hand, they saw the responsibilities of the private sector towards society as equally significant; freedom of enterprise, private property and inheritance rights could all be restricted when public good and social justice were at issue. Finally, the RPP discourse took a clear stance against conservative religious views and reactionary religious groups, which it viewed as major obstacles to economic development and the cultural advancement of the poeple. In this context, the party also attempted to challenge the political influence of the local merchants, intermediaries and notables who were thought to use religion as a means to impede educational and social reform.

In the 1960s and 1970s the policies of accelerated growth were criticised by leading economists such as Myrdal and Singer, who argued that economic growth did not automatically eliminate poverty and social inequality. Others argued that social reforms would not impede but rather speed up economic growth (Hall and Midgley, 2004). Following these ideas and arguments, the centre-left in Turkey proposed that economic resources should be diverted to social programmes aiming at poverty reduction. In its economic policy, the RPP stressed the peoples' sector as both the prime engine of economic growth and an adequate solution to the problem of unemployment and poverty. The peoples' sector was to be developed by the trade unions, cooperatives and local governments as well as through the mobilisation of small savings to spread property ownership, decision making and participation among the working classes. In the rural context, the regime would promote the peoples' sector by setting up core villages well equipped with transportation facilties and basic infrastructural services (Ölçen, 1974; Coşkun, 1978, pp. 147–60). The centre-left assigned government a major role in directing and planning economic and social development. The state was to assume an active and interventionist role in increasing savings and investments through supporting state-owned enterprises and through other etatist measures. The RRP believed that achieving the level of contemporary civilisation was possible through etatism (Bila, 1999, p. 215). Additionally, the centre-left approach to social policy placed a unique emphasis on state provision and state financing of social welfare rather than the private, informal or even the voluntary sectors. In the words of Bülent Ecevit, leader of the RPP; 'Sympathy is a feeling that sensitive people, considerate people would have. What is really necessary however is to leave no one in a situation as to arouse others peoples' pity and sympathy' (Ecevit, 1966, pp. 9, 197).

The party argued for a social-rights-based comprehensive social security system, full employment, unemployment benefits and the elimination of social class inequalities in education. Among the party's policies were also social insurance coverage for the shopkeepers and artisans and priority for investments in Eastern Anatolia. In the 1970s, the majority of working people were still peasants. The RPP defended a comprehensive land reform programme that involved distributing land to farmers and making share-croppers the owners of their farms. It also promised employees in the agricultural sector universal insurance coverage (*CHP*, 1973, pp. 25–38). The creation of educational opportunities for the whole population and removal of all major class inequalities in education were also among the top policy objectives.

A group of politicians in the Republican Peoples Party argued that Atatürk, with his emphasis on national sovereignty, educational and health reform, peaceful and balanced relations between social classes and his highly ambitious modernisation project, paved the way for democracy and established the foundations of a welfare-oriented state (Aksoy, 1977, pp. 39–44; Çeçen, 1984, p. 211). The new RPP leadership under Ecevit (1969) however, saw social policy reforms as even more essential than early Republican political and cultural reforms. They believed that the early Republican reforms had lacked social substance and hence remained ineffective in promoting the welfare of citizens (Koloğlu, 2000). They argued that working people in Turkey were not opposed to the early Republican reforms, but rather indifferent, because they did not contribute significantly to material and social development. The reforms were characterised as fundamentally cultural and superstructural. The RRP's new leaders believed the really necessary reforms were those that would increase the living standards and the social security of the people, those that involved essential changes in the economy and fundamental alterations in social class structure (Ecevit, 1969, p. 69).

Despite this strong ideological commitment to social justice, the RPP lacked specific poverty reduction programmes with regards to malnutrition, health, education, social security and housing. The centre-left came to power only for a short while at a time of severe economic crisis, when the heyday of the Keynesian welfare state was already on the wane and the neo-liberal agenda on the rise. In the 1980s and 1990s, the centre-left's focus on class inequalities and improving social justice was supplanted first by issues of political liberty and democratisation in the 1980s and defending secularism against the Islamist threat in the 1990s. The centre-right and centre-left coalition governments of 1991–5 made no major progress in social policy measures despite their commitment to democratic reforms (Saybaşılı, 1995, p. 52). Such diversions of interest also occurred due to the domination of patronage politics, intense factionalist struggles in the parties and above all the domination of the neo-liberal agenda. In this decade, however, concern about poverty and social justice became a major political objective of the Islamic movement and the Islamic political parties.

Poverty and Islam

In the Quran, the word poor ('*fakr*') refers to a person who fails to meet his basic needs and is therefore dependent on others for his sustenance. Poverty is attributed to forces that are beyond the control of the individual person, such as misfortune involving sickness, old age, death, natural disasters, famine and war. In this conception, poverty is a universal and the poor are found in all societies. The original Islamic sources distinguish between two kinds of dependence and poverty. The first, which is fundamentally economic, entails deprivation in material goods, and the second, religious and spiritual, conceives of all human beings, regardless of economic status, as deficient in various qualities and possessions and hence ultimately dependent on God for their fulfilment. Some Sufi brotherhoods have tried to elevate poverty and asceticism to a spiritually higher status, distancing themselves from worldly concerns to withdraw to a more intense state of religious life that is excessively devoted to God.

In Islam both wealth and poverty are intimately related moral concepts. In the Islamic outlook the individual's family, property and life are all '*emanet*', the trust of God. In other words, human beings cannot be the true owners of poverty. Therefore, wealth should be used according to the dictates of the real owner, God, who decrees that the poor have a share in all property. Hence, there is a powerful urge in Islam for the distribution of wealth. This urge requires an emphasis on charity, on the good deeds of individuals and on helping others. The religious imperative to give to the poor their rightful share involves the rewarding of the benevolent as well as the punishment of the mean. Extravagance, luxury, conspicuous consumption and waste are regarded as violations of God's orders, while helping the poor is seen as submission to God. A good Muslim, therefore, should be prosperous but modest and try to achieve a balance between worship and pursuit of wealth, between this world and the other (Yaman, 2003). In Islam, charity also has an eschatological essence; helping the poor and needy purifies the individual's soul and brings salvation in the eternal world; it involves not only obeying God's orders but also the control of human passions such as avarice, greed and vanity (Bilgin, 2003). Charity entails the blessing of God and therefore is as an integral part of religious faith. In this world, as they undergo a moral test, men of substance are judged according to the extent of their benevolence. The rich are dependent on the help of the poor for salvation in the other world (Baykan, 2003). Islamic groups tend to approach poverty alleviation as a matter of religiously guided benevolence, either in *gemeinschaft*-type local communities or in city-wide, nation-wide or even global networks, giving charity, alms, expiations and maintenance allowances (Cebeci, 2003).

Among Islamic intellectuals and in schools of divinity there is an ongoing debate on the relationship between poverty, wealth and Islam. One powerful trend in Islamic thinking emphasises that private property and acquisition of wealth are clearly recognised in the Koran and are Islamically legitimate concerns. Nevertheless Muslims are warned that Islam is also against acquisitiveness, greed and hoarding of wealth. In other words, the true believer should be aware of the responsibilities that ownership of wealth and property impose on him and lead a sober and modest life. Furthermore, this particular point of view also stresses that poverty is neither a desirable state of being nor one that should be associated with a spiritually higher status in religion. Hence, its advocates are highly critical of other-worldly ascetism and the tendency to withdraw from the world. These scholars hold various Islamic practices that romanticise poverty, and are responsible for a fatalistic outlook that makes individuals overtly passive, submissive and inactive, so that they expect everything from God. Such fatalism is believed to lie at the root of the economic backwardness of the Islamic world and its subordination to the economically powerful Western societies. Recently, these scholars have argued, that Islamic values are changing in the direction of a more positive attitude to work, economic achievement and material prosperity. Poverty, on the other hand, is seen as a threat to decent family life, religion and the moral fabric of society, a social malaise that needs to be eliminated by all means. The faithful Muslim should strive to combine prosperity with modesty, to strike a balance between worship and work, between worldly and other-worldly concerns. Work, prosperity, and economic development, on the one hand, and spiritual strength, religious devotion and social justice, on the other, are regarded as equally essential for an Islamic society. The modernist Islamic point of view also sees Western science and technology as essential for natural development and the elimination of poverty. Islam, in this perspective, is far from being a reactionary force: rather, it is a progressive force that facilitates economic and social development.

The Islamic approach to poverty alleviation tries to strengthen the horizontal ties among individuals, recognising that under the influence of urbanisation and the market economy traditional sources of solidarity are faltering. The population is ageing, more women are taking on outside employment, extended families are splitting into nuclear ones and people are increasingly neglecting to take care of the sick, the poor and the elderly. As a response to such problems, Islamic organisations and networks try to strengthen their grassroots activism. Islamic welfare activity takes two main forms. In the case of vertical paternalist practices, the rich are expected to fulfil their responsibilities towards the poor; in this area the rising Islamic bourgeoisie has become a major donor to Islamic welfare activity. The second approach is to promote and reinforce mutual aid among relatives, friends and neighbours.

At the formal level the Justice and Development Party is highly sceptical of state-centreed welfare policies and the public provision of welfare services. In accordance with the dominant neo-liberal outlook, the JDP government emphasises the inefficiency of state bureaucracies in delivering social welfare and is highly critical of centralised and bureaucratic procedures and methods. The party rejects social policies that necessitate redistributionist economic measures (Akdoğan, 2003; Tekin, 2004). Furthermore, the JDP associates state-based policies with the domination of the modernising elites, identifying their approach as one of abstract policy formulation with little chance of practical applicability. Additionally, the party tends to perceive state-centred welfare activity as a substitute and perhaps even a rival to religious networks of social solidarity. To the extent that the party is supportive of the public provision of services, its tendency is to promote local governments, which in the last two decades have become heavily involved in the distribution of welfare services. In power, the JDP has increasingly come to terms with the liberal model, seeing private provision of welfare as the most preferable option in their efforts to reconcile liberal individualism and traditional Islamic collectivism. Hence, in the JDP approach, the emphasis on welfare gradually shifts towards both the informal and the market sectors.

The Islamically inspired JDP leaders believe in the superiority of voluntary activity, which involves sympathy and love, over bureaucratic expertise. In other words, the party advocates redistribution of wealth through interpersonal and patrimonial relations within a moral framework of religious values and methods. Such Islamic charity has been the subject of extensive media coverage in recent years and the emphasis on show and display is increasing. The main problem with this traditional charitable approach, however, is that the coverage of the Islamic charity organisations and networks is uneven and their accountabilities are unclear. Furthermore, geographically speaking, the voluntary organisations are highly unevenly distributed in the country.

The JDP government has attempted to reform social security institutions in accordance with World Bank and International Monetary Fund guidelines. The Turkish SII has nearly six and a half million active members and provides health services for nearly 34 million people, and, Bağ-Kur has three and a half million active members and a total of sixteen million who benefit from the health services that the institution provides. The deficits of both organisations have been increasing rapidly over the years. The contributions of the members barely suffice to pay old age pensions, as almost nothing is left to cover health service expenditure. The deficits of the two institutions are in the range of ten billion dollars per year. The SII members used to complain about two major problems in access to hospital services. Firstly, they were not allowed to benefit from services provided by the state hospitals, and secondly, unlike the members of Bağ-Kur, were not able to get their medicine from private drugstores. Both deficiencies led to long waiting lists and major delays in health services. The Ministry of Health has now enabled members of the SII to use both state as well as licensed private hospitals on the one hand and to obtain their medicine from private drugstores on the other. Meanwhile, however, the government transferred the ownership of the hospitals to the Ministry, and their personnel, including the doctors, became employees of the government. Finally, as part of the social security reform programme, the existing three social insurance agencies will be united under a new administrative framework where all insured people will be subject to the same set of rules, norms and standards.

Conclusion

In relation to the social policy approaches of the major political party traditions, three general points are evident. Firstly, economic policies and international economic conditions have a deep impact on social policy; for instance, the accelerated industrialisation policies of the 1960s and 1970s and the currently dominant neo-liberal approaches have shaped social policies in Turkey in radically different ways. Secondly, the major political traditions have emphasised and used different instruments of welfare service provision and created different combinations in the social policy mix; traditional and conservative approaches had a stronger bent towards informal provision of welfare, while secular and leftist traditions have been more state-centric in their approach. Civil society and modern voluntary associations have only recently begun to be seen as significant instruments of social welfare. Thirdly, the scope of formal social security tended to expand under all governments. Nevertheless it was primarily the necessity of responding to the urgencies of competitive party politics that led governments to promote social policies. The advancement of the social security system took place in a disorganised, random and haphazard way, resulting in a highly fragmented social security regime. The absence of both a programmatic outlook and a strong commitment to issues of social policy played a significant role in the haphazard development of the social security system in Turkey.

It is possible to conclude by making three general remarks on what I have called the weak political commitment hypothesis, trying to relate these to three central ideas of modernity. Firstly, the welfare state itself is a collectivist undertaking, and its main function is to enable and empower individuals through the extension of substantive freedoms. The enhancement of individual autonomy is the fundamental principle of modernity and the ultimate basis of democracy. Turkey's major political actors and traditions have by and large tended to underestimate the fundamental relationship between the extension of substantive freedoms, democracy and modernity. Secondly, the project of modernity entails increasing human productivity through enhancing the productive powers of the population. According to this perspective, social policy can be seen as the single most significant instrument for developing the human capital of a society. Successive governments in Turkey have been aware of the relationship between the productivity of the population on the one hand and its security, prosperity and welfare on the other. However, neither the political nor indeed the economic elites have been able to introduce an ambitious political project to really advance what Amartya Sen (2001) calls the social preparedness of the country for the market economy. Such a Keynesian urge of modernity has been notoriously absent in Turkey, and its absence remains a very serious problem for sustained economic growth. Finally, one of the greatest challenges of modernity has been the integration of rapidly differentiating and fragmenting societies. In Turkey, until very recently, the creation of an integrated and orderly society was conceived of as the product of state coercion or social control, or discipline by traditional and religious authorities, and sometimes a combination of the two. Recently, there has been a new tendency to regard the market economy and its various elements such as consumption (new fashions in dress, house decoration, cars) and popular culture, that is, football, TV programmes, and music, as almost-sufficient conditions for creating a modern shared culture. Undoubtedly, forces such as the military, the traditional community and the market are significant elements of political and social control. Nevertheless the political parties in Turkey have by and large overlooked the obvious connection between poverty on the one hand, and social exclusion and political unrest on the other, as it became manifest in the case of Turkey's major political challenges such as Islamic radicalism, extreme Kurdish and Turkish nationalism, and the organised crime that has swept the big cities in recent years. Turkish statecraft has hardly ever used social policies and welfare measures as peaceful ways of absorbing, rather than suppressing, social heterogeneity, and generating domestic peace and political stability.

Bibliography

Adalet Partisi (1972) *Millet Hizmetinde Adalet Partisi* (Ankara: Ayyıldız Matbaası).
—— (1977) *Programme ve Tüzük* (Ankara: Doğuş Matbaası).
H. Akder (2004) *İnsani Gelişme ya da Yaşam Kalitesi*. Unpublished paper (Ankara: Middle East Technical University).
Y. Akdoğan (2003) *Muhafazakar Demokrasi* (Ankara: Ak Parti).
M. Aksoy (1977) *Sosyalist Enternasyonal ve CHP* (Ankara: Tekin Yayınevi).
P. Alcock (2002) 'The Subject of Social Policy', in P. Alcock, A. Erskine and M. May (eds) *Blackwell Dictionary of Social Policy* (Oxford: Blackwell Publishing).
E. Baykan (2003) 'Takva Zengini Olmak Yoksulluğu', in A. E. Bilgili and E. Altan (eds) *Yoksulluk* (İstanbul: Deniz Feneri Yardımlaşma ve Dayanışma Derneği).
H. Bila (1999) *CHP: 1919–1999* (İstanbul: Doğan Kitapevi).
V. Bilgin (2003) 'Dinlerin Yoksulluğu Algılayışı Üzerine bir İnceleme', in A. E. Bilgili and E. Altan (eds) *Yoksulluk* (İstanbul: Deniz Feneri Yardımlaşma ve Dayanışma Derneği).
K. Boratav and M. Özuğurlu (2004) *Social Policies and Distributional Dynamics in Turkey: 1923–2002*. Unpublished paper (Ankara: Ankara University Faculty of Political Science).
A. Buğra and Ç. Keyder (2003) 'New Poverty and the Changing Welfare Regime in Turkey' (Ankara: UNDP).
A. Buğra and N. T. Sınmardemir (2004) *Yoksullukla Mücadelede İnsani ve Etkin bir Yöntem: Nakit Gelir Desteği* (İstanbul: Boğaziçi Üniversitesi Sosyal Politika Forumu).

Cebeci, L. (2003) 'Kur'an ve Yoksulluk', in A. E. Bilgili and E. Altan (eds) *Yoksulluk* (İstanbul: Deniz Feneri Yardımlaşma ve Dayanışma Derneği).

CHP (1973) *Ak Günlere; Seçim Bildirgesi* (Ankara: Ajans Türk Matbaacılık Sanayii).

Ü. Cizre (2002) 'From Ruler to Pariah: The Life and Times of the True Path Party', in B. Rubin and M. Heper (eds) *Political Parties in Turkey* (London: Frank Cass).

A. Coşkun (1978) *Cumhuriyet Halk Partisi ve Demokratik Sol* (Ankara: Tekin Yayınevi).

T. Çavdar (2003) *Türkiye Ekonomisinin Tarihi 1900–1960* (Ankara: İmge Yayınevi).

A. Çeçen (1984) *Sosyal Demokrasi* (Ankara: Devinim Yayınları).

T. Çiller (1994) *Vatandaşlarımla Sohbet* (Ankara: Başbakanlık Basın Merkezi).

—— (1995) *Türkiyem* (Ankara: Doğru Yol Partisi).

T. Demirel (2004) *Adalet Partisi İdeoloji ve Politika* (İstanbul İletişim Yayınları).

B. Ecevit (1966) *Ortanın Solu* (İstanbul: Kim Yayınları).

—— (1969) *Atatürk ve Devrimcilik* (Ankara: Tekin Yayınevi).

F. Georgeon (1999) 'Son Canlanış', in Robert Mantran (ed.) *Osmanlı İmparatorluğu Tarihi II* (İstanbul: Adam).

F. D. Güler (2003) *Adalet Partisi* (Ankara: Türkiye ve Orta Doğu Amme İdaresi Enstitüsü).

A. Hall and J. Midgley (2004) *Social Policy for Development* (London: SAGE Publications).

E. Kalaycıoğlu (2002) 'The Motherland Party; Representing the State, the Nation or the Nationalists?', in B. Rubin and M. Heper (eds) *Political Parties in Turkey* (London: Frank Cass).

O. Koloğlu (2000) *Ecevit ile CHP* (İstanbul Büke Yayınları).

Kuruç, Bilsay (2005), 'Refah Devletinin Bugünkü Sorunları ve Türkiye Deneyimi', Erol Tuncer, Sosyal Demokrat Düşünce Platformu, Sosyal Demokrasi Derneği Yayınları, Ankara.

A. Mango (2005) *Türkiye ve Türkler* (İstanbul: Remzi Kitabevi).

A. N. Ölçen (1974) *Halk Sektörü* (Ankara: Ayyıldız Matbaası).

N. Özbek (2002) *Osmanlı İmparatorluğu'nda Sosyal Devlet* (İstanbul: İletişim Yayınları).

K. Saybaşılı (1995) *DYP-SHP Koalisyonunun Üç Yılı* (İstanbul: Bağlam).

A. Sen (2001) *Development as Freedom* (New York: Oxford University Press).

M. Sönmez (2002) *100 Göstergede Kriz ve Yoksullaşma* (İstanbul: İletişim Yayınları).

O. Şahinoğlu (1966) *AP'nin Doğuşundan Bugüne* (Ankara: Seden Yayınları).

C. Talas (1992) *Türkiye'nin Açıklamalı Sosyal Politika Tarihi* (Ankara: Bilgi Yayınevi).

T. C. Başbakanlık, Basin-Yayin and Enformasyon Genel Müdürlüğü (2002) *Elli Dokuzuncu Hukumet Programmei* (Ankara: Basın Yayın ve Enformasyon Müdürlüğü).

T. C. Başbakanlık Devlet Planlama Teşkilatı (DPT) (2003) *İllerin ve Bölgelerin Sosyo-Eknomik Gelişmişlik Sıralaması Araştırması*, DPT Yayın No: DPT:2671 (Ankara: DPT).

Ü. Tekin (2004) *AK Partinin Muhafazakar Demokrat Kimliği* (Ankara: Orient).

S. Tezel (1982) *Cumhuriyet Döneminin İktisadi Tarihi (1923–1950)* (Ankara: Yurt Yayınları).

T. Timur (1971) *Türk Devrimi ve Sonrası 1919–1946* (Ankara: Doğan Yayınları).

D. E. Webster (1939) *The Turkey of Atatürk* (Philadelphia: The American Academy of Political and Social Science).

World Bank (2000) *Turkey: Economic Reforms, Living Standards and Social Welfare Study* (Ankara: The World Bank Poverty Reduction and Economic Management Unit).

G. Yalman (2004) An Evaluation of Poverty Alleviation Programmes in Southeast Anatolia Region (Ankara: Türk Sosyal Bilimler Derneği/UNDP).

A. Yaman (2003) 'Üç Kutsal Kitabın Yoksulluk Tasarımı ve Aldığı Önlemler', in A. E. Bilgili and E. Altan (eds) *Yoksulluk* (İstanbul: Deniz Feneri Yardımlaşma ve Dayanışma Derneği).

T. Yazgan (1974) 'Cumhuriyetin Ellinci Yılında Sosyal Güvenliğimiz', in *Türkiye'nin Sosyal ve Ekonomik Sorunları Semineri* (Erzurum: Atatürk Üniversitesi Yayınları).

M. Yılmaz (1999) *ANAP 2000 Vizyonu* (Ankara: ANAP Teknik Büro).

E. J. Zürcher (1995) *Modernleşen Türkiye'nin Tarihi* (İstanbul: İletişim Yayınları).

11
Forgotten Campaigns: A History of Disease in Turkey

Halis Akder

This chapter examines the history of diseases in Turkey in the late nineteenth- and twentieth centuries and interprets the successful campaigns against these diseases as a modernisation project although the study could not cover all diseases and so some health issues and problems are left out. The following discusses various themes such as medicalisation, external influences, the state-building process, population, agriculture and development. It also attempts to understand why the issue of disease control has been underrated among the achievements of the Turkish Republic in terms of modernisation.

When bubonic plague prevailed in both the Ottoman Empire and in Europe, neither could identify the real cause of the disease.[1] The response in the Empire was to interpret the famine as fate, to tend to the sick and help them in their everyday needs. This response caused the plague to spread. In the West, however, a control system developed, in which the community isolated plague victims and was thus more successful in stopping the spread of the plague. In the Ottoman Empire, the plague lasted almost 500 years, 150 years longer than in Europe. In Austria the plague was last seen in 1716, but it only disappeared in the Ottoman territory around the 1850s.

The Habsburgs created a plague-control zone that covered about half of the provinces of Slovenia and Croatia and set up similar military zones in Transylvania and south of the Danube. All along the frontier, sentry posts, backed up by mobile patrols, had orders to shoot unauthorised travellers. The quarantine sometimes lasted up to 48 days. Trade goods were fumigated. For example, the authorities put suspected raw wool in a warehouse and forced low-status people to sleep there. If plague symptoms appeared, the victims were shot and the wool was burned. Yet the long-lasting, strict quarantine was not simply a matter of time and space. The application of Austrian controls deepened an ideological distinction between the West, which saw itself as plague free and civilised, and the Ottoman Empire, which it viewed as disease-ridden and primitive (Watts, 1997, p. 25). The political abstraction, the metaphor of 'the sick man of Europe' probably developed in the second half of the nineteenth century with the disappearing plague (Panzac, 1997, p. 254) and the arriving cholera epidemics.

This longer-lasting plague had at least one very important consequence for the Ottoman regime. It contributed to the divergence in death rates. There was a continuous and significant increase in population numbers and urbanisation in Europe throughout the nineteenth century. Population numbers in the Ottoman Empire, on the contrary, were stagnant or even decreasing. At the time, population increase meant a stronger army and greater economic and political power. Ottomans lacked both. Reformers and statesmen who advocated better health and hygiene practices did not primarily seek good public health as an end in itself, but as a tool for their immediate political, national security and economic welfare aims. Diseases were severe constraints to their main objectives. From this point of view, it is not surprising that we can track the initial steps towards disease control within the modernisation of the army. Almost all armies were demanding medical improvement and modernisation in the nineteenth century. During the Crimean War and the American Civil War, more soldiers died from disease and deficient sanitation than from battle.

The first important step in medical reform was in the sphere of medical education. The foundation of the military-medical-school (Tıphane-i Amire) in 1827 during the reign of Mahmut II was the starting point of modern medical education in the empire. The newly founded hospitals were a parallel development. Well-known medical doctors were invited as instructors. The medium of instruction was French. The second wave of doctors came from Vienna. The third group came during the Crimean War. These were medical doctors from the UK, France and Piemont-Soveyens. They established the so-called Medical Association of Istanbul. The fourth and last group was that of German medical doctors, who arrived towards the end of the century. Around 1870 the medium of instruction changed to Turkish and those professors who could not speak Turkish lost their positions. Armenian and Greek medical doctors who had been educated in Western countries replaced many of them, but German professors were exempt from the Turkish language requirement. The Crimean War created an international atmosphere among medical doctors in the Ottoman Empire. Later, these links were also important in mediating microbiological advances (Becker, 1993).

The last plague epidemic in Istanbul, during 1836–7, killed around 20,000–30,000 people. A French physician, M. Bulard, used the Leander Tower at the Marmara entrance of Bosporus as a quarantine hospital.[2] The quarantine system established because of cholera was very useful in stopping plague epidemics (Yıldırım, 1985, pp. 1325–6), too. Yet the quarantine does not fully explain the defeat of the plague. In certain parts of the Empire, the plague disappeared before the quarantine practice had been instituted (Panzac, 1997, p. 249) and occasional plague cases continued to be observed in Turkey up until 1947 (Sağlık ve Sosyal Yardım Bakanlığı, 1983, p. 101).

The age of cholera and the Ottoman quarantine

The nineteenth-century modernisation projects concerning health had at least two, interdependent dimensions. The first dimension was the effort to 'catch up' with Europe. The Ottomans were trying to organise (define) their medical system as in Western countries. The modernisation of the medical education system, with developments such as modern hospitals but also better nutrition, sanitation, improved housing and urbanisation, were parts of this effort. The second part of the modernisation project was the effort to keep track of recent, immediate advances in medicine. The disjuncture between these two projects was the main source of discontent. For example, disease became curable, but could not be controlled due to material constraints.

There were six cholera pandemics during the nineteenth century. The challenges posed by cholera were, at the beginning, also new to Western countries. The old quarantine system and the medical knowledge of the time were useless against Vibrio cholerae. Cholera spread out of India in 1817 and arrived in both Istanbul and Britain in the same year, 1831. The real cause of cholera was not known until Robert Koch identified it in Alexandria (Egypt) in 1883. The cure did not come until the 1940s (Watts, 2001, p. 321). Writing in 1831, a highly influential medical man, Bentham's friend Dr Thomas Southwood Smith, claimed that fevers (for him cholera was simply a variant of fever) were caused by immorality (sexual acts and the use of alcohol) and by their victims' general lack of self-reliance and proper habits (Watts, 2001, p. 194). Riots in East London occurred as a response to the confusion caused by the disease. An angry mob, outraged by the death of a young patient, stormed into a hospital and liberated other cholera patients who they believed were at risk of being murdered by medical doctors (Watts, 2001, p. 192).

The first quarantine in Istanbul took place at the Black Sea entrance of Bosporus to block the prevailing cholera epidemics in Russia from spreading to the city (Sağlık ve Sosyal Yardım Bakanlığı, 1983, p. 160). Quarantine policies met with resistance in 1831 in Istanbul. Some traditional people interpreted it as a practice that contradicted aspects of Islam (e.g. burial requirements). This precautionary quarantine was actually not successful. Cholera entered into Istanbul despite it. The same precaution was repeated in 1835 at the Dardanelles, but cholera broke out again. In 1837 the Ottomans established a quarantine assembly, the first preventive health institution in Istanbul. This event can be seen as the breakthrough in the so-called medicalisation process. The Italian practice of plague control, established in the fifteenth century, had evolved into what we call quarantine today. It was not simply a practical precaution against disease, but was strongly ideological. The quarantine was not limited to border crossing. It could be established in any part of the city if cholera was reported. Police then quarantined the house and no one was allowed to enter or leave. At the beginning, even doctors who made examinations had to be 'imprisoned' with their families under quarantine for ten days or more. The quarantine justified intervention into the lives of ordinary people during epidemics, and these ordinary people were usually the poor, who lived in a part of the city with insufficient or no infrastructure. However, quarantine of this sort was not necessarily an efficient practice. The typical number of persons in a household was high and these strict measures discouraged many households from reporting their infected members (Moulin, 1999, p. 181). All these epidemics happened against a background of war, displacement, migration and unplanned urbanisation. So, the Ottomans were not just repeating the plague-quarantine experience of Europe, but were also faced with brand new challenges of their time, and had insufficient modernised medical manpower, infrastructure and finance to deal with them.

The third International Sanitary Conference brought the Ottoman Empire under the spotlight.[3] The conference, which was held in Istanbul between February and September of 1866, could have been called the Cholera Conference, given its focus on the disease.[4] It was a French initiative, launched after the ship-borne importation of the disease across the Mediterranean from Egypt to southern Europe in 1865. Earlier visitations to Europe from 1827 onward had come overland from India, working their way westward through southern Russia and/or Persia (Watts, 2001, p. 329). The Istanbul Conference of 1866 agreed that cholera was propagated by man and spread at the speed of steamboats and railways. From this, it followed that if human movement was blocked, through a cordon of troops, the quarantine of ships or other forceful intervention, a cholera epidemic could be prevented from spreading beyond the locale in which it had first broken out (Watts, 2001, p. 321). The 1865 epidemic in Europe had been closely linked with the Hajj. The pilgrims to Mecca from India were singled out as the most important cause of the spread of cholera to Europe. So the conference recommended the Ottomans begin the organisation of the so-called Hijaz Quarantine (Sarıyıldız, 1996). There were about 80 quarantine stations around Ottoman territory during 1862. After the Istanbul Conference, many more were added (Yıldırım, 1985, p. 1374).

The reaction of European countries was split. They welcomed the quarantines. The industrial revolution was globalising the world, meaning no country alone was in a position to stop epidemics on its own, so international effort was required (Kelly and Richard, 2000). More specifically, they saw Istanbul as the gate to Europe. However, the British, who had signed a free trade agreement with the Ottomans, were reluctant. For them, restrictive sanitary undertakings did not prevent the spread of cholera, but hurt trade and interrupted civil liberties. The Russians were also irritated by Ottoman quarantines. The Ottoman government tried to quell the criticism and ameliorate the lack of expertise of their quarantines by inviting foreign members to their quarantine assemblies. The assemblies evolved to operate with an international management and did not always serve the interests of the Ottomans (Sarıyıldız, 1996). Quarantine regimes were costly and in time they transformed into another kind of capitulation. During the negotiations of the Lausanne Treaty (1923), European countries were still arguing that plague and cholera were endemic in the East, that these diseases were propagated by the Hajj, that Istanbul was the gate to Europe and therefore, in terms of sanitary manpower, Turkey was dependent on Europe. The young Turkish Republic disagreed, and 'nationalised' the quarantine under the Ministry of Health (Sarıyıldız, 1996, p. 10).

Cholera disappeared after 1918, but returned in 1970, bought by workers coming from neighbouring affected countries (Kelly and Richard, 2000, p. 231). There were 384 infected persons in Istanbul and 52 of them died (Sağlık ve Sosyal Yardım Bakanlığı, 1983, p. 87). This seventh pandemic was in some respects different from the nineteenth-century pandemics. It was more geographically widespread and lasted longer (Kelly and Richard, 2000, p. 217). Given the intensity and duration of the pandemic, Turkey's experience, inspection, treatment and prevention measures could be considered adequate.

The Crimean War and syphilis

The arrival of syphilis into the Ottoman Empire is not well documented. Yet the Turkish name of the disease (frengi) indicates a European, particularly French connection: 'the French disease'. The disease has become a serious threat during and after the Crimean War (1853–6). It spread all over the Empire. Migrants from Russian-occupied territories, returning (captive) soldiers from War against Greece, from the Crimean War, the Russian War (1877–8) (Tat, 1982, p. 83), the Balkan Wars (Dağlar, 2004, p. 33) and the prostitution that attended these conflicts were among the main causes. The first brothels in Istanbul opened in 1856–8 (Yıldırım, 1985, p. 1329). Syphilis disease was concentrated in the Black Sea region and the core was Kastamonu province, in the western Black Sea. In contrast to European countries, the disease was more prevalent in small towns and rural areas. There is no single convincing explanation for why the disease concentrated in northwest Anatolia and specifically around Bolu and Kastamonu. A special army force (hassa) recruited the majority of its soldiers from this region, and they were stationed in Istanbul around Galata, where most of the brothels existed. So, the returning soldiers might have brought the disease with them. Another possible explanation points to the proximity of the region to Istanbul for employment and travel opportunities. Again, the workers and travellers might have visited brothels and, returning to Kastamonu, may have carried the disease to their families. Sailors were also stationed at the harbours of the region. Men from the Black Sea region worked in Russia as migrant-workers, especially as bakers. They might have carried the disease from there, too (Kalkan, 2004, p. 71). Those who suffered from the disease remained in rural areas, medically untreated for very long periods, if they survived.

The Ottoman administration started the so-called registration system in 1879 in large towns, first in Istanbul. This was the first attempt to attack syphilis by controlling prostitution. The officers of the municipal police accompanied a physician who inspected the brothels. The infected women were sent to the 'women's hospital'. 'Clandestine' brothels were a serious problem. Because of the capitulations, until 1914 the police could not enter the houses of foreigners. Their controls were limited to a certain section (Beyoğlu and Galata) of the city. This meant that the inflicted prostitutes could escape the control system by looking for customers elsewhere. In İzmir, similar measures were taken. Here, the brothels scattered around the town all moved to a faraway district (Sakızlı). This eased the control. Registration was not applicable in small towns, where there were no brothels. In the rural regions, the responsibility to prevent the disease lay with the 'imam' and 'muhtar'. They were not to allow couples to marry if any of them was suspected of being syphilitic (Kalkan, 2004, p. 73).

The alarm came actually from the army. The German General Baron von der Goltz, who was invited to manage the reorganisation of the Ottoman army in 1883, reported the high incidence of syphilis among new recruits and insisted on appropriate measures. A German specialist in dermatology, Ernst von Düring was invited to help. Düring stayed in Turkey from 1889 to 1902. He made about 14 inspection expeditions throughout Anatolia with a team of physicians (Terzioğlu, 1976, p. 156) and reported 80,000 syphilis victims out of 250,000 inspected persons. During his expeditions, he trained local physicians on diagnosis and treatment and identified the topography of the disease. He made suggestions for an organisation to combat it (Tat, 1982, p. 84) and proposed the location of specialised hospitals with adequate manpower.[5] All these efforts helped to modernise the (delayed) treatment of the disease in rural Anatolia. The treatments were successful when carried out, and to express official appreciation, Düring was rewarded with the title of civil-pasha (mirmiranlık). He returned to Germany in 1902, despite a number of generous offers.

In spite of this success, the outcome was not maintained. During the Balkan Wars and First World War the problem was as severe as it has been in the earlier phase (Dağlar, 2004, p. 34). The main reason for the failure of the prevention regime was poor finance. Another important reason was the requirement of long-term treatment. Poor people with the disease could not afford proper treatment, and certain population groups tried to resist the

Table 11.1   Incidence of syphilis (1926–72) (Cumulative)

Year	Incidence (Cumulative)	New cases (1/100 000)
1926	84.662	31
1930	114.730	87
1935	173.578	127
1940	170.177	101
1945	158.353	162
1950	118.169	50
1955	75.126	32
1960	47.565	15
1965	27.802	2.2
1970	17.420	1.7
1972	13.020	3.6

Source: Sağlık ve Sosyal Yardım Bakanlığı, 1983, p. 96.

control imposed by the strict measures for several reasons. These existing problems and concerns about the decreasing population were transferred to the Republic. Although the topography of the disease had been identified, different forms of resistance were familiar, and suggested solutions were reasonable, financial constraints made the solutions impossible at that time.

In 1921 the National Assembly passed a new law that offered free syphilis treatment. In 1925 a new regulation was put into force. New inspection teams were formed for detecting infected people. The government founded new dispensaries for venereal diseases in Istanbul, Ankara and Izmir in 1927. By the 1980s there were 16 such dispensaries. These kept the identities of the patients secret. A new law made attendance for inspections compulsory. The inflicted ones were also forced to accept treatment (for free) together with their children. Compulsory medical examination before marriage (1913) was reinstated in a 1931 regulation. 2,247,561 persons were checked during 1926–47 and 86,231 (3.8%) were found to be syphilitic. The incidence increased during the Second World War to another peak. The treatment period was reduced considerably after 1964, when new methods for a cure became available (Sağlık ve Sosyal Yardım Bakanlığı, 1983, pp. 93–4). In 1945 there were 30,652 new incidences of the disease, comprising 162 people out of 100,000. New incidences had dropped to 650, a proportion of one person in 100,000, by 1980 (Tat, 1982, p. 85).

Pasteur, rabies, smallpox, diphtheria and microbiology

It is important to stress that the modernisation of medicine diffused into the Ottoman Empire and Turkey quite fast, much faster than general modernisation processes. Advances in microbiological science offer good examples in the late nineteenth century and early twentieth century, when Louis Pasteur and Robert Koch both convincingly demonstrated that living microbes caused many diseases. Koch discovered the cause of cholera in 1883. He had discovered the causal agent of tuberculosis two years earlier. In 1885 Louis Pasteur established a clear relationship between micro-organisms and disease, and formulated the fundamental principles of the germ theory of disease. This approach rejected the miasmas theory, which ascribed disease to bad air (miasmas) from marshes (Faria, 2001). Not all French and German scientists welcomed this breakthrough. Koch and Pasteur opposed each other, creating scientific controversy and generating angry and impassioned public debate. Their antipathy was reflected in the competition between France and Germany, specifically the sentiments of the Franco-German War in 1870. Koch and Pasteur's views were in fact not antagonist, but instead complementary (Priego, 2003). However, scientific development was not free of politics. The diffusion of microbiology science into the Ottoman Empire reflects the ambitions of the main European powers but also the intrigues and manoeuvres of Sultan Abdülhamid II (Huet, 2000).

In 1886, a committee headed by Zoreos Pasha was sent to Paris to learn the anti-rabies immunisation technique that Pasteur had developed in 1885 (Yıldırım, 1995, pp. 91–7).[6] Zoreos Pasha presented the Sultan's donation of 10,000 French francs for the foundation of the Pasteur Institute in Paris and the first-class 'mecidiye' order of Abdülhamit II for successful studies.[7] After his return in 1887, he founded the Rabies Treatment Centre in Istanbul. Zoreos Pasha applied the first anti-rabies vaccination by Pasteur method in 1887 (Yıldırım, 1985, p. 1335). This method continued until 1934. By the 1980s, the number of anti-rabies vaccination stations had increased to 500 (Unat, 1986, pp. 21–3). Yet rabies was actually not necessarily the most important health issue at that time in the empire. The sultan's immediate demand for microbiological technology transfer might have been primarily a quest for international recognition and a justification for the modernity of his regime (Moulin, 1999, p. 179). Another explanation for the closely followed innovations in bacteriology might be the Ottoman Empire's own practices of 'traditional' smallpox inoculation. Edward Jenner developed this inoculation in 1796 in Britain and it was first applied in Istanbul in 1800. There was an attempt to produce the vaccine domestically in 1847, but it was abandoned and instead the vaccine was imported. After several private attempts, the government established the Imperial Vaccine Laboratory in Istanbul in 1892 (Yıldırım, 1985, pp. 1333–5). It should be noted that smallpox is one of the few eradicated diseases in Turkey. Since 1957 no case has been reported (Sağlık ve Sosyal Yardım Bakanlığı, 1983, p. 85).

The serious need for microbiology arose during the cholera epidemic in 1893. The sultan personally requested advice from Pasteur who sent

A. Chantemesse to Istanbul (Nuran Yıldırım, 1995, p. 1336). After his advice, the sultan permitted France to start another 'Pasteur Institute', this one in Istanbul. Chantemesse established the Constantinople Imperial Bacteriology Institute, or 'Bakteriyolojihane-i Şahane', in 1893.[8] Chantemesse was quite successful and vanquished the cholera epidemic. He also brought the diphtheria serum to Istanbul just after its inauguration in the VIII International Hygiene and Demographic Congress (1894) in Budapest (Yıldırım and Bozkurt, 1999).

The first director of the Constantinople Imperial Bacteriology Institute was Maurice Nicolle (1893–1900). He admired Ottoman modernisation but soon experienced great disappointment with its efforts. The French embassy refused his immediate resignation, fearing that German or Austrian experts would replace him. His dilemma pointed to the heart of the problem. The use of the new knowledge of the existence of microscopic organisms and causes of infectious diseases required not only medical expertise, but also social, cultural, industrial and economic development. The diffusion of microbiological technology alone, in the form of a laboratory, was insufficient to combat disease. The microbiological breakthrough had to go hand-in-hand with the widespread use of clean, potable water, improved hygiene, sanitation and proper urbanisation. Besides, the laboratory operated according to the rules of Ottoman bureaucracy and was subject to the arbitrary decisions of the sultan (Moulin, 1999, pp. 169–93). During the same period, the North African Pasteur Institutes were more innovative than the Institute in Istanbul, due to the comparatively more liberal polices of the French government (Huet, 2000, pp. 289–94).

Paul Remlinger replaced Maurice Nicolle in 1900. He was a specialist in rabies and later became a world-class expert on the subject. The third director of the Imperial Bacteriology Institute was Louis Simond, who showed that the plague was transmitted by rat-fleas (Huet, 2000, pp. 289–9). Dr Refik Güran replaced him. In 1913, Refik Bey (Saydam) initiated a reorganisation of the Institute.[9] The last French director was P. Forgeot, who remained in office only briefly due to the outbreak of the First World War.

The experiences of the microbiological advances in various Institutes around the Empire were transmitted and cumulated after the declaration of the Turkish Republic in Ankara. After Refik Saydam became the Minister of Health (1925), he founded the 'Merkez Hıfzısıhha Enstitüsü' the Hygiene Centre in 1928. All these institutions formed the basis of this new Hygiene Centre: the Imperial Vaccine Laboratory, established in Istanbul in 1892, Constantinople Imperial Bacteriology Institute (1894) and the Bacteriology Centre in Ankara (1924). This Institute then became the centre for all health reforms during the early phases of the Republic. After his death (1942), the Grand National Assembly renamed the Institute the 'Refik Saydam Hygiene Centre' as a sign of gratitude.

War and army fever: From empire to nation state

The transitional years from the 1880s to the 1930s, which led to the full medicalisation of the West with the help of microbiology, coincided with the transition from the Ottoman Empire to the Turkish Republic. These were also years of successive wars. The wars, accompanied by the displacement of various ethnic populations, were the cause of serious epidemics throughout the Empire. The death toll of the civilian population due to displacement, war and disease was high.[10] The statistical estimates on the losses to the army during the First World War because of disease are more detailed. The statistics of the Ministry of War, evaluated by Ahmet Emin (Yalman) (Yalman, 1930, pp. 252–3), gives the figure for deaths by disease as 401,859. Deaths by wounds were reported as numbering 59,463 (Dağlar, 2004, pp. 320–1). A more recent study calculates the same statistics, but counts only those who have died in hospitals, with a resulting toll of 330,796 (ATASE; Özdemir, 2005, p. 139). Deaths by disease in the Ottoman army were disproportionately high in comparison to other armies. Ahmet Emin (Yalman) tabulates the distribution of deaths by epidemic diseases as in Table 11.2 (Özdemir, 2005, pp. 120–2, 137–8). The most widespread disease during the war was malaria, but the deadliest were dysentery and typhus.

Typhus was resurgent in all these successive wars. It was nicknamed 'army fever' or 'war fever'. In both the First and Second World Wars, there were serious typhus epidemics not only in the army, but among civilians. Infected lice or fleas carried the disease, and humans were infected by rubbing or scratching the lice faeces into the skin. Poverty, crowding, mass migrations, inadequate housing and malnutrition caused typhus epidemics.[11]

Dr Reşat Rıza (Kor) and Mustafa Hilmi were pioneering physicians in the effort to develop a vaccination against typhus. These two physicians from Gülhane Medical Training School created a typhus vaccine. They experimented with it on themselves, then prepared and published a report. Tevfik Sağlam applied it in the Army in 1915 in the Eastern Front. It was also used on German soldiers. In spite of its limitations, it yielded satisfactory results. Dr Fox developed the final, improved version of typhus vaccination much later, in 1939 (Yıldırım, 1985, p. 1338). The defeat of typhus became possible with the application of DDT during (1943 Sicily) and after the Second World

Table 11.2 Deaths by disease in First World War

Disease	Reported cases	Deaths
Malaria	461 799	23 351
Dysentery	147 000	40 000
Fever	103 000	4 000
Typhus	93 000	26 000
Syphilis	27 000	150

War. During the Second World War typhus was again a great problem in Turkey. The disease became rare thereafter and the last cases were recorded in Turkey in 1966 and 1969 (Sağlık ve Sosyal Yardım Bakanlığı, 1983, p. 99). The development of the Typhus vaccine was an significant breakthrough in the First World War. The Germans replaced the French as Turkey's connection to developments in microbiology during the First War. Their most remarkable success was the vaccination campaign against cholera in Smyrna. The campaign against malaria around Izmir was not as successful, due to a shortage in quinine supplies (Wittern, 1981).

The War of Independence was the breaking point from the Ottoman health policy. The Ottomans had organised health first under the foreign ministry, as the focus was then on quarantines, and later, with microbiological advances, under the Ministry of Interior, as it increasingly involved local governments.[12] During the War of Independence, the new regime reorganised health matters under a separate Ministry of Health and Social Affairs in 1920.[13] Social Affairs now dealt with population, migration, immigration, displacement and all kinds of social problems caused by the war and sudden demographic changes. The ministry was employed with experienced, successful ex-Ottoman military-physicians. Other distinguishing features of the new republican health policy included new legislation and the systematic collection of health statistics. An emphasis on 'the nation', 'the future', 'building healthy national people, women and children' and the increase in population, meant health affairs received increased attention. The medicalisation that had occurred during the Ottoman period had been dependent on Western countries and was very much focused on the army and war. The Republic tried to bring such measures to rural Turkey during a relatively peaceful period. There was, for the first time, a strong break away from external powers in matters of health policy.

Malaria, eucalyptus, agriculture and development

The legacy of early republican health policies started in 1925 with the nomination of Refik Saydam as head of the Ministry of Health. He remained from 1925 to 1937, a record period, in this position.[14] He made preventive public health policies a priority and kept modern bacteriology at a central position. He started a systematic campaign against trachoma, tuberculosis, syphilis and malaria. Some recent studies refer to this early period of the Republic as 'forgotten' and their general criticism that the society asserts 'no appreciation', refers only to these campaigns (Bahadır, 2004, pp. 8–9).

Campaigns against syphilis and tuberculosis restarted after an interruption caused by reorganised legislation and management. Campaigns against trachoma and malaria were new, as very little had been done about these diseases during the Ottoman period. Yet a clear priority and the greatest achievement of the Republic was the campaign against malaria. The period from 1925–37 was only the first phase of the malaria campaign. The second phase came during the war period (1937–44). During those years there was no policy change, but during the war the policies could not be applied due to material constraints, and malaria returned. The next phases are 1945–50, followed by 1950–7. Again, some studies consider 1945–57 to be one period. Those who consider the start of the Marshall Aid important prefer the two-phase approach. 1957 marked the start of the eradication campaign. Malaria incidence reached a historical minimum by 1970, and from then onwards malaria was resurgent again in diminishing cycles (Tekeli and İlkin, 1999, p. 209; Akalın, 1979, p. 187).

Malaria had been a seasonal curse in Turkey (Anatolia) since ancient times. Unlike plague and cholera or syphilis, it did not intrude from outside, instead, it was endemic. The (Anatolian) type of malaria was in many cases non-lethal. A considerable population was suffering though not dying directly from malaria, and those infected were becoming susceptible to other serious diseases as they weakened. Based on the information collected by various Health Directorates, the Ministry prepared a malaria map in 1924 and delivered a report on the 'Geography of Malaria in Turkey' at the first Health Conference 1925. These two documents together give considerable information on the distribution of malaria in Turkey during the 1920s. The disease prevailed in fertile coastal plains, river valleys, and flatlands of rivers. It was also prevalent in Thrace and in the Southeast. It was not so common in areas with relatively high altitude, or in Istanbul. However, this static picture does not reveal everything. The lifestyle of local residents adjusted to the disease. People in coastal regions moved to inland environs with higher altitudes, beyond the reach of mosquitoes, in the late spring and summer season (Tekeli and İlkin, 1999, pp. 221–9).

Malaria does not arise from a virus or bacteria. Prevention or cure via a vaccine (or antibiotic) is not possible. Microscopic parasites that persist in human blood are transferred between human hosts by certain kinds of mosquitoes. As the prevention campaign started in 1925 in Turkey, there were already two opposing views on how to control malaria. After discoveries by Grassi, Ross and others, mosquitoes become the main target of the 'American' approach.[15] Control focused on the reduction or elimination of the mosquitoes (by spraying insecticides). The US government had already used mosquito vector eradication in Cuba (1900) to control yellow fever, and repeated its success in Panama between 1904 and 1914 by eliminating yellow fever and reducing malaria. The other, 'European' position, that dominated until the late 1930s, focused on quininisation of the human host. Among Europeans, the Italians had a broader view. For them, malaria was a rural disease, so they established a social definition of malaria and advocated improved general sanitation, land drainage and reclamation, improved agriculture, plus the regular use of quinine as a therapeutic and prophylactic (Stephan, 2003, p. 27).

The legislation for the anti-malaria campaign was prepared in 1924, and improved and enacted in 1926 in the Turkish National Assembly. The justification for the law was in line with the Italian approach. The government prioritised reducing malaria quite explicitly in the 1923 and 1925 government programmes. According to these, 'Syphilis and tuberculosis were wrongly held in the country as the most damaging diseases. It was actually malaria from which people in Turkey were suffering most!' There are actually no sound statistics for verifying this observation. However, during the First World War malaria was the most common disease among soldiers, it was observed quite frequently during the War of Independence, and in 1923 and 1924 it spread in epidemic proportions around Ankara. However, the justification document prepared by the 'malaria commission' for the 'malaria campaign law' was not based on the immediate developments but on the long-run analysis of the disease.

Before discussing the benefits of the programme, the document defines and describes the campaign against malaria as nationwide action, not solely a concern of the Ministry of Health and health personnel. The campaign asked everyone to participate, and emphasised teaching and learning about the fight against malaria to be part of the general curriculum. The ultimate goal was economic development. Rapid growth was constrained severely by labour shortages. A main cause of the labour shortage (among others) was malaria. Additionally, a considerable proportion of migrants coming from the Balkans, especially from Greece, were infected with malaria. Even if indirectly, malaria was increasing the death rate, especially of children. The weakened survivors could not participate fully in the work force and their children were rarely physically and mentally healthy. Malaria was prevalent in places with higher population densities (near rivers and seas). In order for that state to establish a productive, active population, the campaign against malaria had to be won. The explanation of the law continues by emphasising the additional benefits of land drainage and reclamation that would result in improved agriculture (E. Aydın, 1999, pp. 303–8; Tekeli and İlkin, 1999, pp. 211–13).

Malaria control was actually a scientific, technical activity. It required skilled and dedicated staff with training. Draining marshes and lakes, damming, canalling and land reclamation were all engineering projects. It was the battle against malaria that induced human control over the environment, and this conscious effort to understand and control nature may be considered an important step in the modernisation of Turkey (Tekeli and İlkin, 1999, p. 209).

The Ministry of Health invited two German scientists, experts on tropical medicine, to Turkey in 1925. Professor Martini had started his research on mosquitoes in 1926. The Malaria Institute was founded upon his advice in Adana on the land offered by Adana Municipality and in barracks donated by the German Red Cross.[16] The Institute became the centre of the anti-malaria campaign. At that time, not all mosquito varieties in Anatolia were known. Some new varieties were identified and one of them was named 'Aedes Refiki' after the Minister of Health, as a sign of appreciation and gratitude. The Institute became the centre for education and research.[17]

The Malaria Campaign was organised 'vertically', that is, it operated independently of the rest of the health organisations in Turkey. The malaria campaigners were paid much higher salaries than other health employees. A physician in the malaria campaign received a larger salary than a provincial governor or Member of Parliament.[18] Fieldwork was organised according to regions. A director and laboratory chief headed the project in each malarial region. Each region was further subdivided to sections, and a physician managed each section. Each section consisted of localities (a group of villages). Health officials (specially educated and trained for malaria campaign) directed each locality. There was a dispensary with five to ten beds in each region, and in Adana there was a main malaria hospital. This organisational scheme started first in Ankara, Adana and Aydın in 1925, and in 1926 Konya, Bursa and Balıkesir joined.[19] When the malaria law was enacted, there were already five campaign regions, with 32 sections and 1454 localities. The number of localities increased to 3,453 in 1930 and stagnated from then until 1935 due to the impact of the Great Depression on the Turkish economy. Still, 14 per cent of the population in regions where malaria prevailed most intensively was covered by the campaign in 1935 (Tekeli and İlkin, 1999, p. 237).

During the 1920s, complete mosquito eradication was in Turkey neither practicable nor cost-effective. In the absence of methods to attack mosquitoes directly, the preferred strategy was to reduce breeding sites, that is, to drain swamps and marshes. 25,155 hectares of marshland or wetland were drained for the dual purpose of creating farmland and destroying mosquito breeding sites from 1925 to 1936. Drained territory increased by another 21,363 hectares from 1937 to 1939. Draining and canalling were expensive activities. The state required five days of forced labour from locals (peasants). If marshes were in private estates, then the owner was held responsible for draining. If draining was not feasible in a short period of time, settlements within three kilometres could be resettled elsewhere, if the government could afford it. It was obvious that marshland draining could not be fully accomplished by forced labour alone. This task required increased government involvement in waterworks.

An interesting method of draining was the planting of eucalyptus trees. Throughout the nineteenth century, it was believed that eucalyptus fought malaria simply by disinfecting the ground and air.[20] It was therefore called the 'fever tree' in many countries, and in Turkey it was known as the 'malaria tree'. A report prepared in Turkey (in 1928) indicated clearly that the eucalyptus tree was actually not fighting malaria directly. It was only useful for draining marshes. Poplar trees or willows could be equally useful in this regard. The first eucalyptus forestation (177 hectares) was created in 1937 around Kalkan and another one (670 hectares) in 1939 around Tarsus (Tekeli and İlkin, 1999, pp. 242–3). Drying up wetlands was not necessarily an ecologically sound practice. But only one Member of Parliament criticised such activities in 1946, comparing the practice in Turkey to the Italian example (Tekeli and İlkin, 1999, p. 251).

The use of larvivorous fish was the biological method for fighting mosquitoes. At the beginning of the twentieth century anti-malaria projects were using it in America, as well as in Europe. 'Gambusia' varieties, originally from Hawaii, were the most sought-after fish. They became an anti-malarial tool in many other countries: the US, Brazil, Philippines, Spain and Corsica. It was actually clear from the very beginning that fish never could eradicate larva but they were a useful, a cheap complement to other measures. In 1929, there were early attempts to use fish in Turkey, too. Researchers looked for local fish varieties around Adana. They announced the discovery of five suitable fish species and with four of them conducted certain experiments. The studies also suggested useful information about their transportation and use (Tok, 1929). Later, authorities used fish in the deeper wetlands of Thrace to reduce larva and pupa in 1944 (Tekeli and İlkin, 1999, p. 243).

Malaria also required government intervention for agricultural irrigation management. Rice cultivation came under strict control. A 'discontinued irrigation' method (kesik sulama) was enforced by the 'rice-cultivation-law' (1936). The same law regulated the working hours. Workers were not allowed to start work before dawn, and had to stop one hour before sunset. They had to be supplied with quinine, and their barracks had to be far away from irrigated fields and protected (netted) against mosquitoes.

The other method of the malaria campaign was quinine use. Quinine consumption increased in Turkey from 1314 kg in 1925 to 6217 kg in 1935. This increase should not be understood as merely a straightforward intake of medicine. One of the managers of Adana Malaria Institute assessed the greatest achievement of the Institute in 1938 as the propagation of quinine to the peasants for the cure and prevention of malaria (Fişek, 1987). The propagation of quinine meant a fight against superstition and traditional methods of disease prevention, such as votive offerings to shrines. It was widely believed that malaria could be avoided by fumigation. People used to bind their wrists with cotton threads in the belief that they were cutting up malaria (fever). They also believed that sprinkling a handful of salt into water and wishing that the fever might disappear just as the salt melts down would bring a cure or relief against malaria (Süyev, 1953).

Resurgence, Second World War, aftermath

Turkey stayed neutral in the Second World War, but this choice did not fully protect the country from the damaging effects of the war. Those years

Table 11.3 Budget of Ministry of Health and malaria campaign

Year	Budget of Ministry of Health	Budget of Malaria campaign	Share of Malaria campaign
1925	6.535.362 TL	600.000 TL	9.1%
1930	4.502.216 TL	916.000 TL	20.3%
1935	4.821.587 TL	914.076 TL	18.9%
1940	8.179.424 TL	494.000 TL	6.0%
1945	17.907.024 TL	7.158.000 TL	39.9%
1950	56.721.916 TL	3.449.475 TL	6.0%

Source: B. Akalın, 1979, p. 189.

may be seen as years of strong discontent. Many achievements of the earlier periods of public health work were wiped out. The threat of war absorbed all resources, and import restrictions on medicine due to the war nearly constituted an embargo. The financing of quinine imports was regulated by a revolving fund. In 1935 the Red Crescent became the monopoly for securing cheap imports. Quinine consumption increased in 1940 to 9,548 kg. The use of Atebrin, starting in 1940, exceeded quinine use by 1945 (Tekeli and İlkin, 1999, p. 249) but could not compensate for the overall fallback in access to medicine during the war. The reduced consumption of quinine due to import difficulties and higher prices revived malaria. Anti-larva practices came to a standstill, too. Imports of diesel oil and 'Paris Green' became very difficult. Military movements and the disruption of drainage programmes contributed to the resurgence as well. Drainage programmes continued after the war until 1955.[21] The share of the malaria campaign in the Health Ministry budget may illustrate these developments (Akalın, 1979, p.189).

The problem was not only the lack of chemicals and medicine but the fact that the campaign lacked qualified personnel and equipment, too.

The aftermath of the war saw the start of an 'extraordinary malaria campaign'. In 1946, the campaign was renewed by new legislation and reorganisation. The campaign's coverage increased from 4614 to 16,934 villages. It was ambitious, and the coverage was scaled down to 12,381 villages in 1951. This meant that almost half of the total population of Turkey was affected by the campaign. The government budget share for the malaria campaign increased to a peak, 39.9 per cent (7.158.000TL). Instead of targeting the habitat, the practice of attacking mosquitoes directly came into fashion after the successful eradication programmes of the Rockefeller Foundation in Brazil in late 1930s. By this time, more powerful insecticides such as DDT (dichlorodiphenyltrichloroethane) were available. Before DDT, the even cruder and probably more dangerous Paris Green was used to kill mosquito larvae (Akalın, 1979, p. 188). DDT was applied in Turkey for the first time in 1946. At the beginning, it was extremely diluted[23] and the total amount

Table 11.4 Malaria campaign activities (1930–72)

Year	No of localities	Population[22] (p)	No of blood-tests (b)	No of incidences (i)	(i/b)x 1000	(i/p)x 100000
1930	3 453	2 011 980	370 078	45 653	123	2 269
1935	3 469	2 291 715	594 580	40 842	69	1 782
1940	4 450	3 324 237	586 597	115 683	197	3 479
1945	16 934	7 549 280	63 219	16 739	265	221
1950	11 742	5 307 420	46 038	4 211	91	79
1955	12 812	6 622 135	35 171	1 494	42	22
1960	29 844	16 483 208	1 675 657	3 092	2	18
1965	36 481	30 285 614	1905 218	4 587	2	15
1970	36 799	34 445 165	2 189 875	1 263	1	4
1972	36 970	36 862 865	2 124 015	2 892	1	8

Source: Sağlık ve Sosyal Yardım Bakanlığı, 1983, p. 110.

sprayed in that year was only 2.375 kg. The consumption increased in 1948 to 68 tons, and in 1950 to 109 tons.

Marshall plan aid, WHO, UNESCO, and DDT

For Turkey, the 1950s saw not only a transition to (vector) mosquito control with the intensive use of insecticides, but also a transition from a relatively egalitarian policy to a utilitarian, efficiency-oriented approach. The early Republican policy ranked diseases according to their importance (relative to labour shortage and development objectives). The (malaria) campaign started where the problem was most severe and became more widespread as time passed. The state's objective was to extend the disease-free (equal health status with respect to malaria) geography. Today the health problem is stated from an 'efficiency' point of view: if income or spending on health is reallocated, a higher health status may be reached. The crucial difference between the two approaches is the role of boundaries (rights) and the emphasis on the initial condition (Roemer, 1993).

This transformation began with the influence of international organisations. The Marshall Plan aid programme was not a proper international organisation, but it may be considered as a forerunner to later development projects. Turkey benefited from Marshall aid starting in 1950. The Malaria campaign received 851,000 US dollars in 1951, and this sum increased to 1,855,000 US dollars in 1952 and finally to 1,470,000 US dollars in 1953 (Süyev, 1953). This aid money was spent on insecticides and motor vehicles. DDT consumption jumped to 645 tons in 1952. Total DDT consumption from 1946 to 1972 amounted to 10,896,670 kg (Sağlık ve Sosyal Yardım Bakanlığı, 1983, p. 108). Quinine and atebrin consumption fell alongside

Table 11.5   UNICEF financial contributions by activity (1950–72)

BCG campaign	581.300 US $
Basic public health	2.014.600 US $
Trachoma campaign	509.600 US $
Malaria campaign	7.000.000 US $
Leprosy campaign	70.000 US $
Pasteurized milk project	292.000 US $
Food care for schools	1.173.200 US $
Baby food	788.000 US $
Social services	172.100 US $
Immigration	45.000 US $

Source: Sağlık ve Sosyal Yardım Bakanlığı, 1983, p. 343.

these successful results. In 1956, quinine use had decreased to 2,010 kg and atebrin consumption was only 211 kg. Compared to past efforts, the new campaign was cost-efficient.

The International Conference on Tropical Medicine and Malaria in 1953 took place in Istanbul. The discussions concentrated on malaria eradication. In 1955, the World Health Organisation announced a campaign to eradicate malaria across the globe based largely on the Rockefeller Foundation's precedents.[24] Turkey accepted the call. The government established a malaria eradication programme together with the World Health Organisation and UNESCO. These bodies supported almost all material requirements, such as equipment, medicine and insecticides (See Table 11.5). In 1960 a new 'eradication law' was enacted. By 1968, the disease was to a large extent (in 96% of Turkey's territory) under control but remained a problem in the South East.[25]

From 1971 onwards, the number of malaria cases in the Cukurova and Amikova plains began to increase, reaching epidemic proportions in 1976 and 1977, when 37,320 and 115,512 cases were reported respectively.[26] Many factors contributed to the revival of malaria. Ironically, agricultural development and bad irrigation practices which contributed to it significantly. New road construction activities created water pools that were suitable for mosquito breeding. Insufficient sanitation due to increase in squatter housing was another factor. Insufficient coverage by the anti-malarial campaign played a major role. Many experienced personnel retired and were not replaced, due to the incorrect assumption that malaria had been eradicated (Akalın, 1979, p. 18). Through concentrated effort and at considerable cost, the epidemic was contained. But by 1980 malaria had revived in the southeast. One of the main reasons was again agriculture. Irregular insecticide spraying contributed to insecticide resistance. At the same time, refusals to accept house spraying increased, due to the unpleasant odour of the insecticides. The situation began to improve again in 1997.[27]

Malaria versus tuberculosis

During the Second World War tuberculosis also reached epidemic proportions. Yet there were differences between the anti-tuberculosis and anti-malaria campaigns. In the earlier periods, more resources were devoted to the campaign against malaria. Malaria was always more widespread than other diseases, but tuberculosis was the deadliest. More importantly, as the malaria campaign was a higher priority than those against syphilis and tuberculosis, the chances for curing malaria were higher, and other countries around the Mediterranean were making similar choices. Until the 1950s all efforts against tuberculosis consisted mainly of sanatorium cures conducted by nongovernmental organisations or by the health ministry. Improved social and hygienic conditions and adequate nutrition were required to strengthen the resistance of the body. The sanatorium served two functions: the tubercular patient was isolated, and better care was easily applied.

In the nineteenth century in the Ottoman Empire tuberculosis was as common as in Europe, but unlike malaria, it was more urbanised, later moving from towns to rural areas. Tuberculosis prevailed even at the Palace, taking the lives of at least two sultans and of many more people in the harem (Unat, 1979). The Imperial Bacteriology Institute closely followed the advances concerning tuberculosis cure in Europe. Dr Düring attended the seminar on tuberculin vaccination offered by Robert Koch in Berlin (Terzioğlu, 1976, p. 157). Ottoman specialists followed radiological advances, too. The first Anti-Tuberculosis Association was founded in 1918. The microbiology centre in Ankara developed an oral BCG in 1927 and another (subcutaneous) BCG vaccination in 1948. In 1931, a new law banned the marriage of patients with highly developed tuberculosis. In spite of all advances in the understanding and prevention of the disease, the medicinal cure for tuberculosis was not developed until the end of the Second World War. Although tuberculosis was recognised as an important problem in the early Republic, a campaign against it was impossible due to a lack of material resources (Sağlık ve Sosyal Yardım Bakanlığı, 1983, p. 112), and medical advances. As a cure became available after the 1940s, the campaign started to form.

The new tuberculosis campaign differed considerably from early attempts in one respect. The first campaign from 1925 to 1939 was a 'national' organisation, created at a time when globalisation was weak. The new postwar vaccination campaign against tuberculosis was organised by the WHO and with the material contribution of UNICEF in 1952. About 30 million people (90 per cent of the total population) were vaccinated between 1953 and 1974, and about 16 million microfilms were taken all over Turkey. 622,734 tubercular patients were cured between 1960 and 1975. The campaign was evaluated as a great success, and was even seen as a miracle (Kibaroğul, 2001, pp. 729–33). The tuberculosis campaign is relatively recent and therefore the best-remembered of these public health programmes.

Conclusion

The control of diseases is not present in the collective memory as far as the literature quoted in this study is concerned. It is actually the foundation of the Republic that is remembered and memorialised. The forgotten health campaigns were means to achieving higher developmental modernisation goals. A small group stressing the achievements of the early period, the first 15 years of the Republic, has drawn attention to these efforts. However, the appreciation and gratitude in such studies focuses not on the achievements of the campaigns themselves but on the 'spirit' of the Republic that initiated such campaigns.[28]

This form of remembrance may be classified as 'official' or 'institutional'. These recollections are by nature formal, concern a narrow audience of physicians and refer only to a fraction of the history of the disease and campaign. The Hygiene Centre in Ankara is called 'Refik Saydam Hygiene Centre' after the minister who created it. There is another street in Istanbul named after him. He is commemorated each year by the staff of the Institute. There are also publications on his policies (Sağlık ve Sosyal Yardım Bakanlığı Tanıtma ve İstatistik Birimi, 1982) and in the Institute's garden there is statue of him. Yet, if people sitting in that garden, old and young, were asked about him today, none or very few would know about his achievements in public health campaigns. More importantly, they would be unlikely to see these efforts as part of the security of the state and society, or to associate their health status today with those earlier campaigns.

The lack of public historical appreciation for public health campaigns against diseases is not specific to Turkey.[29] The question posed here focuses not on the past but rather on the individual and society of today. Based on the information that was available to this study, it is not realistic to assume that the rural population simply forgot about these efforts after an earlier period of appreciating them. The question is, rather, why society in contemporary Turkey does not reconstruct a social memory of the campaigns against diseases?

The role of historians of medicine is critical. Medical historians generally make the histories of changes in treatments and biographies of famous doctors their subjects. Their studies are usually very specific and fragmented, and would contribute little material for such a reconstruction. A new history of medicine, including the history of public health and the socio-cultural history of disease, is just emerging in Turkey. The role of physicians is also ambivalent. Their standard evaluation of the early periods is often a kind of apology: 'Given the conditions of that time, it was the best one could achieve!' For many of them, the early malaria campaign made the successful eradication campaign possible, and the early campaign was itself highly efficient if one considers the modest means available. As the diseases are not fully eradicated and new ones have emerged, many physicians probably are reluctant to praise the past. On the contrary they criticise the mistakes of the past in order to justify their recent demands. The lack of a famous artwork (painting) or literature on 'malaria' in Turkey is also puzzling.[30]

One should also not forget that in the past, those who initiated the campaigns against diseases did seek 'good health' as an end in itself, but also saw it as a means of population growth, economic development and national defence. Today, population growth is not desirable, environmentalists criticise the draining of wetlands, the use of DDT is banned because of its potential dangers and the achieved level of economic development in Turkey is still not satisfactory. Moreover, the early malaria campaign, for example, was not necessarily just a medicinal campaign. A significant component of it was 'landscaping' reform concerning agriculture. If drained land was successfully employed in agriculture, the benefits were not necessarily expressed in a disease-health context. The same process may have also produced popular discontent. Peasants had to serve as forced labour in draining activities, and draining wetlands might have negatively affected some traditional crafts and ways of life. One might assume that quinine cure must have produced some public gratitude. But if one recalls the Second World War, when medicine became scarce or available only at black market prices, it is clear that this may not have always been true. Heavy quinine use may cause undesirable side effects. Even during the 1980s, the rate of refusal of house spraying was increasing, due to objections to the unpleasant smell of insecticides. All health campaigns have faced public resistance to some extent. It is unlikely each and every person will believe that these campaigns were for the greater good of the society.

The campaigns were also discontinuous. Staff and institutions were reorganised quite frequently. War was not the only cause of discontinuity. The campaigns were initially organised vertically. They were quite independent from the rest of the public health bureaucracy. The malaria campaigners, for example, were paid much more than the rest of the public health employees. This may have prevented cooperation among health institutions, for example in the joint efforts of health faculties and campaign institutes (Kutlay, 1998, p. 204). Perhaps it created tensions, as well. In periods with restricted finances, the campaigns lost qualified personnel and tried to replace them with less qualified people. The shift towards insecticide use might also have caused expertise and staff change, so intermediaries were lost quite often.

The campaigns against diseases started as national campaigns. After the Second World War, they were increasingly taken over by international organisations. Appreciation and social memory are surely related to participation. Yet cooperation with international organisations strengthened the cooperation among institutions. This formalised acts of commemoration to conferences and publications, and reduced the importance of individual's participation in the campaign. On the other hand, cooperation with international organisations must have evoked appreciation for similar activities before the Republican period. An example might be the French contribution in microbiology: 'Turkey has felt some gratitude towards France for its medical efforts. It organised in 1957 in Istanbul a very congenial celebration for the seventieth anniversary of the Rabies Control Institute, which numerous Pasteur Institute alumni attended' (Huet, 2000, pp. 289–94). There are anniversary books published after similar commemorations of Austrian and German contributions as well (Becker, 1993, p. 156).

One possible reason for the underrating of previous efforts might be the extent of the problems today. Turkey made a jump to a new level of development, becoming a middle-income country. At this level Turkey's health status ranks very low, lower than its income level. From a health point of view, as the problems are: instead of old diseases there are now new ones, such as cancer, HIV/aids, pollution, respiratory infections (like pollution, smoking), and there has been a shift of the disease pattern from rural to urban Turkey. The ways that health problems were perceived and solved at the beginning of the Republic differ considerably from today's methods.

The modernisation of public health in Turkey followed two different paths. One consisted of advances in medicine and their application and diffusion in Turkey. The other path was the complementary developments in infrastructure, sanitation, education, better housing, and urbanisation. Modernisation and improvement in agriculture, in terms of better nutrition, also helps improve many health problems. The development of medicinal advances and their diffusion has always been faster than the latter process, and the main cause of the slow pace on the second path has been poverty. When the pace of development in general catches up with advances in medicine, perhaps these earlier public health campaigns will also be remembered and valued by a much larger proportion of society, along with the appreciation and gratitude they deserve.

Notes

1. Paul-Louis Simond has shown in 1898 that rat fleas transmitted the plague. He has become later in 1911 the third director of the Constantinople Imperial Bacteriology Institute. See Huet (2000).
2. He has published a book on his experience. See Bulard (1839).
3. International sanitary Conferences were organised Paris in 1851 and 1859, Istanbul in 1866, Vienna in 1874, Washington in 1881, Rome in 1885, Venice in 1892, Paris in 1894 and Venice in 1897.
4. The countries represented included: Austria-Hungary, Belgium, Denmark, Spain, the Papal States, France, Great Britain, Greece, Italy, Netherlands, Portugal, Prussia, Russia, Sweden/Norway, Iran, Egypt, and Ottoman Turkey, in Afkhami (1999, p. 125).

5. The syphilis hospitals in Kastamonu, Bolu, Bartın, Düzce and Cide were founded upon his advice. See Yıldırım (1985, p. 1330).
6. The committee consisted of Zoeros Pasha (the president), Dr Hüseyin Remzi and (vetrenarian) Hüseyin Hüsnü.
7. Many donations were received from foreign governments and from national and foreign organisations and individuals that had benefited in some way from Pasteur's works. See Priego (2003, p. 29).
8. In French colonies were similar institutes inaugurated: Saigon (1893), Tunis (1896), Algerie (1900).
9. He did not become the director of the Institute, but the Institute was under his responsibility as he became 'Field Deputy Health Inspector', and he intervened as member of the 'Army Supplies Regulation Inspection Commission'. See Sağlık ve Sosyal Yardım Bakanlığı Tanıtma ve İstatistik Birimi (1982, p. 85).
10. For estimates of civilian losses, see McCarthy (1995).
11. See http://scrab.msu.montana.edu/historybug/typhus.htm.
12. This might also be just the adoption of the Italian example. See Tekeli and İlkin (1999, p. 230).
13. At first 'Bulaşıcı Hastalıklarla Savaş, Sıhhıye ve Muaveneti İçtimaiye Vekaleti' after 1929 'Sıhhat ve İçtimai Muavenet Vekaleti'.
14. The first Health Minister was Adnan Adıvar. Refik Saydam was elected actually in 1921 and 1923 as Minister of Health, too.
15. It was Charles-Alphonse Laveran in 1880, who became the first person to identify the presence of the malaria parasite in human blood. Ronald Ross has observed the life cycle of the parasite. Italian malariologist Giovanni Battista Grassi and Robert Koch issued valuable works that supplied useful knowledge in the combat against malaria.
16. The other scientist was Dr H. Vogel.
17. Prof. Dr E. Martini and Dr H. Vogel, Tropen-Institut Hamburg. SeeUnat (1979, pp. 8–9).
18. See Prof. Dr N. Fişek in Kitaplaşmamış Yazıları – III – 'Sağlık Hizmetlerinde Dr Refik Saydam', available at http://www.ttb.org.tr/n_fisek/kitap_3/31.html.
19. The campaign extended in 1933 to eleven regions covering 24 provinces: Ankara, Eskişehir, Çankırı, Kırşehir, Yozgat, Konya, Afyonkarahisar, Bilecik, Seyhan, İçel, Gaziantep, Antalya, Denizli, Aydın, Muğla, İzmir, Manisa, Balıkesir, Bursa, Kocaeli, İstanbul, Samsun, Amasya. See Cumhuriyeti Sıhhat ve İçtimai Muavenet Vekaleti (1933, p. 47).
20. There were numerous reports worldwide of the success of eucalyptus planting in treating malaria. In 1874, the periodical 'California Horticulturalist' contained such reports. For example, a report from Constantine (Turkey) where eucalyptus had been planted stated: 'The atmosphere is constantly charged with aromatic vapours, the farmers are no longer troubled with disease and their children are bright with health and vigour', in Santos (1997).
21. The aim was land reclamation. Drainage programmes came more and more under criticism after 1990s with growing environmental concerns.
22. Population under malaria control: Number of population measured by the malaria campaign organisation.
23. DDT production started in Turkey after 1945 in small amounts at the Izmit Chlor Factory. See Payzın (1979, p. 62).
24. Actually, at that time it was already evident that mosquito eradication was almost impossible. One may contrast the amounts of DDT use in Turkey to the mosquito

eradication project (not malaria eradication) of the Rockefeller Foundation during the same period in Sardinia. Some 10,000 tons of DDT mixture were doused on Sardinia during 1946–51. The surface of the island was less than Ankara. Malaria was eradicated, yet not all mosquitoes. See Hall (2005).

25. Despite the setbacks, up until 1969, when the global eradication policy was finally abandoned, the following European countries had managed to completely eradicate endemic malaria by interrupting transmission: Hungary, Bulgaria, Romania, Yugoslavia, Spain, Poland, Italy, Netherlands and Portugal.
26. 'Roll Back Malaria in the Who European Region', available at http://www.euro.who.int/malaria/ctryinfo/affected/
27. Roll Back Malaria in the Who European Region', available at http://www.euro.who.int/malaria/ctryinfo/affected
28. Best examples are Bahadır (2004); Ege (1982); Unat (1981).
29. 'the role of illness and the evolution of a modern public health policy have scarcely evoked a footnote in the expanding theme of Iranian modernity'. See Afkhami (1999, p.122). Also 'the lack of appreciation of the human element in disease was connected to what we might call the health of politics'. Stephan (2003, p. 42).
30. In one of the novels of Halide Edip Adıvar, 'Türkün Ateşle İmtihanı' one person is suffering from malaria, but he is not an important character. Yaşar Kemal has a short story titled as 'Mosquitoes' in his book Sarı Sıcak, but it is not about malaria. He has another novel, also arranged as a play, called 'Teneke' about the struggle between and idealist district governor and the landlord. The landlord causes malaria because of illegal irrigation practice. But again, the focus of the piece is not on malaria.

Bibliography

A. A. Afkhami (1999) 'Defending the Guarded Domain: Epidemics and the Emergence of an International Sanitary Policy in Iran', *Comparative Studies of South Asia, Africa and the Middle East*, vol. 19, no. 1, pp. 122–34.

B. Akalın (1979) 'Türkiye'de Dünkü Bugünkü Durumu', in *Sıtma Bilimi Malariologia* (İstanbul: 1. Ulusal Parazitoloji Kongresi, 22–4 Mayıs).

ATASE Arşivi K.1110, D.517, F.2–1, 5

E. Aydin (1999) 'Türkiye'de Sitma Mücadelesi' in *III. Türk tip tarihi kongresi. Kongreye sunulan bildiriler* (Ankara: Türk Tarih Kurumu Basimevi).

O. Bahadır (2004) 'Cumhuriyetin bulaşıcı hastalıklara karşı büyük zaferi (ve büyük unutuluş!)', *Bilim ve Teknik, Cumhuriyet*, 13 November 2004, pp. 8–9.

V. H. Becker (1993) 'Die Medizinische Gesellschaft in Istanbul und Ihre Rolle für die Verwestlichung der Türkischen Medizin im 19. Jahrhundert', in A. Terzioğlu and E. Lucius (eds) *Türk Tıbbının Batılılaşması (Verwestlichung der Türkischen Medizin)* (Istanbul: Arkeoloji ve Sanat Yayınları).

A. F. Bulard (1839) *De la Peste Orientale* (Paris: Locqouin).

O. Dağlar (2004) *War Epidemics and Medicine in the Ottoman Empire from the Balkan Wars through the Great War (1912–1918)*, [Dissertation] (Istanbul: Boğaziçi University).

M. A. Faria (2001) 'Jenner, Pasteur, and Dawn of Scientific Medicine', in *Objective Science*, available at http://www.objectivescience.com/articles/mf_vaccines1a.htm.

N. Fişek (1987) 'Sağlık Hizmetlerinde Dr.Refik Saydam', *Toplum ve Hekim*, no. 45, available at http://www.ttb.org.tr/n_fisek/kitap_3/31.html.

M. Huet (2000) 'The Constantinople Imperial Bacteriology Institute', *Histoire des Sciences Médicales*, vol. 34, no. 3, pp. 289–94.

İ. H. Kalkan (2004) *Medicine and Politics in the late Ottoman Empire (1876–1909)* (MA Thesis) (İstanbul: Boğaziçi University).

L. Kelly and D. Richard (2000) 'Globalization and Cholera: Implications for Global Governance', *Global Governance*, vol. 6, no. 2, pp. 213–31.

E. Kibaroğul (2001) 'Verem Nasıl Bir Hastalıktır, Nasıl Bulaşır, Neden Ortadan Kaldırılamamıştır?', *Yeni Türkiye, Sağlık Özel Sayıs*, vol. 7, no. 39, pp. 729–33.

N. Y. Kutlay (1998) 'Refik Saydam'ın Sağlık Politikası ve Hıfzısıhha Merkezi'nin Bu Politikadaki Yeri', *The New History of Medicine Studies*, no. 4, pp. 187–206.

J. McCarthy (1995) *Death and Exile/The ethnic cleansing of Ottoman Muslims, 1821–1922* (New Jersey: Darwin Press).

A. M. Moulin (1999) 'Kentte Koruyucu Hekimlik: Pasteur Çağında Osmanlı Tıbbı 1887–1908', in P. Dumont and F. Georgeon (eds) *Modernleşme Sürecinde Osmanlı Kentleri* [İkinci Baskı] (İstanbul: Tarih Vakfı Yurt Yayınları).

H. Özdemir (2005) *Salgın Hastalıklardan Ölümler, 1914–1918* (Ankara: Türk Tarih Kurumu).

D. Panzac (1997) *Osmanlı İmparatorluğunda Veba 1700–1850* (İstanbul: Tarih Vakfı Yurt Yayınları).

S. Payzın (1979) 'Sıtmanın Salgınbilimi ve Sıtma Savaşında Önemi', in *Sıtma Bilimi Malariologia, 1. Ukusal Parazitoloji Kongresi, İstanbul, 22–24 Mayıs 1979* (İzmir: Ege Üniversitesi Matbaası).

N. Priego (2003) Microbiology in Mexico and Brazil in the Late-XIX and Early XX Centuries, *Horizontes, Bragança Paulista*, vol. 21, p. 29.

J. E. Roemer (1993) 'Distributing Health: The Allocation of Resources by an International Agency', in M. Nussbaum and A. Sen (eds) *Quality of Life* (Oxford: Oxford University Press).

T. C. Sağlık ve Sosyal Yardım Bakanlığı (1983) *Sağlık Hizmetlerinde 50 Yıl*, Yayın No. 422 (Ankara: Sağlık Bakanlığı).

T. C. Sağlık ve Sosyal Yardım Bakanlığı Tanıtma ve İstatistik Birimi (1982) *Dr.Refik Saydam 1881–1943, Ölümünün 40. Yıl Anısına* (Ankara: SSYB Yayın No. 495).

T. C. Sağlık ve Sosyal Yardım Bakanlığı Tanıtma ve İstatistik Birimi (1982) *Dr.Refik Saydam 1881–1943, Ölümünün 40. Yıl Anısına* (Ankara: SSYB Yayın No. 495).

T. C. Sıhhat ve İçtimai Muavenet Vekaleti (1933) 'Vekaletin On Yıllık Mesaisi', *Sıhhiye Mecmuası Fevkalade Nüshası*, October.

R. L. Santos (1997) available at http://www.library.csustan.edu/bsantos/section2.htm.

G. Sarıyıldız (1996) *Hicaz Karantina Teşkilatı (1865–1914)* (İstanbul: Türk Tarih Kurumu).

N. L. Stephan (2003) 'The Only Serious Terror in These Regions Malaria Control in the Brazilian Amazon', in D. Armus (ed.) *Disease and the History of Modern Latin America* (London: Duke University Press).

M. Süyev (1953) *Sıtma Savaşı Çalışmaları Albümü* (İstanbul: T. C. Sağlık ve Sosyal Yardım Vekaleti Yayınlarından No. 162).

A. L. Tat (1982) 'Türkiye'de Frengi Sorunu', in R. Ege (ed.) *Atatürk ve Cumhuriyet Döneminde Sağlık Hizmetleri* (Ankara: Türk Hava Kurumu Basımevi).

İ. Tekeli and S. İlkin (1999) 'Türkiye'de Sıtma Mücadelesinin Tarihi', in G. E. Kundakçı (ed.) *70. Yılında Ulusal ve Uluslararası Boyutlarıyla Atatürk'ün Büyük Nutuk'u ve Dönemi* (Ankara: Orta Doğu Teknik Üniversitesi Tarih Bölümü).

A. Terzioğlu (1976) *Türk-Alman Tıbbi İlişkileri Simpozyum Bildirileri*, Yeni Seri No. 1 (İstanbul: Istanbul Tıp Fakültesi Tıp Tarihi ve Deontoloji Kürsüsü Yayını).

E. Tok (1929) 'Sıtma Mücadelesinde Külfisaj Balıklar', *Sıhhiye Mecmuası*, vol. 5, no. 26–28, pp. 719–30.

E. K. Unat (1986) 'Son Yüzyılda Kuduz Bilgisindeki Başlıca İlerlemelerin Tarihçesi', *Tıp Tarihi Araştırmaları*, vol. 1, pp. 21–3.

E. K. Unat (1981) 'Türkiye Cumhuriyetinde Atatürk Döneminde Bulaşıcı Hastalıklarla Savaş', *Cerrahpaşa Tıp Fak. Derg*, vol. 12, pp. 383–97.

E. K. Unat (1979) 'Sıtmanın Tarihi', (İzmir: Türkiye Parazitoloji Derneği Yayını No. 1).

E. K. Unat (1979) 'Osmanlı İmparatorluğunun Son 40 Yılında Türkiye'nin Tüberküloz Tarihçesi Üzerine', *Cerr. Tıp. BCG Fak.*, vol. 10, pp. 173–284.

S. Watts (2001) 'From Rapid Change to Stasis: Official Responses to Cholera in British-Ruled India and Egypt: 1860 to c.1921', *Journal of World History*, vol. 12, no. 2, pp. 321–74.

S. Watts (1997) *Epidemics and History, Disease, Power and Imperialism* (New Haven: Yale University Press).

Wittern, R. (1981) 'Dünya Savaşı Sırasında Türkiye'de çalışan Alman Hekimleri', in A. Terzioğlu (ed.) *Türk-Alman Tıbbi İlişkileri* (İstanbul: Istanbul Tıp Fakültesi, Tıp Tarihi ve Deontoloji Kürsüsü Yayını Yeni Seri No. 1).

A. E. Yalman (1930) *Turkey, in The World War* (New Haven: Yale University Press).

N. Yıldırım and S. Bozkurt (1999) 'VIII.Uluslararsı Hijyen ve Demografi Kongresi'nin (1894) Tıp Tarihimizdeki yeri' in *III. Türk Tıp Tarihi Kongresi-20-23 Eylül 1993* (İstanbul, Türk Tarih Kurumu).

N. Yıldırım (1995) 'Zoeros Pasha's Report Presented to the Sultinate on His Return from Paris', *Yeni Tıp Tarihi Araştırmaları*, vol. 1, pp. 91–7.

N. Yıldırım (1985) 'Tanzimattan Cumhuriyete Koruyucu Sağlık Uygulamaları', in *Tanzimattan Cumhuriyete Ansiklopedisi*, vol. 5 (İstanbul: İletişim Yayınları).

Turkey as International Actor

12
Turkey and the Great Powers

Henri J. Barkey

The modern state of Turkey is the successor to what was once a great power. At its zenith, the Ottoman Empire commanded large armies and territory and had an important say in European power politics. In the Middle East, it had no real rival. In his classic *Theory of International Politics*, Kenneth Waltz identifies the Ottoman Empire as a Great Power in 1700 – but by 1800 it had ceased to occupy this status (Waltz, 1979, p. 132). The Ottoman Empire was not the only state to lose this coveted position: by the 1800s, Sweden, the Netherlands and Spain were no longer considered Great Powers either. By the end of the First World War, the Austro-Hungarian Empire had ceased to exist. Over the course of the nineteenth and twentieth centuries, the international system was transformed from a multipolar to a bipolar and, finally, to the current almost unipolar state.

The Ottoman Empire had reached its status like all other empires, through conquest. Its end came about as others encroached on its conquered territories and the people it had subjugated rebelled and exacted their revenge on the Sublime Porte. For most of its dying decades the empire had to contend with dramatic changes in the international system and its immediate neighbourhood without the ability to fashion these developments. Its successor, the Republic of Turkey, also had to devise strategies to survive the uncertainty and insecurity engendered by dramatic shifts in the international system.

This chapter explores how the late Ottoman Empire and Turkey adapted to changing international realities and constraints. It looks at Turkey's relations with the Great Powers. The combination of domestic strengths and external vulnerabilities varied a great deal during the last 200 years of contact with the Great Powers. From an Empire teetering on the verge of collapse to an underdeveloped and poor state on the edge of a global war, to a developing country bordering one of the great expansionist powers of the twentieth century, and now to a middle income and Europe-bound state neighbouring one of the most volatile regions of the world, Turkey has found itself facing these different challenges with equally diverse attributes and resources.

The realist viewpoint, which has been the dominant paradigm in international relations for most of this past century, argues that in the anarchic international system Great Powers pursue power and compete with each other. For realists, this power struggle is a matter of survival. The paradigm expects that mid level powers such as Turkey will behave similarly and face the same general set of insecurities. As a result, they need to join alliances or associate themselves with other powers to balance possible hostile states. In fact, Turkey often perceiving threats, has done exactly that and constructed or joined alliances to ensure its survival. The most important such case is the NATO alliance, which pitted Western states against the Warsaw Pact and its dominant partner, the Soviet Union.

During its long engagement with the Great Powers, Turkey suffered from its relative political, economic and military weakness. Throughout the nineteenth century, the Ottoman Empire, having largely fallen on the defensive, watched almost helplessly as territories it had conquered a few centuries earlier were liberated from its rule. Atatürk's Turkish Republic was born out of the ashes of an Empire devastated by war and economic mismanagement and neglect. It not only had to face the challenges at home attributable to the disintegration of the Ottoman Empire, its poor infrastructure, absence of an economic base, and its religious and ethnic tensions, but had to also negotiate a new course for itself while positioned at the vortex of the great power struggles.

What made Turkey different from the Netherlands, Sweden, Spain, Austria or Italy, to name a few states that lost their so-called great power status, was its strategic location. The major struggles of the last two centuries swirled all around the Ottoman Empire and Turkey. During the nineteenth century, the Ottoman Empire was the object of great power rivalry as the Russian Empire encroached from the north, trying to acquire as much territory from the Ottomans as possible in its own quest to compete with the other European powers. What prevented the Ottoman Empire from collapsing earlier than it did was Britain's desire to contain Russian advances and deny Moscow access to Constantinople and the Mediterranean (Narizny, 2007, pp. 242–4). Similarly, in the twentieth century, Turkey stood in the way of German and Soviet expansionism, and was adjacent to areas of considerable importance to the Great Powers, such as the oil-rich Middle East. Throughout this period, Turkey was considered an important piece in the global chessboard.

If a strategic location makes a state important to others, it also brings about an element of vulnerability. For Turkey, attention came with a deep sense of insecurity, a belief that other powers coveted Turkish territory or resources, even when this may not have been true. The demise of the Ottoman state and division of its territory has had an indelible impact on modern Turkish perceptions. Although the Ottomans had built their empire through conquest, Turks today perceive its demise to be the result of unjust and nefarious plots conjured up by Great Powers and their client states. The

Sevres treaty, the post-First World War treaty that called for the dismantling of the Empire, has been transformed into a political malaise or syndrome of sorts. In a continuing demonstration of the country's vulnerability, it is often invoked in contemporary Turkey as proof of the ill intentions of outside powers. In effect, the Sevres Treaty has become one of the foundational myths of the republic strategically deployed by opponents of improved relations with Western countries (Jung, 2001).

On the other hand, strategic location and importance allow countries to collect 'strategic rents'. Great powers are more likely to disburse funds and other resources, such as military material, to countries they deem critical to their own interests. Such rents, or gains, would not otherwise accrue to a country if it were devoid of any strategic value. These rents are not unlike oil-derived rents and as the rent-seeking literature informs us, countries with access to rents not only seek to maximise them but also end up misallocating them. Since the end of the Second World War, Turkey benefited immensely from strategic rents. It had access to the NATO alliance and more importantly to US aid, both financial and military. The Soviet invasion of Afghanistan and Iran's Islamic revolution further amplified the importance of Ankara in Washington's eyes. The end of the Cold War has been equally kind to Ankara. Many other countries that were no longer front-line states in the struggle against communism found that they occupied a lower place in the priorities of the US. Unrest in the Balkans, the growing importance of Central Asia, the turbulence in the Middle East, and above all Saddam Hussein's ability to survive in Baghdad at a time when the US was adamant in its desire to contain him, all proved beneficial to Turkey.

Turkey emerged from these experiences as a status quo power par excellence. During the Cold War, responding to Soviet threats, Turkey aligned itself with NATO and the US and later joined the Baghdad Pact (and remained within the Regional Cooperation and Development organisation, RCD, that replaced it). As part of the containment policy against the Soviet Union, it kept its distance from against revisionist states in its immediate region. However, for a relatively industrialised country, well-endowed with natural resources and population, strategically well-located, and possessing a powerful military establishment, it has not had any significant influence beyond its immediate neighbourhood. In Turkey two concerns – an ingrained sense of vulnerability and a strong desire for regime survival, as distinct from state survival in the classical sense – account for a lacklustre foreign policy performance. A strong desire for regime survival is not a concern unique to Turkey. Most states in the developing world share this unease. What is distinct about Turkey is the continued resilience of fears regarding the durability of the regime well after the initial transition to democratic rule in 1950.

Turkey's past foreign policy can best be characterised as tactical, defensive and unimaginative. With few exceptions, it has opposed change at home and abroad. When change has come, it has been mainly because of external threats or pressures. One of Turkey's veteran columnists, Mehmet Ali Birand, challenged his readers to find an example of a Turkish leader initiating an important reform or change in policy without foreign pressure. During the Ottoman Empire, battlefield losses forced change, and in modern times, shifting international political circumstances and the pressure of great powers have caused Turkey to alter its course significantly. Today, it is broadly speaking the EU accession process that drives Turkey's economic and political transformation. With the exception of Kemal Atatürk's reforms and Turgut Özal's economic measures, major policy change has almost never been indigenous, but has instead been forced or inspired from abroad.

The current Justice and Development Party (AKP) government led by Recep Tayyip Erdogan, however, is intent on altering this fundamental equation. Erdogan has increasingly charted what appears to be a foreign policy independent of traditional constraints and encumbrances. It is designed to make Turkey a player not just in its immediate region but also globally. This said, it remains to be seen how successful it will be and whether this represents a permanent and fundamental change or an opportunistic attempt at capitalising on the vacuum created by the Bush administration.

Development of foreign policy from the Empire to the Republic

With its imperial heyday a thing of the past, and the threats posed by more dynamic and powerful states encroaching on its territories, the Ottoman Empire reluctantly began to reform itself in the early nineteenth century. War has perhaps been the most important source of political change in history, so it is not surprising that even before the famous 1839 Gülhane edict, the Ottoman Empire introduced a series of reforms starting with its military institutions. Though the reforms managed to delay the eventual collapse of the Empire, they could not stave off this fate forever. Interestingly, what enabled the Empire to survive as long as it did may have had less to do with the military than with a shrewd foreign policy that made the most of the divisions and rivalries among the Great Powers of the day. In effect, the Empire managed to turn its weakness into an asset of sorts, allowing it to manipulate its challengers.

The post-1923 Turkish Republic also sought a foreign policy that would ensure its stability and protection. After suffering through years of war and partial occupation, Mustafa Kemal Atatürk assumed the leadership of a population badly in need of respite. Having learned the lessons of the fall of the Ottoman Empire, he tried to distance his new regime as much as possible from its recent past. While inheriting a territory much more homogenous than the multi-ethnic Ottoman Empire, modern Turkey nonetheless contained a variety of ethnic groups and would be saddled with refugees, as well as newcomers displaced by the population exchanges with Greece. Creating a nation state out of these disparate groups and fashioning a coherent political entity to succeed the Empire was a Herculean task. Atatürk aimed not only to replace religion with Turkish national identity as the main societal bond, but also to marry this new identity with the 'contemporary' civilisational norms of the time. To achieve them he launched into a wholesale transformation of society by imposing a strict version of secularism and trying to affect the everyday life of the citizens by regulating such things as dress codes. As modernist as they may have been, Atatürk's reforms were imposed from above and the one-party state he created was, as Erik Zürcher argued, 'a monolithic system ... [that] left little room for ventilation' (Zürcher, 1993, p. 185).

The Kemalist republic was, in Heinz Kramer's words, 'run by the state bureaucracy and military-turned-civilian politicians led by a caste of urban intellectuals with European-influenced education who entertained an organic understanding of state and society' (Kramer, 2000, p. 8). In the process it institutionalised itself to the extent that its reforms and orientation became an ideology. Upon Atatürk's death, his ideology got sanctified.[1] Kemalism, as most people have come to refer to the state ideology, is a 'mixture of secularism and nationalism which is at the heart of most of Turkey's major policy preoccupations' (Cooper, 2002, p. 118). As Bernard Lewis argues, 'in the hands of lesser men than himself, his authoritarian and paternalist mode of government degenerated into something nearer to dictatorship as the word is commonly understood' (Lewis, 1961, pp. 297–8). This viewpoint informed both domestic and foreign policy. At home, the regime battled both Kurdish demands for recognition and the power of piety in society. The transformation that Atatürk had begun would take much longer than anticipated, partly due to the limited resources at the disposal of an impoverished society. In retrospect, his often-quoted maxim 'peace at home, peace abroad', which has often been interpreted as a type of Turkish isolationism, appears to have had more to do with fear of domestic challenges than with challenges posed by external sources. When faced with a domestic Kurdish insurrection, Atatürk desisted from incorporating Kurdish-inhabited northern Iraqi territory that Turkey had claimed as its own. By contrast, without a domestic challenge, the Kemalist government had no compunction about acquiring Alexandretta away from Syria.

The recognition of Turkey's vulnerability in uncertain times came to the fore during the Second World War. Unlike the First World War, when Enver Pasha's decision to abandon the risk averse and cautious foreign policy by siding with the Germans ultimately brought down the Empire once and for all (Hale, 2000, p. 35), during the Second World War Turkey's leader Ismet Inönü followed a very cautious policy ostensibly intended to preserve the republic. Although historians argue about the very essence of the policy,[2] Turkish neutrality during the war may have prevented it from getting dragged into a conflict it was unprepared for but neither did it help Ankara make many friends. When Turkey finally declared war on the Axis powers in the waning days of the conflict, the Soviets, for one, were unenthusiastic about Turkish participation. Moscow was far more interested in extending its spoils of war to its immediate south, perhaps to the strategic Turkish straits. With the Soviet Union and the Western Alliance emerging as the two poles of the new international system, Turkey found that it had nowhere to go but with the West.

Yet the defeat of Germany, as Hale has argued, was more than a reestablishment of a European balance of power system. The Second World War had been a total war, a war against evil (Hale, 2000, pp. 104–5). Turkey, with its authoritarian system, state controls on the economy and wartime measures against religious minorities, appeared anachronistic as a would-be Western ally. In response to the pressures of the post-war context, President Inönü engineered the transformation of Turkey from a one-party state into a multi-party pluralistic system. He allowed an opposition party, the Democrat Party, to participate in the 1946 elections. These elections were rigged to favour the ruling Republican People's Party, (RPP), which Atatürk had founded and Inönü had taken over. However, ensuing Soviet pressure to incorporate eastern Turkish provinces into its territory made alignment with the West more pressing (Kuniholm, 1980). The pronouncement of the 1947 Truman Doctrine signified the beginning of Turkey's engagement with the US as Washington drew a line against Soviet ambitions in Greece and Turkey. In 1950, the Inönü regime allowed genuinely free elections to take place, and the opposition Democrats swept to power, defeating the party that governed modern Turkey almost since its inception.[3] The Democrat Party, compared with the RPP, was far more private sector oriented and unafraid to befriend the West.

Uneasy relations with the Great Powers

Although Turkey has been firmly implanted in Cold War and post-Cold War Western alliance systems, the irony of modern Turkish foreign policy is the uneasiness that dominates public and government perceptions of Turkey's allies, the US and Europe. This is despite the rhetoric from Ankara regarding its fundamental Western orientation, not just within a security alliance but also philosophically and 'culturally'. Atatürk's admonishment to join 'contemporary civilisation' has been the mantra of successive Turkish governments and of generations of schoolchildren and adults alike. Yet, from the 1950s onwards, the apprehension with which Turkish leaders have approached their allies has been surprising. Disputes aside, the Turkish view of Europe and the US has been saturated with deep suspicion. After 50 years of alliance, one could still find former and experienced prime minister, Bülent Ecevit, easily articulating the darkest fears of many Turks: that the US and the Europeans were only interested in carving up Turkey. At a simpler level, Kenan Evren, the 1980 coup leader and then president of Turkey, upon relinquishing his office in 1989 expressed the general view that 'Turkey has very few friends, and this is why we have to be powerful' (Gönlübol, 1990, p. 614). Paradoxically, both Ecevit and Evren represent facets of the Kemalist vanguard of Turkish society.

What then explains the absence of trust in the West among members of the Kemalist elite?[4] As Ekavi Athanassopoulou convincingly demonstrates, the Turks did not find it easy to gain acceptance as a member of the Western alliance (Athanassopoulou, 1999). Turkey's participation in the Korean War became a primary means to improve its standing with the US and become a member of NATO in 1952 after having previously been rebuffed on a number of occasions. Turks feel that from the NATO membership to the European Union accession negotiations, Turkish interest in membership has always faced unnecessary questioning, prejudice and delay.

Occasionally, classical security issues would become the objects of dispute. The first serious incident was when the US negotiated away the presence of the Jupiter missiles in Turkey during the Cuban Missile Crisis without consulting the authorities in Ankara. This was followed by the infamous 1964 Johnson letter that warned Turkey against intervening militarily in Cyprus.[5] The reluctance of European countries to come to the defence of Turkey on the eve of the 1991 Gulf war as Turks feared that Saddam Hussein would launch non-conventional missiles against Turkish targets did not help improve the standing of the allies. The EU's Common Security and Defence Policy is another issue of contention, because while the Europeans are asking for access to NATO assets, Turkey is kept out of this initiative because it is not yet an EU member state even though its security interests are affected.

During the Cold War, Turkey tended to shy away from active participation in the international system and with the exception of the Cyprus issue proved to be conflict averse. Turkey rarely behaved in a way that was commensurate with its power, given its close and extensive relations with Western powers, from which it derived much of its strength, and certainly its own economic, political and military capabilities. Compared to Egypt or Yugoslavia, which assumed positions of international leadership through the Non-Aligned Movement (NAM), Turkey with its superior capabilities failed to make much of a mark in international politics. This is not to argue that Turkey ought to have joined the NAM (although some in Turkey wanted it to do so) but rather that it could have assumed a more visible position in international institutions, put forward new initiatives and even launched meditative missions abroad. Its efforts to serve on the UN Security Council were for the most part stymied after the 1950s. In the more than 60 years of United Nations history, Turkey has only served on the Council in 1951–2, and 1954–5 and shared a seat with Poland in 1961. It is only after a concerted and wide-ranging diplomatic offensive by the ruling Justice and Development Party (AKP) that Ankara finally managed to secure a seat for the 2009–11 term.

During the course of the Cold War, Turkey also benefited from US military and economic aid. Between 1950 and 1989, the US provided military assistance valued at $8 billion, of which some $4.7 billion were in the form of grants and $3.3 billion were concessional loans (Defence Security Cooperation Agency, 1999). More importantly, the US, sometimes with the help of allies, came to Turkey's rescue at times of deep economic crisis by ensuring that international financial institutions advanced the necessary loans. This was the case in the summer of 1979, when the IMF signed a stand-by agreement with Ankara that enabled an Organisation of Economic Cooperation and Development (OECD) consortium aid package of $1 billion (Krueger and Aktan, 1992, pp. 38–9). The 1979 aid package followed a summit in Guadeloupe earlier that year, at which Presidents Jimmy Carter and Valery Giscard D'Estaing and Chancellor Helmut Schmidt discussed Turkey's difficulties and committed themselves to come to its aid. The summit had coincided with the alarming developments in Iran and Afghanistan. Also, the IMF stand-by package came with the understanding that the government, then led by Ecevit, which was facing a dire foreign exchange shortage crisis, would institute deep structural reforms. His reforms, however, proved to be too moderate and failed to achieve the desired objectives. These were followed by far more radical ones in 1980 implemented by a new government, which included Özal as its economic czar. Despite the promising economic picture, the new government fell victim to a military coup, but the ruling generals kept Özal in his position. Whereas Ecevit symbolised the defensive and status quo-oriented approach, Özal, by contrast, represented a new, opportunistic and assertive vision for Turkey. Turkish exports mushroomed in response to the new economic adjustment programme; Turkish businesses, and especially new ones in the Anatolian hinterland, began to open up to the international market. Özal, who had assumed the premiership with the return to democracy in 1983, further strengthened the reforms and by the end of the decade when the Berlin Wall came down Turkey was ready to play a more important economic role in its immediate region and beyond.

As far as official Turkey was concerned, there never was any doubt after 1947 that the country belonged in the Western alliance. Politicians and opposition members would often speculate on the benefits of greater autarky or a more balanced position between the superpowers, but in reality, despite its mixed feelings about being a secondary actor, Ankara proved to be an erstwhile ally during the Cold War. The potential loss of this privileged, if not completely satisfying, relationship made Turkey fear the aftermath of the Soviet Union's demise. In fact, as Philip Robins argues, Turkey did not experience any of 'the normative euphoria which swept through Europe' at the conclusion of the Cold War (Robins, 2003, p. 13). For Robins, this juncture was not just a lost opportunity, but also an affirmation of how comfortable Turkey felt in its position in the Cold War security architecture. This comfort was not, however, a vote of confidence in the US, but rather in the bipolar system. As a profoundly status quo power, Turkey regretted the end of this system.

The collapse of the USSR sent shock waves through Turkey. At first, it appeared as if the bulwark against Soviet expansionism had lost its most important asset: its strategic location. Turkey quickly tried to refashion itself as a gateway to Central Asia. In reality, Ankara's strategic importance to the sole superpower was about to increase as America shifted focus from the USSR to Iraq and to the rest of the Middle East. Although Iraq did not constitute the same kind of danger to the international system as had the USSR, for over a decade the relationship with Ankara was a critical component of the US Iraq policy. Starting with the first Gulf War in 1990–1, Turkey provided diplomatic and then logistical support to the US in the region. Washington's containment of the Saddam Hussein regime would become significantly dependent on Ankara's cooperation.

Domestic challenges and transformation of foreign Policy

With the end of the Cold War Turkey no longer faced a colossus armed to the teeth with nuclear weapons, but instead a series of neighbouring states, some of which were potentially hostile to its interests. None of these states represented a strategic threat that required the assistance of a great power. Although this change derived in large part from evolving conditions exogenous to Turkey, the fact remains that some 50 years of alliance membership had transformed Turkey into a more robust and somewhat more self assured military power.

The question of Iraq best encapsulates the transformation of Turkish foreign policy. Foreign policy decision-making became a function of domestic rather than foreign insecurities or concerns. With the end of the Cold War, Turkey faced two new challenges as old societal fissures re-emerged. Kurdish nationalism and Islamic reaction kept at bay or dormant during most of the century resurfaced, almost with a vengeance. These were purely domestic in character – though the spillover from Iraq did affect the Kurdish issue – and had a lot more to do with the way in which the Turkish state had been constructed in the first place. At the onset of the republic, Turkish leaders had expended considerable efforts to eradicate Kurdish identity and independent religious orders and forms of expression. The Kemalist republic succeeded in creating a more coherent and developed state where many others such as Egypt or Pakistan failed. Still its hope that 'Westernisation' and modernisation would render issues relating to religion and ethnicity to the dustbin of Turkish history did not materialise.

The domestic challenges, especially the Kurdish one that starting in the mid 1980s mutated with the emergence of formidable insurgent force, the PKK, the Kurdistan Workers' Party (Marcus, 2007), compelled Turkish officials to revert to a foreign policy action programme that was primarily defensive, inward-looking and status-quo oriented. Domestic considerations, in other words, completely dominated its relations with friend and foe. Ironically, this shift also coincided with a new American approach to the Middle East whereby Washington increasingly saw democratic, secular and pro-Western Turkey as a possible model for the Arab world, despite the fact that most Arabs expressed little sympathy or admiration for the Turks. Starting with the Kuwait crisis in 1990–1, Ankara had terrible misgivings about the US Iraq policy. The containment of Saddam Hussein's regime and the creation of the no-fly zones, especially the one protecting Iraqi Kurds over northern Iraq, were received with great trepidation in Ankara. Turkish leaders feared the demonstration effect of the growing Kurdish autonomous entity in Iraq on Turkish Kurds and, with the exception of then President Özal (who died in 1993), would have preferred a return to the status quo ante. Whereas Özal perceived active collaboration with the allies in 1991 as a means of validating Ankara's role in the Western alliance, many of his country's elite, including the powerful military establishment, perceived a re-engagement with the Middle East after seven decades of distancing as betrayal of the Kemalist worldview. Nonetheless Ankara had little choice; with some 500,000 Iraqi Kurdish refugees amassed on its borders it provided facilities for US and British airplanes to patrol the Northern no-fly zone in Iraq and enable the refugees to return home.

Özal would have opted for a closer partnership over Iraq with the US had the Turkish Parliament and military, not to mention the public, been more accommodating. He sought a fundamental change in foreign orientation, providing Turkey with a bigger footprint in world politics, in line with President George Bush's much-heralded 'new world order'. In fact, he wanted to open a second front against Iraq and even send Turkish troops into northern Iraq, but this was seen as a serious departure from the traditional status quo-oriented Turkish foreign policy (Uzgel, 2001, p. 256). As far as Özal was concerned, Turkey had everything to gain from active participation with the US-led coalition. He was reputed to have said, 'we will invest one and receive three in return' (Uzgel, 2001, p. 254). In an unprecedented series of moves, the foreign and defence ministers as well as the chief of staff of the Turkish General Staff resigned to protest Özal's foreign policy management style and ambitions. The clash between Özal and the Turkish establishment over Iraq ended with the president's defeat and to the closing of the debate on the restructuring of foreign policy.

With Özal's demise in 1993, Turkish foreign policy returned once again to reflect domestic worries. The principal issue was the Kurdish question, reflecting the gravity of the PKK challenge at home and Iraq's Kurdish enclave. But the 1995 elections resulted in the formation of a coalition led by the Islamist Welfare party that had hitherto eschewed many of the secular Kemalist republic's ideals, and this brought home to the elite the 'danger' posed by voters from the Anatolian hinterland where people were far more pious and conservative. The rise of the Islamists was actually a response to the ineffectiveness of both centre-right and centre-left parties, which were mired in corruption and lacked political ideas and imagination. It was also an indirect result of the economic changes introduced by Özal that had empowered the Anatolian-based private sector which began to export on its own, bypassing the traditional centres of economic dominance in Turkey, Istanbul and Izmir.

In the post-Özal period, Turkey's relations with its European and American allies came to be dominated by the response to the PKK and the danger it posed to Turkish unity. With more than two million Turks, which include as many as half a million Kurds of Kurdish origin, the Kurdish problem spilled over into the European Union. The PKK found willing adherents and even some political support there, to the great distress of Ankara, which continuously lobbied European governments to clamp down on the organisation's activities. As Turkey opted for tough counter-insurgency tactics and policies that resulted in large numbers of human rights violations and mystery killings and a general onslaught on the freedom of expression, it found its relations with both the US and Europe came under strain. Similarly, the Turkish secular establishment also opted to quash the budding Islamist movement that found expression in the anti-Western Welfare Party of Necmettin Erbakan. The Constitutional Court's decision to ban the party and its successor from politics was roundly criticised in Washington. In the juxtaposition of the state's ideology with the resurgence of Islamic reaction and Kurdish nationalism, what emerged was a new set of vulnerabilities that profoundly affected Turkey's relations with other states and especially the Great Power(s). Ankara interpreted and judged every action of friend or foe through its own narrow prism of Islamic reaction and Kurdish separatism.

At the same time, Turkey continued to pursue its quest for membership of the European Union. In the post-Cold War era, the European Union replaced NATO as the most important international organisation for Turkey. It did not immediately provide security, but instead it opened the door for future prosperity. For Turkish elites, that promised prosperity loomed as an even more important goal, because it offered the prospect of dealing with the twin challenges facing the country. A Europeanised Turkey would become more modern and richer and hence be better placed to handle Islamic reaction and Kurdish nationalism, since both movements had their roots in relative economic deprivation. For elements of the elite, certainly for segments of the business class and intelligentsia, the prospect of Europe was also a route to increased democratisation, whose absence they blamed for the resurgence of both of these problems. Ironically, both Kurds and Islamists would also be won over to the European project, precisely because it promised to bring about greater democratisation and thus political space for the articulation of their platforms. Even the Turkish military – or at least elements of it – perceive accession to the EU as an antidote to the country's

Kurdish problem, according to a recent article (Aydinli, Özcan and Akyaz, 2006, pp. 77–90). Although the US, as the primary champion of Turkey's bid to join the EU, and many Europeans engaged in a discourse that emphasised the importance of solidifying Turkey's place in the Western alliance system, the fact of the matter is that Turks pursued EU membership for reasons that were far more domestic in origin.

As Ankara's post-Cold War foreign policy became an extension of its domestic insecurities, Turkish policy did assume a decidedly frustrating quality, especially when it came to coordination over Iraq with Washington (Barkey, 2003). The one surprising move was the 1998 Turkish military's uncharacteristic move to threaten Damascus with war if it did not expel the PKK leader, Abdullah Öcalan, who had taken up residence there in the early 1980s. Still this threat, which surprisingly compelled President Hafez al-Assad of Syria to expel Öcalan, did not amount to a new coherent foreign policy. The move had been initiated by the military command without political approval and was possibly even a bluff considering that few Turkish forces were positioned on the Syrian border at the time. As Heinz Kramer points out, there was no Turkish 'grand strategy' for its role after the demise of the Soviet Union. Instead, decision-making was quite ad hoc, often rigid and one-dimensional. Ankara combined its inflexibility in what it believed was 'its rightful and legitimate position' with the tactic of 'open or disguised military threat' (Kramer, 2000, pp. 204–12).

Ironically, Ankara's one major and mould-breaking initiative, the rapprochement with Israel in the 1990s, has to also be seen in this light. It was designed as a means to not only put pressure on Syria – a tactic that clearly worked well, as Damascus and Arab capitals were concerned of a possible joint anti-Syrian operation with Israel – but also to solidify its relationship with Washington. The Israeli connection also provided Turkey with access to weapons systems. However, the Turkish leadership never envisaged it as a major realignment, but rather as a medium-term and tactical liaison.

From an American point of view, the expectation of a possible new role for Turkey in the world in the post-Cold War era, as the much-heralded Turkish opening to Central Asia failed to materialise – partly for reasons out of Ankara's control – did not amount to much. For the US, Turkey was a critical player because of its importance to the US aim of containing Iraq. At the same time, the Turkish domestic insecurities outlined above came to worry Washington. As one former US ambassador to Ankara kept repeating, the US mission was to 'help the Turks help themselves'. The US also became vested in Turkish stability, since Turkish failure threatened disastrous consequences for the region as a whole. These factors explain the zeal with which the US pressured the EU to give a fair chance to the Turkish accession application.

Yet its allies' insistence on improving domestic conditions, especially in the areas of human rights and freedom of speech, have tended to mar Turkish perceptions of the US and Europe. Turkish politicians often accuse these allies of being insufficiently sensitive to the country's domestic challenges and equate foreign intrusions with the infamous Sevres Treaty. The Sevres syndrome has come to dominate much of the discourse on the nationalist right and left of the political spectrum reinforcing the distrustful approach to allies.

Even on the question of the Turkish minority on the island of Cyprus, Ankara has operated with domestic considerations in mind. By and large, with the exception of Özal – again – all Turkish prime ministers have given complete support to the veteran Turkish Cypriot leader Rauf Denktash and his maximalist demands (Wilkinson, 2003, p. 193). Denktash could command a formidable bloc of support in the Turkish public and parliament. On this issue, he could dominate Ankara's preferences by reserving the right to go above the head of Turkish politicians. Although the prospect of EU membership for the whole island of Cyprus entailed very significant gains for the Turkish Cypriots, neither Ankara nor Denktash could reconcile themselves to the European guarantees. Change only came when the Turkish Cypriots decided to part company with their leader on the issue of a UN-sponsored unification plan.

Into the future: The advent of the AK Party and the new foreign policy

The Justice and Development Party came to power following a resounding victory at the polls in November 2002. For the first time since the 1980s, one party dominated parliament and could form a government without coalition allies. The AKP's advent heralded not only the emergence of a majority government, but also new thinking in foreign policy. The AKP leadership owed its intellectual roots to Erbakan's Islamist movements, such as the Welfare and Virtue parties, which had been banned by the state courts in the 1990s. Having broken with Erbakan, Recep Tayyip Erdogan and Abdullah Gül, the two architects of the AKP, also distanced themselves from the more militant aspects of their former mentor's ideological approach. Gone from their discourse was any anti-US or anti-European Union rhetoric. On the contrary, the AKP made a point of speeding up the EU accession process by introducing a series of previously stalled reforms. Far more significant, though, was a new underlying foreign policy approach. When Gül was Erbakan's right hand foreign policy person in the mid 1990s, he had helped engineer an opening to the Muslim world, including the creation of a new organisation, the D-8 or Developing Eight, which had brought together economically significant Muslim counties (Robins, 1997). Though motivated by a sense of Islamist thinking and solidarity, this opening stemmed from a desire to become more relevant in the world of diplomacy.

The AKP has taken this process one step further. It does not only aim to increase its influence in the Muslim world, but to take advantage of Turkey's strategic location in order to make it a far more important player in general

(Erdogan, 2006). As such, it has a coherent goal. Here, the success in starting negotiations with the EU has given Ankara an important boost: Turkey can now legitimately claim to be on the way to becoming a member of the world's most economically advanced club. Undoubtedly, Erdogan and Gül's most influential foreign policy advisor, Ahmet Davutoglu, articulated this more encapsulating vision before joining the Turkish foreign ministry. He argued that Turkey's challenging environment entailed a great number of risks as well as opportunities. However, in his view, the correct approach to these challenges required Turkey to be proactive rather than reactive. Turkey has the obligation to influence its immediate region and beyond in order to improve its security situation (Davutoglu, 2001). Davutoglu also believes that it would be a mistake for Turkey to rely solely on the EU; a Turkey that does not solidify its position in Asia cannot aspire to being anything more than a minor player in Europe (Davutoglu, 2001, p. 562).

The new AKP government, for no fault of its own, got off to a rocky start: as soon as it took power, it was confronted with the US decision to invade Iraq. Washington wanted to deploy a significant force in northern Iraq that would have first had to traverse through Turkish territory. In some respects, the situation appeared to be a repeat of 1990–1, when Özal had been willing, mostly on his own initiative, to engage with the US in Iraq. This time, mindful of the possible economic dislocations that a war in Iraq would entail, Ankara, agreed to go along with the US request to open a second front only after protracted negotiations in which Washington promised a significant economic compensation package.

The package deal was met with a great deal of ambivalence in Turkey. Public sentiment was overwhelmingly opposed to the war in Iraq, and the military and the government each tried to shift the responsibility for an unpopular decision on to the other. The memorandum of understanding signed with the US had envisaged a large contingent of Turkish troops entering northern Iraq with the explicit purpose of managing any refugee flow that could result from the war. Turkey was anxious to have a presence in the north because it feared the consequences of the war on Iraq's Kurdish population specifically its desire to secede from Baghdad's domination.

When the measure to authorise the stationing of American troops on Turkish soil came to a vote in the Turkish parliament, on 1 March, it failed by the smallest of margins. This was an embarrassing defeat for the government, which had been confident of passage.[6] In reality, the AKP leadership, just as like other segments of society, was deeply troubled and ambivalent about supporting the US military campaign. In view of the disastrous 2001 economic crisis and Turkey's relative economic weakness, the new government believed it could not take any chances with a Bush administration determined to go to war. Moreover, the AKP feared Kurdish separatist tendencies in northern Iraq and did not want to be accused of standing by. Here again, a foreign policy decision was solely determined by Turkey's vulnerabilities.

The vote on 1 March, however, would turn out to be a watershed event in the evolution of Turkish foreign policy. For the AKP it proved to be a liberating vote; the government had pushed for the measure but its failure to pass was due to inexperience rather than volition. The leadership had failed to anticipate the defections in its own ranks, but given public opposition, and especially opposition among the AKP rank and file, it was not unhappy with the final outcome. The vote did set Turkey on a separate course from the US; events since the vote, such as the round up of Turkish special forces personnel by US troops in the Iraqi Kurdish town of Suleymaniyah on suspicion of plotting the murder of the Kirkuk governor, confirmed suspicions in Turkey that the US would exact a price for Turkish uncooperativeness in the Iraq war. In reality, the US was anxious to maintain a significant level of cooperation with Ankara on Iraq. Although the large economic package offered in exchange for the troop deployment was withdrawn, the Bush administration succeeded in getting a sceptical Congress to pass a much smaller aid package designed to cushion the blows of the Iraq war.

With Turkish economic conditions visibly improving despite the war, the AKP government found more room to manoeuvre in foreign policy. It discovered that with inflation under relative control and a growing economy, Turkey was no longer as vulnerable to external shocks as it had been in the past. It could even afford to turn down the US aid offer when the US Congress attached conditions to the aid package deemed unacceptable to Turks.

The turnabout on Cyprus policy engineered by Erdogan and Gül was the first serious demonstration of the AKP leadership's willingness to take risks in order to free itself from the static and defensive policies of the past and improve its chances at EU membership. There is no doubt that the AKP's new Cyprus posture was critical in getting the EU to agree to start membership negotiations with Turkey in December 2004. AKP was not alone in this. A referendum on the Turkish side of the island resulted in an overwhelming vote of approval for the UN process while the Greek Cypriot side rejected the UN deal with almost equal vehemence. Equally significant was Denktash's exit from the political scene and his replacement by Mehmet Ali Talat, a new leader far more willing to compromise with his Greek Cypriot neighbours.

The AKP government has fervently tried to inject itself into the Arab-Israeli conflict and US-Syrian disputes by proposing that Turkey become an intermediary. Claiming to have a special relationship with the countries and peoples of the region, the AKP government first injected itself into the Lebanese–Syrian dispute by engaging Syrian President Bashar al-Assad at a time when the UN, the US and the French were attempting to isolate him. Erdogan even claimed credit for Assad's decision to remove Syrian troops from Lebanon, a claim that was not well received in Washington. Similarly, following the Palestinian elections Turkey became the first country outside the Arab world to invite the Damascus-based hard-line leader of the victorious Palestinian movement Hamas to visit. In the absence of any Turkish leverage on Hamas, it was an act of supreme self-confidence as the AKP tried to demonstrate – despite the chorus of criticism from Israel, the US and Europe – that it could moderate the harsh views of this group. The AKP's Hamas opening was significant because it showed a new modus operandi: the belief that through ambitious and unconventional diplomatic efforts it could gain credence and a role in international politics. The AKP would ultimately refer to this as the soft power foundations of Turkey's new foreign policy. Turkey aimed at having good relations with all its neighbours and its clout in the Middle East was anchored in the fact that it was the one country that had good relations with Arabs and Israelis.

But how different was this from that of Özal's earlier initiatives? While both were efforts at making Turkey a pivotal country, Özal was more interested in doing so in conjunction with the US. Despite his very devout upbringing, he was comfortable in European and American company and envisaged Turkey's eventual ascendancy in the world as grounded on a combination of laissez faire-based economic prosperity and alliance with the US and Europe. He too tried to change Cyprus policy and made progress in putting together a domestic scheme aimed at winning internal peace, especially with the Kurds. His, however, was a policy anchored in the West and Western values. By contrast, the AKP leadership, despite its pro-European stance, has set its sights in anchoring itself in a non-first world axis. This vision is as much anti-status quo as it is anti-Özalian. Unlike those of previous generations, the new Turkish government has little attachment to NATO and the other institutions and remnants of the Cold War and, therefore, feels no particular closeness to the US.[7]

The 2007 parliamentary elections resulted in an even more impressive victory for the AKP as it won a greater share of the popular vote (47 per cent versus 34 per cent in 2002) despite threats of a military coup. Erdogan and the AKP felt vindicated at home and abroad. This did not stop the judiciary from trying to ban the AKP and banish its leaders. The AKP avoided this gauntlet as well. These successes enabled the AKP to also change Turkey's traditional approach to northern Iraq; instead of approaching the Kurdistan Regional Government with suspicion, the AKP, much to the consternation of nationalist elements in the military and society, adopted some of the policies Özal had advocated.[8] It slowly improved relations with the Kurds and began to discuss policy options that would lead to the dismantling of the PKK infrastructure in northern Iraq.

Turkey benefited from the decline of US influence in the world and in the Middle East in particular, as well as from the vacuum created by the Bush administration's policies in the region. The Erdogan government arranged for secret negotiations between Syria and Israel, an effort that drew praise in Europe and the US. Although it was always clear to all participants in these negotiations that ultimately a final deal would require the presence of the US, Turkey had earned a seat at the table.

When the Georgia crisis erupted, Erdogan was one of the first to jump into the fray to talk to all the parties involved. The notable aspect of this endeavour was that he did not seem to have consulted his allies in Brussels and Washington before engaging the parties in what would turn out to be an unsuccessful effort. Even with Europe, the Erdogan government has been flexing its muscles on issues such as the proposed gas pipeline project, Nabucco, which is presumed, if built, to carry Azeri gas to Europe. At a time when Europeans are concerned over their over-reliance on Russian gas, Turks have been stalling on Nabucco to build, among other things, 'diplomatic leverage with respect to the European Union' (Socor, 2009). The 2009 Gaza crisis saw Erdogan capturing world headlines as he walked off stage at a Davos meeting after virulently criticising the Israeli president Shimon Peres. He became an instant celebrity in much of the Middle East as he continued to lambaste Israel for its use of excessive force. This said, he also provided the unmistakable impression that he was siding with Hamas. He made a case for Europe and the US to stop considering Hamas a terrorist organisation and suggested that Turkey would represent Hamas' positions at the UN Security Council (Ülsever, 2009). These positions represented a departure, not just from the past policies of the Turkish republic but also from the consensus stances of its alliance partners.

It remains to be seen whether the AKP's policy changes and activism will win the respect of its Great Power allies. Pragmatism in northern Iraq and Cyprus has been welcomed in both Brussels and Washington. On the other hand, Turkey's credibility and room to manoeuvre would be severely diminished were Erdogan and the AKP to overreach. The US under President Barack Obama is likely to refill the vacuum that had been created by his predecessor. The return of the US to the Middle East in particular is bound to come at the expense of Ankara. In the meantime, the global economic crisis will not only make it all the more difficult for the Europeans to contemplate an expansion of the EU but it is also likely to reduce Turkey's attraction to them. Finally, the domestic problems in Turkey have not receded; the Kurdish question, despite some important reforms, remains a festering sore. How the AKP confronts this challenge may be of greater consequence to its relations with the Great Powers than any new foreign policy initiative. It was Atatürk, whose motto 'peace at home, peace abroad' adopted and bandied about by the Turkish elite without ever achieving peace at home, might prove to be most prescient.

Notes

1. Zürcher argues that Kemalism was flexible enough that people of different persuasions could take up the mantle. Nonetheless he acknowledges the indoctrination in schools and the military and its assumption of cult-like characteristics, see Zürcher (1993, pp. 189–90).

2. Hale argues that Turkey played the classic game of pitting one power against another to cover up for its military weaknesses, see Hale (2000, p. 103). By contrast, Frank Weber is far more critical of Turkey's role, arguing that it should have lived up to its commitments to Britain and entered the war. Nevertheless he thinks that Turkey's neutrality inadvertently helped keep the Germans out of the Middle East, see Weber (1978). Finally, Selim Deringil argues that Turkish leaders were not only resourceful but also very farsighted with respect to post-war developments. See Deringil (1998).

3. Some authors claim that external events cannot explain the decision to transition to a multi-party system, see Koçak (1996, p. 561). Hale argues that while the West did not make any demands on Inönü, he was sensitive to the fact that democratic countries had emerged victorious; see Hale (2000, p. 111). Ekavi Athanassopoulou, on the other hand, points to the increasing frustration in Turkey with the European refusal to bring Ankara into their security arrangements and argues that the liberalisation of politics had a great deal to do with the pressure emanating from the opposition Democrats. See, Athanassopoulou (1999, p. 145).

4. To be sure, not all of the elite harbours deep suspicions of the West. Many in the business community have been at the forefront of improved ties and the accession to the European Union. On the other hand, traditionally it has been the anti-Kemalist groups who have carried the mantle of anti-Westernism. The pro-Islamist groups fundamentally object to the alliance and economic relationship on cultural grounds, although they may often articulate their views in more political terms.

5. Turkey did not have the wherewithal to conduct an amphibious landing on the island and the Johnson letter most probably saved the Turkish government from an embarrassing political or military failure.

6. On the morning of the vote, the AKP conducted a straw poll in which its own parliamentarians voted largely in favour of the measure and, therefore, assured the leadership that it would succeed. However, a number of deputies not only changed their minds and voted against the measure a few hours later, but under Turkish law, the votes of those who abstained but remained in the chamber were recorded as negative, thereby dooming the measure. More than 100 of the over 360 deputies in the governing party, including cabinet members, voted against the resolution.

7. There is some irony here in that Washington was quite forceful in criticising the Turkish authorities for jailing the then mayor of Istanbul, Recep Tayyip Erdogan.

8. For a discussion of Turkish diplomatic and military moves in northern Iraq, see Barkey (2009).

Bibliography

E. Athanassopoulou (1999) *Turkey and Anglo-American Security Interests 1945–1952* (London: Frank Cass).

E. Aydinli, N. Özcan and D. Akyaz (2006) 'The Turkish Military's March Toward Europe', *Foreign Affairs*, vol. 85, no.1, pp. 77–90.

H. J. Barkey (2003) 'The Endless Pursuit: Improving U.S–Turkish Relations', in M. Abramowitz (ed.) *Friends in Need: Turkey and the United States after September 11* (New York: The Century Foundation).

H. J. Barkey (2009) *Preventing Conflict over Kurdistan* (Washington, DC: Carnegie Endowment for International Peace).

M. Cooper (2002) 'The Legacy of Atatürk: Turkish Political Structures and Policy-Making', *International Affairs*, vol. 78, no. 1, pp. 115–18.

A. Davutoglu (2001) *Stratejik Derinlik: Türkiye'nin Uluslararasi Konumu* (Istanbul: Küre Yayinlari).

Defence Security Cooperation Agency (1999) *DSCA Facts Book*, available at http://www.dsca.osd.mil/data_stats.htm.

S. Deringil (1989) *Turkish Foreign Policy during the Second World War* (Cambridge: Cambridge University Press).

R. T. Erdogan (2006) *Anadolu Ajansi*.

M. Gönlübol (1990) *Olaylarla Türk Dis Politikasi, 1919–1990* (Ankara: Alkim Kitabevi Yayinlari).

W. Hale (2000) *Turkish Foreign Policy 1774–2000* (London: Frank Cass).

D. Jung (2001) 'The Sevres Syndrome: Turkish Foreign Policy and its Historical Legacies', in B. Møller (ed.) *Oil & Water: Cooperative Security in the Persian Gulf* (London and New York: I.B. Tauris Publishers).

C. Koçak (1996) *Türkiye'de Milli Sef Dönemi* (vol. 2) (Istanbul: Iletisim Yayinlari).

H. Kramer (2000) *A Changing Turkey: The Challenge to Europe and the United States* (Washington, DC: Brookings Institution Press).

A. O. Krueger and O. H. Aktan (1992) *Swimming Against the Tide: Turkish Trade Reform in the 1980s* (San Francisco: International Centre for Economic Growth, Press).

B. Kuniholm (1980) *Origins of the Cold War in the Middle East* (Princeton: Princeton University Press).

B. Lewis (1961) *The Emergence of Modern Turkey* (London: Oxford University Press).

A. Marcus (2007) *Blood and Belief* (New York: New York University Press).

K. Narizny (2007) *The Political Economy of Grand Strategy* (Ithaca: Cornell University Press).

P. Robins (1997) 'Turkish Foreign Policy under Erbakan', *Survival*, vol. 39, no. 2, pp. 82–100.

P. Robins (2003) *Suits and Uniforms: Turkish Foreign Policy Since the Cold War* (Seattle: University of Washington Press).

V. Socor (2009) 'Turkey's Stalling on Nabucco Hurts Europe, Azerbaijan, and Itself', *Eurasia Daily Monitor*, vol.6, no. 42.

I. Uzgel (2001) 'ABD ve NATO'yla Iliskiler', in B. Oran (ed.) *Türk Dis Politikasi* [vol. 2] (Istanbul: Iletisim Yayinlari).

C. Ülsever (2009) 'Yeni Dönemde Türkiye-ABD Iliskileri', *Hürriyet*, 3 March.

K. Waltz (1979) *Theory of International Politics* (New York: McGraw Hill).

F. Weber (1978) *The Evasive Neutral: Germany, Britain and the Quest for a Turkish Alliance in the Second World War* (Columbia and London: University of Missouri Press).

J. Wilkinson (2003) 'Cyprus the Last Act', in M. Abramowitz (ed.) *Friends in Need: Turkey and the United States after September 11* (New York: The Century Foundation).

E. Zürcher (1993) *Turkey: A Modern History* (London: I. B. Tauris).

13
The Evolution of Turkish National Security Strategy

Ian Lesser

From the early days of the republic, Turkey has been a security-conscious state, with internal security concerns often at the top of its agenda. The Kemalist tradition emphasised the preservation of a unitary state, and favoured non-intervention in regional conflicts. These elements, together with a strong sense of nationalism and close scrutiny of sovereignty-related matters, continue to shape the Turkish strategic debate at the opening of the twenty-first century. The modern Turkish approach to national security issues has been conservative, traditional, and NATO-centric.

But there have also been powerful elements of change influencing Turkish strategic thinking in recent years – and these elements are becoming structural, shaping how Turks see the world, and how the world sees Turkey.[1] The domestic scene is changing in ways that affect security policy on matters ranging from the Kurdish issue to Islamic politics. There are now competing influences, including a vigorous private sector, and ethnic 'lobbies', participating in the foreign and security policy debate. The military establishment no longer has exclusive influence over strategic decisions. As elsewhere, the very concept of national security is being redefined to embrace aspects of economic security, human security, security of identity, and other 'soft' security matters.

At the same time, the regional and international security environment has changed in ways that have caused Turkey's leaders to rethink their approach. Ankara has engaged in a strategic détente with Greece, with declining strategic interest in Cyprus. Turkey has been an active multilateral player in successive Balkan interventions. Russia remains a long-term worry, but also a leading economic partner. Above all, Turkey has come to see the Middle East as a leading centre of risk – including risks of terrorism, separatism and proliferation – and is willing to act unilaterally as needed in this region. The uncertain future of Iraq, with implications for both domestic and regional security as seen from Ankara, has emerged as a leading driver of Turkish strategy. Developments in the Caucasus and Central Asia have also spurred new thinking.

Turkey's large standing military establishment has been modernised – although not at the pace envisioned a few years ago – and is increasingly capable of projecting power on a regional basis. This capacity is especially notable in the area of airpower, which has been supported by the emergence of a close defence-industrial and operational relationship with Israel. Although the Turkish–Israeli relationship has come under increasing political strain, the defence-related aspects are proving durable. In terms of military power and potential, Turkey is now a more capable partner for the West, and a more potent factor in regional security.

Finally, Ankara's alliance partnerships are in flux. Despite decades of close cooperation in NATO, Turkey has maintained a wary, sovereignty-conscious approach to security cooperation measures, including the provision of access to Turkish facilities. Frictions over Iraq are just the latest example of this tendency. Barring a dramatic reversal in Turkey's relations with the Europe – a development that cannot be ruled out – Turkish national security strategy may well shift toward a more European, less Washington-centric orientation as the EU develops a more active and distinctive security policy. This reorientation will pose uncomfortable dilemmas, and new strategic challenges and opportunities for Ankara.

'Pre-History' and the modern Republic

Strategists and military historians are fond of exploring the cultural and geopolitical roots of strategic tradition. The centuries-long confrontation between European Christendom and the Ottoman Empire – a conflict that has been described by Adda Bozeman as the 'first Cold War' – had a marked effect on the strategic culture of Turkey's neighbours in Europe, as well as on Russia. Much less effort has been devoted to thinking about the effect of this extended confrontation on Turkish security perceptions, or to considering the even earlier experience of Turkic migration westward into Anatolia and beyond. From a sweeping perspective across these centuries of conquest and retrenchment, several points emerge, each with relevance to contemporary problems.

First, the Turkish strategic tradition is solidly *continental* in orientation. This is a tradition Turkey shares with Russia, Germany and China. It is distinct from the maritime orientations of societies like Britain, Holland, Portugal and Greece, or the 'mixed' strategic traditions of France, or the US. This is not to say that Turkey has lacked interests or engagement in the Mediterranean, the Black Sea or the Red Sea – far from it. But the centre of gravity of Turkish strategic thinking has been continental rather than maritime, an emphasis that continues to shape Ankara's security priorities, and goes a long way to explaining the prominent place of the Turkish land forces in Turkish society and policy. This orientation is also one of the leading asymmetries in the strategic relationship between Turkey and Greece.

Second, Turkish strategic culture has displayed a marked conservatism, rooted in a *realpolitik*, even geopolitical approach. There is little that can be described as revolutionary in the strategic outlook of Ottoman Turkey or the Republic. Prior to the end of the seventeenth century, Ottoman policy could be characterised as an expansionist, 'offensive *realpolitik*'. As the Ottoman Empire faced challenges and reverses in Europe, this orientation shifted toward a 'defensive *realpolitik*', aimed at containing threats to the empire at its margins. In the later Ottoman period, this strategy was bolstered by the major powers in Europe, who sought to avoid a precipitous collapse of Ottoman power in the face of Russian pressure (Karaosmanoglu, 2000, p. 201).[2] Modern Turks are the heirs to this late Ottoman tradition of cautious attention to regional balances and coalitions. The experience of the First World War, the loss of empire, and the emergence of the modern republic from the shadow of external intervention and ethnic rift, have left a legacy of close attention to national sovereignty and the preservation of the unitary state. In Kissingerian terms, Turkey is a *status quo* state par excellence.

In contemporary Turkey, this orientation has led to a preference for non-intervention as a component or foreign policy, and as an aspect of Turkey's economic and political development – building Kemalism in one country, to borrow the Soviet terminology. It has also encouraged a widespread wariness and suspicion of foreign intentions regarding Turkish territory and interests, a lingering fear of containment and dismemberment that still influences Turkish perceptions of the country's relations with neighbours and allies. Indeed, Turkish analysts have coined a term – the Sevres syndrome – to describe this vein of geopolitical paranoia.[3] It is not surprising that territorial defence remains a key component of Turkish foreign and security policy, and a key measure of the effectiveness of Turkish security institutions.

A third, enduring area of continuity has been the relationship between modernisation, including military modernisation, Westernisation and internal change. The long decline of Ottoman power in Europe and the Mediterranean was, at least in part, a result of a changing correlation of forces in Europe and the Mediterranean. As Turkey's European adversaries developed more advanced military technologies and became more adept at organising society and military establishments for war, Ottoman Turkey could no longer rely on its own traditional resources and approaches. The Ottoman military consciously sought access to Western European military technology and techniques, a process of modernisation that spurred reforms in other sectors. Turkish strategic thought has long been sensitive to the importance of modernisation and Westernisation as factors contributing to national power and potential. In the late nineteenth- and earlier twentieth centuries, this impetus toward modernisation drove a close relationship with Germany. In contemporary terms, this awareness shapes Turkish perceptions and policies toward Europe, the US, and Israel. Just as Turkey's NATO partners have moved to reduce the size of their land forces in favour of greater attention to modernisation and the ability to project military force beyond the country's borders, the Turkish General Staff has also endorsed this approach.[4]

To say that Turkey's contemporary strategic outlook has been shaped by longstanding geopolitical, even cultural, forces is hardly a novel observation. But it is worth special attention as a counter to the widespread tendency among Western analysts to reduce national strategies to the objective and the generic. Turkey has its share of strategic thinkers steeped in concepts of game theory and deterrence, yet it remains a place where historical images and geography retain their full force for both policymakers and the public.

The influence of domestic developments

The Turkish domestic scene has experienced extraordinary change over the last decade, a pace of change that shows few signs of abating. Whereas ten or even five years ago, Turkish and foreign observers debated the erosion of Kemalism, it is now unclear what is actually left of Turkey's modern republican ideology. Today, the traditional tenets of Kemalism may be more recognisable in Turkey's external rather than its internal posture but it is clear that internal change over the past few years has transformed the way in which Turkish security policy is made and debated. Internal developments are changing the way Turks see the world and respond to it in security terms.

Internal security remains a leading component of Turkey's strategic outlook, shaping attitudes toward a range of issues in Turkey's region and beyond. In almost every sphere, however, these internal concerns are in flux. The AKP (Adalet ve Kalkinma Partisi, Justice and Development Party) government, with one eye (perhaps both eyes) on the country's EU candidacy, has vigorously extended a programme of reform aimed at managing Turkey's Kurdish problem. Yet the problem, influenced by developments in Iraq and elsewhere, refuses to go away, despite the progress that has been made on the cultural front. An effective approach to Kurdish political integration remains elusive, and the Kurdish insurgency, virtually dormant two years ago, has revived and taken new forms. For at least a decade from the late 1980s, the PKK (Partiya Karkerên Kurdiston, Kurdiston Workers' Party) insurgency centred in southeastern Anatolia was the leading security challenge facing Turkey, and was the lens through which much of Ankara's regional policy was viewed. The struggle against the PKK was also a significant influence on Turkey's relations with the EU and the US. Many Turks saw the 1990–1 Gulf War as a catalyst for Kurdish separatism, a stimulus to Kurdish identity and activism in Northern Iraq, and a strongly negative influence on Turkish security. Indeed, Turkish suspicion and scepticism regarding the first Gulf War encouraged an armslength approach to US policy in the most recent war in Iraq.

The insurgency and counter-insurgency in the south-east in the 1990s claimed perhaps 40,000 lives, greatly complicated Ankara's defence relationship with key allies, including Germany and the US, and had an inhibiting effect on the overall evolution of Turkey's political ties with Europe. The war in the south-east also imposed immense costs, and led to the rise of a distorting war economy in south-eastern Turkey and northern Iraq. By the end of the 1990s, the better-trained and better-equipped Turkish armed forces and gendarmerie had largely contained the PKK insurgency, by a strategy of fighting the war, to the extent possible, across the border in northern Iraq. Towards the end of this period, and prior to the capture of PKK leader Abdullah Ocalan in 1999, Ankara came close to open conflict with Syria over the issue of the regime's continued support for the PKK. Ankara's postures toward Iraq and Iran were, similarly, driven by the overriding imperative of containing Kurdish separatism. In the continuing crisis in Iraq, Ankara's policy – and Turkish public opinion – is strongly influenced by the perception that Washington has disregarded Turkey's concerns about Kurdish separatism and irredentism. Stronger measures against PKK fighters based in Iraq are at the heart of Ankara's current agenda in security relations with Washington. The results, from a Turkish perspective, continue to be disappointing, as American policy remains focused on mounting challenges elsewhere in Iraq.

Turkey was fortunate in having an almost five-year respite from Kurdish political violence inside Turkey, a period coinciding with rapid progress in Ankara's relations with the EU. Without this lull, given the demonstrated isolating effect of internal strife, it is questionable whether Turkey's EU aspirations would have advanced so far, so quickly. Moreover, Turkey itself would have found it far more difficult to undertake the sweeping political reforms of recent years against a background of internal security imperatives. The recent upsurge in Kurdish political violence inside Turkey raises the question of whether Turkey is headed for a new round of insurgency and counter-insurgency.[5] The remnants of the PKK, and other successor organisations, may well adopt different tactics, going beyond a rural and regional insurgency to incorporate terrorist attacks in major urban areas (along the lines of the hotel bombings in Istanbul in August 2004), a tactic the PKK had largely avoided in the 1990s. Whatever the trajectory of post-Iraq War Kurdish activity in Turkey, this dominant internal security concern is likely to remain at the core of Turkey's strategic outlook, and could bolster the waning influence of the military in Turkish politics, and a more nationalistic outlook across the board. It is, in short, a key 'wild card' at a particularly delicate juncture in Ankara's foreign and security policy.

Turkey's second traditional internal security concern – Islamism – is also in flux. When the Refah Party led the government, concern about political Islam in Turkey, much of it ascribed to Saudi and Iranian activities, was at or near the top of the security agenda as described by Turkey's military leadership. Indeed, protection of the secular state has been part of the Turkish strategic doctrine, and the perceived role of the military, since the Ataturk years. This concern reached its high point in the 'soft coup' that ended the

Erbakan government and the subsequent pressure on Islamists of varied stripes, a development that enjoyed the backing of Turkey's secular, civilian establishment. Today, this aspect of Turkey's security debate is a mixture of tolerance and renewed concern. In its first years, the Erdogan government, with its 'recessed' religious orientation, secured widespread acceptance from Turkey's sceptical secular establishment, both civilian and military. Against a background of European aspirations, political movements that might once have been viewed as an internal threat are now treated as more normal actors in Turkish politics. Moreover, reforms of the past few years place new constraints on the ability of the military to intervene in politics via decisions of the National Security Council. A return to the more confrontational stance of the 1990s is still possible if AKP policy takes a more radical turn, or if developments in other spheres embolden hard-liners within the military. But for the moment the focus of concern is Islamic terrorism waged from the margins of Turkish society, rather than the risk of a national drift away from secularism.

Until quite recently, Turkey's Islamic extremists were more active and visible in Europe than in Turkey itself. Multiple terrorist bombings in Istanbul in 2003, with alleged connections to Al Qaeda as well as Turkey's own Hizbullah and IBDA-C (Islami Büyükdoğu Akincilar Cephesi, Great Eastern Islamic Raiders' Front) movements, suggest a new kind of threat, along the lines that have reshaped strategic debates in the US, Britain and elsewhere. The struggle against terrorist networks of this kind, however marginal, is now a leading priority for Ankara's intelligence and security forces, and a leading topic for cooperation with external partners. An important, open question is how Islamic terrorism in urban Turkey might interact with the resurgence of Kurdish violence in the south-east and elsewhere. There are already some links, including Turkish Hizbullah's reported roots in the counter-insurgency policies of the early 1990s, and the significant number of Kurds among the alleged conspirators in the 2003 Istanbul bombings. A possible nexus between extreme nationalism and Islamism could also emerge at the margins, if Turkish society as a whole moves in the direction of more polarised and confrontational politics.

Developments on the domestic scene are shaping Turkey's national security outlook in other important ways, with a new set of actors in the policy debate, and a vastly increased role for public opinion. For most of the history of the modern republic, Turkish security thinking was shaped by a relatively small group of military leaders, foreign ministry officials and secular elites (including a handful of influential outside 'analysts'), with a shared ideology of secularism, Westernisation and nationalism. Not surprisingly, this group, led by the Turkish General Staff, took a very traditional 'hard power' view of Turkey's regional and alliance relations, a view fostered and reinforced by the formative experience of two world wars and a traditional wariness of Russian intentions. The West, for its part, looked to these security elites as the interlocutors of choice in relations with Ankara. Whereas Western governments generally view their high civilian officials as the key players in foreign and security policy, the corresponding civilian officials in the Turkish Ministry of National Defence have, in practical terms, been subordinate to the Turkish General Staff – a situation that has begun to change only very recently. Thus, Turkey's model of civil–military relations has not only affected internal politics, but has shaped the country's dialogue with Europe and the US. This pattern persists in relations with Washington, long after the emergence of more diverse and competing actors with foreign and security policy interests. Indeed, this anachronistic practice of 'talking to the generals first' played a role in Turkish–US friction over the war in Iraq.

Strategic perspectives within the Turkish military have never been monolithic and a diversity of views has been evident on such issues as Cyprus and the Aegean, Iran and northern Iraq. More importantly, changes in Turkish society and the Turkish economy in recent years have given rise to a far wider range of actors with an interest in strategic affairs. Turkey's alternative elites, more traditional and conservative businessmen and politicians from Anatolia – a mainstay of the AKP government – have their own perspectives. In some cases, such as policy toward the EU, these views have been in the mainstream. In other cases, notably on relations with Israel and the US, their perspective is more critical than the norm. Even within the secular establishment, private sector organisations, from TUSIAD (the Turkish Businessmen's and Industrialists' Organisation) to civilian think tanks, have become more active in debating national security issues and offering recommendations. Given the significant interplay between the military leadership and the Istanbul-based business sector, it is not surprising that Ankara's policies toward a range of issues, including Cyprus and Greek Turkish relations, increasingly display a synthesis of military and private sector perspectives.

Public opinion has emerged as a substantial factor in Turkish national security policy. Twenty years ago, public opinion was essentially reactive and policy was set by a small security-conscious elite. By the 1990s, this was no longer the case, and public opinion is now a force to be reckoned with in the Turkish strategic debate. The expansion of the private media has reinforced this trend and journalists and opinion shapers of all kinds now play a significant role in mobilising opinion over events in the Balkans, the Caucasus and, above all, the Middle East. Groups that wish to influence Turkish policy toward regional conflicts now seek to influence public opinion directly, often with the media as part of the equation, as in the Imia/Kardak crisis with Greece, or the 1996 hijacking of a Black Sea ferry by Chechen extremists – the resolution of which was actually negotiated by journalists on the deck of the ship. The net effect of this increasingly active public discourse has been to bring the Turkish strategic debate closer into line with Western norms. At the same time, it has exposed the country to a wider range of terrorism and political violence aimed at capturing public attention, and has complicated crisis management for Turkey's security bureaucracy. The AKP's openly populist orientation places clear limits on what Ankara can and cannot do in places such as Iraq. But this orientation has also been successful to the extent that it reflects contemporary Turkish reality. The last decade has also seen the rise of distinct ethnic 'lobbies' in Turkey. These groupings are now a real factor in the Turkish calculus in Bulgaria, Bosnia, Kosovo, on Nagorno-Karabakh and Cyprus, and of course, with regard to the Turkmen in Iraq. Even the question of the Uighur Turks in China, or that of the Tatars in Russia and the Ukraine, can be influenced by a combination of affinity politics and media attention, a development with important implications for Turkey's future strategy.

As elsewhere, in Turkey strategists, policymakers and the public have begun to redefine the question of national security in broader terms. Turkey is far from being at the cutting-edge of this phenomenon, and retains a relatively traditional, military-centric view of security policy – a natural approach, perhaps, for a state with large standing forces and a wide range of 'hard' security risks on its borders. Yet Turkish national security thinking is becoming more comprehensive, encompassing questions of economic security, energy security, human security, and security of identity in ways that have become common in Europe. Turkish thinking along these lines has been strongly influenced by the experience of financial collapse and tenuous recovery, as well as the heavily-reported problems of human trafficking, drug smuggling and refugee flows over Turkey's borders.

By Western standards, Turkey is a security-conscious society (in this respect, it more closely resembles the US than most of its European partners), and for most of the country's modern history, internal security has been at the top of the strategic agenda, with key regional issues viewed through the lens of domestic stability. This remains the case, although changes on the domestic scene have significantly reshaped the national security debate, with more and more diverse actors, and a wider range of security-related interests.

A revolution in regional strategy?

Alongside internal security concerns, Turkish strategists pay close attention to regional relations and the correlation of forces on Turkey's borders. Over some eight decades, Turkey's regional security perceptions have evolved substantially, with change occurring at a very fast pace over the last decade. In the early years of the republic, the principal strategic challenge was the consolidation and protection of the new Turkish state's territorial integrity in the face of direct and proxy interventions. The leading risks emanated from Greece (until the Ataturk-Venizelos détente), the European powers with interests in the Levant, and in a less direct, long-term fashion, the Soviet Union. By the late 1930s, the overarching strategic problem for Ankara was to preserve the country's freedom of action and integrity in the face of a vast

European and, ultimately, global confrontation, in which Turkey's resources and lines of communication were seen as a prize by all sides. By 1945, Turkey found itself confronting Soviet power in Eurasia, and for the next 40 years the containment of the Soviet Union was the centre of gravity for Turkish strategy – and for Western strategic thinking about Turkey. In practical terms, the Cold War began in the eastern Mediterranean, and Ankara was a participant in several of the key episodes in this confrontation, including the Korean War and, indirectly, the Cuban missile crisis. Throughout this period, Turkish strategy was firmly rooted in the realities of NATO nuclear and conventional doctrine, and membership in the NATO 'club' served as the country's most visible badge of membership of the West. As a result, and with few exceptions, Ankara's security policies were oriented toward stability in Europe, and defence cooperation with the US, rather than regional developments in the Middle East or elsewhere.

In fact, Turkey's leading regional interest in Cyprus and the Aegean was in tension with American policy for decades, and most strikingly in the 1960s and 1970s, when Turkish policy on Cyprus brought Ankara to the brink of estrangement from Washington and other NATO allies. The 1974 invasion of Cyprus left a legacy of wariness between Ankara and Washington (especially in the US Congress) that has only recently been overcome. For many years, and despite close defence ties of all kinds, Turkish policymakers complained about the existence of a *de facto* American arms embargo – an exaggeration, perhaps, but true enough on occasion.

A snapshot of Turkish strategic perceptions in the mid-1990s reveals a transformed environment. Russia was now regarded as a significant but long-term geopolitical competitor, with the prospect of further instability in Russia's 'near abroad' seen as almost as much of a risk to Ankara as to Moscow. Iran was viewed with suspicion as a potential exporter of Islamic revolution, but not a direct threat to Turkey. Iraq, Turkey's leading trading partner prior to the Gulf War, had become a zone of instability – at least in the north – and a leading stimulus to Kurdish separatism. Syria, a strategic backwater in Turkish perception, had moved to the forefront of Turkish security concerns as a result of its government's support for the PKK.

Greece remained the leading, proximate source of risk for Turkish planners in the immediate post-Cold War period (and Turkey certainly remained the overwhelming threat in Greek perceptions). In retrospect, and despite some very real points of friction over Cyprus, the Aegean and Thrace, it appears that a good deal of Turkish–Greek antagonism in this period was based on the momentum of the past. That said, Turkey very nearly clashed with Greece on several occasions in the 1990's, most notably in the Imia/Kardak crisis during the winter of 1996.[6] Had these adversaries come to blows, the outcome would probably have turned on the speed and character of American or European intervention. In operational terms, Turkey possessed – and continues to possess – an advantage in land forces and in the air. At sea, in the Aegean, the forces have been more evenly matched, with perhaps a slight Greek advantage in force structure and forward deployment.

In this same period, Turkish strategists began to consider the problem of potential coalitions aligned against Turkey in Eurasia and the Middle East, alignments that could spell trouble, even for Turkey's formidable and expanding armed forces. Most notably, retired ambassador Sukru Elekdag suggested that Turkey required a 'two and a half war' strategy to address potential conflict in the Aegean, with Syria or elsewhere in the Middle East, and against the PKK in Turkey and northern Iraq (the half-war).[7] Turkish observers were also quick to see a Russian hand in the eastern Mediterranean, particularly in connection with the Russian sale of surface-to-air missiles to Cyprus, although the missiles were never deployed.

Successive crises in the 1990s engaged Turkish interests and public opinion, and Turkey has a strong interest in regional stability, the preservation of existing borders, and the prevention of spillovers affecting Turkish security (including the interruption of the country's overland trade links to Europe). On the whole, contemporary Turkish security engagement in the Balkans has been restrained and multilateral. Ankara has been a leading contributor to SEEBRIG (the South-Eastern European Brigade) and has participated in most of the major peacekeeping and peace enforcement operations in the southern Balkans. Turkish aircraft flew in NATO operations in Bosnia and Kosovo, and Turkish humanitarian airlifts have been conducted across Greek airspace – a stark contrast to concerns about Greek–Turkish conflict in the Balkans in the early years of the Yugoslav crisis.

In the Caucasus and Central Asia, Turkish ambitions – much diminished since the early 1990s – have focused on trade, investment and diplomacy rather than defence entanglements. This policy reflects Ankara's continued wariness of geo-strategic competition with Moscow, and a very real stake in economic relations with Russia, Turkey's largest trading partner. In Chechnya, despite some public sympathy for separatism, Ankara has taken an arms-length approach, encouraged, no doubt, by Turkey's own exposure to separatist violence.

A similar *tour d'horizon* in 2004 reveals further substantial change in Turkish national security perceptions and policy. In the eastern Mediterranean, Turkey is engaged in a policy of détente with Greece, a reflection of strategic reality on both sides. Above all, it is a product of Ankara's increasingly European outlook, in which the country's long-term strategic interests are no longer held hostage to narrower regional frictions with Athens. In defence terms, military disengagement with Greece (both countries are now exploring formal force reductions in the Aegean and elsewhere) has left Turkish planners free to address more pressing challenges emanating from the Middle East, and to develop forces better-suited to participation in European and NATO missions. Given parallel changes in Greek policy, and the essential de-coupling of Cyprus from the bilateral relationship,

Turkish-Greek détente appears to be 'structural', and durable. The residual security issues in a Greek-Turkish setting are increasingly seen as part of a wider 'eastern Mediterranean security complex', in which Athens is as likely to play the role of partner as adversary (Dokos and Tayfur, 2004, p. 13; Lesser, 2005). Turkey's strategic commentators are now far less inclined to describe Cyprus as a place of strategic importance. Until a few years ago, it was not uncommon for Western analysts to hear the island portrayed as a vital strategic interest for Turkey and for other actors in the region and beyond. While it is true that the Baku-Ceyhan oil pipeline and the prospect of a return to full use of the pipelines from Iraq to Turkey's Mediterranean coast make Turkey a more important energy *entrepot*, there are few real threats to the sea lanes in the area. Cyprus may be a useful location for signals intelligence aimed at the Middle East. But it plays no truly unique and indispensable role, a reality acknowledged in the Turkish General Staff's spring 2004 decision to support moves toward a political settlement on the island, even if this would imply sharp reductions or the elimination of Turkey's military presence.

In the Middle East, tense security relations with Syria have improved significantly since 1999, and Syria is now far less of a factor in Turkish strategic planning. It is likely to remain a secondary concern, barring a very unlikely revival of Syrian support for the PKK. The PKK factor is also an important dimension in perceptions of Iran. Here too, the perception of risk is much reduced compared to that of the 1990s, with the exception of measured concern about Iranian nuclear and ballistic missile programmes. Indeed, new intellectual currents within and around AKP, including pressure for a more diverse (read 'less Euro-Atlantic') international engagement, and a more active policy in the Muslim world, have led the Erdogan government into a closer strategic dialogue with Iran, Syria and Saudi Arabia. The 'strategic depth' concept articulated by Ambassador Ahmet Davutoglu, a key advisor to Prime Minister Erdogan and the AKP, is very much part of this trend. Turkish and Western analysts are now engaged in a vigorous debate about whether these developments amount to a strategic shift in Ankara's security ties, or a short-term experiment in diversification.

The experience of Iraqi Scud attacks in the first Gulf war, and occasional Iraqi threats to retaliate against Incirlik and other targets on Turkish territory, reminded Turks of the country's growing exposure to weapons of mass destruction deployed in the Middle East. Indeed, Turkey is highly exposed to ballistic missiles of increasing range. Many of Turkey's population centres are within range of systems based in Iran and Syria, and its leaders view the prospect of new nuclear arsenals in the region with concern. That said, their concern is relatively muted, certainly in comparison to prevailing views in Washington.

This measured response can be ascribed to several factors. First, Turkey has faced nuclear risks in the form of Soviet and later Russian arsenals for decades.

It is nothing new. Second, with Iraq out of the equation and improved relations with Syria, Turks see few threats of confrontation with Middle Eastern neighbours. Third, there is a widespread sense among Turkey's security establishment that the NATO security guarantee and the prospect of a closer defence relationship with Europe are sufficient conditions to deter the use of such weapons against Turkish territory. To the extent that Turks fear the use of weapons of mass destruction, they are inclined to see this risk as a product of potential American, European or Israeli action against Iran or elsewhere. In the event that the NATO guarantee wanes or becomes unpredictable, or if Turkey is estranged from its Western security partners, the issue of deterrence in a missile and nuclear-armed region will become more pressing. Under these conditions, it is not unimaginable that Turkey would develop WMD programmes of its own – but these conditions are far from current reality (Lesser, 2004).

Turkey's strategic relationship with Israel, which developed rapidly in the 1990s, has come under increasing pressure both from public opinion and an AKP government that is less inclined to overlook Palestinian–Israeli dynamics. The political dimensions of the relationship may be in decline, but the defence-related aspects have not yet been seriously disrupted. Israel has become an important supplier of defence goods and services, alongside a well-developed programme of training, exercise, and intelligence sharing. Whether the security dimension of the relationship will prove durable in the face of other pressures, including strong public reaction to Israeli operations in Lebanon, remains an open question.

New concerns – and new capabilities

Turkey possesses the second largest standing security establishment in NATO, and is engaged in a long-term programme of defence modernisation aimed at streamlining the force structure and giving the country a greater capacity for power projection beyond its borders (Demir, 2004). Turkey's long-term military procurement programme, although scaled back from the very ambitious plans fashioned prior to the financial crisis in 2000, still includes the co-production of modern main battle tanks and attack helicopters, new refuelling and airlift capability, and more sophisticated command, control and communications systems.[8] New frigates and submarines are also on the agenda.[9] In 2006, there has been discussion of cancelling the planned upgrade of Turkey's ageing F-4 fighters by Israeli Aircraft Industries in favour of a new round of F-16 co-production in Turkey. These new purchases would bolster forces that have already seen steady improvements in power and mobility since the time of the Gulf War. The experience of 1990–1 was interpreted by the Turkish military as a clear demonstration of the need for Turkey to acquire more modern equipment for its large but somewhat antiquated forces. In this context, Turkey benefited from large-scale 'cascading' of surplus NATO equipment removed from central front arsenals as a result of the CFE (Conventional Forces in Europe) treaty.

As noted earlier, Turkish strategists express measured concern about the growing missile capability arrayed on Turkey's borders, although to date, Turkey has only acquired short range, tactical missile systems. Looking ahead, with increasing proliferation pressures and the possibility of new nuclear weapons states in Turkey's neighbourhood, the development of a more ambitious Turkish medium-range missile programme, capable of holding at-risk targets in Iran and Syria, cannot be ruled out. In general, any Turkish response to regional WMD threats can be expected to influence strategic perceptions and balances beyond the Middle East – a significant Turkish missile capability would certainly worry Greece, Armenia, and Russia. For the moment, Ankara's plans focus on enhanced intelligence, warning and air defence, including participation in American and Israeli missile defence initiatives.

As a large-scale purchaser of defence goods and services, Ankara has long been concerned about the reliability of its defence supply relationships. Since 1945, the US has provided the bulk of Turkey's military equipment and training, with somewhat smaller amounts provided by German and other European suppliers. Beginning in the mid-1960s, and with greater severity after the 1974 invasion of Cyprus, Turkey has faced periodic limitations on arms sales from American suppliers, the result of Congressional concerns about Greek-Turkish relations and human rights. These de-facto sanctions have not been a serious problem in recent years but worries about American (and German) reliability have encouraged Turkey to diversify its sources of defence goods and services. Since the 1990s, Russia and, above all, Israel, have emerged as important suppliers. At the same time, military training and intelligence cooperation, once largely focused on the US, has also been diversified. Turkish officers are now as likely to train with European or Israeli forces, and to attend war colleges outside of the US. This changing pattern of defence cooperation could well have longer-term implications for Ankara's strategic orientation, and could reinforce an increasing focus on Europe in the economic and political sphere.

The Turkish armed forces need new equipment and new doctrines oriented toward power projection to address tangible security risks emanating from the Middle East and the Black Sea regions. But these enhancements are also aimed at enhancing Turkey's ability to participate in a range of multinational military operations, from UN and NATO-led interventions, to deployments for peacekeeping and civil emergency planning. Turkey has participated in a number of such missions in recent years, including the UN operation in Somalia and, most recently, NATO operations in Afghanistan (the latter was under Turkish command in 2003). Ankara may also deploy forces in Lebanon as part of an enhanced UN peacekeeping operation in the south of the country. While Turkey has demonstrated a willingness to use military force unilaterally, in Cyprus, in the Aegean, in northern Iraq, and very nearly in Syria, the contemporary thrust of Turkish strategy is multilateral and oriented toward power projection on and beyond the country's borders.

Turks, like many others, are fond of describing themselves as a 'bridge' between regions and civilisations. For some of Turkey's international partners, Turkey's central role might more accurately be described as that of a 'barrier' to instability on the European periphery. Whether bridge, barrier, or neither, Turkey is certainly emerging as a more capable security actor in multiple regions. In this sense, Turkey plays a trans-regional role, and Turkish national security policy is increasingly influenced by non-traditional, trans-regional problems.

Like the proliferation of longer-range weapons capable of reaching from the Middle East or Eurasia to Europe, terrorism is a threat that cuts across traditional regional boundaries. In the years ahead, it is likely that Turkey, together with much of southern Europe and the Mediterranean, will focus much of its national security planning on challenges that have little to do with the conventional defence of borders. Safeguarding the security of an increasingly complex web of oil and gas pipelines and terminals around the Black Sea and the Mediterranean is one task of this kind; monitoring and preventing nuclear smuggling is another (Turkey has been a leading venue for low-level nuclear trafficking incidents in recent years). These challenges of adjustment are by no means unique to Turkey, but Turkey may well be unique in the range and diversity of risks affecting its security.

Alliance relationships in flux

For most of the past 50 years, Turkey has been among the most orthodox members of the Atlantic alliance. Indeed, it would not be inaccurate to describe Turkish military and foreign ministry officials as NATO 'fundamentalists', adhering to a traditional conception of the Alliance's mission and area of responsibility. With tangible security problems on its borders, persistent concerns about Russian power, and limited resources to address multiple demands, it is not surprising that Turkish strategists were wary of the idea of NATO enlargement and reform. Turks still cite NATO's tardy response to Ankara's request for air reinforcements in 1990 – an experience repeated in the run-up to the Iraq War – and worry about any dilution of NATO security guarantees. Yet Turkish perspectives have evolved considerably in the past few years, and Ankara has emerged as a supporter of enlargement, especially in areas of special interest such as the Balkans. Not surprisingly, Turkey is also among the most vigorous advocates for NATO involvement in counter-terrorism and missile defence. Overall, Turkey has a strong stake in the continued viability of NATO, and views the increasingly distant attitude of Washington toward the Alliance with concern.[10] A dysfunctional NATO would affect Turkish perceptions and options in key areas, including deterrence vis-à-vis potential Middle Eastern adversaries. Turkey's traditionally close security relationship with Washington is also in flux (Lesser, 2006). To be sure, Turkish–US defence cooperation has seen many stresses and strains over the past decades, particularly on bilateral rather than NATO matters. Much has been made of frictions over policy before and after the American-led intervention in Iraq. In reality, after Ankara's very cooperative stance during the 1990 Gulf War, the US was never again given unrestricted use of Turkish facilities for Middle Eastern contingencies. Incirlik airbase, once home to a substantial American tactical air presence, has been the source of repeated disagreements, especially in the context of Operation Northern Watch (now disbanded). Turkey has been, and continues to be, extremely sensitive to issues of national sovereignty, and the Turkish constitution prohibits the permanent deployment of foreign forces on Turkish soil. Access to Incirlik and other facilities for NATO and other multilateral purposes has been an easier issue for successive Turkish governments to grapple with, and to justify to the Turkish public. Purely American (or US–British) uses have been a more difficult 'sell'.

Against this background, it is hardly surprising that the negotiations prior to the most recent Iraq war left all sides bitter and dissatisfied. The anatomy of the disagreement is worth summarising briefly, as it sheds light on what may well be a troubled future for Turkish–US security relations.[11] American policymakers made unfounded assumptions about the predictability of Turkish cooperation in Iraq, and took, at least in Turkish perception, a cavalier approach to Ankara's sovereignty concerns. The relatively new AKP government faced sceptical elites in the military and elsewhere, and a public strongly opposed to military intervention (a view that was solidly present in the European mainstream). Moreover, the proposed deployment of as many as 60,000 American troops through Turkish territory to open a northern front in Iraq, together with requests for base access and over-flight, pushed the limits of what Turks could tolerate. These were extraordinary demands in the context of Turkey's history and national sensitivity to foreign intervention. Even for sophisticated, Western-oriented members of the country's security establishment, the prospect of a deployment on this scale, outside the NATO context and without a clear UN mandate, was difficult to accept. Moreover, many Turks, recalling the 1990 experience and the PKK threat, felt that Washington was not prepared to take Turkey's own strategic concerns seriously. Given this overwhelming combination of negative factors, it is surprising that legislation on US–Turkish cooperation in Iraq very nearly succeeded in the Turkish parliament.

Security cooperation remains the centre of gravity in Turkish–US relations. Despite Washington's significance in IMF decision-making and other issues of critical concern to Ankara, the relationship is not as diversified or broadly 'strategic' as both sides profess. Relations with the EU take precedence in economic matters and increasingly in political terms. American planners have discussed the redeployment of a tactical air wing from Germany to Incirlik. On paper, this makes good logistical sense. But in practical terms, it is difficult to envision shifting forces to Turkey in the absence of an agreement about regional strategy and policy. If anything, the American military presence in Turkey looks set to decrease further in the coming years. Turkish scepticism regarding American policy in Iraq and elsewhere in the Middle East appears undiminished. Under these conditions, there remains a possibility of more active Turkish intervention in northern Iraq, to counter renewed PKK operations, to protect the interests of ethnic Turkmen, or both.

The acceleration of Turkey's EU ambitions is also affecting the security realm. Turkish policy is already far closer to Brussels than Washington on a range of security-related foreign policy questions, most notably on Iran and Iraq. In the run-up to key EU decisions regarding Turkey's candidacy, Ankara was keen to champion the country's potential contribution to emerging European security and defence initiatives. Turkey's large military establishment and geopolitical position bring advantages to an EU in search of defence weight (Emerson and Tocci, 2004). On the other hand, those Europeans inclined to be critical of Turkey's EU ambitions pose the question of whether Europe really wants to acquire new borders with Iran, Iraq and Syria – conveniently leaving aside NATO's existing commitment to defend Turkey in Middle Eastern as well as European contingencies.

Even with the uncertain future of Turkey's candidacy, Turkey will almost certainly continue its convergence with European norms and policies in many sectors, including security policy. If, at the same time, Europe develops a more active and independent foreign and security policy, Ankara's own national security thinking is likely to take on an increasingly European character. If this comes against a background of unresolved transatlantic friction, Turkey's security relationship with Washington may well take second place. The most problematic scenario for Turkey would arise from a stalled or 'hollow' EU candidacy, with Washington going its own way on issues of concern to Turkey. This outcome would pose difficult dilemmas for Turkey, with real security risks on its borders requiring American participation, and the possibility of further pressures for cooperation in regional crises. In this case, and even in more favourable European and transatlantic scenarios, Turks will likely opt for an independent and sovereignty-conscious approach.

Conclusions

This analysis points to several important areas of continuity and change in Turkish national security thinking, with recent developments driven by a combination of internal and external forces.

First, Turkey has a strong strategic tradition informed by Ottoman and Republican experience. This tradition is conservative and geopolitical in nature, with a pronounced continental and *realpolitik* flavour. In this, as in other ways, it is possible that within the EU, Turkey would subtly shift the balance of European strategic thinking at a time when European strategy is in flux.

Second, the last few years have seen truly revolutionary changes in Turkey's relations with Greece, with significant implications for the country's national security planning. If Greek–Turkish détente proves durable – and it shows every sign of becoming structural – it will allow an important shift of resources and doctrine from this traditional problem to new risks in the Black Sea and the Middle East.

Third, Ankara's short-term strategy will almost certainly be driven by deepening challenges emanating from the Middle East and, in particular, the return of PKK violence and its implications for Turkish internal security and cohesion. Risks in this area will also shape the prospects for conflict and cooperation with Syria, Iran and, not least, the US.

Fourth, Turkish thinking with regard to long-term risks and strategies will no doubt remain focused on Russia, an historic adversary and geopolitical competitor. If Russia's relations with the West become more confrontational, this competition will no longer be in the centre of Europe, but rather on the European periphery, and in Turkey's neighbourhood. Ankara's future security posture is likely to reflect this concern, whether in a transatlantic, European or unilateral context.

Fifth, Turks are fully in the Western mainstream in terms of the changing debate about functional security issues – from proliferation and energy security to human security – and the very definition of security is evolving to encompass unconventional challenges, cutting across traditional regional lines. The Turkish position is distinctive in that it reflects a wide range of new and 'soft' security problems, alongside a large number of persistent 'hard' security risks. Few countries are as security conscious, in the broadest sense – and few face such a tangible array of concerns.

Finally, Turkish security and strategy are inextricably bound up with the country's European prospects. Turkey has arguably always been part of the European system, above all in security terms. Ankara aspires to be a European and transatlantic, not a Middle Eastern ally. The nature of Turkey's European role over the next few years – whether moving rapidly toward membership, converging with Europe in a formal and distant manner, or even becoming estranged from EU partners – is likely to be the single most important factor shaping the country's security outlook. Whatever the outcome, Turkey will remain an independent-minded actor, with an eye on its own strongly felt national interests – an important but difficult partner in its alliances.

Notes

1. Several recent volumes treat Turkish foreign and security policy in historical perspective. See Robins (2003); Hale (2000); Larrabee and Lesser (2003); and Martin and Keridis (2004).

2. See also Inalcik (1996).
3. The Treaty of Sevres (1920) would have led to a much smaller and weaker successor to the Ottoman state. Its provisions were never implemented, but the experience is often cited by Turkish politicians and observers as evidence of Western intentions toward Turkey.
4. The newly appointed Chief of Staff, General Buyukanit, has made the drive for smaller, more modern forces a leading priority.
5. In the summer of 2003, the PKK opted to infiltrate back into Turkey from bases in northern Iraq and Iran. Some 2000 PKK fighters may now be back on the ground in Turkey, bolstered by weapons from Iraqi depots and recently obtained shoulder-fired surface-to-air missiles. Armed contact between the PKK and Turkish security forces has increased steadily since June 2003. See Cagaptay and Koknar (2004).
6. The crisis was defused, in large measure, by last minute American diplomacy, including telephone calls from President Clinton. Former US Assistant Secretary of State for European Affairs, Richard Holbrooke, famously described his efforts 'while Europe slept'.
7. This thesis was elaborated in a series of articles in *Milliyet* in 1994. See discussion in Robins (2003, pp. 171–2).
8. Turkey has a sophisticated defence industry of its own, led by Turkish Aircraft Industries (TAI). TAI has co-produced hundreds of F-16s for its own use and for export.
9. Initial plans called for some $31 billion to be spent over a 10-year period, with as much as $150 billion in new procurement over 25 years. See Robins (2003, p. 193).
10. Turkish aircrews were aboard the NATO AWACS aircraft deployed to the US to monitor airspace after the September 11 terrorist attacks – a fact few American politicians chose to highlight.
11. For a discussion of this episode, see Candar (2004, pp. 47–62). See also Lesser (2003, pp. 166–74).

Bibliography

S. Cagaptay and A. Koknar (2004) 'The PKK's New Offensive: Implications for Turkey, Iraqi Kurds and the United States', *Policywatch*, No. 877 (Washington: Washington Institute for Near East Policy).
C. Candar (2004) 'Turkish Foreign Policy and the War on Iran', in L. G. Martin and D. Keridis (eds) *The Future of Turkish Foreign Policy* (Cambridge: MIT Press).
S. Demir (2004) 'Turkey's Security Needs and Policy on the Threshold of the 21st Century', *Turkish Policy Quarterly*, 2004, pp. 111–9.
T. Dokos and F. Tayfur (2004) 'Greece and Turkey', *EuroMeSCo Paper*, no. 28 (Lisbon: Euromesco Secretariate).
M. Emerson and N. Tocci (2004) *Turkey as Bridgehead and Spearhead: Integrating EU and Turkish Foreign Policy* (Brussels: Centre for European Policy Studies).
W. Hale (2000) *Turkish Foreign Policy 1774–2000* (London: Frank Cass).
H. Inalcik (1996) 'The Meaning of Legacy: The Ottoman Case', in L. C. Brown (ed.) *Imperial Legacy: The Ottoman Imprint on the Balkans and the Middle East* (New York: Columbia University Press).
A. L. Karaosmanoglu (2000) 'The Evolution of the National Security Culture and the Military in Turkey', *Journal of International Affairs*, vol. 54, no.1, pp. 199–216.
F. S. Larrabee and I. O. Lesser (2003) *Turkish Foreign Policy in An Age of Uncertainty* (Santa Monica: RAND).

I. O. Lesser (2006) 'Turkey, the United States and the Delusion of Geopolitics', *Survival*, vol. 48, no. 3, Autumn, pp. 83–96.

I. O. Lesser (2005) *Security and Strategy in the Eastern Mediterranean*, Policy Paper, no. 5 (Athens: ELIAMEP).

I. O. Lesser (2004) 'Turkey, Iran and Nuclear Risks', *Turkish Policy Quarterly*, Summer, pp. 81–100.

I. O. Lesser (2003) 'Playing Turkey', *Aspenia* (Rome), no. 21–22, pp. 166–74.

L. G. Martin and D. Keridis (eds) (2004) *The Future of Turkish Foreign Policy* (Cambridge: MIT Press).

P. Robins (2003) *Suits and Uniforms: Turkish Foreign Policy Since the Cold War* (Seattle: University of Washington Press).

14
Turkey's Engagement with Europe: A History of Mutual Management

Nuri Yurdusev

This chapter examines Turco-European relations over a historical period from the Ottoman era to the present with an emphasis on the broader picture. It aims at taking a broad view not only in terms of time span, but also in respect of its principal focus. The chapter deals with diplomatic engagement. In line with the stated broad perspective, diplomatic engagement has been analysed in terms of both the mainstream conceptualisation of the term as an activity of the recognised state agents and within the context of the mutual identity perceptions between Europeans and Turks. Thus, while examining the question of whether Turkey was part of the modern European system, both the actual diplomatic practices and mutual identity perceptions have been taken into consideration. Similarly, when dealing with relations between Turkey and the EC/EU, the chapter addresses on the one hand the requirements of prudence and on the other hand the impact of cultural factors.

Adopting a wiser perspective, the chapter avoids reductionist accounts of Turco–European relations as expressed in terms of the historical dichotomy of *Dar-al-Islam* versus *Dar-al-Harb*, or the Kemalist version of the oppressed peoples versus the imperialists, or the identical treatment of Turkey and the West in the Cold War period. It will be argued that Turkey's engagement with Europe exhibits features of *confrontation, mutual management* and *cooperation*. These processes do not follow a historical chronology, rather, they have been in operation at all times. Having said this, I shall argue that in Turco–European relations, a policy of managing each other has been prevalent and the story remains one of mutual management.

The conventional account

Historically one may see the beginning of Turkish engagement with Europe as early as the early fourteenth century when the Ottoman Turks crossed the Dardanelles and stepped on to the European continent. One may go even further back to the encounter between various Turkic bands of warriors and the Crusaders. Of course such a view is largely a result of the retrospective reading of history. In the period of the Crusaders or in the early fourteenth century, neither was it meaningful to speak of Europe as an entity and nor did the Turks exhibit the characteristics we now attribute to them as a nation. Yet, perhaps just like all conventional statements, this has some truth in it. Turks were a people that had recently adopted Islam and Turkey and the Turkish nation of today identified themselves with those people who founded the Ottoman *Beylik* (principality) and expanded into the lands of the Christians or Franks. Europe, though it had been no more than a vague geographical designation in the fourteenth century, came to signify a land inhabited by Christians in the fifteenth century and more importantly began to be used as an appellation for social identity and political entity from the mid-seventeenth century on. More significantly, the term 'European' is said to have been used for the first time in connection with the Turks. Pope Pius II in his letter to Mehmed II in 1458 used the 'European' interchangeably with the 'Christian'. From then on, it is said, the words European and Europe began to be used in connection with or in contrast to, the Turk (Hay, 1968, pp. 83–7). Thus the Christian European and the Muslim Turk were positioned as adversaries and Turkey's engagement with Europe during the Ottoman period until the late eighteenth century was conventionally described as one of confrontation.

From the fifteenth century onwards, the dissolution of the medieval system in Europe and the subsequent emergence of sovereign territorial states led to the formation of what came to be called the European state system. It is a commonplace argument that the European state system, composed of sovereign territorial states, began to emerge from the mid-fifteenth century onwards (Wight, 1977). It is held that the principal institutions of the European state system began to emerge in fifteenth-century Italy. They were then adopted by the monarchies north of the Alps in the sixteenth century and by the mid-seventeenth century they were more or less Europe-wide. In the eighteenth and nineteenth centuries they became more institutionalised and gradually expanded into non-European parts of the world.

With the conquest of Istanbul in the mid-fifteenth century, the Ottoman Empire can conveniently be considered to have been an imperial system. From its emergence as a power at the beginning of the fourteenth century, the Ottoman Empire expanded at the expense of Europe. It occupied, controlled and administered one quarter to one-third of the European continent from the fourteenth century to the late nineteenth century. As already pointed out, the modern European state system is conventionally said to have emerged from the fifteenth century onwards and consequently the Ottoman Empire was in Europe when the European system came into being. From its emergence as a formidable power, the Ottoman Empire had been a continuous consideration for the Europeans. Thus, the modern European state system and the Ottoman imperial system were never isolated from each other. The Ottomans actively and intensively engaged in European affairs. It can rightly be asserted that the Empire played a major part in the formation and working of the European state system and this shows that a process of mutual dependence operated between the two systems, despite the historical prejudices of the Europeans towards the Turks and the pretensions of self-sufficiency on the part of the Ottomans.

Nevertheless the conventional account (Anderson, 1993, p. 71; Hurewitz, 1961, pp. 145–6; Lewis, 1964, pp. 30–2; Naff, 1963, pp. 296, 299, 314; Kuran, 1988, pp. 10–11) holds that normal peaceful diplomatic relations were exceptions, confrontation or a state of permanent war was the rule between Turkey and Europe. According to the prevalent view, the Ottomans, faithful to Islamic precepts, distanced themselves from the infidel Europeans and adopted a negative attitude toward Europe. The Ottoman refusal to send resident missions to the European capitals until the late eighteenth century was taken as an indication of this. Whereas, the argument goes, the major European states sent their resident ambassadors to Istanbul from the sixteenth century onwards as soon as resident embassies became common Europe-wide. The Ottomans had to reciprocate and establish resident embassies as part of its reform attempts only when the Empire had lost its strength in comparison to the European powers. As the European ambassadors were received by the Sublime Porte, but not vice versa; if there was any Ottoman diplomacy it was only a unilateral diplomacy. As an Islamic empire, so it is argued, she carried out her relations with the Europeans on the basis of a conception of a permanent (actual or potential) state of war. These interpretations are based upon the assumption that the Ottomans adopted an orthodox version of Islam. They had a vision of the world in terms of *Dar al-Islam* versus *Dar al-Harb* dichotomy. Since the Ottoman polity was defined by religion, it was not, so it is argued, easy for the Ottomans to transcend the Islamic exclusivism and consequently establish diplomatic relations with non-Muslims. Therefore, one cannot expect normal peaceful relations and the reciprocal exchange of resident representatives between the Ottoman Turks and Europeans.

The conventional view, that the Ottoman Empire was a strictly Islamic empire and the Ottoman Turks were striving for perpetual *ghaza* and that engagement with the Europeans was based on permanent confrontation, is a reductionist account and, as I have argued elsewhere (Yurdusev, 2004), cannot be sustained with reference to the historical record on three grounds: firstly, the Ottoman Empire was not an orthodox Islamic polity but an imperial system combining diverse traditions; secondly, there had been extensive engagement between the Ottomans and the Europeans involving not just confrontational but also cooperative interactions from the very beginning; and thirdly, it was not just the Ottomans that observed the precepts of religion but also the Europeans that enjoyed the idea of the *common corps of*

Christendom in their relations and thus excluded the Ottomans. Let us first see how Islamic the Ottoman Empire was.

The Ottoman imperial system

Although the Ottoman Empire officially defined itself as Islamic, Ottoman practice was rather pragmatic. The precepts of Islam were pragmatically interpreted especially with regard to external affairs. The Ottomans did not only make use of the *Aman* system or the system of *Ahdname* internally, involving granting safe passage and autonomy of subject populations who were non-Muslims, but also followed a similar approach in their external relations. They did not in practice pursue a policy of permanent war, observing the 'existing customs' and 'agreements'. When Mehmed II granted the Capitulations to the Venetians in 1454, it was stated that the decision was taken according to the existing custom, by which it was meant the previous capitulatory agreement between the Byzantine Empire and the Venetians (Sousa, 1933, p. 16). The respect for existing customs (agreements made should be honoured) can be seen in the practice and implementation of the *Aman* system (İpşirli, 1999, pp. 4–5). After the fall of Istanbul, Mehmed II granted the Greeks, Genoese and Latins *Aman* and when Selim I later wanted to get rid of some Byzantine notables in Istanbul due to their suspected efforts to re-establish the Byzantine Empire, the Sultan was reminded of the *Aman* given by Mehmed II and he retreated from his compulsory conversion or expulsion policy. Similarly, Suleiman the Magnificent, in his *firmans* to the *Beys* of Bosnia and Buda, stressed that the Beys must observe the *Ahd-u Aman* of the Sultan.

Islam did not prevent the Ottomans from reaching or making agreements with non-Muslims. It is true that such agreements were considered to be unilateral truces rather than bilateral treaties. Yet they signed truces for long periods and they were more or less automatically renewed, so that, in practice, there was a permanent state of peace with a considerable number of states. As İnalcık (2004, p. 71) showed us, as early as the time of Beyazid II, an agreement was made between the Sultan and Pope Innocent VIII. In this pact, Beyazid II promised to deliver the City of Jerusalem to the French King after it was captured from the Mamluks, in return for the King keeping his brother Jem in custody in France instead of sending him to the enemies of the Ottomans. This is most striking. Beyazid II, known to be one of the most religious sultans, was to deliver the City of Jerusalem, sacred for Muslims, to the King of France, king of the infidels, after he captured it from the Mamluks, a Muslim state! What could demonstrate better than this that the Ottomans behaved according to self-interest rather than the strict requirements of religion?

In the second half of the eighteenth century, it was heavily debated within Ottoman circles if the alliance with Prussia was compatible with Islam. In the end, a *fetva* affirmed that it was. Similarly, Ottoman policymakers did not have any difficulty in securing a *fetva* for the alliance between the Ottomans and the Austrians against the Russians. On the other hand, Frederick the Great had a hard time in his efforts to explain the alliance with the Ottomans (Beydilli, 1984, 1985). Many other examples could be found demonstrating that the Ottomans did not strictly abide by a policy which the conventional account would have us believe they did. But there is no need to rehearse them. What we know historically is that the Ottomans were quite pragmatic and observed the rules of expediency. The Ottoman Empire was not then an orthodox Islamic polity.

The Ottoman Empire was first and foremost an empire, an imperial system deriving from many sources, as richly argued in the Ottoman historiography. These sources included Islamic civilisation (Wittek, 1938), Byzantine heritage (Gibbons, 1916), Turkish and nomadic traditions (Köprülü, 1992; Lindner, 1983) and Inner Asian origins (Togan, 1991). No doubt the Empire, in time, borrowed from Europe. The Capitulations developed, on the one hand, as part of the *Aman* system of Islam, and as a continuation of the Byzantine tradition, on the other. Similarly the relations of the *Ulama* and the Grand Mufti to the Sultan reflected both the Sunni path and practice of Islam and the position of the Patriarchate in the Byzantine Empire. The Ottoman sultans were not only referred to as the *Padishah of Islam*, but also as *Sultan-ı İklim-i Rum* (Emperor of the Realm of Rome). The infiltration into the frontier zones and subsequently their administration and the entrusting of the young princes with the government of some provinces derived from the nomadic and Turkic heritage. The interrelationships of these different sources and influences meant the Empire enjoyed a rich culture and diversity in its composition and administration. As it grew from a small frontier *beylik* to a worldwide empire, the diversity increased and it came to comprise multiple peoples, ethnic groups, religions and vast territories. Logically speaking, it could have been possible to confine a small *beylik* to a single tradition, say, nomadic; but it is not possible to confine and reduce a large and diverse empire within the limits of a single tradition or religion such as Islam. In other words, by definition, it is hard to define the Ottoman Empire as an 'Islamic' or *Shari'a* polity. By the nineteenth century, the Empire came to adopt the governmental, military and diplomatic techniques common to European nation states.

To summarise so far, the Ottoman Empire was not a consolidated polity like the one which began to emerge first in Renaissance Italy and later in Europe. As an imperial system, the Ottoman Empire had all the notions and, perhaps, pretensions of universalism and self-sufficiency. Yet the Ottoman Empire was born and grew alongside Europe when the European states were beginning to emerge and it had an extensive engagement with the European state system.

The Ottoman engagement with the European state system

The Ottoman engagement with the collective affairs of the Europeans can first be observed vis-à-vis the Italian city state system, which is traditionally considered as the forerunner of the modern European system. As early as the first stage of the Italian Wars from 1494 onwards, the Ottoman Empire was an important actor in the Italian system and for their part the Italian courts maintained diplomatic relations with the Porte. In 1494, faced with the first French triumphs in Italy, Naples and the Papacy negotiated with the Sultan for help against Charles VIII. In order to keep France out of Italy, when the Second Holy League was signed in 1495 with an almost Europe-wide participation, Mattingly (1955, pp. 136–7) tells us, an ambassador of Sultan Beyazid II was present, in a sense, as an observer at the signing ceremony.

The historical record shows that the Ottoman Empire became an active participant in the emerging European balance system in the sixteenth- and seventeenth centuries. The sixteenth-century Ottoman historian Sinan Çavuş, for instance, argued for the alliance between Turkey and France in order to prevent France from aligning with the Pope and the Emperor against the Ottomans (İnalcık, 2001). The sultans thus pursued a conscious policy of balance vis-à-vis the European powers so that the rise of the nation states was to a certain degree facilitated. The Ottomans encouraged and supported the English and Dutch in the period after 1580 when these nations proved to be the champions of European resistance to the Habsburgs' attempts at hegemony. In the sixteenth- and seventeenth centuries, support for the Protestants and Calvinists was one of the fundamental principles of Ottoman policy in Europe. The Ottoman pressure on the Habsburgs was an important factor in the spread of Protestantism in Europe. The Westphalian settlement of 1648 became possible through this pressure on the Habsburgs as observed by Watson: 'The Habsburg bid to establish a hegemonial system in Christian Europe was defeated, decisive Westphalian formulation of the anti-hegemonial nature of the European states system was made possible by the Ottoman pressure on the Habsburgs' (Watson, 1992, pp. 177–8, 216).

Similarly, the European sovereigns took into account the Sublime Porte in their calculations of the balance in Europe and did not hesitate, from time to time, to align with the Sultan against each other. According to Dehio (1962, pp. 40–1), the Ottoman Empire became a counter weight to the unifying tendency represented by Charles V. The introduction or intervention of the Empire into the European balance of power system and the European diplomacy played a most significant part in preserving the freedom of the system of states. Indeed the contemporary Europeans recognised and accepted the Ottoman engagement with European affairs from the early sixteenth century on and saw the Ottoman Empire as part of a European balance system well into the nineteenth century. In the early sixteenth century Francis

I admitted that the Ottoman Empire was the only force to prevent the emerging states of Europe from being transformed into a Europe-wide empire by Charles V. In the late sixteenth century, when Queen Elizabeth I established relations with the Ottoman Empire, one of her motives was certainly the expansion of trade but she was also driven by the idea that the Sultan could balance the Habsburgs in the East and consequently relieve Spanish pressure upon England. Elizabeth I even stressed that Protestantism and Islam were equally hostile to 'idolatry' (Catholicism). In granting Capitulations to the English and the Dutch, the Sultan, too, considered that these nations were the champions of the struggle against the idolaters (Rodinson, 1987, pp. 43–5; İnalcık, 1974, pp. 52–3). In the late eighteenth century, the place of the Ottomans in the European balance system was acknowledged in the British Parliament. Similarly it has been reported that Catherine the Great of Russia explicitly recognised it (Butterfield, 1966, p. 143; Davison, 1996, p. 175). It seems obvious that the Ottoman Empire was within the European balance system from very early on. While Vaughan (1954) speaks of a 'pattern of alliance' between the Turks and Europe, Goffman (2002) makes the point that the Ottomans were an indispensable part of, and fully integrated into, the European diplomatic system.

What one can draw from the foregoing analysis of the mutual positions of the emerging European international system and the Ottoman imperial system is that the two systems were closely interwoven and were in constant interaction. This analysis of the mutual dependence between the Ottoman Empire and the European international system in its formative (and, of course, later) centuries unequivocally leads us to conclude that the two systems were not isolated. They had frequent relations with each other and the nature of these relations was not always warlike. The Europeans and the Ottomans did not always aim at plundering each other, they were not in a permanent state of war as the orthodox understanding of the *Christendom* versus *non-Christendom* or *Dar-al-Harb* versus *Dar-al-Islam* dichotomies would have us believe. In light of all those contacts, wars, conflicts, alliances, agreements and commercial exchanges between the Ottoman Empire and Europe, and given the actual control, administration and government of one quarter to one third of the European continent for half a millennium, 'the logical conclusion ought to be', as Naff puts it, 'that the Ottoman Empire was, empirically, a European state. The paradox is that it was not. Even though a significant portion of the Empire was based in Europe, it cannot be said to have been of Europe' (Naff, 1984, p. 143). Despite the existence of extensive relations so as to form 'a pattern of alliance' between Europe and the Turks, the fact that the Empire was considered *in* Europe but not *of* Europe shows that a rift remained. The initial positioning of the Christian European and the Muslim Turk as adversaries did not disappear but continued, frequently emerging until this day. This was because, despite the intensive engagement in the process of making the modern European identity, as I have argued elsewhere (Yurdusev, 2007) the Turk was 'otherised'. A summary here of that argument might be useful.

European identity and the Turk

It is widely held that the Turk has been one of the most significant 'others' of Europe in the modern period. While Bosworth (1980, p. 25) argued that more than any other empire since the early period of Arab conquests and expansion 'the Ottoman Turks struck terror into the hearts of Christian Europe', Yapp (1992, p. 84) notes that 'of all the negatives known to Europe the nearest, the most obvious and the most threatening has been the Islamic Near East, represented from the fourteenth century onwards by the menace of the Ottoman Empire'. The historian Butterfield (1951, p. 22) agrees with Yapp in Turks being considered the greatest menace to the European civilisation until well into the eighteenth century and Neumann (1999) summarises that the Turk has been 'the dominant other in the history of the European state system'. That the Turk has been the dominant and significant other of Europe in the modern period is not just held by present scholars, but it was the opinion held by the contemporary Europeans from the statesmen and scholars to the preachers and the masses.

Pejorative descriptions of Turks may be found in European discourse from the time of the Crusades onwards. The Norman minstrel Ambroise, on the Third Crusade, writes of 'the best Turks one could find in heathendom' (Bartlett, 1994, p. 254). The Turk was considered as a heathen by Ambroise in the thirteenth century. About 200 years later when informed of the fall of Constantinople, King Christian I of Denmark declared that 'the grand Turk was the beast rising out of the sea described in the Apocalypse' (Schwoebel, 1967, p. 4). In the early sixteenth century, Sir Thomas More, imprisoned in the Tower of London before his execution, was not so much worried about his own predicament, as disturbed by the Turkish threat to the Christendom (Wight, 1977, p. 36). One can even find negative references to the Turk in the course of European expansion into the Americas. In a popular book of romance published in Seville (1525), with the title *Las Sergas del Virtuoso Cavallero Esplandin* ('Exploits of the virtuous cavalier Esplandian'), it was told that a mythical eastern emperor, defending Constantinople against the Turks, was succoured by an army of Amazons led by their queen (Morrison, 1974, p. 617). The Turks were disapproved of to the extent that even the Amazons, who themselves did not receive a positive treatment by the Spaniards, were posed against them.

The pejorative portrait of the Turk further increased from the sixteenth century on. For the Elizabethan historian Richard Knolles, the Turks were 'the present terror of the world' and, for the English Consul, Paul Rycaut, incapable of feeling friendship to a Christian (Lewis, 1968, p. 40). According to Rousseau (1913, p. 109), Turks were the barbarians who conquered the civilised Arabs. Burke (1910, pp. 123, 256) told the House of Commons that the Turks were 'worse than savages' and that 'any Christian Power was to be preferred to these destructive savages'. One should not confuse the late French monarchy with the 'barbarous anarchic despotism' of the Turks whose government was 'oppressive to human nature'. When classifying humanity into three categories of the civilised, the barbarian and the savage, the nineteenth century Scottish lawyer James Lorimer (1883, pp. 10–12) defined two subgroups of savage, the progressive and non-progressive. On the Turks, he said that they did not even belong to the progressive races of humanity. In the view of Sir Elliot (1965, p. 16), writing at the beginning of the twentieth century, the Turks had been a destructive force; they destroyed a great deal and constructed nothing. From the late seventeenth century to the beginning of the nineteenth century, there occurred various proposals for universal peace in Europe, projects of the European Union in the present sense. Until Kant, almost all authors justified their proposals with the need to unite against the Turkish peril (Hinsley, 1963). With all these characterizations and representations, the Turks have been used to serving as a means of affirmation for the Europeans. The Turk was the 'perfect barbarian' for the Europeans in order to readily affirm the civilised nature of Europe.

The first and perhaps most important reason for the 'otherisation' of Turks by the Europeans was the Turk's having a strong religious tradition (Islam), a religion which was historically regarded as heresy. The second reason can be found in the fact that the Turk was in Europe and expanding at the expense of the Christian peoples and countries. In other words, the Turk was not a Muslim people somewhere in the world, say, like the Malays, but they were at the heart of Christendom or what had once been Christendom. Furthermore, they were not like earlier invaders. Not like the Hungarians who were Christianised nor like the Huns who were short-lived. Just like the earlier Muslim invaders, or the Saracens, that conquered and kept control of once Christian lands in the Middle East, North Africa and Spain for long centuries, the Turk was in Europe to stay and the Europeans were not able to come to terms with this.

That the Europeans were not able to come to terms with the presence of the Turks in Europe has already been shown via the statements of people from Sir Thomas Moore in the sixteenth century to Sir Charles Elliott in the early twentieth century. And this has not only been the view of the writers, but some statesmen as well. The crusading spirit against the Turks was maintained until the late seventeenth century. From the late eighteenth century onwards the policy of expelling the Turks from Europe was expressed and implemented with the famous Eastern Question (Anderson, 1966). The Allied Powers during the First World War, in a communication to the US President Woodrow Wilson on 11 January 1917, specified that among their war aims was their common goal of expelling the Ottoman Empire from Europe, which had been totally alien to Western civilisation (Toynbee, 1922,

p. 328). Nor was this just the opinion of the statesmen who were technically and actually at war with the Turks. When the War was already over, an eminent historian such as Henri Pirenne (1939, pp. 588, 592–3) had this to say: 'wherever the [Turkish] invaders advanced they brought with them economic ruin and moral decadence. All those peoples who were subjected to the Turkish Yoke – Bulgars, Serbs, Rumanians, Albanians, and Greeks – relapsed into a state verging upon barbarism, from which they never emerged until the beginning of the 19th century. ... Barbarians they [Turks] were and barbarians they remained. ... It is astonishing to think that the industrious and inoffensive Moors of the Kingdom of Granada were driven back into Africa at the end of the 15th century and that the Turks are still in Constantinople in 1918'.

Given that the Turk was, on the one hand, the principal other in modern European identity formation and, on the other hand, actively engaged in the European state system, the result was (is) what Naff called the paradox of being in Europe but not of Europe.

The paradox of being *in* Europe but not *of* Europe

Naff's observation with regard to the Ottoman Empire was shared in debates in the British Parliament during the 1790s. The Ottoman Empire was considered within the European balance system to some extent although not fully. With the Paris Peace Treaty of 1856, the Ottoman Empire was admitted into the Concert of Europe, the then European Union. Nevertheless both the provisions of this Treaty and the legitimacy of the Ottoman entry into the Concert of Europe and thus her Europeanness, have frequently been subjected to discussion (Lorimer, 1883, p. 102; Temperley, 1932).

From the late nineteenth century, the Turkish engagement with Europe increased with a stress on the 'European' character of Turkey. Modern Turkish identity has been defined with reference to Europe. Even the Ottoman sultans considered themselves as the Emperors of Rome. From the mid-nineteenth century onwards they were European sovereigns. When the German Emperor visited Istanbul in November 1889, Sultan Abdulhamid II met Emperor William not just as Caliph of Islam, but also as a European sovereign (Haslip, 1958, p. 190). From the eighteenth century onwards, in response to a decline in military strength the Turkish statesmen embarked upon a policy of modernisation/Westernisation which is, one could rightly say, still going on. In this process, the West or Europe was used in defining modern Turkish identity. With the modernisation project culminating in the Republican reforms, Turkey defined itself as part of the 'civilised world', which was represented first and foremost by Europe. Even the majority of the Republican elite rejected the imperial past.

Despite this, questions and doubts about the European character of Turkey are constantly raised in many European quarters. For example, on the fourth of March 1997, six centre-right leaders (of Belgium, Germany, Ireland, Italy, Luxembourg and Spain), at the meeting of European Union of Christian Democrats in Brussels, were reported to have agreed to intensify efforts to create a special relationship with Turkey built around the existing Customs Union. However, they agreed unanimously that Turkey's human rights record, its size, and implicitly, the Islamic strain in its society made it impossible for the European Union to contemplate admitting the country into the European Union. Mr Wim van Welzen, president of the European Union of Christian Democrats, said that the EU had cultural, humanitarian and Christian values that were different from Turkey's (*Financial Times*, Wednesday, 5 March 1997). While the European Christian Democrats approved the place of Turkey in Europe under the framework of the existing Customs Union agreement, they could not contemplate Turkey entering into the European Union and becoming a part of Europe. The reason why Turkey cannot be a European country can be found, for the Christian Democrats, in different cultural values of which religion constitutes an essential part. Perhaps the Christian Democrats at that time publicly declared what many Europeans implicitly or explicitly agreed. Nowadays they still oppose Turkish membership of the European Union, yet they suggest an 'enhanced partnership'. Although the idea of Turkey's full membership of the EU appears to have been accepted by EU leaders at the Helsinki European Council in December 1999 and accession negotiations actually started on 5 October 2005, it cannot be said that the debates about the Europeanness of Turkey have come to an end. Turkey remains in but not of, Europe.

The state of being in Europe but not of Europe may be seen both from the European and Turkish sides. On one side, the Europeans do not deny the place or significance of Turkey in/for Europe, even if they do not usually consider her as European. First and foremost, as shown above, Turkey has been in Europe from the very beginning. Turkey has been in Europe in terms of physical occupation as observed by Naff. When Europe is defined in geographical terms, Turkey is in it. Turkey was and is in Europe not just by its physical presence but also human presence. Turkey was and is in Europe as an actor and element that had/has to be taken into consideration when Europe-wide policies need(ed) to be designed. Turkey is again in Europe at present, with her economy largely integrated into Europe, her membership of various political organisations of European origin such as NATO, the Council of Europe, OECD, and the OSCE, and her Association Agreement, Customs Union and slow but continuing accession process with the EC/EU. Turkey today is in Europe with Turkish communities living in various European countries as guest workers or migrants numbering now about four million, larger than the total population of several countries in Europe. The cultural differences may prevent Turkey from being accepted as European, but they cannot prevent her from being a part of Europe.

From the other side, Turkey does not just want to be in Europe but of Europe as well. She claims to be a European country and aspires to full EU membership. This desire and aspiration has been expressed on every occasion for the last 150 years. On 19 April 1855, Ali Pasha, the then Foreign Minister, expressed the aspiration to join the Concert of Europe (in a drafted treaty article for a possible peace treaty to end the Crimean War) as follows: 'The Contracting Powers, wishing to demonstrate the importance they attach to assuring that the Ottoman Empire participate in the advantages of the concert established by public law among the different European States, declare that they henceforth consider that empire as an integral part of the concert and engage themselves to respect its territorial integrity and its independence as an essential condition of the general balance of power' (Türkegeldi, 1987, pp. 601). Davidson (1996, p. 184) rightly detects four basic aspects of Ottoman policy represented in Ali Pasha's statement: a) the importance of Ottoman independence and integrity; b) observance by the contracting (great) powers of those rights; c) acknowledgment of the Empire as a member of the Concert of Europe; and d) acknowledgment that the Empire was essential to the European balance of power. The Treaty of Paris of 1856 comprised three of those proposals apart from the last one. What is striking among these proposals is that Ali Pasha explicitly stated the Ottoman desire for entering into the Concert of Europe and with the consequent treaty, the Empire became a member of the Concert system.

Just as Ali Pasha expressed that Ottoman Turkey shared the public law system of Europe, the policy makers of Republican Turkey have always declared that Turkey shares Western (European) ideals and wants to be a part of Europe. In 1989 when Turkey applied to the European Community for full membership, Turgut Özal (1989, p. 6), then Prime Minister, boldly said that Turkey's relations with the West could not be reduced to military alliance and her strategic location. Above this, Turkey shared Western ideals. From Ali Pasha to the present-day Turkish statesmen, it has been persistently claimed that Turkey is a European state though not considered as such by the Europeans. On the one hand, Europeans recognise that Turkey is in Europe but do not approve of her as European. On the other hand, Turkey publicly declares herself to be a European state without advancing policies to comply with the criteria for being European. The paradox of being in Europe but not of Europe continues. This paradox may result from different values as Mr Van Welzem declared; or from the 'two equally formidable bulwarks of religious ideology and culture – one Christian, the other Muslim, both reinforced by ignorance, prejudice, and hostility', as argued by Naff (1984, p. 143); or from 'Turkish inadequacy' in complying with European standards as most Europeans see it; or from 'European double standards' in dealing with Turkey as most Turks understand it.

The main reason is, as I have shown, Turkey was involved in European affairs from the emergence of Europe itself so cannot be said to be outside

Europe. On the other hand, cultural difference enforced by religion has remained effective and there has been mutual otherisation in the making of both the modern European and Turkish identities so that it is not easy to say that they share a common heritage. That the Europeans historically otherised the Turks because of their being Muslim and in Europe, is a well-established argument as I have outlined above. The question is whether Europeans are still doing this and more importantly whether this is because of Islam. The answer to these questions seems to be in the affirmative, even in so-called post-Christian secular Europe.

The Turk: Still the other

Various reasons may be given for why a considerable number of Europeans still, to some extent, consider the Turk as the other. They may include the economic problems faced in many European countries, lack of knowledge of the general public and the hugeness of Turkey being somewhat over-whelming for the man in the street. However, one reason is, I argue, that the Europeans have not yet come to terms with Islam as a normal religion, like Christianity, nor with Turkey's Ottoman past. The late Edward Said, in his seminal work (Said, 1979, p. 343), made the point that European fear and hostility towards Islam in one way or another persists to the present day, 'both in scholarly and non-scholarly attention to an Islam which is viewed as belonging to a part of the world – the Orient – counterposed imaginatively, geographically, and historically *against* Europe and the West'. Similarly, when Edward Mortimer (1990) reviewed the contemporary European perceptions of Islam and Turkey in a newspaper article, he found them to be echoing the early European writers cited above and made the point that 'for good or ill the Christian legacy remains a key component of European identity'. These observations by two eminent scholars may be followed both in general public perceptions and elite attitudes and even in some official circles, especially after the September 11 attacks.

A recent study by the International Helsinki Federation for Human Rights (IHF) covering eleven EU member states found that Muslims in Europe have faced increased discrimination since September 11. According to the report of the IHF, 'pre-existing patterns of prejudice and discrimination have been reinforced and Muslims have increasingly felt that they are stigmatised because of their beliefs'. A report by the EU race watchdog confirmed similar findings. One sees widespread use of the phrases such as 'Islamic terrorism' or 'Muslim terrorists' in media coverage. Even some statesmen have made otherising statements about Islam. Italian Premier Silvio Berlusconi's remark on the superiority of Western civilisation over the Islamic culture (*Independent*, 27 September 2001) is perhaps the most striking one. The law banning Islamic headscarves from French state schools is a prime example of the development of official policies towards Muslims.

We can even find the impact of European uneasiness with Islam in the descriptions and decisions of European institutions. In reference to Bulgaria (a candidate country), the EU website (visited in June 2002) claims that '85% of Bulgarians are Christian Orthodox, whereas 13% of the population profess Islam' (EU, 2002). While Orthodox Christianity is considered something that one simply *is*, Islam must be *professed*. In other words, Islam does not sound as normal as Christianity. In the regular reports prepared by the European Commission on the progress of Turkey, the EU has not been favourable towards religious freedoms or freedoms of expression when it comes to Muslims. While the demands of the non-Muslim communities and the minority Alevi community have been salient concerns in the reports, the demands of the majority Sunni population have consistently been neglected. For example, when the Turkish university authorities undertook a disciplinary investigation against some Kurdish students petitioning for the teaching of Kurdish in 2002, this was immediately covered in the EU regular report, even though in the end, no student was subjected to disciplinary measures. In contrast, the EU consistently refused to cover the actual disciplinary penalties against the students who wanted to attend universities wearing headscarves. Similarly, the European Court of Human Rights has been quite restrictive in its decisions regarding the cases brought by Muslims from Turkey. While the Court always rejected the decisions of the Turkish Constitutional Court banning the Kurdish and socialist parties, it upheld the decision of the Turkish Constitutional Court banning the Islamist Welfare Party, in spite of there not having been any evidence of the Party being linked to violence or that it posed a threat to democratic society (Refah Paritisi, Erbakan, Kazan and Tekdal vs. Turkey No. 41340/98). The Court also upheld one case on the headscarf ban at Turkish universities, despite the fact that there is no such ban at the universities of any other state signatory to the European Convention on Human Rights (*Leyla Şahin* v. *Turkey*, No. 44774/98). These instances indicate that European institutions share the otherising practices of militant Turkish secularism towards Islam.

These examples, from public perceptions to the descriptions of the elite to the decisions of institutions, clearly show that Europe has not yet fully come to terms with Islam as a feature of normality, like Christianity or any other religious, ethnic and ideological discourse. Although the EU has come to open membership negotiations with Turkey, in many quarters Turkey's Muslim character continues to be a concern. The often referred to 'cultural difference', as everybody knows, actually refers to the difference of religion. Mortimer's observation that the European identity of Turkey has been judged by religious criteria has not yet been persuasively falsified since then.

Furthermore, Turkey's Ottoman past as a great Muslim power is frequently being referred to on the basis of a one-sided reading of Turco-European relations when assessing Turkey's bid for EU membership. According to Pope Benedict XIV, in one of his statements when he was Cardinal Joseph Ratzinger, the Ottoman Empire threatened Vienna and fought wars in the Balkans and thus 'Turkey has always represented a different continent, in permanent contrast to Europe' (as was reported by Reuters News agency on 11 August 2004). In October 2004, the Dutch Commissioner Frits Bolkenstein declared that 'the liberation of 1683 would have been in vain' if Turkey was given a date for the start of membership talks at the forthcoming meeting of the Brussels European Council (Reynolds, 2004). On the eve of the official start of negotiations, the Austrian Member of the European Parliament, Johannes Swoboda in an interview with a Turkish newspaper explained Austria's opposition to Turkey's EU membership by claiming that Austrians have not yet been able to forget the siege of Vienna (*Akşam*, 30 September 2005). Writing at the same time when membership talks between the EU and Turkey officially started, a European observer pointed out that 'the Turks have always been the Other, a common foe useful to Europeans for stimulating alliances against them and, by contrast, for defining identity' (Tonge, 2005, p. 120). There is no need to extend these examples. One can find many such instances and one can also find historical explanation. However, a different reading of history is possible. For example, one may refer to Turkish support for the Netherlands (Bolkenstein's country!) when the Dutch rebelled against Spain in 1568. One may cite the wars Turks fought in the Balkans and at the same time, one may also remember the role of the Turks in the preservation of the distinctive identities of the Balkan peoples.

It is evident that history still hinges on Turco–European relations. Scholars and preachers from the Archbishop of Canterbury and Richard Knolles in the late sixteenth- and early seventeenth centuries, through to Burke, Lorimer and Elliot in the late eighteenth- and nineteenth centuries, to the present-day Christian Democrat politicians and Cardinal Joseph Ratzinger, have consistently made the case for the Turkish peril. Yet, the 'most Christian King' and the 'Great Queen' in the sixteenth century, English and Dutch diplomats at Carlowitz in the late seventeenth century and the British Parliament in the late eighteenth century, Anglo-French politicians in the nineteenth century and contemporary European statesmen have formed various channels of friendly relations with Turkey such as alliances, exchanges, treaties and common organisations. As is well known, in its later centuries, the Empire was considered 'the sick man of Europe'. It was not just 'a sick man'; it was 'the sick man *of* Europe'. All this shows that Turkey is in Europe and to some extent of Europe. No matter how suspicious they have been, the Europeans have never been able to exclude Turkey from Europe. Since both sides are so interwoven vis-à-vis each other, and their respective identity formations have historically involved a process of mutual otherisation, the result has been a consistent policy of each managing the other.

Managing each other

During the first few centuries of Turco–European engagement, relations can be described as reflecting a policy of mutual management in terms of strength and balancing of power. This policy continued in later centuries, albeit with increasing suspicion. Ever since the Eastern Question, formulated from the late eighteenth century on, the Turks have been suspicious that Europeans wanted to destroy the unity and integrity of Turkey. Paradoxically, one remedy to this suspicion has been the Turkish attempt to be part of Europe. For Turks, then, the 'Eastern Question' has become a 'Western Question' (Yurdusev, 2005). During most of the nineteenth century, Europeans did not consider Turkey a European country. However, due to the requirements of *raison d'état*, Turkey was admitted into the Concert of Europe. This was the way Turkey was managed for the time being. On the other hand, Turkey, in the face of the Russian threat, introduced reforms and thus claimed to be a European state. This was the way Turkey managed Europe at that time.

The picture and the strategy have not significantly changed today. Republican Turkey introduced swift modernising reforms. In Turkish intellectual discourse during the Republican period, the concepts of modernisation, secularisation, Westernisation and Europeanisation have been understood as interchangeable and used as such. As a complementary policy to its internal reforms, in its external relations, the Republican policymakers have been very keen on being a member of international organisations of Western/European origin. Aside from the ideological negation of the imperial past, this was indeed a continuation of the policy adopted by the late Ottoman statesmen. Turkey adopted European style laws and political institutions at home and became a member of organisations like NATO, the OECD, the Council of Europe, and the OSCE abroad. In 1963, she signed an Association Agreement with the then European Community with a view to future membership, a view which has yet to be realised.

The Europeans for their part seemed to have welcomed the European orientation of Turkey and did not much hesitate in including Turkey in those European institutions. Of course the bipolar structure of the international system in the twentieth century and the consequent ideological confrontation of the Cold War years made the European statesmen adopt a policy in line with the principle of *raison d'état* rather than the politics of identity. In spite of Turkey's flirtation with the Soviet Union during the inter-war years, Britain and France guaranteed Turkey's security in 1939. After WWII, the Europeans did not exclude Turkey from their international organisations and institutions. The politics of identity did not come onto the scene till the late 1970s, or so it seemed according to those security perceptions of the Cold War years.

Nevertheless the issue of identity has never faded away. For the Turkish administrative and intellectual elite all this was a confirmation of Turkey's modern/European identity. It has been an escape from the imperial past, the 'other' of the Republican identity. As Çalış (2006) has persuasively showed, the Turkish policy towards Europe and European institutions has been basically determined by an effort to confirm the European character of Turkey. For the Europeans, too, the issue of identity has always been in the background. In 1962, when the Turkish diplomat Feridun Cemal Erkin met De Gaulle in Paris to ask his support for the Association Agreement, the French President implicitly referred to differences of identity between Europe and Turkey in terms of culture and history (Erkin, 1976).

By the 1990s, unlike the homogeneity of the early Republican elite, a heterogeneous political class including Kemalists, nationalists, leftists, liberals, and pro-Islamists had appeared in Turkey. For the Kemalists and the nationalists from the Right to the Left, the contemporary European policy of 'support' for the Kurdish people is reminiscent of the Eastern Question and the unratified Sèvres Treaty of 1920. For the pro-Islamists, the European upholding of the rights of Kurdish and leftist dissidents but disregarding the rights of Muslims, is no different from when nineteenth century Europeans intervened on behalf of non-Muslim minorities of the Empire. As the homogeneity of the early Republican elite disappeared, the view of Europe as the cradle of civilisation and Turkey's ultimate destiny has no longer been held by the Turkish elite uniformly. Though all opinion polls show that a sizable majority of the Turkish people are in favour of EU membership, the established Kemalist elite seems to have strong reservations.

On the other hand, relieved from Cold War necessities and united with their natural brethren in Central and East Europe, the Europeans began to openly question the Europeanness of Turkey, 'a large Muslim country'. Both the 'Christian legacy' and the historical legacy of the Turk as the principal other of Europe remain. The Europeans are no longer worried about Turkish troops as they are not likely to appear at the outskirts of Vienna any more, but they are quite concerned with the nearly four million Turks living in Europe and about 70 million Turks in Turkey with a higher population growth than the average in Europe. The findings of survey after survey by the Eurobarometer show that the majority of the European public is against Turkey's membership of the EU. Both the Europeans and the Turks thus have mutual suspicions and reservations, yet they cannot simply turn their backs on each other due to a logic of culture and a logic of *raison d'état*. The result is then the ongoing policy of management.

The examples of this policy of management can be found in the relations between Turkey and the EC/EU. On 14 April 1987, Turkey presented its application for membership to the European Community. The European Commission issued its opinion on the Turkish application on 18 December 1989, more than two and a half years later. The Commission concluded that 'it would not be useful to open accession negotiations with Turkey straight away'. The Commission gave both economic and political reasons and it also noted 'the negative effects' of the disputes between Greece and Turkey and 'the situation in Cyprus'. In its opinion of 1989, the Commission concluded that it would not be useful to open accession negotiations straight away, an opinion that was to be held until 2004. This opinion of the Commission revealed the management policy of the EU since a simple 'No' to Turkey's application would not have been feasible for well-known reasons. Morocco applied for membership of the Community a year before Turkey and the opinion of the Commission on this application came shortly after. Rabat was simply told that the Community was open only to Europeans and that was it. Though both Turkey and Morocco were Muslim countries, the latter was easily turned down because neither logic of culture and identity nor *raison d'état* had ever deeply penetrated relations between modern Europe and Morocco as had been the case between the Europeans and the Turks. The Europeans cannot be indifferent to Turkey, even though they cannot admit her straight away. They are thus compelled to manage her.

At the European Council in Luxembourg in December 1997, Turkey was not declared to be a 'candidate country' due to its lack of civilian democracy and respect for and protection of human rights by European standards. Two years later, in December 1999, European Council in Helsinki declared Turkey as a candidate country. What happened between the time of the Luxembourg and Helsinki Councils in terms of the objections advanced at the former? Nothing much had changed but the situation was accepted by the EU authorities. Both of the Progress Reports of 1998 and 1999 before the Helsinki Council are full of examples to show how far Turkey was away from satisfying those concerns voiced at the Luxembourg Council. In the 1999 Report, for example, it was clearly expressed as follows: 'Generally speaking, since the last report, the situation concerning civil and political rights in Turkey has not evolved significantly ... Moreover, certain administrative measures taken in the aftermath of the Öcalan affair show a more restrictive attitude by the Turkish authorities as regards freedom of expression'. Surprisingly, based on this report, the EU Council in Helsinki extended candidate status to Turkey. In an interview with a Turkish journal (*Liberal Thought*, Winter 2000), the then EU Ambassador to Turkey, Karen Fogg also said that no significant improvement took place in Turkey in terms of democracy, rule of law and the human rights, except perhaps the rather symbolic removal of judges with military backgrounds from the State Security Courts. Only one third of European public opinion was in favour of Turkey's EU membership according to results of a Eurobarometer survey in July 1999. From 1997 to 1999 no significant reforms were realised in Turkey and the majority of the European public was against the accession of Turkey. Why, then, did the EU designate Turkey as a candidate at Helsinki?

The reason can be found in the EU's policy of managing Turkey. The Europeans realised that the Luxembourg formula was not an adequate way to manage Turkey since the latter suspended the political dialogue between the EU and Turkey. A new formula was needed to manage Turkey and that was the Helsinki formulation. Speaking to Turkish press, the French Minister for Foreign Affairs, Hubert Vedrine (who is said to have been decisive for the Helsinki summit's conclusions recognising Turkey as a candidate) explicitly stated the policy of management. According to M. Vedrine, the Europeans had two concerns at Helsinki: the fact that Turkey was still far away from fulfilling the Copenhagen criteria and a lack of trust in Turkish policymakers making the necessary reforms. However, 'the Europeans finally realised that it would not be possible to find any solution if they remained firm on those two points. It was admitted that a dynamic process would come out by recognising the candidate status ... Due to those unresolved questions many countries were against Turkey being a candidate. We told them that those questions could be resolved later. We must start by extending candidate status to Turkey' (*Milliyet*, 15 December 1999). Indeed in Helsinki, as expressed by M. Vedrine, Turkey was declared to be a candidate country as a result of the search for a new formulation for managing Turkey.

From the Helsinki Summit of December 1999 to the Accession Partnership Document, adopted by the European Council on 8 March 2001, the Progress Reports of the EU on Turkey again revealed the policy of managing Turkey. In those reports, it was repeatedly stated that Turkey had not yet met the Copenhagen political criteria. One of the persistent themes of these reports was the lack of effective civilian control over the military and the latter's frequent intervention in political affairs with detailed examples. Despite the detailed instances given in the reports, the Accession Partnership Document simply required that the National Security Council be reformed as an advisory body in accordance with EU practice. No detail about civilian control of the Army was given in this detailed document. Unlike previous reports, the Accession Partnership document seems to have been prepared so as not to offend the Turkish Armed Forces (TSK). This shows the strategy of management. This policy of managing Turkey in respect of TSK still continues. The EU officials from time to time speak highly of the TSK. When Olli Rehn, the Enlargement Commissioner, warned the TSK over its intervention in the presidential voting in late April 2007, he added that they respected the 'professionalism' of TSK (Rehn, 2007). One may wonder how professional an army based upon conscription and a heavy indoctrination can be. It is clearly a reflection of the policy of management.

The policy of management is also seen on the part of Turkey. After her application for full membership of the EC/EU, despite the high public support and the professed enthusiasm of the elite and policymakers, Turkey did not make the necessary reforms to fulfil the Copenhagen political criteria until the second half of 2004. Even then, the Commission said that Turkey just 'sufficiently fulfilled' the political criteria. Turkey was criticised for human rights violations, not just in the EU reports but also in the reports of Amnesty International and Human Rights Watch. After the so-called Soft

Coup of 28 February 1997, the military increasingly infiltrated the domain of the civilian government. In the words of Heath W. Lowry: 'Between the State (*Devlet*) and the elected government (*Hükümet*), the balance has clearly swung in favour of the Devlet' (Lowry, 2000, p. 44). Despite all those criticisms coming from the EU and the increasing militarisation of civilian political life, the issue of civilian control of the military was not addressed in the Turkish National Programme for the Adoption of the *Acquis*, adopted by the Government on 19 March 2001. The Accession Partnership simply spoke of the reform of the NSC as an advisory body to meet European standards of practice. The Turkish National Programme did not even refer to it. Similarly, in the Accession Partnership, the issues regarding the Cyprus question and Greece were treated under 'Political Criteria'; the National Programme included them in the 'Introduction'. Unlike the Accession Partnership, the National Programme did not mention the free usage of the 'mother tongue' by all Turkish citizens and the right to television broadcasting in the mother tongue. With such escape clauses Turkey tried to manage the EU in its National Programme for the Adoption of the *Acquis*. The Turkish policy in response to calls for reforms coming from the EU and other democratic circles was sometimes to ignore and sometimes to do just enough.

One can observe that in order to manage each other, both European and Turkish policymakers made use of their fellow countries and fellowmen. For years, some European states like Germany and France made use of persistent Greek objections as an easy way of managing Turkey. Similarly, Turkish policymakers made use of the so-called threat of fundamentalist Islam coming to power in Turkey as leverage in their argument for Turkey's membership of the EU. The former Prime Minister Mrs. Tansu Çiller told a journalist from *Time* in the run up to the Customs Union Agreement that a failure by the European Parliament to admit Turkey would lead to the Islamist Welfare Party coming to power (*Time*, 20 November 1995). Mesut Yılmaz, Prime Minister after Çiller, also used the same argument in the German Press, saying that the failure by the EU to admit Turkey would only strengthen the two pro-Islamist parties. By echoing the historical 'other' of Europe, Turkish secular politicians actually tried to manage the EU. Since Greek governments began to support Turkey's EU membership and the so-called Islamists in Turkey began to follow pro-EU policies, there has not been much room left for management by some European policymakers and the secularist Turkish elite. Yet, given the historical legacy and the rivalry between different groups within Europe and inside Turkey, the mutual policy of managing the other will likely persist for some time to come.

Bibliography

M. S. Anderson (1966) *The Eastern Question 1774–1923: A Study in International Relations* (London: Macmillan).

M. S. Anderson (1993) *The Rise of Modern Diplomacy 1450–1919* (London: Longman).

R. Bartlett (1994) *The Making of Europe: Conquest, Colonization and Cultural Change 950–1350* (Harmondsworth: Penguin Books).

K. Beydilli (1985) *Büyük Frederik ve Osmanlılar: XVIII. Yüxyılda Osmanlı-Prusya Münasebetleri* (*Friedrich the Great and the Ottomans: Ottoman-Prussian Relations in the Eighteenth Century*) (İstanbul: İstanbul Üniversitesi Yayınları).

K. Beydilli (1984) *Osmanlı-Prusya İttifakı: Meydana Gelişi-Tahlili-Tatbiki* (*Alliance between the Ottomans and Prussia: Its Development, Analysis and Implementation*) (Istanbul, Günyay).

C. E. Bosworth (1980) 'The Historical Background of Islamic Civilization', in R. M. Savony (ed.), *Introduction to Islamic Civilization* (New York: Cambridge University Press).

E. Burke (1910) *Reflections on the Revolution in France* (London: J. M. Dent).

H. Butterfield (1966) 'The Balance of Power', in H. Butterfield and M. Wight (eds) *Diplomatic Investigations: Essays in the Theory of International Politics* (London: George Allen and Unwin).

H. Butterfield (1951) *History and Human Relations* (London: Collins).

Ş. H. Çalış (2006) *Türkiye-Avrupa Birliği İlişkileri: Kimlik Arayışı, Politik Aktörler ve Değişim* (*Relations between Turkey and the European Union: Search for Identity, Political Actors and Change*), third edition (Ankara: Nobel Publications).

R. H. Davison (1996) 'Ottoman Diplomacy and Its Legacy', in L. Carl Brown (ed.) *Imperial Legacy: The Ottoman Imprint on the Balkans and the Middle East* (New York: Columbia University Press).

L. Dehio (1962) *The Precarious Balance: Four Centuries of the European Power Struggle* (New York: Alfred A. Knopf).

C. Elliot (1965) *Turkey in Europe*, second edition (London: Frank Cass and Co.).

EU (2002) available at http://europa.eu.int/comm/enlargement/bulgaria/index.htm.

F. C. Erkin (1976) 'Ortak Pazara İlk Adım' [The First Step to the Common Market], *Milliyet*, 14 September 1976.

H. Gibbons (1916) *The Foundation of the Ottoman Empire: A History of the Osmanlis 1300–1403* (Oxford: Oxford University Press).

D. Goffman (2002) *The Ottoman Empire and Early Modern Europe* (Cambridge: Cambridge University Press).

J. Haslip (1958) *The Sultan: The Life of Abdulhamid II* (London: History Book Club).

D. Hay (1968) *Europe: The Emergence of an Idea* (Edinburgh: Edinburgh University Press).

F. H. Hinsley (1963) *Power and the Pursuit of Peace* (Cambridge: Cambridge University Press).

J. C. Hurewitz (1961) 'Ottoman Diplomacy and the European States System', *The Middle East Journal*, vol. 15 (Spring), pp. 141–52.

H. İnalcık (2004) 'A Case Study in Renaissance Diplomacy: The Agreement between Innocent VIII and Bayezid II on Djem Sultan', in Nuri Yurdusev (ed.) *Ottoman Diplomacy: Conventional or Unconventional?* (Basingstoke: Palgrave Macmillan).

H. İnalcık (2001) 'Avrupa Devletler Sistemi, Fransa ve Osmanlı: Avrupa'da "Geleneksel Dostumuz" Fransa Tarihine Ait bir Olay' ('European States System, France and Turkey: An Incident in the History of France – "the Traditional Friend of Turkey"') *Doğu Batı*, vol. 4, no. 14, pp. 122–42.

H. İnalcık, (1974) 'The Turkish Impact on the Development of Modern Europe', in K. H. Karpat (ed.) *The Ottoman State and Its Place in World History* (Leiden: E. J. Brill).

M. İpşirli (1999) 'Osmanlı Devletinde 'Eman' Sistemi' (the *Aman* System in the Ottoman Empire), in İsmail Soysal (ed.) *Çağdaş Türk Diplomasisi: 200 Yıllık Süreç*

(*Contemporary Turkish Diplomacy: The Course of Two Hundred Years*) (Ankara: TTK Basımevi).

M. F. Köprülü (1992) *The Origins of the Ottoman Empire*, trans. and ed. Gary Leiser (Albany: State University of New York Press).

E. Kuran (1988) *Avrupa'da Osmanlı İkamet Elçiliklerinin Kuruluşu ve İlk Elçilerin Siyasi Faaliyetleri, 1793–1821 (The Establishment of the Ottoman Resident Embassies in Europe and the Political Activities of the First Ambassadors, 1793–1821)* (Ankara: Türk Kültürünü Araştırma Enstitüsü Yayınları).

B. Lewis (1968) *The Emergence of Modern Turkey* (London: Oxford University Press).

B. Lewis (1964) *The Middle East and the West* (London: Weidenfeld and Nicholson).

Rudi P. Lindner (1983) *Nomads and Ottomans in Medieval Anatolia* (Bloomington, IN: Indiana University Press).

J. Lorimer (1883) *Institutes of the Law of Nations*, 2 vols (Edinburgh and London: William Blackwood and Sons).

H. W. Lowry (2000) 'Betwixt and Between: Turkey's Political Structure on the Cusp of the Twenty-First Century', in M. Abromowitz (ed.) *Turkey's Transformation and American Policy* (New York: The Century Foundation Press).

G. Mattingly (1955) *Renaissance Diplomacy* (Harmondsworth: Penguin Books).

S. E. Morrison (1974) *The European Discovery of America: The Southern Voyages 1492–1616* (New York: Oxford University Press).

E. Mortimer (1990) 'Is This Our Frontier', *Financial Times*, 3 April.

T. Naff (1963) 'Reform and the Conduct of Ottoman Diplomacy in the Reign of Selim III, 1789–1809', *Journal of the American Oriental Society*, LXXXIII, pp. 295–315.

T. Naff (1984) 'The Ottoman Empire and the European States System', in H. Bull and A. Watson (eds), *The Expansion of International Society* (Oxford: Clarendon Press).

I. B. Neumann (1999) *Uses of the Other: The East in European Identity Formation* (Manchester: Manchester University Press).

T. Özal (1989) 'Turkey in the Southern Flanks', *Brassey's Defense Yearbook*.

H. Pirenne (1939) *A History of Europe: From the Invasions to the XVI Century*, trans. Bernard Miall (London: George Allen and Unwin).

O. Rehn (2007) available at http://www.trt.net.tr/wwwtrt/hdevam.aspx?hid=175181&k=2.

P. Reynolds (2004) 'Anlaysis: EU's Turkish Challenge', available at http://news.bbc.co.uk/1/hi/world/europe/3719418.stm.

M. Rodinson (1987) *Europe and the Mystique of Islam* (London: I. B. Tauris).

J. J. Rousseau (1913) *The Social Contract and Discourses* [trans. G. D. H. Cole, Everyman edition] (London: J. M. Dent and Sons).

E. W. Said (1979) *Orientalism* (New York: Vintage Books).

R. Schwoebel (1967) *The Shadow of the Crescent: The Renaissance Image of the Turk* (Nieuwkoop: B. De Graaf).

N. Sousa (1933) *The Capitulatory Régime of Turkey: Its History, Origin, and Nature* (Baltimore: The John Hopkins Press).

H. Temperley (1932) 'The Treaty of Paris of 1856 and Its Execution', *Journal of Modern History*, vol. 4, pp. 387–414, 523–43.

I. Togan (1991) 'Ottoman History by Inner Asian Norms,' *Journal of Peasant Studies*, vol. 18, no. 3–4, pp. 185–210.

D. Tonge (2005) 'How Western is Turkey?', *Europe's World*, vol. 1, pp. 120–3.

A. J. Toynbee (1922) *The Western Question in Greece and Turkey: A Study in the Contact of Civilizations* (London: Constable and Company).

A. F. Türkegeldi (1987) *Mesail-i Muhimme-i Siyasiyye*, vol. 1, second edition (Ankara: TTK Basımevi).

D. M. Vaughan (1954) *Europe and the Turk: A Pattern of Alliances, 1350–1700* (Liverpool: Liverpool University Press).

A. Watson (1992) *The Evolution of International Society: A Comparative Historical Analysis* (London: Routledge).

M. Wight (1977) *Systems of States* (Leicester: Leicester University Press).

P. Wittek (1938) *The Rise of the Ottoman Empire* (London: The Royal Asiatic Society).

M. E. Yapp (1992) 'Europe in the Turkish Mirror', *Past and Present*, no. 137, pp. 134–55.

N. Yurdusev (2004) 'The Ottoman Attitude toward Diplomacy', in Nuri Yurdusev (ed.), *Ottoman Diplomacy: Conventional or Unconventional?* (Basingstoke: Palgrave Macmillan).

N. Yurdusev (2005) 'From the Eastern Question to the Western Question: Rethinking the Contribution of Toynbee', *Critique: Critical Middle Eastern Studies*, vol. 14, pp. 323–32.

N. Yurdusev (2007) 'Re-visiting the European Identity Formation: The Turkish Other', *Journal of South Asian and Middle Eastern Studies*, vol. 30, no. 3, pp. 62–73.

Part II Society and Culture in Flux

The Republic in Culture and Arts

15

"Westernisation against the West": Cultural Politics in the Early Turkish Republic

Orhan Koçak

'European civilisation will have a beneficial effect on us, not only with its science and technology, but also in matters of taste and morality. But this influence is permissible only to the extent that it helps dismantle the Persian one. The moment it attempts to supplant what it destroys, it has itself become harmful and should be resisted' (Gökalp, 1995, p. 15). Written at the end of the First World War, these words of Ziya Gökalp revealed with utmost clarity (too explicitly, perhaps, even for a reluctant inheritor of a defeated empire) the ideological and psychological mainsprings of the newborn Turkish nationalism. Today, at a century's remove, we hear much the same idea reiterated in different sectors of the Turkish political and cultural elite: to be part of Europe so as not to be part of the Middle East, or, more often, to be part of Europe *if only not to be bogged down* in the Middle East. In the long interval, Gökalp's ideas have come to define the terms of the relevant debate, not only providing the spiritual core of early Republican cultural politics, but perhaps more significantly, forcing even his opponents to begin with his formulation of the problem at hand: how ought the long-submerged and now re-emerging Turkish national identity be understood and lived in relation to Ottoman culture on the one hand, and the modern, scientific–rational civilisation of the West on the other? And no cultural agent of importance, whether official or oppositional, has been able to entirely escape the call of the indicated, if fantastic, answer: Westernisation in defiance of the West, in order to be freed of Persian and Arab influences.[1] At the time, the immobilising double-bind involved in such a stance seems to have gone largely unnoticed.

Of course, over a period of more than 70 years, there have been fluctuations in the fixity of this basic formulation of both the question and the answer. The 1950s, when an initially more liberal offshoot of the Republican Party was in power, saw the relaxation of government intervention in cultural affairs, allowing sectors of the population to once again reach back to their 'Eastern' or 'Alla Turca' past. The 1960s were years of jubilant expectancy, giving rise to Turkey's first mass socialist movement, contemporaneously with the emergence of an autonomous art and literature, the first of its kind. With the partial exhaustion of experimentational and revolutionary energies by the end of the 1970s old formulas reappeared in slightly changed appearance: 'Turkish-Islamic synthesis' or less frequently, 'Turkish-Islamic-Western synthesis'. And even in the formative era extending from the birth of the Republic to 1950, we can and should distinguish between two periods. The first, lasting until Atatürk's death in 1938, I would characterise as the moment of Ziya Gökalp, with the emphasis on religion *partly* lifted;[2] the second has been more unanimously called the period of 'humanist culture'. If the former was more a time of expurgation, then the latter was one of relative restoration. However, the ideological and institutional groundwork laid during the earlier period also limited the extent of any reparative effort: all government-sponsored action on 'the cultural front' would have a defensive character, reflecting the crippling effects of the original double-bind, that is, Westernisation against the West. Every major cultural policy pursued by the new Republican regime would bear the mark of this contradictory injunction, just as every significant artistic or intellectual breakthrough would prove to have shaken loose its hold – an unshackling itself made possible only by an initial internalisation and working-through of the original dispossession that had given rise to that double-bind. I shall take my examples mostly from the early Repuclican debates on poetry, not only because until recently poetry has been the dominant genre in artistic terms, but also because the discourse on poetry has long acted as a cipher of Turkey's engagement with modernity.

'Western-style' national literature

As the nineteenth century drew to a close, Ottoman poetry (*Divan*) abdicated, relinquishing its age-old pre-eminence in the intellectual makeup of the Turkish elite in favour of a new, as yet nonexistent, 'Western-style' national literature. The keepers of a hieratic tradition were thus reduced to and/or displaced by literary infants learning to speak. This change was part of a more sweeping process of putative Westernisation initiated by the Ottoman state itself, whose late-nineteenth-century reformist guardians saw *Divan* poetry, with its inconsequential intricacies, as *the* emblem of Ottoman decay.[3] On the other hand, it was also an acknowledgement of intellectual defeat before a long-disdained enemy, a defeat that left the prospective national poet, more or less a clean slate now, wide open to the influence of de-nationalising ('cosmopolitan') currents. And these currents were not slow in coming. Halit Ziya Uşaklıgil (1866–1945), a novelist from the second generation of 'Western-style Turkish writers', in his hugely influential novel *The Blue and the Black* (1897), described the new poet in his fascinated slide toward French models:

> And so all the drafts were burnt ... together with the pieces written in the manner of Fuzuli, Baki, or Nedim ... At first, they were inclined to

follow a chronological order ... but attempting to read the Iliad and the Odyssey, they left the books unfinished ... They were in a hurry to come down to modern times. So they went forward until they reached Goethe, Schiller, Milton, Byron, Hugo, Musset ... He knew that by following only his own impulses he would be confining his thinking inside too narrow a space ... and that the poet had to stimulate his emotions by ever new marvels of poetry. Thus he plundered his friend's library, and carried to his tiny retreat works by those who came after Hugo and Musset; all the Parnassians, the Symbolists, the Decadents ... And he was struck by the subtlety the art of poetry had gained in the half century leading to Verlaine.

This was both what the original Westernisers intended, and what they would come to abhor. There was an aspect of unstoppability to the whole process: the futurity of the new source of influence, calling from an ever-changing locus, seemed to leave no time for consolidation. This was the curse of belatedness. The new model, the new point of comparison, would always appear to be signalling from the future – its foreignness, its arrival as part of what compelled the Ottoman state to alter itself in the first place, imparting a tantalising quality to its action. It would recurrently give fresh impetus to innovation, but like an ever-receding threshold, would also frustrate the innovator. This was the original instance of the double-bind, its first moment: *Be like me*, the new foreign model seemed to be whispering to the poet – adding, *as you know full well that you cannot*. Already before the turn of the century a more apprehensive feeling had set in, a preliminary stage of that state of 'unhappy, internally divided consciousness' described by Hegel, which would soon lead to a real division within the ranks of the Westernising intelligentsia itself, with those recoiling from the bolder versions of the 'Western style' irresistibly drawn toward the disgruntled traditionalists who had been suppressed or left aside by the first wave of Westernisation – thereby jointly forming a veritable pool of ressentiment.[4] Namık Kemal had already attacked his reformist masters in the Sublime Porte for their excessive Westernisation and disrespect for the Islamic heritage, just as his protégé Ahmed Midhat (1844–1912) would later heap accusations of 'decadence' and 'depravity' upon the second generation of the Western-influenced poets. But the decisive reaction came around the time of the Balkan Wars, with a National Literature Movement taking the stage as the vanguard of the emerging Turkish nationalism. Its leading exponent was Ziya Gökalp.

A much-respected senior member of the Union and Progress party that took power just before the Balkan Wars, Gökalp had come to resent the woolly ideas of his fellow nationalists. He felt he had to provide a rigorous, scientific answer to the still unsettled question of Turkish national identity. The systematic character of his answers has been well noted by both contemporaries and later writers. Taha Parla, the author of a critical study of Gökalp's political and economic ideas, praises him for having 'laid the only plausible comprehensive cognitive map for Turkey's passage from an age-old empire to a new nation-state'. For Parla, Gökalp 'stands out in Turkey as the one person who was able to go beyond narrow ideological blueprints to a systematic theoretical construction. With him, and in contrast to the Young Turks, loose ends come together; eclecticism is replaced by synthesis' (Parla, 1985, p. 22).

I believe synthesis is the keyword here, the magical word, the source of Gökalp's enduring appeal, even for those who have never heard of him. Gökalp gave several versions of what he meant by synthesis, but I think they can all be reduced to his simplest and best-known formula, which states that human culture is a synthesis of national culture and international civilisation. The idea would seem bland in retrospect, based on a very diluted version of the nineteenth-century German distinction between civilisation and culture, with all the cutting edges blunted and the tension removed. But this simplicity was all the better, for at a time of imperial dissolution and defeat, when things seemed to fall apart and the educated public felt itself to be torn between irreconcilable ideals, this idea held out the promise of being whole again, even without regard to the nature of the elements to be pieced together. What Gökalp offered, however, was meant to be more than a narcissistic recompense. His formula registered the famously irreducible cleavages of a post-Enlightenment world, to which he traced the opposing demands of various sections of the population, thereby according them some measure of legitimacy, while also promising to mend the rift.

Gökalp defined culture as the 'ensemble of institutions that bind all the members of a society to each other' and civilisation as 'those institutions and practices that connect the upper stratum of a society to their counterparts in other societies'. Civilisation was the product of 'conscious, voluntary and methodical efforts by individuals', while culture was a spontaneous formation 'just like the organic evolution of plants and animals'. The products of civilisation, namely techniques, concepts, and to some extent, political institutions, were transferable from one society to another by imitation. Those of culture were not: culture was precisely what remained inimitable, the spiritual essence of a unique national community (Gökalp, 1995, p. 11).[5]

Gökalp scholars have made a point of stressing his debt to the French school of sociology, to Durkheim and Gabriel Tarde. Few have mentioned the similarity of his thoughts to those that were in circulation in Germany and East Europe. However, Gökalp was not really trying to compare 'our' superior (because spontaneous and spiritual) culture with 'their' inferior (because artificial and material) civilisation. In fact, he took pains to sidestep just this sort of comparison, trying to show instead that these two concepts belonged to different levels of experience. This was the gist of Gökalp's accomplishment: to differentiate culture and civilisation, to define them as noncomparable entities, so as to make them combinable, synthesisable. This was what allowed him to state that Turks can and must borrow from Western civilisation, that they can and must be a part of that civilisation. At this point in Gökalp's argument, the concepts of form and essence, or method and content, took over from the previous two, culture and civilisation. Form and method would be borrowed from the West, but not essence or content. The quote is from a pre-war essay:

> What separates us from Europe is above all religion. Europe will remain Christian, just as we will keep to our faith. On the other hand, there is nothing wrong with learning from Western theology. For theology is a science that furnishes us with positive and objective procedures of studying religion, any religion ... We shall not even take the end products of positive sciences, we shall only adopt the sciences themselves. Thus, instead of imitating the works of European composers, we shall take principles of structure like harmony in order to apply them to the tunes sung by our common folk.
>
> (Gökalp, 1980, pp. 41–2)

Elsewhere he would write: 'Let our poets read the whole of European poetry, beginning with Homer ... But let them be content with taking only the techniques, stopping short of adopting other nations' tastes also' (Gökalp, 1995, p. 17). Here Gökalp sounds very different from German thinkers indeed, if not entirely like the French either. He never considered the hermeneutic relation, that very 'German' relation, between form and content, technique and application. Of course, Gökalp had little time for such leisurely considerations: he was writing under pressure, at a moment when everything seemed in the balance for a nation yet to be born. The struggle for survival had to be both registered and naturalised, assumed and neutralised. Thus Gökalp had to contend that the culture–civilisation dichotomy was a perennial feature of Turkish history, that Turkish culture had in the past freed itself from Chinese civilisation, only to fall under the influence of the Iranians and Arabs, and that just as it had to fight its way out of their civilisations, it now faced the task of surviving the influence of the European one (Gökalp, 1995, p. 14).[6]

It may be said that so embattled a vision of culture and civilisation mocks any idea of synthesis. But it was also what made synthesis a matter of life and death: 'Either we master Western civilisation,' wrote Gökalp near the end of the war, 'or become subjugated by Western states – there is no other choice' (Gökalp, 1980, p. 40). The context also gives the subtext of the whole argument, even of the entire project that would come to be called Kemalism: a deep anxiety about survival. In his marvellous study of the Greek national imaginary, Stathis Gourgouris wrote: 'In every nation, antiquity coexists with modernity but also with infinity; no nation can imagine its death' (Gourgouris, 1996, p. 15). True enough; but it can imagine a life permanently at the brink of death. According to Renan, the existence of a nation was predicated 'on the fact of having suffered together'. He wrote: 'Suffering in common unifies more than joy does. Where national memories are concerned, griefs are of more value than triumphs, for they impose duties'. In the Turkish case, however, this sentiment seems to be less a matter of past grief than of future loss, less about remembrance and reparation than about projection and vigilance. If the existence of Renan's nation was a daily plebiscite, then the existence of Gökalp's nation would be more like an hourly mobilisation. For the danger, in the form of a grudgingly admired enemy, a model and point of comparison, was already part of the national imaginary itself, sowing there the seeds of permanent strife. If my language sounds a bit colourful here, that of the nationalist elite was not any less so. Thus Enver, the future leader of the war-time empire, wrote in a letter to a European lady friend while he was fighting the Italians in Tripoli in 1911: 'Your civilisation, it is poison, but a poison that awakens, and one cannot, one does not want to sleep anymore. One feels that if one were to close one's eyes, it would be for dying' (Göçek, 1996, p. 117). The sense of conflicted fascination was there already, in advance imparting a rearguard quality to Gökalp's laboured formulations of synthesis.

So this was the second moment of the double-bind, given a further twist by having been introjected and then projected – ejected, as it were. *Do like them, but remain one of us,* Gökalp was saying to the prospective national poet. And given the poets' predilection for divagation, there was no reason, no artistically compelling reason, why they should not read this contradictory injunction as: *Do like them, if you can, and then see if you still manage to remain one of us.*

Neither-this-nor-that: Literature in the early republic

In a letter to Walter Benjamin written in 1937, Erich Auerbach, who was teaching at Istanbul University at the time, complained of an atmosphere of unremitting vigilance, deriving from a 'neither-nor' state of mind:

> But Kemal Ataturk had to force through everything he did in the struggle against European democracies on the one hand and the old Mohammedan-Pan-Islamic sultan's economy on the other; and the result is a fanatically anti-traditional nationalism: rejection of all Mohammedan cultural heritage, the establishment of a fantastic relation to a primal Turkish identity, technological modernization in the European sense, in order to triumph against a hated and yet admired Europe with its own weapons. Hence, the preference for European-educated emigrants as teachers, from whom one can learn without the threat of foreign propaganda.[7]

Gökalp would not have been happy, either, had he lived to see that his formula of *both-this-and-that* had effectively been interpreted as *neither-this-nor-that*. The notion of a culture–civilisation dichotomy may have been dug up from the annals of the German reaction to Napoleonic conquest, but the Turkish cultural nationalists, in marked contrast to the efforts of nineteenth-century German canonisers, seemed bent on exclusion rather than inclusion in their attempts at compilation and anthologising. The famous 'homesickness' of the German Romantics tended to assume a drastically abridged quality when transposed into a Turkish nationalist context, having been received by way of its Wilhelmine travesty. This foreshortening is evident in Gökalp's conception of Romanticism:

> The [Christian] Reformation ... was the first emergence of national consciousness in the realms of religion and morality ... Then a second reaction against Classicism followed, in which there was a revival of the ancient legends, old folktales, and epics which had survived from the ethnic stage and lived through oral traditions of the people. From this reaction arose the the movement of thought which we call Romanticism ... the second manifestation of national consciousness within literature and art ... As to Turkish Romanticism, this could only rise from Turkish nationalism because Romanticism means the expression of the national spirit in literature.
>
> (Berkes, 1959, pp. 145–7)

In retrospect, this rejection of Classicism in favour of Romanticism seems only a pretext for denouncing 'cosmopolitanism', the real enemy, for elsewhere Gökalp would commend European Classics as an antidote against the pernicious influence of post-Romantic literature: 'Our aesthetic sense should be cultivated by translating Western classics into our own language. The classical literature of Europe is a healthy literature. The kind of literature created by decadents and phantasists is morbid. The Ottomans [i.e., the second generation of Westernisers] copied this sick literature because Ottoman society was senile. The Turkish nation, which has emerged intact out of its ruins, is young, even in its infancy' (Berkes, 1959, p. 268).[8] Here, Gökalp's views seem to foreshadow the Stalinist condemnation of 'sick art', even as his distinction between cosmopolitanism and internationalism resonates with a whole tradition of socialist rationalisation. Cosmopolitanism was bad because it considered humanity as a single 'civilisation, common to all men, whose members are not nations but individuals'. Internationalism, on the other hand, was the 'opposite' of cosmopolitanism, for it was predicated on the existence of separate nations. An internationalist could appreciate other cultures, but only to a certain extent: 'We shall build our own culture for our own taste and enjoyment', Gökalp wrote, 'Our enjoyment of other cultures will not go beyond the limits of an exotic interest. For us, anything

French or English or German or Russian or Italian may only have an exotic beauty. Although we admire it, we shall not be captivated by it. Our hearts are given to our own culture' (Berkes, 1959, pp. 280–3).[9] A *neither–nor* stasis was bound to follow. Ottoman culture was unacceptable because 'it became cosmopolitan and put class interests above national interests ... The Ottomans regarded themselves as the ruling nation and looked down on their Turkish subjects as a subjugated nation'. And the Westernising Tanzimat literature was also under attack, as it had moved from an initial Ottomanism to an equally unacceptable (because cosmopolitan) 'humanism'.[10] Yet, the national literature of the last decade apparently could not mollify the nationalists, as is evident from the damning pronouncement of Fuat Köprülü toward the end of the 1920s:

> Some minor exceptions aside, no work in our contemporary literature strikes the eye as being clearly different from that of the recent past ... We would look in vain to find a period in our whole literary history that is as noxious, as so foreign to the national spirit as the literature of the last decade. Our theatre is busy adapting the French drama of 'prostitution and adultery', just as our publishing industry has been insinuating novels of the same sort into the sanctuary of our families. Our supposedly 'national' story writers have flooded the market with the most trivial copies of this filthy literature ...The protagonists are mostly pathological types devoid of national character ... The scenes these novel depict are either dilapidated neighborhoods where old traditions drag on, or the meaningless 'smart set' of the ridiculously Europeanized Levantine Turks ... And our poets are no different in this respect, intent as they are on not expressing the truly original and vigorous aspects of Turkish existence.
>
> (Fuad, 1981, pp. 131–3).[11]

Neither the dilapidation of the old, nor the meaninglessness of the new and nor the triviality of the 'supposedly' national present: too often tacitly assumed or obliquely approached, this state of perpetual discontent has of late been made the direct object of critical inquiry by a number of writers. In a compelling Girardian account of Turkish nativism, Nurdan Gürbilek has described, with reference to Köprülü himself, the entanglement of the quest for 'the original Turkish spirit' with an ultimately failed mourning for an original lack: 'Criticism in Turkey – not only social, but also literary criticism – is mostly the criticism of a lack, a critique devoted to what Turkish society, culture, or literature lacks. Thus statements of a lack ("We don't have a novel of our own") are typical of a critical stance that ... [regards itself to be] convincing only when it talks about something the "others" have but "we" don't' (Gürbilek, 2003). An obsessively 'comparativist' stance (as Gürbilek names it), but often without a precise picture of the 'other' point of comparison – since too close a look would entail the risk of pollution – had thus been established as the most basic act of the critical response, with things local apparently never measuring up to standard.

Lately, there have been attempts to redescribe the making of Turkish nationalism as a kind of Occidentalism, or Orientalism-in-reverse, emphasising the fact that Turkey's confrontation with its West has been a defining feature of its self-representation. The quote is from a recent piece by the sociologist Meltem Ahıska:

> I offer the term Occidentalism to conceptualize how the West figures in the temporal/spatial imagining of modern Turkish national identity. From its initial conception in the process of defining the Turkish national identity in the late nineteenth century right down to this day, 'the West' has been contrasted to 'the East' in a continuous negotiation between the two constructs. 'The West' has either been celebrated as a 'model' to be followed or exorcised as a threat to 'indigenous' national values ... Labeled by both outsiders and insiders as a bridge between the East and the West, Turkey has ambivalent relation not only to the geographical sites of the East and the West, but also to their temporal signification: namely, backwardness and progress. It has been trying to cross the bridge for more than a hundred years now, with a self-conscious anxiety that it is arrested in time and space by the bridge itself.
>
> (Ahıska, 2003, p. 353)

I have doubts about the ultimate accuracy or even the heuristic value of the concept of Occidentalism, as it seems to reduce the prior term Orientalism to its narrowest and most immediately geopolitical sense, from which Edward Said saw reason to extricate his own position. Perhaps Orientalism-in-reverse is a better option, given the fact that Orientalism was a hegemonic discourse, at once the means and the record of a real enough mastery, an effective mastery – whereas what is called Occidentalism is merely reactive. Nevertheless these new interdisciplinary conceptualisations have the great merit of laying bare the tormented inner workings of the Turkish national imagination, forcing it to display its self-deceptive negotiations. Ahıska and others have also called attention to 'a certain stasis' throughout this whole debate, a frozen core making for an intellectual paralysis as evidenced in the controversies around the EU. The critic Murat Belge, in particular, has grappled with what he termed 'the central complex' of the Turkish national imagination, a set of partly conscious ideas that cut across the political spectrum, lately leading to the convergence of sections of the left and right on many issues, from the Cyprus or Kurdish questions to the use of foreign languages as the medium of teaching in Turkish universities. In Belge's account, the most visible effect of this formative complex is extreme xenophobia – to which I would only add, so as to make it a more rounded picture, an ingrained sense of futility, an inability to truly appreciate what is actually at hand.

It is this paralysis, a result of the original double-bind, which eluded the outsider-insiders like Auerbach. They could not see the non-hegemonic character of Turkish nationalism, even as Turkey's contemporary neo-nationalists cannot see the merely defensive nature of the cultural policies of the 1930s, the moment in time to which they would like to revert. Claims to sovereignty were cut short by the meagre means of a greatly impoverished society, leading the cultural establishment to lapse into fantastic solutions for real problems.

The Language Reform is a case in point. Gökalp's formula of 'Turkish culture inside Western civilisation' had facilitated the adoption of the Latin script,[12] but when it came to the question of a total overhaul of the language, the synthetic formula itself would begin to show its seams. In 1930, Atatürk declared: 'Turkish language is one of the richest, provided it is developed and refined with discretion. The Turkish nation, which proved able to pro-tect its land and its independence, must also liberate its language from the yoke of foreign languages'. Commenting on these words in his humour-ously damning account of the language reform, subtitled *A Catastrophic Success*, Geoffrey Lewis wrote: 'The second sentence unleashed the reform. If more people heeded the first, the success of the reform could have been unqualified'.[13] Unfortunately, the premises of the reform did not allow for such an outcome. Some of Lewis' comments would also lead one to believe that the extravagances of the reform had more to do with the idolatrous behaviour of Atatürk's cultural lieutenants than with anything program-matical. But with all due respect, I would insist that the whole affair was underwritten by the original synthetic idea, both the grounds and the limits of which were determined by the belated character of Turkish nationhood.[14] The process that had been transpiring in Germany, since the time of Luther's translation of the Bible, had here to be compressed into the lifespan of two generations. The often bizarre aspect of the linguistic experimentation, aptly termed a 'wild etymology' by Lewis, exposed the shaky foundations of the whole culture–civilisation dichotomy as a guide to action: if getting out of one 'civilisational circle' through a drastic linguistic cleansing seemed easy enough at the time, then replacing a real reservoir of conceptual capability with another one (as yet purely prospective) would prove near impossible. The flights of fancy were a way of getting the better of the double-bind – to take the easy way out, as it were, without a real elaboration of its terms. Two quotations underline this point, the first one from Lewis:

One should not be shocked at the apparent disingeniousness or self-deception that still allows some Turks to look one in the eye and insist that all the neologisms are entirely home-grown and uninfluenced by the for-eign words that have manifestly inspired them; to swear, for example, that the resemblance between *okul*, 'school', and the French *école* is fortuitous. One's first thought is, who do you think you're fooling? But when anyone except the most unregenerate of reformers says such a thing, it means no more than 'But it *could* have a Turkish etymology, couldn't it?

(Lewis, 1999, p. 44)

The second is a central passage from Melih Cevdet Anday's memoirs, hardly more propitious:

> I have no intention of reviewing all the intellectual currents of the Republican era; I only wished to convey the impression of rapid flow that this period has left on me. This state of affairs must have led all of us to believe that we could achieve much even if we knew very little ... I should add that this sense of easiness still forms the basis of our culture. Just mention the name of Mevlana at a meeting: someone is sure to come up and read his famous poem beginning with the words *bâzâ bâzâ*, 'come, come'. But this poem is not by Mevlana ... We say that science was born in Anatolia, and take pride in it as part of our own history. A commendable attitude! But while no one attempts to translate Heraclitus, everyone is content with repeating his words, *pante rei*, 'everything flows' ... We wanted to live at a haste both the Renaissance and the Enlightenment, as well as the modern age, all at once in the Republican era. And we did indeed! For we were in a hurry.
>
> (Anday, 1984, pp. 148–9)

Restoration and recovery: After the Sun-Language

Anday belonged to a generation that came of age after Atatürk's death, in the second stage of the period under discussion, a time of relative restoration, of recovery. An immediate sign of the sea change was the abandonment of the most fantastic aspect of the language reform, the Sun-Language Theory, which asserted that Turkish was the primal language of mankind. A second, much less noted indication is the sudden resurgence of Istanbul literature – memoirs or essayistic pieces on 'Istanbul *vécu*', Istanbul as it was lived. This genre had emerged in late-Ottoman times with writers like Ahmet Rasim (1867–1932) but had largely been dropped during the Atatürk period, a sign of the political exigencies of the time.[15] Now the old town was once more available for eulogising, even if nostalgically and still with much circumspection. At this point, the work of Yahya Kemal (1884–1958), the poet of Istanbul, assumes a significance that goes well beyond the confines of a narrowly conceived literary history.

Most often regarded as a revivalist harking back to Ottoman glory, Yahya Kemal was in fact well aware of the impossibility of real revival, even a strictly cultural one. One of his unfinished pieces, titled 'Reviving the Past', shows him to be quite explicit on this point: '95 per cent of all literature', he wrote, 'is based on the past. But it is naive to assume that literary works, just because they are based on the past, are thereby trying to revive it ... For there is an aura to every past age, which no one could bring back' (Kemal, 1984, pp. 311–12). On the other hand, Yahya Kemal was highly critical of the formulations of his friend Gökalp, especially those concerning poetry. The nationalists had discredited the cosmopolitan poets like Tevfik Fikret – but this was more a political victory than a poetic one: all along, a poetry not confined by Gökalp's formulas had kept coming forth. At this point, Yahya Kemal adopted a dual strategy. On the one hand, he turned back the accusation of 'foreignness' to Gökalp himself, dismissing the works of the National Literature group as an aberration. The quote is from an influential essay of the late 1930s:

> It was Ziya Gökalp who, with his theories, attempted to sweep aside Fikret and his movement. But despite all his deficiencies, Fikret belonged to our own poetry. He had come at a time when poetry was about to take a Westward turn, assuming a leading role in the process. He has done his job, and is now forever a part of our literature, both with his work and his personality. Ziya Gökalp was a scientist who remained outside our poetry. His theoretical knowledge of poetry, his sense for the national, could not help him in this regard; therefore he played no role in the rejuvenation of our poetry ... The National Literature movement did not bring a new sound, a fresh taste. Their poems were merely the products of a scientific recipe designed by Ziya.
>
> (Kemal, 1986, pp. 22–4)

On the other hand, Yahya Kemal also dismissed Tevfik Fikret – but unlike the Nationalists, he did this on aesthetic grounds. In the same essay, he had disparaged Fikret for remaining at the level of 'a Coppée', the nineteenth century French poet François Coppée: 'Fikret understood nothing of the profounder aspects of the French poetry of his time, from Baudelaire to the Symbolists. The poets he understood were Sully Prudhomme, Coppée, and the like'. It was Yahya Kemal's seemingly pure aesthetic judgement that finally did the Nationalists' political job for them: the 'merely a Coppée' pronouncement, to be reiterated to this day, finished Fikret as a poetic model.

It is precisely this dual action that I had in mind when I spoke of an elaboration or working-through of the original double-bind. And what gave weight to Yahya Kemal's position was the double-acting quality of his own poetry, a poetry which at once deliberately assumed the Westward drift of Turkish literature *and* held out the promise of arresting it. Simply put, his proposition was *Back to our Classics, by way of the Western Moderns*. A longish quote again, from his account of his poetic itinerary:

> I had left the cruder sides of Hugo. I stayed for quite a while with the Légende, his true poem ... I had just begun to appreciate the finer

qualities of Romanticism, when I read Baudelaire's poetry, which left me enthralled ... After Baudelaire I began to see Verlaine in a different light ... On the other hand, those literary historians who would find a temporal progress in poetry are deceiving both themselves and their readers. Though I understood Gautier, though I had a frenzied passion for Baudelaire and Verlaine, though the works of Maeterlinck and Verhaeren were not unknown to me, it was nonetheless on José Maria de Heredia that my tastes would finally come to rest, a poet regarded as quite backward compared to the others. Heredia was not an innovator; he was a classical artist, if a very belated one ... Through him, I had a taste of classical Greek and Latin poetry too. And it was in this way that I realised I had come very close to the new Turkish I had long sought: Our spoken Turkish was something like that *white language* found in Latin and Greek poetry. Thus I began to sense the wisdom behind the beauty of our Divan verses.

(Kemal, 1976, pp. 106–8)

After the catastrophe of dispossession, the promise of a double patrimony, with each alleviating the other's burden of anxiety: if one looked to foreign models, it was only for the sake of recovering what is most oneself; and if the ancient Divan masters were once again evoked, it was done with the reassuring knowledge that they had long been rendered powerless, sublimated into merely aesthetic phenomena precisely by the gaze that had first looked elsewhere. This was an undeniable victory over both the 'excessive Westernisers' and the followers of Gökalp, all the more compelling because it seemed to be ironically resonating with the Gökalpian formula itself: the form, the method, or the enabling principle might well be West-inspired, but the substance would be something supremely local – the record of an *erlebnis*, a lived experience. With the original double-bind losing much of its stigma as it was translated into something like *Do like them, you will encounter yourself*, the curse of belatedness also seemed to be lifted, allowing a less conflicted and more self-confident attitude towards Western culture. The passage I will now quote also sums up the basic idea behind the cultural policies of the 1940s:

When one speaks of the need to turn to ourselves, to what is ours, this is hastily interpreted as an obligation to be finally done with the French poetry and prose we have enjoyed, even to forget it, and retreat to Anatolia, to the old neighborhoods of Istanbul, Bursa and Edirne, so as to entirely close in upon ourselves. This is a misconceived idea. A nation's need for learning never ends. Especially in this century, shrinking away from the intellectual currents of other nations is in any case impossible. If one does not conceive turning to ourselves from such a wrong perspective, then one must say that within the circle of European civilisation every nation has a specific identity, and that we also seek to be an identity within that circle.

(Kemal, 1984, pp. 297–8)

Hasan Ali Yücel and Yahya Kemal

Yahya Kemal watched the debates of the first decades of the Republic mostly from the sidelines. But some of his disciples and colleagues from the pre-Republican years were already part of the cultural establishment by the 1930s. Foremost among these was Hasan Ali Yücel, who became Minister of Culture the year Atatürk died. Despite his misgivings about Yahya Kemal's complete disregard of the language reform, Yücel largely embraced the poet's critique of Gökalpian prescriptions. Already in 1937, he had objected to Gökalp's formula of 'Turkification, Islamicisation, Modernisation': 'The present Turkish revolution', Yücel wrote, 'is holistic and systematic, not eclectic. We don't wish to be three things at once, as Ziya Bey prescribed: what we want is to be one thing'. And his views on the East–West divide also reflected Yahya Kemal's influence: 'I see no East-West divide. The diversity of human works have more to do with differences in method ... I read Mevlana's *Fihi Ma Fih* in the same way as I read Goethe's *Conversations with Eckermann*. Were I not accustomed to reading the latter, I might have failed to understand the former' (İnsel, 2001, pp. 394–7). The notion of a world literature, first put forward by Goethe in his talks with Eckermann, was thus the formative idea behind the 'translation mobilisation' of the 1940s, Yücel's pet project. At the Turkish Publication Conference in 1939, Yücel introduced the 'Translations from World Literature' series of the State Publishing House as follows: 'Republican Turkey, in its resolve to become a distinguished member of the Western cultural and intellectual community, needs to ... invigorate its spirit by acquainting itself with the diverse sensibilities of the whole world'. In the general preface to the series, he also stressed the idea of 'humanism', relating it to the efforts of 'a nation to repeat the the literature of other nations in its own language, or rather, in its own mind'.

Of the 109 works translated during the first three years of publication, 39 were classical Greek, 38 French, ten German, eight English, six Latin, five Islamic or Eastern, two Russian, and one Scandinavian, namely Ibsen. Reviewing the whole project during the early Eighties, one nationalist critic would write that 'a few Islamic classics were also sprinkled onto the series as showpieces' (Ayvazoğlu, 1989, p. 245). I believe the pertinent point of comparison is not an imaginary situation in which all the Islamic classics would be translated, but the preceding period, the Atatürk era, when the whole idea of 'Eastern-Islamic' culture was being suppressed. On the other hand, the same critic is probably right when he points to the incongruity of making a 'humanist' out of Mevlana. There was a definitely facile aspect to Yücel's conception of world literature. The naivety of taking Goethe too literally, of seeing 'world lit' as something already existing rather than a projection, indicated the persistence of the fantasising tendency noted by Lewis, the habit of not tarrying with real constraint. The difference between Yücel's and Yahya Kemal's emphases should make this clear, as in a last quotation from the latter: 'Passing beyond the stage of copying a civilisation proves to be possible only when that civilisation is thoroughly digested. Taking technique and science does not suffice here; maturity in this regard entails the adoption of what really creates the new life, i.e. taste, morality, and manner of thinking' (Kemal, 1984, p. 296). Yücel could not bring himself to use so stark a phrasing. Words like 'copying' and 'maturation' were better left unstressed. He was in office, unlike his master, anxious to get his own reforms passed. We were in a hurry, as Melih Cevdet put it.

I have taken Gökalp and Yahya Kemal as political figures, but also as tropes, rhetorical shorthands which in their turnings and exertions also revealed the possibilities and the constraints of Turkish modernity, its continuities and its fractures. Gökalp's thought was a desperate response to Turkish belatedness, a necessarily premature response: at once too early and too late. His syntheses had a too-stiff, too-laboured quality: designed to preempt a comparison between Western civilisation and national culture, these formulations had the paradoxical effect of rendering the comparison all the more insistent, with the fractured nature of the emerging Turkish national imagination unduly exposed. 'We didn't want to be three things, we wanted to be one thing'. The irony was not lost on Yahya Kemal, a latecomer with the benefit of hindsight. Less self-deceptive than most of his followers, he also seemed to have an unencumbered trust in time's passage. He sensed that it was a matter of time for this whole question of earliness and lateness to work itself out. He believed it was great works that mattered, not programmes or prescription. He knew that these great works, these severe poems, are often made from the deficiencies of their times, but once made, they would become their own condition, their own origin – and the source of a new history. But perhaps it is with his passing that Yahya Kemal best reveals the basic developmental law of Turkish modernity. Against his predeccessors, he made use of a process of elimination by comparison, the 'merely a Coppée' method I have mentioned. And he would fall victim to the same process. The Westward drift he wanted to arrest was the condition of his victory, just as it would be the cause of his eventual downfall. His own manoeuver and negotiations still had a defensive, therefore non-hegemonic character. Even as he tried to break out of the originary double-bind by energising and manipulating its own terms, Yahya Kemal still had to station himself at a 'backward' site out there: 'Heredia' this time, instead of 'Coppée'. It was not long before he was unseated in turn, and his poetry regarded as defencless against the onslaught of prose, of the prosaic – the true sign of modernity.

Notes

1. Though current as a leitmotif throughout much of the Republican era, a first enunciation of the expression is found in Niyazi Berkes' 1964 account of Turkish secularism: 'Mustafa Kemal's drive "towards the West in spite of the West" by methods contrary to Western liberalism was merely the logical consequence of his belief that the struggle for national liberation was one between advanced nations and nations that allowed themselves to be exploited by their insistence on their medievalism'. See Berkes (1998, p. 464).

2. I say 'partly', because Republican laicism could never entirely suppress the Islamic element in its conception of Turkish national identiy, as I will try to show with reference to the episode of 'Christian conversions' of the late 1920s. For a recent study of Turkish experiment in secularism, see Davison (1998).

3. This was the verdict of Namık Kemal (1844–88), arguably the most influential figure among late-Ottoman intellectuals. 'Comparing the progress made by our literature with the West's literary culture', he wrote near the end of his life, 'is like comparing the few words managed by an infant with the [expressive] powers of a man of learning', in Kemal (1996, p. 344). Overlooking the fact that the concept of 'progress' was quite irrelevant to Ottoman poetic discourse (its near-homologue being 'mastery'), Kemal could not see that any progress he would assess must be that of his own time, with his own works as the centerpiece. In the same fateful essay, an introduction to his play *Celaleddin Harzemşah*, Kemal also stated that 'our [traditional] poetry consists of disconnected visions deriving from a realm of illusion with no relation to reality and nature'. No one before Kemal had dared to belittle a whole tradition. For a cogent account of the discrediting of Ottoman poetry, together with a close reading of its last great work, see Holbrook (1994).

4. For a fascinating – and nowadays increasingly relevant – portrayal of the discontented late-nineteenth-century Ottoman poet, see Mardin (2000, pp. 107–32).

5. See also Berkes (1959, pp. 104–9).

6. For a more lenient account of the evolution of 'Turkish culture' through different 'civilisations', see Berkes (1959, pp. 268–79).

7. Quoted in Barck (1992, p. 82).

8. Translation slightly changed.

9. To date, no commentator has wondered at the absence of the 'Hungarian' one among those exotic cultures, or the 'Spanish'.

10. The nationalists seemed to be especially enraged by an insipid line by the poet Tevfik Fikret (1867–1915), the leading figure of the *Servet-i Fünun* (The Riches of Learning) group which took the stage after the generation of Namık Kemal: 'My home is the [expanse of the] earth, my people the humankind'.

11. Fuat Köprülü (1890–1965), generally regarded as the one person who introduced philology and the historical method to Turkish scholarship, had made his debut as a minor 'Western-style' poet, before he became a fervent nationalist under the influence of Gökalp. Although he had misgivings about some of the later nationalist (i.e. Kemalist) undertakings, such as the adoption of the Latin alphabet and the seemingly wholesale rejection of Ottoman culture, Köprülü stood out as one of the harshest critics of 'cosmopolitanism', with a belligerence that even his increasing cooperation with international Oriental societies could not alleviate.

12. Some of the more conservative figures among Atatürk's original circle, such as General Kâzım Karabekir, opposed the script change, on the grounds that it

would 'have placed a splendid weapon in the hands of all Europe', which would thus get the chance to 'declare to the Islamic world [that the Turks] have accepted a foreign alphabet and turned Christian' – this being the 'diabolical idea with which our enemies are working'. See Lewis (1999, p. 32). But what the Minister of Education said at the time of the alphabet change showed that Gökalp's views had come to pass: 'The question of alphabet will naturally be solved according to the principles accepted by the civilised world'. See Levend (1972, p. 400).

13. Quoted by Lewis (1999, p. 42). At the time, the most immediately 'foreign' languages seemed to be Arabic and Persian. The journalist Falih Rıfkı Atay, a protégé of Atatürk's, would later make this point clear in his reminiscences about the language reform: 'With these reforms, we were for the first time assuming our Turkishness ... Westernisation also meant being saved from Arabification [Araplaşmak], it meant being Turkified'. Atay (1969, p. 446).

14. The notion of belatedness was explicitly taken up by some of the founding figures. Thus Mehmet Izzet, a student of Levy-Bruhl's who was teaching at the University of Istanbul at the time, wrote in 1927: 'Ever since it entered the stage of world history, the distinguishing mark of the Turkish race has been the will to dominate. But I am not a one to believe in historical fatedness; I cannot believe that races are but actors who have already memorized their roles. As in every stage, there are actors in the historical stage too, who are late to their roles, or who get confused and fail to deliver', in Kaplan (1981, p. 208). Less passionately, Gökalp had observed in 1913 that 'the ideal of nationalism appeared [in the Ottoman Empire] first among the non-Muslims, then among the Albanians and Arabs, and finally among the Turks'. See Berkes (1959, p. 71).

15. There were two, perhaps three, interconnected circumstances involved. Istanbul was the seat of Ottoman power. Many of the influential writers and journalist based in Istanbul were believed to have collaborated with the occupying forces after the war. And for the first five years of the Republic, the colonial powers refused to move their embassies to Ankara, probably in the belief that the new regime was not likely to last long, to which refusal Atatürk responded by not visiting Istanbul until 1927.

Bibliography

M. Ahıska (2003) 'Occidentalism: The Historical Fantasy of the Modern', *The South Atlantic Quarterly*, vol. 102, no. 2/3, pp. 351–80.

M. C. Anday (1984) *Akan Zaman, Duran Zaman* [Time Flowing, Time Stopped] (İstanbul: Adam).

F. R. Atay (1969) *Çankaya* (İstanbul: Doğan Kardeş Yayınları).

B. Ayvazoğlu (1989) *İslam Estetiği ve İnsan* (İstanbul: Çağ Yayınları).

K. Barck (1992) 'Walter Benjamin and Erich Auerbach: Fragments of a Correspondence', *Diacritics*, vol. 22, no. 3–4, pp. 81–3.

N. Berkes (1998) *The Development of Secularism in Turkey* (London: Hurst).

N. Berkes (ed.) (1959) *Turkish Nationalism and Western Civilisation: Selected Essays of Ziya Gökalp* (New York: Columbia University Press).

A. Davison (1998) *Secularism and Revivalism in Turkey: A Hermeneutic Reconsideration* (New Haven: Yale University Press).

M. K. Fuad (1981) 'İnkilab ve Edebiyat' [The Revolution and Literature], in I. Enginün, M. Kaplan, N. Birinci and Z. Kerman *Atatürk Devri Fikir Hayatı* II [Intellectual Life in the Atatürk Era] (İstanbul: Kültür Bakanlığı Yayınları).

S. Gourgouris (1996) *Dream Nation: Enlightenment, Colonization and the Institution of Modern Greece* (Stanford: Stanford University Press).

F. M. Göçek (1996) *Rise of the Bourgeoisie, Demise of the Empire: Ottoman Westernisation and Social Change* (Oxford: OUP).

Z. Gökalp (1995) *Hars ve Medeniyet* [Culture and Civilisation] (İstanbul: Toker Yayınları).

Z. Gökalp (1980) *Makaleler* IX [Essays] (İstanbul: Kültür Bakanlığı Yayınları).

N. Gürbilek (2003) 'Dandies and Originals: Authenticity, Belatedness, and the Turkish Novel', *The South Atlantic Quarterly*, vol. 102, no. 2/3, pp. 599–628.

V. Holbrook (1994) *The Unreadable Shores of Love: Turkish Modernity and Mystic Romance* (Austin: University of Texas Press).

A. İnsel (ed.) (2001) *Modern Türkiye'de Siyasi Düşünce:Kemalizm, vol. 2* (İstanbul: İletişim).

I. Enginün, M. Kaplan, N. Birinci and Z. Kerman (1981) *Atatürk Devri Fikir Hayatı* I (Istanbul: Bakanlığı Yayınları).

Y. Kemal (1984) *Edebiyata Dair* (Istanbul: İstanbul Fetih Cemiyeti Yayınları).

Y. Kemal (1986) *Siyasi ve Edebi Portreler* (İstanbul: Istanbul Fetih Cemiyeti Yayınları).

Y. Kemal (1976) *Çocukluğum, Gençliğim, Edebi ve Siyasi Hatıralarım* (İstanbul: Istanbul Fetih Cemiyeti).

A. S. Levend (1972) *Türk Dilinde Gelişme ve Sadeleşme Evreleri* (Ankara: TDK).

G. Lewis (1999) *The Turkish Language Reform: A Catastrophic Success* (Oxford: OUP).

Ş. Mardin (2000) *The Genesis of Young Ottoman Thought* (Syracuse, NY: Syracuse University Pres).

T. Parla (1985) *The Social and Political Thought of Ziya Gökalp* (Leiden: E. J. Brill).

K. Yetiş (ed.) (1996) *Namık Kemal's Writings on Turkish Language and Literature* (İstanbul: Alfa).

16
The Turkish Novel: From Model of Modernity to Puzzle of Postmodernity

Nüket Esen

What we call the Turkish novel appeared in the second half of the nineteenth century, during the 1870s. This was a time of weakness and disintegration for the Ottoman Empire; for the past 200 years, the empire had fought a series of losing wars and had lost its economic stability. In the hope of saving the empire from total ruin, the government and intellectuals of the day sought social and political changes that took the shape of Westernisation. Actually, the process of Westernisation had started in the eighteenth century, when the empire decided that acquiring technical knowledge from the West for the sake of the military was a necessity.

A number of sultans tried to carry out reforms to different aspects of the empire, but did so mainly in the military and educational institutions, by taking the West, that is to say, Europe, as an example of success. Erik J. Zürcher (1998, p. 41) writes, 'The policies of Sultan Mahmut II from 1826 onwards determined the direction which Ottoman reform efforts would take for the next eighty years ... [The reforms] were ultimately aimed at the strengthening of the central state through the building of a modern army ... Better communications were needed to extend government control and new types of education to produce the new-style military and civil servants the sultan needed' (see Mardin, 1974). These new types of education brought with them a new infusion of European culture.

In the nineteenth century, people who had been educated in the new Western style schools became state officials, and Westernisation slowly spread, first among the upper classes, then gradually down to the common people. One of the favourite topics of early Turkish novels was the criticism of superficially Westernised people who were caught between a West they did not really know and an East they could not really break away from.

This East/West dichotomy is a recurring theme in the Turkish novel right from the start. In order to see the emergence and the chronological development of the Turkish novel, I shall first examine its beginnings at the end of the nineteenth century, then move on to the time of its technical development at the start of the twentieth century. From around 1910, the novel became a force for contributing to the nation-building process of the new Turkish Republic. From then until the 1950s, Turkish novels reflected the Westernisation project underway in Turkey. I shall look at the two separate lines of development in the novel after 1950: a strong line of village novels focusing on issues concerning social inequality and social injustice, and a weaker line of novels featuring individual crises, mostly of the intellectuals. After 1980, the Turkish novel escaped from realism and developed an inclination towards 'post-modern' narration. Orhan Pamuk's novels can be taken as representative of the contemporary Turkish novel, with their varying narrative techniques and continuing concern with issues the Turkish novel has featured since the very beginning. I shall therefore, briefly discuss Pamuk's novels one by one, before mentioning other contemporary novels.

The beginnings

In the 1870s the Ottoman Empire was imitating the West in almost all aspects of life; literature could not escape a similar fate. Modernisation in Turkish literature emerged with the introduction of new genres, such as modern poetry, plays, short stories and novels. Introduction to new, Western concepts called for new, Western genres in literature. When we look at the emergence of the novel in particular, we can say that there was, of course, a tradition of storytelling in Islamic-Ottoman culture. These were stories told in verse form in classical literature, mainly in the form of the Persian *mathnawi* (Turkish *mesnevi*). There were also popular folk stories, either oral or written, which took the form of either love stories or tales of heroism in addition to a variety of mystic literature in Anatolia, since Sufism was widespread, especially in rural areas. But although there was a tradition of storytelling in traditional Ottoman culture, the first novelists started writing novels in imitation of the Western literary genre of the *roman*, which they had read mostly in French. It is from the French *roman* that the same Turkish word for novel comes from.

Before the appearance of the novel in the Ottoman Empire, however, there were 'threshold texts', writings that hovered on the threshold between traditional storytelling and the new genre called the novel. Aziz Efendi (?–1798) from the island of Crete, wrote such a text in 1796 entitled *Muhayyelat* (Imaginations), which is made up of three seemingly unrelated stories called 'hayal' (image, dream). These pieces add up to a whole in such a way that the text becomes something between a fairy tale and a fantasy novel. In 1851 and 1852 Hovsep Vartan Paşa (1813–79), an Armenian, published *Akabi Hikayesi* (The Story of Akabi) and *Boşboğaz Bir Adam* (A Blabbermouth), respectively. They were simple love stories told in prose, interestingly written in Ottoman Turkish, but with the Armenian alphabet and therefore probably only accessible to Armenian Ottomans and not to the general reading public. The same problem of audience exists for the 'novel' by Evangelinos Misailidis (1820–90), an Ottoman of Greek background, who wrote *Temaşa-i Dünya* (Viewing the World), published in 1871–72. The book was written in Ottoman Turkish, but with Greek letters, and was actually the translation and expansion of a shorter Greek 'novel' of the previous century. The first novels that appeared in Turkish with the Arabic alphabet, which was the mainstream alphabet of the Ottoman Empire, were translations from eighteenth-century European novels, mostly French, with Fénelon's *Télémaque*, Hugo's *Les Misérables*, Defoe's *Robinson Crusoe* and Dumas Pere's *Monte Cristo* among them. (See Strauss (2003), for a discussion of all literary developments in the different languages of the empire).

Following these developments, Turkish intellectuals of the period started writing novels themselves. Mainly state officials and journalists, these writers wrote only one or two novels each, as if to give examples of a new genre of literature. Only Ahmet Mithat (1844–1912) was a dedicated novelist, writing about 35 novels and numerous short and long stories. He also considered himself the foster-father of the first Ottoman-Turkish woman novelist, Fatma Aliye Hanım (1864–1936). Hanım was the daughter of Ahmet Cevdet Paşa, one of the empire's top politicians and historians, but she could only become a writer with the help and approval of the famous novelist Ahmet Mithat.

The Turkish novel at this time was mainly an imitation of the eighteenth-century romantic French novel and was technically quite primitive and piecemeal. The Turkish novelists of the time used the form as a vehicle for educating the public about new ideas drawn from the West. The novels criticised the corrupt ways of Ottoman social life, such as household slavery and arranged marriages. These novels also introduced and discussed new Western ideas, and sometimes even new Western technology like the telephone. The novel was used for teaching and interpreting new ideas to the reading public, and therefore its content was important.

The novel had no socio-political background in Ottoman society, as it had in Europe. One of the conditions existed; there were middle-class people living in Istanbul who were willing to read novels that talked about their everyday lives and problems. But the novel is based on the notion of the importance of the individual. A prominent literary critic and novelist, Ahmet Hamdi Tanpınar (1901–62), believed that in Islamic cultures the inner feelings of individuals were not important, and that there was no psychological curiosity in Islam. He (Tanpınar, 1988, pp. 28–30) argued that this was due to the fact that an individual in Islamic culture was never faced with life alone – he lived as part of the community, of the congregation. He did not have to make decisions by himself; he did not have to choose. Islam had decided and chosen for him. There is an absolute belief in fate, and so an individual can do little to direct the course of his life. If Tanpınar's argument was correct, it would have made it difficult for a Western-style hero to appear in early Turkish novels. (See Finn (1984) and Evin (1983), for information on early Turkish novels in English.)

The last 20 years of the nineteenth century was a time of oppression in the Ottoman Empire. As the country became weaker economically and politically, Abdülhamid II (1876–1909) resorted to sentences of imprisonment and exile against the intellectuals who wanted to establish constitutional monarchy. Constitutional monarchy had been established in 1876, but abolished by the sultan in less than a year. There was a general feeling of hopeless pessimism among writers of the time, and this was reflected in their novels. Although censorship meant social and political problems could not be written about, these writers depicted individuals who were suffering for different reasons. Subject matter turned to personal feelings, feelings of love and melancholy, through which the depiction of the individual finally appeared in the Turkish novel.

The twentieth century

With these developments, the technical improvement of the novel at the turn of the century began. In 1900 Halit Ziya Uşaklıgil (1866–1945) wrote *Aşk-ı Memnu* (Forbidden Love), which is still regarded as one of the best Turkish novels. This novel has a totality of its own; it is woven together very strongly, like a good nineteenth-century realistic novel, and it is at this stage, that real individual characters appear in a Turkish novel for the first time. The main female character in the novel, Bihter, has married a man much older than herself. She falls in love and has an affair with her husband's young nephew. In previous novels, such a character would have been depicted as a woman with low morals and condemned by the author from the start. But here we sympathise with her dilemma and her feelings of guilt, which in the end lead her to suicide.

The nineteenth-century Turkish novel criticised the old and introduced the new; it had a mission to accomplish and for this purpose used stereotypes instead of characters. But at the beginning of the twentieth century, the novels developed technically and the characters in them became unique individuals with their own psychological make-up. These new realistic novels reigned for a very short period. In the 1910s a long period of war began, and with the Balkan War, World War I and the Turkish War of Independence, the Turkish novel entered a new stage of politicisation. The novels written at this time were called 'nationalistic novels', and in them social problems again came to the fore, now with a new political dimension. At this time, novels contributed to the nation-building process. After the establishment of the second constitutional monarchy in 1908, the concept of 'popular sovereignty' emerged. Before this time, the state had always been in the hands of an elite group. With the establishment of a parliament representing the people as a whole, the idea that ordinary people should contribute to state affairs emerged for the first time.

As a part of this nationalistic culture, a movement called 'towards the people' emerged in Turkish literature of this period, in the form of trends simplifying language, reflecting local lifestyles and using forms of popular Anatolian literature, since these were the national resources in Ottoman-Turkish literature before Arabic, Persian and much later French factors influenced it. The novels at this time consisted of observations of contemporary life and were written in simple Turkish. They were set around the country and not just in Istanbul, as was the case with almost all Turkish novels before the 1910s.

Halide Edip Adıvar (1884–1964) was an important novelist during this stage. Her first novels were about family life and women's issues. Later she fought in the War of Independence; she was a corporal in the army and wrote war novels at this time. After the war she turned to social novels that dealt with the workings of Istanbul society in the face of Westernisation. The novels of this era were issue-oriented again, and seemed to be written in a great hurry, with language that was usually careless, in order to provide for the needs of a newly emerging Republic.

After the 'towards the people' movement and the War of Independence, an important political and cultural stance emerged, focusing on the problems of Anatolia, those who had fought in the War, and on villagers and peasants. During the 1950s, following this trend, village novels started to appear. Until this time, novels had almost always depicted the intellectuals, first of Istanbul, then of Ankara. The village novels, however, portrayed the clash between the big landowner, or Ağa, and the ordinary poor villager. Many such novels were written, most of them using the same cliché of the good peasant versus the evil Ağa.

But among the village novelists of the 1960s there was one special writer whose novels stood out, because what he produced within the known formula was somehow quite universal. Yaşar Kemal's (1923–) novels were about Anatolia, where he grew up and about the poor Turkish villager, but they were also about being human. In a very simple, pure and poetic language, Kemal depicted human existence, our shared human weaknesses and strengths, within the frame of the Turkish peasant's life. Kemal's humanism is reflected in the fact that his novels have been translated into many languages around the world.

The important Turkish literary critic, Berna Moran (1921–93), has argued (2003, p. 9) that the three short stages of the Turkish novel I have identified – that is, the crude beginnings at the end of the nineteenth century, the technical development at the turn of the twentieth century, and the years of nationalism just before and after the wars – can all be seen as constituting the first phase of the Turkish novel. According to Moran, the novel in its first 80 years, up to the 1950s, dealt mainly with Westernisation, with modernisation, or with what we can call the East–West problematic.

In the 1950s, with the emergence of the Anatolian village novel, a new issue was introduced into the Turkish novel. At this time, social-class formations were becoming apparent in the new Republic. Apart from the

Anatolian villagers, the newly developing industrial activity was producing a working class in and around the big cities. During this period, therefore, the novel started to address the issue of social inequalities.

At the same time that these village novels were being written, another important novelist was writing novels about intellectuals and about city life in Turkey. In the middle of the twentieth century, Ahmet Hamdi Tanpınar appeared on the literary scene in Istanbul. He was a professor of Turkish Literature at Istanbul University who wrote poems, short stories, essays, literary articles and novels. His novels dealt with aesthetics, cultural issues, and Ottoman-Turkish national identity. His was the voice of the life and culture of the Ottoman and Turkish intellectuals who were trying to carve out an identity for themselves after the establishment of the new Turkish Republic. Tanpınar considered the culture of the Ottoman Empire to be the epitome of Eastern civilisation and tried to portray a continuity between the glorious Ottoman past and the new Turkish Republican present in his famous novel *Huzur* (A Mind at Peace, 1949/2008).

In the 1970s, after the military coup of 1971, social and political novels appeared in which individuals were portrayed confronting the political situation in the country. Most of these novels showed imprisoned Marxist intellectuals writing about their experiences in prison while re-evaluating their individual place and responsibility within the new political framework. These novels mainly discussed the position of Turkish society in relation to socialism. It is interesting to note that most of the prominent novelists of this period were women, the most famous being Adalet Ağaoğlu (1929–).

Around the same time, Turkey saw the emergence of another important novelist, who died at the young age of 43. Oğuz Atay (1934–77) dealt with the personal psychology of the bourgeois intellectual without directly discussing the intellectual's political stance. Where Tanpınar had reflected the pain of the intellectual trying to establish his identity, Atay explored similar issues with parody and playfulness in his famous novel *Tutunamayanlar* (The Failures, 1971).

Up until the 1980s, the Turkish novel had developed from its technically humble beginnings in the second half of the nineteenth century into what we may call a realistic novel form, where the novel was expected to, and did, hold a mirror up to real life. Ottoman and then Turkish society and politics were reflected in these novels. These novels usually had a message to give; most of the time they had a clear socio-political stance. They could be read as sociological novels giving us a clear picture of the history of the country.

In the 1980s the global picture started to change. Left-wing governments were collapsing everywhere, and in the face of overly complicated social and economic problems, novelists abandoned classical realistic approaches that tried to solve such challenges in favour of playing games and making pleasure out of literature. Moran (2003, p. 9) argues that with the de-politicisation of Turkish society in the 1980s, despite another military coup, the themes of an unjust social order and exploitation that had been prominent in novels of previous periods lost their strength. Trying to change the world became a futile effort, and so writers in Turkey started developing a new kind of narrative, one they found in translations of such writers as Marquez, Borges, Eco, and Calvino.

The 1980s in Turkey saw the emergence of Latife Tekin (1957–) who wrote about life in the shantytowns sprawling around Turkish urban centres. She wrote about the downtrodden, doubly so because she depicted the pain of growing up in a shantytown as a woman. The hybrid language she created in her novels belongs to these women, as in *Berci Kristin Çöp Masalları* (Tales from the Garbage Hills, 1984/1993). Migration to the slums that appeared around the big cities was the ground on which Tekin built her placeless, language-less subjectivities, mostly women. She created the voice of the 'subaltern' in the use of language and silence by these women, who developed strategies in which they used magic, jinn (fairy) stories and hearsay to build collective, alternative subjectivities for themselves. Tekin's novels depicted a different experience of modernity, lived by different subjectivities, in a language distinct from the mainstream experience of modernity.

Orhan Pamuk's novels

In the 1980s, following in the footsteps of Tanpınar and Atay, Orhan Pamuk (1952–), appeared as the voice of the intellectual, writing novels that did not have an immediate correlation with social problems and political issues, but instead gave only an indirect indication of them. Pamuk's novels eschew direct socio-political messages in favour of refined clues to these problems. This tendency was atypical of the Turkish novel in general, which usually had a very clear political stance. Writing in the last 20 years of the twentieth century, Pamuk showed a strong political commitment to human rights and freedom of speech in his country and in the world, but this was usually expressed in his commentary outside the novel form. In his novels he deals with substantial and universal human issues, addressing man's very being. As the first novelist writing in Turkish to achieve world stature, his novels are translated into many languages today, and he received the Nobel Prize for Literature in 2006.

Pamuk's novels involve intelligent games, playful narration, and technical refinement. So far he has written eight novels with different narrative techniques. The first was *Cevdet Bey ve Oğulları* (Cevdet Bey and Sons, 1982), which has the format of a classical realistic novel. This is a family novel telling the story of three generations of a bourgeois Istanbul family. It is a *Bildungsroman* like Thomas Mann's *Buddenbrooks* and Charles Dickens' *Great Expectations*, in which we follow individual characters as they grow up and mature. In *Cevdet Bey ve Oğulları*, events take place between 1905 and 1970, with 65 years of Turkish culture and society as the background to the family depicted in the novel. Pamuk uses quotations from daily newspapers of the time to contribute to the semblance of reality in the novel. This is the story not only of individuals within a family, but also of a country, or rather of the development of the bourgeois class in the country after the formation of the Republic.

Pamuk's second novel was *Sessiz Ev* (The Silent House, 1983), in which he used a new narrative technique: plural narration. Events are not told from the point of view of a single narrator but from the consciousness of different characters. This technique comes close to Mikhail Bakhtin's idea of polyphony, which he attributed to Dostoyevsky (see Bakhtin, 1984). In *Sessiz Ev*, five characters tell the same story separately, from their own viewpoints with a first person singular narration. The novel is the compilation of these narratives, to be put together in the mind of the reader. In *Sessiz Ev*, the actual time span of the novel is just one week, but flashbacks present the reader with almost a century of this particular family's history, and of Turkish life in general. Here again, we have an indirect vision of society. Pamuk does not talk about the society directly, but by combining the pieces told by five different characters, the reader can construct a picture.

Beyaz Kale (The White Castle, 1985), Pamuk's third novel, is an historical novel that takes place in the seventeenth-century Ottoman Empire. There is a frame to this novel; it starts with a preface by Faruk Darvınogˇlu, an historian who was one of the narrator-characters in *Sessiz Ev*. *Beyaz Kale* is supposed to be a rewriting of a manuscript Faruk Darvınogˇlu had found in the old archives. The narrator, who uses a third person singular point of view, interprets incidents that are presented as having taken place a few centuries before.

In this novel East faces West in the form of two characters, the Hodja, an Ottoman scholar, and his Venetian slave. They sit facing each other across a table in the Hodja's house in Istanbul and discuss and compare the two cultures. They both try to answer the question 'Who am I?', as their search for identity becomes obvious. They eventually change places, and thus master becomes slave and slave becomes master. The two men look exactly alike, as if identical twins. Here, of course, we have a *doppelgänger* story of twins. The relationship between the two characters who represent the East and the West is a relationship between master and slave, between I and the Other. At some point in the novel we see how they will eventually change places; how the master will gradually become the slave and the slave the master. At the end of the novel, fact and fiction, reality and representation, reader and writer are indistinguishable from each other because the text turns its gaze on itself, on its own production, and thus becomes meta-fiction. At the beginning of the novel, the narrator, the Venetian slave, tells us of a scene he remembers from his childhood: 'peaches and cherries lay on a tray inlaid with mother-of-pearl upon a table, behind the table was a divan upholstered with straw matting strewn with feather cushions the same colour as the green window-frame' (Pamuk, 1990, p. 30).

At the end of the novel, an Italian traveller reads a book given to him by the person who is either the Hodja or the slave (we cannot tell the difference any more) and realises that what he is reading in the book is exactly what is happening around him at that moment. That is to say, what he is witnessing at that moment is already depicted in the book he is reading. It is, of course, the same book we are holding in our hands. The following is from the very last two pages of the novel:

> I left him alone, I went out into the garden and sat down on the divan covered with straw matting where I could see him through the open window ... Then he turned and gazed blankly out of the window, resting and trying to digest what he'd read. I watched with delight as he looked first at some infinite point in the emptiness, as people do in such situations, at some non-existent focal point, but then, then, as I had expected, his vision focused: now he was looking at the scene through the frame of the window ... As I had thought he would, he began to turn the pages of my book greedily, searching, and I waited with excitement till at last he found the page he was looking for and read it. Then he looked again at the view from that window overlooking the garden behind my house. I knew exactly what he saw. Peaches and cherries lay on a tray inlaid with mother-of-pearl upon a table, behind the table was a divan upholstered with straw matting, strewn with feather cushions the same colour as the green window-frame.
>
> (Pamuk, 1990, pp. 160–1)

Pamuk's fourth novel is *Kara Kitap* (The Black Book, 1990), in which he writes of Istanbul as James Joyce wrote of Dublin. The story of the novel refers to a number of traditional Eastern texts that use frame stories and tell mystical tales. One such text that the novel refers to is Rumi's *Mesnevi*. As an intertextual novel, *Kara Kitap* uses the Eastern traditions of the story of a journey, of a quest in search of the beloved, of God, and creates a novel of small stories within frame stories. The main character looks for his lost wife and his writer cousin, who have disappeared. As he strolls through Istanbul looking for them, we understand that he is also looking for his identity as a Turkish individual and as a writer. Here again we have the search for identity, this time the identity of a writer, as the main character eventually becomes one. One of the questions the novel asks is 'how to be oneself', and this novel, following in the footsteps of *Beyaz Kale*, in which East and West came face to face with each other, reflects the dilemma of Turkish identity caught between the two.

Orhan Pamuk's fifth novel is *Yeni Hayat* (The New Life, 1994), another quest novel. The main character travels the country in search of his beloved, the writer of the book 'New Life' and of the meaning of life and death. The novel begins like a detective story but it eventually becomes obvious that the real aim of life is this perpetual search. The background to this search is the Turkey of the 1980s. The main reference in this novel is to Dante's *New Life* and to his beloved Beatrice, the person for whom the main character has been searching. Again, like most of Pamuk's novels, the story turns in on itself and becomes a meta-fiction. As the story of this quest is told, the novel refers to things it has said a few pages before and the characters become aware of the fact that they are characters in a novel. In the end, we understand that the writer of the book 'New Life' in the novel, is actually the writer of the novel *New Life* that we are reading, that they are the same book. This novel offers us puzzles to solve, references to connect in a circular, spiral structure. This is the most playful novel Pamuk has written so far.

Pamuk's sixth novel, *Benim Adım Kırmızı* (My Name is Red, 1998), is another historical novel, taking place in sixteenth-century Istanbul. But it is also a love story and a murder tale at the same time. Here Pamuk deals with the Ottoman-Islamic tradition of representing the world in miniatures as opposed to the Western depiction of life in realistic paintings. The differences between Eastern and Western ways of seeing the world and representing it in visual art functions as a metaphor for how totally different the two worldviews are. *Benim Adım Kırmızı* is divided into 59 chapters, in each of which a different character or object tells the story from his, her or its point of view. Thus in each chapter the narrator's consciousness is limited; he or she knows and cares about different things and concentrates solely on them. Even when the story returns to the same narrator, Pamuk ensures it is from a different temporal perspective and the narrator's consciousness has shifted. Thus, the totality of the story takes shape only in the mind of the reader.

Pamuk's seventh novel is *Kar* (Snow, 2002), both a love story and a political thriller. The setting of the novel is the far-away Eastern Turkish city of Kars and the events of the novel take place in 1992. The protagonist is Ka, a poet sent by a newspaper to write about the widespread suicides among fundamentalist Islamic women in the town. Ka falls in love with a young woman in Kars, and through his roaming in the small city he meets different groups of people with distinct political affiliations. He also witnesses a military coup. As it is winter, the city of Kars is snowed-in (*kar* is the Turkish word for 'snow') and all communication with the outside world is cut. Pamuk presents the reader with a microcosm of Turkey, frozen for a short time in a small town. Ka meets religious zealots, Westernised intellectuals and secular Kemalists. Here again, Pamuk deals with the identity problem with a particular emphasis on the conflict between Islamic fundamentalists and secular Kemalists during the 1990s. The narrator in the novel uses a third person singular point of view. But towards the end of the novel, this changes into a first person singular narrator, who turns out to be a writer from Istanbul and an old friend of Ka's, called Orhan. Orhan has found Ka's notebooks and has travelled to Kars to find out about Ka's adventures in this city, and Orhan's reconstruction becomes the story we are reading.

Masumiyet Müzesi (Museum of Innocence, 2008) is a long novel about love and obsession depicting upper-middle-class life in Istanbul in the 1970s. The main focus of the novel is on time, remembering and objects, based on the fact that the past comes to life with old objects because they carry past moments with them into the present. Orhan Pamuk is actually building a museum in Istanbul called the 'museum of innocence' which the novel keeps referring to in order to exhibit the objects the main character in the novel collects/steals. Once completed, the 'museum of innocence' will make a fresh contribution to the age-old debate on the fact–fiction dichotomy in the novel genre.

A theme running through many of Orhan Pamuk's novels is that of Westernisation in Turkey. It has been and remains one of the most popular subjects for Turkish novels. But Pamuk tries to deconstruct the binary opposition of East and West from the standpoint of a twentieth-century Turkish intellectual writer caught within this binary opposition. Many of his novels are about a quest, a quest for one's identity, for the beloved, for the meaning of life. The search for identity has also been an important issue in the Turkish novel in general. But Pamuk turns this search for identity into a playful search for the meaning of life and of writing. Many of his novels are about the act of writing itself, about the art of storytelling.

Pamuk uses many different techniques, as indicated above. The narrative technique of each novel is appropriate for the content of that particular novel. There is also a thin thread of connection running through his novels because many of his novels talk about each other. intertextuality is an important characteristic of these works. In addition, Pamuk has a good knowledge of Turkish and world literature and makes references to or parodies of both Eastern and Western literary texts.

Pamuk's narrators in each novel have different positions. He is a contemporary novelist in that he never uses an omniscient, authoritative narrator. It is obvious that in a world where cause and effect relationships are no longer clear and where the narrator can no longer control the narrative, the authority of the narrator will disappear. A narrator will narrate something and the reader will have to put the pieces together to construct a story in his or her mind, resulting in a far from clear picture. In these reader-oriented narrations, the reader is not a passive receiver but an active creator. Since the reader has to contribute to the creation of the narration, reading becomes a tiring process. Pamuk's novels are not easy to read, because they require this active participation. This has been the case for most Turkish novels written since 1980.

Other late-twentieth-century novelists

In the last 20 years of the twentieth century, the Turkish novel developed what we might call contemporary narratives. Among them are İhsan Oktay Anar's (1960–) novels, which are historical novels that deal with their own creation. Unlike traditional historical novels, which are about the sultans and the palace, or military commanders and wars, Anar's novels deal with ordinary men in the streets of Istanbul during the time of the Ottoman Empire. Anar uses a historical and/or fantasy basis for his stories, and this enables him to produce a meta-fictional world where he can question reality. For him, harmony and balance belong with stasis and death. He joyously invites the reader to recognise and enjoy a world of incommensurability and miracles.

Turkish novels after 1980 usually have a frame story and many small stories within that frame. Intertextuality has become very popular, and novels refer to other texts of both Western and Eastern traditions. The role of the reader has become very important in that he or she has to be active in creating meaning and thus in creating the novel. Most novels today are meta-fictional in that they deal with themselves; they are about themselves. Hasan Ali Toptaş's (1958–) novels are good examples of such works, where the pain and pleasure of writing are combined. Toptaş has written four novels so far, and each is more 'postmodern' than the one before. He starts with the loss of identity and the search for the self, moves on to blurring the line between fact and fiction and ends up with characters who know they belong to a fictional world.

Another prominent new novelist is Elif Şafak (1971–), who has been writing novels that are simultaneously intellectual and enjoyable. She wrote her fifth novel in English, while she was living and working for a Ph.D. degree in the US. Her novel was then translated into Turkish. This language switch may be a way to overcome the difficulty of writing in a language that is not internationally widespread.

Most of the Turkish novels mentioned in this paper, except of course Yaşar Kemal's and Orhan Pamuk's novels, need to be translated into different languages to be recognised by the world. All of these novels reflect the Westernisation process that Turkey has been going through for the last 140 years. They tell the story of the people of this country enduring a painful and perpetual process of engagement with modernity, as a people caught between the East and the West. As depicted in this paper, the novel as a genre emerged in Turkish as late as the 1870s and has developed into a contemporary narrative within the last century and a half. The story of the Turkish novel is an interesting example of 'belated modernity' in the field of literature.

Bibliography

O. Atay (1972) *Tutunamayanlar* (Istanbul: Sinan).
A. Efendi (2007) *Muhayyelat-ı Aziz Efendi* , (ed. A. Kabaklı) (İstanbul: TEV Yayınları).
M. M. Bakhtin (1984) *Problems of Dostoevsky's Poetics* (trans. C. Emerson) (Minneapolis: University of Minnesota Press).
A. Evin (1983) *Origins and Development of the Turkish Novel* (Minneapolis: Bibliotheca Islamica).

R. Finn (1984) *The Early Turkish Novel, 1872–1900* (Istanbul: ISIS).

Ş. Mardin (1974) 'Super-Westernisation in Urban Life in the Ottoman Empire in the Last Quarter of the Nineteenth Century' in P. Benedict, E. Tümertekin and F. Mansur (eds) *Turkey: Geographic and Social Perspectives* (Leiden: E. J. Brill).

E. Misailidis (1988) *Seyreyle dünyayı [Temaşa-i dünya ve Cefakâr u Cefakeş]* (eds R. Anhegger and V. Günyol) 2nd Revised Edition (Istanbul: Cem).

B. Moran (2003) *Türk romanına eleştirel bir bakış 3: Sevgi Soysal'dan Bilge Karasu'ya* (İstanbul: İletişim Yayınları).

O. Pamuk (1990) *The White Castle* [trans. Victoria Holbrook] (London and Boston: Faber and Faber).

O. Pamuk (1998) *The New Life* [trans. Güneli Gün] (New York: Vintage).

O. Pamuk (2001) *My Name is Red* [trans. E. M. Göknar] (New York: Alfred A. Knopf).

O. Pamuk (2004) *Snow* [trans. Maureen Freely] (New York: Knopf).

O. Pamuk (2006) *The Black Book* [trans. Maureen Freely] (New York: Vintage).

O. Pamuk (2008) *Masumiyet müzesi* (Istanbul: İletişim).

J. Strauss (2003) 'Who Read What in the Ottoman Empire (19th–20th centuries)?', *Middle eastern literatures*, vol. 1, no. 1 (January), pp. 39–76.

A. H. Tanpınar (1988) *XIX. asır Türk edebiyatı tarihi* (Istanbul: Çağlayan Kitabevi).

A. H. Tanpınar (2008) *A Mind at Peace* [trans. E. Göknar] (New York: Archipelago Books).

L. Tekin (1993) *Berji Kristin: Tales from the Garbage Hills* [trans. R. Christie and S. Paker] (London and New York: Marion Boyars).

H. Z. Uşaklıgil (2001) *Aşk-ı memnu* (Istanbul: Özgür).

P. Vartan (1991) *Akabi hikâyesi* (İstanbul: Eren).

E. J. Zürcher (1998) *Turkey, a Modern History* (London: I. B. Tauris).

17

The Turkish Music Reform: From Late Ottoman Times to the Early Republic

Emre Aracı

'The speed with which a nation can transform itself is related to how well it can adapt to new styles in music', declared an impatient Mustafa Kemal [Atatürk] during one of his keynote parliamentary speeches in Ankara in November 1934 (Saygun, 1981, p. 49). What he meant by 'new styles in music' was of course a suitable adaptation of the key principles of the Western classical tradition – its harmony, melody and form – to the indigenous music of Turkey, thus creating a balanced fusion fit for the new emerging Turkish state. Only after this transformation could the national music of Turkey, in his opinion, possibly be elevated to a universal musical level. 'New Turkish Music', in other words, was going to play an important role in the transformation of the country. All the young and promising composers of the republic were expected to fulfil their duties by writing music to serve the needs of the new regime, rooted of course in Turkey's national heritage.[1]

The search for a new identity through the music of Europe was no novelty in Turkish lands. Since the Ottoman times, the systematic introduction of Western music occupied the minds of many rulers from Mahmud II (1807–39) onwards. It is therefore no coincidence that under Mahmud's rule, one of the first educational establishments to be inaugurated in Constantinople after the abolition of the corrupt janissary corps in 1826 was a Military School of Music, which offered training in European principles and rudiments. Two years after that, Giuseppe Donizetti, the elder brother of the famous opera composer Gaetano Donizetti, was appointed *Istruttore Generale delle Musiche Imperiali Ottomane* (Donizetti, 1897, p. 54). The reformist sultan also made great attempts to introduce Western music at his court. Pianofortes were ordered from Vienna for the ladies of his harem (*Le Ménestrel*, 1836) and according to *The Musical World* of London, a concert was given at one of the royal palaces in the summer of 1839 'to the fair ones, at which a young Turk, who had acquired his education in Paris, played among other pieces one of Beethoven's sonatas with variations, which enraptured the assembly and drew down thunders of applause' (*The Musical World*, 1839, p. 91).

Mahmud's passion for European music was very much shared by his sons and successors Abdülmecid (1839–61) and Abdülaziz (1861–76). The former not only welcomed famous European virtuosi of the time, such as Franz Liszt and Leopold de Meyer, for private concerts at his court, but also supported the annual Italian opera season in the city, and built an imperial theatre within the grounds of his new palace, Dolmabahçe.[2] Famous composers of the time, including Rossini and Gaetano Donizetti, also paid him their respects by composing and dedicating ceremonial marches.[3] The young sultan was often seen riding to the mosque for weekly Friday prayer ceremonies, the *Selamlık*, to the strains of either a Rossini or Donizetti march.[4] The *Bayram* festivities at his court were marked with grand choral concerts for which Italian artists were specially engaged, and it became customary for ladies of his harem to follow Italian opera productions with libretti in their hands.[5]

During the reign of Abdülaziz, patronage offered to European opera extended further beyond the Ottoman lands, when the Sultan, along with the rest of the European nobility, became a donor to the funds for the construction of Richard Wagner's Festival Theatre and the first production of the *Ring* cycle at Bayreuth.[6] Sultan Abdülaziz was also a very able composer of European ballroom music, so much so that his short dance pieces for the pianoforte were printed by the Italian music publisher Lucca.[7] The Ottoman regimental bands often played the Sultan's own compositions at ceremonial events, just as the band of the Grenadier Guards did when he visited London in 1867.[8] His nephew Sultan Murad V (1876), who only held the Ottoman throne for three months, was an even more accomplished and productive composer of polkas, mazurkas and waltzes.

In the century following Mahmud II's introduction of European music to his court and armies, it appears that the Ottoman élite and the palace population were all well immersed in the operatic and symphonic repertoire of the period, and some even composed their own music. In 1918, the Ottoman Imperial Symphony Orchestra, the 'Kaiserlich Osmanischen Palastkapelle', as it was advertised, travelled to Eastern Europe for a series of concerts in Berlin, Vienna, Sofia and Budapest, performing Beethoven's *Eroica* Symphony, Weber's *Oberon* Overture and Wagner's *Tännhauser* March among other works (Arman, 1979, pp. 64–5).

After the abolition of the sultanate in 1922 the same orchestra came under the patronage of the Caliph Abdülmecid Efendi (1922–4), who was himself an accomplished pianist, composer and painter.[9] One of his wartime paintings, in fact, entitled *Beethoven at the Harem*, depicts a scene of a Beethoven trio being performed at his summer residence at Çamlıca. It still hangs in the *Resim Heykel Müzesi* in Istanbul.

For the Ottomans, the practice of European music at their court was simply another trend in an already mixed musical tradition, which was still principally under the influence of the Arabo-Persian convention that had been exposed to Byzantine culture. This was a monophonic tradition based on the principle of a single melodic line with no harmonic accompaniment and its richness came from its complex combination of hundreds of different modes known as *makams*, which included quartertones completely alien to the European diatonic system. To the Western-trained ear, the *makam*-based music of the Orient sounded strange, out of tune and was deemed to be primitive. 'There are amongst the Turks some who affect a taste for music; but they understand not the "concord of sweet sounds", nor comprehend, according to our system, a single principle of musical composition. An ill-shaped guittar, with several wires always out of tune [...] [with] which they continue for hours to torment with a monotony the most detestable' wrote Charles Griffiths in his *Travels in Europe, Asia Minor and Arabia* in the early nineteenth century (Griffiths, 1805, p. 153).

The young republic, under the guidance of Mustafa Kemal, who was greatly influenced by the teachings of the Turkish nationalist thinker Ziya Gökalp (1876–1924), saw the traditional side of its Ottoman musical heritage in the same Orientalist vein as Griffiths. 'The kind of [monophonic] music we are hearing today is far from doing any good for the future of our young nation', Mustafa Kemal warned the delegates of the National Assembly (Saygun, 1981, p. 49). The monophonic tradition, with the dominance of the single melodic line, was seen as backward and primitive. Advancement in the field of music in modern Turkey could only be achieved with the introduction of polyphony and the harmonic dimension to the Turkish folk repertoire. Gökalp had already laid out proposals for this task in his influential book, *The Principles of Turkism*: 'We shall not copy the compositions of European composers, but learn the methods and the techniques of modern music by which we shall harmonise the melodies sung by our people. The aim, therefore, is to arrange our national melodies on the basis of the techniques of modern music and produce our own modern national works of music' (Berkes, 1981, p. 268). So whereas Mahmud II imported the European musical tradition to his court directly from Vienna and Italy and implanted it as an original entity, the young republic was determined to go even further, infusing the methods and techniques of European music into the traditional music of the country and thus into the very fabric of its society.[10]

Thus began a systematic suppression of the Ottoman monophonic court tradition, which also included official bans of this kind of music on radio networks. As it became apparent in later years, this was highly damaging to a musical practice that relied heavily on aural continuity with no available and efficient notation system.[11] But the regime was determined to implement the changes. The term 'national music' would only be applied to works that were composed using Western compositional techniques, and Mustafa Kemal himself took part in the conducting of such experiments. On one occasion, Ahmed Adnan [Saygun][12] – who later became one of the republic's most prolific composers – was invited to the presidential lodge at Çankaya and asked, on the spot, to compose a vocal piece based on a well-known traditional song of the Ottoman period. The words of the song had been translated into the new Turkish language, and Adnan's duty was to provide new music. When the composition was finally finished, Mustafa Kemal took the new song to his guests, remarking: 'Gentlemen! The old words [of the song] were in Ottoman and its music was also Ottoman. These words are Turkish and this new music is Turkish music. New society, new art'.[13]

Although the Kemalist state held a very strong anti-Ottoman sentiment, it was perfectly acceptable to rename and transform old Ottoman establishments to serve the needs of the modern republic. The Imperial Ottoman Orchestra of the last Caliphate, for example, was not disbanded, but instead moved to Ankara and renamed *Riyaset-i Cumhur Orkestrası*, the Presidential Orchestra. Its staff became teachers at the newly founded *Musiki Muallim Mektebi*, the Music Teachers' Training College, where prospective talented candidates were educated to spread the spirit of the music reform across the new republic.[14] Selected students were also sent to European music conservatories to study composition. Paris, Vienna and Berlin proved to be the three most popular destinations. Apart from Ahmed Adnan [Saygun], these included Ulvi Cemal [Erkin],[15] Ekrem Zeki [Ün],[16] Necil Kâzım [Akses][17] and Hasan Ferit [Alnar].[18] With the exception of Ekrem Zeki and the participation of Cemal Reşid [Rey],[19] who had already received his education in Paris before the others, all five composers subsequently joined an unofficial league calling themselves the 'Turkish Five', after the 'Mighty Five' of Russia and 'Les Six' in France.[20] Their collective output dominated the musical fabric of the early republican years.

The implementation of the reform programme also ran into difficulties at times. As in the planning of other reform strategies, Mustafa Kemal first ordered the active musicians of the country to discuss the future of Turkish music and advise sensibly for a future music policy. However, as then aspiring young composer Cemal Reşid observed, some of the discussions were clearly losing touch with reality: 'On the orders of [Atatürk] eight musicians, including myself, were invited by the Minister of Education, Abidin Özmen, to attend a council meeting to discuss the music reforms [...] the Minister of Education abruptly said:

We are supposed to do a reform. How are we going to do it?', which confused all the delegates [...] somebody suggested that monophonic music should completely be banned in the country. I think, to this I said: 'if a shepherd wants to sing a song [...] is he supposed to find another shepherd [...] and ask him to sing in correct counterpoint?'

(İlyasoğlu, 1997, p. 253)

The time had come to seek the advice of a true professional from the Western world and, just as in Ottoman times, a qualified musician was sought through appropriate channels for the post. On the advice of the German conductor William Furtwängler, the Ankara government invited the musician Paul Hindemith. Hindemith arrived in Ankara in April 1935, to 'put Turkish music on its feet' and to prepare reports for the future of music development in Turkey and the formation of a European-style conservatoire in the new capital (Skelton, 1975, p. 128). The visit started with an inspection of the existing musical establishments, including the Presidential Orchestra, whom Hindemith found 'playing too loud and out of tune, but [he] was determined to show what one can do with what there is when one goes about it properly' (Skelton, 1975, p. 129). After conducting one of the orchestra's concerts, he left for Germany in order to engage teachers and to place orders for orchestral material and instruments. Other eminent German instrumentalists joined him, to take charge of teaching at the new conservatoire and also join the Presidential Orchestra; these included Ernst Praetorius (who became the director of the conservatoire as well as assuming the conductorship of the Presidential Orchestra), Eduard Zuckmayer and Licco Amar. The Ankara State Conservatory was officially opened on 6 May 1936. Béla Bartók, Dmitri Shostakovich, Carl Ebert and Ninette de Valois were other famous names employed by the Turkish state in the organisation of its artistic institutions.

In the meantime, the Turkish Five had started producing their early works in line with the guidelines set by the state. Anatolian folk-song harmonisations dominated their early output. Harmonising folk songs had been a regular feature in the works of the Russian and Hungarian schools, mainly with composers like Bartók and Kodály. Kodály's *raison d'être* for arranging folk songs was echoed in the aspirations of the Ankara government:

> to enable the general public to get to know and enjoy folk-song [...] in transferring them from the countryside to the town, some such 'dressing-up' so to speak, was necessary. But since simply to put them into town clothes would make them awkward and ill at ease, we have tried to design a costume which would enable them to breathe freely.
>
> (Eösze, 1962, p. 132)

There was not however, in the Turkey of the 1930s, a tradition of collective singing in the villages, and the first aim of the republic was to encourage the formation of choirs through its networks of *Halkevi*, the People's Houses.[21] The material for teaching these choirs had to be easy-to-sing and familiar to the singers. In this respect, traditional Anatolian folk songs, which the peasants were already familiar with, were extremely suitable. Collections by Adnan Saygun, like *Çoban Armağanı*, Op. 7, *Dağlardan Ovalardan*, Op. 18 and *Bir Tutam Kekik* Op. 22, amounting to 25 songs in all, are all examples of this new genre.

Atatürk implemented reforms at a phenomenal speed. By 1934 it was already time for the creation of the first Turkish opera, which he appears to have seen as the highest and most sophisticated of all Western art forms. Modern Ankara's city development plans also included a new opera building.

In Ottoman times, local composers had written several successful national operas and operettas, such as *Zemiréh*, *Arif* and *Léblébidji Hor-Hor* by Dikran Tchouhadjian (1837–98), an Armenian subject of the sultan. The commission of the republic's first opera, *Özsoy*, went to the 26-year-old Ahmed Adnan [Saygun], who was given a month to compose the music. Mustafa Kemal supervised the libretto himself, as the opera was the key cultural event being organised for the state visit of Reza Shah Pahlavi of Persia to Ankara.[22] Although the performance was successful, *Özsoy* had far too much spoken dialogue for a proper opera, as the composer admitted himself, describing it as more of an 'ouvrage scenique' (Aracı, 2001, p. 71). Nevertheless the republican regime continued with operatic experiments by commissioning more works in this genre, such as Necil Kâzım's *Bayönder* and Ahmed Adnan's *Taşbebek*. But it would be wrong to judge these composers' abilities by their early works in the major forms of the Western classical tradition, as they were often prepared under pressure and with inadequate performance facilities. When Dmitri Shostakovich, accompanied by David Oistrackh and Lev Oborin arrived in Ankara in 1936, he later observed: 'Turkey's musical life was in an embryonic stage [...] when the delegation needed some sheet music to perform – I think it was Beethoven – it couldn't be found in all of Ankara' (Shostakovich, 1981, p. 113).

As time and experience are the two most important factors for artistic maturity, succeeding years saw more substantial works produced by the Turkish Five and their contemporaries. Adnan Saygun's *Yunus Emre* oratorio (1942), for example, a major choral work blending the mystical poetry of the thirteenth-century Sufi poet Yunus Emre with the traditional music of Anatolia, became a symbol of the new Turkish music[23] and drew the attention of international musicians including Leopold Stokowski and Michael Tippett.[24] Stokowski conducted the American premiere of *Yunus Emre* in New York in 1958.[25] 'There is neither the intense musical nationalism, nor the forging of a new idiom through synthesis of the old [...] rather there is a more universal style – a style which is to be associated with that of post-romantic music', wrote the American critic Franklin Zimmerman (1959, p. 99). In 1954 the *Grove Dictionary of Music and Musicians* devoted a large section to the work of the Turkish Five. By 1965 there were some 30 composers in Turkey writing in the Western style (Oransay, 1965). This number had nearly doubled 30 years later (İlyasoğlu, 1998).

Early republican policy also followed an extensive programme for the training of virtuoso musicians. In 1948, the Turkish parliament passed a unique law called 'İdil Biret – Suna Kan Kanunu'. Named after two child prodigies – the former of the pianoforte, the latter of the violin – the new law paved the way for young students to be sent to foreign conservatories for their education from a very young age, accompanied by their parents and with the aid of a full state scholarship. İdil Biret became a pupil of Nadia Boulanger at the Paris Conservatory and studied with Wilhelm Kempff. Suna Kan also attended the Paris Conservatoire, studying under Gabriel Bouillon. Violinist Ayla Erduran and pianist Ayşegül Sarıca also became prominent soloists following their education in the French capital, while soprano Leyla Gencer began to make a reputation for herself at the opera houses of Italy for her *bel canto* singing style and distinctive interpretation of Donizetti solos.

In Turkey today, villagers do not sing polyphonic folk songs harmonised by the Turkish Five, but the symphonic works of the early composers of the republic are still performed at concerts and occasional new recordings of their work appear either in the national market or in international releases by the world's well-known orchestras. As Peter Reed acknowledged in a recent *Sunday Telegraph* article, 'The Turkish Five cast a long shadow on contemporary Turkish music [...] Modern Turkish music is electrifying, original and largely unknown' (Reed, 2004, p. 9). Atatürk's reforms clearly gave birth to a distinctive school of composition, still active and alive today.

Notes

1. In a letter sent on 28 October 1934 to composers working at state schools in Turkey, the Minister of Education observed: 'I regret to say that during my inspections at the state schools I have witnessed that some of the songs composed and taught by certain music teachers, who saw themselves as able composers in this field, lacked any kind of musical or educational value regarding their melody and wording. There is no doubt that this kind of teaching will be extremely unhealthy for the future of our modern Turkish music education based in Western principles, which we are trying to establish [...] There is no doubt that the young music teachers sent to foreign conservatoires at great expenses to the state will fulfill our expectations in this field with great care and sensitivity'; See Aracı (1999, p. 116).
2. The theatre, which opened in 1858 with great pomp and ceremony, sadly burnt down only a few years later during a devastating fire. An engraving of the sumptuous interior of the new theatre was published in *L'Illustration* on 25 June 1859.
3. Donizetti composed his Gran Marcia Militare Imperiale in 1840. Rossini's Marcia Militare was composed and published in 1852. Both composers were awarded the Ottoman Order of Nişan-ı İftihar.
4. During a visit to Constantinople in 1841, Hans Christian Andersen heard the 'merry music of Rossini and Donizetti' which sounded through the streets of the city while 'the troops were marching on, to be paraded between the Serail and the Mosque of Ahmed, whither the Sultan [Abdülmecid] was about to proceed in state'. Trans. Dulcken (1983, p. 833).
5. According to a report in the The Times, when Donizetti's Belisario was performed at the palace of Sultana Valide, one of the apartments was fitted up as a theatre and all the members of the harem were given printed copies of the libretto translated into Turkish: 'The ladies listened very earnestly during the performance and perused the books with great attention. The sympathy of one was strongly excited by the appearance of blind Belisario, and she became

so moved by the representation of his distress, that she started up suddenly, and with expression of pity threw a purse full of gold at him'. See The *Times* (17 February 1843, p. 6).

6. Richard Wagner Archives, Inv. No: 230, 231 and 232; 'Seine Majestaet der Sultan zu Konstantinopel' bought three patronat-shein to the value of 300 thalern each (in total around 21,000 Euros in today's value), all signed by Wagner and dated 23 September 1872; see: Aracı (2004, pp. 29–31).

7. These are entitled Invitation à la Valse, La Harpe Caprice, La Gondole Barcarolle and a polka. Published, c. 1860 by F. Lucca in Milan. For a recording of Invitation à la Valse and La Gondole Barcarolle. See, Aracı, European Music at the Ottoman Court, CD 177, Kalan.

8. La Gondole Barcarolle composed by HIM the Sultan was performed by the bands of the Grenadier Guards under the direction of Dan Godfrey at Marlborough House during the state dinner hosted by the Prince of Wales in honour of Abdülaziz on 13 July 1867; The *Times*, 15 July 1867.

9. The Caliph's 1911 Steinway piano is today housed at Dolmabahçe Palace, in room 48, along with his extensive library of musical scores of major chamber works from the European classical repertoire.

10. According to Stokes: 'In Gökalp's view, the split between culture and civilization could be illustrated by the existence of two quite distinct kinds of music, one pertaining to the Ottoman élite and the other rural *halk*, the folk. The former was the product of Arabo-Persian civilization, of the Byzantines. The latter was the true culture of the Turks'; Stokes (1992, p. 33).

11. Some alleged in later years that the Arabesk musical tradition in Turkey was a result of this ban, when people tuned their radio sets into Egyptian radio: 'The effects of Egyptian film and radio began to be felt in Turkey in the 1930s. Kocabaş and Güngör have argued that this was directly attributable to the ban imposed upon the radio broadcasting of Turkish art music between 1934 and 1936'; see Martin Stokes (1992, p. 33).

12. Ahmed Adnan Saygun (1907–91) studied at the Schola Cantorum in Paris between 1928 and 1931 under Vincent d'Indy, Eugène Borrel, Amedée Gastue and Paul Le Flem.

13. 'Efendiler! o sözler Osmanlıcadır ve onun musikisi Osmanlı musikisidir. Bu sözler Türkçedir ve bu musiki Türk musikisidir. Yeni sosyete, yeni sanat'; see Adnan Saygun (1981, p. 44).

14. The college was founded on 1 November 1924 in the Cebeci district of Ankara, principally to train suitable music teachers for state schools.

15. Ulvi Cemal Erkin (1906–72) arrived in Paris in 1925, studied with Jean Gallon and Isidor Phillip at the Conservatoire, and transferred to École Normale de Musique in 1929, returning to Turkey in 1930.

16. Ekrem Zeki Ün (1910–87) arrived in Paris in 1924, and studied at the École Normale de Musique for six years with Line Talluel, Marcel Chailley, George Dandelot as well as Jacques Thibaud.

17. Necıl Kâzım Akses (1908–92) studied in Vienna from 1926 with Joseph Marx and subsequently with Joseph Suk and Alois Haba in Prague and returned to Turkey in 1934.

18. Hasan Ferit Alnar (1906–78) studied composition with Joseph Marx at the Hochschule für Musik in Vienna between 1927 and 1932.

19. Cemal Reşid Rey (1904–85) was educated in Paris between 1913 and 1923. He attended Marguerite Long's piano classes, later moved to Switzerland during the

outbreak of the World War I, and returned to Paris in 1920 to resume classes with Gabriel Fauré and Henri Defosse.

20. All five composers presented their works at a joint concert given on 19 February 1939 in Ankara. It was after this event that they collectively came to be known as the 'Turkish Five'.

21. Adnan [Saygun] explains this notion in his book on music education at Halkevi, where he says: 'Halkevi should encourage people to sing together. It is important to observe that the Turks do not enjoy singing together as a group. In fact both amongst villagers in Anatolia and students at city-schools, solo-singing is more dominant than group-singing. One of them sings a Türkü [a folk-song] and the others listen. Even occasionally when others join in they often sing out of tune [...] This does not mean to say that the Turk does not have an ear for music, it simply shows that they have not been trained to sing as a group'; in Saygun (1940, p. 13).

22. Based on an old Turco-Persian legend in Firdevsi's Şehname, the opera depicts the lives of Tur and Irac, the twin sons of Feridun, who turn against each other under the spell of Ahriman. Keen to embark on good relations with Iran, Atatürk in fact constructed the libretto in an allegoric style: Tur is the representative of the Turkish nation, while Irac is of the Iranians, and the plot is woven around the fact that these two nations have fought each other for centuries not knowing that they were actually brothers. The second and third acts depart from the mythology and centre on modern Turkey and the War of Independence, reaching a final scene where Feridun asks the whereabouts of Tur and Irac. To this the minstrel on the stage points at Mustafa Kemal and the Shah in the president's box saying: 'Here is Tur and here is Irac'; see Aracı (2001, pp. 68–9).

23. After the premiere in Ankara in 1946, Selahattin Batu wrote: 'Those in the field of arts and music, and those who are not, have all once again witnessed the defeat of the monophonic, primitive eastern music by our new [polyphonic] music. In this work [Yunus Emre] our true spirit, feelings and national identity have all been reflected through an advanced technique [of musical writing]'; see Batu (1946).

24. Saygun and Tippett met in London in 1946. Tippett, though unsuccessful, tried to organize a performance of Yunus Emre with his choir in England. He wrote to Saygun: 'Let me know quickly the exact date of performance of this great work'; see Emre Aracı (2001, p. 133).

25. The concert took place on 25 November 1958 in the General Assembly Hall of the United Nations, with the participation of the Symphony of the Air Orchestra and the Crane Chorus of the State University of New York at Potsdam.

Bibliography

E. Aracı (2004) 'Dolmabahçe'den Bayreuth'a uzanan yardım eli', *Andante*, no. 8, pp. 29–31.

E. Aracı (2001) *Ahmed Adnan Saygun, Doğu Batı Arası Müzik Köprüsü* (İstanbul: Yapı Kredi Yayınları).

E. Aracı (2000) *European Music at the Ottoman Court*, CD 177 (İstabul: Kalan).

E. Aracı (1999) *The Life and Works of Ahmed Adnan Saygun*, [Unpublished Ph.D. Thesis] (Edinburgh: Universuty of Edinburgh).

A. N. Arman (1979) 'Muzika-i Humayun'un Avrupa Seferi', *Yıllarboyu Tarih*, no. 3.

S. Batu (1946) 'Bir Sanat Başarısı' (Ankara: Unknown publishing house).

N. Berkes (ed.) (1981) *Turkish Nationalism and Western Civilization: Selected Essays of Ziya Gokalp* (Westport: Greenwood Publishing Group).

G. Donizetti (ed.) (1897) *Ricordi di Gaetano Donizetti, Esposti Nella Mostra Centenaria Tenutasi in Bergamo* (Bergamo).

H. W. Dulcken (1983) *The Complete Illustrated Stories of Hans Christian Andersen, 'Mahomet's Birthday – A Scene in Constantinople* (London: Chancellor Press).

L. Eösze (1962) *Zoltan Kodaly His Life and Work* [Trans. István Farkas and Gyula Gulyás] (London: Collet's).

J. Griffiths (1805) *Travels in Europe, Asia Minor and Arabia* (London: Printed for T. Cadell and W. Davies).

E. İlyasoğlu (1998) *Contemporary Turkish Composers* (Istanbul: Pan Yayıncılık).

E. İlyasoğlu (1997) *Cemal Reşid Rey* (Istanbul: Yapı Kredi Yayınları).

Le Ménestrel (1836) 18 December.

The Musical World (1839) 6 June.

G. Oransay (1965) *Batğ Tekniğiyle yazan 60 Türk Bağdar* (Ankara: Küğ Yayınları).

P. Reed (2004) 'Synthesis of East and West', *The Sunday Telegraph Review*, 13 June.

A. Saygun (1981) *Atatürk ve Musiki* (Ankara: Sevda Cenap And Vakfı Müzik Yayınlan).

A. A. [Saygun] (1940) *Halkevlerinde Musiki* (Ankara: Cumhuriyet Halk Partisi Yayını).

D. Shostakovich (1981) *Testimony* (London: Robert Hale).

G. Skelton (1975) *Paul Hindemith* (London: Gollancz).

M. Stokes (1992) *The Arabesk Debate* (Oxford: Oxford University Press).

The Times (1843) 17 February.

F. Zimmerman (1959) 'New York: Turkish Music at the U. N.', *The Musical Times*, February.

Media and Popular Culture

18
Fashioning the Turkish Body Politic

Arus Yumul

> *I see a man in the crowd in front of me; he has a fez on his head,*
> *a green turban on the fez, a smock on his back, and on top of*
> *that a jacket like the one I am wearing. ... Now what kind of*
> *outfit is that? Would a civilised man put on this preposterous*
> *garb and go out to hold himself up for universal ridicule?*
>
> —Mustafa Kemal

While fashion permeates almost all forms of social life, including such seemingly rationally inclined and instrumentally governed fields as science and engineering (Blumer, 1968, pp. 341–5), it has attained its comprehensive, institutionalised manifestation in dress, and above all in the dress of women (Davis, 1989, pp. 337–8). In this paper, I shall concentrate on Republican Turkish attempts to 'fashion the body politic' and my focus will be on male rather than female bodies. Bodies are important because the life of the nation is played out through the technical arrangements of clothes, adornment and gesture, as nationalism transforms the body into an imprint and embodiment of the aspired national qualities and practices and into a surface of inscription through which political struggles are expressed. In a nutshell bodies are the essence of the nation. Although the literature on nationalism and gender suggests that men and women are involved differentially in nationalist projects, and that the symbolic representation of the nation usually takes a female form, I argue that not only women but also men are seen as the symbolic bearers of the nation's identity. In the Turkish case men were not only associated with 'masculine' themes like patriotism, bravery, sacrifice and heroism, but also with so-called feminine issues such as the politics of dress and demeanour. Like female bodies, male bodies were simultaneously material and metaphor. Male bodies were discursively produced, becoming surfaces for the inscription of society's ideals, morals and laws. Masculinity, as Kandiyoti notes, is the 'missing dimension in the study of Turkish modernity' (Kandiyoti, 1997).

349

Sartorial reforms directed at men played an important role in the construction of a modern, national Turkish masculinity. Fashion has been conceptualised as a phenomenon historically unique to Western civilisation and the culture of capitalism. As such, it has been distinguished from the clothing behaviour of other cultures, which have been relegated to the realm of costume. The latter as 'pre-civilised' behaviour has been considered in opposition to fashion as traditional, static, and fixed (Craik, 1993, pp. 3–4). It was this understanding of fashion that influenced the Kemalist reformers and their construction of modern male bodies and dress.

In 1922, Elizabeth Harris, an American residing in Turkey for some time, made the following comments on her impressions of Turkey:

> The customs of the Turkish people reflect an age which the average American thinks of as existing only in romance. The Westerner who finds himself as quite removed from the influences of his own civilisation feels that he has dropped back many centuries. [After 18 months of stay in this country I realized that] the expression 'unchanging East is not meaningless'.

For her, one of the most striking differences lay in the matter of dress. She compared Turkish men's dress with that of the Westerners in the following way:

> The men in Turkey are not soberly-dressed individuals such as we see in Europe and America. One is constantly reminded of Joseph and his coat of many colours. Our head-carpenter, [for example] who really dressed quite conservatively, wore bright red slippers, a ziboom (a long, straight garment) usually of darker red silk, a long flowing black coat trimmed with gold braid and a fez.

Let me note, in passing, that the apparent straightforwardness and sobriety of Western male dress code that Elizabeth Harris compared with the Eastern style is a modern phenomenon. Men's clothing in the West, at least for the wealthy, was elaborate and decorative throughout much of European history. It was only in the second half of the eighteenth century that a simpler style of male clothing, which was associated with discipline, reliability, restraint and rationality, emerged in Europe and the Americas.

Contrary to Elizabeth Harris' predictions, the East did change. Mustafa Kemal, the founder of the Turkish Republic, believed that the Turks must dress in 'the ordinary clothes in use among the civilised people of the world'. He wanted to make his countrymen look properly Westernised by giving up their characteristic Ottoman dress in favour of that of the Europeans. To this end, he first wanted to get rid of the fez. In order to introduce the Turks to the hat and convince them of the necessity to embrace Western clothes he went to the Anatolian city of Kastamonu. On 26 August 1925, dressed in Western style and carrying a white Panama hat (without a hatband), Kemal spoke to the people about civilisation, progress, and clothing: 'Is it possible for a nation to be civilised without dressing in a civilised manner?' he asked. The crowd answered 'Never! Never!'. Then he continued, 'Are you ready to be described as uncivilised?'. And again the crowd responded 'Never! Never!' (Volkan and Itzkowitz, 1984, p. 255). Atatürk then likened the people to jewels – but jewels covered with mud. 'In order to see the jewel shine, one must get rid of the mud', he told his audience. Getting rid of the mud, he insisted, meant wearing 'shoes on the feet, trousers over the legs, shirts with neckties under the collar, jackets, and naturally, to complement all of this, a head covering to protect you from the sun'. Then came his most celebrated statement on the dress reforms. Pointing to his Panama hat, he told those present: 'The name of this headgear is "hat". The dress of civilised people is good enough for us', he added, rejecting the idea of a separate national dress code (Volkan and Itzkowitz, 1984, p. 255).

On 25 November, the fez was formally banned. The hat was to become the headdress of the Turks: 'The hat is the common headgear of the Turkish people' the law stated 'and the government forbids habits to the contrary' (Mango, 1999, p. 436). The adoption of the Hat Law led to a number of protests and rebellions throughout Anatolia, which the government suppressed. In his autobiography, Irfan Orga recalls reactions to the Hat Law:

> The men indulgently refused to throw away the fez and it became a usual sight to see fighting taking place between the supporters of the new order and the die-hards of the old. Government officials were the first to give way to Atatürk. They were forced into this position by reason of their work and the streets became full of bowler hats worn with a self-conscious air. The children used to throw stones after them and the police arrested the men who still persisted in wearing the fez, and the street sellers in desperation put fancy paper hats on their heads ... And out in the country places and the villages the men even wore women's hats in order to evade arrest. The old men took to trying handkerchiefs on their heads, placing the offending Christian hat over this, but the police became wise to this ruse and promptly arrested them. Arrested men were hauled to the police station in such great numbers that they could not be dealt with and the white handkerchiefs were pulled off ... the insulting head-gear being firmly clamped over the naked, uneasy heads.
>
> (Orga, 1988, p. 223)

Since Muslims deemed hats to be the insignia of the 'infidel' this was considered to be the most thorny and essential reform by the Kemalists. In the words of a contemporary observer, Lyman MacCallum: 'Kemal Pasha's aide told some of us this year that this was the most difficult and most fundamental of all Kemal's reforms. After the Turk's had crossed that ditch there was no reform that he could not have forced on them' (Padwick, 1958, p. 50). Regarding the Hat Law, Mustafa Kemal said:

> It was necessary to abolish the fez, which sat on the heads of our nation as a sign of ignorance, fanaticism, or hatred to progress and civilisation and to adopt in its place the hat, the customary headgear of the civilised world, thus showing that no difference existed in the manner of thought as in other respects between the Turkish nation and the whole family of civilised mankind.
>
> (Atatürk, 1950–2, p. 895)

In passing let me note that the fez, which was then in use among North African Muslims, had been introduced into the Ottoman Empire only in the nineteenth century by the modernising sultan, Mahmud II. It became the signifier of the modernising Ottoman bureaucracy before it was turned into an emblem of conservatism and religious affiliation (Berkes, 1964, pp. 124–5).

In an attempt to create westernised/civilised bodies, Mustafa Kemal was also keen on introducing ballroom dancing to Turkey. This genre was unfamiliar to Muslims except those living in the Europeanised parts of big cities, especially Istanbul and Izmir. While dance occurs in numerous forms and shapes, it was the social dance – by socialising and incorporating the 'modern individual into a new condition of societal membership' – that provided one of the symbolic bases of the moral order that legitimated the developing political order of emergent modernity in Europe. Social dance has accomplished this task in two distinct ways: 'First, the ordered exercise required by learning its performance provides a training in new forms of self-control required by the new social order. Second, the sociality of that performance – the dances were couple dances and could be watched as spectacle as well as performed – constitute a change in the expressive character of embodiment characterised by social consensuality' (Filmer, 1999, p. 11). There are significant conflicting tensions between folk dance and social dance. Whereas in the former the dancing body expresses the power of the body performatively, in the latter the trained and self-controlled dancing body is a manifestation of the order of society as orchestrated in the body of the sovereign (Turner, 2005, p. 5). It was this very tension between different forms of dances that inspired the politics of dance in the early republican period.

In 1938 Atatürk attended his last ball. He asked the orchestra to play the music of an Aegean folk dance, the *zeybek*.[1] One observer described the event in the following manner: 'And there was Atatürk, prancing through this strenuous dance like a young warrior' (Volkan and Itzkowitz, 1984, p. 338). The zeybek was re-choreographed in 1916 by Selim Sırrı Tarcan who had introduced modern sports to Turkey. It is interesting to note that a major element of Turkish reform agenda involved creating a dignified, masculine Turk in order to overcome the somewhat feminised, aged or feeble image of the Turks epitomised in the phrase 'the Sick Man of Europe'. Tarcan was not pleased with the traditional zeybek performances. For him, they lacked the elegance and sophistication of European dances and required refinement by getting rid of the 'rough' and 'sharp' movements and all kinds of improvisation (Öztürkmen, 2002, pp. 129–30). He had choreographed, in his words, a zeybek dance in a more 'methodological' way with fixed form and movements (Öztürkmen, 2002, pp. 129–30), that is, as a system of formalised and rationalised expression. Subject to the discipline of the civilising process zeybek was transformed from rowdy, spontaneous folk culture into a more polished and stylised spectacle of the Westernised elites. In modern imagination ballroom dancing and folk dance communicate different kinds of physical discourses. Whereas the latter corresponds to the discourse of nature, the former emphasises the cultural or social, as it exemplifies the significance of the corporeal restraint entailed by the civilising process. As Franko notes the corporeal discipline required by the social dance of early modernity 'was in many ways indistinguishable from that required by civility' (Franko, 1986, p. 31). Tarcan's choreography was in fact conceived as a ballroom dance genre that could be performed by mixed couples. In 1925 after watching his performance Atatürk flattered him with the following words:

> Ladies and Gentlemen! Selim Sırrı Bey has given the zeybek dance a civilised form by reviving it. From now on, we can tell the Europeans that we too have an excellent dance and we can perform it in our salons. The zeybek dance can and must be performed with women in all kinds of social occasions.
>
> (Öztürkmen, 2002, pp. 129–30).

Ballroom dancing was now to be appropriated as emblematic of the modern rather than as standing in opposition to masculinity. It was to provide an epistemological metaphor for the attributes required of the new order. It became a site of cultural struggle between forces of tradition and modernity. In modern and progressive settings, ignorance of social dance was associated with backwardness. Dance schools were established for adults teaching dances like the tango, swing, waltz and fox trot, and the magazines of the period contained pieces teaching gentlemen 'the etiquette of dancing' (Mahir, 2005, p. 20).

At a ball he gave in honour of the founding of the Republic, Mustafa Kemal is reported telling a group of young officers that he 'cannot conceive that any woman in the world can refuse to dance with a Turk wearing an officer's uniform' (Kinross, 1995, p. 421). This remark gives important clues about the masculine ideal of Turkish nationalism. Social dancing and military discipline in different ways act upon corporeal containment. The differences between the former and the latter are those between self-control and self-coercion, which are irreconcilable with one another, since 'self-control is more likely to develop in privileged social spaces' than in an institution in which tenets of command and subordination give meaning and direction to life (Kuzmics, 1987, p. 523).

Nilüfer Göle emphasises the need to re-conceptualise attempts at modernisation in non-Western countries as civilising projects (Göle, 1997, p. 84). If we define a modern society as one in which this project becomes its central dynamic, then the society is transformed into one in which individuals are reconstructed as appropriate subjects who carry out this process by becoming civilised and enlightened. This process is not only about ideals, ideas and imagery, but also about bodies. The civilising process, with its accent on public demeanour and appearances, connected civic virtue with 'outward bodily propriety' (Elias, 1994, p. 44). Civility has been depicted using similar expressions to those used for national identity. In the words of Mustafa Kemal the Turkish people who had established the Turkish Republic were 'civilised in history and reality. But ... the people of the Turkish Republic, who claim to be civilised, must show and prove that they are civilised, by their ideas and their mentality, by their family life and their way of living. In a word, the truly civilised people of Turkey ... must prove in fact that they are civilised and advanced persons also in their outward aspect' (Lewis, 1967, pp. 268–9). The Kemalists envisioned an heroic society, an ordered life shaped by will in which the everyday with its heterogeneity and lack of order is to be subdued, resisted or rejected, 'something to be subjugated in the pursuit of a higher purpose' (Featherstone, 1995, p. 55). This higher purpose, for the Kemalists, was 'to reach the level of contemporary civilisation'.

Civilisation can only be signified by what Ernesto Laclau terms an 'empty signifier', that is, a signifier that is not connected to any signified due to the endless sliding of the signifieds under the signifier (Laclau, 1994, pp. 167–78). Just as the West had hegemonised the empty place of the universal, the Kemalist project emerged as the embodiment of the empty signifier that signified civilisation. The discourse of civilisation in Turkey was centred on the figure of the West. The body politic was organised around an imaginary Westernised body. It was to emerge as the local embodiment of Western subjectivity. This single model created an ideal that drew everything back into sameness and erased difference.

In 1935, the Turkish parliament passed a law that made the wearing of clerical garments outside places of worship a punishable offence. The modernising state viewed religious and ethnic identities and their bodily expressions as parochial, provincial and local, thus challenging the claims of universalism made by Turkish reformers. The embodiment of citizenship required a rearrangement of the human body. The aim was to transform the heterogeneous masses, with their diverse traditions, into a homogeneous body, an imagined community, that is, a 'nation' – the embodiment of unity. Those who were marked with a 'surplus corporeality', (Berlant, 1993, p. 176) to use Laurent Berlant's phrase, were banished from the official public sphere. The public sphere had been imagined as an orderly garden in which 'Each person has his own preferences. Some people like gardening and growing flowers. Others prefer to train men. ... He who trains men ought to work like the man who grows flowers,' (Volkan and Itzkowitz, 1984) said Mustafa Kemal in 1937. This gardening ambition, an attribute of the modern spirit, is evocative of Zygmunt Bauman's 'gardening state' (Bauman, 1991, p. 20) – a state that is managed like a garden. A gardening state delegitimises the present-day reality of the population as wild and uncultivated. The plants are not to be left to themselves. Through the will of the gardener they are to be moulded, whereas wild growth, weeds etc. are either removed or tamed to be incorporated into the order of the garden.

The body was detached from the individual lived body, from the concrete embodied habits and routines, and from subjectivity itself and became the abstract object of public supervision in the public realm. The changes related to the body ran counter to the body techniques of most Ottomans, not only of Muslims, but also of non-Muslims. The Western style of clothing, for example, was scarcely compatible with either habitual resting postures, or the furnishings of traditional dwellings. Thus, in remarking on a group photograph of Armenian men in nineteenth-century Anatolia, Ellsworth Huntington observed: 'one has adopted typical European trousers and therefore finds it inconvenient to sit on his knees or cross-legged as the others do' (Zelinsky, 2004, p. 93). Likewise, the hats mismatched the way Muslims perform their daily prayers where believers should touch their foreheads to the ground in the course of praying. Another transformation pertaining to the male body was the removal of facial hair. By the end of the nineteenth century, clean-shaven faces had become the norm in Europe and this norm was to be adopted by the Turks. 'The modern face in the contemporary world is the clean-shaven face. The man with a moustache today is not seen as a modern man', says a Turkish etiquette book written in 1932 (Akçura, 2002, p. 197). For the author of this book, the shaven face was associated with cleanliness, youth and dynamism. And in 1941 a popular magazine asserted that a civilised man shaves his face every day (Akçura, 2002, p. 198). Moustaches became popular again among urbanites only following the 1950 elections, when the more populist Democratic Party replaced the elitist Republican People's Party (Akçura, 2002, p. 203).

Modernisation in the cultural sphere was more a modernisation of the urban public sphere than a process of urban modernisation as such. Outward appearances and life on the street constituted the face of modernisation, the heart of the civil. Men's dress in urban areas, following the European trend, became less elaborate, less decorative, and less variable. In the 1930s, a more homogeneous and standardised look replaced the cosmopolitanism of Ottoman Istanbul. Public populism, by eradicating the difference in appearance between civil servant and citizen, and nationalism, by emphasising patriotism over cosmopolitanism, both attempted to adjust the appearance of urban streets to the European standards of the time (Işın, 1995, p. 159). The street was the setting of the citizen intermingling with other citizens on the national podium of politics and social life via officially sanctioned forms of embodiment.

The government directed its cultural policies of the period mainly at 'high culture', leaving the sphere of popular culture either untouched or constructed through an imaginary 'popular' by the elite (Tekelioğlu, 2004, p. 4) or selected elements of it were enshrined into the treasury of national culture through a process of what Tilman Schiel designates as 'vernacularization' (Schiel, 2005, p. 81) since Westernisation was blended with the revival, and re-enactment of the 'authentic' Turkish culture. It was for this reason that research in folklore coincided with the introduction of ballroom dancing to Turkey. 'Ennoblement' through vernacularisation takes place 'only after scientific research has "purified" the selected elements, has canonised them, has provided experts to "explain" these elements in a "correct" way, experts who also teach this folklore to the people ... in the "scientifically corrected" form' (Schiel, 2005, p. 81). It was in the 1950s that popular culture and its influence began to become more visible in Turkey. The economic policies pursued by the Democratic Party resulted in large-scale rural-to-urban migration, which irreversibly altered the cultural landscape of urban areas. It was in this period that Anatolian tints became visible on the streets of Istanbul. After this shift, the main cleavage in urban centres revolved around the established and the outsider. Since the body emerged as the central concept that represented the spirit of the national political and cultural agenda, and symbolised simultaneously the real, imaginary and symbolic[2] (the body, the nation and civility respectively), conceptions of citizenship became patterned with corporeal assumptions. Those who were deemed to have control over their bodies became real citizens, whereas those who were supposed to be governed by their bodies[3] were designated as the populace, the masses, the common people and were sent into a symbolic exile. This process rendered the latter group invisible, by excluding them from the definition of the nation, yet simultaneously made them visible as the representation of 'Otherness'. 'The people has rushed to the beaches and there is no room left for citizens' the governor of Istanbul remarked in the 1950s, when swimming, which had largely been an elite pursuit, became a popular leisure activity among the migrants from the provinces (Coşkun, 2007a, 2007b).

It was the culture of the periphery that was understood by the modernising elites as popular culture, and it was this very culture that was to sow the seeds of popular opposition in Turkey. For example, *arabesk* culture, as a historical formation of popular culture, emerged, not as a conscious, but as a spontaneous popular response (Tekelioğlu, 2001, pp. 194–215), to the dissatisfactions experienced by squatter populations in the 1960s.[4] As Meral Özbek notes, this 'culture of hybridity' was initially made popular by migrants 'giving voice to experiences shaped by the rapid modernisation of Turkish society since the 1950s' (Özbek, 1997, p. 211). Challenging the characterisation of arabesk by the modernisers as vulgar, tasteless and fatalistic, Özbek defines it as a culture of ambivalence that affirmed and denied, submitted to and resisted modernity.

In the post-1950 period the impact of the culture pole of the culture/civilisation binary opposition that Ziya Gökalp (1976) had constructed, intensified. This process, naturally, influenced the construction of masculinity. On the one hand, in the official view and discourse, 'traditional masculinity' and the 'oppression of women' were being 'portrayed through rural mores and interpreted as a deficit in civilisation' (Kandiyoti, 1997, p. 122). Popular discourse, on the other hand, praised traditional masculine values.

The Turkish melodramas of the period were instrumental in reproducing this nebulous masculine ideal. On the one hand they idealised Westernised, modern-looking, educated men, preferably of Istanbul origin, who had adopted *alafranga* (Western) manners, tastes and life styles; but at the same they were careful to portray these men as individuals honouring patriarchal values, exercising authority over their wives and children, adhering to the precepts of the traditional sexual division of labour, taking their economic responsibilities to their families seriously and refusing to allow their wives to participate in the labour force. These men were represented as courageous, bold individuals, standing up to all challenges and insults and ready to defend the honour of their family even by resorting to violence. Although sexually experienced and the heroes of many love affairs, these ideal men led decent lives after marriage, and knew well the difference between easy women and the woman worthy of marrying. Men lacking any of these qualities were excluded from the category of the ideal man. Those found to be deficient with respect to traditional masculine norms were denigrated by such adjectives as 'molly', 'dandy' and so on, whereas those who were not found to be 'civilised' enough were represented as beasts, the polar opposite of the 'civilised body', by way of such nicknames as 'bear', 'ass' and so on. This hybrid man –'civilised' and 'Western' in outward appearance, but traditional and Eastern in essence – was not the exact equivalent of the rational man idealised by the Enlightenment, who was identified with reason and the mind, and disconnected from his emotions and nature (Seidler, 1994). This disparity was, however, endorsed by many and was explained in terms of the innate characteristics of the 'Mediterranean' people (Yumul, 1999, p. 111).

The parameters of masculine dress, which during the Second World War were influenced by uniforms, started to expand. With the politicisation of society along leftist and rightist lines, clothing became invested with political significance. The style of hair, beard and moustache all became markers of political commitment and religious persuasion. Different costumes indicated different politics. The parka, for example, was emblematic of the leftists, whereas militant Islamists preferred black baggy trousers. Even subdivisions within ideological groupings were reflected: the droop of a moustache, would tell the difference between a Maoist and a Marxist. The politicians of the period, too, had their particular styles of dress, display and bodily performance. Rural-born Suleyman Demirel appropriated the felt hat, emblematic of modernity and urbanity in the Turkish context, and the cloth cap, which had been preferred by rural men since the Hat Law was introduced, was appropriated by urbanite Bülent Ecevit in the 1970s. Thus the cloth cap, which used to be the signifier of provincialism, turned into a symbol of populism in the hands of Ecevit. This development was paradoxical for the line of reasoning of modernisation theory, which, with its rigid distinction between traditional and modern produced remarkably inflexible and unchanging analyses of fashion. As Hasan Bülent Kahraman notes, the relation of bodies to clothes is far deeper than such binary divisions (Kahraman, 2004).

Whereas Ecevit and Demirel's different styles had never violated conventional codes of masculine dress, Turgut Özal was exceptionally relaxed. He did not refrain from inspecting a military honour guard in his shorts when the occasion arose. The post-1980 period represented the third transformation of Turkish society. As migrants with their traditional dresses and behaviour patterns appeared on the streets, what Elijah Anderson (1990, p. 230) labels as 'street etiquette' lost its significance. The newcomers were reluctant to assimilate to urban or urbane ways. They were now self-assured of their way of life and routine. Even the titles of arabesk songs communicated this novel attitude. Whereas in the 1970s some of the most popular arabesk songs were *Batsın Bu Dünya* (Down with This World), *Bir Teselli Ver* (Give me a Consolation), in the late 1990s *Ben de İsterem* (I too Demand for) epitomised the prevailing popular sentiment and taste of the period. Although the former was an expression of the symbolic castration of the deprived and displaced, it still embraced a yearning for popular justice with utopian connotations and 'a democratic resonance' (Özbek, 1997, p. 217). While the right to live in dignity was a common theme in these lyrics, this demand was still filtered through a sense of restraint and moderation, and the fulfilment of pleasures was postponed. The latter, on the other hand, conveyed a sense of urgency and determination in getting a share from worldly pleasures and comforts.[5]

By the 1990s, the heroic society that the Kemalists had envisioned had been replaced by a culture of consumerism and hedonism. This was coupled with the gradual 'de-sacralisation of Kemalism'. The homogeneously imagined and ideologically inspired dominant public sphere had undergone a substantial transformation through the intrusion of, what Nancy Fraser designates, 'subaltern counterpublics' of all sorts.[6] This transformation of the public sphere is well captured in a study comparing the funerals of Mustafa Kemal and Turgut Özal (Seufert and Weyland, 1984). Atatürk's funeral was conceived and carefully planned by the state apparatus as a national stage where the imagined community was to acquire a physical reality as a single body.

Not only were nationwide funeral marches and ceremonies centrally organised to the minute details, but a government circular also prescribed dress to the effect that all participants 'must, if civilians, wear a tail-coat (black jacket and white tie) and hat or top hat, or if they belong to the military, dress uniform and independence medals' (Seufert and Weyland, 1984, p. 78). Only students were exempted from this prescription. Those who were not dressed in the prescribed way were to take their place together with the *people*. The latter referred to those who could not be integrated into any institutional order, that is, the military, the political and bureaucratic establishment, the academia and other educational institutions, financial, commercial and administrative institutions and students (Seufert and Weyland, 1984, pp. 78–9).

Whereas Atatürk's funeral was the visual proof of the harmony and unanimity of the Turkish nation, Özal's funeral showed that the projected uniformity of the nation had given way to heterogeneity. Although the whole nation was present be they Kemalists or Islamists, Kurds, leftists or rightists 'there was no longer any uniformity of symbols, signifiers and simulacra, no military organisation of the society, no fusion into a single body' (Seufert and Weyland, 1984, p. 94). The repressed had returned in many forms and colours. It was not only religious or ethnic identities that were carried from the private to the public sphere, but also the Ottoman past had been reclaimed by the elite through an appreciation of Ottoman *objet d'art*, life styles, cuisine and so on. Moreover from the 1980s onwards, both at state and societal levels, the local had been put on par, if not above, the global/Western. Alongside the Western, the Turkish and the Islamic were celebrated. Turks had learnt to situate themselves in their own past and culture, rejecting to imagine themselves through the derogatory evaluations of the West/Westernised.

Fashion, in the process, was transformed into a combination of fragmentation and identity; it became the perfect foil for a world of fragmented and incommensurate identities and personae, offering a dynamic procession of free-floating signs and symbolic exchanges. The body emerged, once more, at the intersection of hegemony and counter-hegemonic practices, compliance and defiance, authority and subversion, conservative nostalgia and democratic possibilities. The state's concern with bodies was reactivated especially when the official public sphere was in question, for the reason that an embodied politics still locates the nation in an archaic moment, constitutive of the political order it sought to overcome.

The 28 February Measures, dictated by the National Security Council in 1997 to limit the influence of religion on the political and social life of Turkey and bring Islamic activity more tightly under state control, were said to have been triggered when Necmettin Erbakan, the then prime minister and leader of the Islamic Welfare Party, gave a dinner whose participants included sheiks and hojas in religious dress, at the prime minister's official residence.[7] Their presence in the public sphere, with their embodied identities seemed to challenge the body politic of the nation. In the republican imagination their bodies corresponded to the blatant signifiers of a pre-political order coexisting awkwardly with the abstract national membership that had superseded it.

The public sphere had been structured from the onset 'by a logic of abstraction' that provided privilege for supposedly 'unmarked identities' (Warner, 1996, p. 383): 'the civilised', 'the Westernised', 'the normal'. The implicit association of unmarked bodies and the universal subject has a bearing on the constitution of the public sphere. Those who do not measure up to these standards gain admittance to the public sphere only after discarding their concrete embodiments, whether religious, ethnic or local, which have been marked as an unrelenting anachronism, a symbol of the past and of difference that had been incorporated into the nation through citizenship. For example, the candidates who were elected as headmen in Siverek in Sanlıurfa province in the late 1990s were warned by the head of the district election council, not to wear their traditional regional clothes, *şalvar* and *poşu*, and to dress in public in a manner that was befitting the republican regime and the civilised Turkish nation.[8] Embodiment was to emerge as an internal demarcation line not only between the public and the private, but also within the nation.

Civility and urban life have always been associated in the popular imagination. The idea of civility coincides with the creation of the modern public/private distinction (Jervis 1999, p. 41). The public realm contrasts not only with the private sphere, but also with the countryside, designated from ancient Greece onwards (Boyd, 2006, pp. 868–9), as the domain of nature rather than of culture. The discourse of 'civility' and 'civilisation' is still reminiscent of these binary oppositions. Thus in the popular understanding of urbanites, village dwellers, almost inevitably, are less civilised since they are more directly related to the untamed habits and practices that urban civilisation seeks to surmount. They experience social stigmatisation for falling short of norms of how a 'good citizen' should behave, and are regarded as lesser citizens not only by the state but also by 'decent' and 'normal' subjects. They must either assimilate to urbane ways, or remain unseen.

The concern with the civilising process in Turkey gained momentum once more from the 1990s onwards as a result of the rise of the Islamic and Kurdish movements, and especially as Istanbul and other big cities experienced unprecedented levels of migration from the provinces, which not only challenged but also managed to transform the cultural landscape of the city. The bodies of the newcomers inevitably embodied their own cultural and social capital, the acquired knowledge and education, and networks and milieu respectively. It was in this period that the civil rather than the military portrayal of Atatürk, emphasising his civilised manners, habits and lifestyle, gained an unprecedented popularity. In this way, past meanings were reactivated from the early republican tradition that held sway until 1950s. In the opinion of a famous fashion designer, in order to be chic, Turkish men had to shave off their moustaches and take Atatürk as their model (Bali, 2002, p. 182). There were successions of fashion shows especially designed to depict the clothes of Atatürk. Such representations made the contrast between the lives of rural-to-urban migrants and the so-called civilised man more conspicuous. They held a mirror to their faces in the Lacanian sense where the reflection revealed to them that they were the 'Other'.[9]

As far as their visual representations in popular culture are concerned, the bodies of the migrants were constructed in line with Bakhtin's grotesque body: uncontrolled, appetitive, vulgar, dirty and inconvenient, bodies that smell, bleed, laugh, scream, fancy and copulate especially when they are not supposed to (Yumul, 2000, pp. 37–49). Their corporeal disparagement has been best articulated by a columnist who designated the popular beaches and shores of Istanbul as 'The Carnivore Land of Islam', where men swim in their underwear – whom she placed betwixt man and animal – cook meat by the sea and 'ruminate': 'This scene is repeated in every ten meters. At the seashore, our black folk turning their back to the sea, inevitably grill meat on the brazier. It is virtually impossible to see even a single family cooking fish'. In her opinion if they had enjoyed fish and knew how to cook it, they wouldn't have stretched out in their underpants and undershirts, nor scratch themselves, nor ruminate, and belch; neither would they be so stout, have so short legs and long arms, nor would their bodies be covered with black hair (Kırıkkanat, 2005). Not only were their bodies and body techniques taken as fixed indicators of their personality, but their appetite was also targeted. Appetite, it should be noted is different from hunger. Whereas hunger is a biological drive, appetite is associated with taste, and as such is subject to the civilising process (Mennell, 1987; 1985). In the course of the 'civilising of appetite', meat, as a reminder of our animal part, was downgraded in the hierarchy of taste (Fiddes, 1991). In the Turkish case, meat was devalued doubly for it was associated with the kebab, the badge of migrants, especially from the south-east. The above-mentioned column was written following the re-opening of the Caddebostan Beach, one of the popular beaches of Istanbul in the 1950s. The municipality forbade swimming in underclothes albeit to no avail. This was followed by a beach rally organised by the satirical magazine *Leman*, under the banner 'Hold Onto your Underwear'.[10]

It was again in the 1990s that journalists coined two different terms to refer to so-called civilised and uncivilised bodies: 'White' and 'Black Turks', respectively. The racist connotations of these terms are, of course, apparent. These invented categories were represented as the polar opposites of each other. Their bodies were portrayed in terms of a biology of incommensurability. Blackness, here, was not a simple metaphorical allusion to racial categories, but referred to real physicality. A well-known member of Istanbul high society, for example, expressed her views about 'Black Turks' in the following way:

> My humble opinion is that we should provide those of our citizens, one half of whose face is covered with black hair and the other with black moustache, with job opportunities in those regions where they were born and grew up. If our businessmen from the eastern, south eastern and Black Sea regions, in spite of investing in Istanbul and its surroundings, turned towards their own hometowns, neither the moustached would conquer Istanbul ... nor would the 'black-moustached' image remain.
>
> (Kozanoğlu, 1995, p. 14)

Those who adopted the mission of re-civilising Turkish men launched a 'getting rid of moustaches campaign'. This campaign, by freeing the Turkish man from his 'black-moustached' Middle Eastern image, was going to bring him closer to the construct of the 'civilised body'.

What the fez signified for Atatürk came to be signified by the moustache in the 1990s. One columnist resented the stereotypical visual representation of the Turks in the European media always with black moustache in the following way: 'Even if we get rid of our moustache the moustache does not abandon us. It sounds as if the black tassel be it in our heads [referring to the fez] or on our lips, has clung to us like a bur, as if it is our destiny'. (Özkök, 1998). The moustache became the most important obstacle for those who desired to project a modern Turkish image to the West. For this reason, physical appearance gained importance in the eyes of the Westernised elites. The primary aim in this operation of what Rıfat Bali (2002, p. 185) refers to as 'image renovation' was to substitute the black-moustached image of the Turks in Western public opinion with a new one: an image that would not differentiate Turkish men from European men. One journalist urged the then minister of foreign affairs to get rid of his moustache as soon as possible, since in international forums the moustache was associated with the Middle East and as such did not befit the modern image of Turkey (Bali, 2002, p. 182). The new nationalism of the 'White Turks' was an 'aesthetic nationalism' whose codes incorporated narcissism and nurturing which was soon to be mimicked by many, including the ultranationalist Nationalist Action Party. The leadership of the party, in order to embrace the rising nationalism of the 'White Turks' asked from its members and supporters to shave off their moustache, not to wear white socks, use a light fragrance against odour, refrain from eating garlic and onion, smoke less, brush their teeth and shave their face every morning.[11] The party school educated the candidates on politesse and decorum before the 1999 general elections.[12] Although the relinquishment of the bodily symbols of party allegiance – such as long moustache, head-butting as a way of saluting each other – alienated many people within the party and among its supporters, many commentators took these as real signs of change in the militant ultranationalist ideology of the party.[13]

The body once more emerged as a site for political struggle, as the outward expression of internally upheld republican virtue when Onur Öymen, the deputy leader of the Republican People's Party, the stronghold of Kemalism, after referring to the balls organised by Mustafa Kemal, claimed that it was inconceivable for Tayyip Erdoğan, the Prime Minister and the leader of the Islamic Justice and Development Party, to host a ball and invite any woman attending, to dance.[14] Erdoğan responded by inviting Öymen to play *horon* (a folk dance of the eastern Black Sea region performed by males) with him.[15] Erdoğan's body is taken as a text to decipher social change in the periphery. Although he dresses in Western fashion, in defiance of the imperative to express a fixed inner nature through clothing, he refrains from wearing tuxedo or performing Western dances. His body extends far beyond the faculty of the codified maps of difference to confine it. One columnist who joined the debate after referring to Louis de Cahusac, who in the eighteenth century had drawn attention to the relation between modernity and dance along with the performing arts, declared the person who could perform tango and waltz could easily 'play folklore', whereas the vice versa was not likely (Kırıkkanat, 2005). That Bülent Ecevit as a prime minister never danced had not become a point of concern, since in the 1970s he had emerged as the populist leader of the working classes, at a time when bourgeois bodies and practices in the intellectual circles had been associated with capitalism and therefore denigrated. It was perhaps after the introduction of the concept of the public sphere to the Turkish reading public that Turkish intellectuals realised the significance, for democratic theory, of the bourgeois public sphere and its corollary bodily practices that the 'White Turks' had appropriated in different forms and degrees. Urban, educated upper and middle class individuals, who have adopted Western lifestyles and manners, primarily represent 'White Turkishness'. In the achievement of 'White Turk' status, physical characteristics play an important role. In this context, attractiveness, youth, fair complexion and a clean-shaven face gain importance. Such physical features are associated with refinement and elegance. On the other hand, a dark complexion suggestive of Eastern origins, and consequently of provinciality and unrestrained drives, is associated with bestiality. Let me note in passing that blondness and fair complexion have always been privileged by the Westernised urban elites. In Recaizade

Mahmut Ekrem's nineteenth century novel *Araba Sevdası* [Carriage Love], the protagonist Bihruz Bey is pre-disposed to fall for a blonde. When he sees a woman with blonde hair he is struck by her and this 'blonde woman becomes the object of his fantasies and is transformed into an image' (Büker, 2002, p. 151).

The particular construction of civilised bodies in the Turkish modernisation/Westernisation project, by creating certain privileged binary oppositions between the modern and the traditional, the urban and the rural, the 'civilised' and the 'uncivilised', tried to reject and suppress any traces of the Orient. To modernise, Kemalists reasoned they had to Westernise. Ironically 'the very nature of Westernisation meant Orientalisation' (Sayyid, 1994, p. 270), for the West had constructed its identity in its opposition to the Orient. That is, the 'Other' in opposition to which identity is constructed had to be created from within the very nation that the Kemalist project of Westernisation attempted to modernise/civilise. Thus to be Western involved more than the rejection of the Oriental; the rejection 'involved a certain metaphorical surplus: the rejection of the impossibility of being the other'; it entailed the (re)production of the Oriental subject (Sayyid, 1994, p. 270). This led to a situation, which Bauman calls the 'internalisation of ambivalence' (Bauman, 1991, p. 128). It was perhaps for this reason that many Westernised Turks felt proud when Westerners told them that they did not resemble Turks. For them, it seemed like a promotion from the inferiority and backwardness of their own communally confined peculiarity, to adherence to superior, progressive and universal human standards. A sense of revulsion and embarrassment in their co-nationals was the price of joining the good society. Today, urban Turks from Western Turkey often express resentment towards their 'backward' and 'embarrassing' compatriots, who they say give all the Turks, even the well-integrated, modern ones, an ill repute. As Frantz Fanon puts it 'every people in whose soul an inferiority complex has been created ... finds itself face to face with the language of the civilising nation' (Fanon, 1967, p. 18).

Despite these ideal–typical contrasting representations of White and Black Turks, the reality has always been more complex. Although the aim of the Kemalist elites was to create an imaginary embodied position of a pure Westernised subject, this position however paved the way for a myriad of impending subject positions to be articulated around it. These corresponded to more hybridised subjectivities that were able to articulate, in diverse embodiments, Eastern and Western elements. Most wedding parties of the so-called White Turks, for example, start with a tango and end with belly dancing or a regional folk dance. Although the body had emerged as the coordinating conjunction of the real, imaginary and symbolic, through the course of history their stuffing was made and re-made through adjustment, ambiguity and compromise, in a way that was not foreseen by the Kemalist elite. In a flexible appropriation of an infinite and unpredictable range of items of fashion and bodily performances, these hybridised subjectivities, who have learnt to construct themselves from the reflections they see in the hall of mirrors in which they find themselves, have shown a surprising ability to transform the Kemalist project. Orhan Gencebay, the 'King of Arabesk', for instance, has started to perform in clothes identical to those used by Atatürk. Although the encounter between the abstract and the concrete, or the universal and the particular is usually ignored, 'the subject', according to Slavoj Žižek, 'exists only within this "failed encounter" between the Universal and the Particular – it is ultimately nothing but a name for their constitutive discord' (Žižek, 1991, p. 46).

As new social actors, such as Islamists, appropriate the public sphere, we see the proliferation of new forms of publicity. Their previously excluded bodies now refract elements from Eastern and Western cultures through a process of exchange, appropriation, imitation and incorporation. This body conveys a set of seditious messages. This proliferation, however, should not be read as a trouble-free and an undemanding enhancement of the public sphere. Binary oppositions, classifications and categorisations are rooted in the psychic landscape of modernist wisdom. The emerging hybridised subjectivities of the new social actors, as the embodiment of ambivalence, are allied to the abject – the indeterminate, fluid borderline area between certainties, between self and other – an in-between, confusing, composite area associated with the relativity of cultural absolutes, with a deplorable, alarming difference, the difference of rival possibilities and lifestyles and thus the grounds for anxiety and aversion (Kristeva, 1982). The abject, which lies beyond the range of the acceptable, the possible, the imaginable, is a realm outside culture and in the eyes of its critics, by disrespecting orders, ranks and conventions, threatens to reduce culture (that is western/'civilised' embodiments and lifestyles, and the republican political order with its emphasis on secularism and unity) to chaos. It was the same apprehension that was expressed by a columnist when he portrayed the voters of the Justice and Development Party as what he deemed the uneducated masses who 'never read', 'never think' as 'the man who scratches his belly', and contrasted them with the 'bright' (read 'enlightened') faces of Turkey who took to the streets against the danger of political Islam before the 2007 presidential elections (Coşkun, 2007a; 2007b). Evocative of Bakhtin's grotesque body, where the 'lower stratum' conspires against the codes of order and rationality issued by its 'head', (Hitchcock, 1998 p. 85) his representation of 'the man who scratches his belly' who, in his words, 'will never scratch his head' is reminiscent of the Cartesian mind/body split and the deep-seated predisposition since the early modern period to imagine human beings as principally cognitive or rational subjects, reducing the body to 'a machine, a mere physiochemical container for the rational *cogito*' (Gardiner, 1998, p. 140).

Following the Western example (Huyssen, 1986, p. 47), the centre from the beginning had been constructed as representing the rational, the logical, that is the masculine. The periphery, the masses on the other hand, represented the Eastern, the irrational, the emotional, that is the feminine. As the infiltration of the periphery into the centre have reached unprecedented levels and as the centre has lost its apparent unity and homogeneity, the principle challenge confronting state elites will be to re-conceptualise the embodied citizen for the current stage of the civilising process.

Notes

1. In this dance, traditionally performed by males, the dancers go around, arms raised, kneeling on one knee at regular intervals.
2. For a psychoanalytic treatment of body, see Pile (1996).
3. For the 'controlled over body' versus 'controlled by body' demarcation line in connection to citizenship, see Bacchi and Beasley (2002).
4. Squatter houses, or *gecekondus* – literally placed (built) overnight – were constructed from mid-1940s onwards at the outskirts of cities by rural-to-urban without proper permissions, usually by illegally occupying vacant land. In time, shantytowns have been incorporated into the very fabric of big cities and became an inseparable part of metropolises.
5. For an excellent comparison of the arabesk lyrics of the 1990s with the lyrics of the 1970s, see Gürbilek (1999).
6. By 'subaltern counterpublics' Fraser means 'parallel discursive arenas where members of subordinated social groups invent and circulate counter-discourses to formulate oppositional interpretations of their identities and needs' where public discourse has been understood purely as a 'single, comprehensive, overarching public'. Fraser (1996, pp. 122–3).
7. See *Sabah* (2006) (Turkish daily), 12 February.
8. See *Hürriyet* (1999) (Turkish daily), 9 May.
9. The image reflected in the mirror was similar to those that Mustafa Kemal, Mahmut II and Selim III had seen in their comparison of Western and Eastern embodiments.
10. See, http://www.kenthaber.com /Arsiv/Haberler/2005/Ağustos/28/Haber_81359.aspx.
11. See *Hürriyet* (2001) 13 April.
12. See *Sabah* (2002) 8 April.
13. See for example, Özkök (2000).
14. See *Vatan* (2005), 10 October.
15. *Milliyet* (2005), 20 October.

Bibliography

G. Akçura (2002) *Ivır Zıvır Tarihi III: Uzun Metin Sevenlerden Misiniz?* (İstanbul: Om Yayınevi).

E. Anderson (1990) *Streetwise: Race, Class and Change in an Urban Community* (Chicago: University of Chicago Press).

K. Atatürk (1950–2) *Nutuk*, vol. I (Ankara: MEB).

C. L. Bacchi and C. Beasley (2002) 'Citizen Bodies: Is Embodied Citizenship a Contradiction in Terms', *Critical Social Policy*, vol. 22, no. 2, pp. 324–52.

R. Bali (2002) *Tarz-I Hayat'tan Life Style'a* (İstanbul: İletişim).

Z. Bauman (1991) *Modernity and Ambivalence* (Oxford: Polity Press).

N. Berkes (1964) *The Development of Secularism in Turkey* (Montreal: McGill University Press).

L. G. Berlant (1993) 'National Brands/National Body: Imitation of Life', in B. Robbins (ed.) *The Phantom Public Sphere* (Minneapolis: University of Minnesota Press).

H. Blumer (1968) 'Fashion', in *International Encyclopedia of the Social Sciences* (New York: Macmillan).

R. Boyd (2006) 'The Value of Civility', *Urban Studies*, vol. 43, no. 5/6, pp. 863–78.

S. Büker (2002) 'The Film does not End with an Ecstatic Kiss', in D. Kandiyoti and A. Saktanber (eds) *Fragments of Culture: The Everyday of Modern Turkey* (London: I. B. Taurus & Co Publishers).

B. Coşkun (2007a) 'Göbeğini Kaşıyan Adam', *Hürrriyet*, 3 May.

—— (2007b) 'Göbeğini Kaşıyan Adam Kafasını Kaşıdığında', *Hürriyet*, 3 October.

J. Craik (1993) *The Faces of Fashion: Cultural Studies in Fashion* (London: Routledge).

F. Davis (1989) 'Of Maids' Uniforms and Blue Jeans: The Drama of Status Ambivalences in Clothing and Fashion', *Qualitative Sociology*, vol. 12, no. 4, pp. 337–8.

N. Elias (1994) *The Civilising Process: The History of Manners and State Formation and Civilisation* [trans. E. Jephcott] (Oxford: Blackwell).

F. Fanon (1967) *Black Skin, White Masks* (New York: Grove Press).

M. Featherstone (1995) *Undoing Culture: Globalization, Postmodernism and Identity* (London: Sage Publications).

N. Fiddes (1991) *Meat: A Natural Symbol* (London: Routledge).

P. Filmer (1999) 'Embodiment and Civility in Early Modernity: Aspects of Relations between Dance, the Body and Sociocultural Change', *Body & Society*, vol. 5, no. 1, pp. 1–16.

N. Fraser (1996) 'Rethinking the Public Sphere: A Contribution to the Critique of Actually Existing Democracy', in C. Calhoun (ed.) *Habermas and the Public Sphere* (Cambridge, MA: MIT Press).

M. Franko (1986) *The Dancing Body in Renaissance Choreography: 1416–1589* (Birmingham, Ala: Summa Publications).

M. Gardiner (1998) 'The Incomparable Monster of Solipsism: Bakhtin and Marleau-Ponty', in M. Mayerfeld Bell and M. Gardiner (eds) *Bakhtin and the Human Sciences* (London: Sage).

Z. Gökalp (1976) *Türk Medeniyeti Tarihi* (Ankara: Kültür Bakanlığı Yayınları).

N. Göle (1997) 'The Quest for the Islamic Self within the Context of Modernity', in S. Bozdoğan and R. Kasaba (eds) *Rethinking Modernity and National Identity in Turkey* (Seattle and London: University of Washington Press).

N. Gürbilek (1999) 'Ben de İsterem', *Defter*, vol. 37(Summer), pp. 23–32.

P. Hitchcock (1998) 'The Grotesque of the Body Electric', in Michael Mayerfeld Bell and Michael Gardiner (eds) *Bakhtin and the Human Sciences* (London: Sage).

A. Husseyn (1986) *After the Great Divide: Modernism, Mass Culture, Postmodernism* (Bloomington: Indiana University Press).

E. Işın (1995) *İstanbul'da Gündelik Hayat* (İstanbul: İletişim).

J. Jervis (1999) *Transgressing the Modern* (Oxford: Blackwell).

H. B. Kahraman (2004) *Tarih Kültürü affetmez: Türkiye'de 1990 'lar ve kültürel dönüsüm sorunsalları* (İstanbul: Agora Kitapları).

D. Kandiyoti (1997) 'Gendering the Modern: On Missing Dimensions in the Study of Turkish Modernity', in S. Bozdoğan and R. Kasaba (eds) *Rethinking Modernity and National Identity in Turkey* (Seattle and London: University of Washington Press).

M. G. Kırıkkanat (2005) 'Oni Yesin Ninesi ha bu Diyar Valsi', *Vatan*, 14 October.

M. G. Kırıkkanat (2005) 'Halkımız Eğleniyor', *Radikal* (Turkish daily), 27 July.

P. Kinross (1995) *Atatürk: The Rebirth of a Nation* (London: Phoenix).

C. Kozanoğlu (1995) *Pop Çağı Ateşi* (İstanbul: İletişim).

J. Kristeva (1982) *Powers of Horror: An Essay on Abjection* (New York: Columbia University Press).

E. Kuzmics (1987) 'Civilisation, State and Bourgeois Society: The Theoretical Contribution of Norbert Elias', *Theory, Culture & Society*, vol. 4, no. 2/3, pp. 515–31.

E. Laclau (1994) 'Why do Empty Signifiers Matter to Politics?', in J. Weeks (ed.) *The Lesser Evil and the Greater Good: The Theory and Politics of Social Diversity* (London: Rivers Oram Press).

B. Lewis (1967) *The Emergence of Modern Turkey*, 2nd edn (London: Oxford University Press).

E. Mahir (2005) 'Etiquette Rules in the Early Republican period', *Journal of Historical Studies*, vol. 3, pp. 15–32.

A. Mango (1999) *Atatürk* (London: John Murray).

S. Mennell (1987) 'On the Civilising of Appetite', *Theory, Culture and Society*, vol. 4, no. 2–3, pp. 373–403.

S. Mennell (1985) *All Manners of Food: Eating and Taste in England and France from the Middle-Ages to the Present* (Oxford: Basil Blackwell).

İ. Orga (1988) *Portrait of a Turkish Family* (London: Eland).

M. Özbek (1997) 'Arabesk Culture: A Case of Modernisation and Popular Identity', in S. Bozdoğan and R. Kasaba (eds) *Rethinking Modernity and National Identity in Turkey* (Seattle and London: University of Washington Press).

E. Özkök (2000) 'Merkez bu kadar Partiyi Kaldırır mı?', *Hürriyet*, 9 November.

E. Özkök (1998) Dizney Köyünde Bıyıklı bir Cim Bom', *Hürriyet*, 12 July.

A. Öztürkmen (2002) 'I Dance Folklore', in D. Kandiyoti and A. Saktanber (eds) *Fragments of Culture: The Everyday of Modern Turkey* (London: I. B. Taurus).

C. E. Padwick (1958) *Call to İstanbul* (London: Longmans, Green).

S. Pile (1996) *The Body and the City: Psychoanalysis, Space and Subjectivity* (London: Routledge).

B. Sayyid (1994) 'Sign O' Times: Kaffirs and Infidels Fighting the Ninth Crusade', in E. Laclau (ed.) *The Making of Political Identities* (London: Verso).

T. Schiel (2005) 'Modernity, Ambivalence and the Gardening State', *Thesis Eleven*, vol. 83 (November), pp. 78–89.

V. J. Seidler (1994) *Unreasonable Men: Masculinity and Social Theory* (London: Routledge).

G. Seufert and P. Weyland (1984) 'National Events and the Struggle for the Fixing of Meaning: A Comparison of the Symbolic Dimensions of the Funeral Services for Atatürk and Özal', *New Perspectives on Turkey*, vol. 11 (Fall), pp. 71–98.

O. Tekelioğlu (2004) 'Çevre Modernleşmeleri Tarihi ve Popüler Kültür', *Varlık*, vol. 71 (June), pp. 3–7.

O. Tekelioğlu (2001) 'The Rise of Spontaneous Synthesis: The Historical Background of Turkish Popular Music', *Middle Eastern Studies*, vol. 32, no. 1, pp. 194–215.

B. S. Turner (2005) 'Introduction – Bodily Performance: On Aura and Reproducibility', *Body & Society*, vol. 11, no. 1, pp. 1–17.

V. D. Volkan and N. Itzkowitz (1984) *The Immortal Atatürk: A Psychobiography* (Chicago: The University of Chicago Press).

M. Warner (1996) 'The Mass Public and the Mass Subject', in C. Calhoun (ed.) *Habermas and the Public Sphere* (Cambridge MA: MIT Press).

A. Yumul (2000) 'Bitmemiş bir Proje Olarak Beden', *Toplum ve Bilim*, vol. 84 (Spring), pp. 37–49.

A. Yumul (1999) 'Scenes of Masculinity from Turkey', *Zeitscrift für Türkeistudien*, vol. 1, pp. 107–17.

W. Zelinsky (2004) 'Globalization Reconsidered: The Historical Geography of Modern Western Attire', *Journal of Cultural Geography*, vol. 22, no. 1, pp. 83–134.

S. Žižek (1991) *For They Know Not What They Do: Enjoyment as a Political Factor* (London: Verso).

19

Two Faces of the Press in Turkey: The Role of the Media in Turkey's Modernisation and Democracy

Şahin Alpay

Turkey's democracy is well known for its many shortcomings. Substantial restrictions on basic rights and freedoms, and serious human rights violations have been the rule rather than exception since the introduction of multiparty politics in 1946. At the turn of the twenty-first century, however, Turkey also has an impressive record of at least half a century of regularly held free elections and parliamentary rule. The democratic regime has survived at least four military interventions of different kinds since 1960, violent clashes between ultra rightist and leftist groups that approached the level of a civil war in the 1970s, and an armed separatist insurgency lasting most of the 1980s and 1990s. Turkish democracy may still not be fully consolidated, but few would doubt its durability.

The Turkish media may be said to display a similar paradox. The media in Turkey at the turn of the twenty-first century is far from being a respected and trusted institution. The part it has played in military interventions, its openness to manipulation by state authorities and corporate interests, and its involvement in corruption that brought the country to the brink of financial bankruptcy have contributed to its rather dismal standing in public opinion. And yet the media in Turkey is impressively diverse and vibrant, and functions as the main voice of a civil society that is in general poorly organised and weak. It is the main means of political communication, a major agent of political socialisation, and has assumed an increasingly important role in the political process. Turkey may be said to be a 'media democracy' or 'mediacracy', a polity in which the media plays a decisive role in the shaping of public opinion and in the political decision making process.

This paper will provide an historical overview of the role the media has played in Turkey's modernisation and democratisation in the twentieth century. It will attempt to provide an account of what may be called the 'two faces' of the media in Turkey at the turn of the twenty-first century, that is, its serious failings and problems on the one hand, and the positive role it plays in the democratic process on the other. The analysis presented below is based on available research in the field, as well as participant observation by the author, who has worked in the Turkish press as an editor and columnist for over 20 years.

Historical overview

The origins of the press in Turkey coincide with the initial efforts to modernise the Ottoman state. The first printing presses in the Ottoman Empire were set up by Jewish refugees from Spain in Istanbul and Salonica at the end of the fifteenth century, not much later than the first printing shop set up by Johanness Gutenberg in Germany in 1450. An Armenian printing shop was established in Istanbul in the middle of the sixteenth century, and a Greek one in the early seventeenth century. However, the regime prohibited printing in Turkish or Arabic until as late as the eighteenth century. The imperial edict allowing the establishment of a Turkish printing house was first issued in 1727, but the house only published 17 books before it was closed down in 1742. The uninterrupted development of printing in the Ottoman Empire did not begin until after 1784 (Lewis, 1961, pp. 50–1).

That year, the Constantinople correspondent of the prestigious *Gazette de Leyde* wrote that whereas in most European monarchies 'there is at least a public journal which keeps the nation informed about current events from the government point of view', there was no such publication in the Ottoman Empire (cited in Keane, p. 22). A 'public journal' or official bulletin was first established in Istanbul in 1831. *Moniteur Ottoman* in French and its Ottoman-language equivalent *Takvim – i Vekai* (Calendar of Events) were founded as part of the *Tanzimat* reforms initiated by Sultan Mahmut II in order to modernise and strengthen the state (Zürcher, 1993, p. 45). The first privately owned newspaper in Ottoman Turkish, *Ceride – i Havadis* (Chronicle of Events), was established in 1840 by an Englishman called Churchill. Like the *Takvim – i Vekai*, it largely covered official news, but gave more space to international events.

The birth of a civil society based Ottoman press can be traced back to the 1860 foundation of the journal *Tercüman – ı Ahval* (Interpreter of Conditions), edited by Ibrahim Sinasi, a modernist intellectual attached to liberal ideas. *Tercüman – ı Ahval* was the first of the newspapers published by the Young Ottomans, a group of intellectuals led by Namik Kemal who tried to merge liberal European ideas and Islamic tradition, and whose opposition to authoritarian government policies and demand for representative and constitutional rule led to the introduction of the Ottoman Constitution in 1876 (Zürcher, pp. 70–4). It can be said that the Young Ottoman press, despite its limited reach, led the way to the creation of 'public opinion' in the Ottoman Empire.

The Constitution remained in force little over a year before Sultan Abdulhamit II established absolutist rule, which was to last for 30 years. The press, which became increasingly professionalised and reached a much larger public, faced severe censorship that suppressed discussion of political issues, especially after 1888 (Zürcher, 1993, pp. 82–3). According to Bernard

Lewis, 'even the emasculated and ineffectual newspapers of the Hamidian era, however, made some contribution to the modernisaiton of Turkey, if only by increasing more Turks to the European habit of reading the news every day' (Lewis, 1961, p. 188).

Opposition to Hamidian autocracy organised around the Committee of Union and Progress (CUP), which in 1895 began to publish in Paris the newspaper *Meşveret* (Consultation) in both Ottoman and French. The Young Turk press was highly instrumental in spreading the opposition movement that succeeded in forcing the sultan to restore the Constitution in July 1908. The Young Turk Revolution heralded a period of unprecedented freedom of thought, expression, press and association in the empire. 'In the few years of freedom that followed the ending of Abdulhamid's autocracy, there was an opportunity for discussion and experiment such as the country had never known before ... And even though the discussions ended in silence and the experiments in dictatorship, new hopes and new appetites had been created which could not be indefinitely denied' (Lewis, 1961, p. 213).

This period of 'liberty' ('Hurriyet') came to an end in January 1913 when the CUP seized power through a *coup d'etat*. The press was the main forum for intellectual debate in the period that culminated in the founding of the Turkish Republic in 1923, following the collapse of the Ottoman Empire at the end of the First World War, and the victory of the independence war led by Kemalist nationalists. Freedom of the press, however, soon fell victim to the Law on Maintenance of Order, proclaimed following the Kurdish rebellion two years after the founding of the Republic. This law, which empowered the government to prohibit any organisation or publication it deemed necessary, effectively started the era of authoritarian single-party rule by the Kemalist Republican People's Party (CHP) led by Mustafa Kemal Atatürk. All oppositional organisations, including the Progressive Republican Party founded in 1924 by some former leaders of the independence movement who were critical of the Kemalist leadership's radical, centralist and authoritarian tendencies, were closed down. Similarly, all oppositional newspapers and periodicals were banned and their writers imprisoned, exiled or otherwise silenced. The remaining press was mobilised to support the Kemalist regime and its modernising reforms.

Cumhuriyet (the oldest newspaper in Turkey and still active today), which was established in Istanbul in May 1924 by Yunus Nadi, a close associate of Mustafa Kemal, and *Ulus*, which began publishing in Ankara in 1930 as the semi-official organ of the government party, assumed the role of mouthpiece of the Kemalist regime. The entire press was kept under strict government control throughout the period of single-party rule, which lasted until the end of the Second World War, and during the transition to multi-party politics in the mid 1940s.

While Turkey followed a policy of non-alignment during the Second World War, sympathies for the Axis and Allied powers were reflected in the

Turkish press. Newspapers like *Tan*, *Vatan* and *Akşam* supported the Allied powers, while others like Cumhuriyet, by then edited by Yunus Nadi's son Nadir Nadi, sided with the Axis powers. Allegations have also been leveled against the publishers of Cumhuriyet, for receiving financial support from Nazi Germany in the early 1940s.

By the end of the Second World War, the government of İsmet İnönü, who assumed the leadership of the CHP upon Atatürk's death in 1938, had become greatly unpopular. Internal and external pressures led İnönü to start a process of democratisation. In 1946 political parties were allowed to organise and the press law was liberalised to allow for criticism of the government. The introduction of multi-party politics resulted in a landslide victory for the main opposition, the Democratic Party led by Adnan Menderes. Soon after coming to power the DP further liberalised the press. The new law enacted in 1950 lifted licensing requirements for publications and introduced for the first time social security measures for press employees. Liberal press policies were, however, shortlived and the government adopted measures for increased political control of the press as early as 1953. In 1957, the import of newsprint was put under state monopoly and arbitrary allocation of official advertisements and announcements was used as a carrot-and-stick policy towards the press (Gevgilili, 1983, pp. 2002–20).

Despite these restrictions on press freedom, the 1950s witnessed significant developments in the press. Mass newspapers employing modern printing technologies and popular styles like *Hürriyet, Yeni Sabah*, and *Milliyet* attained unprecedented levels of circulation with over 100,000 copies, and reached ever broader sections of society. The political weekly *Akis*, edited by Metin Toker (son-in-law of the CHP leader İsmet İnönü) which was the main publicist of opposition to the DP policies, also managed to sell over 100,000 copies per week, becoming the political weekly with the largest circulation ever in the history of the Turkish press.

The DP's increasingly repressive policies towards the opposition and the press were among the factors that paved the way for the military intervention of 27 May 1960. The military junta which seized power moved to ease restrictions on press freedom, and even introduced broad social rights for press employees, facilitating the rise of a professional class of journalists. The adoption of Turkey's most liberal constitution in 1961 broadened the scope of freedom of expression and the press on an unprecedented scale. Socialists were allowed to organise in the Turkish Labour Party, and the press was able to reflect nearly the entire political spectrum, from the far right to the far left. The constitution also provided for the autonomy of the state radio and television institution (Türkiye Radyo Televizyon Kurumu, TRT). However, laws introduced during the single-party period prohibiting propaganda for communism, ethnic separatism and against the secular nature of the regime remained strictly in force.

By the 1960s, mass circulation newspapers reached even the remotest areas of the country and *Hürriyet* became the first newspaper to achieve a circulation of more than a million copies. The 1960s also witnessed the rise of popular newspapers called 'boyalı basın/painted press' or 'bulvar basın/ boulevard press', which made extensive use of colour, visual material and pithy, tabloid coverage.

Periodicals continued to be the main forum for political debate during the 1960s and 1970s. The political weeklies *Yön* (Direction), published between 1961–67, and later *Devrim (Revolution)*, published between 1969–71, both of which were edited by journalist and economist Doğan Avcıoğlu, were clearly the most influential publications among the Turkish intelligentsia of the 1960s and made a deep impact on Turkey's domestic politics.

If *Yön* had served as the instrument for the development of a platform for the 'revolution for national liberation' Avcıoğlu and his group were seeking, *Devrim* became the instrument which implicitly called for a revolutionary takeover by the 'progressive' forces in the military. A military junta that conspired to seize power on 9 March 1971 and establish a Ba'ath-like regime failed, however, and the intervention by the top military command on 12 March 1971 took quite a different course, leading to the arrests of Avcıoğlu and some of his cclosest collaborators, including prominent columnists like İlhan Selçuk of *Cumhuriyet* and İlhami Soysal of *Milliyet*, alongside a number of military officers. The members of the 'leftist junta' were held in custody for several months by the military authorities, before being acquitted by a military court in 1973, possibly due to fears that a complete disclosure of the conspiracy could implicate certain members of the high command and destabilise the entire armed forces. The story of *Devrim* and its relationship with the 'leftist junta' is best told by Hasan Cemal, one of the two managing editors of the journal and currently a senior columnist for *Milliyet* (Cemal, 1999). The military command pushed the elected government out of office by imposing an ultimatum in March 1971, and installed a handpicked government in its place. It then initiated a substantial revision of the Constitution of 1961 which ended the autonomy of the TRT, and re-introduced restrictions on the press.

The most important development concerning the press in the 1970s was the rapid spread of television, which adversely affected not only the circulation of newspapers but also their incomes, by claiming a growing share of advertising revenue. As the newspaper industry began to require larger capital investments, a trend began that saw the concentration of media ownership. Another significant development was the experiment initiated by the chief editor of *Milliyet*, Abdi İpekçi, to transform the paper, which had been founded in the early 1950s into a quality reference journal. The experiment failed however, when Abdi İpekçi (like many other fellow journalists) was shot and killed by ultra rightist gunmen in 1979. The violent clashes between the left and right wing extremists in the latter half of the 1970s paved the way for the seizure of power by the military high command on 12 September 1980.

The military rule that was established in 1980 put a stop to the violence by means of brutal suppression of all dissent, and radically restructured the political system before handing power back to civilians in 1983. The constitution that was adopted by a referendum in November 1982 stipulated that basic rights and freedoms could be suspended or restricted on grounds of national security, national interest and the presence of a danger to the republican order. It stated in its preamble that 'No protection shall be given to thoughts or opinions that run counter to Turkish national interests, the fundamental principle of the existence and indivisibility of the Turkish state and territory, the historical and moral values of Turkishness, or the nationalism, principles, reforms and modernism of Atatürk'. The laws enacted by the military prohibited the publication of statements that 'threaten the internal and external security of the state', 'incite people to violate the law', 'make people unwilling to serve in the military' or 'publicly insult or ridicule the moral personality of the Republic, the Parliament, the Government, ministers of state, the military or security forces or the judiciary', suggest 'that minorities exist in the Turkish republic based on national, religious, confessional, racial or language differences', and 'insult or curses the memory of Atatürk'. These laws were used extensively to prosecute and imprison journalists, intellectuals and politicians in State Security Courts presided over by military judges. The use of the Kurdish language in any context was banned.

Semi-liberal if not illiberal Turkish democracy increasingly assumed the nature of a national security state, dominated behind the scenes by the military, where the protection of the state and its interests took priority over the protection of individual citizens' rights and liberties. The national security state developed in parallel with the struggle against the armed Kurdish separatist uprising led by the PKK (Kurdish Workers Party) between 1984 and 1999. Due to armed clashes between the security forces and the insurgents, many of the southeastern and eastern provinces of the country were subjected to emergency rule (which was to be gradually lifted, finally ending in 2003).

During this period, which witnessed the growth of covert military and policing agencies, the state (especially in the provinces under emergency rule but also in the country as a whole) increasingly resorted to censorship of the press, ranging from prior restraint in the form of warnings, threats and instructions delivered by telephone and the issuing of mandatory guidelines, to post-publication censorship in the form of confiscations, bans and arrests. Journalists were forced to choose between their professional interests and their critical opinions of the security agencies dominated by the military.

The 1980s witnessed the beginnings of a radical restructuring of the Turkish media scene. Prime Minister Turgut Özal, in order to win over the political support of the mainstream media, provided the big media bosses with business interests in banking, insurance, tourism, and marketing, and subsidies in the form of low interest rate credit and tax exemptions, amounting to an estimated sum of three billion dollars (see *The Economist*, 7 April 2001). In this new era, newspapers were no longer owned by families with a sole interest in publishing but by businessmen who had acquired their capital in other sectors and were now racing to acquire media outlets in order to promote their business interests. Businessmen who owned media outlets exchanged political support for favours and privileges (in the form of various subsidies such as inexpensive credit, tax exemptions, cheap state land, public tenders and the sale of privatised public companies and banks, etc.) from the Ankara government.

One of the most remarkable developments in the Turkish press in the 1980s concerned the daily *Cumhuriyet*. Hasan Cemal, appointed editor-in-chief in 1981, attempted to steer the paper away from the domination by the 'old guard' editors and columnists led by İlhan Selçuk, who were attached less to liberal democratic ideals than to a peculiar mix of Kemalism and Marxism. Cemal wanted to reform *Cumhuriyet* into a liberal left reference paper modelled on Western European newspapers. Cemal's efforts led to a substantial increase in the paper's readership throughout the 1980s, but eventually failed. The power struggle that broke out following the death of the paper's publisher Nadir Nadi between the 'old guard' columnists led by Selçuk, the 'new guard' of younger editors and columnists led by Cemal, ended in the former's victory and Cemal's resignation in early 1992 (Cemal, 2005).

The early 1990s witnessed steps towards broadening the scope of freedom of expression and the press. The ban on the Kurdish language was lifted in 1991, although the anti-terror law adopted that year introduced harsh punishments for propaganda 'against the indivisible unity of the state'. The most important step towards liberalisation of the media regime in the 1990s was the lifting of the state monopoly on radio and television that year. Private broadcasting had a profound impact. Television broadcasts started by the TRT in the late 1960s had adversely affected the spread of the habit of reading newspapers and consequently led to the stagnation of the total newspaper circulation at around three million copies in a country with a population of over 60 million. The ending of the state monopoly on broadcast media resulted not only in sharpened competition between newspapers, but also in the integration of print and broadcast media under an increasingly oligopolistic ownership structure (Gür, 1995, pp. 145–8).

The competition for market share between newspapers led to ingenious marketing tactics in the 1990s. Initially lottery ('lotaryacılık') campaigns were utilised, in which television sets, cars and even aeroplanes were rewarded in draws among customers who had sent in coupons. Lotteries were later replaced by giveaway campaigns ('promosyon savaşları') in which items ranging from toothpaste, soap, etc. to full sets of encyclopaedias were handed out to customers in return for coupons collected (Akar, 1995, pp. 140–1). These marketing tactics managed to increase the total newspaper circulation to over six million in the mid-1990s but hardly helped increase newspaper readership, which was estimated to be remain at around three million (Koloğlu, 1995, pp. 134–40).

By the 1990s, two media conglomerates, Doğan Holding and Medya Holding, both of which had grown huge on government subsidies, dominated the sector. Aydın Doğan, the owner of the Doğan Group, controlled nine newspapers (including five major dailies, *Posta, Hürriyet, Fanatik, Milliyet and Radikal*), 31 magazines, two major TV stations (Kanal D and CNN – Turk), three radio stations, the major newspaper distribution company, alongside a bank and companies in energy, fuel distribution, tourism, publishing, internet and other sectors. Dinç Bilgin, the owner of the Medya (or Sabah) Group owned several dailies, including *Hürriyet's* main competitor, *Sabah*, the ATV channel, several magazines and Etibank, a medium-sized bank which was purchased from the state in the context of a privatisation campaign. Competition between the two main groups found its reflection in the rivalry between the two main parties on the centre-right. The Doğan Group developed a close relationship with the Motherland Party led by Mesut Yılmaz, while the Sabah Group courted the True Path Party chaired by Tansu Çiller. The two groups periodically engaged in 'media wars' to discredit each other or made cartel agreements to promote their common interests against governments and employees.

Media barons in Turkey have a record of being highly supportive of the military authorities. In the 1980s, the relationship between the military and the media was described by the former publisher of *Hürriyet*, Mr. Erol Simavi, in the following terms: 'In most democracies there are three powers: the legislative, the executive and the judiciary. But in Turkey there are only two; the military and the press. The press calls for a military intervention, and the military intervenes' (Barutçu, 2004). The mainstream press staunchly backed the military interventions of 1960, 1971 and 1980. The two big media groups were the main promoters of the military's campaign to force the resignation of the coalition government composed of the Islamist Welfare and centre-right True Path parties in 1997.

The military authorities did not only exert influence over the editorial policy of newspapers through behind-the-scenes pressures on publishers, but resorted to disinformation campaigns to discredit oppositional journalists. When Nazlı Ilıcak, a member of parliament from the Islamic-oriented Virtue Party and a prominent columnist, disclosed in 2000 such a campaign, the army made an unusual admission. It admitted that in 1998 the army intelligence division had spread false information about leading journalists, including Mehmet Ali Birand and Çengiz Çandar, accusing them of being on the outlawed PKK's payroll. Some of the journalists lost their jobs and others were instructed by the media bosses 'not to antagonise the military'.

When Cengiz Çandar wrote a column asking the military officers who were responsible for the smear campaign to be punished, Sabah, the newspaper he worked for, refused to publish it, alleging in print that Çandar's column violated the law by insulting the military. A patronage relationship developed beginning in the 1980s between increasingly powerful media owners and the political establishment, in what has been called the 'vicious triangle of collaboration between media, politicians and business'. This relationship was one of the main sources of the rampant corruption that was partly responsible for the financial crisis that broke out in February 2001, when the Turkish Lira slipped by more than 80 per cent in value against the dollar and tens of thousands of employees including over 3,000 media sector workers lost their jobs (Sönmez, 2003). In April 2001 Dinç Bilgin, the owner of the Sabah Group, was arrested on charges of siphoning off millions of dollars from Etibank, and all of his holdings were eventually seized by the authorities. Sabah Group's media holdings were leased by the state to a company owned by Turgay Ciner, a rising media baron with stakes in various industrial and financial investments, who was eventually to take over the ownership of the Sabah Group. Seventeen television stations, ten newspapers and six periodicals belonging to bankrupt media owners were seized by the authorities, giving rise to a peculiar phenomenon of state-owned and controlled private commercial media. These media outlets were eventually auctioned to private companies, resulting in an even greater concentration of media ownership in two large groups.

The nature of the relationship in the late 1990s between media control on the one hand and commercial and political power on the other is perhaps best demonstrated by the case of a businessman named Korkmaz Yiğit. Mr Yiğit, after winning the public tender for the privatisation of the state owned Turkish Trade Bank (Türk Ticaret Bankası) in 1998, moved to purchase two national dailies (one from each of the two big media groups, *Milliyet* and *Yeni Yüzyıl*) and two television stations. Soon after being arrested on charges of having links to organised crime, he stated that he had been encouraged to buy the media outlets by Motherland Party ministers, anxious to have a media group that would loyally support them. The scandal led to the resignation of the government led by Prime Minister Mesut Yılmaz in 1998. Mr Yılmaz was tried by the Constitutional Court on corruption charges, and eventually acquitted due to a statute of limitation before the case came to trial.

What may be said to be the 'classical' example of how newspaper editors were obliged 'to pursue the business affairs' of media owners is the case of *Hürriyet* editor-in-chief Mr Ertuğrul Özkök. His story is best told by Andrew Finkel, a foreign journalist who has worked for the media in Turkey for many years:

A telling example of the press' wavering integrity before financial inducement is a well documented incident where an editor – in – chief was revealed to have made contacts with a state minister to help secure industrial incentives for a packaging company that owned his newspaper. He first objected that the evidence against him was the result of an illegal wire trap, despite the fact that his own newspaper had itself recently tried to expose misdeeds through phone taps ... The editor's second argument was even more outrageous and worth quoting at length: 'I admit the conversations were mine. I said nothing to give offence or to cause me to feel ashamed. As well as being the editor-in-chief of *Hürriyet*, I am a president of the executive board. At the same time I am one of the two most senior executive directors of the Doğan Publications Holding Company. Therefore as a Director I have an obligation to pursue the business affairs of the group...'. The notion that an editor-in-chief can pursue both editorial independence and the financial interests of his employers is, to say the least, inconsistent with most understanding of the basic ethical requirements of the profession.

(Finkel, 1999, p. 158)

Mr Özkök's admission that financial interests take precedence over protecting editorial independence did not lead to his resignation from any of his posts.

Aydın Doğan, dubbed a 'Turkish Rupert Murdoch' by *The Economist*, is known to have used his close relationship with the government led by Mesut Yılmaz to amend the Law on the RTÜK (Supreme Board of Radio and Television). Amendments adopted in 2002 lifted the restrictions that prohibit media owners with more than 10 per cent share in radio and television stations from competing in government tenders and conducting business on the Stock Exchange, thereby enabling media owners in general and Mr Doğan in particular, to legally and publicly own what they already controlled in violation of the law.

The most flagrant example of the way media barons have used their media outlets to enhance their political interests is Cem Uzan, who founded the hardline nationalist Youth Party (Genç Parti) in 2002, when he mobilised his eight television and radio stations and two newspapers (The Star Group) to support his bid for political power, in full violation of broadcasting regulations barring media owners from using their networks in the service of their political or business interests. The Youth Party failed, however, to pass the 10 per cent threshold to win seats in the parliament and soon after all of Mr Uzan's holdings were seized by public authorities on charges of extensive financial fraud (Purvis, 2004).

While often used by owners to advance their interests, the Turkish media has also helped expose incompetence and corruption in government. The case of the so-called Susurluk affair is perhaps the best example of the power of the media in exposing corruption in government and its limits. One evening in November 1996, the media broke the news that that a senior police chief, a wanted ultra rightist gangster and his former beauty-queen girlfriend had died and a member of parliament and Kurdish tribal leader had suffered injuries in a car crash that took place outside a small town called Susurluk in western Turkey. The identities of the people involved in the crash were most likely leaked by the intelligence services, and the media pursued the incident to unravel Turkey's biggest political scandal to date, involving connections between politicians, security forces, and heroin smugglers. The interior minister Mehmet Ağar resigned after the media linked his name to underworld figures. The 'Susurluk affair' investigation eventually ended up with only a few policemen sentenced to imprisonment but the media succeeded in showing the existence of a 'deep state' or a 'state within the state' in Turkey (*Financial Times*, 4 November 1997).

The paradoxes of the Turkish media are well described by Stephen Kinzer, the Istanbul bureau chief of the New York Times between 1996 and 2000:

> In no other country does so much liberty coexist with such sustained viola-tion of elemental human rights. Of all the countries with bad human rights records, Turkey is the freest. To put it the other way, Turkey has the worst human rights record of any free country. This is its deepest and most trou-bling contradiction ... The irony is that today, public discourse in Turkey is astonishingly free. Politicians attack each other virulently, newspapers cam-paign loudly against abuses of power, and late – night television programs feature intense debates over national issues. For all its failings, the Turkish press is the great platform for its civil society, and there are some among Turkish journalists who would be heroes in any country. But all Turks who speak out in public understand the limits, explicit and implicit.
>
> (Kinzer, 2001, pp. 143–7)

'Two Faces' of the press at the turn of the twenty-first century

The central question of the public debate on the media in Turkey at the turn of the twenty-first century is whether it is part of the problem or part of the solution to the shortcomings of Turkish democracy. Some argue that part of the blame for Turkey's status as a largely illiberal democracy lies with the mainstream media, which has increasingly allied itself with the holders of political, administrative and economic power. Others claim that the media, and the press in particular, is a major force in Turkey's democratisation. Both arguments may be equally valid. The media in Turkey can be said to have 'two faces'. An understanding of the 'two faces' of the media in Turkey requires an examination of the legal, structural and cultural environment within which it operates.

Liberal democratic theory assumes that citizens are sufficiently well informed 'to vote for the wisest, the most honest, the most enlightened of their fellow citizens' (Bobbio, p. 19). Democracy works when it involves the participation of an informed electorate. 'The importance of an informed, knowledgeable electorate dictates that democratic politics must be pursued in the public arena (as distinct from the secrecy characteristic of autocratic regimes). The knowledge and information on the basis of which citizens will make their political choices must circulate freely, and be available to all' (McNair, 1995, p. 18).

In democratic regimes, the media is expected to fulfil the following functions: it has to inform the citizens of fact in the country and the world. In order to do so, it must be free to write and to speak out without being subject to censorship by state authorities or media owners and have access to information in the possession of public authorities. The media also has to educate the citizenry as to the meaning and significance of the facts. This aim requires that journalists be committed to editorial independence and avoid conflict of interest in order to be able to provide their readers with objective assessments of events. The media must investigate and expose acts by the holders of political, administrative, economic or cultural power that violate the rule of law (the 'watchdog' or the Fourth Estate role) and moral principles. The media must also provide a platform for political debate, and serve as a channel for the advocacy of different viewpoints so that the public is able to form an independent opinion on political issues.

Nowhere in the world of democracies is the media perfectly able to fulfil all these functions in accordance with liberal democratic theory. A number of factors render the media in Turkey even less able to fulfil its democratic obligations. The Turkish media at the end of the twentieth century is very diverse and vibrant, with at least 35 national dailies, 16 national and 260 local television stations, and over 2500 national, regional and local radio stations representing a broad spectrum of political leanings and social subcultures. Television and radio broadcasts reach even the remotest parts of the country. Print media, however, has fallen far behind. The total daily circulation of national newspapers remained at around 4.7 million copies in a country with a population of about 70 million people in the year 2000. There were only about 20 dailies with a circulation exceeding 40,000 copies. According to a survey conducted by the State Institute of Statistics in June 2003, only about 7 per cent of potential newspaper readers were actually reading newspapers (Tunç, 2003, p. 3). Aside from a few newspapers published in İzmir and Bursa, there exists no local press worth mentioning. Turkey at the turn of the century appeared to be the country with the lowest rate of newspaper readership in Europe. Television broadcasts, dominated by commercial stations that provide mainly entertainment programmes with limited coverage of domestic and world affairs, remain the main source of information for the vast majority of Turkey's population.

The extent to which the media fulfils its democratic functions is highly dependent on the legal framework within which it operates. The decision of the Helsinki European Council in December 1999 to declare Turkey a candidate for membership of the European Union constituted a turning point towards political and media liberalisation in Turkey. In order to fulfil the 'Copenhagen Political Criteria', a precondition for starting membership negotiations, successive governments have adopted reform packages stipulating extensive constitutional and legislative amendments, which have substantially eased restrictions on basic rights and liberties in general and on the freedom of expression and the press in particular. The parliament also adopted in 2004 a Freedom of Information Act, which, despite many restrictions, provides for access by citizens (and among them journalists) to information held in the files of public authorities. Reforms led the state radio and television to start in the summer of 2004 broadcasts in 'languages traditionally used by Turkish citizens in their daily lives', among them Kurdish. Thanks to EU-inspired reforms the number of journalists arrested or imprisoned have steadily decreased. The non-violent expression of certain political views is, however, still restricted by a variety of laws, and the implementation of the reforms have remained 'uneven' despite the fact that Turkey started membership negotiations with the EU in 2005.

At the turn of the twenty-first century, censorship and interference in the work of journalists by media owners constitutes a greater ill than censorship and interventions by state authorities. Commentators in the Turkish press often express radically critical views on issues of domestic and foreign policy but there are few if any who dare challenge the decisions and actions of their employers. Most media owners take freedom of the press to mean their freedom to acquire and control the means of communication and have little or no respect for editorial independence of journalists. They often treat their media holdings as public relations offices for the promotion of the image of their companies and even families and use the political influence afforded by their media outlets to promote their business interests.

With most of its rivals bankrupt or in financial trouble or disgraced, the Turkish media scene is currently dominated by the Doğan Group, which controls nearly half of the daily newspaper circulation, and collects two-thirds of advertising revenues. According to *The Economist* the Doğan group has 'ballooned into a near-monopoly, with the potential to undermine Turkey's wobbly democracy' (*The Economist*, 2002). Doğan has argued that his investments in various other businesses 'do not bring a conflict of interest, but editorial and economic freedom' for his media outlets. His rivals, according to Doğan, invest in the media to use it as a 'weapon' to promote their commercial agendas (Boulton, 2001). The concentration of media ownership is perhaps the most serious threat to freedom of expression and the press in Turkey at the turn of the twenty-first century (Sönmez, 1996).

The April 2001 arrest of Dinç Bilgin, the main rival of Doğan, raised hopes that the era of patronage between the political establishment and media moguls might have come to an end and that the latter could no longer be able to count on politicians for protection. These hopes were bolstered when the state authorities seized the media holdings and started prosecution of a number of businessmen who had engaged in shady business dealings. Some regard the landslide victory of the Justice and Development Party, AKP, in the national elections of November 2002 (despite strong opposition from the mainstream press) as marking the end of deals between government and the big media to mutually support each other. Others speculate that this is just a realignment in the relationship between political and media power holders.

Big media owners have in general employed a highly discriminative wage policy. In order to secure their loyalty to employers, top editors and senior columnists are paid extravagant salaries and transfer payments, while rank and file journalists (earning an average of only about 500 dollars a month) are among the lowest-paid professionals in the country. Some of the highly paid strata of editors and columnists are believed to serve as links between media owners and the political establishment in their under-the-table dealings. The highly discriminative wage policy has been very effective in breaking down any kind of solidarity among higher and lower levels of media employees. The poor wages for the vast majority of employees has made the media sector among the least attractive sectors for the better educated and talented university graduates. A widespread complaint about employers' policies is that investments in state of the art technology are made at the cost of neglecting investment in human capital, which partly explains the generally poor level of journalism in the Turkish media.

Until the 1990s, the Journalists Union of Turkey (Türkiye Gazeteciler Sendikası, TGS) negotiated with the Turkish Newspaper Owners Union (Türkiye Gazete Sahipleri Sendikası) collective agreements with most of the major dailies on the basis of the law governing relations between employers, which grants special benefits to journalists, such as early retirement and high minimum wages. From the 1990s onwards, however, media magnates pressured their employees to sign contracts on the basis of the labour law as ordinary workers and to quit union membership (EFJ, 2002). Union membership has thus gradually faded away from the media. According to the Ministry of Labour and Social Security statistics, only about 5 per cent of approximately 10,000 employees were members of the journalists' union at the turn of the decade (TGS, 2002).

Self-censorship by journalists is perhaps a greater problem for press freedom in Turkey than in other democracies. Most Turkish journalists tend to abide by the 'national/official truth' rather than the 'objective truth'. They are known to avoid issues concerning such 'sensitive' subjects as the role of the military in Turkey's politics and economy, the Kurdish question, the 'Armenian genocide' issue, Atatürk's legacy and similar matters, although recent years have witnessed increasingly daring reporting and commentary on such issues. Turkish editors and columnists eagerly accuse the editors and columnists of rival newspapers of conflicts of interest or violation of journalistic ethics but almost never dare criticise their own publishers and editors for such behaviour. Despite efforts by professional organisations such as the Journalists Association and the Press Council to publish and enforce codes of ethics for journalists, violation of professional ethics is rampant, partly because professional organisations of journalists are also controlled by journalists who are closely affiliated with the media magnates. The Code and Board of Ethics set up by the Doğan Group in 1999 does not have much credibility, being seen by journalists as nothing more than window dressing.

One of the strongest attributes of the Turkish media, however, is that it is able to reflect nearly the entire political spectrum in the country. Most mainstream newspapers with large circulations published by the 'big' media groups are committed to the Kemalist nationalist secularist ideology of the state authorities. The non-mainstream papers with limited circulation published by smaller companies tend, on the other hand, to reflect the views of marginal political groups, ranging from ultra Turkish (and Kurdish) nationalism to Islamic fundamentalism.

It needs to be emphasised that the Turkish media has displayed a remarkable propensity to adopt modern communications and printing technologies. It may also be said to the benefit of the Turkish media that recent years have also witnessed improvements in the general quality of journalism with the rising educational level of journalists. Most major newspapers produce regular business, foreign news and culture pages, which did not exist prior to the 1980s. Despite manipulations by the big media bosses, who often intervene in the editorial policy of their outlets, objectivity in news reporting has been improving. Mainstream newspapers pay greater attention to diversity of opinion by employing columnists of diametrically opposed political leanings. The mainstream press is flooded with columnists. According to one count, there were in the year 2000 at least 400 columnists in the major newspapers with circulations over 40,000, most of whom contribute on a six-days-a-week basis. Although the press in general allocates much space to opinion, few papers feature 'op-ed' pages.

Despite positive developments during the recent decades, the lack of even a single serious quality, reference paper remains a conspicuous characteristic of the Turkish press. All Turkish newspapers are broadsheet in form but in substance even the most serious among them provide mixtures of tabloid and broadsheet journalism, with coverage of political and economic issues combined with sensational exclusives, nationalist hype and backpage pin-ups. Popular papers (called 'bulvar/boulevard') which publish mostly fabricated news, sex and crime stories with colour photographs, have succeeded in enlarging their share of the total circulation. Even in the most serious of newspapers, the distinction between news and opinion is often blurred. Leaks by state authorities have so far been the main source for what passes for investigative journalism in the Turkish context, although the passing of the Freedom of Information Act in 2004 has raised hopes that the situation may improve. Private television and radio stations are dependent on and steered by advertising revenues. Most are dominated by entertainment programmes, some mixing information with entertainment ('infotainment') in their news coverage, although a few stations like NTV and CNN-Turk, founded in the late 1990s, provide extensive news coverage and debate programmes. The state broadcasting institution TRT, established in early 1960s as an independent public service broadcasting institution, lost its autonomous status in the 1970s and has since turned increasingly into a mouthpiece for state authorities. The lack of independent, non-commercial public service broadcast media is a major shortcoming of the Turkish media. Factors discussed above partly explain the low level of credibility the Turkish journalistic corps seems to suffer from at the beginnings of the twenty-first century. Surveys indicate that journalists rank among the least respected and trusted professional groups in the country (Adaman, Çarkoğlu and Şenatalar, 2001).

Concluding remarks

Whereas press freedom was established in the West in the eighteenth century, censorship laws prevailed in the Ottoman Empire until the 'Constitutional Revolution' of 1908. The right to publish without prior permission was not guaranteed until the constitution adopted in 1961. The presence of a more or less independent press in Turkey, on the other hand, enjoys a history that goes back to the appearance of privately owned papers in the 1860s.

Throughout its history, the Turkish press and its tradition of opposition and criticism has played an important role in the social and political modernisation of Turkey. Journalists have been instrumental in introducing liberal democratic ideas and values to Turkish society, both in the Ottoman Empire and Republican Turkey and the press has been influential in securing democracy despite the many reversals in the maintenance of democratic rule since its introduction in the late 1940s.

It may be said that the commitment of Turkish journalists to democratic principles and institutions has grown stronger following the bitter experiences of military interventions, which were all supported by the mainstream media. The mistrust of parliamentary democracy that was widespread in the 1960s and 1970s has lost its vigour. At the turn of the twenty-first century there seems to exist a broader consensus among journalists that solutions to the social and political problems of the country should and can be found in the context of a liberal democratic regime (Alpay, 1993). The majority of Turkish media and journalists of various political inclinations have strongly supported Turkey's bid for membership of the European Union. The media, despite its many failings discussed at some length in this paper, is a strong force for further liberalisation and democratisation in Turkey.

Technological innovations in the communications sector have also broadened the reach of the media, although there seem to be limits to this. Satellite television broadcasts and broadening internet access have significantly contributed to improvements in the quality and depth of coverage of world news. The media provides a rich forum for the discussion of issues concerning domestic and foreign policy. Newspapers from across the whole ideological spectrum provide readers with dozens of columnists, most of whom write on a daily basis, to criticise with great vigour the holders of political, administrative and economic power. The much-needed increase in the quality and credibility of the Turkish media, however, depends upon improvement in journalistic standards and ethics, as well as increased competition in the sector.

Bibliography

F. Adaman, A. Çarkoğlu and A. Şenatalar (2001) *Hane halkı gözünden Türkiye'de yolsuzluğun nedenleri ve önlenmesine ilişkin öneriler* (İstanbul: Türkiye Ekonomik ve Sosyal Etüdler Vakfı (TESEV).

R. Akar (1995) 'Basında 'Herkese' Dönemi', in *Cumhuriyet Dönemi Türkiye Ansiklopedisi*, vol. 11 (İstanbul: İletişim Yayınları).

Ş. Alpay (1993) 'Journalists: Cautious Democrats', in M. Peper, A. Öncü and H. Kramer (eds) *Turkey and the West: Changing Political and Cultural Identities* (London: I. B. Tauris).

İ. Barutçu (2004) *Babıali Tanrıları: Simavi Ailesi* (Istanbul: Agora Kitaplığı).

N. Bobbio (1987) *The Future of Democracy* (Oxford: Polity Press).

L. Boulton (2001) 'A Media Magnate Strikes Back for His Empire', *Financial Times*, 6 June.

H. Cemal (1999) *Kimse Kızmasın, Kendimi Yazdım* (İstanbul: Doğan Kitapçılık).

H. Cemal (2005) *Cumhuriyet'i Çok Sevmiştim: Cumhuriyet Gazetesi'ndeki 'İç Savaş'ın Perde Arkası* (İstanbul: Doğan Kitapçılık).

A. Finkel (1999) 'Who Guards the Turkish Press? A Perspective on Press Corruption in Turkey', *Journal of International Affairs*, vol. 54, no. 1, pp. 147–66.

D. Franz (2000) 'Tackling Entrenched Corruption in the Turkish Economy', *The New York Times*, 12 November.

A. Gevgilili (1983) 'Türkiye Basını', in *Cumhuriyet Dönemi Türkiye Ansiklopedisi*, Cilt 11 (İstanbul: İletişim Yayınları).

A. Gür (1995) 'Sermaye Yapısında Değişim ve Dergiler', in *Cumhuriyet Dönemi Türkiye Ansiklopedisi*, Cilt 11 (İstanbul: İletişim Yayınları).

European Federation of Journalists (EFJ) Report (2002) *Journalism and the Human Rights Challenge to Turkey: Putting Union Rights and Press Freedom on the Agenda.* Report of the IFJ/EFJ mission to Turkey 26–30 April (Brussels: IFJ/EFJ).

J. Keane (1991) *The Media and Democracy* (Cambridge: Polity Press).

S. Kinzer (2001) *Crescent and Star: Turkey between Two Worlds* (New York: Farrar-Strauss-Giroux).

Koloğlu, O. (1995) 'Liberal Ekonomi Düzeninde Basın Rejimi', in *Cumhuriyet Dönemi Türkiye Ansiklopedisi*, Cilt 11 (İstanbul: İletişim Yayınları).

B. Lewis (1961) *The Emergence of Modern Turkey* (Oxford: Oxford University Press).

B. McNair (1995) *An Introduction to Political Communication* (London and New York: Routledge).

T. Meyer and L. Hinchman (2002) *Media Democracy: How the Media Colonize Politics* (Malden: Blackwell).

A. Purvis (2004) 'Not Just Business as Usual', *Time Europe*, 4 August.

M. Sönmez (1996) 'Türk Medya Sektöründe Yoğunlaşma ve Sonuçları [Concentration in the Turkish media and its Consequences] *Birikim*, no. 92, pp. 76–86.

—— (2003) *Filler ve Çimenler: Medya ve Finans Sektöründe Doğan* [Anti – Doğan Savaşı] (İstanbul: İletişim).

The Economist (2002) 'Face Value: "A Turkish Rupert Murdoch"', 16 February.

A. Tunç (2003) 'Faustian Acts in Turkish Style: Structural Change in National Newspapers as an Impediment to Quality Journalism between 1990–2003', in O. Spassov and C. Todorov (eds) *New Media in Southeast Europe* (Sofia: SOEMZ, European University Viadrana (Frankfurt-Oder) and Sofia University).

Türkiye Gazeteciler Sendikası (TGS) (2002) *Briefing Note by TGS for the IFJ – EFJ Mission to Turkey*.

E. Zürcher (1993) *Turkey: A Modern History* (London: I. B. Tauris).

20
Rapid Commercialisation and Continued Control: The Turkish Media in the 1990s

Ayşe Öncü

The 1990s have been a *fin de siecle* decade in Turkey in at least one important respect: the realm of media has undergone a profound transformation. The overall story is familiar (1). Since the deregulation of the state broadcasting monopoly in 1990, as an integral part of the government's economic liberalisation and privatisation programme, commercial television has expanded at a frenzied pace. The broadcasting industry has become a hotbed of mergers and acquisitions, with growing concentration of corporate control within and across various commercial-media markets. In short order, two media giants have been consolidated, with powerful production and distribution networks in newspaper publishing, television and radio. As the struggle for domination among these two giants and their lesser competitors continues, the trend is clearly in the direction of horizontal linkages into domestic film production and the music recording industries. At the same time, the potential for the expansion of cable and digital satellite networks has begun to attract new players into the communication field, aggressively moving to establish joint ventures with global telecommunication giants. Thus, while the privatisation of television and the emergence of new communication technologies have already changed the face of the Turkish media scene almost beyond recognition, the present configuration appears far from settled. The first decade of the new millennium portends yet another round of mergers and acquisitions, as established media giants seek new partners in the international arena and continue to spread their tentacles by crossing over into new sectors of the national consumer market.

In its bare outlines, this story is one that has been repeatedly told in a variety of national settings, ranging from India and Australia to Italy (2). As such, it cannot be divorced from the encompassing transnational trends that have, in one country after another, undermined state monopoly over broadcasting. Most immediately, the growing accessibility of satellite technologies have eroded the ability of national states to police their airwaves. More broadly, the complex set of forces set in motion by neoliberal capitalism at the turn of century have dramatically restricted the capacity of states to sustain economies in which production, consumer markets, or monetary transactions are essentially national phenomena. To the extent, then, that deregulation and commercial expansion in media markets are propelled by the demands of an increasingly transnational world economy, the 'Turkish case' is but one specific instance of a global phenomenon. When couched in very abstract and general terms, the metamorphoses wrought by the neoliberal turn are 'everywhere' the same: the decline of public service broadcasting and newspaper readership; the explosive growth of commercial media; the extension of corporate control of media institutions and the concentration of ownership.

At the same time, of course, the unfolding of such processes as 'deregulation', 'commercialisation', and 'conglomeration' cannot occur apart from socially grounded, politically embedded actors. As the growing literature on the subject makes it abundantly clear, the workings of transnational pressures and incentives are dependent upon the very national frontiers they transgress(3). They operate through various 'national' institutional arrangements, from legislative acts to firms, which are subject to power struggles among contending players in the domestic arena, including the state. So transnational networks are multi mediated, re-deployed, 'domesticated' and resisted wherever they come to rest. And depending upon timing, place and context, they assume historically contingent forms. It is also the case, then, that unfolding changes in Turkish media markets constitute a unique story, one that involves a distinctive set of historical mediations and dilemmas.

In what follows, my aim will be to map out the emergent configurations of the past decade in the media realm in Turkey. Throughout, my emphasis will be on the manner in which prevailing trends in the transnational arena have become intertwined with the complexity of ongoing politico-economic events on the ground, to shape the media scene in Turkey in particular ways. My purpose is thus to engage with the particular and the specific, rather than with generalities. The attendant danger, of course, is to become entrapped in an endless descriptive account so I have organised the discussion below around themes commonly used to compare various national media systems. This method will, I hope, provide a convenient compass, one which will allow me to dwell upon the distinctive aspects of the Turkish media scene, without losing sight of 'world-wide' trends.

The erosion of public service broadcasting

In taking stock of the past decade, one of the most striking features of the Turkish media scene seems to be the swift and dramatic decline of public television in terms of audience share, finances and programme production/ acquisition. Available evidence suggests that within a span of three years after the introduction of private TV – between 1990 and 1993 – the market share of the state-funded TRT channels declined to less than 10 per cent in terms of total advertising revenues and audience share. Needless to say, public broadcasting has everywhere suffered declines in the face of competition from commercial television, along with cuts in public spending. But in most countries, public TV corporations seem to have proved more resilient in the face of competition. In Italy, for instance, the combined RAI channels continue to rate better than the combined commercial channels; in India the state-funded Doordarshan has retained a significant share of the market despite commercial competition; and in Australia the ABC has consistently improved its ratings. Irrespective of fluctuations in up-to-date statistics, the overall pattern in Europe points toward a more or less even split in the market share of commercial and public channels.

The vulnerability of state broadcasting in Turkey and its counterpoint, the enthusiasm with which Turkish audiences and advertisers have embraced private-commercial channels, were the outcomes of several contributing factors. The timing and mode of deregulation in media markets played a significant part. The year 1990 – when a satellite venture, beaming from Germany, broke through state monopoly – coincided with an upward spiral in the broader economy. The banking and advertising industries, which spearheaded Turkey's 'opening' to international markets from the early 1980s onwards, were already integrated into global markets through partnerships and joint ventures. And Turkish consumer markets were flooded with goods and brand names from distant corners of the world. In the exuberant consumer market of the 1980s however, the major beneficiary of the growing 'advertising cake' (to translate a phrase from Turkish) was TRT (Türkiye Radyo ve Televizyon Kurumu, Radio and TV Institution of Turkey), the state broadcasting company. Advertising on state television, initially introduced in the mid-1970s, had evolved into an increasingly important source of revenue, such that licence fees were abandoned entirely in the mid-1980s. The significance of television as a venue for advertising in a growing consumer market where newspaper circulation is very low (total daily circulation of around four million in a country with a population of more than 70 million) is self-evident. By contrast, more than 60 per cent of Turkey's 11 million households owned colour television sets in 1991, with the proportion reaching up to 99 per cent in large metropolitan centres. So the 'timing' of deregulation in 1990 was most opportune from the vantage point of commercial interests with an eye on media markets.

The fact that Turkey's first commercial/private channel was launched by the incumbent Prime Minister Turgut Ozal's own son was also important, beyond the impact of sheer nepotism, that is. It signified a planned move, one that was consistent with Turgut Ozal's overall strategy of implementing deregulation in various other sectors of the economy. From the moment he came to power as prime minister in 1983, Turgut Ozal took advantage of the powers newly vested in him by the 1982 constitution to surround himself with an inner circle of young and self-confident economic advisors, directly responsible to the office of the prime minister. This structure enabled him to by-pass the parliament, as well as the cumbersome bureaucratic-legal machinery of the state apparatus and directly implement a series of rapid-fire measures which dismantled the existing customs barriers in financial and consumer markets. The long-term implications of such a strategy – deregulation in the absence of state reforms – are beyond the scope of this article. Suffice to say that the mode of deregulation in the media sector was consistent with this overall strategy. It meant that private broadcasting became an accomplished fact (with 11 nation-wide commercial channels and some 200 local TV stations on the air) long before parliamentary battles over the relevant article of the constitution culminated in an amendment, in August 1993 – six months after Turgut Ozal's death. It took yet another year of intense political negotiation to reach a compromise on the stipulations of a new broadcasting law, which went into effect in 1994.

The four years between 1990 and 1994 became a period of wide-open opportunity for entering commercial media markets. It was also a moment of unbridled competition, when a series of new satellite ventures, launched one after another, vied for a share of lucrative advertising revenues by under-cutting each other. For TRT, with its stringent controls over advertising airtime and content, as well as its above-the-board, uniform pricing policies, this four-year-long period spelled a drastic decline in revenues. Equally immediate and dramatic in its consequences was the exodus of TRT's experienced, professional cadres – from technical experts and programmers, to news anchors – who were lured away by attractive financial offers from the commercial sector.

TRT has not recovered since. Its programming strategy in the face of commercial competition has been, in a word, suicidal. It has progressively 'diluted' the range and quality of its entertainment programming, trying to produce in-house dramas, game shows, and music programmes that copy those broadcast on commercial infotainment channels. Combined with 'serious-official' newscasts – dominated by canned footage from ceremonial events of the day and authoritative statements by governmental dignitaries – the outcome has been deadly from the perspective of audience ratings. Since any sparkle of new talent or innovative programming ideas are quickly 'transferred' by commercial competitors, public broadcasting continues to function as a stepping stone to the lucrative infotainment sector. In 2001, TRT resembled an overblown but incapacitated giant, with a vast bureaucratic apparatus with seven public channels on the air, but a withering audiences.

The question of whether TRT can still fight back to increase its ratings is not easy to answer, given the historical legacy of public broadcasting in Turkey and the predicaments posed by commercialisation in a context where the vast majority of audiences are 'semi-literate'. Public television would seem to have three distinct programming strategies in the face of commercial competition. Firstly, it could choose to compete on the same ground and on the same terms as its commercial competitors. But if public television is a copy of commercial television, there remains no justification for its existence, let alone its public funding. The opposite strategy would be to go for a high quality and a distinctive programming menu, one catered to programme types that commercial television sidelines. This might include extended foreign news and current affairs, or certain kinds of original drama or documentaries. The problem with this approach, especially in the Turkish context, is that it is a minority audience strategy. Perhaps the most viable strategy for public television is to maintain a full range of programme types from drama to sports and quiz shows, but to aim for quality and distinctiveness by promoting the best of all kinds of programme. Such a strategy however, necessitates major and long-term political support, which has not been forthcoming in Turkey. So far, TRT's emergent programming policies have been shaped by default more than anything else. And the resultant configuration – entertainment programming which mimics commercial television, accompanied by news and current affairs programmes which promote governmental policies in the name of 'national interest' – continues to marginalise both the institution and its programmes.

The paradoxes of ex-post-facto re-regulation

In so-called mixed broadcasting systems, public broadcasting constitutes the most important single countervailing force against the market-led logic of commercial television. Commercial broadcasting is everywhere driven by the pressure to maximise audiences and programme popularity above all else. The competition among commercial networks, however, does not seem to increase the range and quality of programming but rather the reverse, so that at any given moment the viewers' choice of programmes is very limited. Formats across networks are very similar, since programming is pitched to the lowest common denominator of audience taste. The political logic of 'mixed-systems' resides in counterbalancing such unbridled commercialism through public broadcasting – the assumption being that regulatory legislation over commercial networks, important as it may be, is not enough to ensure political accountability, access, quality and diversity of programming. In the Turkish context, the problems posed by the erosion of 'public interest' broadcasting have been compounded by the 'ineffectiveness' of regulation over commercial networks.

Among the aims of the new broadcasting law of 1994 was restrictions on cross-media ownership and the reduction of common control of newspapers, television and radio. It has been effective in discouraging foreign investors from entering Turkish media markets. But ensuring the compliance of domestic investors with the statuary maximum of 20 per cent has proved impossible to implement and monitor in practice. So while the ownership restrictions of Turkish broadcasting law are similar to many other countries, which follow some variation of the percentage method, they remain ephemeral in practice. The enactment of the law in 1994 did little more than to trigger a spate of buying and selling, a game of musical chairs in which stations and newspapers changed hands, leaving an increased concentration of ownership on the ground.

The most significant outcome of the 1994 broadcasting law was the creation of a supervisory body, the RTUK (Radio and Television Supreme Council). Empowered to allocate frequencies and licences, and authorised to monitor broadcasting content, the council's composition and powers became a source of public controversy from day one. Its practices have since been condemned for political favouritism as well as heavy-handed censorship. A variety of amendments to the existing law have been proposed by journalists' associations, media interests, and various political parties. But while there seems to be a consensus that RTUK *must* change, reconciling the demands of divergent interest groups has so far proved impossible.

Part of the problem stems from the fact that the RTUK is empowered to impose black-outs (temporary or permanent) on commercial channels and radios, but not financial penalties. In practice, this has given RTUK the power to clamp down on a variety of regional and local television stations and radios defined as 'damaging to the national interest' – either for promoting Kurdish separatism or Islamic fundamentalism. But as far as mainstream-commercial channels are concerned, 'blackouts' have proved to be a very blunt instrument for ensuring political accountability. In contrast to monetary fines, which penalise commercial networks for specific kinds of programming, 'blackouts' attract much public attention, but their justification remains obscure as far as audiences are concerned. So blackouts on nation-wide commercial channels invariably invite accusations of outright political censorship on the part of RTUK, which in turn means that it can only be used very selectively, that is, where 'national interest' is at stake.

The broader picture I have drawn above suggests that neither of the two major vehicles for promoting 'public interest' in media markets have been particularly effective in the Turkish context. The first of these, public service broadcasting as an alternative in the face of increased commercialisation, appears to have lost its viability, because it is out of touch with audiences. The second, legislation that regulates commercial markets in the name of 'public interest', appears ephemeral on the ground – apart from incidents of direct censorship.

The prelude to conglomeration: Press-wars of the 1980s

Throughout much of the history of the republic, the sin-qua-non of newspaper ownership was a background in journalism and in the case of major national dailies, 'ownership' often implied several generations in the publishing business. The stories of such notable press families – such as the Simavi or Karacan families, for instance – remain beyond the scope of this paper. Suffice to say that the advent and consolidation of mass-circulating dailies in Turkey was intertwined with these illustrious family names. But unlike the 'press barons' of nineteenth-century Britain or America for instance, the names of Turkey's press families were never blemished by a murky history of accumulation through laissez-faire capitalism. On the contrary, there was an aura of sanctity attached to these family names, which were imbued with heroism in struggles against state censorship, as well as a journalistic ethos of 'independence' from the vicissitudes of party politics. Moreover, given the vagaries of publishing markets in Turkey and the very narrow circulation base of daily newspapers, Turkey's press families were never able to amass the kind of wealth and economic power accumulated by the rising industrial tycoons of the post-WWII decades. What they lacked in economic capital, however, they made up for with the immense influence they wielded in the intellectual and political life of the country.

The first signs of impending changes in the world of newspaper publishing became apparent in the mid-1980s, when state investments in communications technology expanded the reach of television and TRT began to broadcast in colour. For daily newspapers already limited to a very narrow readership base, the increasing reach of television spelled disaster. Evidence of just how limited the newspaper reading public was, even before the phenomenal growth of commercial television, is clear in the results of a national survey conducted by PIAR-Gallup in 1990. Among the adult population surveyed, close to 70 per cent *never* read newspapers. The comparable Euro-average is 14 per cent. When gender differences are taken into account, the differences are even more dramatic. Only 11 per cent of the women sampled read (looked at) newspapers on a daily basis; those responding *never* was 79.9 per cent. The comparable figures are higher for men, 29.5 per cent and 56.4 per cent respectively, although still very low by European averages.

The implication of these figures for advertising is hardly worth reiterating. Newspapers in Turkey do not reach women – the most important single target group in an expanding consumer economy. By contrast, more than 60 per cent of Turkey's 12 million households had acquired colour television sets by 1990 – in large metropolitan centres this figure had reached to 99 per cent.

In trying to compete with the growing reach of state television throughout the 1980s, all major daily newspapers resorted to tabloid formats in the layout of their front and back pages, sandwiching all 'serious' content in between. This competition rapidly transformed into a full-blown war of attrition, as each newspaper increased the number of pages devoted to entertainment and sports, and began to offer magazine supplements, as well as 'free' encyclopaedia leaflets for school children. Promotional campaigns became more and more extravagant as competitors retaliated. Attempts to entice readers with lotteries was soon abandoned in favour of issuing daily 'coupons' which could be exchanged for kitchen implements, cutlery, tableware or television sets. With more than ten national dailies trying to out-sell one another by announcing ever more exorbitant promotional schemes, the entire newspaper industry seemed headed for an imminent market collapse. And since total figures for circulation had become stabilised around four million, it appeared that only a couple of the largest dailies would survive into the 1990s.

As events turned out, the denouement of the 1980s press-wars was not a market collapse, but the elimination of Turkey's notable press families from the publishing field. The consolidation of two giant media conglomerates in the early part of the 1990s allowed most of the daily newspapers to survive through vertical linkages with commercial broadcasting. The press wars of the 1980s thus metamorphosed into a battle for television ratings in the 1990s. Symbolising this transformation was the movement of Istanbul's publishing industry from the Cagaloglu district, long synonymous with Turkish journalism, to new high-tech media towers outside the city limits.

The consolidation of two rival media empires

Giant holding companies, composed of vertically and horizontally linked firms operating in different sectors of the economy (manufacturing, finance, trade and distribution) have been a dominant feature of the Turkish economy since the 1960s. Conglomeration in the so-called culture industries however, is a post-1990 phenomenon.

The initial consolidation of two rival conglomerates in the Turkish media scene in the early part of the 1990s coincided with a booming consumer economy and an unprecedented expansion in advertising markets. This context made investments in commercial broadcasting highly attractive, given the technical feasibility of satellite broadcasting and the absence of constraints on cross-media ownership. Thus a series of commercial networks were launched in rapid succession, followed by a spate of buying and selling of stations to gain common control of newspapers, television and magazines. By 1994, when the first economic crisis of the decade hit advertising markets, the media sector was already dominated by two rival conglomerates, with cross-ownership in television, major daily newspapers and the glossy magazine market.

From a broader comparative perspective, one major consequence of such early and rapid conglomeration in Turkish media markets has been to effectively discourage investment by global broadcasting corporations. With the notable exception of Hearst in magazine publishing and a more recent joint venture with CNN to establish a news channel, there has been no influx of foreign investment. Turkey's media empires have remained primarily domestic entities, consolidating their financial power by branching out into a variety of commercial activities, ranging from condominium construction and tourism, to distribution and banking. This expansion has enabled them to undertake major capital investments in broadcasting technologies, and to expand their reach to the diaspora populations in Europe as well as to the Central Asian republics. The Dogan Group, for instance, which owns Channel D as well as *Hurriyet*, Turkey's largest circulating daily, embarked on a new EuroD channel in 1996, broadcasting most of its programming content from its domestic output. In tandem with EuroD, the daily sales of *Hurriyet's* European edition (published in Frankfurt) jumped from 110,000 copies to 160,000. The rival conglomerate, Medya Group, immediately followed suit by establishing a similar operation in 1997, ATV Avrupa, once again relying mostly on its domestic ATV channel for programming content. After the introduction of ATV Avrupa, the European sales of *Sabah*, Turkey's second largest newspaper, increased from 8000 to 38,000. Thus, in both cases, direct broadcasts to Europe have promoted the sale of newspapers, as well as the other products of the conglomerates.

In domestic media markets, the meteoric rise and growing political influence of two rival media empires has closed off all possibilities for 'independent' ventures in TV broadcasting. At the same time, however, a series of powerful conglomerates based in other sectors of the economy, have discovered the advantages of acquiring their own TV stations and newspapers. Thus Bayindir Holding, a construction giant with major contracts in Russia and the post-Soviet Republics in central Asia and Eastern Europe, owns and operates its own television channel, BRT. Similarly, Dogus Holding, which brings together a vast number of manufacturing-cum-commercial enterprises under its umbrella, including two major banks (Garanti and Osmanli), owns NTV – a major news channel which currently has higher audience ratings than CNN-Turk. The political advantages of owning a television station are self-evident – it enhances influence in 'Ankara circles' because for top bureaucrats and 'lowly' parliament members alike, exposure to commercial TV audiences implies instant celebrity status. But it also makes good 'market sense' since it provides an advertising venue for a multitude of products and services within the rubric of the same conglomerate. It is rumoured, in journalistic circles for instance, that Dogus Holding subsidises its television channel, NTV, to the tune of 15 million dollars per annum. But so long as the total annual advertising budget of the conglomerate (given the vast array of firms under its umbrella) exceeds this figure, investing in a television channel, with its in-house production capabilities, becomes financially feasible and in the specific instance of NTV, profitable.

From the perspective of Turkey's popular culture industries – publishing, music, as well as film – the rivalry between the two media giants has left few areas untouched. The competition between mainstream commercial channels has rapidly initiated Turkish audiences in the seductions of round-the-clock infotainment and the fascination with tabloid news – with roughly three quarters of audiences tuning into these channels on any single night. Infotainment programming has spurred an explosion of new sounds and music videos, giving birth to a new generation of blended 'Turkish-pop' celebrities and hence to a major consolidation in favour of large recording companies in Unkapani – the district associated with music production in Istanbul. For the popular actors and actresses of Turkey's declining film industry – which ground to a halt in the 1980s – the insatiable demand of infotainment channels for 'domestic' series and serials has opened new doors of employment – albeit secondary to the young and nubile TV stars of the moment. From around the mid-1990s onwards, the possibilities of financial backing by major TV channels has allowed scope for a new generation of emergent talent from the advertising and media industries to try their hand at full-length feature films. By combining fast-paced, televisual narrative techniques with 'domestic' content, and relying upon the publicity value of television celebrities in their casting, such films have achieved phenomenal box-office success – playing side by side with the latest imports from the global bestseller market. Thus at the turn of the new millennium – a moment when commercial television has entered into 99 per cent of homes – Turkish cinema has acquired a second breath of life.

Most importantly, of course, has been the transformation of journalism itself. Commercial television has created a select group of celebrity-journalists who make regular appearances on television talk shows, as well as writing daily columns in mainstream newspapers owned by the same media conglomerate. The exclusive contracts of such celebrity-journalists have reached figures comparable to those of entertainment stars and football players. At the same time, the possibilities of instant celebrity through live reporting on television news programmes, has given many young journalists a chance to write under their own names in newspapers. But among the rank and file – the enormous number of 'invisible', nameless cadres employed in a vast range of publications under the rubric of the rival media empires – the job market has become progressively precarious. Both poorly paid and also immediately dispensable at the first inkling of an economic crisis, they remain hopelessly trapped in what has become, for all outward appearances, the most glamorous profession in Turkey.

Negotiating the parameters of alternative-Muslim broadcasting

Turkey's first nationwide 'alternative/Islamic' channel (TGRT) came on the air in April 1993, beaming via satellite from England. It was sponsored by the owner of Turkey's largest conservative/Islamic daily newspaper, *Turkiye*, affiliated with the Naksibendi order. The second Muslim channel, (STV) sponsored by the Nur order, began broadcasting a year later. Since then, two other channels have joined them – Channel 7, affiliated with the Islamist Refah Party and MESAJ TV, sponsored by the Kadiri order.

Despite differences in their sectarian affiliations and emergent programming strategies, these channels share a number of broad commonalties.

They are 'private' but not 'commercial' in the sense that they are subsidised by religious orders and hence are not dependant upon advertising revenues (i.e., audience ratings) for survival. They define themselves as 'civil initiatives' against the 'moral degeneracy' of infotainment channels on the one hand and the official 'secularism' of the state broadcasting agency on the other. This is signified through such self-referential terms as *'milliyetci-maneviyatci'* (nationalist-moralist), *'milliyetci-mukaddesatci'* (nationalist-follower of the Holy) or as *muhafazakar-musluman* (conservative-Muslim) channels. Last, but most importantly, all four channels have evolved, over time, as part of an interlocking set of organisations which include commercial enterprises, financial houses, educational institutions and publishing interests, all based upon communitarian networks. STV for instance, is owned and operated by the Feytullah community, which is also the owner of a major conservative-religious national daily and a publishing company. The community has set up dormitories for tens of thousands of poor students and founded more than 300 prestigious high schools in the Balkans, the Caucasus and Central Asia, where teaching is in the national language as well as Turkish and English. The owner of TGRT, Enver Oren, is a businessman with 'Islamic' credentials who began in the 1980s as the publisher of the conservative daily Turkiye. Since then, he has developed a powerful network of business organisations under the umbrella of Ihlas Holding, which includes for instance, an Islamic bank (Ihlas Finanse), a cola company (Kristal Kola) and imports Kia automobiles from Korea, all of which are lavishly advertised on his TGRT. Channel 7, affiliated with the Refah/Fazilet Party, has developed in close connection with local municipalities as well as government circles.

Initially, each of the four Muslim channels began broadcasting during prime time, with a couple of hours of religious/edifying programming. Thus, for instance, TGRT went on the air with a programme prepared and presented by a notable scholar and divinity professor, Orhan Kurmus, who read passages from the Koran in the original Arabic, then translated and explained them, educating viewers in the high culture of scriptural Islam. Very rapidly, however, the predicaments of religious education during prime time in a multi-channel, competitive environment became apparent. For the viewer, zapping between infotainment channels, where fast-paced commentary and on-the-scene footage of live events turn 'news' into riveting drama and anchors are young and good looking, the talking head of Orhan Kurmus looked old, tired and lifeless. When STV went on the air a year later with a discussion format – several men engaged in 'religious conversation' – the results proved to be equally pedantic and boring.

These early broadcasts brought into the foreground two dilemmas which subsequently shaped and transformed the programming content of all Muslim channels. The first dilemma was one which provoked widespread debate among Muslim intellectuals in the Islamic press. Does being a devout Muslim prohibit enjoying sports, music and good drama? Is there no room for gaiety, enjoyment, leisure activities in Islam? Or as the question was formulated in the popular press, 'don't Muslims have fun?' (*Muslumanlar eglenmez mi?*) The implied 'other' in these questions – those who enjoy sports, music, laughter – are obviously not foreign, Christian Westerners, but rather middle class urbanites who tune into infotainment channels. The questions themselves are very much a product of metropolitan life, where leisure, entertainment and consumption fuse into one another to define a middle-class way of life. The predicament facing all Muslim channels was how to reconcile the strictures of orthodox Sunni Islam – particularly its emphasis on the invisibility and inaudibility of women in the public realm – with the demands of nationwide broadcasting.

A second, equally 'sensitive' issue, as it turned out, stemmed not from the scriptural orthodoxy of Sunni Islam, but its language, that is Arabic. On the landscape of television, Arabic language and script as the holy language of the Quran proved to be a double-edged sword. Its sanctity notwithstanding, Arabic spoken on television is a 'foreign' language in present day Turkey, totally unintelligible to typical average viewers, whether they are devout Muslims or not. The assumption that a sizeable segment of Turkish audiences, given the choice, would immediately tune in to Islamic channels to hear Quranic recitations in original Arabic, proved to be false.

Faced with the danger of becoming restricted to a very narrow viewer base, all four alternative/Muslim channels began to progressively introduce more diversified and sophisticated programming in an attempt to broaden their audience appeal. The first thing to go was 'religious education' during prime time, replaced by domestic and international news with live footage. The focus of panel discussions and tele-debate programmes soon shifted from scriptural interpretations to current affairs and political events of the moment. To meet the voracious demands of material for round-the-clock broadcasting, all four channels have inevitably resorted to Hollywood archives of the 1940s and 1950s, ranging from Humphrey Bogart re-runs, to Westerns (where female actresses wear long sleeves and floor length gowns) during late hours. The litmus test of concessions to mainstream audience tastes however, hinged upon 'light entertainment'. Among the four channels, TGRT has made the greatest concessions in this direction, setting up its own in-house production company to introduce a variety of show programmes featuring popular female stars and singers of the moment. Currently, TGRT has evolved into 'a family channel which Muslim believers can watch without shame or embarrassment' according to its own self-definition. Channel 7, sponsored by Refah Party, has progressively shifted its programme mix to news coverage during evening hours and sharpened its critical stance as the voice of political opposition in the national arena. STV and Mesaj TV continue to draw the line at female singing (and anchorwomen), confining themselves to 'serious' music sung by male voices. But they have had to introduce an 'internationalised' soundtrack to punctuate the programme flow, given the difficulties of adapting Turkish music (classical or folk variety) to the fast-paced rhythms of television broadcasting. So regardless of differences in programming content, the atmospheric presence of 'Western' rhythms have permeated the sights and sounds of all alternative/Muslim channels, including advertising jingles, ever since the introduction of commercial breaks by one channel after another in rapid succession.

Thus during evening hours, the programming content of the Muslim channels has become increasingly divergent between them – although they have all avoided tabloid news, paparazzi programmes or reality shows which are standard fare on commercial infotainment channels during prime time. Daytime programming on alternative/Muslim channels however, is an entirely different matter. For together with increasing broadcasting time and more diversified programming during evening hours, the onus of 'religious-conservative' education has shifted towards women and children during mornings and afternoons. Programmes developed for daytime audiences deliberately eschew straightforward Quranic education. Instead, the conventional genres and formats of daytime television, ranging from documentaries, cartoons, to health and cookery programmes, are used to convey the omnipresence of Allah in all walks of life. Thus for instance, a vast array of documentaries on wildlife, wonders of nature, or explorations in space (bought on the international market place) are carefully re-edited and dubbed to underscore Allah's generosity in creating them. Stories for children dwell upon the lives and deeds of holy men from Islamic history. Theologians answer questions and give advice on matters of daily religious observance, ranging from bodily ablutions to the use of nail polish, or the most auspicious prayers for particular occasions.

The picture I have depicted above suggests that despite considerable 'mainstreaming' in terms of their programming content, Turkey's conservative-Muslim channels continue to define themselves as 'alternative' to the commercial-infotainment sector. At the same time, the sectarian/religious networks which subsidise these channels have reached into various sectors of the economy over the past decade, to become 'conglomerates' in their own right. So far from being 'independent', Turkey's conservative-Muslim channels have become a major vehicle of 'empire building' – through overlapping political and economic connections – in the so-called Islamic sector. This has in turn been refracted into the popular culture industries, transforming what was a consumer niche barely ten years ago, into an 'Islamic public sphere' – with its own newspapers, magazines, documentaries, advertisements, films etc.

Concluding comments: The 1990s in retrospect

In the account above, I have focused on the reconfiguration of media markets in Turkey in the political conjuncture of the 1990s. My emphasis has been upon the ways in which 'politics' and 'markets' have interacted, at a particular historical moment in time, to lend specificity to the emergent 'mixed-system'. Needless to say, these developments cannot be divorced from broader forces of neoliberal capitalism which have swept across media markets in various parts of the world, North and South. The 1980s and early 1990s have been periods of deregulation and re-regulation of broadcasting in most parts of the world. Viewed with the bird's eye view of the cosmopolitan expert, the general contours of the emergent picture in Turkish media markets are far from unique. In one national context after another, the advent of 'mixed-systems' has been accompanied by a decline in 'public interest' broadcasting, along with conglomeration and corporate control in news media and culture industries. Yet as the reconfiguration of media markets in Turkey illustrates, such general trends yield highly variable outcomes in different national contexts, contingent upon the political configurations which underpin and shape them.

In summarising the ramifications of the emergent configuration in Turkish media markets of the 1990s, three aspects seem worth reiterating, at the risk of oversimplification: firstly, the marginalisation of public sector broadcasting, together with the ineffectiveness of regulatory legislation over commercial networks, has meant that state intervention in the name of the 'public interest' has become synonymous with monitoring and censorship of media content. Secondly, the rapid consolidation of corporate control across various media markets, with linkages into different sectors of the economy, has attracted major investment into the broadcasting industry and fostered a media boom, while simultaneously blocking market opportunities for new entries and posing serious questions about 'influence peddling' in the wider political arena. Thirdly, increasing segmentation in the public/political domain, between a hegemonic 'mainstream-infotainment' media sector on the one hand and 'religious-conservative' media on the other, has meant that the existing critique of the status quo has been translated into Islamist politics.

The configuration I have described above appears far from settled. In retrospect, the frenzied expansion of the commercial media markets in the 1990s seems like distant history. The current spate of bankruptcies, including the collapse of one of the two established media conglomerates that were consolidated over the past decade, has triggered a new round of mergers and acquisitions, portending further concentration of ownership in major media markets. What can safely be predicted, without engaging in mere conjecture, is that the coming shape of Turkish media markets in the first decade of the millennium will be shaped as much by power struggles in the national political arena, as by transnational trends in global markets.

Bibliography

A. Bugra (1999) *Islam in Economic Organizations* (Istanbul: Tesev Yayinlari).
D. Catalbas (1998) 'Broadcasting Deregulation in Turkey: Uniformity within Diversity', in J. Curran (ed.) *Media Organizations in Society* (London: Arnold).

R. Colin (1994) 'National Broadcasting and the International Market: Developments in Australian Broadcasting Policy', in *Media, Culture & Society*, vol. 16, no. 1, pp. 9–30.

W. S. Hastings (1996) 'Foreign Ownership of Broadcasting: The Telecommunications Act of 1996 and Beyond', *Vanderbilt Journal of Transnational Law*, vol. 29, pp. 817–55.

M. Milikowski (2000) 'Exploring a Model of De-Ethnicization: The Case of Turkish Television in the Netherlands', *European Journal of Communication*, vol. 15, no. 4, pp. 443–68.

A. Oncu (2000) 'The Banal and the Subversive: Politics of Language on Turkish Television', *European Journal of Cultural Studies*, vol. 3, no. 2, pp. 296–318.

A. Oncu (1995) 'Packaging Islam: Cultural Politics on the Landscape of Turkish Television', *Public Culture*, vol. 8, no. 1, pp. 51–73.

M. Pendakur and K. Jyotsna (1997) 'Think Globally, Program Locally: Privatisation of Indian National Television', in M. Bailie and D. Winseck (ed.) *Democratizing Communication? Comparative Perspectives on Information and Power* (London: Creskill Champton Press).

K. Robins and A. Aksoy (1997) 'Peripheral Vision: Cultural Industries and Cultural Identities in Turkey', *Environment and Planning*, vol. 29, no. 1, pp. 1937–52.

H. Sahin and A. Aksoy (1993) 'Global Media and Cultural Identity in Turkey', *Journal of Communication*, vol. 43, no. 2, pp. 31–41.

Social and Urban Histories

21

From 'Cubic Houses' to Suburban Villas: Residential Architecture and the Elites in Turkey

Sibel Bozdoğan

As any first-time visitor to Istanbul would immediately observe, a dense conglomeration of reinforced concrete medium to high-rise apartment blocks constitutes the overwhelming fabric of contemporary Turkish urbanscape. The majority of Turkey's urban population lives in apartments, which range from mid-rise, spacious and relatively well-designed examples, to generic blocks on small urban lots produced for a speculative market and the substandard, often illegal 'squatter apartments' of the poorer urban fringes. Regardless of differences in size, height or quality, apartment blocks represent the most pervasive residential typology in modern Turkish architecture, reflecting the forces of modernisation at work in the country, especially since the 1950s.[1]

The same visitor will soon discover, however, that a different and more recent residential typology is also on the rise, marking the period since 1980 as a distinctly new phase in modern Turkish architecture: namely, the gated community (*site*) and the suburban villa with a garden. As an architectural concept, the detached single-family house or villa in a garden is not new. The ontological 'other' of the much-despised high-rise apartment and the cherished symbol of healthy lifestyles, it has been the singularly most idealised residential typology, at least since the early republican period. Many such modern villas were built in the 1930s for the modernising elites of the republic. Today, while the last few surviving examples of these so-called cubic houses/villas are abandoned to neglect and oblivion, waiting for the highest-bidding developer in the fervent construction boom that has gripped the country since the 1980s, the concept of the 'villa in a garden' has made a spectacular comeback, offering the post-Ozal elite exclusive lifestyles closer to nature and away from poorer urban crowds.

The definition of who constitutes 'the elite' in Turkey has changed dramatically, from the predominantly bureaucratic, military and state-connected elite of the early republic to the business, finance and media-connected elite of the present. Conceptions of what modern home and domestic life is all about and how it should relate to the rest of the society have shifted along with them. The professional and ideological profiles of the architects serving this elite clientele, and the prevailing norms of architectural design, practice and construction, have also changed along the way. In this paper, I will offer a synthetic overview of some of these historical shifts over three periods, corresponding to three distinct typologies in residential architecture: the idealised 'cubic villas' of the early republic (1923–50), the proliferation of apartments in the following period of multi-party democracy (1950–80) and the suburban gated communities of the current era (1980–present).[2] While drawing contrasts between the early republican period and the present, I will suggest that the intervening period contains some important lessons and lost opportunities that could have opened up a 'third space', so to speak, between an architectural ideal based upon an authoritarian and homogenising project of modernity on the one side and one that represents a total surrendering of that project to globalisation and postmodernity on the other.

1923–50: Modern house as a national ideal

For the modernising elites of the new republic, the modern house was, first and foremost, a 'civilisational' concept that included a major pedagogical function. They viewed the house as both a symbol and an instrument of the Kemalist modernity project – a highly idealised architectural container that would accommodate (even dictate) the modern, secular and Western-oriented lifestyle prescribed by the Kemalist reforms. As I have discussed extensively elsewhere (Bozdoğan, 2001), official publications, popular magazines and architectural journals of the time, charged the modern house with a 'civilising mission'. Residential architecture had the potential, they argued, to transform a traditional population into the citizens of a modern nation by turning their traditional lifestyles into the modern *wohnkultur* ('domestic habits' or 'culture of dwelling') of the nuclear family (Figure 21.1).[3]

During the 1930s, the emerging architectural profession seized this opportunity for social engineering with enthusiasm. Young Turkish architects (who were the first graduates of the Istanbul Academy of Fine Arts after its curriculum was radically transformed along modernist lines in the late 1920s) presented themselves as 'agents of civilisation', making the design of the modern house the centrepiece of their professional legitimacy. In the inaugural issue of *Mimar*, the professional journal that started publication in 1931, Aptullah Ziya articulated this new definition of the architect as follows:

> The whole world admits today that the architect is not simply a builder who constructs our houses to shelter us from rain and sun. He is an intellectual leader to guide our social life and a thinker concerned with our comfort, hygiene and health. He deals with the interior design of our homes, as much as, if not more than, the exterior.
>
> (Ziya, 1931, p. 19)

Yurdumuzun her köşesini böyle güzel yuvalarla dolu görmek istiyoruz.

Birkaç haftadanberi neşretmekte ol- | şı gösterdiği alâkayı da öğrenmiş olu- | ev nümunelerini bu sayfada neşre de-
duğumuz İstanbul ve civarının güzel ev | yoruz. Şunu da söyliyelim ki bu nümu- | vam edeceğiz. Bu münasebetle okuyu-
fotoğrafları her tarafta alâka uyandır- | neler yalnız İstanbul evlerine inhisar | cularımızdan yeni ev yaptıranlardan bu
dı. Bunu bize gelen mektuplardan anlı- | etmiyecektir. Güzel yurdumuzun her kö- | sayfada neşredilmek üzere evlerinin re-
yoruz ve halkımızın modern inşaata kar- | şesinden elde ettiğimiz yeni ve modern | simlerini göndermelerini diliyoruz.

Figure 21.1 The modern house. The caption reads: "We want to see all corners of our country adorned with such beautiful homes"

The most cherished characteristics of the modern house were comfort, hygiene, economy, functionality, simplicity and the avoidance of ostentatious display of wealth and luxury. Reiterating the canonical modernist argument that rationalism and functionalism are indifferent to and independent of class and wealth, early republican architects portrayed the modern dwelling (*mesken mimarisi*, as they called it) as the precise expression of the ideals of modern democratic societies. 'Modern needs are the same for everyone' wrote Behcet Unsal in 1939: 'maximum beauty, economy and comfort are as much desired in a worker's house as in a large villa' (Unsal, 1939, p. 60). A series of 'small house' projects by Bekir Ihsan, published in 1933 in *Mimar*, illustrate this ideal of a homogeneous nation without class conflicts. In these small single-family dwellings for the employees of the State Railroads, the house of a lower-rank employee and that of a director differs only in size, otherwise sharing similar formal features and the same undecorated simplicity (Ihsan, 1933, pp. 53–4).

The fact that modern architecture entered popular parlance in early republican Turkey under the rubric of 'cubic architecture' (*kubik mimari*) underscores the primacy of exterior form in a country eager to project a modern, Western image. As a stylistic signifier, the term 'cubic' designated a distinct and pervasive modernist aesthetic: geometric, asymmetrical volumetric compositions, wide balconies and terraces, metal railings, rounded corners, flat roofs and most significantly, the avoidance of luxury and exuberant ornamentation (Figure 21.2). It applied equally to single-family houses or villas, apartment buildings or the so-called 'rental houses' (*kira evi* – a multi-unit residential building with a single owner) and even to furniture and interior design (*kubik esya*). Yet the ideal residential typology in early republican architecture was, by a wide consensus, the detached, low-rise single-family house or villa, which was celebrated for its proximity to nature, sunlight and healthy living. The early republican distaste for apartments and urban life (coupled with an idealisation of the 'garden city' experiments in interwar Europe) was framed within an overtly nationalist and anti-cosmopolitan discourse. Many early republican leaders, intellectuals and architects portrayed the apartments in Sisli, Nisantasi, Taksim and other fashionable districts of Istanbul in a negative light, not just on scientific grounds (their alleged unhygienic nature, lack of sunlight, air and

Figure 21.2   A quintessential 'cubic house' of the 1920s and 30s

ventilation) but also increasingly ideologically (as the architectural expressions of greed and excessively Westernized or cosmopolitan and therefore 'unpatriotic', lifestyles). 'Apartments have turned us into nomads without home and hearth' wrote Huseyin Cahit Yalçın in 1937 (Yalçın, 1938, p. 5). 'Apartments are symbols of rootlessness, transience and modern nomadism' repeated Vedat Nedim Tor, 'whereas a house in a garden represents roots, continuity and commitment to the homeland' (cited in Balamir, 1994, p. 31).

The early republican elites who commissioned the canonical modern villas of the 1930s were government bureaucrats, high-ranking military officers and members of the Republican People's Party (RPP), judges, engineers, doctors and professors. These were the people who identified most closely with the regime and who perceived themselves as representatives of the regime's ideals. Like Hakki Bey, the character in Yakup Kadri Karaosmanoglu's paradigmatic 1934 novel Ankara, they 'took the lead and built the first examples of the so-called cubic houses' (Karaosmanoglu, 1991, p. 141). To be the owner of an architect-designed, well-built modern house carried a prestige and pride literally etched in stone by the fact that these buildings are still identified with the names of their original owners: *Devres Villasi, Agaoglu Evi, Tuten Apartmani* and so on. At the same time, although paradigmatic, 'cubic' was by no means the only stylistic choice available to the early republican elite. Sedad Hakki Eldem and his associates formulated a nationalist critique of 'cubic architecture' and instead advocated a modernist reinterpretation of the traditional timber-frame Ottoman/Turkish house.[4] While 'cubic villas' proliferated in the newly developing suburbs on the Anatolian side of Istanbul (Moda, Goztepe, Suadiye and Erenkoy in particular), Sedad Hakki Eldem's modern *yali*s continued a centuries-old tradition along the shores of the Bosphorous (Figure 21.3). To this day, these *yali*s constitute the most exclusive, privileged and timeless residential typology associated with the old Istanbul elite.

Figure 21.3   A modern waterfront 'Yalı' on the Bosporus, Architect: Sedad Hakkı Eldem

Ultimately, however, in spite of recurrent references to the democratic and progressive connotations of modernism, the early Republic largely failed to produce anything like the massive housing schemes, or *siedlungen*, of Weimar Germany that were so admired by republican leaders, architects and planners. The absence of comprehensive planning and land appropriation policies, the poverty of the building industry and the lack of a strong private sector able to undertake large scale, standardised and rationalised production of housing were key reasons for this gap between ideals and reality. In the absence of these material conditions, the actual built examples of 'cubic houses' remained limited to a handful of custom-designed and custom-built villas for the bureaucratic, military and professional classes. Almost exclusively, they were designed by modernist Turkish architects, particularly Zeki Sayar, Abidin Mortas, Behcet Unsal, Seyfi Arkan and Bekir Ihsan.[5]

Equally significant in explaining the absence of large-scale modern housing schemes in the 1930s is the fact that urban housing was not yet a pressing 'problem' (*konut sorunu*) in the early republican period, in the way it would be after 1950. In spite of all the idealised images of an industrial nation and all the proud publicity about the new factories built by the republican regime, this period did not see a massive industrialisation capable of triggering real urbanisation and social mobility. Overall, modernisation was still 'a project' and its primary direction was from the city to the countryside rather than the other way around. By and large, the peasants stayed in their villages while RPP leaders, architects and planners sought to take modernity and civilisation to them, 'colonising the countryside' as Zeki Sayar called it, without a hint of irony (Sayar, 1936, p. 47).

1950–80: Populist modernism and the apartment block

The early republican period came to a decisive end with the election victory of the Democrat Party in 14 May 1950. Abandoning the secular authoritarianism, statist economic policies and nationalist isolationism of the previous two decades, the DP regime promoted populist democracy, private enterprise and a more ambitious regional role for Turkey in a sharply divided Cold War world. The Western-oriented cultural politics of Kemalism continued into the 1950s, but the 'Western' model shifted from Europe to that of America. Two major American imports, 'modernisation theory' in social sciences and 'international style' in architecture, began to shape perceptions of democracy, modernity and the 'good life'. After two decades of relative insignificance with respect to Ankara, Istanbul was revitalised as the spectacular site of the DP's massive urban modernisation schemes under the personal directive of Prime Minister Adnan Menderes, as well as the pole of attraction for massive waves of migration from rural Anatolia. As a result, housing became a very real, pressing problem in Turkey, rather than a theoretical dimension of its modernity project.

The paradigm shift from the single-family villa in a garden to a multi-unit apartment block, the dominant residential typology after the 1950s, is best understood in this larger context. The canonical Atakoy Cooperative Development in Istanbul was one of the first experiments undertaken with credit from the newly established Emlak Kredi Bank (Figure 21.4).

Figure 21.4   An iconic block of flats from the 1950s: Ataköy, in the western suburbs of Istanbul

Architecturally quite successful, with good design and landscaping, proper angles of sunlight and ventilation, the Atakoy blocks have been widely criticised for catering to the affluent upper middle classes rather than responding to the needs of the urban poor. The paradoxical and distinctly American ideal of democratising comfort and luxury permeated the entire discourse on the modern home in the 1950s. In the pages of *Arkitekt*, German interwar concepts of minimal dwelling (*existenzminimum*), rationalist and functionalist simplicity (*neuesachlichkeit* or new objectivity) and above all, the idealised garden city model (*siedlungen*) were out. American homes, that is, large kitchens with electric appliances, dishwashers, refrigerators and family dining corners, were in. In a remarkable change of mentality from the early republic, the nationalist, anti-cosmopolitan criticism of apartment living gave way to a more positive attitude, even aspiration, towards apartment life across the social spectrum. The image of spacious, well-designed and luxurious urban apartments quickly became the preferred residential typology for the new Turkish elite, whose fortunes were accumulated in the growing private sector and through connections with the DP government in power.

The concomitant transformation of architectural culture and professional practice was equally phenomenal. During the early republican period, the state had been the exclusive patron of architecture. Even when individuals hired architects to design their cubic houses or apartments, it was still a relationship between an architect and a client who both worked for the state in one way or the other. After 1950, although the practice of providing major public architectural and planning services within the state bureaucracy continued, the emergence of independent private clients, especially for residential and commercial architecture, led to the emergence of what architectural historians consider to be the first truly private architectural firms and partnerships, the pioneers of the corporate model in architectural practice. The 'Insaat ve Mimarlik Atelyesi' (Construction and Architecture Studio) of Maruf Onal, Turgut Cansever and Abdurrahman Hanci, established in 1951 and the partnership of Haluk Baysal and Melih Birsel, established in 1952, were among the architecturally most successful.[6] In 1954, the Turkish Chamber of Architects was established as a licensing and regulating body, affirming the profession's autonomy and relative independence from the State.

Although ultimately ineffective against the magnitude of the housing problem, the sense of aesthetic refinement and careful conceptual experimentation that some of these architects put into apartment design remained unmatched for a long time afterwards. The practice of Baysal and Birsel is paradigmatic in that respect, beginning with their Birkan Apartment in Bebek (Figure 21.5), a well-designed and spacious apartment building illustrative of the 'domestication' or 'naturalisation' of international modernism into the familiar aesthetic of apartment blocks in Turkey.[7] In their apartment block for the Lawyers' Cooperative (*Hukukcular Sitesi*, 1958–61), one of the canonical projects of modern Turkish architecture, Baysal and Birsel took the basic

Figure 21.5 The 'Birkan Apartment' in Bebek, Architects Baysel and Birsel

multi-story slab block and with explicit indebtedness to Le Corbusier's l'Unite in Marseilles (1946–52), worked with the section to create duplex units stacked within the main grid of the reinforced concrete frame.[8] Later, they elaborated the same concept into a flexible schema that could accommodate considerable morphological variation – as for example, in a later low-rise, high-density project in Yesilkoy in which they transformed the corridor into an open-to-sky multi-level street, resulting in one of the most interesting but isolated episodes in modern Turkish architecture (Figure 21.6). Collectively, such projects make a convincing case that a certain sense of comfort, luxury and aesthetic satisfaction was not necessarily a monopoly of the detached, single-family villa and could in fact be embodied in high density urban schemes as well.

It was, however, not these few architectural experiments of quality, but rather the socio-economic realities of the country that would shape the physical fabric of Turkish cities in this period and afterwards. Today these custom-designed early apartments are hardly visible within the anonymous modern vernacular of lesser examples built with inferior technical and financial means. Murat Balamir writes that, rather than being a preferred residential typology, 'apartmentalisation' in Turkey (*apartmanlasma*) is the consequence of external factors like lack of capital, the shortage of available urban land and so forth (Balamir, 1994). Especially after the condominium or flat ownership legislation of 1965 (*kat mulkiyeti kanunu*), it has become a convenient model

Figure 21.6   A path unexplored: Low-rise residential flats by Architects Baysal and Birsel

Figure 21.7   Rent-generated urbanscapes in the suburbs of the Asian side of Istanbul

for small investors to pool their resources into a housing cooperative or for a small contractor (*yap-satçı müteahhit*), the new actor on the building scene, to tear down an older house and replace it with a multi-unit block. In the course of this speculative apartment boom, designs have become increasingly more generic and the resulting urbanscape, increasingly more faceless (Figure 21.7). Today, while a spacious and luxurious apartment in Tesvikiye or Bebek is still the mark of wealth and status (in the same way that the exclusive Bosphorus mansions of Sedad Eldem and his followers are and will be for a long time), a younger generation of wealthy and aesthetic-conscious Turks are seeking new residential patterns away from the city or at least insulated from its perceived environmental, social and aesthetic ills.[9]

1980–Present: The rise of the gated suburban community

Recent shifts in residential preferences of the wealthier classes go hand-in-hand with the phenomenal social, economic and cultural transformation of Turkey after 1980, when the country opened up to the forces of globalisation under the late President Turgut Ozal. It is hard to miss the conspicuous impacts of these developments on architecture and urbanscape in major Turkish cities, especially Istanbul, effectively 're-branded' as a global city. The proliferation of five star hotels, supermarket chains, shopping malls and office towers have transformed the fabric, the skyline and the social panorama of the city in ways that would have been inconceivable before 1980. In contrast to the more or less homogeneous society of the previous decades, differences of class, culture and background are now very widespread, and so are the different residential choices of the elites. Some are rediscovering the cosmopolitan richness of Istanbul's historically most Europeanised sections (Galata, Pera, Cihangir and the Bosphorus shores in particular), putting their money into increasingly more fashionable gentrification projects within the city. Many others are moving into newly constructed gated communities within the city ranging from medium rise 'mixed-use developments' as in the case of Etiler Maya Residences (Figure 21.8) to slick, corporate-looking residential towers like the Elite Residences in Sisli, or the more recent residential lofts of Kanyon in Levent. The most paradigmatic and pervasive development, however, is the increasingly fashionable gated suburban community, comprised of detached, single-family villas.

Although the idealisation of the villa in a garden is not new, important differences separate Turkey's recent villa boom from the cultural, social and political meaning of the villa in the early republic. First, unlike the cubic villa of the 1930s, the new suburban villa carries no larger national ideal or a 'civilising mission': it is an unapologetically displayed object of private consumption (Figure 21.9). The tastes and lifestyles that it represents are unequivocally those of a privileged and wealthy subset of society, without any claims to be relevant for the nation as a whole. The idea is to withdraw from the rest of the society rather than to lead it by example. The inhabitants of Kemer Country or Kasaba, two of the most paradigmatic exclusive suburbs, have no problem with the fact that they probably have more in common with the inhabitants of Seaside, Florida in the US than with those of Umraniye or Bakirkoy in Istanbul. They are part of an unprecedented new trend towards *the privatisation of space* in general – a conspicuous retreat of the wealthy and the privileged behind well-guarded perimeters and hermetically

Figure 21.8 A mixed use development in Etiler (Maya Residences), Architects: Skidmore, Owens and Merril

Figure 21.9   The new suburban villa in the 1990s

sealed SUVs (including, in some cases, the employment of a bodyguard) in order to better insulate themselves from poorer and 'conspicuously Muslim' urban crowds and from the messiness of an increasingly contested 'public space'.[10]

In stark contrast to the early republican emphasis on homogeneous national communities, avoidance of conspicuous luxury and ostentatious display of individualism, it is precisely the promise of exclusiveness – physical and social separation from the masses – that the potential customers of suburban villas are after. While functionality and comfort are still important in advertising their architectural qualities, new keywords like pleasure (*keyif*), quality of life (*yasam kalitesi*) and exclusiveness (*ayricalik*) feature most prominently as the most effective marketing points.[11] In fact, the term 'white Turks' (*beyaz Turkler*), implying connotations of race and class distinction that would have been anathema to early republican modernisers, is now a common expression in everyday parlance designating the owners and inhabitants of these exclusive residences – a predominantly well-educated, internationally well-connected, technologically-savvy and mostly young population of wealthy professionals, business executives, corporate managers, finance wizards, stockbrokers, journalists and media celebrities.[12]

Secondly, the very premise of a gated community – a secure boundary with guards and surveillance systems to exclude those who do not belong, is by definition anti-urban. While early republican distaste for dense urban living was often explained in terms of a quest for health, hygiene, sunlight and air (i.e. the *scientific* demands for a healthy body and a healthy nation), the new 'white Turks' link this to the larger pursuit of pleasure and quality of life. They cite the environmental degradation in the city – congestion, pollution, traffic, noise and lack of greenery – as the primary reasons for which they move to the suburbs in search of a more tranquil and more aesthetically refined life. It is an ironic twist of modern Turkish history that while the early republic criticised urban and apartment life as cosmopolitan and excessively Westernised, it is the cosmopolitan and excessively Westernised Turks who are now escaping from the city – or more precisely, from the poorer, more traditional, less cultivated urban crowds, and especially from the increasing presence of Islam in public space. Whereas the early republic sought to re-conceptualise the city as a 'garden city', the post-Ozal elite is leaving the city altogether, creating their own surrogate 'urban centres' in their suburban communities – 'village squares' and 'social centres', as they are typically called. In reality, the density in most suburban communities is much higher than what one would expect from their developers' promises of tranquillity, personal space and connection to nature. Some actually replicate urban densities, albeit within a more controlled perimeter. Bahcesehir (or Garden City) is a good example: an exclusive suburban development to the west of Istanbul, it is neither a 'garden' nor a 'city'.

Beyond these ideological differences that separate the two periods, there are also important shifts in the design and production process of residential construction. The villas of the early republic were almost invariably commissioned from individual architects by individual clients and were built by small contractors using conventional techniques (masonry or brick walls in conjunction with reinforced concrete slabs, cantilevers and structural frames). By contrast, recent gated communities and suburban developments are designed and built by large construction firms, often with international design and development teams and cutting-edge technological capabilities. Large finance capital and leading banks have now entered the construction sector (e.g., Is Bankasi in the case of both Kasaba and Optimum, two of the recent and most exclusive suburban developments) and the scale, complexity and corporate structure of these developments have reached a level undreamt of in the early republican period, even in the case of public buildings. Whereas the cubic villas of the 1930s were entirely the work of Turkish architects, it is not uncommon today to find the stamp of prominent international designers – as for example in the Maya Residences in Etiler, designed by Skidmore, Owings and Merril, the American corporate giant whose work in Turkey goes back to the Istanbul Hilton in the early 1950s. Similarly, the third phase of Kemer Country bears the signature of the prominent Florida firm of Duany and Playter-Zyberk which introduced neo-traditionalist 'New Urbanism' to Istanbul in the early 1990s (Figure 21.10).[13]

Meydanın çevresindeki evler için geleneksel
Türk mimarisi örnek alındı. Evler avlulu ve cumbalı

Figure 21.10   Suburban desires: Kemer Country, Architects: Playter-Zyberk

Today, following the example of Kemer Country, the most pervasive and seemingly most successful stylistic choice available in the upper scale housing market appears to be some version of the traditional 'Ottoman/Turkish house' with tile roofs, wide overhangs, modular windows and projecting window bays on the upper floor (Figure 21.11). With rhetorical references to Ottoman *konaks* (in Beykoz Konaklari), *mahalles* (in Kemer Country) and *yalıs* (in Bosphorus City, a newer development in Halkalı Küçükçekmece replicating the Bosporus in a 'theme park' version), these developments package themselves as remedies to the destructiveness of modern urbanism and a much-desired return to the architectural and urban qualities of traditional environments. The affinities between these recent villas and Sedad Hakki Eldem's canonical work in the 1930s are hard to miss (See Figure 21.3). However, unlike Sedad Hakki Eldem's lifelong and meticulous typological studies and his extensive theoretical arguments for national expression in modernism, these recent stylistic references to tradition are often only skin-deep – a postmodern façade architecture employed to lend distinctiveness and historical/cultural relevance to what is in fact a generic luxury suburban villa. The fact that the traditional Turkish house is just one among many other stylistic possibilities – including American log cabins (in Kemer Country) – testifies to the subordination of architecture to the forces of market and the whims of fashion. Architectural style is no longer

Figure 21.11 Ottoman references in high-rise residential flats of the 1990s

the visual expression of some larger idea or programme: such as modernity (cubic villas) or national identity (Sedad Eldem villas). It is a marketing tool targeting a particular group and appealing to the tastes, lifestyles and desires of that group. Or as Anna Klingman puts it, it is a form of 'branding' characteristic of the 'experience economy' where customers are in search of brands and lifestyles rather than use value (Klingman, 2007).

The popularity of 'neo-traditional Turkish houses' notwithstanding, a recent suburban development, the Optimum Houses near Omerli Dam on the Anatolian side of Istanbul, proves that in this pluralistic and relativistic market, there is as much room for a late modernist aesthetic as for other styles (Figure 21.12). Advertised as providing 'the best designed houses in Turkey', designed by one of the young stars of contemporary Turkish architecture, Han Tumertekin, and constructed as a result of the collaboration of Is Bankasi with EMTA (Integrated Engineering Designs Company), the primary selling point for Optimum is its aesthetic distinction from other suburban developments like Kemer Country or Kasaba. 'It is not a typical housing development', says the publicity brochure, 'it is a land development project that takes the private needs of its inhabitants seriously, responds to them with *boutique* solutions [my italics] and devotes utmost care and attention to details'.[14]

Figure 21.12   The 'neo-traditional' Turkish house, Architect: Han Tümertekin

Indeed, next to the neo-traditional style of Kemer and Kasaba, the four different types of Optimum houses ranging from 236 to 360 metre squares distinguish themselves with their slick modernism, elegant minimalist details, three-dimensional spatial conception (a double height living room with two story-high glass walls), tasteful colour schemes and the high quality of its interior fittings, kitchen and bathroom fixtures (Figure 21.13). It also has a more integrated, densely planned social centre with a swimming pool, sports hall, cinema, café, solarium, recreation centre and children's club. Overall, it testifies to a further differentiation within the high-end of the housing market, to cater to a more discerning, educated and sophisticated clientele.

Visiting one of the model homes in Optimum, I could not help thinking about yet another comparison with early republican architectural culture – one that concerns the historically problematic relationship between the architect and the inhabitants of the modern dwelling. Every inch of the Optimum villa was so thoroughly designed (perhaps over-designed) and every piece of designer furniture and every accessory so carefully selected and put in place that it was very hard to imagine moving into these villas with one's own personal furniture and belongings without impairing the aesthetic elegance of the space. This observation reminded me of Adolf Loos' highly pertinent, turn-of-the-century criticism of total design (*gesamkunstwerk*)

Figure 21.13 Interior of the 'neo-traditional' Turkish house

as an oppressive ideal of the modernist architect – one that violates the ultimately personal and homely (*heimlich*) character of the domestic interior (Loos, 1988). The irony is that these villas are marketed with the promise of 'letting you be yourself in your home, accommodating your hobbies and allowing you the freedom to use the house as you desire – to turn the garden into a workshop, the kitchen into a small gourmet restaurant and the top floor room into an amateur observatory'.[15]

By contrast, early republican architects made no secret of their enthusiasm for social engineering, for prescribing lifestyles and for *gesamkunstwerk*. The perspective sketches illustrating Aptullah Ziya's 1931 essay I have mentioned earlier depicted thoroughly Westernised interiors with modern furniture, Bauhaus inspired lighting fixtures, glossy surfaces, and in one corner, the inevitable piano – the perennial symbol of Turkish Westernisation since the late Ottoman period. Yet photographs of real interiors from the 1930s suggest that many families were unwilling to dispense with inherited period furniture and family paraphernalia even when they moved into the new modern houses and apartments. The domestic interior was far more resistant to the penetration of modernism than architects hoped for.[16] It seems to be a curious irony of Turkish modernity that whereas early republican architects actually intended to dictate lifestyles but could not do so in the way they envisioned, contemporary architects, while criticising the authoritarian and prescriptive social agenda of modernism, seem to be more successful in dictating their tastes and design choices to an elite clientele infatuated with expensive designer objects.

Conclusion

The same residential typology, that is the single-family house or villa in a garden, signifies diametrically opposed visions in the early republican period and in contemporary Turkey. Between the authoritarian and prescriptive modernism of the former, and the exclusivist, elitist and consumerist post-modernism of the latter, we look in vain for the opening up of a 'third space'. I have also suggested that the period in between (i.e., 1950–80), the period of so-called populist modernism typically associated with the ills of rapid urbanisation – especially the much-despised apartment boom (*apartmanlasma*) and development of squatter communities (*gecekondulasma*) – actually contains some important but under-appreciated architectural lessons for precisely such a possible opening.[17] It is in this period that Turkish architectural culture began to address the defining paradox of modernism for the first time – namely, the conflict between a socially concerned view of housing as the central question of modern democracies (a question of shelter) and at the same time, an aesthetic preoccupation with the dwelling as a designed product to accommodate the 'good life' (a question of quality). More than ever before, a small number of architects realised that the modern dwelling had to be conceptualised as inseparable from the question of urbanism and by and large, refused to escape either to the 'garden city' anti-urbanism of the early republic or to the anti-urban exclusivism of today's gated community. It was a moment in time when architecture was released from its larger-than-life civilisational mission under the sponsorship of an authoritarian state and had not yet surrendered to the demands of the market and to the fashionable residential formulas of the global theme park. It was a brief moment, to which we look back somewhat nostalgically today.

Notes

1. For a comprehensive discussion of urbanisation in Turkey, see Sey (1998).
2. For a broader discussion of the transformation of Turkish architectural culture along these three periods, see Bozdoğan (1997).
3. Particularly illustrative are the 'model homes' sections of popular journals and illustrated family magazines like Yedigun, Muhit and Modern Turkiye Mecmuasi.
4. See S. Bozdoğan et al. (1987) and Eldem (2009).
5. Turkish architects claimed houses as their primary domain, while important public commissions of the republican regime went to German and Central European architects, who built Ankara as a modern capital and transformed architectural education in Turkey. On these foreign architects, see Nicolai (1998).
6. See Kacel (2007) and Kortan (1997).
7. In her 'Rethinking Ordinary Architecture in Postwar Turkey' (paper presented to the Docomomo Conference, New York, September 2004), Ela Kacel challenges the common opposition between 'high' and 'anonymous' modernism and convincingly argues how projects like Birkan Apartments 'transformed the international into ordinary modern architecture'.
8. For another remarkable example of the similarly conceived modernist block of duplex units in Ankara, see Cengizkan (2002).
9. In his 'The New Middle Class and the Joys of Suburbia' (in D. Kandiyoti and A. Sanktanber, 2002) Sencer Ayata broadens this new pattern to include a larger sector of the society what he calls a 'new middle class', giving examples from suburban developments around Ankara. While this larger spread of the trend is certainly a most interesting research topic, my analysis is limited to the upper end, exclusive suburbs of Istanbul, which are more visible as trendsetters and as canonical *architectural* experiments.
10. For a critical discussion of Kemer Country, see Genis (2007).
11. 'Optimum bir Yasam' (An optimum life): the publicity booklet of recently completed Optimum Houses, an exclusive suburban development in Istanbul by EMTA Integrated Engineering Designs Inc.
12. On the emergence, tastes and lifestyles of the 'white Turks', see Bali (2002).
13. Basically, neo-traditionalist New Urbanism represents a nostalgic 'return' to the traditional values of small towns before what its proponents see as the onslaught of modern urbanism. The town of Seaside, Florida, designed by Duany and Playter-Zyberk, is the paradigmatic built example of this idea, extensively criticised by modernist architects and publicly championed by conservative celebrities like Prince Charles.
14. Optimum Publicity Brochure showing plans of four different units.
15. Optimum Publicity Brochure showing plans of four different units.

16. On the dialectic of modernism and domesticity, see Heynen (2005).
17. The most insightful general analyses of Turkish architecture and housing after 1950 can be found in the writings of Ugur Tanyeli and Ihsan Bilgin in Turkish, such as the essays they have contributed to Sey (1998). Unfortunately there are no English translations of these discussions.

Bibliography

M. Balamir (1994) 'Kira Evinden Kat Evine Apartmanlasma' [Apartmanization from rental houses to flats], *Mimarlik*, no. 260, pp. 29–33.

S. Ayata (2002) 'The New Middle Class and the Joys of Suburbia', in D. Kandiyoti and A. Sanktanber (eds) *Fragments of Culture* (New Brunswick: Rutgers University Press).

R. Bali (2002) *Tarzi Hayattan Life Style'a: Yeni Seckinler, Yeni Mekanlar, Yeni Yasamlar* (From *Tarz-I Hayat* to Life Style: New Elites, New Spaces, New Lives) (Istanbul: Iletisim, 2002).

S. Bozdoğan (2001) *Modernism and Nation-Building: Turkish Architectural Culture in the Early Republic* (Seattle: University of Washington Press).

S. Bozdoğan and R. Kasaba (eds) (1997) *Rethinking Modernity and National Identity in Turkey* (Seattle: University of Washington Press).

S. Bozdoğan, S. Özkan and E. Yenal (1987) *Sedad Eldem: Architect in Turkey* (Singapore: Concept Media).

A. Cengizkan (2002) 'Cinnah 19: Utopik Mi, Gercek Modern Mi?' [Cinnah 19: Utopia or real modern?] in *Modernin Saati* (The Hour of the Modern) (Ankara: Mimarlar Dernegi).

S. Genis (2007) 'Producing Elite Localities: The Rise of Gated Communities in Istanbul', *Urban Studies*, vol. 44, pp. 771–98.

S. H. Eldem (2009) *Retrospective* [exhibition catalogue] (Istanbul: Ottoman Bank).

H. Heynen (2005) 'Modernity and Domesticity: Tensions and Contradictions', in *Negotiating Domesticity: Spatial productions of gender in Modern Architecture* (New York: Routledge).

B. Ihsan (1933) 'Kucuk Ev Projeleri'i (Small house projects), *Mimar*, vol. 3, no. 2.

E. Kaceli (2007) 'Fidusyer: Bir Kollektif Dusunme Pratigi' (*Fidusyer*: A Collective Practice), in M. Cengizkan (ed.) *Haluk Baysal – Melih Birsel* (Ankara: TMMOB Mimarlar Odasi Yayinlari).

Y. K. Karaosmanoglu (1991) *Ankara* (Istanbul: Iletisim Yayinlari).

A. Klingman (2007) *Brandscapes: Architecture in the Experience Economy* (Cambridge: MIT Press).

E. Kotran (1997) *1950 ler Kusagi Mimarlik Antolojisi* [Anthology of the 1950s Generation of Architects] (Istanbul: YEM Yayinlari).

A. Loos (1988) 'Story of the Poor Rich Man', in *Spoken into the Void* (Cambridge: The MIT Pres).

B. Nicolai (1998) *Moderne und Exil: Deutschsprachige Architekten in der Turkei 1925–1955* (Berlin: Verlag fur Bauwesen).

Z. Sayar (1936) 'Ic Kolonizasyon', *Arkitekt*, vol. 6, no. 2.

Y. Sey (ed.) (1998) *75 Yilda Degisen Kent ve Mimarlik* [75 Years of Architecture and Urbanism] (Istanbul: Tarih Vakfi).

B. Unsal (1939) 'Kubik Ev ve Konfor' [Cubic House and Comfort], *Arkitekt*, vol. 9, no. 3–4.

H. C. Yalçın (1938) 'Ev ve Apartman', *Yedigun*, vol. 9, no. 265.

A. Ziya (1931) 'Binanin Icinde Mimar' [The Architect in the House], *Mimar*, no. 1.

22

Tin Town to Fanatics: Turkey's Rural to Urban Migration from 1923 to the Present

Jenny B. White

The story of urbanisation in Turkey has three storytellers: the individual migrant, the state, and the scholarly observer. Their three visions or interpretations have to a large extent defined and shaped one another, although their interests and aims are not the same. All are subject to the opportunities and barriers thrown up by history, and have responded to political and intellectual currents from abroad. The Marshall Plan, for instance, reshaped the existence of the individual farmer in Turkey. The introduction of multi-party politics changed the nature of interaction between the government and illegal squatters, who became voters to be wooed. Each stage in the urbanisation of Turkey has been accompanied by scholarly analysis, shaped and reshaped by intellectual currents from abroad. And, finally, the media and the market continue to shape new urban identities today.

When the Turkish Republic was declared in 1923, the city of Ankara stretched from the hill below the Byzantine citadel to the train station. The town consisted of traditional mahalle buildings like those described by Yakup Karaosmanoğlu in his 1935 novel, *Ankara*: one and two-story houses with tile roofs, no running water; muddy, unpaved roads with open sewers; grazing animals wandering about in the daytime and shut into stalls at night. Water came from public fountains. People worked in a variety of occupations, often more than one at a time (Şenyapılı, 1985, p. 6). The newcomers to Ankara were the *yaban*, the strangers, who could not under-stand the locals' language or customs. They were members of the urbanised, Western-educated Ottoman bureaucratic class whose lifestyles, habits and worldview had been shaped in Europe and the cosmopolitan city of Istanbul (Duben and Behar, 1991). It seemed to one witness that the locals would have been glad to see the departure of the new government (Atay cited in Şenyapılı, 1985). But the Kemalist government stayed, built a new city that encompassed the old one, and set about modernising it. In 1926, Ankara got its first telephone exchange. By 1925 it already had a professional fire brigade. In 1936 the Çubuk I Dam went into service. As land became dear, large, well-constructed multi-storey apartments were built to house the middle- and upper classes. Many had shops on the ground floor. In 1928, the Jansen plan, named after the German city planner Hermann Jansen (1869–1947), won the competition to design the expansion of the city. It foresaw large boulevards, well-planned homes with gardens, and a green belt (Nalbantoğlu, 1997).

In the first quarter of the twentieth century,[1] Ankara's population only grew by between 20,000 and 30,000 people, retaining a balance with the surrounding countryside, which, given the agricultural technology of the day, could not support more (Şenyapılı 1985, p. 43). Agricultural needs required that people remain on the land, and this, combined with few employment opportunities in the cities, limited migration. Also, rural migrants had no money to rent or build in the increasingly expensive capital city. The city itself was unable to make provisions for the migrants, so they found nowhere to stay. The Jansen plan and the municipalities formed after 1930 had made no provisions for rural migrants.

As economic opportunities opened up, in the garden sector or in small industry, poor people from the surrounding countryside came and settled on Altındağ hill, which had been excluded from the Jansen plan as being uninhabitable. They began to build on empty, marshy or otherwise undesirable land outside Ankara. In Istanbul, on the other hand, there were economic opportunities in the city centre, in places like Eminönü, as well as on the outskirts, where industries had settled along the Sirkeci rail line. Migrants to Istanbul settled in shared rooms within the city and built illegal housing in the fields, especially along rail lines.

The authorities believed this wave of labour migration to be a temporary phenomenon. Migrant workers were a solution for the new government, which needed workers but had no resources to provide housing. Nor did migrants have the political clout to demand it. This initial phase of urbanisation was substantively different from the wave of migration that began in 1945. It was much smaller in scale and looked upon more kindly by the authorities.

In 1927, three quarters of Turkey's population of 13.6 million people lived in rural areas. Today three quarters live in cities, some of which have almost as many inhabitants as the entire 1927 population. How did this come about? What were the reactions of city dwellers, the state and scholars since the first migrations in the early Republican period? Scholarly discussion, official response, and public reaction were shaped by both the severity of the problem and by popular theoretical approaches to similar phenomena in the West. The phenomenon of migration itself also continued to change. In the 1950s single men worked in the city before returning to their villages with a few liras, having left no lasting mark on city life. The present-day third and fourth generations, city-born and city-bred, have invented a new urbanism.

Tin-can towns

Between 1930 and 1940, migrants built cheap tin-roofed huts (*barakalar*) in shantytowns, nicknamed tin-can towns (*teneke mahalleleri*). Their numbers increased after the 1929 global economic crisis, which affected Turkey's agricultural exports. As farmers grew poorer, they moved to the cities, adding between 5000 and 6000 inhabitants a year. Ankara's population in 1927 was 75,000; by 1935 it was 123,000 (Şenyapılı, 1985, p. 203). The Turkish government's first development plan implemented in 1934 did not include Ankara, but projects foreseen for Ankara in later plans centred around agriculture-related industries like beer and wine factories. A cement factory was opened in 1937. Although the government founded banks and established state agencies to oversee trade and industrial development during this period, it lacked a housing policy to deal with the problem of workers in the planned industries. The municipalities had no resources to protect or develop the land under their aegis. Rather, the state made efforts to give the capital a 'modern' appearance by developing architectural plans (Bozdoğan, 2002). Between 1930 and 1933, Ankara was Turkey's most expensive city (Şenyapılı, 1985, p. 50). Rents and land prices reflected the shortage of housing.

As the city grew beyond the capacity of its official agencies and construction industry, illegal construction increased, often under the guise of extending existing structures for which permission had been obtained (Şenyapılı, 1985, p. 56). Low-income and lower middle-class residents, however, were unable to take part in this expansion, since it required at least the capital to build, as well as some property to build on. The expansion of the railroad and industry also led to an increase in *baraka* construction. While state financing was available for the middle classes to build cooperative housing, no solutions were at hand for the poor, so they found their own.

In 1934, Interior Minister Şükrü Kaya told parliament that there were three Ankaras: the new Ankara, which was being developed according to a public works plan; the old Ankara, which had been included in both the Jansen plan and the government's seven-year plan; and the third Ankara, which was composed of 'houses built by the people in one night and sold for between 4 and 15 liras' (Şenyapılı, 1985, p. 58). He agreed that living in such houses was better than lacking a roof over one's head in winter and acknowledged that the results of razing them were painful. However, he argued, the alternative was worse, since the areas lacked roads, water and services. He and his colleagues saw illegal housing not as a systemic problem, but a neighbourhood problem that could be solved at any time simply by demolition. The first official documents ordering the razing of illegally built *baraka* housing were issued in 1933. In 1934, the municipality tore down 199 illegal structures (Şenyapılı, 1985, p. 57).

Early research on migration was funded by a wary yet sympathetic state. These studies were concerned with the questions of who moved and why, how they got on in the city, and what kind of work they found. Much was written about the flimsy houses the migrants constructed, also called 'spontaneous housing'. Ankara, after all, had just been elaborately planned according to European models. Migrants were perceived as a threat to this new modern order in a literal sense, yet also as necessary labour for developing industry that required cheap, mobile workers. There was a pattern of state management (and also state definition) of the 'problem': freezing rents, alternately tearing down and legalising illegally built homes, building cooperatives, absorbing squatter areas into municipalities, and using state banks to issue credit so people could build their own homes. Abatement practices, accommodation and punishment through razing lagged behind the sheer numbers arriving every day. The state passed laws that were not or could not be implemented, creating the conditions for local initiatives that were illegal, but tolerated in practice. Illegal housing became legal when convenient, as politicians handed out land deeds before elections, leading to massive construction of new squatter houses during campaign seasons. Selective implementation resulted in a kind of housing lottery. A squatter might eventually gain legal status even if his house was torn down several times. This became a viable alternative route to city home ownership, arrived at by ducking through and around holes in the law and spaces between the law and its implementation. The ultimate touchstone was political expediency.

The quilt on their backs

In the aftermath of the world economic crisis of the 1930s, in order to ensure self-sufficiency Turkey turned inward and expanded its state-led economic model, developing industries in a variety of sectors. World War II deepened Turkey's economic distress. As raw materials became scarce, Turkish industries closed down and farm production declined. After 1945 the Marshall Plan financed widespread changes in agricultural technology that pushed peasants from the land and precipitated a stream of migration to the cities. Land became a commodity and agriculture a form of commercial production, leading to the specialisation and diversification of agricultural labour and the movement of workers to areas where their skills were needed or cash could be earned to supplement farm income (Akşit, 1993). It was at this point that urban populations increased exponentially. There were few industrial jobs in the cities, however, and the migrants congregated in the informal sector. Unemployed and low-wage migrants were forced to build their own shelters.

Şenyapılı identifies three types of migrants building squatter housing between 1940 and 1950:

- First, those with low-level jobs and money for basic materials who settled in best-situated areas and within a short time were able to obtain services like electricity and a public fountain.

- Second, those from surrounding villages who came to the city to work for a limited time and whose income supplemented farming income. These mostly rented.
- Third, those forced to leave their land and unable to bring with them anything more than 'the quilt on their backs'. They settled on the least desirable land and dug holes and covered them with wood or kilims, or made huts from found materials. They found employment as occasional workers in the marginal sector (Şenyapılı, 1985, pp. 80–1).

The increase in migrant numbers initiated debate in parliament about the need for a housing policy. Members of parliament argued that tearing illegal homes down would lead to suffering and leave the poor without a roof over their heads. Instead, they suggested that only the worst slums be torn down and their residents helped to find suitable housing or to buy cheap land on credit. This solution was also meant to be applied in Istanbul. The Emlak Bank was directed to help make Turkish citizens homeowners. In other words, the government's first response to the growth in illegal housing was not simply to tear the buildings down, but to find housing alternatives. State lands on which squatters had built illegal housing were put under the jurisdiction of the Ankara municipality. Private land taken over by squatters was compensated for with a small payment. The municipality was to distribute this land to homeless people for a small fee, paid interest-free over a period of ten years. In order to avoid land speculation, the new owners were required to begin building within a year and finish within three. The mortgage would serve as collateral for bank loans under favourable conditions with the municipality as guarantor. Beneficiaries of this law had to have lived in the city at least a year and could not own land or a home (Şenyapılı, 1985, p. 87). Any squatter houses built after the law was in force were to be razed (Law 5218).

Debate raged in parliament about whether legalising existing squatter houses would solve the basic social problems behind such settlements, and deputies also expressed worry about the heavy financial burden on municipalities. In the end, the law was extended to the entire nation (via Law 5228) on the assumption that the phenomenon of illegal construction was basically a housing problem, rather than a social problem having origins in the developing countryside or urban unemployment. Housing seemed an easier issue to solve, despite the financial cost, than the latter problems.

Şenyapılı argues that although the municipality distributed cheap land, it did not do enough to hinder land speculation, nor did banks provide sufficient credit. What the laws did do was accept and legalise the existence of squatter areas and transfer state lands to local administrations for this purpose. The laws did little to help the masses of landless peasants flooding the city. However, as she points out, the mostly middle class Yenimahalle neighbourhood was founded in 1950 under Law 5228 (Şenyapılı, 1985, p. 91).

Squatter areas (*Gecekondu*)

As squatter areas grew, they created environmental problems and thus, became a health risk for the population. Laws existed that allowed the government to tear down illegal housing that had not been absorbed by the municipality, but these laws were not consistently applied. Throughout the 1950s, researchers and the government (which often hired the researchers) still perceived migration as basically a housing question, rather than a broader socioeconomic problem requiring different kinds of solutions. The state and municipal governments joined forces to develop cooperative projects for self-contained neighbourhoods. Prospective homeowners drew lots and received mortgages. Once the houses were built, however, residents subdivided them and rented them out, greatly increasing the population density of these carefully planned communities. Early squatter and cooperative homes were two and three-storey houses set inside small gardens. In 1948, owners obtained legal permission to build upward, increasing population density. In Ankara, rapid construction further undermined the Jansen plan despite the government's attempts to maintain its basic principles (Şenyapılı, 1985, p. 108).

During this period, migrants who had lived for some time in the cities became adept at understanding and manipulating the contradictions and weaknesses of municipal policies and control, and bettered their lot by pushing the boundaries of legality. The increasing middle class population density in cooperative housing provided some job opportunities, especially for squatter-area women who could work as servants, laundresses and child minders. The economy improved and roads built under the Marshall Plan brought produce to market and producers to the city as cheap labour. They found work in the marginal sector and the growing service sector. The urban population soared. Twenty-five per cent of Turkey's population was urbanised in 1950; 32 per cent by 1960 (Şenyapılı, 1985, p. 118). Between 50,000 and 60,000 poor migrants lived in Ankara's squatter areas between 1940 and 1950. In the end, cities like Ankara were unable to provide them with cheap land. Government sponsored housing meant for the squatter population, land ended up in the hands of those able to make long-term payments to banks. Migrants without a steady income were unable to pay rent, much less mortgages. Speculators profited by renting out or selling the land instead of developing it.

Toward the end of the decade, factory jobs became available in state-run factories manufacturing flour, beer, sugar, motors, turbines, tractors and other farm machinery. The construction sector grew, while agriculture declined in importance. This meant that, for the first time, not only was the countryside 'pushing' migrants out, but the city was also 'pulling' them in with jobs (Şenyapılı, 1985, p. 121). Housing, however, remained a problem, and prices soared beyond the means even of some civil servants. Rents that had been frozen in 1939 and 1947 were set free to rise (Şenyapılı, 1985, pp. 122–3). Zeytinburnu in Istanbul and Altındağ in Ankara became enormous, iconic squatter areas. Zeytinburnu had 80,000 inhabitants in 1960, half of them migrants from Yugoslavia, Bulgaria, Greece and Romania. Most of the rest came from Turkey's Black Sea region. About half 'owned' their homes, three quarters of them without a deed to the land. They had built on land belonging to individuals (41 per cent), a foundation (39 per cent), and the state (12 per cent). Sixty-one per cent of these residents were workers employed in the same area where they lived. While 81 per cent had electricity, 96 per cent had no sewage connection. On the Anatolian side of Istanbul, squatter areas mostly arose on state land (half), more squatters 'owned' their houses (95 per cent), and most were internal migrants (96 per cent; half from the Black Sea coast). In 1963, 40 per cent of Istanbul homes were squatter houses, in which 45 per cent of the city's residents lived (T. C. Imar ve Iskan Bakanlığı (IIB), 1966).

From the 1950s on, migrants increasingly brought their families to the cities and became politically active. Their quality of life gradually improved. New migrants came with not just quilts on their backs, but with an address in hand of a relative or person from their village already there. Informal relations helped newcomers find housing and jobs. Illegal settlements began to become permanent. All stages of the process, from taking over the land to supplying building material and labour, became organised and professionalised. Transportation networks in the new neighbourhoods grew (Tekeli, 1991). Tin towns became established neighbourhoods. Some residents improved their financial lot by renting out their old squatter homes and constructing new ones, or by building shops into the lower levels to rent out. In this regard, some of the squatter landlords were better off than middle-class salaried professionals, especially those that rented.

After the introduction of multiparty politics in the 1950s, politicians began to view squatter populations as voters to be wooed. Political parties distributed deeds to land in supportive neighbourhoods and improved their infrastructure. Thousands of squatters built homes right before elections when the deeds were handed out. Orders to raze houses that did not 'meet health standards' were often given right after elections. Newspapers carried reports of heart-wrenching scenes of people standing in the way of bulldozers. While the media and some scholars increasingly saw illegal settlement as a problem of poverty, the government still treated it as a housing problem, to be fixed either through legalising or demolishing settlements. Although squatter areas remained illegal, government housing policy accepted them as a fact and continued to respond in three basic ways: amelioration, clearance and prevention. The idea behind housing and squatter-related laws, policies and projects developed since the 1960s was that the state should make land available, finance low-cost alternative housing, enable citizens to obtain credit, and thereby prevent the spread of squatter areas (Şenyapılı, 1985, p. 27).

Squatter area residents organised to petition for neighbourhood (*mahalle*) status (Şenyapılı, 1985, p. 174). To speed things up, squatter area residents shared cost and labour with the municipality, modelled after the village custom of *imece* (shared labour) in order to set up services like electricity, water, roads and sewers (Şenyapılı, 1985, p. 176).

A 1964 study of a squatter area in Ankara found that squatter 'owners' included people like policemen and low-level municipal civil servants (*zabita* and *fen memuru*), some of whom were charged with preventing squatter building. By 1964, 59 per cent of Ankara's population lived in squatter areas (Antakya 32 per cent, Erzincan 53 per cent, Erzurum 35 per cent, Iskenderun 38 per cent, Istanbul 45 per cent, Samsun 36 per cent, Izmir 32 per cent, Bursa 27 per cent). Half of these residents were 'owners' and half renters (IIB, 1966, pp. 15–16, 19).

Nevertheless in Turkey's 20 largest cities in 1960, 24 per cent of homes had no electricity, 55 per cent no city water, and 97 per cent no gas connection (IIB, 1966, p. 10). Of the neighbourhoods on Istanbul's Anatolian side, only 18 per cent of squatter areas were connected to city sewers, 37 per cent had electricity, and 19 per cent city water (IIB, 1966, p. 53). Fifty-seven per cent of squatter homes had been constructed by the owner, often with cheap or old materials. Thirty-five per cent of buildings in Ankara squatter areas had walls of sun-baked brick, and 53 per cent had earthen floors. Built quickly in a state of fear, the houses were built to a much lower standard than village houses (IIB, 1966, pp. 16–17). T. Kurucu describes typical squatter housing in 1962 as follows: once a roof was put on, the residents would move in a bed, a crib and a stove, put a brazier by the door on which is bubbling a pot, and hang a picture of Ataturk on the wall. That way, not much would be lost if the structure were to be torn down (cited by Şenyapılı, 1985, p. 132).

Pure peasants, polluting slums

In the 1960s, the state sponsored studies of migrants' sociocultural characteristics (Yasa, 1966). Some studies were influenced by Western research that viewed slums as a source of social problems and delinquency, and argued that a certain family culture and personality were linked to poverty. The issue of illegal settlement was increasingly seen as a political problem requiring state-sponsored solutions, like Western slum clearance projects. Squatters retained their village habits. They baked their own bread, grew vegetable gardens, and raised chickens and cows, even on upper-story apartment balconies. They retained strong ties with their villages, returning to help with the harvest. Cities, it was said, were becoming 'villagised' (Keleş, 1972, p. 44).

At the same time that scholars portrayed the rural migrant as a force potentially polluting urban culture, health, water and air; peasant life itself was romanticised as pure (*saf*), simple, naïve. Some scholars believed that villagers lived in a more open environment with stronger social ties and social controls and, therefore, had lower resistance against illness and various 'behavioral vices' encountered in the cities (Yörükan, 1968, p. 71). This tendency was supposedly exacerbated by poor living conditions and other problems hindering their adjustment to city life. Yörükan described poverty, disease, a high birth rate, crime and sexual crimes among migrants in the cities, arguing that returning migrants then brought these problems back to the village. He recommended that a variety of ministries step in to build squatter-area roads, bridges, pavements, schools, libraries, health clinics, and job training centres.

Interestingly, Yörükan's own statistics do not bear out his claim of spreading vice, nor was there much evidence of delinquency in other studies. A 1971 study by Birsen Gökçe also raised the red flag of juvenile delinquency in squatter areas (Gökçe, 1976). Migrant youth problems, she argued, were caused by the contradictions of 'traditional behaviour' and expectations, on the one hand, and the desire of youths to identify with city life, on the other. When group consciousness decreased, social controls were weakened and social problems resulted (Şenyapılı, 1985, p. 21). Gökçe described squatter youths' work characteristics, habits and 'behavioural mistakes'. She pointed out, for instance, that their nutrition contained inadequate amounts of protein. However, 75 per cent of the youth in her study claimed never to smoke, 94 per cent never drank alcohol, and 91 per cent did not use drugs. Crime was also in short supply. Furthermore, squatters had a higher literacy level than villagers (Gökçe, 1976, pp. 126–9, 137), see also Table 22.1.

Forty per cent of girls and 44 per cent of boys said they would rather study than work. They mostly wanted to become teachers, doctors, pharmacists, or engineers and architects (139). And most said they would model themselves not on a family member, but on a friend (45 per cent). Although dissatisfied with their neighbourhoods, 92 per cent were happy to be living in the city: life was easier; you could find everything, there was a possibility of education and fun. In their free time, 45 per cent read (novels, stories, illustrated magazines) and 19 per cent went to the movies. Religion played a minor role. Only 12 per cent of respondents read religious works and 5 per cent listened to religious radio programs (Gökçe, 1976, p. 149).

While Western slums were characterised by low literacy and education, in Turkey the slum-produced crisis had not actually occurred, although the

Table 22.1 1971 literacy levels in urban and rural areas

	Men	Women
City	82.2%	54.2%
Country	63.4%	27.0%
Total	70.2%	37.3%

Source: Gökçe (1976, p. 137).

literature had assumed it would and suggested plans to prevent or alleviate it. Like Yörükan, Gökçe concluded that, as in the West, social centres should be built to meet the psychological and socioeconomic needs of migrant youth and their families and help them pass the time in a 'productive' way and overcome 'culture lag' on the way to modernity.

Orhan Tuna, in his 1977 study of Istanbul squatter areas, suggested that the psychology of rural people was more closely tied to religious beliefs and traditions than that of urbanites (Tuna, 1977). He argued that the different moral values and economic and social characteristics of the city created an impetus for change, so that after coming to the city, migrant families became smaller. What they needed to complete the transition to modernity, he argued, was a little help, a living wage, and the ability to build a house with a garden to grow vegetables and where children could play. All this, Tuna wrote, was foreseen in government plans, but never implemented. Önder Şenyapılı also wrote about the poverty of urbanising villagers, laying their lack of integration squarely at the door of an unjust distribution of income (Şenyapılı, 1978).

The middle class concentrated in downtown apartments until the spread of car ownership in the 1960s allowed first the upper, and then the middle classes to build at the city's edge, in less-crowded *banlöyü* areas far from environmental and cultural pollution. Even in areas tied to city services, environmental degradation, pollution and the lack of green space were severe. Inadequate water, electricity, sewage disposal, garbage collection and roads caused health problems. Between 1970 and 1971, of the 4000 residents of Abidin Paşa squatter neighbourhood in Ankara (in a study based on a 10 per cent sample), 51 per cent of families had lost a child and 85 per cent of women had suffered a miscarriage (reported in Şenyapılı, 1985, p. 196).

The 1970s literature on squatter areas focused on another kind of pollution, that of disorder, the disruption of city planning, parking and food distribution mechanisms. The emphasis was on the city as an ecology or system, with each part of the population playing a role within the larger capitalist economy that needed the participation of different social groups. Tekeli, Gülöksüz, and Okyay wrote about burgeoning squatter populations and mass high-rise buildings as forces overwhelming the city as a plan and the city as an economy. The solution, they suggested, was not to bow down by legalising illegal housing and small-scale informal businesses, nor by forbidding, outlawing or harassing them, but to accept them as a necessary part of the urban system and to order their activities. They suggested, for instance, that the state organise neighbourhood vegetable sellers or small tradesmen in small open markets and regulate the shared taxis that had grown up to service far-flung squatter areas. The alternative, they insisted, should not be whatever model produced the most votes (Tekeli, Gülöksüz, and Okyay, 1976, p. 239).

A member of the Ankara Chamber of Architects jokingly suggested the organisation give its1971 book on urbanisation the title *Praise to*

Industrialisation because the heart of the argument contained within was that the lack of healthy urbanisation can be traced to a lack of industrialisation and the ensuing organisation of workers into groups, associations, unions, and political parties (Ankara Chamber of Architects, 1971). That is, failed urbanisation was the result of a failure to transform passive residents into active workers. This continued passivity, the architects argued, resulted in cultural and economic underdevelopment. They placed much hope in the double power of urbanisation and industrialisation to catapult peasants and small producers into capitalist relations that would make individual men into active, modern urbanites.

These and other studies had been influenced by two preoccupations in the Western literature on urbanisation and modernisation in the first half of the twentieth century. One group of writers gave precedence to capitalism, industry and class formation, the other to urbanism as a path to modernity. Foremost among the latter were Daniel Lerner's *The Passing of Traditional Society* (Lerner, 1958), Louis Wirth's *Urbanism as a Way of Life* (Wirth, 1938), Oscar Lewis' folk and urban ideal types (Lewis, 1959), and Gideon Sjoberg's proposed path from pre-industrial to industrial society (Sjoberg, 1955). Juvenile delinquency was but one symptom to be expected of incomplete urbanisation, these authors contended, with youth succumbing to the contradictions and the temptations of the city as they presumably lost their traditional bearings but had not yet entered into a contract with modernity.

The fanaticisation of the city

Scholars writing in the 1980s saw peasants in the cities as an example of the periphery challenging the centre (IIB, 1966; Şenyapılı, 1981). Urbanisation was linked to social change, and reflected in economic and social relations. Many of the articles in Kağıtçıbaşı examine the effect of urbanisation on family structure, sex roles, and community (Kağıtçıbaşı, 1982). From the 1980s on, squatter areas also became a cultural problem, instead of simply a social class issue requiring economic solutions. Rather, rural values and lifestyle were juxtaposed to urban life. Did squatter residents have a 'culture of poverty'?

Scholars closely examined survival mechanisms of migrants and squatters in the cities. 'Traditional' rural cultural values and practices, particularly family structure and relationship webs, played important roles in compensating the effects of poverty (Kıray, 1998). Strong communities allowed less deviance and crime. My own early work, *Money Makes us Relatives* focused on the neighbourhood relational webs and the concept of *imece*, a village custom of mutual obligation that, in the city, often disguised capitalist exploitation (White, 2004). Güneş-Ayata (1996) pointed to the continuing family and social solidarity of the migrant urban family, a direct challenge to predictions by Wirth and Lerner that urbanisation would lead to a loosening of family ties and atomisation of the individual. Instead, community relations were diversified and more 'modern' forms of association added to traditional ones. Güneş-Ayata suggested that such continuing solidarity and networking is responsible for strong urban communities that help keep deviance in crime to a minimum despite poverty. Kiray described conservatism as a survival strategy that brought security to migrant communities. She, like the Ankara Chamber of Architects, wondered whether factory work would eventually cause this to change. The assumption was that conservative social mores would, indeed had to, change. Urbanisation led to modernity, after all. State-sponsored studies continued to measure squatter resident attitudes and behaviours on a traditional-to-modern continuum, the modern end of the scale characterised by 'free thought and behaviour' and membership of organisations.[2] In this period, squatter life also became the setting for popular novels like *Berji Kristin: Tales from the Garbage Hills* and *Dear Shameless Death*, both by Latife Tekin (1996 [1984]); 2001 [1983]).

Were squatters alienated from urban society? Or were they using extra-legal means to establish a place in city life that threatened its integrity? Some called this the fanaticisation (*yobazlaşma*) of urban culture (Kongar, 1982). The stated or unstated counterpoint to 'traditional' practices was the array of 'modern' relations: membership of formal organisations, labour unions, neighbourhood associations and political parties (Gökçe et al., 1993). The 1990s boom in literature documenting the spread of civil society in Turkey fed a desire to map a globally accredited modernity onto Turkey's variegated face, veiled and smiling and now right down the street.

The new urbans

The 1996 proceedings of a retrospective conference on 50 years of Turkish urbanisation concluded that migration continued unabated and that the most important problems for migrants remained poverty, shelter and integration into urban life. Yet the report also mentioned 'the new urbans' – young, dynamic, no longer affected by the social texture of rural life (Ekonomi Forum, 1996). They were throwing themselves into the social and political life of the cities.

High-rise living at the heart of the city had replaced early one-story squatter homes set within gardens at the city's edge. The architecture of living had set into play changes in relationships among family members, neighbours, and regional countrymen. The anonymity brought some women freedom from surveillance. As Sencer Ayata put it, in his insightful analysis of squatter apartment dwellers, 'The atmosphere of the apartment is freedom' (Ayata, 1989). Middle class developments encroached on former squatter areas. In a 2001 article, Sevilay Kaygalık concluded that urban poverty had spread to include the urban salaried population.[3] Sema Erder describes the working-class district of Ümraniye in Istanbul, not as a homogenous squatter area, but as a varied, changing, highly mobile metropolis full of unexpected relationships (Erder, 1996).

In the 1990s, the increasingly differentiated cityscape made it impossible to speak of squatter districts. The term *varoş* came into use, replacing gecekondu or squatter area. The concept of varoş for the first time acknowledged that this was no longer a rural phenomenon, the peasantisation of the city, although the varoş was viewed as equally polluting. The varoş was a site of fanaticisation, associated with a politicised Islamic religiosity that showed itself in a clash of symbolic markers having the power and qualities of amulets in urban public space – the veil versus Ataturk's image.

For the first time also, observers understood that the solution to poverty, housing, and environmental problems that had plagued the cities would be in the hands of the very people whom many secular city dwellers had viewed as the problem. Poor, working-class urbanites, many with rural origins, voted conservative, religious politicians into power. However, Kaygalık and others posed the following questions. Was this population politically active on the basis of social class? Did the poor reject capitalism and the logic of the market or did they embrace its potential? Or did migrant families enter the political fray on the basis of sociocultural, religious, ethnic or regional differences – a conservatism and in-group politics that rejected secular, liberal urban values and lifestyle? Who exactly had come to power?

Identity politics

A popular approach to understanding this increasingly politically powerful and socially visible conservative urban population was to analyse it as a form of identity politics (Ayata, 1997). This analysis focused particularly on the conspicuous lifestyles and new fashions of conservative urban Muslims. Women and *tesettür* veiling were central to this analysis. The tesettür style of veiling has become a fashion with its own styles that change annually, and its own runway shows, companies and markets, some global (Navaro-Yashin, 2002). It differs substantially from Ottoman veiling styles, although tesettür clothing companies refer to Turkey's Ottoman heritage to add distinction to their products. Tesettür also bears little resemblance to rural forms of covering. As a fashion, it changes year by year and has merged in style and colour with Western-style secular fashions sold in the same markets. In 2004, I saw for the first time a see-through headscarf that clearly revealed hair and ears. The young woman thus 'covered' was dressed in jeans and a matching tightly fitted long jeans overcoat.

The identity politics approach posited that wearers of tesettür are engaged in a bid to acquire elite status for an Islamic lifestyle that would compete with a Western lifestyle in the definition of social status (Göle, 1996; Saktanber, 1997). Until the 1980s, the Western, secular Kemalist elites determined what behaviours and clothing counted as urban and modern and, thus, socially desirable. The conservative urban population now challenged that monopoly of status and style – and, in so doing, ultimately contested the right to define what is modern. The identity politics approach also assumes that the flaunting of Muslim identity in the former power centres of secular society – the city, markets and other public arenas – makes it a political act, a challenge to the old elites from those positioning themselves as alternate, new elites. The 'new Islamic woman' was educated, professionally and politically active, and both physically and economically mobile. She stood for a politically aggressive and increasingly socially popular 'modern Muslim' identity that arguably took shape among the ambitious offspring of urban migrants.

This explanation, however, does not deal directly with social class differences (other than status markers) or with in-group allegiances. An interesting example of the different approaches to the varoş/gecekondu is that of Nalan Türkeli, a working-class woman who kept a diary of her struggle to survive economically and socially in such a neighbourhood. Her diary was published with the title *To be a Woman in the Varoş: A Diary* (Türkeli, 1996) and Türkeli was paraded at meetings of liberal intellectuals and journalists as a success story – a woman from the 'other Istanbul' who had engaged in modern self-reflection and publication. While liberal elites defined Türkeli in terms of 'varoş'/city identity politics, she herself wrote and spoke primarily of the economic problems she faced as a 'gecekondu' resident.

Like social class, group solidarity continues to be an important factor in Turkish society, whether the group is based on religiosity, region, or social class. Erder, for instance, argues that in-group localism and networking takes on increasing importance as urban life becomes more diverse and competitive (Erder, 1999). Güneş-Ayata also suggests that regional ties in squatter areas compete with other forms of organisation (Güneş-Ayata, 1990). Social class and lifestyle differences create divisions among secularists, and among conservative urbanites, rather than just dividing secular elites from migrants. Salaries of secular professionals and civil servants continued to decline over the 1990s, while some conservative devout Muslims became wealthy and developed lifestyles – living in gated communities, for instance, and shopping for couture veils – that alienated them from other conservative Muslims who remained in the large working-class neighbourhoods that had replaced their parents' squatter areas. Islamist elites joined secularist elites in fleeing the inner city for luxury gated communities on the green outskirts of the city. It is unclear which 'identity' is being hailed in 'identity politics'. Islamic and secularist middle-class property owners have more interests in common than they share with their working-class or rural ideological fellows. It can be argued that the Islamist elite does not represent the rest of the devout Muslim population, and that not all women have the financial wherewithal to live the lifestyle of the 'New Islamic Woman', beyond the wearing of a down-market version of tesettür, ironed often and replaced once a year.

Staging the local and the global

What is clear is that as of the 2000s, migrants and their offspring – of all classes – had *become* the city, at least a large part of it. This has caused anxiety over political control of the nation as a whole and the city in particular. An ongoing debate has revolved around the question of how much power local administrations should wield. Local administrations were addressed in the government's seventh Five-Year Plan (1996–2000). The plan proposed a fundamental transfer of authority and resources from the central government to the municipal levels, along with greatly increased capacity-building and accountability of local authorities and more citizen participation in local government. But how well do local administrations represent 'local' concerns? And what exactly *is* the local? How much of what the city or the local represents is the will and needs of the people and how much is big business? (Şengül, 2001). When people speak of '*We, the city*', who is *we*?

The literature influencing recent debates about the identity of the city discusses identity in terms of globalisation, history, memory, and postmodernity (influenced by such scholars as Jonathan Boyarin, Michael Herzfeld and David Harvey). Whose history is being preserved? Whose past is represented by urban heritage and conservation? It is a truism that identities are shifting, becoming globalised. The city is a competitive staging ground for enactments of history and memory (Keyder, 1999; Özyürek, 2006). Islamists make street theatre of the conquest of Byzantium by the Muslim Turks and proposed building a mosque in Taksim, the centre of Istanbul's modern entertainment centre. Secularists lay wreaths at the feet of Ataturk's statue in Taksim Square and clink glasses of potent raki at outdoor restaurants in Beyoğlu (Bartu, 1999).

But the major actor – or enactor – in urban identity theatre is arguably business. What is one to make of such transformations of the urban landscape as French Street (ironically, formerly named Cezayir, or Algeria, Street), the newly 'renovated' street in Istanbul's historic centre? Its working-class residents removed, French Street has become a theme park of global urbanism, with Francophile sidewalk cafes and indoor restaurants serving bad American-style food (cheese balls and French fries). Other 'traditional' buildings and entire neighbourhoods have been renovated and turned into hotels or sanitised cultural experiences for elite shoppers and tourists. The culture of rural life has been turned into urban conservation couture.

The story does not end here. Some migrant families, unable to survive the unemployment and high cost of urban living, have begun to return to their villages. The countryside also is becoming suburbanised as elites leave the city centres to the middle and lower classes. Satellite suburbs are magnets for certain types of populations, in effect creating lifestyle-segregated communities dominated by either secular Kemalist or conservative Muslim populations. In other upscale housing areas, Muslim and secular lifestyles have begun to blur around bourgeois desires for certain types of housing, commodities, fashion, leisure activities and status brands. In other words, while social class continues to be a basic differentiating condition of urban populations, class no longer can be matched to rural versus urban origin, local versus global outlook, religiosity versus secularism, or differences in taste and lifestyle. New identities – Euro-centric, ethnic, hybrid – are continually emerging and being tried on for urban fit.

Notes

1. This discussion of early Republican migration is taken largely from Şenyapılı (1985).
2. See, for instance, Gökçe, Acar, Ayata, Kasapoğlu, Özer and Uygun (1993); and Onat (1993).
3. Kaygalık, Sevilay (2001) 'Yeni Kentsel Yoksulluk, Göç ve Yoksulluğun Mekansal Yoğunlaşması: Mersin/Demirtaş Mahallesi Örneği', *Praksis* Spring, no. 2, pp. 124–72.

Bibliography

Akşit, B. (1993) 'Studies in Rural Transformation in Turkey 1950–1990', in P. Stirling (ed.) *Culture and Economy: Changes in Turkish Villages* (Hemingford, UK: The Eothen Press).

Ankara Chamber of Architects (1971) *Türkiyede Kentleşme* (Ankara: Ankara Chamber of Architects).

A. Ayata (1997) 'The Emergence of Identity Politics in Turkey', *New Perspectives on Turkey*, Fall, no. 17, pp. 59–73.

S. Ayata (1989) 'Toplumsal Çevre Olarak Gecekondu ve Apartman', in *Toplum ve Bilim*, vol. 46–7, pp. 101–27.

A. Bartu (1999) 'Who Owns the Old Quarters? Rewriting Histories in a Global Era', in C. Keyder (ed.) *Istanbul Between the Global and the Local* (Oxford: Rowman and Littlefield).

S. Bozdoğan (2002) *Modernism and Nation Building: Turkish Architectural Culture in the Early Republic* (Seattle: University of Washington Press).

A. Duben and C. Behar (1991) *Istanbul Households: Marriage, Family and Fertility, 1880–1940* (Cambridge: Cambridge University Press).

Ekonomi Forum (1996) *Türkiye'de Gecekondunun 50. Yılı: Barınma Ihtiyacından Kentsel Rant Paylaşımına Dönüşen Bir Sürecin Ekonomik, Sosyal ve Politik Boyutları*. (Istanbul: Friedrich Ebert Foundation).

S. Erder (1996) *Istanbul'a Bir Kent Kondu: Ümraniye* (Istanbul: Iletişim).

S. Erder (1999) 'Where Do You Hail From? Localism and Networks in Istanbul', in C. Keyder (ed.) *Istanbul Between the Global and the Local* (Oxford: Rowman and Littlefield).

B. Gökçe (1976) *Gecekondu Gençliği: Ankara* (Ankara: Hacettepe University Publications).

B. Gökçe, F. Acar, A. Ayata, A. Kasapoğlu, I. Özer and H. Uygun (1993) *Gecekondularda Ailelerarası Geleneksel Dayanışmanın Çağdaş Organizasyonlara Dönüşümü* (Ankara: Turkish Prime Ministry, Women and Social Services Administration).

N. Göle (1996) *The Forbidden Modern: Civilization and Veiling* (Ann Arbor: University of Michigan Press).

A. Güneş-Ayata (1990) 'Gecekondularda Kimlik Sorunu, Dayanışma Örüntüleri ve Hemşehrilik', *Toplum ve Bilim*, vol. 51–52, 89–101.

A. Güneş-Ayata (1996) 'Solidarity in Urban Turkish Family', in G. Rasuly-Paleczek (ed.) *Turkish Families in Transition* (Frankfurt am Main: Peter Lang).

Imar ve Iskan Bakanlığı, Ministry of Public Works and Habitation (IIB) (1966) *Şehirleşme, Gecekondular ve Konut Politikası* (Ankara: Ministry of Public Works and Habitation).

Ç. Kağıtçıbaşı (ed.) (1982) *Sex Roles, Family and Community in Turkey* (Bloomington: Indiana University Turkish Studies).

S. Kaygalik (2001) 'yeni kentsel yoksulluk, Göç ve Yoksulluğun Mekansal Yoğun laşmasli Mersin/Demirtaş Mahallesi Örneği', Praksis, Spriny, no. 2, pp. 124–72.

R. Keleş (1972) *Türkiye'de Şehirleşme, Konut ve Gecekondu* (Istanbul: Gerçek Yayınevi).

Ç. Keyder (1993) 'The Genesis of Petty Commodity Production in Agriculture', in P. Stirling (ed.) *Culture and Economy: Changes in Turkish Villages* (Hemingford, UK: The Eothen Press).

Ç. Keyder (ed.) (1999) *Istanbul Between the Global and the Local* (Oxford: Rowman and Littlefield).

M. Kıray (1998) *Gecekondu: Az Gelişmiş Ülkelerde Hızla Topraktan Kopma ve Kentle Bütünleşememe, Kentleşme Yazıları* (Istanbul: Bağlam).

E. Kongar (1982) 'Kentleşen Gecekondular Ya Da Gecekondulaşan Kentler Sorunu', in *Kentle Bütünleşme*, Turkish Development Foundation no. 4, pp. 23–46.

D. Lerner (1958) *The Passing of Traditional Society: Modernizing the Middle East* (New York: The Free Press).

O. Lewis (1959) *Five Families: Mexican Studies in the Culture of Poverty* (New York: Basic Books).

G. B. Nalbantoğlu (1997) 'Silent Interruptions: Urban Encounters with Rural Turkey', in Sibel Bozdoğan and R. Kasaba (eds) *Rethinking Modernity and National Identity in Turkey*, pp. 192–210 (Seattle: University of Washington Press).

Y. Navaro-Yashin (2002) 'The Market for Identities: Secularism, Islamism, Commodities', in Deniz Kandiyoti and A. Saktanber (eds) *Fragments of Culture: The Everyday of Modern Turkey* (London: I. B. Tauris).

Ü. Onat (1993) *Gecekondu Kadının Kente Özgü Düşünce ve Davranşılar Geliştirme Süreci* (Ankara: Turkish Prime Ministry, Women and Social Services Administration).

E. Özyürek (2006) *Nostalgia for the Modern: State Secularism and Everyday Politics in Turkey* (London: Duke University Press).

A. Saktanber (1997) 'Formation of a Middle-Class Ethos and Its Quotidian: Revitalizing Islam in Urban Turkey', in A. Öncü and P. Weyland (eds) *Space, Culture and Power: New Identities in Globalizing Cities* (London: Zed Books).

G. Sjoberg (1955) 'The Preindustrial City', *American J. of Sociology*, no. 60, pp. 438–45.

T. Şengül (2001) 'Türkiye'de Yerel Yönetimler: Deneyim ve Söylemin Dönüşümü', in *Kentsel Çelişki ve Siyaset* (İstanbul: Demokrasi Kitaplığı).

Ö. Şenyapılı (1978) *Kentlileşen Köylüler* (Istanbul: Milliyet Yayınları).

T. Şenyapılı (1981) *Gecekondu: 'Çevre' Işçilerin Mekanı* (Ankara: Middle East Technical University Department of Architecture).

T. Şenyapılı (1985) *Ankara Kentinde Gecekondu Gelişimi (1923–1960)* (Ankara: Batğkent Konut Üretim Yapı Kooperatifleri Birliği).

I. Tekeli (1991) 'Development of Intra-Urban Trips and Their Organization in Ankara', in M. Kıray (ed.) *Structural Change in Turkish Society* (Bloomington: Indiana University Turkish Studies).

I. Tekeli, Y. Gülöksüz and T. Okyay (1976) *Gecekondulu Dolmuşlu Işportalı Şehir* (Istanbul: Cem Yayınevi).

L. Tekin (1996 [1984]) *Berji Kristin: Tales from the Garbage Hills* (London: Marion Boyars).

L. Tekin (2001 [1983]) *Dear Shameless Death* (London: Marion Boyars).

O. Tuna (1977) *Istanbul Gecekondu Önleme Bölgeleri Araştırması* (Istanbul: Istanbul University Publication No. 2300a).

N. Türkeli (1996) *Varoşta Kadın Olmak: Günlük* (Istanbul: Gökkuşağı).

J. B. White ([1991] 2004) *Money Makes Us Relative: Women's Labour in Urban Turkey* (Second Edition) (London: Routledge).

L. Wirth (1938) 'Urbanism as a Way of Life', *American J. of Sociology*, vol. 44, no. 1, pp. 1–24.

I. Yasa (1966) *Ankara'da Gecekondu Aileleri* (Ankara: Health and Social Services Ministry).

T. Yörükan (1968) *Gecekondular ve Gecekondu Bölgelerinin Sosyo-Kültürel Özellikleri* (Ankara: Ministry of Public Works and Habitation).

23
Oral History and Memory Studies in Turkey

Leyla Neyzi

Itself a relatively new interdisciplinary field, oral history and memory studies is a fledgling research area in Turkey. This provides a contrast with history, a well-established, hegemonic discipline historically allied with the state. While many academics in the field of oral history and memory studies outside Turkey were trained in history, and through their work challenged and transformed traditional historiography, in Turkey, practitioners of oral history tend to come from other disciplines such as folklore, anthropology, sociology, literature and women's studies. As a new field, oral history and memory studies is weakly institutionalised in academe: few universities offer courses in oral history and/or memory studies, usually on the inititative of individual academics based in other programmes. In recent years, though, with the rise of identity politics and widespread debate in the media on national history, academics as well as NGO's, informal groups and individuals are turning to oral history as a means of rediscovering and reinterpreting the past.

In this chapter, I briefly review the history of oral history and memory studies in Turkey, and provide a case study to show that this methodology and interdisciplinary field has the potential to change the way the recent past is studied and represented both within academe and in society as a whole.

The rise of oral history

Oral history is defined as spoken memories about the past recorded by oral historians in a dialogue with individuals providing testimony. Oral history often examines events and experiences not recorded (or differently recorded) by written history, and shows that historical events may be alternately interpreted by individuals who embody the past in the present (Portelli, 2001). Over time, oral history developed into the wider interdisciplinary field of memory studies, which studies memory with or without recourse to oral history interviewing *per se* (Hodgkin and Radstone, 2006).

Key to the rise of oral history was the development of mobile voice recording devices and a perspective that valued the experience and viewpoint of the ordinary person. In the US, a landmark event was the decision in the 1940s of historian Allan Nevins of Columbia University to record interviews with individuals who knew former presidents of the US. Nevins felt that, with the advent of new technology, information that previously would have been sent by letter was transmitted over the telephone, no longer being available as a source for historians. Nevins realised that individuals who had known past presidents were key historical sources themselves, and set about interviewing them. Allan Nevins' research led to the creation of the Columbia University Oral History Research Office, one of the first oral history programmes in the world, with one of the largest collections of oral history interviews (Columbia University Oral History Research Office).

Oral history also developed rapidly in the UK, particularly in the years following World War II. It was particularly those on the left, and/or feminists, who became dissatisfied with traditional history's ability to convey the experience of the powerless and marginal, including the working class, women, minorities, and immigrants. As traditional history was based on written documents in archives, social history, including women's history, required a fine-tooth comb to trace the silenced experience of the non-literate or not-so-literate (Steedman, 2007). Oral history interviews made it possible to fill in the gaps of a historiographical tradition which overwhelmingly represented the experience of upper class white men (Chamberlain, 2009).

Oral history was used in particular to study the Holocaust, the numerous genocides of the twentieth century, and recent violence and trauma in diverse contexts including Latin America, South Africa, Ireland, India, and Africa (Rogers and Leydesdorff, 2004; Robben, 2005; Das, 2007). Early practitioners celebrated oral history as a means of giving voice to the silenced or subaltern, and oral history methodology resembled anthropological fieldwork in providing a bottom-up view of society. It also demonstrated a particular focus on the subject, on emotions and on the senses. Yet it soon became evident that oral history was no panacea. Methodological dilemmas, particularly concerning power relations between the researcher and the subject(s), led to discussions of ethics and reflexivity. Similar methodological and epistemological debates took place in feminist studies and anthropology. The methodological and theoretical questions raised by oral history research led to the emergence of the field of memory studies, which moved beyond oral history interviewing to develop its own theoretical tools and was enriched by discussions in history, psychiatry, literature, anthropology, sociology, and women's studies. Memory studies is not limited to oral history interviewing: memory is studied in media as diverse as oral tradition, material culture, art, film, photography, letters, fiction, autobiography, architecture, ritual, performance, and popular culture. Recent textbooks on memory studies and a new journal of the same name are signs of a field that is rapidly coming into its own (Rossington and Whitehead, 2007; Hoskins et al., 2008).

Given its interest in everyday life and the ordinary person, and its history of political commitment, oral history tends to have one foot inside and one foot outside academe. While oral history and memory studies is taught in many universities, it tends to be associated with interdisciplinary institutes or programmes that bridge traditional disciplines. In addition, oral history methodology tends to be readily practiced outside the academe, by associations, groups, networks or individuals, with or without the support of public funds (International Oral History Association).

The development of oral history in Turkish academia

Oral history's introduction to Turkey was as late as the 1990s. Is it a coincidence that practically all academics working in the field of oral history and memory studies in Turkey are non-historians and women? A key figure is folklorist and oral historian Arzu Öztürkmen. Receiving her doctorate in folklore from Pennsylvania University in 1990, Arzu Öztürkmen became possibly the only oral historian to be based in a history department in Turkey. Since the early 1990s, she has offered undergraduate and graduate courses in oral history at Boğaziçi University. As a member of the International Oral History Association Council, Arzu Öztürkmen played an important role in making Istanbul the venue for the XIth International Conference of the International Oral History Association in 2000. In her work, Öztürkmen focuses on the linkages between oral tradition, folklore, performance and oral history (Öztürkmen, 2003). Historically, research on oral tradition formed part of the Republican state's nation building process. However, the development of folklore as a field was curtailed when key researchers were marginalised from the system (Öztürkmen, 2005). Orality remains an important means of cultural transmission in Turkey in the twenty-first century, deserving further research.[1] An emerging area of research is Kurdish oral tradition. The lack of recognition of the Kurdish language by the Turkish state throughout the twentieth century led to a heightened consciousness about language, oral tradition, music and performance (Kevirbiri, 2005; Kızılkaya, 2000).

Oral history plays a central role in the re-evaluation of recent history on the basis of personal memories. In Turkey, national history taught in schools excludes many events experienced by the peoples of the country. In addition, historical events that do form part of the national canon may be recounted and interpreted differently by individuals. There is a gap between individuals' experiences at home and within communities and at school or through the media, which, until recently, was controlled by the state. Fear remains an important factor leading parents to choose not to transmit their experiences to their children. In other cases, individuals may be raised to live in parallel worlds, or parallel contexts, each of which may be associated with different narratives. This results in complex, divided subjectivities and a convoluted, tortured and often traumatic relationship to the past.

The coup of 12 September 1980 was a major watershed in Turkish history. Despite (or because) of the political repression, and under the impact of global trends, there was a turn to cultural and subjective identities. The emergence of private media opened up new channels of communication in the public sphere. Beginning in the 1980s, and continuing into the present, Turkish society turned to its recent past, furiously debating national history. History has acquired tremendous significance for the present (and future), as contemporary issues are discussed in relationship to the past and the past in relation to the present. The country is increasingly divided into conflicting groups whose differences vis-a-vis contemporary issues are linked to different interpretations of the past.

Interest in the recent past has meant that particular historical events have come under renewed scrutiny in the present. These include the Armenian genocide of 1915, the 'War of Independence' (1919–23), the establishment of the Turkish Republic in 1923, the exchange of populations between Greece and Turkey in 1923, the attacks against Jews in Thrace in 1934, the massacre of the Alevi/Kurds of Dersim in the 1930s (known as Dersim 1938), the conscription of non-Muslim soldiers into labour battalions during World War II, the pogroms against non-Muslims on 6–7 September 1955, the 1960, 1971, and 1980 military coups, the massacre of Alevis in Maraş in 1978, the conflict between the PKK and the Turkish state from 1984, the Marmara earthquake of 1999, and the murder of Armenian journalist Hrant Dink in 2007, among others.

It is no coincidence that many events that were omitted from national history and sometimes from transmission within families were violent, traumatic events associated with conflict between communities which marked Turkish society irreparably even (or because of) through silence. Trauma studies constitutes an important subfield of oral history and memory studies, and theoreticians continue to debate whether traumatic memory constitutes a distinct form of memory (Radstone, 2005). While there is a specialised literature on the Holocaust and genocide, research on violence and trauma in Turkey from a memory studies approach is relatively new. Several factors have precipitated research in this long taboo area. Hrant Dink's murder in 2007, along with several nations' decision to recognise the Armenian genocide, has led to widespread debate on and interest in the history and memory (and postmemory) of 1915. The experience of the Marmara earthquake of 1999 in which thousands died, resulted in widespread NGO activity and made trauma an ordinary experience for many. The emergence of the PKK and the ongoing violent conflict between Kurdish guerillas and the Turkish military touches the lives of millions as soldiers and civilians are killed, thousands are forcefully displaced, and conscripts and volunteers on both sides and their families are traumatised.

Oral history research in Turkey in recent years has tended to focus on a number of key themes or topics. These include women's experiences (Dur-akbaşa and İlyasoğlu, 2001; Çakır, 2006; Bora, 2005; Akal 2003), the experiences of elites educated in republican institutions (Tan et al., 2007; Özyürek, 2006; Akşit, 2005), migration, the urban experience (Cantek and Funda, 2003), urban poverty (Erdoğan, 2002) and ethnic/religious identity, including Islamist (İlyasoğlu, 1994), Alevi (Neyzi, 2002), and Kurdish (Çağlayan, 2007; Özgen 2003) identity. Few and far between are studies carried out in rural settings (Hart, 2007; Candan, 2007).

Whereas early work tended to rely on oral history interviewing, the 2000s evidenced the emergence of memory studies. In 2003, sociologist Meltem Ahıska organised a workshop at Boğaziçi University at which Andreas Huyssen, an important figure in the field of memory studies, was the keynote speaker. Meltem Ahıska has made an important contribution to memory studies through her discussion of the concept of Occidentalism (Ahıska, 2006). According to Ahıska, the lack of value accorded to archives in republican Turkey is no mere oversight but derives from a deep sense of unease with the past. Esra Özyürek and Yael Navaro-Yashin, anthropologists teaching in the US and the UK respectively, have also contributed to research on memory studies in Turkey. Esra Özyürek showed how the early republican period was represented differently by secularists and Islamists vying for political power, and how republican iconography such as Atatürk's photographs and statist rituals such as the commemoration of the establishment of the republic, were privatised and commodified (Özyürek, 2006). Navaro-Yashin showed how Atatürk is mythologised in popular culture, continuing to live on in the Turkish psyche as a kind of sacred ancestor (Navaro-Yashin, 2002). Current research on memory studies in Turkey is expanding to encompass new topics such as fiction, architecture, monuments, commemoration, museum and heritage studies.

To date, oral history and memory studies remains weakly institutionalised in Turkish universities. Courses, in so far as they are available, are offered by a small number of academics based in a variety of disciplines. Sabancı University, a relatively new private university structured on the basis of interdisciplinary degree programmes, has incorporated oral history and memory studies into its undergraduate and graduate curriculum (Sabancı University Cultural Studies Program). An oral history archive and oral history website were created to archive and showcase the oral history research of students (Sabancı University Oral History Website).

Currently, many students from Turkey are studying in graduate programmes in the US, Canada and the UK, and growing interest in the recent past suggests that research on memory in Turkey will increase in the near future. It is to be hoped that this will lead to the establishment of oral history and memory studies teaching programmes and research institutes, greater collaboration between oral historians and traditional historians, more courses on oral history and memory studies in history programmes, and a more interdisciplinary and reflexive approach to historiography in history departments in Turkey.

Oral history in the public sphere in Turkey

Since the 1980s, with the expansion of the public sphere, the media, NGO's, private institutes, networks and individuals have begun to use the term 'oral history' to refer to a wide variety of projects concerned with memories of the recent past. The History Foundation played a seminal role in introducing the term 'oral history' to Turkey. An NGO founded in 1991 by a group of intellectuals, including academics based in universities, the History Foundation, expressed among its planned activities oral history, history education, local history, cultural heritage management and publishing. Its aims vis-a-vis oral history included oral history research, the creation of an oral history archive, organising oral history workshops and publishing books on oral history (The History Foundation).

In 1993, the History Foundation invited Paul Thompson, the renowned British oral historian, to its first oral history workshop. Many other workshops followed, including training workshops carried out in different locations in Turkey. In 1993, with the support of the Ministry of Culture, the Foundation initiated its first oral history project. For this project, key witnesses to the early years of the Turkish Republic were interviewed on videotape. In 1998, to commemorate the seventy-fifth anniversary of the republic, a series of documentary films titled 'Memories of the Republic' were produced. Other oral history projects initiated by the History Foundation include 'Voices from a Silent Past' (on Turkey's African heritage), 'A Thousand Witnesses to History' (on memories of the elderly), 'People's Views from Mardin' (on memories of the people of Mardin in Southeastern Turkey), and 'Memories of Istanbul/Mediterranean Voices' (on the transformation of Istanbul neighbourhoods). Many additional oral history interviews were carried out as part of regional history or institutional history projects.

The History Foundation also published books on oral history, beginning with a Turkish translation of Paul Thompson's *The Voice of the Past* (Thompson, 1999). Other books followed (Neyzi, 1999a; Danacıoğlu, 2001; İlyasoğlu and Kayacan, 2006; Böke, 2006). The History Foundation played a key role in putting oral history on the map in Turkey. However, because the Foundation is an NGO that depends for its maintenance on a number of short-term projects, these tend to be carried out relatively quickly, usually by volunteers rather than professionals. There is often little time or funding available to sufficiently prepare for, transcribe, index and analyse interviews, disseminate results or evaluate projects. Despite its enthusiasm, given that oral history is such a new and unfamiliar field in Turkey, the History Foundation may have unwittingly done some harm to the field through the way it has represented oral history. It is particularly unfortunate that few trained historians associated with the Foundation are involved in oral history projects, which frequently rely on the labour of young, and usually female, volunteers.

Istanbul University Women's Issues Research Center (İstanbul Üniversitesi Kadın Sorunları Araştırma Merkezi) and the Women's Library and Information Center Foundation (Kadın Eserleri Kütüphanesi ve Bilgi Merkezi Vakfı) are two other institutions that helped introduce oral history in Turkey. In 1995, The Women's Library organised a workshop and brought together a group of women who carried out a pilot project and who worked as a group to discuss key issues such as the rights and responsibilities of interviewees and interviewers, power issues, ethics and reflexivity (Öztürkmen, 2001/2). As Öztürkmen points out, such a necessary focus on the research process would be rarely found among the many projects titled 'oral history' in the public sphere thereafter.

In the post 1980 period, with the expansion of private media and the emergence of new, privately funded museums and art and cultural centres, journalists, documentary filmmakers and museum professionals also became interested in oral history. For example, the documentary filmmakers' association (BSB) organised and took part in oral history training workshops, and many filmmakers in this network consider their work as a form of oral history (Balay and Ocak, 2006). Another institution which purports to use oral history is the Mithat Alam Film Centre at Boğaziçi University. The Centre interviews significant personalities in the history of Turkish cinema, making their work available in DVD format (Mithat Alam Film Merkezi). The Boğaziçi Performance Arts Group is another NGO that relies on oral history interviewing in the course of its performative work (Boğaziçi Gösteri Sanatları Topluluğu).

Oral history is also used in museums. Meltem Ahıska and Zafer Yenal, both from Boğaziçi University, used personal narratives as a means of organising exhibitions on the topics of human rights and changing personal identities respectively (Ahıska and Yenal, 2004; 2005). In an intriguing case of personal initiative, Hakan Gürüney, a private individual, created the Bozcaada Local History Museum on the island of Tenedos in the northern Aegean. The museum's activities include oral history interviews with elderly residents of Bozcaada, and the tapes of the interviews and their transcripts are archived in the museum (Bozcaada Müzesi).

Among the many NGOs and informal networks that emerged in Turkey in the post-1980 period, an important subsection had their roots in the leftist movements of the 1960s and 1970s. Among these, the Turkish Social History Research Foundation (TÜSTAV) has been particularly active in archiving its own history. For example, autobiographies of key participants in the movement are published in a book series titled 'The Yellow Notebooks'. An experimental book in this series, *The Konca Correspondence*, for example, incorporates the autobiographical writings individuals formerly imprisoned in the Konca military prison in Istanbul shared with one another through an Internet group (Karataş et al., 2005).

Since the 1990s, many NGOs, groups and informal networks have organised on the basis of cultural identities. Alevi, Kurdish, Assyrian, Laz, Circassian, Pomak, African, Armenian, Jewish, Greek-Orthodox, Muslim are among the many ethnic/religious/linguistic identities that are in the process of being rediscovered in the public sphere in the present. In the course of this rediscovery, many groups turn to oral history. However, while many NGOs and informal groups make claims about doing oral history research, few have disseminated their results. On the other hand, given their commitment to researching the Kurdish experience, an informal network known as 'The Middle East History Academy Collective', has produced two books. This group used interviews with family members to narrate the stories of Kurdish fighters who died in the conflict between the PKK and the Turkish military (ODTAK, 2006). The group also interviewed families who experienced forced migration as a result of this conflict.

One of the differences between academic research and projects carried out by NGOs, the media, or informal groups in the public sphere, is that the latter tend to equate oral history with interviewing and transcription. The results of much non-academic oral history work, in so far as it is available, tends to be in the form of transcribed interviews, usually prefaced by a brief introduction. Academic publications, on the other hand, particularly in the field of memory studies, tend to be more analytical, including lengthy discussions of theoretical and methodological issues, using the research material to make an argument contextualised within a wider literature. With such an approach, transcripts come to be viewed vis-a-vis a methodological and theoretical minefield across which the researcher/author must venture at her/his peril. Concern with 'mere' content is replaced by a focus on complex issues of representation, construction, interpretation and meaning. The authority of the researcher/writer to represent the viewpoint of the narrator(s) is problematised, the text resembling an ethnography in so far as the researcher/author is as much the subject as the subject the author or collaborator. Having said this, academic work in oral history and memory studies in Turkey has a long way to go. This is due to the lack of academic oral history programmes, the lack of an organisation or association representing oral history in the public sphere, the distancing of the history establishment from oral history, the misrepresentation and misperception of oral history as a kind of seat-of-the-pants conversation-making rather than a professional field requiring training, and the subsequent unavailability of courses, training workshops and reference materials in Turkish for those interested in carrying out professional research in oral history.

From ethnography to oral history: A personal journey

As a means of illustrating the value of oral history in providing (an often alternate) means of approaching the past, I would like to discuss briefly how I discovered oral history, and provide a case study based on my own research. I became interested in the recent past, and its relationship to the present, during the course of my dissertation research among the Yörük (pastoral nomads) of Southern Turkey (Neyzi, 1991). My impetus for working in the countryside was to explore what was unfamiliar to me – what *was* familiar was the cosmopolitan heritage of the Ottoman Empire and the urban middle class culture of republican elites (Neyzi, 1999b). Although the problem I had set myself concerned the adaptation of transhumant pastoralists to intensive agriculture and tourism as new forms of livelihood, I found that I could not solve this puzzle without going farther back in time. It was the narratives my interlocutors told about the exploits of their parents and grandparents (and my sense that this differed considerably from official history – though my informants felt no compunction in using the latter when it suited their purposes) that provided the key to understanding my informants' behaviour, interpretations and emotions in the present. It was during the latter end of eighteen months' fieldwork that I began to tape the lifestories of informants, whose dialect differed considerably from my own Istanbul Turkish. Transcripts of these conversations would largely guide the thesis I eventually wrote.

As a trained anthropologist affiliated with a cultural studies programme, I currently teach anthropology, oral history, and memory studies. In fact, I view oral history interviewing as a form of ethnographic research (Neyzi, 1999a). Over the last two decades, my research has focused on Turkish nationalism, cultural identity and subjectivity. I have conducted lifestory interviews with individuals from a variety of ethnic/religious/linguistic backgrounds, disseminating the results of my research in media ranging from Turkish newspapers, video documentaries, popular books in Turkish, and academic articles in English and Turkish. Rather than focus on one particular group, I have chosen to interview members of different communities as a means of better understanding the way subjects experience Turkish nationalism and the state. The identities I have become most familiar with include Sabbateanism, Turkish Jewish identity, Alevi/Kurdish identity and Arab/Christian identity. Over time, I have become increasingly interested in the question of subjectivity in its own right.

My work gradually led to a study of Turkish national identity from within. I am currently completing a research project on the oral history of a neighbourhood in Istanbul. This neighbourhood, Teşvikiye, was established in the late nineteenth century by decree of the Ottoman Sultan. The neighbourhood became identified with a Turkish Muslim bourgeoisie in the course of the transition to the Turkish Republic. For this project, I am interviewing three generations of neighbourhood residents. I am interested in how neighbourhood identity is defined, and how the neighbourhood has changed – and is perceived to have changed – since the turn of the twentieth century. I am as interested in the history of the neighbourhood as in its accelerated transformation in the present; for it has become a showcase for Istanbul's new image as a global metropolis. Today, economic, social and cultural inequality and conflict characterise everyday life in the neighbourhood, where the economic and cultural elite ironically perceive themselves as living under siege (Neyzi, 2007).

Building on an interest in generational identity (Neyzi, 2001), I am currently planning a new project on childhood and youth. Oral history tends to be associated with the elderly: it is assumed that it is the elderly who have built up a fount of experience and who remember the historical events historians are interested in. But why not apply the methodology of oral history to the study of childhood and youth? We know by now that memories tell us as much about the present as the past. In the twenty-first century, we tend to be more preoccupied with the past than with the future (Huyysen, 2003). In the field of anthropology, childhood and youth studies is experiencing a revival (Durham, 2008). Given that much of the population of Turkey is under the age of 25, it is crucial to understand the ways children and youth construct the past. This can provide significant clues to how they experience the present and will shape the future. For this project, I plan to conduct oral history interviews with young people from diverse cultural and class backgrounds – and with disadvantaged young people in particular – in metropoles, rural areas, and the diaspora. My aim is to explore the subjectivities of children and young people in and from Turkey through their memories and representations of the past.

A case study: Why oral history?

In this section, I would like to present a case study in order to discuss the ways oral history can contribute to understanding the recent past. In the late 1990s, an interdisciplinary network of scholars from Greece and Turkey came together with the aim of studying our 'shared history'. The peoples of Greece and Turkey had lived together under the Ottoman Empire, but nationalism rent them apart. Greek and Turkish national histories interpret the same events in bipolar, mirror-image fashion (Özkırımlı and Sofos, 2008). The group decided to study an important event in the recent history of the two countries to compare how it was narrated in national history and remembered and represented in the present. Because of its significance in the international literature, and differential treatment in the national histories of the two nations, the event chosen was the burning of Smyrna/Izmir in September 1922. This event, which sealed the 'Asia Minor catastrophe', as it is known in Greek history, played a central role in the construction of modern Greek national identity. On the other hand, while symbolising the 'liberation' of the city of Izmir, this event tended to be downplayed, if not forgotten, in modern Turkish history (Kırlı, 2005).

The task the oral historians in the group set themselves was to interview ordinary Greeks and Turks who were old enough to have experienced this event to see how they remembered and narrated this period (Neyzi, 2008). According to Greek (and Armenian) history, it was the Turks who burned Smyrna/İzmir. The Turks, on the other hand, blamed the Greeks and/or the Armenians. How would ordinary individuals remember? Would this event be central to Greek lifestory narratives? Would it be underplayed/discounted in Turkish narratives? To what extent would lifestory narratives conform to/diverge from national chronology and official ideology? Were alternate accounts available, and if so, how were they reconciled/conflicted with national history? We also wanted to know how contemporary events and issues influenced the way our informants remembered and represented the past. Was the rapproachement between Greece and Turkey, and nostalgic memories of the cosmopolitan heritage of the Ottoman Empire, changing understandings and representations of the histories and identities of Greece and Turkey, viewed for so long in bipolar terms?

I would like to briefly discuss the findings of my research. During 2001–3, I recorded four lengthy oral history interviews with Gülfem İren, one of the few Turkish Smyrniotes/İzmirians old enough to remember the burning of Smyrna/Izmir. Born in 1915, Gülfem İren was seven years old in 1922. Today, she is 94 years old. During my interview with her, she stated that although she was very young, the trauma of the burning of Smryna/İzmir (and the prior burning of the town of Manisa, which she also experienced) resulted in the engraving of the experience in her mind as if it was an image. İren also said that as she is now aged and physically infirm – but strong in mind – she spends most of her days remembering and reliving the past, particularly the days of her childhood.

My life history interview with Gülfem İren did not begin with or even focus on the burning of İzmir, the event I was interested in. Rather, I chose to let İren tell me the story of her life in the order and way of her choosing. Over the course of several meetings, I got to know the main contours of her life and the events and themes that she considered significant to her life. It turned out that the burning of İzmir – and perhaps even more, the earlier burning of Manisa, were among these.

Gülfem İren belongs to a family native to İzmir, and her forebears were local landlords and powerholders who both collaborated with and rebelled against the Ottomans. At the same time, as urban elites, the family shared a history with the diverse inhabitants of the city that included Muslim, Christian and Jewish communities. Most important in her account – and highly relevant to my research – was how these relationships were affected when nationalisms began to set neighbours against one another.

Gülfem İren was raised in a period of transition from the Ottoman Empire to the Turkish Republic. Through her mother and many older siblings (her father died when she was young), she learned about the traditions of İzmir, including the relationship between neighbours of different cultural backgrounds. Attending Republican schools, she also learnt the history of İzmir's 'liberation'. The juxtaposition of these different contexts and narratives is what made her lifestory narrative of particular value. For example, when I first asked Gülfem İren who burnt İzmir, she automatically replied, 'the Greeks'. When I came back to the subject later, she began to debate with herself, and with the few surviving acquaintances from her age cohort. When we spoke about the aftermath of the burning of İzmir, and her years growing up, she spoke of the 'necessity' of the burning of İzmir. She said: 'You could not have such a cosmopolitan Republic'. At the same time, comparing her world as a young girl with that of her elder siblings when they were of the same age, she decried the loss of an older, cosmopolitan İzmir. In this context, the term 'cosmopolitan' acquired a different, more positive connotation. She spoke with nostalgia of the everyday life of the 'knowledgeable' people of İzmir, the Armenians, Greek Orthodox, Levantines and Jews. When the issue of responsibility for the fire came up, she also spoke differently in different contexts. When speaking as a citizen of the new Republic, she blamed the Greek invaders of İzmir – and the native Christians – for collaborating with the invaders. Speaking as a native İzmirian, on the other hand, she mourned the loss of the beautiful city of the past and blamed the Republican leaders – themselves outsiders to İzmir – suggesting that if they had not actually burnt the city, then they had done nothing to stop the fire once it had begun as a result of the fighting between the Muslims and Christians.

My experience of interviewing Gülfem İren raises a number of key issues concerning oral history. First of all, doing oral history does not amount to delegitimising national or official history and simply replacing it with an alternative, subaltern account. Ordinary people are tremendously influenced by such macro discourses, and tend to internalise and incorporate them in their accounts. At the same time, individuals and communities also develop their own syncretic accounts of the past, which may differ, conflict with, and coexist with hegemonic accounts. This is why the contexts within which narratives are recounted are central, and a strength of oral history is its ability to shed light on the contexts within which narratives are shaped.

Concerning the history of the burning of Smyrna, what I learned from interviewing Gülfem İren is that, as might be expected given our knowledge of recent history, the burning of İzmir was not much talked about in Turkey in the aftermath. When the event was talked about, particularly in the public sphere, the national narrative predominated: 'it was the Greeks/Armenians that did it'. Gülfem İren suggested, in a rather guarded way even after all these years, that there was silencing about the event, possibly due to fear of the state – the former soldiers of the Greco-Turkish War then administering the city. She also suggested that while the natives of İzmir celebrated the liberation, they also saw their liberators as outsiders, just as they did the rulers that came before them. Although she initially repeated the usual 'the Greeks/Armenians did it' line, Gülfem İren, once she began to debate the issue with herself, with her few surviving age-mates and me, she actually stated that the administration of the time, and the governor of İzmir in particular, was responsible for the fire, directly or indirectly. She suggested that if the administration did not start the fire, then they were probably guilty of letting it burn itself out, as a handy means of getting rid of the Greeks and the local Christians they saw as outsiders and traitors who had no place in the Turkish nationalist project. The degree of silencing involved in Gülfem İren's narrative has no doubt to do with the widespread violence between Christians and Muslims and the bloodletting that occurred at the end of Turkey's 'War of Independence' that made the Turks, first victims, then perpetrators, want to forget their suffering, and subsequently their guilt, for what they made others suffer. It is, in a nutshell, the story of modern Turkey – and remains so. Unfortunately, today's internecine violence between Turks and Kurds is a repeat performance in contemporary disguise.

An important aspect of oral history interviewing concerns the relationship between the past and the present. Oral history illuminates not only the past but also the present. For example, at the time I was interviewing Gülfem İren, Turkish society was beginning to re-evaluate its relationship with Greece. The rediscovery of the recent past in Turkey resulted in a discourse of nostalgia, particularly concerning the cosmopolitan life of metropolises such as İstanbul and İzmir. As an avid follower of the media, Gülfem İren was affected by this process. For example, she shared with me novels and memoirs written by Greek authors of Smyrniote origin that Turkish publishers were beginning to translate and publish. My sense is that her present-day experience was beginning to soften the edges of the nationalist narrative that she grew up with, though the latter still shaped her account in particular contexts.

I hope to have demonstrated that oral history can make an important contribution to the study of the recent past as well the present. It is impossible to interview documents, yet it is possible to ask a living person about their motivations, feelings, senses, dreams and hopes. I was not only able to ask Gülfem İren to tell me the story of her life, to find out which events and aspects of her life she deemed important enough to speak to me about, but I was also able to ask 'why'? As in ethnography, in oral history, it is possible to view our subjects as not only subjects but theoreticians in their own right. I was able to discuss with Gülfem İren not only what happened, but how she viewed the history of İzmir and why she thought/felt the way she did. And this interaction and process, showed that there was no simple answer to the question of 'what happened in Smryna?'. Let me add that my own identity, and my relationship to Gülfem İren, also played a role in the story she told, for it was out of our relationship and dialogue that her history of İzmir was shaped.

Conclusion

As I hope my case study has demonstrated, it is important not to view the fields of oral history and history as incompatible or even opposed: they are similar in many ways and also different. Oral history relies on history in going about its work. Oral history is also a major means of studying recent history. On the other hand, unlike traditional history, oral history is also about, and studies, the present. An oral history approach can also complicate the way we understand history, particularly at the subjective level, and how it should be studied.

An important means of remedying the misperception and misrepresentation of oral history in the public sphere is to produce high quality original research and to make accessible work on oral history in the international literature in Turkish. The History Foundation initiated this important work. İş Bankası Kültür Yayınları, the publishing house of İş Bank, is in the process of launching a new book series on memory studies. The series will publish new research on Turkey, translations of classics and of pathbreaking new studies.

Between 31 January and 1 February 2009, Garanti Bank's Ottoman Bank Museum and Research Centre, an important cultural centre in Istanbul, planned to offer a training workshop in oral history. To date, interest in the workshop has been overwhelming: over 200 people, of diverse backgrounds and interests, from all over Turkey, have applied to take part. The workshop will be followed by regular meetings to support oral history research groups. The goal is to enable professional oral history research, to create an oral history archive, and to disseminate results in the form of exhibits, websites, and books. The Ottoman Bank Museum and Research Center also plans to initiate its own oral history project on urban memory of Istanbul as part of Istanbul 2010: Cultural Capital of Europe. It is to be hoped that this new venture will open the way for additional activities and further collaboration between academic institutions and centres, networks and individuals interested in oral history.

Oral history and memory studies is a newly emerging field in Turkey. From an academic standpoint, recent Turkish history awaits further study from a memory studies perspective. The country's tortured relationship with its past makes it a particularly challenging context within which to study recent history. At the same time, oral history research can contribute to debates on history in the public sphere, and Turkey's democratisation process. Many conflicts and impasses of the present have their roots in events of the past and in the perceptions and representations of them. If Turkish society is able to come to terms with its taboos about the past, to face its fears, and to re-examine its present in terms of its experience and memory, it may have the chance of building a more democratic, participatory society for the future.

Notes

1. For an intriguing study of the relationship between literacy and orality in contemporary Turkey, see Schick (2008).

Bibliography

M. Ahıska and B. K. Kırlı (2006) 'Editors' Introduction', *New Perspectives on Turkey*, vol. 34, pp. 5–8.

M. Ahıska (2006) 'Occidentalism and Registers of Truth: The Politics of Archives in Turkey', *New Perspectives on Turkey*, vol. 34, pp. 9–29.

M. Ahlska and Z. Yenal (eds) (2005) *Aradığınız Kişiye Şu An Ulaşılamıyor: Türkiye'de Hayat Tarzı Temsilleri, 1980–2005* (İstanbul: Osmanlı Bankası Arşiv ve Araştırma Merkezi Yayınları).

M. Ahıska. and Z. Yenal (eds) (2004) *Hikayemi Dinler misin? Tanıklıklarla Türkiye'de İnsan Hakları ve Sivil Toplum* (İstanbul: Tarih Vakfı Yayınları).

E. Akal (2003) *Kızıl Feministler: Bir Sözlü Tarih Çalışması* (İstanbul: TÜSTAV Yayınları).

E. E. Akşit (2005) *Kızların Sessizliği: Kız Enstitülerinin Uzun Tarihi* (İstanbul: İletişim Yayınları).

B. Balay and E. Ocak (2006) 'Sözlü Tarih Çalışmalarında Video Teknolojisinin Kullanılması', in A. Ilyasoğlu and G. Kayacan (eds) *Kuşaklar, Deneyimler, Tanıklıklar: Türkiye'de Sözlü Tarih Çalışmaları Konferansı* (İstanbul: Tarih Vakfı).

Belgesel Sinemacılar Birliği available at http://www.bsb.org.tr/

Boğaziçi Gösteri Sanatları Topluluğu available at http://www.bgst.org/bgst/

A. Bora (2005) *Kadınların Sınıfı: Ücretli Ev Emeği ve Kadın Öznelliğinin İnşası* (İstanbul: İletişim Yayınları).

Bozcaada Müzesi available at http://www.bozcaadamuzesi.com/sozlutarih.htm

P. Böke (2006) *İzmir 1919–1922 Tanıklıklar* (İstanbul: Tarih Vakfı Yurt Yayınları).

A. B. Candan (2007) 'Remembering a Nine-Thousand-Year-Old Site', in E. Özyürek (ed.) *The Politics of Public Memory in Turkey* (Syracuse: Syracuse University Press).

Ş. Cantek and L. Funda (2003) *Yaban'lar ve Yerliler: Başkent Olma Sürecinde Ankara* (İstanbul: İletişim Yayınları).

M. Chamberlain (2009) *Family Love in the Diaspora: Migration and the Anglo-Caribbean Experience* (New Brunswick: Transaction Publishers).

Columbia University Oral History Research Office, available at http://www.columbia. edu/cu/lweb/indiv/oral/index.html.

H. Çağlayan (2007) *Analar, Yoldaşlar, Tanrıçalar: Kürt Hareketinde Kadınlar ve Kadın Kimliğinin Oluşumu* (İstanbul: İletişim Yayınları).

S. Çakır (2006) 'Sözlü Tarih Projelerinde Yöntemsel ve Etik Sorunlar ve Bu Sorunları Çözme Yolları', in A. Ilyasoğlu and G. Kayacan (eds) *Kuşaklar, Deneyimler, Tanıklıklar: Türkiye'de Sözlü Tarih Çalışmaları Konferansı* (İstanbul: Tarih Vakfı).

E. Danacıoğlu (2001) *Geçmişin İzi: Yanıbaşımızdaki Tarih İçin Bir Klavuz* (Istanbul: Tarih Vakfı Yurt Yayınları).

V. Das (2007) *Life and Words: Violence and the Descent into the Ordinary* (Berkeley: University of California Press).

N. K. Dinç, M. Toptaş Kömürcü, A. Isık and S. Bozkurt (2008) *Göç Hikayeleri* (İstanbul: Göç-Der).

A. Durakbaşa and A. İlyasoğlu (2001) 'Formation of Gender Identities in Republican Turkey and Women's Narratives as Transmitters of 'Herstory' of Modernization', *Journal of Social History*, vol. 3, no. 1, pp. 195–203.

D. Durham (2008) 'New Horizons: Youth at the Millennium', *Anthropological Quarterly*, vol. 81, no. 4, pp. 945–57.

N. Erdoğan (ed.) (2002) *Yoksulluk Halleri: Türkiye'de Yoksulluğun Toplumsal Görünümleri* (İstanbul: İletişim Yayınları).

K. Hart (2007) 'Weaving Modernity, Commercializing Carpets: Collective Memory and Contested Tradition in Örselli Village', in E. Özyürek (ed.) *The Politics of Public Memory in Turkey* (Syracuse: Syracuse University Press).

The History Foundation, available at http://www.tarihvakfi.org.tr/

K. Hodgkin and S. Radstone (eds) (2006) *Memory History Nation: Contested Pasts* (New Brunswick: Transaction Publishers).

A. Hoskins, A. Barnier, W. Kansteiner and J. Sutton (2008) 'Editorial', *Memory Studies*, vol. 1, no. 1, pp. 5–7.

A. Huyysen (2003) *Present Pasts: Urban Palimpsests and the Politics of Memory* (Stanford: Stanford University Press).

A. İlyasoğlu and G. Kayacan (eds) (2006) *Kuşaklar, Deneyimler, Tanıklıklar: Türkiye'de Sözlü Tarih Çalışmaları Konferansı* (İstanbul: Tarih Vakfı).

A. İlyasoğlu (1994) *Örtülü Kimlik* (İstanbul: Metis Yayınları).

International Oral History Association, available at http://iohanet.org/

İstanbul Üniversitesi Kadın Sorunları Araştırma ve Uygulama Merkezi, available at http://www.istanbul.edu.tr/merkezler/webkaum/1htm.html

Kadın Eserleri Kütüphanesi ve Bilgi Merkezi Vakfı, available at http://www.kadineserleri.org/

A. B. Karataş, E. Alçınkaya, E. Çakar, G. Basyurt, H. Öztürk, H. Gencer, M. Alçınkaya, M. Müstecaplioğlu, N. Kur, N. Cingirt, Ö. Gündoğan and S. Ceylan (2005) *Konca Yazışmaları* (İstanbul: TÜSTAV).

S. Kevirbiri (2005) *Bir Çığlığın Yüzyılı Karapete Xaco* (İstanbul: Elma Yayınları).

B. K. Kırlı (2005) 'Forgetting the Smyrna Fire', *History Workshop Journal*, vol. 60, no. 1, pp. 25–44.

M. Kızılkaya (2000) *Kayıp Diwan: Sözlü Kürt Kültüründen Üç Örnek* (İstanbul: İletişim Yayınları).

Mithat Alam Film Merkezi, available at http://www.mafm.boun.edu.tr/

Y. Navaro-Yashin (2002) *Faces of the State: Secularism and Public Life in Turkey* (Princeton: Princeton University Press).

L. Neyzi (2008) *Türkiye'de Bellek Çalışmaları* (İstanbul: İş Bankası Kültür Yayınları).

L. Neyzi (2008) 'Remembering Smyrna/Izmir: Shared History, Shared Trauma', *History & Memory*, vol. 20, no. 2, pp. 106–27.

L. Neyzi (2007) 'Urban Regeneration, Memory and Subjectivity in a Neighborhood in the Global City of Istanbul'. Paper presented at Session on Local Transitions to and from the European Union, 106th Annual Meeting of the American Anthropological Association, Washington DC, 28 November–2 December.

L. Neyzi (2002) 'Embodied Elders: Space and Subjectivity in the Music of Metin-Kemal Kahraman', *Middle Eastern Studies*, vol. 38, no. 1, pp. 89–109.

L. Neyzi (2001) 'Object or Subject? The Paradox of 'Youth' in Turkey', *International Journal of Middle East Studies*, vol. 33, pp. 411–32.

L. Neyzi (1999a) *İstanbul'da Hatırlamak ve Unutmak: Birey, Bellek ve Aidiyet* (İstanbul: Tarih Vakfı Yurt Yayınları).

L. Neyzi (1999b) *Küçük Hanım'dan 'Rubu Asırlık Adam'a: Nezihe Neyzi'den Oğlu Nezih Neyzi'ye Mektuplar 1947–1948* (İstanbul: Sel Yayıncılık).

L. Neyzi (1991) *Beyond Tradition and Resistance: Kinship and Economic Development in Mediterranean Turkey* (Unpublished Ph.D. Dissertation, Cornell University) [1992 Malcolm H. Kerr Dissertation Award in the Social Sciences].

Orta Doğu Tarih Akademisi Kollektifi (2006) *Ben Öldüm Beni Sen Anlat: Savaşın Tanıkları Anlatıyor* (İstanbul: Vate Yayınevi ve Belge Yayınevi).

H. N. Özgen (2003) *Van-Özalp ve 33 Kurşun Olayı: Toplumsal Hafızanın Hatırlama ve Unutma Biçimleri* (İstanbul: TÜSTAV Yayınları).

U. Özkırımlı and S. A. Sofos (eds) (2008) *Tormented by History: Nationalism in Greece and Turkey* (New York: Columbia University Press).

A. Öztürkmen (2005) 'Folklore on Trial: Pertev Naili Boratav and the Denationalization of Turkish Folklore', *Journal of Folklore Research*, vol. 42, no. 2, pp. 185–216.

A. Öztürkmen (2003) 'Remembering through the Material Culture: Local Knowledge of Past Communities in a Turkish Black Sea Town', *Middle Eastern Studies*, vol. 39, no. 2, pp. 179–93.

A. Öztürkmen (2001/2002) 'Sözlü Tarih: Yeni Bir Disiplinin Cazibesi', *Toplum ve Bilim*, vol. 91, pp. 115–21.

E. Özyürek (ed.) (2007) *The Politics of Public Memory in Turkey* (Syracuse, NY: Syracuse University Press).

E. Özyürek (2006) *Nostalgia for the Modern: State Secularism and Everyday Politics in Turkey* (Durham: Duke University Press).

A. Portelli (2001) 'What Makes Oral History Different', in A. Portelli (ed.) *The Death of Luigi Trastulli and Other Stories: Form and Meaning in Oral History* (Albany: State University of New York Press).

S. Radstone (2005) 'Reconceiving Binaries: The Limits of Memory', *History Workshop Journal*, vol. 59, pp. 134–50.

A. Robben (2005) *Political Violence and Trauma in Argentina* (Philadelphia: University of Pennsylvania Press).

K. L. Rogers and S. Leydesdorff (eds) (2004) *Trauma: Life Stories of Survivors* (New Brunswick: Transaction Publishers).

M. Rossington and A. Whitehead (eds) (2007) *Theories of Memory: A Reader* (Baltimore: Johns Hopkins University Press).

Sabancı University Cultural Studies Program, available at http://www.sabanciuniv.edu/ssbf/cult/eng/

Sabancı University Oral History Website, available at http://www.sabanciuniv.edu.tr/sozlutarih/

I. C. Schick (2008) 'Bedensel Hafıza, Zihinsel Hafıza, Yazılı Kaynak: Hat San'atının Günümüze İntikalinin Bazı Boyutları', in L. Neyzi (ed.) *Türkiye'de Bellek Çalışmaları* (İstanbul: İş Bankası Kültür Yayınları).

C. Steedman (2007) *Master and Servant: Love and Labour in the English Industrial Age* (Cambridge: Cambridge University Press).

M. G. Tan, Ö. Şahin, A. Bora and M. Sever (2007) *Cumhuriyet'te Çocuktular* (İstanbul: Boğaziçi Üniversitesi Yayınevi).

P. Thompson (1999) *Geçmişin Sesi: Sözlü Tarih* (İstanbul: Tarih Vakfı).

Selected Bibliography

F. Adaman, A. Çarkoğlu and A. Şenatalar (2001) *Hane halkı gözünden Türkiye'de yolsuzluğun nedenleri ve önlenmesine ilişkin öneriler* (İstanbul: Türkiye Ekonomik ve Sosyal Etüdler Vakfı (TESEV).

H. E. Adıvar (1935) *Conflict of East and West in Turkey* (Lahore: Ashraf Press).

——— (1930) *Turkey Faces West* (New Haven: Yale University Press).

——— (1928) *The Turkish Ordeal* (New York: The Century Co).

M. Ahıska and Z. Yenal (eds) (2005) *Aradığınız Kişiye Şu An Ulaşılamıyor: Türkiye'de Hayat Tarzı Temsilleri, 1980–2005* (İstanbul: Osmanlı Bankası Arşiv ve Araştırma Merkezi Yayınları).

F. Ahmad (1977) *The Turkish Experiment in Democracy 1950–1975* (Boulder, CO: Westview press).

R. Akar (1995) 'Basında 'Herkese' Dönemi' in *Cumhuriyet Dönemi Türkiye Ansiklopedisi*, Vol. 11 (İstanbul: İletişim Yayınları).

E. D. Akarlı with G. Ben-Dor (eds) (1975) *Political Participation in Turkey: Historical Background and Present Problems* (İstanbul: Boğaziçi University Press).

N. Akman (2004) *Gurbette Fethullah Gülen* (İstanbul: Zaman Kitap).

G. Akçura (2002) *Ivır Zıvır Tarihi III: Uzun Metin Sevenlerden Misiniz?* (İstanbul: Om Yayınevi).

Y. Akdoğan (2003) *Muhafazakar Demokrasi* (Ankara: Ak Parti).

M. Aksoy (1977), *Sosyalist Enternasyonal ve CHP* (Ankara: Tekin Yayınevi).

M. S. Anderson (1993) *The Rise of Modern Diplomacy 1450–1919* (London: Longman).

——— (1966) *The Eastern Question 1774–1923: A Study in International Relations* (London: Macmillan).

E. Anderson (1990) *Streetwise: Race, Class and Change in an Urban Community* (Chicago: University of Chicago Press).

S. Andreski (1968) *Military Organization and Society* (Berkeley and Los Angeles: University of California Press).

E. Aracı (2001) *Ahmed Adnan Saygun, Doğu Batı Arası Müzik Köprüsü* (İstanbul: Yapı Kredi Yayınları).

——— (2000) *European Music at the Ottoman Court*, CD 177 (İstabul: Kalan).

A. F. Arat (ed.) (1998) *Deconstructing Images of The Turkish Woman* (New York: St. Martin's Press).

Y. Arat (1989) *The Patriarchal Paradox: Women Politicians in Turkey* (New Jersey: Fairleigh Dickinson University Press).

F. Atacan (1990) *Sosyal Değişme ve Tarikatlar: Cerrahiler* (İstanbul: Hil Yayınları).

——— (1999) 'A Portrait of a Naqshbandi Sheikh in Modern Turkey' in E. Özdalga (ed.) *Naqshbandis in Western and Central Asia: Change and Continuity* (London: Curzon Press).

F. R. Atay (1969) *Çankaya* (İstanbul: Doğan Kardeş Yayınları).

E. Athanassopoulou (1999) *Turkey and Anglo-American Security Interests 1945–1952* (London: Frank Cass).

E. Aydınlı, N. Özcan and D. Akyaz (2006) 'The Turkish Military's March Toward Europe', *Foreign Affairs*, vol. 85, no.1, 77–90.

B. Ayvazoğlu (1989) *İslam Estetiği ve İnsan* (İstanbul: Çağ Yayınları).

R. Bali (2002) *Tarz-ı Hayat'tan Life Style'a* (İstanbul: İletişim).

H. J. Barkey (2009) *Preventing Conflict over Kurdistan* (Washington, DC: Carnegie Endowment for International Peace).

R. Bartlett (1994) *The Making of Europe: Conquest, Colonization and Cultural Change 950–1350* (Harmondsworth: Penguin Books).

İ. Barutçu (2004) *Babıali Tanrıları: Simavi Ailesi* (İstanbul: Agora Kitaplığı).

Z. Bauman (1991) *Modernity and Ambivalence* (Oxford: Polity Press).

N. Berkes (1963) *The Development of Secularism in Turkey* (Montreal: McGill University Press).

—— (ed.) (1959) *Turkish Nationalism and Western Civilization: Selected Essays of Ziya Gökalp* (New York: Columbia University Press).

H. Bila (1999) *CHP: 1919–1999* (İstanbul: Doğan Kitapevi).

A. E. Bilgili and E. Altan (ed.) (2003) *Yoksulluk* (İstanbul: Deniz Feneri Yardımlaşma ve Dayanışma Derneği).

M. A. Birand (1995) *Demirkırat* (İstanbul: Milliyet Yayınları).

—— (1987) *The Generals' Coup in Turkey* (London: Brassey's Defence Publishers).

N. Bobbio (1987) *The Future of Democracy* (Oxford: Polity Press).

T. Bora (1999) *Türk Sağının Üç Hali* (İstanbul: İletişim).

C. E Bosworth, E. van Donzel, W. P. Heinrichs and the late G. Lecomte (1997), Encyclopedia of Islam, Vol. IX, (Leiden : Brill)

S. Bozdoğan (2001) *Modernism and Nation Building: Turkish Architectural Culture in the Early Republic* (Seattle: University of Washington Press).

S. Bozdoğan and R. Kasaba (eds.) (1997) *Rethinking Modernity and National Identity in Turkey* (Seattle: University of Washington Press).

S. Bozdoğan, S. Özkan and E. Yenal (1987) *Sedad Eldem: Architect in Turkey* (Singapore: Concept Media).

L. C. Brown (ed.) *Imperial Legacy: The Ottoman Imprint on the Balkans and the Middle East* (New York: Columbia University Press).

M. van Bruinessen (1992) *Agha, Shaikh and State: The Social and Political Structures of Kurdistan* (London: Zed Books).

A. Buğra (1999) *Islam in Economic Organizations* (İstanbul: Tesev Yayınları).

A. Buğra and Ç. Keyder (2003) *New Poverty and the Changing Welfare Regime in Turkey* (Ankara: UNDP).

A. Buğra and N. T. Sınmardemir (2004) *Yoksullukla Mücadelede İnsani ve Etkin bir Yöntem: Nakit Gelir Desteği* (İstanbul: Boğaziçi Üniversitesi Sosyal Politika Forumu).

A. B. Candan (2007) 'Remembering a Nine-Thousand-Year-Old Site' in E. Özyürek (ed.) *The Politics of Public Memory in Turkey* (Syracuse: Syracuse University Press).

H. Cemal (2005) *Cumhuriyet'i Çok Sevmiştim: Cumhuriyet Gazetesi'ndeki 'İç Savaş'ın Perde Arkası'* (İstanbul: Doğan Kitapçılık).

—— (1999) *Kimse Kızmasın, Kendimi Yazdım* (İstanbul: Doğan Kitapçılık).

S. Çakır (1993) *Osmanlı Kadın Hareketi* (İstanbul: Metis Yayınları).

T. Çavdar (2003) *Türkiye Ekonomisinin Tarihi 1900–1960* (Ankara: İmge Yayınevi).

A. Çeçen (1984) *Sosyal Demokrasi* (Ankara: Devinim Yayınları).

A. Davison (1998) *Secularism and Revivalism: A Hermeneutic Reconsideration* (New Haven: Yale University Press).

A. Davutoğlu (2001) *Stratejik Derinlik: Türkiye'nin Uluslararası Konumu* (İstanbul: Küre Yayınları).

L. Dehio (1962) *The Precarious Balance: Four Centuries of the European Power Struggle* (New York: Alfred A. Knopf).

T. Demirel (2004) *Adalet Partisi İdeoloji ve Politika* (İstanbul: İletişim Yayınları).

H. Demirel (1977) *12 Mart'ın İçyüzü* (İstanbul: Yeni Asya Yayınları).

S. Deringil (1998) *The Well-Protected Domains: Ideology and the Legitimation of Power in the Ottoman Empire 1876–1909* (London: I. B. Tauris).

—— (1989) *Turkish Foreign Policy during the Second World War* (Cambridge: Cambridge University Press).

H. Dosdoğru (1993) *6–7 Eylül Olayları* (İstanbul: Bağlam Yayınları).

A. Duben and C. Behar (1991) *İstanbul Households: Marriage, Family and Fertility, 1880–1940* (Cambridge: Cambridge University Press).

A. Durakbaşa (2000) *Halide Edip: Türk Modernleşmesi ve Feminizm* (İstanbul: İletişim Yayınları).

B. Ecevit (1969) *Atatürk ve Devrimcilik* (Ankara: Tekin Yayınevi).

—— (1966) *Ortanın Solu* (İstanbul: Kim Yayınları).

C. Elliot (1965) *Turkey in Europe* (London: Frank Cass and Co.).

M. Emerson and N. Tocci (2004) *Turkey as Bridgehead and Spearhead: Integrating EU and Turkish Foreign Policy* (Brussels: Centre for European Policy Studies).

N. Erdoğan (ed.) (2002) *Yoksulluk Halleri: Türkiye'de Yoksulluğun Toplumsal Görünümleri* (İstanbul: İletişim Yayınları).

L. Erdogan (1995) *Fethullah Gülen Hocaefendi: 'Küçük Dünyam'* (İstanbul: AD Yayınları).

B. B. Ersanlı (1992) *İktidar ve Tarih: Türkiye'de 'Resmi Tarih' Tezinin Oluşumu (1929–1937)* (İstanbul: Afa).

P. Evans, D. Rueschmeyer, and T. Skocpol (eds) (1985) *Bringing the State Back In* (Cambridge: Cambridge University Press).

A. Evin (1983) *Origins and Development of the Turkish Novel* (Minneapolis: Bibliotheca Islamica).

N. Falay, E. Kalaycıoğlu and U. Özkirimli (1996) *Belediyelerin Mali Yönetimi: İktisadi ve Siyasal Bir Çözümleme* (İstanbul: TESEV Yayınları).

R. Finn (1984) *The Early Turkish Novel, 1872–1900* (İstanbul: ISIS).

B. C. Fortna (2002) *Imperial Classroom: Islam, the State, and Education in the Late Ottoman Empire* (Oxford: Oxford University Press).

F. W. Frey (1965) *The Turkish Political Elite* (Cambridge, MA: MIT Press).

F. Georgeon (2003) *Abdulhamid II: Le sultan caliphe* (Paris: Fayard).

H. Gibbons (1916) *The Foundation of the Ottoman Empire: A History of the Osmanlis 1300–1403* (Oxford: Oxford University Press).

D. Goffman (2002) *The Ottoman Empire and Early Modern Europe* (Cambridge: Cambridge University Press).

S. Gourgouris (1996) *Dream Nation: Enlightenment, Colonization and the Institution of Modern Greece* (Stanford: Stanford University Press).

F. M. Göçek (1996) *Rise of the Bourgeoisie, Demise of the Empire: Ottoman Westernization and Social Change* (Oxford: OUP).

Z. Gökalp (1995) *Hars ve Medeniyet* (İstanbul: Toker Yayınları).

—— (1980) *Makaleler IX* (İstanbul: Kültür Bakanlığı Yayınları).

—— (1976) *Türk Medeniyeti Tarihi* (Ankara: Kültür Bakanlığı Yayınları).

—— (1990) *Türkcülügün Esaslari* (Ankara: Kültür Bakanlığı Yayınları).

N. Göle (1996) *The Forbidden Modern: Civilization and Veiling* (Ann Arbor: University of Michigan Press).

M. Gönlübol (1990) *Olaylarla Türk Dis Politikasi, 1919–1990* (Ankara: Alkım Kitabevi Yayınları).

F. D. Güler (2003) *Adalet Partisi* (Ankara: Türkiye ve Orta Doğu Amme İdaresi Enstitüsü).

W. Hale (2000) *Turkish Foreign Policy 1774–2000* (London: Frank Cass).

—— (1994) *Turkish Politics and the Military* (London: Routledge).

Ş. Hanioğlu (1995) *The Young Turks in Opposition* (Oxford: Oxford University Press).

J. Haslip (1958) *The Sultan: The Life of Abdulhamid II* (London: History Book Club).

V. Holbrook (1994) *The Unreadable Shores of Love: Turkish Modernity and Mystic Romance* (Austin: University of Texas Press).

S. P. Huntington (1968) *Political Order in Changing Societies*. (New Haven and London: Yale University Press).

E. Işın (1995) *İstanbul'da Gündelik Hayat* (İstanbul: İletişim).

E. İlyasoğlu (1998) *Contemporary Turkish Composers* (İstanbul: Pan Yayıncılık)

A. İnan (1981) *Atatürk Hakkında Hatıralar ve Belgeler* (Ankara: Türkiye İş Bankası Kültür Yayınları).

―――― (1958) *Herkesin Bir Dünyası Var* (Ankara: Türk Tarih Kurumu Basımevi).

A. İnsel (ed.) (2001) *Modern Türkiye'de Siyasi Düşünce: Kemalizm, vol. 2* (İstanbul: İletişim).

Ç. Kağıtçıbaşı (ed.) *Sex Roles, Family and Community in Turkey* (Bloomington: Indiana University Turkish Studies).

D. Kandiyoti and A. Saktanber (eds) (2002) *Fragments of Culture: The Everyday of Modern Turkey* (London: I. B. Tauris).

M. Kaplan, I. Enginün, N. Birinci and Z. Kerman (1981) *Atatürk Devri Fikir Hayatı I* (İstanbul: Kültür Bakanlığı Yayınları).

K. H. Karpat (2001) *The Politicization of Islam: Reconstructing Identity, State, Faith, and Community in the Late Ottoman State* (Oxford: Oxford University Press).

―――― (ed.) (2000) *Ottoman Past and Today's Turkey* (Leiden: Brill, 2000).

Ç. Keyder (ed.) (1999) *Istanbul Between the Global and the Local* (Oxford: Rowman and Littlefield).

P. Kinross (1995) *Atatürk: The Rebirth of a Nation* (London: Phoenix).

S. Kinzer (2001) *Crescent and Star: Turkey between Two Worlds* (New York: Farrar-Strauss-Giroux).

C. Koçak (1996) *Türkiye'de Milli Sef Dönemi* (İstanbul: Iletisim Yayınları).

O. Koloğlu (2000) *Ecevit ile CHP* (İstanbul: Büke Yayınları).

C. Kozanoğlu (1995) *Pop Çağı Ateşi* (İstanbul: İletişim).

M. F. Köprülü (1992) *The Origins of the Ottoman Empire* (Albany: State University of New York Press).

H. Kramer (2000) *A Changing Turkey: The Challenge to Europe and the United States* (Washington, DC: Brookings Institution Press).

A. O. Krueger and O. H. Aktan (1992) *Swimming Against the Tide: Turkish Trade Reform in the 1980s* (San Francisco: International Center for Economic Growth, Press).

S. Ladas (1932) *The Exchange of Minorities: Bulgaria, Greece and Turkey* (New York: Macmillan Company).

F. S. Larrabee and I. O. Lesser (2003) *Turkish Foreign Policy in An Age of Uncertainty* (Santa Monica: RAND).

D. Lerner (1958) *The Passing of Traditional Society: Modernizing the Middle East* (New York: The Free Press).

G. Lewis (1999) *The Turkish Language Reform: A Catastrophic Success* (Oxford: OUP).

B. Lewis (1961) *The Emergence of Modern Turkey* (London: Oxford University Press).

R. P. Lindner (1983) *Nomads and Ottomans in Medieval Anatolia* (Bloomington, IN: Indiana University Press).

A. Mango (2004) *The Turks Today* (London: John Murray).

―――― (1999) *Atatürk: The Biography of the Founder of Modern Turkey* (Woodstock and New York: The Overlook Press)

A. Marcus (2007) *Blood and Belief: The PKK and the Kurdish Fight for Independence* (New York: New York University Press).

Ş. Mardin (2000) *The Genesis of Young Ottoman Thought* (Syracuse, NY: Syracuse University Press).

—— (1989) *Religion and Social Change in Modern Turkey: The Case of Bediüzzaman Said Nursi* (New York: State University of New York Press).

—— (1975) 'Centre-Periphery Relations: A Key to Turkish Politics?' in E. D. Akarlı with G. Ben-Dor (ed.) *Political Participation in Turkey: Historical Background and Present Problems* (İstanbul: Boğaziçi University Press).

L. G. Martin and D. Keridis (eds) (2004) *The Future of Turkish Foreign Policy* (Cambridge: MIT Press).

M. Meeker (2002) A *Nation of Empire: The Ottoman Legacy of Turkish Modernity* (Berkeley: University of California Press).

Y. Navaro-Yashin (2002) *Faces of the State: Secularism and Public Life in Turkey* (Princeton: Princeton University Press).

L. Neyzi (2008) *Türkiye'de Bellek Çalışmaları* (İstanbul: İş Bankası Kültür Yayınları).

—— (1999a) *İstanbul'da Hatırlamak ve Unutmak: Birey, Bellek ve Aidiyet* (İstanbul: Tarih Vakfı Yurt Yayınları).

—— (1999b) *Küçük Hanım'dan 'Rubu Asırlık Adam'a: Nezihe Neyzi'den Oğlu Nezih Neyzi'ye Mektuplar 1947–1948* (İstanbul: Sel Yayıncılık).

İ. Orga (1988) *Portrait of a Turkish Family* (London: Eland).

İ. Ortaylı (1995) *İmperatorluğun En Uzun Yüzyılı* (İstanbul: Hil Yayınları).

N. Özbek (2002) *Osmanlı İmparatorluğu'nda Sosyal Devlet* (İstanbul: İletişim Yayınları).

E. Özbudun (2000) *Contemporary Turkish Politics: Challenges to Democratic Consolidation* (Boulder, London: Lynne Rienner).

—— (1992) *1921 Anayasası* (Ankara: Atatürk Kültür, Dil ve Tarih Yüksek Kurumu, Atatürk Araştırma Merkezi Yayınları).

E. Özdalga (ed) (1999) *Naqshbandis in Western and Central Asia: Change and Continuity.* (London: Curzon Press).

A. Özdemir and K. Frank (2000) *Visible Islam in Modern Turkey* (London: Macmillan).

H. Özdemir (1989) *Rejim ve Asker* (İstanbul: Afa Yayınları).

U. Özkırımlı and S. A. Sofos (eds) (2008) *Tormented by History: Nationalism in Greece and Turkey* (New York: Columbia University Press).

E. Özyürek (ed.) (2007) *The Politics of Public Memory in Turkey* (Syracuse, NY: Syracuse University Press).

—— (2006) *Nostalgia for the Modern: State Secularism and Everyday Politics in Turkey* (Durham: Duke University Press).

C. E. Padwick (1958) *Call to İstanbul* (London: Longmans, Green).

T. Parla (1985) The *Social and Political Thought of Ziya Gökalp* (Leiden: E. J. Brill).

O. Pamuk (2008) *Masumiyet müzesi* (İstanbul: İletişim).

O. Pamuk (2006) *The Black Book* [trans. Maureen Freely] (New York: Vintage).

O. Pamuk (2004) *Snow* [trans. Maureen Freely] (New York: Knopf).

O. Pamuk (2001) *My Name is Red* [trans. E. M. Göknar] (New York: Alfred A. Knopf).

O. Pamuk (1998) *The New Life* [trans. Güneli Gün] (New York: Vintage).

O. Pamuk (1990) *The White Castle* [translated by Victoria Holrook] (London and Boston: Faber and Faber).

İ. Parlatır and N. Çetin (eds) (1999) *Genç Kalemler Dergisi* (Ankara: Türk Dil Kurumu Yayınları).

H. Poulton (1997) *Top Hat, Grey Wolf and Crescent: Turkish Nationalism and the Turkish Republic* (London: Hurst).

P. Robins (2003) *Suits and Uniforms: Turkish Foreign Policy Since the Cold War* (Seattle: University of Washington Press).

R. D. Robinson (1963) *The First Turkish Republic: A Case Study in National Development* (Cambridge: Harvard University Press).

D. A. Rustow (1959) 'The Army and the Founding of the Turkish Republic', *World Politics*, vol. 11, no. 4, 513–52.

E. W. Said (1979) *Orientalism* (New York: Vintage Books).

K. Saybaşılı (1995) *DYP-SHP Koalisyonunun Üç Yılı* (İstanbul: Bağlam).

A. Saygun (1981) *Atatürk ve Musiki* (Ankara: Sevda Cenap And Vakfı Müzik Yayınlan).

G. Seufert (1997) *Politischer Islam in der Türkei. Islamismus als symbolische Repräsentation einer sich moderniesierenden muslimischen Gesellschaft* (Stuttgart: Fraz Steiner).

D. Shankland (1999) *Islam and Society in Turkey* (Huntingdon: Eothen Press).

S. Shaw and E. K. Shaw (1977) *History of the Ottoman Empire and Modern Turkey, Vol. II* (London: Cambridge University Press).

S. A. Somel (2001) *The Modernization of Public Education in the Ottoman Empire, 1839–1908: Islamization, Autocracy and Discipline* (Leiden: E. J. Brill).

N. Sousa (1933) *The Capitulatory Régime of Turkey: Its History, Origin, and Nature* (Baltimore: The John Hopkins Press).

M. Sönmez (2002) *100 Göstergede Kriz ve Yoksullaşma* (İstanbul: İletişim Yayınları).

M. Stokes (1992) *The Arabesk Debate* (Oxford: Oxford University Press).

O. Şahinoğlu (1966) *AP'nin Doğuşundan Bugüne* (Ankara: Seden Yayınları).

C. Talas (1992) *Türkiye'nin Açıklamalı Sosyal Politika Tarihi* (Ankara: Bilgi Yayınevi).

M. Tamkoc (1976) *The Warrior Diplomats* (Salt Lake City: University of Utah Press).

M. G. Tan, Ö. Şahin, A. Bora and M. Sever (2007) *Cumhuriyet'te Çocuktular* (İstanbul: Boğaziçi Üniversitesi Yayınevi).

Ş. Tekeli (1982) *Kadınlar ve Siyasal-Toplumsal Hayat* (İstanbul: Birikim Yayınları).

Ü. Tekin (2004) *AK Partinin Muhafazakar Demokrat Kimliği* (Ankara: Orient).

S. Tezel (1982) *Cumhuriyet Döneminin İktisadi Tarihi (1923–1950)* (Ankara: Yurt Yayınları).

P. Thompson (1999) *Geçmişin Sesi: Sözlü Tarih* (İstanbul: Tarih Vakfı).

T. Timur (1971) *Türk Devrimi ve Sonrası 1919–1946* (Ankara: Doğan Yayınları).

B. Toprak (1981) *Islam and Political Development in Turkey* (Leiden: Brill).

Toptaş, Hasan Ali (2005) *Uykuların Doğusunda* (Istanbul: İletişim Yayınları).

_____ (1995) *Gölgesizler* (Istanbul: İletişim Yayınları).

A. J. Toynbee (1922) *The Western Question in Greece and Turkey: A Study in the Contact of Civilizations* (London: Constable and Company).

B. Turam (2007) *Between Politics and the State: The Politics of Engagement* (Stanford: Stanford University Press).

N. Turfan (2000) *Rise of the Young Turks – Politics, the Military and Ottoman Collapse* (London: I. B. Tauris)

D. M. Vaughan (1954) *Europe and the Turk: A Pattern of Alliances, 1350–1700* (Liverpool: Liverpool University Press).

V. D. Volkan and N. Itzkowitz (1984) *The Immortal Atatürk: A Psychobiography* (Chicago: The University of Chicago Press).

F. Weber (1978) *The Evasive Neutral: Germany, Britain and the Quest for a Turkish Alliance in the Second World War* (Columbia and London: University of Missouri Press).

D. E. Webster (1939) *The Turkey of Atatürk* (Philadelphia: The American Academy of Political and Social Science).

J. B. White ([1991] 2004) *Money Makes Us Relative: Women's Labor in Urban Turkey* (Second Edition) (London: Routledge).

_____ (2002) *Islamist Mobilization in Turkey: A Study in Vernacular Politics* (Seattle: University of Washington Press).

P. Wittek (1938) *The Rise of the Ottoman Empire* (London: The Royal Asiatic Society).

A. E. Yalman (1930) *Turkey, in The World War* (New Haven: Yale University Press).

Y. Navaro-Yashin (2002) *Faces of the State: Secularism and Public Life in Turkey* (Princeton: Princeton University Press).

H. Yavuz and J. Esposito (eds) (2003) *Turkish Islam and the Secular State: The Gülen Movement* (Syracuse: Syracuse University Press).

H. Yavuz (2003) *Islamic Political Identity in Turkey* (Oxford: Oxford University Press).

K. Yetiş (ed.) (1996) *Namık Kemal's Writings on Turkish Language and Literature* (İstanbul: Alfa).

N. Yurdusev (ed.) (2004) *Ottoman Diplomacy: Conventional or Unconventional?* (Basingstoke: Palgrave Macmillan).

Y. Zihnioğlu (2003) *Kadınsız Inkılap* [Revolution without Women] (İstanbul: Metis Yayınları).

E. J. Zürcher (2004) *Turkey: A Modern History* (London: I. B.Tauris).

——— (1993) *Turkey: A Modern History* (London: I. B.Tauris).

Index